MOON

W9-ANW-285

LAKE VILLA DISTRICT LIBRARY

3 1981 00592 5197

BLUE RIDGE
PARKWAY
Road Trip

JASON

Lake Villa District Library
Lake Villa, Illinois 60046
(847) 356-7711

PENNSYLVANIA

Morgantown

Cumberland

Hagerstown

MARYLAND

Canaan Valley
National Wildlife
Refuge

The
Shenandoah
Valley

Winchester

FRONT
ROYAL

George Washington
National Forest

WASHINGTON
DC

Alexandria

WEST
VIRGINIA

Monongahela
National Forest

Luray

Manassas
National
Battlefield Park

Harrisonburg

Stanley

Elkton

Shenandoah
National Park

Fredericksburg

WAYNESBORO

Charlottesville

White
Sulphur
Springs

Green Springs
National Historic
Landmark District

George Washington
National Forest

VIRGINIA

RICHMOND

Jefferson
National Forest

Lynchburg

ROANOKE

Petersburg

Virginia
Blue Ridge

Danville

Winston-
Salem

GREENSBORO

Durham

Rocky
Mount

Salisbury

NORTH
CAROLINA

RALEIGH

Greenville

Uwharrie
National
Forest

Goldsboro

CONTENTS

Discover The Blue Ridge Parkway....6

Planning Your Trip 8
Where to Go............................8
When to Go 9
Before You Go 9
Driving Tips 11

Hit the Road 12
The 14-Day Blue Ridge Parkway Road Trip 12
Four Days from Washington DC 17
Five Days from Knoxville 19
Music of the Blue Ridge 22

The Shenandoah Valley.............25
Washington DC..........................31
Manassas Battlefield National Park 57
Front Royal.............................58
Shenandoah National Park 62
Waynesboro 81
Charlottesville.......................... 84

Virginia Blue Ridge.................. 97
Rockfish Gap (MP 0.0)................... 103
Humpback Rocks (MP 5.9)................ 103
Wintergreen Resort (MP 13.7)............ 104
Sherando Lake (MP 13.7) 104
Crabtree Falls (MP 27.2) 105
Whetstone Ridge (MP 29) 106
Yankee Horse Ridge (MP 34.4) 107
Bluff Mountain (MP 53.1) 107
Otter Creek (MP 60.8).................. 107
James River Overlook (MP 63.2) 109
US-501 West: Natural Bridge (MP 63.7) 109
Apple Orchard Mountain (MP 76.5) 111

Peaks of Otter (MP 85.9)...................112
VA-43 South: Bedford (MP 86)...............114
Purgatory Overlook (MP 92.1)............ 120
Great Valley Overlook (MP 99.6) 120
N&W Railroad Overlook (MP 106.9) 121
Roanoke................................121
Virginia's Explore Park (MP 115) 133
Mill Mountain and the
   Roanoke Star (MP 120)..................135
Roanoke Mountain (MP 120.4) 137
Roanoke Valley Overlook (MP 129.6) 137
Devils Backbone Overlook (MP 143.9) 137
Smart View (MP 154.1) 137
VA-8 North: Floyd (MP 165.2)............. 138
VA-8 South: Fairy Stone
   State Park (MP 165.2) 141
Rocky Knob Recreation Area (MP 167)...... 142
Chateau Morrisette Winery (MP 171.5) 143
Mabry Mill (MP 176.1) 144
Primland (MP 177.7) 145
Groundhog Mountain (MP 188.1)........... 145
Fancy Gap (MP 199.5) 146
US-52 South: Mount Airy (MP 199.5) 146
Sugarloaf Mountain (MP 203.9) 152
Blue Ridge Music Center (MP 213) 152
VA-89 North: Galax (MP 215) 152

North Carolina High Country......157
Cumberland Knob (MP 217.5) 162
US-21 South: Roaring Gap
   to Elkin (MP 229)....................... 163
Stone Mountain State Park (MP 229) 164
Doughton Park (MP 238.5) 166
Sally Mae's on the Parkway (MP 259) 170

NC-163 West: West Jefferson (MP 261) 170
The Lump (MP 264.4) 174
E. B. Jeffress Park (MP 272). 174
US-321 North: Boone (MP 291.9). 175
Blowing Rock (MP 291.9) 181
Moses H. Cone Memorial Park (MP 294) 187
Julian Price Memorial Park (MP 297.1) 188
Linn Cove Viaduct (MP 304.4) 190
Grandfather Mountain (MP 305). 191
Beacon Heights (MP 305.2) 193
Flat Rock (MP 308.3) 194
Linville Gorge (MP 316.3) 194
US-221 South: Linville Caverns (MP 317.4) . . . 196
Chestoa View (MP 320.8) 196
McKinney Gap (MP 327.5) 196
Museum of North Carolina
    Minerals (MP 331) 197
NC-226 West: Penland School
    of Crafts (MP 331) 197
Little Switzerland (MP 334) 197
Crabtree Falls (MP 339.5) 199
Mount Mitchell State Park (MP 355.3) 199
Craggy Gardens (MP 364.6). 200

**Asheville and the
    Southern Blue Ridge** **203**
Folk Art Center (MP 382) 209
Asheville (MP 382.5) 210
Blue Ridge Parkway
    Visitor Center (MP 384) 233
US-Alt 74 East: Chimney Rock (MP 384.7) . . . 234
North Carolina Arboretum (MP 393) 235
Lake Powhatan (MP 393) 235
Mount Pisgah (MP 408.6). 242

Cold Mountain Overlook (MP 412) 243
US-276 South: Pisgah Ranger District
    and Brevard (MP 412) 244
Looking Glass Rock Overlook (MP 417) 249
Graveyard Fields Overlook (MP 418.8) 249
Devil's Courthouse (MP 422.4) 250
US-215 North: Cold Mountain (MP 423.2) . . . 251
Richland Balsam Overlook (MP 431.4) 252
US-74 East: Waynesville (MP 443.1). 252
Waterrock Knob Visitor Center (MP 451.2). . . 255
US-19 North: Maggie Valley (MP 455.7) 256
Soco Gap (MP 455.7). 258
Big Witch Gap Overlook (MP 461.9) 258
Southern End (MP 469.1) 258
US-441 South: Cherokee (MP 469.1) 258
US-19 South: Bryson City 264

Great Smoky Mountains **271**
Great Smoky Mountains National Park 277
Gatlinburg 307
Pigeon Forge and Sevierville 316
Knoxville 324

Essentials **335**
Getting There 335
Road Rules. 337
Travel Tips 341
Health and Safety. 342
Information and Services 343
Suggested Reading 344
Internet Resources 344

Index **347**

List of Maps **358**

DISCOVER
The Blue
Ridge Parkway

F or the 15 minutes it took the sun to hide behind the mountains, we were silent. A crowd of strangers, we'd gathered car by car at Waterrock Knob at Milepost 451 on the Blue Ridge Parkway because something in the shape of the clouds hinted at a sunset we shouldn't pass by.

Summer was in full swing and the mountains seemed 80 shades of green, but when the sun's crepuscular rays shone through gaps in the clouds, they rinsed all color away, then washed the landscape in gold. It was the kind of light that had texture, like the finest silk draped over the mountains.

The birds quieted and the crickets ceased their call. The valleys darkened. The ridges gleamed like blades. The evening mist began to rise from the deepest and most secret hollows and coves.

This sunset was singular; a moment that, once it passed, would be gone from the world. So we watched. We held our breath. We waited until the last possible moment to break the spell with the click of a camera shutter, the soft glow of a cell phone screen.

Then it was gone. One minute the mountains around Cherokee were bathed in golden light; the next they were night dark. Birds called—doves roosting, an owl preparing to take wing—and the insects returned. First came the quiet fireflies, blinking their coded messages to one another, then the crickets filling in the silence.

That wasn't the first sunset I'd seen from the Blue Ridge Parkway, but it was the one that left the deepest mark. Yours is waiting. Your sunset. Your sunrise, when the mountains go from predawn blue to the faintest green. Your moonlit night. Your shooting star. Your moment of nature—so pure and true your throat catches when you try to describe it later.

Go find it. Get in the car and drive the Blue Ridge Parkway. Because somewhere along these ridges, somewhere in the Smoky Mountains, somewhere in the long valleys of the Shenandoah, there are a thousand moments like this. All you have to do is find them.

PLANNING YOUR TRIP

Where to Go

The Shenandoah Valley
Shenandoah National Park and **Skyline Drive** form the northern cap to this monumental mountaintop ride. Here, wide valleys and rivers give the landscape an interesting character. Hike a leg of the storied **Appalachian Trail** or discover the interesting character of the region underground at **Luray Caverns.** Nearby, the **monuments, museums,** and vibrant culture of **Washington DC** beckon.

Virginia Blue Ridge
This stretch of the Parkway is the **easiest to drive.** As the Blue Ridge Mountains give way to plains, the views are long, with many a rolling hill, pasture, and bucolic farmhouse or church in the distance. **Small towns** like Floyd and

Bedford offer big attractions like Floyd's unforgettable **Friday Night Jamboree.** Orchards and **wineries** dot the hills around **Roanoke.**

North Carolina High Country
As you enter North Carolina, you begin to climb, and the mountains take center stage. The peak of **Grandfather Mountain** looms high over the Blue Ridge Parkway, and places like **Blowing Rock,** a stunning outcrop where snow falls upside down, add to the magic of the region. The spectacular **Linn Cove Viaduct,** which seems to float off the mountainside, is part of the commute, and countless **waterfalls** are just a short hike away.

Asheville and the Southern Blue Ridge
Between Asheville and Cherokee is the **highest and most crooked part of the drive.** Here, the mountains are tall and steep, making for **dramatic views** from hikes and overlooks. Many small towns remained relatively isolated until the early 20th century and are rich with

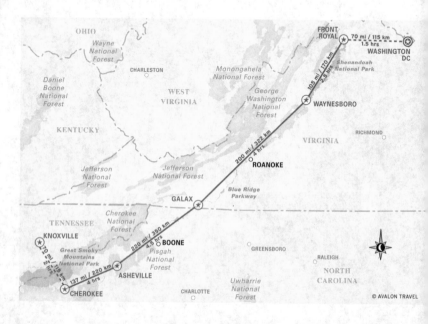

history and culture. Asheville is home to the lauded **Biltmore Estate** and some of the best **restaurants** in the South. **Cherokee,** where the Blue Ridge Parkway ends, is the ancestral home of the Eastern Band of the Cherokee Nation.

Great Smoky Mountains

Great Smoky Mountains National Park is the **most-visited national park** in the country. The scenery and **wildlife**— rounded peaks and jagged mountain-tops, crystal-clear trout streams and white-water rivers, elk and bear, morning mist and evening firefly shows—explain why. The tourist towns of **Gatlinburg** and **Pigeon Forge** welcome millions of visitors who flock to **Dollywood** and the park. **Knoxville,** one of the nation's top outdoor towns, is fun in any season.

When to Go

The obvious season to visit the Blue Ridge Parkway is **autumn.** The leaves blaze with color from the end of September through October. The timing for peak color varies by region, but you're just about guaranteed a great color show anywhere October 5-20. Expect mild weather, with warm days and chilly evenings (you'll be fine in long sleeves and a vest or jacket).

Winter along the Parkway is tricky as the high elevations and exposed ridge-lines are especially susceptible to snow and ice. Only a few sections of the Parkway (the ones that also double as public roadways) are plowed and salted during winter, so long stretches and point-to-point segments are closed from November through spring. The Blue Ridge Parkway maintains a live link of road closures available at www.nps.gov/blri (select "Road and Facility Closures").

Spring is lovely, though trails can be muddy. There's a great payoff to spring rains, though: wildflowers and water-falls. It's also the time you may see young

animals trailing their mothers across the road or along the wood's edge.

Summer draws big numbers of visitors taking advantage of warm weather and vacation days. The elevation keeps the Parkway cooler than the flatlands, and the overlooks are rich with the deep green of summer leaves.

Before You Go

If you're visiting from outside driving distance, you'll likely fly into one of the **airports** in Washington DC, Baltimore, or Knoxville. **Pack** your hiking boots for the miles of trails along the drive. Swimsuits are recommended for enjoying the waterfalls and mountain streams, and rain gear and binoculars are a good idea. A tripod and zoom lens are handy for landscape or wildlife photography. **Reservations** are recommended (and sometimes required) at **campgrounds** in both national parks and along the Blue Ridge Parkway, especially during the peak seasons of summer and fall. Reservations for **hotels and B&Bs** along the route are recommended during peak times as well.

The Blue Ridge Parkway and Great Smoky Mountains National Park are free to visit and use. An **entrance fee** ($25 per vehicle, $20 per motorcycle, $10 pedestrians and cyclists; admission good for one week) is required for Shenandoah National Park, payable at any of the four entrances to the park along Skyline Drive.

Weather can be a factor when visiting any spot along this route. In any season you may face thick fog and sudden storms, though most rain is of the springtime or summer thunderstorm variety. Hail is not unheard of, especially at higher elevations, which are also vulnerable to snow and ice during late fall, winter, and early spring. Sections of the Blue Ridge Parkway and Skyline Drive are apt to be **closed or restricted** due to weather

Clockwise from top left: Linn Cove Viaduct, North Carolina; berries at a summer farm stand; Chimney Rock State Park.

in any season. Check road conditions at www.nps.gov/blri (select "Road and Facility Closures"). In North Carolina, Ray's Weather (www.raysweather.com) offers highly localized weather reporting and forecasting, often including color reports in the autumn.

Note that **cell phone reception** can be very spotty, especially as the route ventures away from more populated areas.

Driving Tips

Both the Blue Ridge Parkway and Skyline Drive are organized by **mileposts.** Markers, signs, and pillars note each mile, and waypoints include directions like "Blue Ridge Parkway Milepost 52.6." This system makes it easy to anticipate where the next sight, visitors center, or hike may be. On Skyline Drive, you'll travel from mile 0 in Front Royal, Virginia, to mile 105.5 at Rockfish Gap, near Waynesboro, Virginia. At Rockfish Gap, the Blue Ridge Parkway begins with mile 0, then carries on down the mountain chain to Cherokee, North Carolina, and mile 469.

You can drive your own car the 740-mile length of the Skyline Drive-Blue Ridge Parkway-Great Smoky Mountains National Park route, or you can pick up a **rental car** at or near the airport or train station where you begin your journey. Do check that you will have a place to turn in the car at the other end if you plan on taking a one-way trip, and note that some companies levy hefty fees for this service.

Gasoline is available at only one place along Skyline Drive and nowhere on the Blue Ridge Parkway. You'll need to fuel up at the towns, cities, and waysides off the Parkway. Fuel availability is noted at the beginning of relevant chapters in this guidebook, but as a rule, you'll find a gas station near any town or major route that crosses the Parkway.

The **speed limit** on the Parkway is 45 miles per hour, though it slows to 35 or even 25 in certain areas. Along Skyline Drive, the speed limit is 35 miles per hour. You'll encounter a great deal of wildlife along the drive. At any faster than the speed limit, you pose a threat to animals and yourself, as you may not have adequate time to stop if you encounter an animal. It comes as a surprise to some, but the National Park Service can pull you over and issue tickets (and you're not likely to talk your way out of this one), so keep your speed appropriate to the traffic and weather. Traffic slows considerably during peak seasons. During autumn, you may never reach the speed limit.

Many locals choose to travel a segment of the Parkway, then **return home via interstates** to reduce travel time. If you fly into one of the travel hubs in this guidebook, you'll likely travel one way, north or south, along the route and depart from an airport on the other end. Otherwise, you may do like the locals, traveling the Parkway one direction and a faster route on the return trip.

HIT THE ROAD

The 14-Day Blue Ridge Parkway Road Trip

Tracing the ridges and hillsides of the Blue Ridge Mountains, the Blue Ridge Parkway hosts millions of visitors every year, lured by the hum of tires on the road and the whisper of mountain winds through the trees. In just two weeks, you can drive the 716 miles from Washington DC to Knoxville, via one of the greatest scenic roads in the nation. You can also easily reverse this route by beginning in Knoxville and ending in DC.

Day 1
ARRIVE IN WASHINGTON DC
Settle in to your hotel, then spend the rest of the day at museums of your choice. The museums of the Smithsonian Institution, including the **National Air and Space Museum, National Portrait Gallery,** and **National Museum of Natural History** are fascinating, as are the **Newseum** and **Phillips Collection.** Try dinner at **Sfoglina** or **Hill Country Barbecue** before catching a jazz concert at **Columbia Station** or an indie band at the **Black Cat,** or go for a **nighttime bicycle tour** of the Mall.

Day 2
EXPLORE WASHINGTON DC
Go to the moving and enlightening **National Museum of African American History and Culture,** then cross the river to **Mount Vernon,** George Washington's home, or **Arlington National Cemetery,** or both. For dinner, head to **Rasika,** which will transform the way you look at Indian cuisine.

Day 3
WASHINGTON DC TO SHENANDOAH NATIONAL PARK
70 miles; 1.5 hours
Head to the **National Mall,** a grand grassy avenue lined with the museums of the Smithsonian Institution, the most iconic monuments—**Washington Monument, Lincoln Memorial, Vietnam Veterans Memorial**—and, of course, views of the **United States Capitol** and **White House.** Have lunch at **Ben's Chili Bowl,** a DC institution, or one of the many ethnic restaurants like **Rasika,** or hit the road and dine in **Front Royal,** at the entrance to **Skyline Drive** and **Shenandoah National Park.** Along Skyline, **75 overlooks** in the park give a sense of the vast wilderness that once blanketed the countryside. Hike to **Dark Hollow Falls,** and spend the night inside the park at **Big Meadows Lodge** or **Skyland Resort.**

Day 4
SHENANDOAH NATIONAL PARK TO WAYNESBORO AND CHARLOTTESVILLE
160 miles; 4.5 hours
Head outside the park to the spectacular **Luray Caverns,** one of the best cave systems in the nation. When you're finished, drive down to **Waynesboro,** near the end of Skyline Drive and the start of the Blue Ridge Parkway, and check in at **Iris Inn.** Then take I-64 east for 24 miles to **Charlottesville.** Tour **Monticello,** Thomas Jefferson's home, only a few miles from downtown, then walk the grounds of the **University of Virginia,** which was founded by Jefferson and bears his architectural mark. If you have time, a **wine tour** will take you to some of the region's best wineries. Try dinner at **C&O Restaurant** or **Fleurie Restaurant,** or eat at **The Fishin' Pig** in Waynesboro and prepare for the Parkway on the morrow.

Best Hikes

Hen Wallow Falls in Great Smoky Mountains National Park

Skyline Drive

- **Mary's Rock Trail (MP 33.5):** Views from Mary's Rock are some of the best along Skyline Drive, with full panoramas of the mountain chain stretching off into the distance (page 70).

- **Dark Hollow Falls (MP 50.7):** This short but taxing trail in Shenandoah National Park leads to a beautiful 70-foot waterfall (page 73).

Blue Ridge Parkway

- **Linville Falls Trail (MP 316.3):** Take in three views of one of the most beautiful waterfalls in what's called the "Grand Canyon of the East" (page 194).

- **Craggy Gardens Trail (MP 364.6):** Venture out on this moderate hike through rhododendron tunnels reminiscent of a fairy-tale forest (page 201).

Great Smoky Mountains National Park

- **Andrews Bald:** Wildflowers abound in this bald, a high meadow in Great Smoky Mountains National Park (page 287).

- **Alum Cave Bluff to Mount LeConte:** This strenuous hike has a huge payoff as you take in the views from the top (page 288).

- **Hen Wallow Falls Trail:** A short trail leads you to a photogenic 90-foot waterfall that starts out only 2 feet wide but spreads to 20 feet at the base (page 296).

Day 5
WAYNESBORO TO ROANOKE
132 miles; 4 hours

Have breakfast at Iris Inn, then start your journey south along the **Blue Ridge Parkway.** Make your first stop the **Humpback Rocks** (MP 5.9) and take the one-mile trail to the eponymous rocks. Stop at the **James River Visitor Center** (MP 63.6), the lowest point on the Parkway, and stretch your legs on one of the short walks that detail the history of the river or the diverse plant life here.

At Milepost 86, detour off the Parkway for lunch in **Bedford.** You can spend the afternoon in Bedford, taking a docent-led tour of the **National D-Day Memorial** followed by fruit-picking at a nearby **apple orchard,** or head to the **Peaks of Otter** (MP 85.9) for a quick but strenuous hike to the peak of **Sharp Top** (2.5-3 hours). Afterward, continue south to **Roanoke.** Enter the city via the Mill Mountain Parkway at Milepost 120 and pass by the famous **Roanoke Star,** then rest up at one of the **B&Bs** in town before heading to **River and Rail Restaurant** for dinner.

Day 6
ROANOKE TO FLOYD
56 miles; 1.5 hours

It's a short day today, so you have time to explore Roanoke. Have a biscuit at **Scratch Biscuit Company** or an egg sandwich from **Texas Tavern,** then wander over to the **Market Square,** where the farmers market will be in full swing any day of the week. Look in at the **Taubman Museum of Art** or shop at the downtown boutiques before heading for **Floyd.** Have lunch near Floyd at **Chateau Morrisette,** one of the oldest wineries in Virginia, before checking into **Ambrosia Farm Bed & Breakfast.** Time your visit to coincide with Floyd's weekly **Friday Night Jamboree,** and have a traditional country dinner at **The Historic Pine Tavern Restaurant** before you hit the Jamboree for an evening of dancing.

Day 7
FLOYD TO STONE MOUNTAIN STATE PARK
85 miles; 2.5 hours

The drive from Floyd to the North Carolina state line is one of the most beautiful on the Parkway. Stop at **Mabry Mill** (MP 176.1) for legendary buckwheat pancakes and a look at a working waterwheel-powered gristmill and sawmill. At **Groundhog Mountain** (MP 188.1), enjoy spectacular views from the observation tower. Learn how country and bluegrass music originated in these very hills at the **Blue Ridge Music Center** at the state

line. Camp at **Stone Mountain State Park** and squeeze in a quick hike to the top of the namesake bald granite dome. Head into nearby **Elkin** for dinner and drinks (just be back before the park is locked for the night).

Day 8
STONE MOUNTAIN TO BLOWING ROCK
75 miles; 2.5 hours

North Carolina's High Country is no joke. The mountains are steep, and the road grows aggressively curvy, making for unworldly views as you round corners with nothing but space and the Blue Ridge Mountains in front of you. Stretch your legs on the 30 miles of trails in **Doughton Park** (MP 238.5), which also has a picnic area, or hike the **Cascade Falls Trail** at E. B. Jeffress Park (MP 272). Stop at the **Moses H. Cone Memorial Park** (MP 294.1) for a look at a turn-of-the-20th-century manor house that's home to the gift shop of the **Southern Highland Craft Guild. Blowing Rock** is just a few miles away, and so are your accommodations at **The New Public House & Hotel,** as well as dinner at **Storie Street Grille.**

Day 9
BLOWING ROCK TO ASHEVILLE
93 miles; 3 hours

Before heading to Asheville, check out the **Blowing Rock,** where you'll have sweeping views of peaks, including Grandfather Mountain. Back on the Parkway, prepare yourself for one of the road's most striking stretches: the **Linn Cove Viaduct** (MP 304.4). Just past the viaduct, drive to the top of **Grandfather Mountain** and take the **Mile High Swinging Bridge** to one of its lower peaks for 360-degree views of the Blue Ridge. Have lunch here, then continue down the road. Just off the Parkway at Milepost 316.3 is the entrance to **Linville Falls.** This waterfall requires a short hike to see and a slightly longer one for postcard views, but it's worth the effort. At

Clockwise from top left: somber and beautiful Arlington National Cemetery; mountain laurel; Grandfather Mountain's mile-high swinging bridge.

Milepost 364.6, stop at **Craggy Gardens** to take in the summertime blooms of rhododendrons and flame azaleas, then continue to the **Folk Art Center** (MP 382), just outside Asheville.

In Asheville, spend the night in the mountains at the **Sourwood Inn** or downtown at the swank **AC Hotel by Marriott Asheville Downtown**. Dinner can be fancy or affordable; there's no shortage of places to eat in this town. Spend a late night downtown checking out the breweries and bars and listening to a little music.

Day 10
EXPLORE ASHEVILLE
Start the day in Asheville with breakfast downtown, then head over to the **Biltmore Estate.** Tour the home, walk the gardens, take lunch in the former stable, then head to the estate's **winery** and wine-tasting room (it's the most-visited one in the nation). Sample some wine and head back to your accommodations to freshen up before hitting town again for excellent barbecue at **Buxton Hall Barbecue** and late-night cocktails and snacks at **Sovereign Remedies.**

Day 11
ASHEVILLE TO CHEROKEE
137 miles; 4 hours
The winding section of the Parkway between Asheville and the southern terminus in Cherokee is quite beautiful. Before you hit the road, down a giant biscuit at **Biscuit Head.** Continue down the Parkway and take in the view of **Mount Pisgah** (MP 408.6) and hike to **Devil's Courthouse** (MP 422.4)—a short hike that's not as fearsome as it sounds and has a view you won't want to leave. **Richland Balsam Overlook** (MP 431.4) is the highest point on the Blue Ridge Parkway, so stop here and mark your trip with a selfie. Stop at the **Waterrock Knob Visitor Center** (MP 451.2) for a four-state view and panorama of the **Great Smoky Mountains.** At Milepost

461.9, you'll reach **Big Witch Overlook,** the last overlook before the Parkway terminates at Milepost 469.1. Take one last long look before heading into **Cherokee** for the night. Spend the night at **Harrah's Cherokee Casino Resort,** where you can gamble, visit the spa, and grab a bite in one of the casino's restaurants.

Day 12
CHEROKEE TO GREAT SMOKY
MOUNTAINS NATIONAL PARK
43 miles; 1.5 hours
Today you'll drive Newfound Gap Road through Great Smoky Mountains National Park. Before you start your drive, visit the **Qualla Arts and Crafts Mutual** in Cherokee. Stop at the **Oconaluftee Visitor Center** for a park map and to check out **Mountain Farm Museum.** The twisting **Newfound Gap Road** is popular with motorcyclists and is stunning in fall; along the way, you'll likely see black bears and white-tailed deer. Stop along the way at any of the overlooks—in a landscape this stunning, there are no bad views. Before you leave the park, drive out to **Cades Cove,** a one-time mountain community, where you might spy bears lounging in the remnants of an apple orchard. Check into a hotel in **Gatlinburg,** then take a walk down the main drag of this tourist haven. Grab some moonshine at **Sugarlands Distilling Company** and dinner at **Mama's Chicken Kitchen** or get dolled up and go to the four-course dinner at **Buckhorn Inn.**

Day 13
GATLINBURG TO KNOXVILLE
30 miles; 45 minutes
Head straight from your Gatlinburg hotel to **Dollywood,** where mountain music, mountain crafts, mountain food, and mountain folks are interspersed with roller coasters. Spend the day here, then head to Knoxville (45 minutes away) for the night. Walk the **World's Fair Park** and climb to the top of the **Sunsphere** for the best view in town. Then, take in a concert

at the historic **Tennessee Theatre.** Dinner at **Not Watson's Kitchen + Bar** will put you in the center of downtown, where you can explore to your heart's content.

Day 14
KNOXVILLE BACK TO WASHINGTON DC
487 miles; 7 hours
You'll definitely want to make better travel time on the return drive to Washington DC. Take I-81 north through Tennessee and Virginia to I-66 east, which will carry you right into DC. This route is doable in a day, rather than two or three at Parkway speeds.

Four Days from Washington DC

Get a taste of Washington DC's history and culture, hit the trail in Shenandoah National Park, spend a night under the stars, and see the homes of two former presidents, all in one mini-expedition.

Day 1
WASHINGTON DC TO SHENANDOAH NATIONAL PARK
70 miles; 1.5 hours
Begin your trip in DC at one of the most recognizable structures in town: the **Lincoln Memorial.** Step out to the landing where Martin Luther King Jr. delivered his "I Have a Dream" speech. Then take the short walk to the **Martin Luther King Jr. Memorial** and continue your walk along the Mall toward the **Capitol.**

Grab an early lunch at **Duke's Grocery** before heading west to **Manassas Battlefield National Park,** site of the First and Second Battles of Bull Run. From Manassas, continue west to the town of **Front Royal,** where you can grab lunch if you didn't do so in DC. Downtown Front Royal is only about a mile from **Shenandoah National Park** and the start of incredibly scenic

105-mile **Skyline Drive,** which bisects the park and will be your route for the next couple of days. Camp at **Matthews Arm Campground,** the first campground in the park as you travel south, or **Big Meadows Campground,** or stay at one of the park's two famous lodges, **Skyland Resort** or **Big Meadows Lodge.** Get dinner at either lodge, then sit back and watch the sunset.

Day 2
SHENANDOAH NATIONAL PARK TO WAYNESBORO
110 miles; 3 hours
Cook yourself a camp breakfast or dine at your lodge of choice, then head out on Skyline Drive. Your first stop is **Dark Hollow Falls,** a short hike to a 70-foot waterfall that spills over a ferny cliff, with a steep ascent on the way back. Afterward, if you're hoping for a hiking reprieve, make the easy jaunt to **Blackrock Summit,** 30 miles south, for enormous views of the countryside. If you're in the mood for more trail time, hike the **South River Falls Trail,** which leads to an 83-foot waterfall, one of the largest in the park.

Continue south to **Waynesboro** and your room or cabin at the mountaintop **Iris Inn.** Have dinner in town at **The Green Leaf Grill.**

Day 3
WAYNESBORO TO CHARLOTTESVILLE
28 miles; 30 minutes
After yesterday's day on the trail, it's time for a day in the city. Just a few miles east is **Charlottesville,** home of the **University of Virginia** and site of **Monticello.** After touring Jefferson's home, stop by a few of the wineries on the **Monticello Wine Trail** to sample some of Virginia's best and a have bite to eat.

Check in at **200 South Street Inn** in the heart of town, and make reservations at **Peter Chang China Grill,** or try **Mas Tapas** for some unexpected flavors.

Views from the Top

autumnal view from Waterrock Knob

Along Skyline Drive and the Blue Ridge Parkway are a number of **overlooks** and **roadside attractions.** In every instance below, it's worth pulling over for an eyeful:

Skyline Drive

- **Hogback Mountain Overlook (MP 20.8):** The longest overlook on Skyline Drive gives you expansive views of mountains and valley (page 67).

- **Crimora Lake Overlook (MP 92.6):** Expect big views centered around Crimora Lake, a remnant of a manganese mining operation (page 80).

Blue Ridge Parkway

- **Peaks of Otter (MP 85.9):** Get to the summit of Sharp Top via either a strenuous hike on the Sharp Top Trail or an easy shuttle ride, then enjoy views of the Parkway, the lights of Bedford, and Abbott Lake (page 112).

- **Mabry Mill (MP 176.1):** This picturesque millhouse with waterwheel is one of the most photographed on the Parkway (page 144).

- **Groundhog Mountain (MP 188.1):** The view of the observation tower is lovely but nothing compared to the view from it (page 145).

- **Beacon Heights (MP 305.2):** Whether you stay at the car and admire the view of Grandfather Mountain or take the short hike to a rocky bluff with massive views, you won't be disappointed (page 193).

- **Richland Balsam Overlook (MP 431.4):** From the highest point on the parkway, you'll have great views of several mountain ranges (page 252).

- **Waterrock Knob Visitor Center (MP 451.2):** This is the perfect vantage point for taking in the sunset and star-filled sky (page 255).

Day 4
CHARLOTTESVILLE TO MOUNT VERNON AND DC
131 miles; 3 hours

Don't leave Charlottesville without a bagel from **Bodo's Bagels.** On the way back to DC, avoid the congestion of the interstate and take **US-29** through the countryside until you get back to Manassas Battlefield National Park.

From here, head east to **Mount Vernon,** the riverside home of our first president, just a couple of miles south of Alexandria and only 15 miles from DC. Tour Mount Vernon and have lunch alfresco at one of the many charming restaurants and cafés in **Old Town Alexandria.** Then return to DC. For a relaxed dinner, try **Birch & Barley,** or try some Filipino dishes at **Bad Saint.**

Five Days from Knoxville

With just five days, you can explore Knoxville, traipse into Dollywood, log some quality trail time, explore Great Smoky Mountains National Park, catch an amazing firefly display, ride a steam train…and drive a short, but beautiful, section of the Blue Ridge Parkway.

Day 1
KNOXVILLE TO DOLLYWOOD
43 miles; 1 hour
Grab a tasty breakfast at **The French Market** in Knoxville, then head over to the **Sunsphere** for a selfie in front of the city's golden-crowned monument. Get a feel for the people and culture of East Tennessee and the Smoky Mountains at the **East Tennessee History Center** downtown, then hit the road, following US-441 south toward the mountain towns of **Pigeon Forge** and **Gatlinburg.** Spend the day at **Dollywood,** where you can grab lunch and a few roller coaster rides, before freshening up at **The Inn on the River** and heading out for dinner at **Local Goat New American Restaurant** and riding go-karts at **SpeedZone Fun Park.**

Day 2
DOLLYWOOD TO GREAT SMOKY
MOUNTAINS NATIONAL PARK
44 miles; 2 hours
Have breakfast at the **Pancake Pantry** in Gatlinburg, then follow US-441

south two miles into **Great Smoky Mountains National Park,** stopping at the **Sugarlands Visitor Center** to pick up maps and park tips. Set up camp in the **Elkmont Campground.** Here, for a two-week window in the summer, one of only four colonies of synchronous fireflies in the United States puts on a dazzling show, so reserve your site early. Drive a loop around **Cades Cove,** which was once home to a mountain community. At the various buildings throughout the community, you can stop and hike, so pick up a map at the visitors center, select a couple of hikes, and hit the trail. **Wildlife viewing** is awesome here, with massive herds of deer and black bears playing in the boughs of apple trees. Good dinner options are located in Gatlinburg and Pigeon Forge.

Day 3
GREAT SMOKY MOUNTAINS
NATIONAL PARK TO CHEROKEE
47 miles; 1.5 hours
After breakfast, begin your cross-park drive via **Newfound Gap Road.** You'll find trailheads all along this twisting mountain road, but for a hike with impressive views, save yourself for **Clingmans Dome,** the highest peak in Tennessee and GSMNP. You'll see signs for Clingmans Dome as Newfound Gap Road crests the Smokies. Head down this spur road to "climb" to the top (the summit is accessible via a walkway and concrete observation platform, not much of a climb) for jaw-dropping views. From here, a 1.75-mile trail leads to **Andrews Bald,** the highest such meadow in the park. In summer, the trail is bombarded with flame azalea and rhododendron.

After hiking to Andrews Bald, get back to Newfound Gap Road and descend into North Carolina and the town of **Cherokee.** Browse the **Qualla Arts and Crafts Mutual,** then stop in at the **Museum of the Cherokee Indian**

Where to Spot Wildlife

All along Skyline Drive and the Blue Ridge Parkway and in Great Smoky Mountains National Park, you'll have the chance for some spectacular wildlife viewing (if you keep your eyes peeled).

a young elk grazing

- **Hawksbill Mountain:** From this peak in the Shenandoah National Park you can see a number of raptors—hawks, falcons, eagles, and the like—riding thermals and hunting the hillsides (page 72).

- **Big Meadows:** The largest meadow along Skyline Drive is visited by dozens of white-tailed deer each morning and evening (page 73).

- **Grandfather Mountain:** On Grandfather Mountain you'll find a small zoo with native animals (including a cougar and pair of bald eagles), but at the Mile High Swinging Bridge, you'll see a number of raptors and vultures riding thermals, and, if you're lucky, a raven or two playing on the wind, flying upside down or holding on to one another as they soar overhead (page 191).

- **Cataloochee:** The Blue Ridge Mountains were the home of elk until the species was hunted out. Today you can see reintroduced herds of elk at Cataloochee Valley, a lovely spot on the north end of Great Smoky Mountains National Park (page 292).

- **Elkmont:** At Elkmont you'll see one of the rarest sights in the world: synchronous fireflies. In a meadow here for approximately two weeks each summer, swarms of fireflies blink in unison at groups on the ground, who blink back (page 301).

- **Cades Cove:** Deer graze the fields and bear laze in the remnants of the apple orchards in this onetime mountain community in Tennessee's Smoky Mountains (page 303).

across the street or **Oconaluftee Indian Village** just up the hill. Spend the night at **Harrah's Cherokee Casino Resort** or opt for a cabin at **Panther Creek Cabins.**

Day 4
CHEROKEE TO BRYSON CITY AND CATALOOCHEE
69 miles; 2 hours

Try your hand at the nickel slots on your way out of Harrah's (you never know) before stopping at **Granny's Kitchen** for a country breakfast buffet. Your next stop is the nearby town

of Bryson City for a mountainside ride aboard the **Great Smoky Mountains Railroad.** You can pair your train ride with a little white-water rafting or ziplining, or you can keep it tame and simply enjoy the scenery.

Backtrack to Cherokee and hop on the **Blue Ridge Parkway.** Today, you'll traverse 25 miles of the Parkway, including some of the road's most rugged mountains and impressive overlooks. After following the Parkway for a short ways, exit onto the Great Smoky Mountains Expressway (US-441) and

Clockwise from top left: gardens at the National D-Day Memorial; Smoky Mountains morning; stunning fall colors lining the Blue Ridge Parkway.

head north toward Waynesville, where you can grab lunch before connecting with I-40 and making your way to the beautiful **Cataloochee Campground** on the North Carolina side of GSMNP. Cataloochee is another former mountain community, but this one has a few residents: **elk.** Cataloochee is a prime spot to see them. Be sure to bring in something to cook; it's a bit of a drive back out for dinner.

Day 5
CATALOOCHEE TO KNOXVILLE
96 miles; 2 hours
If you missed the elk last night, get up early and watch the tree line at the edge of the fields. You'll see them eating their way around the perimeter. Take a little time this morning to check out the haunting and picturesque old church and hike among the other structures in Cataloochee.

When it's time to leave, I-40 will carry you right back into Knoxville in time to get lunch at **Stock & Barrel, The Tomato Head,** or any other restaurant on Knoxville's **Market Square.**

Music of the Blue Ridge

Music plays a major role in defining the culture of the Blue Ridge Mountains. Country music was born in these hills, and bluegrass found its way down from these mountains. Today, musicians perform old-time, gospel, bluegrass, and country music, but you'll also find a vibrant community of progressive musicians and college rock. For some of the best live music, stop in and discover something new.

Washington DC and Charlottesville
Washington DC's legendary **9:30 Club** hosts some of the best acts in the nation. From free shows featuring up-and-coming DC musicians to

concerts by the opera and symphony, the **Kennedy Center** is an American icon in performance. And at the historic **Jefferson Theatre,** you can catch some of Charlottesville's biggest college bands as well as national alternative and rock acts.

Virginia Blue Ridge
Every Friday night in the small town of Floyd, the Floyd Country Store transforms from mercantile to bluegrass concert and dance hall for the **Friday Night Jamboree. FloydFest,** held every summer, is a weekend celebration of music, life, and the mountains. Every August in Galax, listen to that high, lonesome sound of bluegrass and old-time music at the **Old Fiddler's Convention,** a weeklong gathering of musicians, dancers, and string bands.

Free concerts and interactive displays document the history of country and bluegrass music at the **Blue Ridge Music Center** near the Blue Ridge Parkway. Along the **Crooked Road Music Trail,** explore the roots of bluegrass, country, and old-time music via concerts at storied venues, recordings of influential musicians, and waysides that reveal the history of American music.

North Carolina High Country
MerleFest brings together some fabulous roots, Americana, old-time, bluegrass, country, folk, and rock acts.

Asheville
One of the best venues for live music in North Carolina, Asheville's **Orange Peel Social Aid and Pleasure Club** brings in the very best musicians in every genre. A huge **drum circle** forms every Friday night in Pritchard Park.

Knoxville and Vicinity
You'd expect to hear some great music at Dolly Parton's theme park, and hear it you will. Parton herself performs at **Dollywood** from time to time, but the

Fabulous Fall Foliage

As you cruise along Skyline Drive and the Blue Ridge Parkway during October, the height of autumn color, be prepared for two things: a slower pace and a feast for the eyes. You can pull over at any **overlook** for a frame-worthy photo, but check out the list below for the best lookouts, hikes, and vantage points for fall color on the rolling and wrinkled hills of the Blue Ridge and Smoky Mountains.

Skyline Drive

+ **Range View Overlook (MP 17.1):** From here, look down a long stretch of the Blue Ridge with Stony Man Mountain at the far end, and see why the valley adjacent was once called "the Great Wagon Road" (page 67).

+ **Big Run Overlook (MP 81.2):** It's an iconic view for a reason: scenic, breathtaking, and with horizon-to-horizon leaves in fall. On the best days, you'll see veins of quartz twinkling on Rocky Top Ridge across the valley (page 79).

+ **Crimora Lake Overlook (MP 92.6):** Crimora Lake shines from the middle of a sea of fall colors, a gorgeous reminder of what was once a manganese mining operation (page 80).

Blue Ridge Parkway

+ **Rockfish Valley Overlook (MP 2):** Start your trip down the Parkway with a stop looking over the Rockfish River (page 103).

+ **James River Visitor Center (MP 63.6):** The lowest point on the Parkway showcases fall leaves reflected in the wide, placid James River and makes a lovely place for a picnic (page 109).

+ **Peaks of Otter (MP 85.9):** Abbott Lake reflects Flat Top and Sharp Top, the Peaks of Otter, near Bedford (page 112).

+ **Mabry Mill (MP 176.1):** See for yourself why this millhouse and waterwheel is one of the most-photographed places on the Parkway (page 144).

+ **Chestoa View (MP 320.8):** The sweeping views of Linville Gorge are just a short walk from the parking area (page 196).

+ **Orchard at Altapass (MP 328.3):** Admire the views as you pick apples in this historic orchard (page 196).

+ **Looking Glass Rock Overlook (MP 417):** The slick stone face of Looking Glass Rock makes quite the contrast to the green, red, and yellow ridges around (page 249).

+ **Graveyard Fields Overlook (MP 418.8):** The view is lovely from the overlook, but it's even better on the hike to Lower Falls or through the color-studded fields (page 249).

+ **Devil's Courthouse (MP 422.4):** A great view from the overlook only improves when you take the short, steep hike to the knob of rock that is Devil's Courthouse (page 250).

shows by house bands and local and national acts are the true stars. Knoxville's legendary **Tennessee Theatre** has been hosting acts since 1928. Bands, Broadway plays, and symphony concerts are just some of what you'll hear.

The Shenandoah Valley

Bordered to the west by the sharp peaks of the Allegheny Mountains and to the east by the gentle crest of the Blue Ridge, the Shenandoah Valley cuts a slash along Virginia's western border.

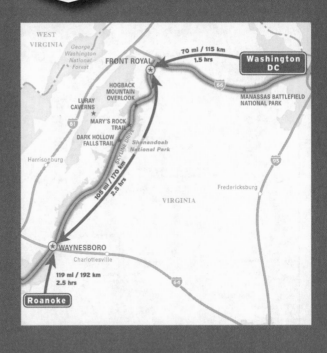

WEST VIRGINIA
George Washington National Forest
FRONT ROYAL
70 ml / 115 km
1.5 hrs
Washington DC
HOGBACK MOUNTAIN OVERLOOK
MANASSAS BATTLEFIELD NATIONAL PARK
LURAY CAVERNS
MARY'S ROCK TRAIL
DARK HOLLOW FALLS TRAIL
Shenandoah National Park
SKYLINE DRIVE
Harrisonburg
105 ml / 170 km
2.5 hrs
Fredericksburg
VIRGINIA
WAYNESBORO
Charlottesville
119 ml / 192 km
2.5 hrs
Roanoke

The Shenandoah Valley

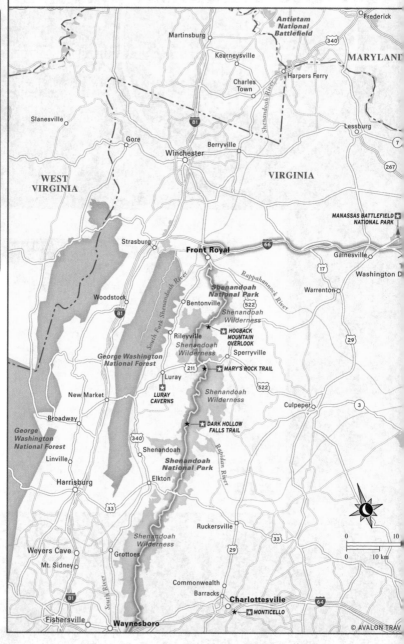

© AVALON TRAV

Highlights

★ **United States Holocaust Memorial Museum:** This moving memorial illustrates the rise of Nazi Germany and the atrocities perpetrated upon European Jews and other ethnic and social groups during World War II (page 40).

★ **National Museum of African American History and Culture:** This museum catalogs the pains and glories of African Americans with exhibits that are as moving as they are enlightening (page 40).

★ **Arlington National Cemetery:** The second-oldest national cemetery contains the Tomb of the Unknown Soldier and the gravesite of JFK, among its monuments to patriotic sacrifice (page 44).

★ **Manassas Battlefield National Park:** The site of two bloody battles during the Civil War, this battlefield is the place where General "Stonewall" Jackson earned his nickname and the Confederate army earned two early victories (page 57).

★ **Hogback Mountain Overlook:** From here you can spot 11 bends of the Shenandoah River and mountains as far as you can see (page 67).

★ **Luray Caverns:** Just west of Skyline Drive, these caverns were discovered in the 1870s and found to contain human bone fragments embedded in a stalagmite (page 69).

★ **Mary's Rock Trail:** This moderate trail leads to a beautiful rock outcrop with sweeping views of the countryside (page 70).

★ **Dark Hollow Falls Trail:** This short trail leads you to a beautiful 70-foot waterfall just off Skyline Drive (page 73).

★ **Monticello:** Thomas Jefferson designed his plantation and primary residence just outside Charlottesville. Today, you can visit his home and his grave (page 87).

The Great Valley, as the Shenandoah Valley is known today, wore the moniker "the Great Wagon Road" for nearly a century as the United States emerged from colonial rebellion and began to form a nation unto itself. Early settlers found it to be an easier route into the unknown interior of the fledgling states than direct routes west.

Hikers on the storied Appalachian Trail experience these seemingly endless ridgelines firsthand (or firstfoot, as it were), much like the early settlers. Traveling stunning Skyline Drive, which runs the length of Shenandoah National Park, gives you a taste of the mountains, and you can even follow the Appalachian Trail for a ways. Hiking in Shenandoah National Park reveals the true wild nature of this place: secluded waterfalls, overlooks with hundred-mile views, caves of unplumbed depths, black bears and white-tailed deer, the hush and hum of nature.

Just 75 miles to the east of Shenandoah National Park's entrance is Washington DC, our nation's capital. Here, museums like those of the Smithsonian Institution are repositories for much of what the United States holds dear and significant in our nation's history, and monuments honor George Washington, Abraham Lincoln, and Martin Luther King Jr. But museums and monuments are only part of the DC experience. Thanks to the influence of diplomats, immigrants, and international visitors, Washington DC has amazing international cuisine and a vibrant culture. You can always find some sort of visual or performing arts to watch, listen to, or take part in yourself.

Washington DC is also a great place to start your 700-mile road trip south along Skyline Drive, the Blue Ridge Parkway, and on to Great Smoky Mountains National Park. On this segment of your journey, from Washington to Front Royal and on to Charlottesville near the start of the Blue Ridge Parkway, you'll pass by the homes of George Washington and Thomas Jefferson as well as Revolutionary and Civil War battlefields. As you travel Skyline Drive through Shenandoah National Park, look out over the countryside. With a little imagination, you can picture this view through the eyes of those settlers, patriots, or Civil War soldiers who marched into battle on their home soil. It's beautiful, wild, and steeped in history.

Planning Your Time

You could spend as little as two days or as much as a week on this stretch of your drive. Washington DC alone is worth a week's stay, and it would be no problem to spend two or three days exploring Shenandoah National Park and then another two or three in Charlottesville.

For the quickest route, spend a day in Washington seeing the monuments and touring your museum of choice, then jump on the road to Front Royal and drive south along Skyline Drive until you reach your campground or room at Big Meadows Lodge or Skyland Resort. The next morning, get in a quick hike and drive through to the end of Skyline Drive, then head to the busy college town of Charlottesville (30 minutes east) or laid-back Waynesboro (5 minutes west) for dinner and to spend the night before starting the Blue Ridge Parkway on the morrow.

Hikers will want to spend more time in Shenandoah National Park, logging some trail miles and enjoying the waterfalls, peaks, and wide views. Wine lovers will want to linger around Charlottesville and tour the wineries there. Monuments, historic sites, and stories line every mile of this route. History buffs will want to slow down and soak them in.

Best Restaurants

★ **Ben's Chili Bowl, Washington DC:** This DC institution, open since 1958, has served the likes of President Obama (page 53).

★ **Bad Saint, Washington DC:** Sample Filipino dishes in an intimate dining room (page 53).

★ **Rasika, Washington DC:** Hit up this spot to taste lesser-known Indian dishes and wine off a renowned list (page 54).

★ **Sfoglina, Washington DC:** Experience Italian dining taken to new heights (page 55).

★ **Mas Tapas, Charlottesville:** Dip into a large menu of small plates at this Spanish- and Mediterranean-inspired restaurant, where many ingredients are locally sourced (page 92).

★ **Fleurie Restaurant, Charlottesville:** Here you'll find outstanding French dining with exceptional tasting menus (page 92).

★ **C&O Restaurant, Charlottesville:** Savor meat-heavy, French-inspired dishes in elegant surroundings (page 92).

THE SHENANDOAH VALLEY

Seasons in this region are gentle. In summer, temperatures sometimes rise into the 90s, though heat like this is uncommon in all but the densest urban areas. Thunderstorms may pop up from time to time, and higher elevations may experience hail and lightning. Watch the weather forecast and plan around oncoming storms.

Driving Considerations

In winter, the region receives snow, but blizzards are nonexistent and shutdowns of major roads or even surface streets are rare in the cities and towns of the region. The exception is Skyline Drive, which, unlike the Blue Ridge Parkway, remains open all winter, except when snow accumulation outpaces the park's ability to maintain roadways. Along Skyline Drive, fog can pop up in any season. If it does, slow down or stop if you need to.

Gasoline is readily and plentifully available along this leg of the route; however, the **Big Meadows Wayside** (MP 51.2) is the only place to fuel up on Skyline Drive.

Getting There

If you're following the full 740-mile route prescribed in this guide, you'll begin in **Washington DC**, the major travel hub on the northern end of your monumental road trip. From here, you'll travel west for **70 miles** along **I-66** to **Front Royal**, Virginia. **Skyline Drive** originates here, meaning that Front Royal is the true start of your journey through the national park's lands.

Skyline Drive heads south through **Shenandoah National Park** for **105.5 miles**, ending in **Rockfish Gap** where the **Blue Ridge Parkway** begins.

The nearest **major travel hubs** to this region are Washington DC; Richmond, Virginia; and Charlottesville, Virginia.

Car

To get to Washington DC from **Richmond**, Virginia, it's a 110-mile, two-hour drive north on I-95. To get directly to Front Royal from Richmond, take I-95 north and I-66 west for a total of 130 miles (2.5 hours).

To get to DC from **Charlottesville**, Virginia, take VA-20 north and I-95 north for a total of 120 miles (2.5 hours). To go straight to Front Royal from

Best Accommodations

★ **Hamilton Hotel Washington DC:** Convenient to transportation lines, this hotel offers comfortable and cozy accommodations (page 57).

★ **Morrison-Clark Historic Inn & Restaurant, Washington DC:** This Civil War-era Victorian mansion is conveniently located for sightseeing (page 57).

★ **Clarion Collection Hotel Arlington Court Suites, Arlington:** Relax in modern suites that are enormous by Washington DC standards (page 57).

★ **Iris Inn, Waynesboro:** Enjoy gorgeous views from your mountaintop room, cabin, or cottage (page 84).

★ **200 South Street Inn, Charlottesville:** Sleep in an 1800s home with Jeffersonian connections, in a great location to boot (page 94).

★ **Arcady Vineyard Bed & Breakfast, Charlottesville:** Wine tour and massage packages make this a perfect home base for a getaway (page 94).

Charlottesville, take US-29 north, VA-231 north, and US-522 north for a total of 75 miles (1 hour, 45 minutes).

Several major interstates—**I-95, I-81, I-64, I-270, I-66**—serve as vehicular arteries for the region, with most roads (excepting I-81 and I-64) leading to Washington DC.

You'll find the offices of most car rental agencies in any of the airports or at Union Station in DC. Available agencies include **Alamo** (844/357-5138, www.alamo.com), **Enterprise** (855/266-9565, www.enterprise.com), **Hertz** (800/654-3131, www.hertz.com), **National** (844/393-9989, www.nationalcar.com), and **Thrifty** (800/344-1705, www.thrifty.com).

Air

A quartet of major airports serves the region: **Washington Dulles International Airport** (IAD, 1 Saarinen Circle, Dulles, Virginia, 703/572-2700, www.flydulles.com) and **Reagan National Airport** (DCA, 2401 Smith Blvd., Arlington, Virginia, 703/417-8000, www.flyreagan.com) in Washington DC, **Baltimore Washington International Airport** (BWI, 7050 Friendship Rd., Baltimore, 410/859-7111, www.bwiairport.com) in Baltimore, and **Charlottesville Albemarle Airport** (CHO, 100 Bowen Loop, Charlottesville, 434/973-8342, www.gocho.com). **Richmond International Airport** (RIC, 1 Richard E. Byrd Terminal Dr., Richmond, 804/226-3000, www.flyrichmond.com) is another option as it's only 116 miles south of DC and is served by American Airlines, Delta, Jet Blue Airways, Southwest, and United.

Taxis are readily available at each airport. Fares vary according to traffic and time. Trips to DC generally cost around $15 from Reagan, $70 from Dulles, and close to $100 from Baltimore. You can use **Supershuttle** (800/258-3826, www.supershuttle.com, around $15 from Reagan, $30 from Dulles, and $40 from Baltimore) to get to downtown DC from any airport.

Train and Bus

Amtrak (800/872-7245, www.amtrak.com) pulls into DC's **Union Station** (50 Massachusetts Ave. NE, 24 hours daily), with trains arriving and departing from destinations all over the Eastern Seaboard. Amtrak services include the Acela Express, Northeast Regional, Silver Service/Palmetto, Cardinal/Hoosier State, Crescent, Vermonter, Capitol Limited, and Carolinian/Piedmont. Via Amtrak, you're 3.75 hours from New

York City, 2.25 hours from Philadelphia, 1.25 hours from Baltimore, Maryland, and 3.25 hours from Richmond, Virginia.

The Amtrak line connects directly to the **Maryland Area Rail Commuter (MARC)** system (410/539-5000 or 866/743-3682, www.mta.maryland.gov), a Monday-Friday commuter service with dozens of trains connecting the Baltimore-Washington corridor, southern Maryland counties, and northeastern West Virginia. It also connects to **Virginia Railway Express** (703/684-1001, www.vre.org), which runs to Manassas and Fredericksburg.

At **Charlottesville's Amtrak station** (CVS, 810 W. Main St., 434/296-4559 or 800/872-7245, www.amtrak.com, 6am-9:30pm daily), the Cardinal/Hoosier State, Crescent, and Northeast Regional lines pass through daily.

Greyhound Bus Lines (202/289-5141 or 202/289-5118, www.greyhound.com) serves Washington DC, arriving and departing from **Union Station** (50 Massachusetts Ave. NE, 24 hours daily). The **Charlottesville Greyhound station** (310 W. Main St., 434/295-5131, www.greyhound.com, 8am-10pm daily) is just a few blocks from the Amtrak station.

Washington DC

Despite all the partisan bickering that goes on in the capital of the United States, there's one thing every political party can agree upon: This city is one of the best in the world. There's great food from far-flung foreign cuisines to Texas barbecue, shopping both vintage and haute couture, and more museums and monuments than you can count. Washington DC is a treasure trove of culture, history, art, and architecture.

At any time of day, the city has beautiful sights to behold: rowing crews slicing down the Potomac at dawn, food vendors undertaking morning rituals at markets across the city, crowds visiting museums and coming out more enlightened for it, monuments lit at night. Casual sightseers will find most of what they came for centered around the National Mall. Explorers looking for the neighborhood treats and DC-only surprises will find what they seek on the side streets away from the busy center of town. The mix of immigrants and emissaries, Congressional staffers and corporate lobbyists, and residents and visitors is the glue that holds the city together.

Getting Around

Most of the major sightseeing highlights in central DC—the National Mall, White House, a bevy of monuments and memorials, the Smithsonian museums, Holocaust Memorial Museum, and Newseum—are within walking distance of one another. Other sights, like Arlington National Cemetery and neighborhood-specific destinations, are simple to get to, thanks to an easy-to-use, efficient rail and bus system. Since so much of what visitors clamor to see is located on or within a block or so of the National Mall, many opt for bike tours or to work their way from sight to sight on foot.

You can drive around the city, but if you're not familiar with the odd diagonal streets, the circles, and a secret place to park near your destination, you're better off with public transportation or a cab. Once you get your bearings and can identify a few landmarks around you, navigating the city is pretty simple.

Metro

The Washington Metropolitan Area Transit Authority (WMATA) operates the DC subway system called the **Metrorail** (202/673-7000, www.wmata.com, 5am-midnight Mon.-Fri., 7am-3am Sat., 8am-midnight Sun.) or simply "the Metro." It covers the downtown area and the suburbs, and expansion is almost constant. Metro stations are identified by a large letter "M" atop a black pylon. For as chaotic as DC can get, the

One Day in Washington DC

Even if you're eager to start your drive, you need to give DC at least a day.

Morning

Start your day by visiting the **National Mall,** where the majority of the Smithsonian's museums line the perimeter. Pick a pair to speed through, or select one to savor with a longer visit. If you're visiting only one museum, make it the **National Museum of African American History and Culture**—but if you aren't lucky enough to get one of the sought-after tickets, the **National Air and Space Museum** is a solid second choice. If you have time for two, add the **National Museum of Natural History,** where you can see everything from the Hope Diamond to Egyptian mummies.

Afternoon

When it's time for lunch, walk east on the Mall toward the Capitol where you can snap a few shots of our seat of government on the way to **We the Pizza.**

After lunch, find a Metro station and take a ride to **Arlington National Cemetery,** where you can pay your respects to John F. Kennedy and countless other American heroes and heroines. While you're there, visit the **Tomb of the Unknown Soldier** to witness the ceremonial changing of the guard.

Evening

On your way back into town, stop by the **Kennedy Center** for one of their **free concerts** held nightly at 6pm on the Millennium Stage, or take a three-hour **nighttime bicycle tour** of the National Mall and monuments with **Bike and Roll.** Then hop in a cab and head to Georgetown for dinner at **DAS Ethiopian Cuisine,** or stick close to the Mall and try **Rasika,** a top-notch, award-winning Indian restaurant with a tasting menu that's out of this world.

Metro system is surprisingly fast, clean, and efficient.

Fares range from $2 to $6 depending on the distance you're traveling and whether you're traveling during peak commute times. There are trains every 5-6 minutes during peak times and every 10-15 minutes at other times. One-day passes are $14.75, and seven-day passes are $38.50 (Short Trip Pass) or $60 (Fast Pass). Make sure you get on the correct side of the tracks for your destination: Look at the maps located by the fare machines and at the digital displays on the various platforms, showing which trains are coming and how soon.

Bus

Metrobuses, run by WMATA, connect with Metrorail stations for travel to outlying areas. Fares are $2-4.25 per trip (exact change only); transfers from the Metrorail are free. One-week passes are $17.50. Buses run on roughly the same schedule as trains. Rail-to-bus and bus-to-bus transfers are possible—simply hand your bus-transfer pass, which you must purchase for each transfer, to the driver of the second bus.

The **DC Circulator** (202/671-2020, www.dccirculator.com) bus system runs six loops:

- **Dupont Circle to Georgetown to Rosslyn** (6am-midnight Sun.-Thurs., 6am-3am Fri., 7am-3am Sat., 7am-midnight Sun.)

- **Georgetown to Union Station** (6am-midnight Mon.-Thurs., 6am-3am Fri., 7am-3am Sat., 7am-midnight Sun.)

- **National Mall Route** (7am-8pm Mon.-Fri., 9am-8pm Sat.-Sun.)

- **Potomac Ave Metro to Skyland** (winter 6am-7pm Mon.-Fri., summer 6am-9pm Mon.-Fri. and 7am-9pm Sat.)

- **Union Station to the Navy Yard** (winter 6am-7pm Mon.-Fri., summer 6am-9pm Mon.-Fri. and 7am-9pm Sat.)

- **Woodley Park to Adams Morgan to McPherson Square** (7am-midnight Sun.-Thurs., 6am-3:30am Fri.-Sat.)

Buses pass every 10 minutes, and tickets are $1.

Taxis and Ride-Hailing Services

Taxicabs in DC operate on time- and distance-based meters. Fares start at $3.25 plus $0.27 for each one-eighth of a mile, with wait time costing $35 per hour (counted fractionally and charged when cab is stopped or slowed less than 10 miles per hour for more than one minute). There are other fees as well: a $0.25 passenger surcharge; $1 for each additional passenger; $2 for telephone dispatch; $15 for a declared snow emergency. It can add up, especially in the oft-heinous traffic here. Top cab companies include **Yellow Cab** (202/544-1212, www.dcyellowcab.com) and, if you're traveling to and from Virginia, **Red Top Cab of Arlington** (703/522-3333, www.redtopcab.com). You can also try **Taxi Transportation Service** (202/398-0500, www.dctaxionline.com, or download their app for your phone or tablet), a cab service with a network of more than 16 cab companies on call in the area.

Ride-hailing services **Uber** (www.uber.com) and **Lyft** (www.lyft.com) have become staples of transportation in DC, and are especially handy for visitors who may be unfamiliar with the Metro or find themselves on a search for some of the District's best sips and bites.

Sights
National Mall

In the midst of the hard urban landscape of Washington DC is a green space to end all green spaces: the **National Mall** (www.nps.gov/nama). When Pierre L'Enfant began planning the future city of Washington DC, his designs included a mile-long, garden-lined boulevard stretching away from the Capitol building. He never knew that this lawn would be the gathering place for Martin Luther King Jr.'s "I Have a Dream" speech, protests against the Vietnam War, the site where the AIDS quilt was first displayed, and many other historic events.

Activism notwithstanding, the National Mall is a popular spot for visitors and residents of the greater DC area. On sunny days, Congressional staffers, FBI types, families, college kids, young professionals, and people from all walks of DC life gather to eat lunch and take in the fresh air, peeling off shoes and socks to feel a little grass between their toes. More than 25 million people visit the National Mall each year. Considering that it's the site of some of the most iconic monuments and memorials—the Washington Monument, reflecting pool, Lincoln Memorial, and the Vietnam War Memorial—and the museums of the Smithsonian Institution, which form its outer border, it's a wonder that number isn't larger.

The National Mall stretches west nearly two miles from the Capitol to the Lincoln Memorial; the Washington Monument stands sentinel in between. At its widest, the Mall is nearly 1,600 feet side to side; at its most narrow, it's still twice the size of a football field. There are a number of free attractions on the Mall. For more information, you can stop a ranger during your visit, or contact the Park Superintendent (900 Ohio Dr. SW, 202/426-6841 or 202/485-9880).

Lincoln Memorial

The **Lincoln Memorial** (2 Lincoln Memorial Circle NW, 202/426-6841, www.nps.gov/linc, 24 hours daily, free), completed in 1922, stands at the west end of the National Mall. Consisting of three iconic parts—the reflecting pool between this memorial and the Washington Monument, the Colorado

The National Mall

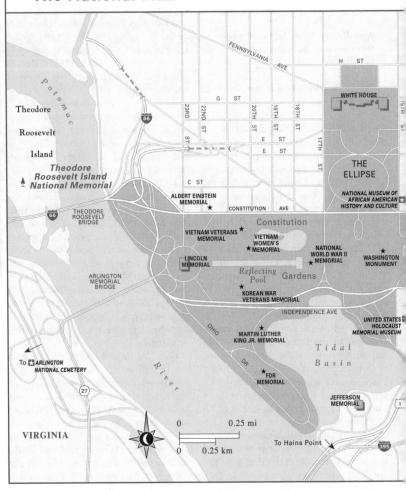

Yule marble exterior resembling a Greek temple, and the 19-foot-tall statue of a seated Abraham Lincoln inside—the Lincoln Memorial is a presence. Part of that palpability comes from Lincoln himself (savior of the Union, breaker of the shackles of American slavery, assassinated in office) and part from its deep significance to the Civil Rights Movement. Martin Luther King Jr. delivered his famous 1963 "I Have a Dream" speech to a crowd of 250,000 strong from these steps, and, on that same day, contralto Marian Anderson performed for the second time in this important spot. Her first performance marked another milestone in Civil Rights history, though one lesser known. In 1939 she was scheduled to perform for the Daughters of the American Revolution in nearby Constitution Hall. They refused to allow a woman of color to take the stage. First

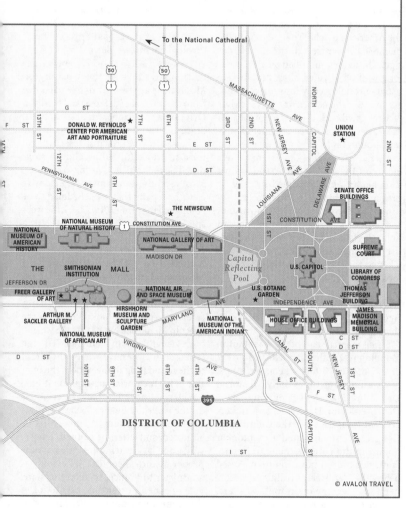

To the National Cathedral

© AVALON TRAVEL

Lady Eleanor Roosevelt and a cadre of like-minded women resigned from the organization over the flap, but Roosevelt took it a step further and arranged an Easter Sunday performance on the steps of the Lincoln Memorial featuring none other than Marian Anderson. Anderson sang that day to a nationwide radio audience and live crowd of 70,000 gathered at the foot of the steps and around the reflecting pool.

Vietnam Veterans Memorial

The evocative **Vietnam Veterans Memorial** (5 Henry Bacon Dr. NW, 202/426-6841, www.nps.gov/vive, 24 hours daily, free) is a simple, but revolutionary, structure, described by designer Maya Lin as "a rift in the earth." Rather than trumpeting the glory of struggle or the legacy of some lauded general, the memorial lists the names of more than 58,000 service members who died in the

Vietnam War. At the time of the memorial's completion in 1982, the war was nearly a decade gone, but still fresh in the American psyche. The response to the memorial was mixed, due to its bold design. The names, inscribed on a 492-foot-long wall of polished black granite, are listed chronologically in order of death. As you read the names, you can see your face reflected back. At the foot of the wall are flowers, flags, tokens, mementos, letters, photographs, and offerings left for the dead. To witness a Vietnam veteran visit the wall, rest his hand against a name, and bow his head in grief or prayer is crushing. It's an important reminder of the power of war, and also of the power that art and monuments can hold. Registers at either end of the wall list the names alphabetically and provide a key to their location for those who are looking for a specific one.

Washington Monument

According to federal law, no structure in the capital can be built higher than the 555-foot tapered shaft of the **Washington Monument** (2 15th St. NW, 877/444-6777 or 877/559-6777 for tickets, www.nps.gov/wamo, 9am-10pm daily Memorial Day-Labor Day, 9am-5pm daily Labor Day-Memorial Day, free but tickets are required). In 1783, the Continental Congress first suggested a monument honoring the nation's inaugural president, but more than a century passed before the idea became reality; from cornerstone to completion took 40 years. During one embarrassing interlude from 1854 to 1876, the obelisk languished as an unsightly stump of 150 feet, described by Mark Twain as "a factory chimney with the top broken off."

When work began again, the marble originally drawn from a Maryland quarry had been exhausted; thus the noticeable change in shade of the remaining 400 feet. The monument finally opened in 1888, with women and children dutifully trudging up the 898 steps (the elevator was considered patently dangerous, braved only by men). Today everyone rides the elevator, ascending to 360-degree views of the capital's historic heart through narrow windows.

Tickets (877/559-6777, www.recreation.gov) to visit the Washington Monument are free, available each day from the kiosk at 15th Street and Madison Drive on a first-come, first-served basis. Since they tend to go quickly, get there early—as in 7am—or just reserve them for a small fee ($1.50) by phone or online. The monument is prone to closures. Most recently, it was closed for extensive elevator repairs that are scheduled to be completed in spring 2019. Check the website for updates.

Jefferson Memorial

A little ways off the Mall proper, the **Jefferson Memorial** (southern end of the Mall, next to the Tidal Basin, 202/426-6841, www.nps.gov/thje, 24 hours daily, free) has an iconic look similar to the Lincoln Memorial, but it lacks the weight, both visually and in its impact. Though Jefferson was immeasurably important to the foundation of the nation, the interior of his memorial lacks the emotional punch you find in Lincoln's. Inscriptions on the walls are long passages from the Declaration of Independence, bills he authored, and letters he penned. They're stuffy and lackluster unless you have the proper historical context. Jefferson was a minister to France, secretary of state, vice president, president, negotiator of the Louisiana Purchase, writer, architect, inventor, and all-around fascinating guy, so to get an idea of his import, try to visit the memorial when park rangers and staff are offering interpretive **tours** (every hour on the hour 10am-11pm daily). This memorial, which opened on April 13, 1943, on the 200th anniversary of Jefferson's birth, is jaw-droppingly beautiful in the spring when the cherry trees that line the Tidal Basin in front of it are in full bloom.

Martin Luther King Jr. Memorial

Not far from where he delivered his impassioned "I Have a Dream" speech, Martin Luther King Jr. stands memorialized in stone. The **Martin Luther King Jr. Memorial** (near intersection of West Basin Dr. SW and Independence Ave. SW, 202/426-6841, www.nps.gov/mlkm, 24 hours daily, free) opened in 2011, 48 years to the week after that famous speech. The memorial's entrance is a monstrous granite slab, cleaved in two as a symbol for the despair felt by African Americans under segregation and Jim Crow laws. Inside the memorial, curved walls inscribed with quotes from King surround you, and a 28-foot-tall statue of King himself emerges from a rough-hewn rock known as the Stone of Hope. It's a fascinating monument and increasingly relevant.

National Gallery of Art

One of the finest collections in the world, the **National Gallery of Art** (600 Constitution Ave. NW, 202/737-4215, www.nga.gov, 10am-5pm Mon.-Sat., 11am-6pm Sun., free) is housed in two separate facilities. In the 1930s, the museum's west wing sprang full-grown from the wallet of rapacious banker Andrew Mellon, who wisely declined to append his name to the edifice. I. M. Pei designed the angular east wing, which was built in 1978 and boasts one of the sharpest corners you'll ever see on a building. Both wings are constructed of pink Tennessee marble, but there the similarity ends: the east displays 20th- and 21st-century works by the likes of Miró, Magritte, and Matisse, while the homier, more crowded west wing is the domain of classic art by the likes of Raphael, Rembrandt, and Renoir.

Historians of the presidency are invariably drawn to the west wing, which sits

Top to bottom: cherry blossoms framing the Washington Monument; National Museum of Natural History; the courtyard at the National Portrait Gallery.

over the bones of the old B&P Railroad Station where, in 1881, President James A. Garfield was shot twice in the back by Charles Guiteau. Across 7th Street from the west wing is a pleasant **sculpture garden** (10am-7pm Mon.-Thurs. and Sat., 10am-9:30pm Fri., 11am-7pm Sun., free) full of whimsical works.

The **Gallery Shops** at the National Gallery of Art have an extensive collection of art books that range from pricey coffee table books to nonfiction books about artists, and a great selection of children's books and art activities. Some great, affordable takeaways are unframed prints, postcard books, calendars, magnets, stationery, and select jewelry pieces.

Smithsonian Institution

When English chemist James Smithson passed away in 1829, he willed to the United States 105 bags of gold sovereigns to found "at Washington, under the name of the Smithsonian Institution, an establishment for the increase and diffusion of knowledge." This was no small sum of money: in fact, it was his entire estate, totaling around $500,000, which, at the time was one-sixty-sixth of the total budget for the United States. After several long conversations, Congress accepted the gift in 1836, but it wasn't until 1846 that President James K. Polk signed an act of Congress to establish the Smithsonian Institution. The resulting museums are some of the most important in the world, holding troves of artifacts and relics relevant not only to U.S. history but also to the development of human culture as a whole.

Nineteen museums, galleries, gardens, and zoos in DC operate under the **Smithsonian Institution** (administrative offices at 1000 Jefferson Dr. SW, 202/633-1000, www.si.edu). Most of them are on the National Mall or within a few blocks of it. The hours of individual museums differ, but generally museums are open 10am-5:30pm daily (except Dec. 25); check before you visit. Best of all, they're

National Air and Space Museum

free, meaning anyone can bask in the "increase and diffusion of knowledge" Smithson envisioned.

The **National Museum of Natural History** and **National Air and Space Museum** are two of the most popular Smithsonian museums. Others include the **Smithsonian Castle** (1000 Jefferson Dr. SW, 202/633-1000, www.si.edu, 8:30am-5:30pm daily, free), **National Museum of American History** (14th St. and Constitution Ave. NW, 202/633-1000, www.americanhistory.si.edu, 10am-5:30pm daily, free), **American Art Museum** (8th St. and F St. NW, 202/633-1000, www.americanart.si.edu, 11:30am-7pm daily, free), **National Museum of African Art** (950 Independence Ave. SW, 202/633-1000, www.africa.si.edu, 10am-5:30pm daily, free), the **National Museum of the American Indian** (4th St. and Independence Ave. SW, 202/633-6644, www.nmai.si.edu, 10am-5:30pm daily, free), the **National Zoo** (3001 Connecticut Ave. NW, 202/633-4888, www.nationalzoo.si.edu, 10am-6pm daily Apr.-Oct., 10am-4:30pm daily Nov.-Mar., free), the **Freer Gallery of Art and the Arthur M. Sackler Gallery** (1050 Independence Ave. SW, 202/633-1000, www.asia.si.edu, 10am-5:30pm daily, free), and the **National Portrait Gallery** (8th St. and F St. NW, 202/633-8300, www.npg.si.edu, 11:30am-7pm daily, free), among others.

National Museum of Natural History

The **National Museum of Natural History** (10th St. and Constitution Ave., 202/633-1000, www.mnh.si.edu, 10am-5:30pm daily, open late select dates, free) is just one small part of a larger set of facilities around the United States (and in a few foreign locales) that collect, analyze, and exhibit items that tell the story of our world, inside and out. The museum's holdings are impressive—126 million specimens and artifacts, including 30 million insects, 7 million fish, 4.5 million plants, and 2 million cultural artifacts from around the globe.

Only a small portion of the awesome and extensive collection is on display, but what is shown at the National Museum of Natural History is a wonder. Take a look at the Hope Diamond, a 45.52-carat diamond (it's the size of a walnut) with a long and twisting history that includes a possible curse; it's just one part of a spectacular display of gems. There are also displays on ocean life (including a living coral reef), a butterfly pavilion, mummies from ancient Egypt (including a mummified cat), and rotating displays and exhibits that often include some of the best wildlife and cultural photography from every corner of the globe.

National Air and Space Museum

From the moment you walk through the door of the **National Air and Space Museum** (Independence Ave. and 6th St. SW, 202/633-2214, www.airandspace.si.edu, 10am-5:30pm daily, open late select dates, free), you're immersed in the

technology and boldness that allowed humankind to take to the sky and explore outer space. Rockets, satellites, and spy planes hang from the ceiling. In each of the 20 or so exhibition halls, you'll find everything from the Wright Flyer to space suits to a moon rock you can touch. There's the Apollo 11 Command Module, Sputnik, and a collection of WWI and II aircraft. This is the most popular museum in the United States, seeing more than eight million visitors a year here and at the **Steven F. Udvar-Hazy Center** (14390 Air and Space Museum Pkwy., Chantilly, Virginia, 703/572-4118, www. airandspace.si.edu, 10am-5:30pm daily, free), so expect company no matter when you visit.

★ United States Holocaust Memorial Museum

Nothing prepares you for a visit to the **United States Holocaust Memorial Museum** (100 Raoul Wallenberg Pl. SW and Independence Ave., 202/488-0400, www.ushmm.org, 10am-5:20pm daily, free), and in truth, it's hard to comprehend this historical black mark either before or after a visit. But it's a required sight if for no other reason than the adage "those who don't know history are destined to repeat it" holds more truth than we may like to admit.

The building exterior was designed to resemble the high brick ovens used to dispose of the bodies of millions of European Jews. Inside, exhibits methodically trace the rise of Nazi Germany and the systematic implementation of its policy of genocide. Visitors witness many depictions of horrific atrocities, but perhaps the most affecting items are the heaps of personal effects the Nazis collected from those they murdered, including piles of shoes, brushes, and hair.

You'll need a **timed pass** to visit the permanent collection. A limited number are distributed at the museum each morning; otherwise, you can order passes and make reservations for your tour for a nominal fee (www.ushmm.org, $1). Allow at least 3-4 hours to visit. The permanent exhibition is not recommended for children under age 11.

★ National Museum of African American History and Culture

The **National Museum of African American History and Culture** (1400 Constitution Ave. NW, 844/750-3012, www.nmaahc.si.edu, 10am-5:30pm daily, free) cuts a striking figure, simultaneously boxlike and organic. The building itself is a statement about the legacy of African Americans. Look closely at the facade and you'll see a design built into it, which was inspired by ironworks made by enslaved Africans.

The exterior is only part of the story, though. The rest is told inside, some of it through architecture. The first exhibit hall is three floors underground, and as you move through eras of African American history, the exhibit halls get larger, more open, and lighter. As you move to the top floor, you're finally in the sun. Gripping displays explore African American contributions to literature and art, music, sports, and culture, and thousands of artifacts and photographs tell the African American story from enslavement through the Civil Rights Movement to today.

The museum's **Sweet Home Café** (202/633-6174, 10am-5pm daily, $8-18), the last stop for many visitors, puts a stamp on the experience by revealing the broad influence African Americans have had on the nation's culinary development. With four dining stations telling the distinct food stories of the Agricultural South (with Gullah-style dishes), the Creole Coast (think po'boys and shrimp and grits), North States (smoked turkey, pepper pot), and the Western Range (pan-roasted trout, beef brisket), it's one more way to measure the breadth and depth of African Americans' influence on the development of American culture.

There's only one problem with the

museum: It's popular, meaning tickets are notoriously difficult to procure. Timed passes are released online for visits 3-4 months out; these tickets are free, but limited to six per transaction, and are up for grabs beginning at 9am Eastern on the first Wednesday of the month. Same-day tickets are available online beginning at 6:30am Eastern daily. A limited number of walk-up tickets are available at the ticket counter on weekdays beginning at 1pm, but you can only get one per person using this method. Try for your tickets well in advance, and if that doesn't work, try online the day of your visit or get in line early (and with everyone from your party) to get those walk-up tickets. However you procure yours, this museum is well worth the effort and the wait.

The White House

First occupied by John Adams, the mansion at 1600 Pennsylvania Avenue NW was known as the President's House until it was whitewashed to cover smoke damage from the 1814 British burning of the city. It's not nearly as accessible today as it was during Jefferson's time, when the president examined mastodon fossils in the East Room and enthusiastic dairymen would bustle in to deposit huge cheeses. Nevertheless, it's the only chief executive's abode in the world that is open to tourists. When visiting the **White House** (1600 Pennsylvania Ave. NW, 202/456-7041, www.whitehouse. gov, by tour only), don't step across the boundary ropes or make other foolish moves—those friendly folks patrolling the halls can turn serious quickly.

Tours (7:30am-11:30am Tues.-Thurs., 7:30am-1:30pm Fri.-Sat., free) are available, though on a very restricted schedule. For tickets to the self-guided tour, contact your member of Congress; foreign citizens must submit tour requests through their Washington DC embassy. Requests for tickets can be submitted up to six months in advance and no less than

21 days before your visit. Submit your request early as this is a very popular tour. Also, it *is* the White House, so tours can be canceled on a moment's notice.

United States Capitol

Any first-time visitor to DC should take advantage of the opportunity to peek into the **Capitol** (east end of the National Mall, 202/226-8000, www. visitthecapitol.gov, by tour only) and see our elected congressional officials at work. The small but well-appointed Senate chamber offers each senator a private desk separate from the rest, whereas House representatives are jammed together in long, curved pews. The rest of the building presents its own peculiar charms: niches and rotundas stuffed with statues, long marble halls, paintings and frescoes everywhere. A word of warning: Much of the Capitol is off-limits to non-officeholders, and visitors must heed the guidance of Capitol police.

Visiting the Capitol on a guided **tour** (free) is much easier than securing a ticket for a White House tour. You still need to schedule a tour in advance, through your Senator or Representative, or online, though there are some same-day tour passes available. There is also a **Visitor Center** (8:30am-4:30pm Mon.-Sat.) at the Capitol. If you're interested in observing the Senate or House of Representatives when they're in session, you can get a pass from your Senator or Representative that will allow you access to the balcony galleries in their respective chambers.

Sightseeing Tours

One of the best ways to see the monuments and museums on the National Mall is by bicycle. Though most of DC's surface streets lack bike lanes (and what city-biking novice wants to negotiate that traffic?), around the Mall, you'll find biking easy. **Bike and Roll** (955 L'Enfant Plaza SW, 202/842-2453, http://bikeandrolldc.com, tours daily Mar.-early Dec., bike tours $40-45 adults, $30-35 children, Segway tours $49-65 adults only, call for age and height requirements) leads a number of guided excursions to see the sights and hear tidbits of DC trivia on the Mall via bike or Segway.

Outside the Mall
Newseum

It's easy to spend hours at the **Newseum** (555 Pennsylvania Ave. NW, 202/292-6100, www.newseum.org, 9am-5pm Mon.-Sat., 10am-5pm Sun., $25 adults, $20 seniors, $15 ages 7-18, free 6 and younger), one of the best museums in DC. Seven floors of interactive exhibits display some of the most famous newspaper front pages in history as well as artifacts, photographs, newsreels, and firsthand accounts, helping you understand the importance of journalism (the so-called "fourth estate") and our First Amendment rights.

Downstairs, there's a long section of the Berlin Wall and a guard tower that once watched over it. Upstairs, the 9/11 Gallery contains a piece of the spire from the World Trade Center's North Tower and a wall of front pages from every major paper around the globe as they relayed word of the attack; it's an overwhelming exhibit. On the main floor, a gallery containing all of the Pulitzer Prize-winning photographs gets to the heart of what constitutes great journalism.

Inside the excellent **gift shop,** you'll find journalism-related gifts (so, lots of coffee mugs). They also have books of award-winning photography and essays, and headline bloopers.

The Phillips Collection

The Phillips Collection (1600 21st St. NW, 202/387-2151, www.phillipscollection.org, 10am-5pm Tues.-Sat., 11am-6pm Sun., open until 8:30pm on first Thurs. of the month, museum collection by donation Tues.-Fri., ticketed exhibitions and extended Thurs. hours $12 adults, $10 students and seniors, free 18

and under), America's first museum of modern art, opened in 1921. Housed in a beautiful 1897 Georgian Revival house in the Dupont Circle neighborhood, The Phillips Collection contains some remarkable pieces by Vincent van Gogh, Pierre-Auguste Renoir, Henri Matisse, Paul Cézanne, Winslow Homer, Paul Klee, Mark Rothko, Willem de Kooning, and Jackson Pollock.

International Spy Museum

Live out your secret agent fantasies at the **International Spy Museum** (800 F St. NW, 202/393-7798, www.spymuseum.org, 10am-6pm daily, $22 adults, $16 seniors, military, and law enforcement, $15 ages 7-11, free 6 and under), where interactive exhibits include the tools used by spies the world over, information on tradecraft, famous spy capers and incidents, and a series of stations where you, under cover as a spy with an assumed name and backstory, have to use what you've learned to evade capture by counterintelligence agents. Fee-based extras up the ante, including Operation Spy ($15), an interactive spy mission, and Spy in the City ($15), a GPS-led walking tour of the neighborhood. The **Spy Museum Store** (www.spymuseumstore.org, museum admission not required) has a ton of fun toys, games, and spy gadgets.

National Portrait Gallery

The **National Portrait Gallery** (8th and F Sts. NW, 202/633-8300, www.npg.si.edu, 11:30am-7pm daily, free) tells the story of America through the individuals who helped shape its history and culture. Exhibitions of portraits, sculptures, and busts include ones dedicated to key figures and events 1600-1900, 20th-century Americans, performing artists, sports figures, pop-culture icons, and presidents. The National Portrait Gallery is connected to the **Smithsonian American Art Museum** (8th and F Sts. NW, 202/633-1000, www.americanart.si.edu, 11:30am-7pm daily, free), where you can see some absolutely astounding pieces of fine and folk art. Between the two buildings is the lovely and restful Kogod Courtyard (where there's free Wi-Fi and decent coffee).

Sightseeing Tours

City Segway Tours (502 23rd St. NW, 202/626-0017, www.citysegwaytours.com, $75) zips you around to the museums, monuments, and memorials on those fun little two-wheeled vehicles. If you've never ridden one, this is a good place to try it. If you're more comfortable on a bike, the company has daytime and nighttime monument tours on standard (from $49) and electric (from $79) bikes.

DC Ducks (Union Station, 50 Massachusetts Ave. NE, 866/754-5039, www.dcducks.com, $39 adults, $29 children 12 and under) takes you on a tour of the city in these strange World War II amphibious vehicles we call "ducks." Your driver will be part historian and part comic, which makes the ride lots of fun. At the end, you'll head into the Potomac River to ride to a point near Reagan National Airport.

Old Town Trolley Tours (Union Station, 50 Massachusetts Ave. NE, 844/356-2603, www.trolleytours.com, $39-59 adults, $29 children age 4-12, free 3 and under) offers hop-on, hop-off sightseeing that takes you all around the city, making 20 stops along the way. Stops include Arlington National Cemetery, the National Cathedral, Georgetown, the National Mall, and a ton of monuments.

The **Potomac Riverboat Company** (703/684-0580 or 877/511-2628, www.potomacriverboatco.com) has a small fleet that plies the waters around the capital. There is a 40-minute narrated sightseeing tour to Alexandria (departures 11am, noon, and 1pm Tues.-Fri. Mar.-Aug., hourly 11am-8pm Sat.-Sun.

Top to bottom: the Tomb of the Unknown Soldier at Arlington National Cemetery; colorful homes in Georgetown; Dupont Circle.

Sept.-Oct., $12 adults, $6 children); another boat runs between the Alexandria and Georgetown docks (every 1-2 hours daily Mar.-Sept., every 1-2 hours Sat.-Sun. Oct., $24 adults, $12 children round-trip). You can also take a cruise to Mount Vernon and Alexandria (departures from Alexandria at 10:30am, Gaylord National Hotel at 11am, and National Harbor at 11:10am, Apr.-late Oct., $15-32).

★ Arlington National Cemetery

The country's second-oldest national cemetery, **Arlington National Cemetery** (across Memorial Bridge from the Lincoln Memorial, Arlington, Virginia, 877/907-8585, www.arlingtoncemetery.mil, 8am-7pm daily Apr.-Sept., 8am-5pm daily Oct.-Mar., free, parking $2 hour), spreads over 624 acres of rolling hills across the Potomac from DC. The resting place for more than 400,000 active-duty service members, veterans, their families, heads of state, and others whose service to our

country is unheralded, Arlington is a beautiful and somber place to visit. The gravesite of John F. Kennedy and the elaborate Changing of the Guard at the Tomb of the Unknown Soldier attract visitors wishing to pay their respects to the sacrifices made by the individuals interred here.

History

Arlington National Cemetery began as a thousand-acre plantation owned by George Washington Parke Custis, grandson of Martha Washington and adopted son of George Washington. The centerpiece was Arlington House, built as a memorial to our first president. In 1857, the property came into the hands of Custis's daughter, Mary, and her husband, General Robert E. Lee. When General Lee accepted command of Virginia's army at the onset of the Civil War, he resigned his commission with the U.S. Army and left, never to return to Arlington House. After a brief

Arlington National Cemetery

occupation by Virginia militiamen, the house and estate were taken and held by Union forces.

In 1864, the 1,100-acre estate was confiscated by the federal government when Mary couldn't appear in person to pay the property taxes. Quartermaster General Montgomery Meigs, a Georgian who had remained loyal to the Union, considered Lee the worst kind of traitor and came up with a scathing revenge: the burial of Union dead, literally, in Lee's backyard. Meigs crossed the Potomac to personally oversee the interment of the first Union soldiers in Mary's rose garden. Eventually, 16,000 Civil War soldiers were buried in the fields around Arlington House.

After the war, Lee's grandson, George Washington Custis Lee, sued the U.S. government for possession of the estate and won after taking the case to the Supreme Court. In 1883, he sold it back to the government for $150,000 (more than $3 million in today's dollar). Two hundred surrounding acres were set aside to start the cemetery.

Visiting the Cemetery

Your first stop should be the **Welcome Center** (by the cemetery entrance, 877/907-8585, www.arlingtoncemetery. mil, 8am-7pm daily Apr.-Sept., 8am-5pm daily Oct.-Mar.), where you can view displays detailing the history of the cemetery and, more importantly, grab a map. You'll need it, as the cemetery can be confusing, and it's a hike between commonly visited sites—namely the Kennedy graves and the Tomb of the Unknown Soldier. The cemetery also offers free shuttle service for individuals to visit a specific gravesite. If it's hot, you're tired, or you're traveling with little ones or seniors, the **Arlington National Cemetery Official Tour Company** (866/754-9014, www.arlingtontours.com, 8am-5pm daily Oct.-Mar., 8am-7pm daily Apr.-Sept., $13.50 adults, $10 seniors ages 65 and up, $6.75 children ages 4-12) takes a small bus to the major spots in the cemetery.

The most visited spot in the cemetery is the Kennedy graves. Situated on a grassy knoll that has magnificent views of the National Mall across the Potomac are the graves of President **John F. Kennedy,** his wife **Jacqueline Kennedy Onassis,** and their two infant children, with an **Eternal Flame** burning at their heads. Nearby are the graves of Senators **Robert Kennedy** and **Ted Kennedy.**

On the hilltop above the Kennedys sits **Arlington House** (703/235-1530, www. nps.gov/arho, 9am-6pm daily Apr.-Sept., 9:30am-4:30pm daily Oct.-Mar., free), a Greek Revival mansion and former home to Robert E. Lee.

Look for the white marble **Memorial Amphitheater** and pass behind it to reach the **Tomb of the Unknown Soldier.** This tomb holds the remains of unidentified soldiers from World War I, World War II, and the Korean War. Dating back to 1926, the tomb was built from more than 50 tons of white Yule marble from

Colorado. Guards from the Army's 3rd Infantry, called the Old Guard, keep a constant vigil. These tomb sentinels march 21 unerring steps back and forth, then snap their heels and recouch their rifles at every turn. Crowds gather for the **changing of the guard** (every 30 minutes daily Apr.-Sept., every hour daily Oct.-Mar.) and watch in awed silence as the on-duty officer inspects and gives orders to the sentinel going on duty and the one coming off. For a moment, they march in unison, looking like reflections of each other. The tomb also held the remains of an unknown Vietnam War veteran until 1998, when DNA evidence revealed his identity as Lieutenant Michael Blassie, an Air Force pilot shot down in 1972. Blassie was disinterred and reburied closer to home.

Two more memorials of note are worth seeing. The **Women in Service Memorial** (www.womensmemorial.org), at the entrance to the cemetery, pays tribute to the women who have served in all five armed services as well as the affiliated women's auxiliaries like the WAVES and WACS of World War II. The **U.S. Marine Corps War Memorial** (www.nps.gov/gwmp) depicts in bronze the iconic photograph of a group of marines raising the American flag on Iwo Jima in World War II and honors all marines who've given their lives in service to the United States since the inception of the Corps.

Mount Vernon

Just 15 miles southwest of DC is **Mount Vernon** (3200 Mount Vernon Memorial Hwy., Mount Vernon, Virginia, 703/780-2000, www.mountvernon.org, 9am-5pm daily, $20 adults, $16 seniors, $9 ages 6-11, free under 5), the riverfront plantation of George Washington. The property includes Washington's 1735 manor; manicured gardens and wooded grounds; outbuildings and working buildings; and the tombs of George and Martha Washington. From the bluff nearly 200 feet above the Potomac River,

the mansion overlooks the countryside of Maryland. A few miles west are Washington's distillery and gristmill. In 1799, Washington's distillery was the largest in the country, producing nearly 11,000 gallons of whiskey.

In the mansion and Donald W. Reynolds Museum and Education Center are impressive collections of furnishings and artifacts, including the key to the Bastille and even some of Washington's false teeth. You'll see for yourself (you read it here first!) that they're not made of wood.

A variety of themed tours are available, including garden tours, a tour about slave life, and a tour detailing canine life at Mount Vernon. From mid-March into fall, you can take a **Potomac River Tour** ($10 adults, $6 ages 6-11, free 5 and under) with the **Potomac Riverboat Company** (877/511-2628, www.potomacriverboatco.com).

Guided bus tours from **Gray Line** (202/779-9894, www.graylinedc.com, from $39) and **On Board Tours** (301/839-5261, www.washingtondctours.onboardtours.com, $80 adults, $70 children) will bring you to Mount Vernon and Alexandria. Bikers can pedal to the estate on the 18-mile-long **Mount Vernon Trail,** though the 36 miles round-trip from Arlington to Mount Vernon is taxing. By car, take the George Washington Memorial Parkway, which passes right by Arlington National Cemetery and Reagan National Airport, along the Potomac, through Alexandria, and right to Mount Vernon. **Potomac Riverboat Company** (877/511-2628, www.potomacriverboatco.com, $42 adults, $22 ages 6-11, Mount Vernon admission included) offers tours of the Potomac with a four-hour stopover at Mount Vernon.

Entertainment and Events
Nightlife
Bars and Clubs
ChurchKey (1337 14th St. NW, 202/567-2576, www.churchkeydc.com, 4pm-late

Day Trip to Old Town Alexandria

For a great day trip from DC, visit **Mount Vernon,** the home of our first president, then stop in **Alexandria** (www.visitalexandriava.com) on the way back for dinner and shopping. In Alexandria, you'll find a charming downtown, a lovely waterfront, and an impressive collection of shops, restaurants, and sights. The center of it all is charming Old Town Alexandria, which stretches back a few blocks from the Potomac River.

Grab a bite to eat at **Gadsby's Tavern** (138 N. Royal St., 703/548-1288, www.gadsbystavernrestaurant.com, 11:30am-3pm and 5:30pm-10pm Mon.-Sat., 11am-3pm and 5:30pm-9:30pm Sun., $15-30), where George Washington celebrated his 66th birthday; **Taverna Cretekou** (818 King St., 703/548-8688, www.tavernacretekou.com, 11:30am-2:30pm and 5pm-10pm Tues-Fri., noon-10:30pm Sat., 11am-3pm and 5pm-9:30pm Sun., $12-36), a Greek restaurant with lovely outdoor seating; or **Nasime** (1209 King St., 703/548-1848, www.nasimerestaurant.com, 5pm-10pm Tues.-Thurs., 5pm-10:30pm Fri.-Sat., 5pm-9:30pm Sun., $48), a Japanese restaurant serving a five-course tasting menu.

There are a number of high-end shops and boutiques to check out. **Bishop Boutique** (815-B King St., 571/312-0042, www.bishopboutique.com, 10am-7pm Mon.-Sat., 11am-5pm Sun.) has shoes and accessories; **An American in Paris** (1225 King St., Suite 1, 703/519-8234, www.anamericaninparisoldtown.com, 11am-8pm Mon.-Fri., 11am-7pm Sat.-Sun.) is filled with one-of-a kind, stylish pieces of clothing. Consignment shops include **Mint Condition** (103 S. Saint Asaph St., 703/836-6468, www.shopmintcondition.com, 11am-7pm Tues.-Sat., noon-6pm Sun.) and **Current Boutique** (1009 King St., 703/549-2272, www.currentboutique.com, noon-8pm Mon.-Fri., 11am-8pm Sat., 11am-6pm Sun.).

Other spots to check out are the **Torpedo Factory Art Center** (105 N. Union St., 703/838-4565, www.torpedofactory.org, 10am-6pm Fri.-Wed., 10am-9pm Thurs., individual studio hours vary), a former torpedo factory filled with galleries, studios, and workshop spaces; and any of the dozen galleries and studios along the waterfront and a block or two back.

Mon.-Fri., 11:30am-late Sat.-Sun.), upstairs from Birch & Barley restaurant, serves a small menu of tasty snacks and small plates ($8-25), but it's the beer that brought you here. They have five cask ales, 50 beers on draft, and 500 bottles at any given time, and they've designed their beer menu with headings like "Fruit & Spice," "Roast," and "Tart & Funky," so that you can easily find a beer you'll like. I prefer dark, heavy beers or sours, lambics, and wild ales, and ChurchKey has plenty to offer someone with my palate. They also have an awesome array of IPAs, lagers, and ales.

Jack Rose Dining Saloon (2007 18th St. NW, 202/588-7388, www.jackrosediningsaloon.com, 5pm-2am Sun.-Thurs., 5pm-3am Fri.-Sat.) keeps a cheeky counter on their website that tallies the number of "Bottles of whisk(e)y on the wall" of their establishment. A visit here will reveal bottles of bourbon, scotch, whiskey, whisky, rye, and other spirits on the wall. They also have beers and wine, but brown liquor is where it's at. You can build your own flights from an incredible range of rare and exotic spirits or talk to one of the bartenders and have one built for you around your tastes and budget.

Number Nine (1435 P St. NW, 202/986-0999, www.numberninedc.com, 5pm-late Mon.-Fri., 2pm-late Sat.-Sun., happy hour 5pm-9pm Mon.-Thurs., 2pm-9pm Sat.-Sun.) is a chic gay bar in the heart of Logan Circle. The second floor (cleverly called 9 1/2) is a video bar where they show select sports, but more often movies and music videos by the club's VJs. On the first floor, you'll find a plush, well-appointed, modern bar with extensive seating options. The bartenders know their stuff, and though you can go up and order a classic cocktail, it's more fun to try a bartender's choice or one of the house specials.

Live Music
At **Columbia Station** (2325 18th St. NW, 202/462-6040, www.columbiastationdc.com, 5pm-2am Tues.-Thurs., 5pm-3am Fri.-Sun.) in the Adams Morgan neighborhood, you can hear live jazz every night it's open. This is a popular spot and known for staging some of the top regional jazz acts, so check their schedule and pick a show.

You can't write about live music in DC without including the **9:30 Club** (815 V St. NW, 202/265-0930, www.930.com, box office noon-7pm Mon.-Fri.; show nights noon-11pm Mon.-Fri., 6pm-11pm Sat., and 6pm-10:30pm Sun., show times vary), DC's most popular small venue for rock bands and artists from a range of genres. The stage is visible from just about everywhere in the club, and with four bars, you never have to wait long for a drink. My advice is to arrive early and find a spot up by the stage so you can listen to a few songs up close. Don't be alarmed if you see kids; 9:30 is an all-ages club (except for specified shows).

Black Cat (1811 14th St. NW, 202/667-4490, www.blackcatdc.com, box office 6:30pm-midnight Mon.-Fri., 7pm-midnight Sat.-Sun., show times vary, cash only) is a fantastic venue for live music, stand-up comics, and more. Bands tend toward the indie-rock side of things, and you'll catch both known and up-and-coming acts here. This place is cash only.

Madam's Organ (2461 18th St. NW, 202/667-5370, www.madamsorgan.com, 5pm-2am Sun.-Thurs., 5pm-3am Fri.-Sat.) features blues, R&B, rock, bluegrass, salsa, and just about every genre of music under the sun every night of the week. Four floors, five bars, and an enormous mural of the Madam herself on the outside of the building make this place hard to miss. Redheads take note: They love a redhead here, so there's always a half-price drink special just for you.

Performing Arts
The John F. Kennedy Center for the Performing Arts
The crown jewel of the DC performing arts scene is without a doubt **The John F. Kennedy Center for the Performing Arts** (2700 F St. NW, 202/467-4600 or 800/444-1324, www.kennedy-center.org). You can go on a free **tour** (10am-5pm Mon.-Fri., 10am-1pm Sat.-Sun.) of the Kennedy Center, visiting the center's three grand performance halls, the Hall of States and Hall of Nations, and ending on the rooftop terrace. You have the option of dropping in for a walk-in tour or reserving a group tour (if you're traveling with 20 of your closest friends).

The tours are nice, but the best way to see the Kennedy Center is to take in a performance. Various theatrical performances, concerts, and events occur throughout the year, so check the calendar to see who and what will be there while you're in town.

The Kennedy Center is home to the **National Symphony Orchestra (NSO)** (www.kennedy-center.org/nso), founded in 1931 and consistently performing 175 or so concerts a year. The **Washington National Opera** (www.kennedy-center.org/wno) also calls the Kennedy Center home, as does **The Suzanne Farrell Ballet** (www.kennedy-center.org/sfb). Ticket prices vary by performance, but it's a good idea to reserve tickets well ahead of time if you're interested in taking in a major production. If you're more inclined to a free performance, which could be anything from a concert to a comic to a dance troupe, check out the **Millennium Stage,** which hosts free events nightly at 6pm.

Other Venues

Probably the most famous of all theaters in DC, or even the United States, is **Ford's Theatre** (511 10th St. NW, 202/347-4833, www.fordstheatre.org). Here, the assassin John Wilkes Booth shot President Abraham Lincoln, who was sitting in his box enjoying a production of *Our American Cousin*. Take in a performance here and sit within feet of that infamous balcony box, or **tour** (9am-4:30pm daily, free) the theater with a guide or a park ranger. You can also do a self-directed tour. Check their calendar for exact tour times; tickets are free at the door, or you can get advance tickets ($2.50) by calling the theater.

The elegant **National Theatre** (1321 Pennsylvania Ave. NW, 202/628-6161, www.thenationaldc.org) is the third-oldest theater in the country, and the longest in continuous operation in DC. Just two days after opening its doors on December 7, 1835, they staged their first production, *Hamlet*. Plays like *West Side Story* and *Hello, Dolly!* premiered here. If you want to catch a show, check the schedule to see what's playing, and know that the balcony seats are quite steep and narrow, so you may want to spring for orchestra seats.

If you're a fan of Shakespeare, then the **Folger Theatre** (201 E. Capitol St. SE, 202/544-7077 or 202/544-4600, www.folger.edu) and **Shakespeare Theatre Company** (450 7th St. NW, 202/547-1122, www.shakespearetheatre.org) deliver exactly what you're looking for. The Folger Theatre is an extension of the Folger Shakespeare Library, and they stage several performances each year of works by the Bard and other fantastic playwrights. The Shakespeare Theatre Company also stages plays by Shakespeare as well as excellent contemporary playwrights.

The Capitol Steps (www.capsteps.com) comedy troupe likes to say they "put the 'mock' in Democracy," and they do. Very well. The Capitol Steps are equal-opportunity offenders, performing a 90-minute musical satire that targets the funniest situations, sound bites, and personalities from either side of the aisle. Songs have included "Obama Mia," "Ballad of the Queen Berets," and other pointed political tunes. It's all in good fun and they seek only to point out the absurdity around us. In DC, shows go on every Friday and Saturday night at the **Ronald Reagan Building** (1300 Pennsylvania Ave. NW, 202/312-1555; tickets 202/397-7328, www.ticketmaster.com, $36).

To see some of the best stand-up comics in the nation, head over to the **DC Improv** (1140 Connecticut Ave. NW, 202/296-7008, www.dcimprov.com). This comedy club opened in 1992 and showcased several notable newcomers (Ellen DeGeneres, Dave Chappelle, and Brian Regan, to name a few) to kick off a long and laugh-filled tenure as *the* place to see live comedy in DC. Top national comics (think Todd Glass, Bill Burr, Bert Kreischer) stop here and play, as do rising stars in the comedy world. Buy your tickets well ahead of time as the major comics tend to sell out fast.

Festivals and Events

In spring, DC becomes a stunning pink palette as millions of blossoms on the city's famous cherry trees open for the world to admire. The **National Cherry Blossom Festival** (877/442-5666, www.nationalcherryblossomfestival.org) commemorates the 1912 gift of 3,000 cherry trees from the mayor of Tokyo to the city of Washington DC. The first two trees were planted by First Lady Helen Herron Taft and Viscountess Chinda, wife of the Japanese ambassador, on the north bank of the Tidal Basin in West Potomac Park. This three-week festival usually begins around the third week of March, and includes musical entertainment, fireworks, the Blossom Kite Festival, a parade, a Japanese street festival, the crowning of the Cherry Blossom Queen, and more parties than you can count. It's the biggest annual event in DC.

June brings **Capital Pride** (www.capitalpride.org), a District-wide LGBTQ+ festival. The festival is growing every year, with a crowd of more than 400,000 attending 30-some events including block parties, the Pride Parade, concerts, and a daylong festival on Pennsylvania Avenue. Events vary by price and type, so check the Pride schedule before planning your celebration.

If you're looking for one of the premier **Independence Day** (www.nps.gov/foju, www.july4thparade.com) celebrations, you've come to the right city. Every July 4, an ocean of people flood the National Mall for a parade, food, live music, and, of course, fireworks. Events start bright and early with historical reenactors reading the Declaration of Independence at the National Archives. Then there's a parade along Constitution Avenue. And the fireworks. If you can't get a seat on the National Mall, don't worry. There are other great spots across the river in Arlington, where you'll have a broad view of the monuments lit up and the fireworks exploding overhead. Try the hill near the Marine Corps War Memorial or the grassy slope by the Air Force Memorial; those are prime spots.

Other than the Cherry Blossom Festival and Independence Day celebrations, no DC event is as well-known as the **National Christmas Tree Lighting and Pageant of Peace** (www.thenationaltree. org). Somewhere around the second week of December, the president lights the National Christmas Tree on the Ellipse in front of the White House. The first national tree was lit with some 2,500 bulbs by President Coolidge in 1923; today, the tree uses LED lights numbering in the tens of thousands. On the day of the lighting, there's a concert of both musical and choral acts. Along with the lighting of the tree is the Pageant of Peace, a four-week holiday celebration. Trees decorated by every state and territory are lit up around town, and there are a wide range of concerts, gatherings, and to-dos.

Shopping

In the heart of the Capitol Hill neighborhood is the **Eastern Market** (225 7th St. SE, 202/698-5253, www.easternmarket-dc.org, 7am-7pm Tues.-Fri., 7am-6pm Sat., 9am-5pm Sun.), where you'll find everything from flowers and fresh produce to bakery products, butchers, cheese, pasta, and seafood. This market has been a DC fixture since 1873, and on weekdays, you'll find it to be a gourmet farmers market. On weekends, it comes alive with music and even more farmers and food purveyors, as well as artists, craftspeople, and antiques sellers.

Tiny Jewel Box (1147 Connecticut Ave. NW, 202/393-2747, www.tinyjewelbox.com, 10am-5:30pm Mon.-Sat.) has a fantastic slogan: "If it's not special, it's not here." The store started tiny, opening its 100-square-foot storefront in 1930, selling antique jewelry. Now it has four floors of outstanding jewelry and gifts. You'll still find plenty of antique and estate jewelry pieces, but now that selection is augmented by a floor of current and trendsetting designers; the third floor features watches and men's accessories; and the top floor holds all sorts of desk accessories, pens and pencils, and other corporate-type gifts.

At **Union Station** (50 Massachusetts Ave. NE, 202/289-1908, www.unionstationdc.com, 10am-9pm Mon.-Sat., noon-6pm Sun.), there are more than a few shops worth your time. Names you'll recognize—like Papyrus, H&M, and The Body Shop, to name a few—mix with DC-only shops. **America's Spirit** (202/842-0540) sells mementos, clothing items, keepsakes, home decor, and gifts featuring all of the DC iconography you can imagine. It's the one-stop tourist gift shop for DC. **Appalachian Spring** (202/682-0505, www.appalachianspring. com) sells wonderful handmade gifts. You'll find jewelry, art glass, elegant wooden boxes, birdhouses, pottery, and scarves, all made by regional artisans and craftspeople.

While you're in **Georgetown** (www.georgetowndc.com/explore/fashion), be sure to wander a bit. You'll find more than 150 fashion stores ranging from local boutiques to well-known brands; 70 or so home decor, art, and design shops; 40 salons, spas, and beauty-related spots; and countless other shops. Every Sunday, the **Georgetown Flea Market** (1819 35th St. NW, 202/775-3532, www.georgetownfleamarket.com, 8am-4pm Sun.) brings in bargain hunters, browsers, and sharp-eyed shoppers.

If you're into handmade and vintage items, then **Analog** (716 Monroe St. NE, Studio 5, www.shopanalog.com, noon-7pm Wed. and Fri., noon-2pm Thurs., 11am-5pm Sat.) belongs on your list. In addition to handmade stationery and paper goods, they carry an assortment of kitschy home goods and vintage clothes and accessories. Fans of vintage boutiques should be sure to stop by **Mercedes Bien Vintage Clothing and Decor** (2423 18th St. NW, 202/360-8481, noon-6pm Sat., noon-5pm Sun.) on a weekend day. This store has a carefully curated selection of vintage clothing and accessories for women as well as home decor goods from yesteryear.

Every museum in DC has a **gift shop.** Most of them are good, but a few are exceptional, especially those at the **International Spy Museum** (admission not required) and **Newseum** (admission not required, tell the front desk you're there for the gift shop), as well as the **Gallery Shops** at the **National Gallery of Art** (free).

Sports and Recreation
Biking
One of the more popular bike trails is the **Capital Crescent Trail** (202/610-7500, www.cctrail.org), a former railroad bed that leads from the western end of Water Street NW in Georgetown, DC (right underneath the Whitehurst Freeway and Key Bridge) to Silver Spring, Maryland. The trail is mostly paved, though there is a crushed stone section, but it's nothing to worry about. For the first few miles, it follows the Potomac on a beautiful little northwestern course before it moves northeast toward Silver Spring. Be aware that the trail is mixed use, so you'll see runners here; be sure to use proper etiquette. Other popular bike trails are found within **Rock Creek Park** (3435 Williamsburg Ln. NW, park headquarters 202/895-6000, visitor information 202/895-6070, www.nps.gov/rocr, dawn-dusk daily, free).

Capital Bikeshare (www.capitalbikeshare.com) has more than 2,500 bikes at unstaffed stations around the city. The bikes are built for function, so they're not exactly sleek. It's an interesting concept and one that's gaining traction here and in other cities. To ride, you have to become a member (sign up online) and select your plan. Visitors will want a 24-hour ($8) or three-day ($17) pass, then you'll have to pay the rental fee on bikes (first 30 minutes free, $2 each additional 30 minutes, $8 each additional 30 minutes beyond 90 minutes). **Bike Washington** (www.bikewashington.org) has some great maps, routes, and tips for bicycling the city, so if you're doing a freestyle tour, you may want to get some ideas here before starting out. In addition to leading guided bike tours, **Bike and Roll** (955 L'Enfant Plaza SW, 202/842-2453, http://bikeandrolldc.com, bike rental: adults $16-30/two hours, children $10/two hours) rents a variety of adult and kids' bikes.

Parks
Washington DC is one of the fittest cities in the nation, thanks to a top-notch series of parks, trails, and activities in and around downtown. One of the most recognizable is **Rock Creek Park** (3435 Williamsburg Ln. NW, park headquarters 202/895-6000, visitor information 202/895-6070, www.nps.gov/rocr, dawn-dusk daily, free), one of the largest forested urban parks in the nation. You'll

see a bevy of animals—white-tailed deer, foxes, rabbits, squirrels, raccoons, hundreds of bird species, and even coyotes—living in the remarkably thick forest that covers the park's 2,700 acres. Rock Creek Park sits on the fall line between Virginia's Piedmont and the Atlantic coastal plain, and the park shows the dramatic changes in geology as a result. In the rocky northern end you'll find steep little canyons, hillsides, and gullies. The southern end, closer to the city, eases into a broad, flat plane as Rock Creek empties into the Potomac River. There are many miles of **hiking** and **biking** trails, and the park is quite popular for these activities. There's also a **Nature Center** (9am-5pm Wed.-Sun.), where many ranger-led activities begin; an equestrian program through **Rock Creek Park Horse Center** (5100 Glover Rd., 202/362-0117, www.rockcreekhorsecenter.com, $42); **tennis** (16th St. and Kennedy St. NW, 202/722-5949, www.rockcreektennis.com, $15/hour); **golf** (202/882-7332, www.golfdc.com, par 65, $15-25 with pull cart, rental clubs available); and plenty of space to just relax in nature.

Theodore Roosevelt Island (700 George Washington Pkwy. between Key and Roosevelt Bridges, 703/289-2500, www.nps.gov/this, 6am-10pm daily, free) is an even bigger break from the noise and modernity of DC than Rock Creek Park. This thickly forested island has beautiful city views, but turn your back and you're in the woods. Three short trails lead around the park, giving you the chance to walk on something other than concrete. Though the island is heavily forested and looks very natural, you may be surprised to learn that it was once home to a mansion where one of Virginia's oldest families lived, then a Union field hospital during the Civil War, at which time the whole of the forest was felled. Thanks to Frederick Law Olmsted, who planted close to 30,000 trees here and removed all nonnative flora, the island looks like virgin forest.

Spectator Sports

Located in the heart of Chinatown, the **Verizon Center** (601 F St. NW, 202/628-3200, www.verizoncenter.monumentalsportsnetwork.com) is not your typical sports venue. Home to the **NHL's Washington Capitals** (www.capitals.nhl.com), the **NBA's Wizards** (www.nba.com/wizards), and the **WNBA's Mystics** (www.mystics.wnba.com), the center features a video center showcasing historic moments in athletics, a sportscasters' hall of fame, and a gift shop; you can also see a variety of concerts and other performances here.

Washington's NFL franchise (www.redskins.com)—officially called the Washington Redskins, a name that many find offensive and that some publications refuse to use—moved out of DC in 1996 and now play their games at **FedEx Field** (1600 Fedex Way, Landover, Maryland). Washington fans are rabid and loyal, hoping every year for a winning season. For some reason, this team gets it together for a season, then falls apart for the next few seasons; even so, the 79,000-seat FedEx Field is packed on game day.

The **Washington Nationals** (www.mlb.com/nationals), known locally as the "Nats," are the city's Major League Baseball franchise. The team plays at **Nationals Park** (1500 South Capitol St. SE, www.washington.nationals.mlb.com/was/ballpark) in southeastern DC, a great stadium that shows off the personality of the city in both its architecture and its attitude.

Opened in 2018, **Audi Field** (100 Potomac Ave. SE, 202/337-9642, www.audifielddc.com) hosts the city's pro soccer team, **DC United** (www.dcunited.com). DC United is the most successful sports franchise in town, having won three U.S. Open Cups and four Major League Soccer Cups since the team's founding in 1995.

Food

Washington DC is a foodie town. Between the unbelievable array of international cuisine and ethnic restaurants, there are spots catering to vegetarians and vegans, burger fiends, those searching for the best pizza (outside of New York), farm-to-fork fanatics, and barbecue aficionados.

Outside the Mall
Burgers and Sandwiches

The DC area is rife with outstanding burgers, beyond the original Five Guys Burgers and Fries—the nationwide chain that has hosted the likes of President Obama. **Duke's Grocery** (1513 17th St. NW, 202/733-5623, www.dukesgrocery. com, 11am-late Mon.-Fri., 10am-late Sat.-Sun., kitchen closes 10pm Sun.-Tues., 1am Wed.-Thurs., and 2am Fri.-Sat, $8-15) makes burgers and sandwiches that are turning first-time customers into evangelists with one bite. The Proper Burger takes your standard cheeseburger and tosses in charred red onion, Thai sweet chili, and garlic aioli. Add in their take on a cheesesteak, the duck confit sandwich that's mouth-watering to the last bite, and their Cubano, and you have a sandwich shop that's a must-stop.

Burger, Tap & Shake (2200 Pennsylvania Ave. NW, 202/587-6258, www.burgertapshake.com, 10am-11pm Mon.-Thurs., 10am-1am Fri., 11am-1am Sat., 11am-9pm Sun., $6-9) grinds their meat on-site throughout the day to get the freshest, most flavorful burger possible. They serve beef, turkey, chicken, and salmon burgers, but also a crispy falafel patty topped with pickled veggies and feta if you're not in a meaty mood. Staying true to their name, they have around two-dozen beers on draft and serve shakes. If you wish to combine your milkshake with something a little stronger, try one of their Shaketails.

Contemporary American

★ **Ben's Chili Bowl** (1213 U St. NW, 202/667-0909, www.benschilibowl.com,

6am-2am Mon.-Thurs., 6am-4am Fri., 7am-4am Sat., 11am-midnight Sun., $4-9) has been around since 1958 and is a legend in DC. Hang out here long enough and you'll see just about every city politician, Capitol Hill VIP, and celebrity in town come in for a half-smoke (a delicious, spicy sausage) or a burger. A meal never sets you back more than $10 here.

Hill Country Barbecue (410 7th St. NW, 202/556-2050, www.hillcountry-wdc.com, 11am-10pm Mon.-Thurs., 11am-11pm Fri., 11:30am-11pm Sat., 11:30am-9:30pm Sun., $7-28) is Texas barbecue at its finest. You'll find the full cadre of Texas barbecue delights: brisket, beef shoulder, beef ribs, pork spareribs, sausages, smoked turkey, beer-can chicken, and more sides than you could imagine. The brisket is an absolute knockout, and you have to try the Kreuz sausages. They sell more Shiner here than anywhere outside of Texas, and you can get $20 pitchers every day, but the real treat is a Shiner Float—your choice of Shiner's beer and a couple of scoops of Blue Bell ice cream.

Birch & Barley (1337 14th St. NW, 202/567-2576, www.birchandbarley.com, 5:30pm-10pm Tues.-Thurs., 5:30pm-11pm Fri.-Sat., 11am-3pm and 5pm-8pm Sun., $16-30) has incredible food and an unreal collection of 555 craft and artisanal beers. The ever-changing menu is filled with items like lamb loin from the Shenandoah Valley; grouper caught off the coast of Maryland and Virginia; and vegetables from local suppliers. If you can't decide, get the tasting menu ($65 pp, another $30 for beer pairings). At those prices, you're getting some great beer and excellent food for less than you'd spend on yourself at many other DC eateries.

Filipino

Named as one of the best new restaurants of 2016 by *Bon Appétit* magazine, ★ **Bad Saint** (3226 11th St NW, 202/733-4507, www.badsaintdc.com, 5:30pm-10pm Mon. and Wed.-Thurs., 5:30pm-11pm Fri., 5pm-11pm Sat., 5pm-10pm Sun., $12-32) delivers a phenomenal, authentic Filipino meal in an intimate space. Their dining room is minuscule, seating just 24 guests at a time. They don't take reservations, so plan to line up well before they open.

Ethiopian

DC is the home of an Ethiopian community, and that means there are some fantastic Ethiopian restaurants. **DAS Ethiopian Cuisine** (1201 28th St. NW, 202/333-4710, www.dasethiopian.com, 11am-11pm daily, $8-22), possibly the best of the bunch, is white-tablecloth, elegant dining in Georgetown. A beautiful dining room and a handful of alfresco tables start to set this restaurant apart, but it's the food that does the rest of the job. The well-curated menu has a great mix of vegetarian and meat entrées, from flaxseed *wat* (pureed or roasted flaxseed in spicy sauce) to beef *awaze fitfit* (*injera* flatbread soaked in a peppery sauce with beef).

Indian

★ **Rasika** (633 D St. NW, 202/637-1222, www.rasikarestaurant.com, 11:30am-2:30pm and 5:30pm-10:30pm Mon.-Thurs., 11:30am-2:30pm and 5pm-11pm Fri., 5pm-11pm Sat., $9-36) is Sanskrit for "flavors," and there are plenty of them here. The restaurant serves up *twa* (griddle), *sigri* (open barbecue), and familiar tandoori dishes as well as a number of regional delicacies, exposing diners to more than the expected Indian cuisine. Try the Grand or Chef's Table tasting menus ($50-75, wine pairings $40-50), which come in both vegetarian and nonvegetarian versions. Rasika is renowned for its wine list.

Bindaas (3309 Connecticut Ave. NW, 202/244-6550, www.bindaasdc.com, 5pm-10pm Mon.-Thurs., 5pm-11pm Fri., 11am-11pm Sat., 11am-9pm Sun., $7-16),

Ben's Chili Bowl, a DC classic

sister restaurant to Rasika, has been making waves since James Beard award-winning chef Vikram Sundaram opened the doors. The emphasis is on street food, and that's part of the draw—that, and the lower prices and exceptional flavors.

Italian and Pizza

★ **Sfoglina** (4445 Connecticut Ave. NW, 202/450-1312, www.sfoglinadc.com, 4pm-10pm Mon., 11:30am-10pm Tues.-Thurs., 11:30am-10:30pm Fri., 10:30am-10:30pm Sat., 10:30am-9pm Sun., $9-65), pronounced sfoal-yee-nah, is among the best Italian restaurants in the city, with handmade pasta, regional dishes, and big, shareable plates. The octopus is exceptional, as is the romesco-drizzled spicy calamari (grilled, not fried). The pasta tasting—a selection of three from the menu—is a family-style feast, but dishes like their 72-hour beef short ribs may just keep your meal pasta-free.

We the Pizza (305 Pennsylvania Ave. SE, 202/544-4008, www.wethepizza. com, 11am-11pm daily, $3-20), by *Top Chef* contestant Spike Mendelsohn, elevates traditional pizza to something more akin to his fine-dining establishments. The Forest Shroomin' Pie, with wild forest mushrooms, truffles, fresh mozzarella, thyme, and parmesan, is something you'll return for. Mendelsohn and his chefs are creating new pies that reflect different food traditions. The China Poblano Spicy Mexican Pie is laced with chipotle and cilantro; the Cajun Chicken & Andouille is a taste of New Orleans; and the Regal Pepper Farm is a peppery blast inspired by some choice Florida cuisine. They also have wings, salads, and an interesting selection of sodas.

Spanish

Some locals claim **Boqueria** (1837 M St. NW, 202/558-9545, www.boquerianyc. com, 11:30am-10:30pm Mon.-Thurs., 11:30am-11:30pm Fri., 10:30am-11:30pm Sat., 10:30am-9:30pm Sun., $6-42) is the best brunch spot in DC. This Spanish restaurant serves up a bevy of classic and reinterpreted tapas dishes as well as an impressive cheese and charcuterie selection. If you love tapas, the prix-fixe brunch ($39) is for you. Unlimited tapas, drinks, and sweets are right there at your fingertips, so long as everyone at the table orders them; otherwise, you're going à la carte.

Vegetarian

Founding Farmers (1924 Pennsylvania Ave. NW, 202/822-8783, www. wearefoundingfarmers.com, 7am-10pm Mon., 7am-11pm Tues.-Thurs., 7am-midnight Fri., 8:30am-midnight Sat., 8:30am-10pm Sun., $11-37) is known for eclectic, Southern-inspired food created with seasonal products acquired as locally as possible. They serve steaks, chops, and seafood, but their vegetarian and vegan dishes are top-notch. Try the trumpet mushroom "scallops" or the grilled cauliflower steak to see what the kitchen is capable of. Of course, you can also fill up on the fantastic salads and a number of excellent small plates.

Arlington

German

It's not clear if **Lyon Hall** (3100 N. Washington Blvd., 703/741-7636, www.lyonhallarlington.com, 11:30am-3pm and 5pm-10pm Mon.-Thurs., 11:30am-3pm and 5pm-11pm Fri., 9:30am-3pm and 5pm-11pm Sat., 9:30am-3pm and 5pm-10pm Sun., $8-29) is German or German-ish, but it does serve schnitzel and features a two-page beer menu. The food here is excellent. The Bohemian sausage platter gives you a trio of sausages, along with pork belly, herb spätzle, kraut, and house-made condiments. The mussels are exceptional, and the cheese and charcuterie selection is as interesting as it is delicious.

Mediterranean

Yayla Bistro (2201 N. Westmoreland St., 703/533-5600, www.yaylabistro.com, 11am-9pm Sun.-Thurs., 11am-10pm Fri.-Sat., $6-25) incorporates Turkish and Greek food traditions. Flatbreads with Turkish sausage and cured beef, falafel and moussaka, and baklava and the Turkish rice pudding known as *sutlac* grace the small menu. But don't let the size of the menu fool you—the food is outstanding.

Accommodations

Finding a place to stay in or around DC is not hard: There are hundreds of hotels, inns, and bed-and-breakfasts. The problem is price. This is an expensive city, and the hotels here are especially expensive. Lucky for you, the city has a great public transportation system and is easy to navigate with the most rudimentary of maps. With that in mind, and thinking of the road trip ahead, I looked at lodging on the more affordable end of the spectrum.

Outside the Mall

$100-150

In what used to be an apartment building overlooking Rock Creek Park, the **Windsor Park Hotel** (2116 Kalorama Rd. NW, 202/483-7700, www.windsorparkhotel, $95-158) offers guests beautiful city or park views. More than that, the Windsor Park offers convenience, as Dupont Circle and the shops, restaurants, and bars there are within easy walking distance.

Adam's Inn (1746 Lanier Pl. NW, 202/745-3600 or 800/578-6807, www.adamsinn.com, $90-179) consists of three brick town houses and a carriage house hidden away on a leafy residential street two blocks from the heart of Adams Morgan. Built around 1913, the inn has a definite Victorian feel, with some modern touches. The common rooms are equipped with TV and computers for Internet access. A lavish continental breakfast is included in the price of your stay. A total of 26 rooms are available. As elsewhere in Adams Morgan, parking is limited, though there are four spots available at the inn for $25 a night.

Staying at the **Hotel Harrington** (436 11th St. NW, 800/424-8532 or 202/628-8140, www.hotel-harrington.com, $135-219), you may think you're Batman (their logo is more than a little caped crusader-ish), but don't expect the lavish digs Bruce Wayne would stay in. Here, the rooms are much smaller and not nearly so elegant. What makes this place special, though, is the location. It's just a couple of blocks from the Smithsonian museums and the National Mall, and that, plus the price, makes it a popular spot for budget-conscious international travelers. Parking is $23 per day at a garage four blocks away.

$150-200

At the **Washington Marriott Wardman Park** (2660 Woodley Rd. NW, 202/328-2000, www.marriott.com, $180-239), you'll be within walking distance of restaurants, the National Zoo, and the

Naval Observatory, and steps away from a Metro stop. Rooms are large and comfortable; suites are even larger. This hotel is a big one, but separate towers and convention facilities give it a smaller feel without sacrificing on quality.

Over $200

The ★ **Hamilton Hotel Washington DC** (1001 14th St. NW, 202/682-0111 or 877/270-1393, www.hamiltonhoteldc. com, $115-354) has more than 300 guest rooms that are cozy, both in size and appointments, but they're so comfortable that you won't mind the diminutive size. Larger rooms are available in the Guest Suites and on the Concierge Level if you'd like to spread out a little. One interesting offering of The Hamilton is a women-only floor catering to female business travelers. The Hamilton's concierge is excellent and quick with suggestions for how to make the most of your visit to DC. Additionally, the hotel is convenient to the Metro train and bus lines, and adjacent to a park that's lined with food trucks each day for lunch.

Downtown DC's ★ **Morrison-Clark Historic Inn & Restaurant** (1015 L St. NW, 202/898-1200 or 800/332-7898, www.morrisonclark.com, $215-260) is only a block from the convention center and close to a host of restaurants and sights. This Victorian mansion was built during the Civil War and is something of an anomaly in a neighborhood busy with office buildings. Rooms here are elegant—high ceilings, ornate crown moldings, antique bedding and furniture, much of it true to the period of the inn—but not ostentatious.

Arlington
$150-200

The ★ **Clarion Collection Hotel Arlington Court Suites** (1200 N. Courthouse Rd., Arlington, 703/524-4000, www.arlingtoncourthotel.com, $129-239) has comfortable, monstrously spacious suites in a location that's convenient to the Metro

and just a few minutes' ride to the heart of DC. The smallest suites are ample and the largest more than double the size of the biggest rooms in DC (excepting, of course, those coveted Presidential Suites). It's common to see groups of business travelers here, some wearing military uniforms.

Information and Services

For a comprehensive list of restaurants, attractions, activities, and accommodations, let **Destination DC** (www.washington.org) be your guide. The site is filled with links, itineraries, and trip ideas. The excellent team in the **Arlington Convention and Visitors Service** (www.stayarlington.com) has put together a great site that will lead you around Arlington and DC (but only to the major attractions).

George Washington University Hospital (900 23rd St. NW, 202/711-4000, www.gwhospital.com) is one of several hospitals and clinics providing emergency care and other medical services.

★ Manassas Battlefield National Park

The gently rippled hills north of Manassas—still almost as rural as they were in the 1860s—saw two major Civil War battles. The First Battle of Bull Run, in 1861, opened the war with a horrific bang. The Second Battle of Bull Run, in 1862, set the stage for Lee's abortive invasion of the North in 1863. Any visit to the **Manassas Battlefield** (703/361-1339, www.nps.gov/mana, dawn-dusk daily, free) should start at the **Henry Hill Visitors Center** (6511 Sudley Rd., 8:30am-5pm daily), on Route 234 south of its intersection with Route 29. The park movie, *Manassas: End of Innocence,* which runs about 45 minutes, is free. You can pick up tour maps of the battlefields and check the daily schedule for ranger-led programs. Walk the loop trail of First

Manassas in about 45 minutes, passing reconstructed houses and a muscular statue of Jackson commemorating his bold stand. During the First Battle of Bull Run (as the First Manassas is more commonly known) in 1861, General "Stonewall" Jackson earned his nickname when he inspired Confederate troops to stand tall against Union attacks, earning a victory for the Confederacy. Nine sites of Second Manassas are linked by a driving tour. The Second Battle of Bull Run took place a year later, when Confederate troops again routed Union forces.

To get to Manassas Battlefield National Park, head west from DC on I-66; the park is 35 miles (about 45 minutes) outside the city. From Front Royal, the park is 37 miles (about 38 minutes) east on I-66.

Front Royal

The northern gateway to Skyline Drive and Shenandoah National Park, as well as the Blue Ridge Parkway, is Front Royal, in Warren County. The sleepy little burg was known as Hell Town during its frontier days, and many think it was unintentionally renamed by an exasperated colonial drill sergeant, who repeated orders for his troops to "Front the royal oak!" in the center of town (oaks were considered the royal tree of England).

The Shenandoah River runs through town, offering opportunities for fishing, tubing, and canoeing. Downtown is very attractive, with a town hall that looks like part of a movie set, many boutiques, and several restaurants.

A long bridge over the Shenandoah leads to tree-lined Royal Avenue (US-340). Turn left onto East Main Street at the Warren County Courthouse to reach

Manassas Battlefield National Park

the Village Commons with its gazebo, big red caboose, and the town visitors center.

Getting There

I-66 runs by Front Royal just outside of town limits; Washington DC is 70 miles to the east, and I-81 is 15 miles to the west. Winchester, Virginia, is only 30 minutes north via I-66 and I-81 or by taking US-340 north. The town of Luray, Virginia, is 24 miles to the southwest on US-340. There is no train service or bus service to Front Royal, nor is there an airport of any consequence.

Sights

The **Warren Rifles Confederate Museum** (95 Chester St., 540/636-6982, 9am-4pm Mon.-Sat., noon-4pm Sun. Apr. 15-Nov. 1, by appointment Nov. 2-Apr. 14, $4) contains a large collection of arms, uniforms, flags, pictures, and personal items that evoke the Civil War exploits of Stonewall Jackson, Mosby's Rangers, J. E. B. Stuart, and Robert E. Lee. There

are also artifacts from the famous Civil War spy Belle Boyd.

Practically across the street from the Warren Rifles Confederate Museum is the **Belle Boyd Cottage** (101 Chester St., 540/636-1446, www.warrenheritagesociety.org, 10am-4pm Mon.-Sat. Apr.-Oct., 10am-4pm Mon.-Fri. Nov.-Mar., $3). Boyd was a charming spy who helped Stonewall Jackson capture Front Royal in 1862. She was well known among Union forces, reported for suspicious activity more than 30 times, arrested a half-dozen times, and even spent a little time behind bars. For a while, Front Royal was her base of operations, and you can learn more about her spy exploits here.

Opened to the public in 1939, **Skyline Caverns** (10344 Stonewall Jackson Hwy./US-340, 540/635-4545 or 800/296-4545, www.skylinecaverns.com, 9am-5pm Mon.-Fri., 9am-6pm Sat.-Sun. Mar. 15-June 14; 9am-6pm daily June 15-Labor Day; 9am-5pm Mon.-Fri., 9am-6pm Sat.-Sun. Labor Day-Nov. 14; 9am-4pm daily Nov. 15-Mar. 14; $22 adults, $11 ages 7-13, free 6 and under) were discovered a few years earlier by means of a giant sinkhole where the parking lot now sits. The highlights of these caves, otherwise overshadowed by their southern neighbors, are glittering calcite formations called anthodites. These delicate spikes are found in only one other cave in the United States (and there in much smaller quantities). They grow one inch every 7,000 years, either pure white or stained brown by iron oxide. Skyline Caverns' crop sprouted in a vacuum left by a receding underground pool. Throughout the rest of the cave, high, smooth passages evoke the slot canyons of the American Southwest. Kids love the Skyline Arrow ($6 ages 3 and up, free 2 and under), an outdoor miniature train that crawls near the entrance. There's also a mirror maze ($6 ages 5 and up, free 4 and under). The caverns are on US-340, about one mile south of Route 55.

Entertainment and Events

There's very little nightlife to speak of in Front Royal. Most of the bars are attached to restaurants, so don't expect any out-till-dawn evenings. There are, however, four fun festivals in town. In May, the one-day **Virginia Wine and Craft Festival** (historic downtown Front Royal, 540/635-3185, www.wineandcraftfestival. com, admission free, tasting tickets $25 in advance, $30 day of) draws two dozen Virginia wineries to dole out samples; more than 100 vendors, artists, and crafters; and tons of fair food.

The **Warren County Fair** (Fairgrounds Rd., 540/635-5827, www.warrencountyfair.com, $40 weekly tickets) comes to town for a week in early August, bringing with it concerts, 4-H events, a demolition derby, a tractor pull, ATV drag racing, and everything you'd expect to find at a county fair.

In late September, the **Brew & Blues Festival** (historic downtown Front Royal, 540/635-3185, www.brewandblues.com, tasting tickets $20-25) brings blues music and beer tastings from 50 or so microbreweries to downtown Front Royal. Area restaurants and food purveyors will be on hand to serve up munchies and plates of food that should make all that beer tasting go a little easier.

The Warren Heritage Society holds their annual fundraiser, the **Festival of Leaves** (historic downtown Front Royal, 540/636-1446, www.warrenheritagesociety.org) in mid-October. Bluegrass, blues, rock, and country acts perform throughout the day; there's a parade and vendors selling food and crafts, and a kids area.

Shopping

When you're searching for something to take home, stop by **Ole Timer's Antiques** (220 E. Main St., 540/636-9444, 10am-5pm Mon. and Wed.-Sat.), *the* place for assorted treasures, junk, and crafts. Alternately, you can shop for antiques of all sorts at **Arleen Brown Antiques** (301 E. Main St., 703/789-1245, 11am-5pm Mon. and Wed.-Sat., noon-5pm Sun.) and **Roger's Antiques** (112 E. Main St., 540/622-2055, www.hbrefinishing.com, 11am-5pm Mon.-Sat., noon-5pm Sun).

The **Royal Oak Bookshop** (207 S. Royal Ave., 540/635-7070, www.royaloakbookshop.com, 10am-6pm Mon.-Sat., noon-5pm Sun.) stocks thousands of rare, used, out-of-print, and new books. Visit with Willa Catter, the bookshop cat, while you're there.

Sports and Recreation

Several local outfitters take advantage of the fact that one of Virginia's favorite rafting rivers flows practically through their backyard. Most operate campsites down the South Fork of the Shenandoah for overnight visitors during the floating season of March-November. Prices should include equipment, brief instruction, maps, and shuttle service.

The **Front Royal Canoe Company** (8567 Stonewall Jackson Hwy., 540/635-5440 or 800/270-8808, www.frontroyalcanoe.com, 9am-6pm Mon.-Fri., 7am-7pm Sat.-Sun., from $33) runs canoe, raft, and kayak trips, with longer excursions of 2-3 days also available. Tubing ($24) is also popular. You can also rent canoes ($50/day), kayaks ($30/solo, $50/tandem per day), and stand-up paddleboards ($40/day) to explore the river on your own.

Take a guided horseback ride with **Royal Horseshoe Farm** (509 Morgan Ford Rd., 540/636-6375, www.royalhorseshoe.com, starting at $35). They lead trail rides year-round and can tailor an excursion to fit your skill level and desire for adventure.

Mountain bikers will find several challenging trails nearby. At the **Elizabeth Furnace Trail**, experts will find quite the adventurous track to ride. Located 11 miles west of Front Royal in the Lee Ranger District of **George Washington National Forest** (www.fs.usda.gov/gwj), the 15-mile trail starts with an easy uphill climb on a fire road before a long, rough downhill with a dozen or so water crossings, rock outcrops, technical trail sections, and rock gardens. At the **Shenandoah River State Park** (350 Daughter of Stars Dr., Bentonville, 540/622-6840, park at www.dcr.virginia.gov, 8am-dusk daily, parking $5-7 Virginia residents, $7-9 out-of-state visitors), 9 miles southwest of Front Royal, there is a 13-mile network of trails better suited to less-experienced mountain bikers. Most of these trails are wide and smooth, though there are a few challenging climbs. Plus, there are great views of the river from many trails. Find trail maps at www.virginiaoutdoors.com.

Food

L Dee's Pancake House (522 E. Main St., 540/635-3791, www.ldeespancakehouse.com, 6am-2pm Mon. and Wed.-Sat., 7am-1pm Sun., $2-14) offers breakfast all day, with fantastic French toast and great omelets. Their lunch menu is of the burger and sandwich variety that you'd expect at a little diner-like restaurant such as this.

Element (317 E. Main St., 540/636-1695, 11am-3pm and 5pm-9pm Tues.-Sat., $6-18) serves up a spread of refined food for lunch and dinner that will leave you full and won't empty your wallet. Whether you choose something casual—wings, calamari, fish-and-chips—or upscale—mussels in white wine sauce, tuna Nicoise salad, pan-roasted salmon with soba noodles—you'll find a dish worth returning for.

For something quick and filling, hit **Spelunker's Burgers & Frozen Custard** (116 South St., 540/631-0300, www.spelunkerscustard.com, 11am-10pm daily, $2-10). Their name says it all: They have handmade burgers and ice cream and frozen custard made daily. The burgers are big and the ice cream toppings are numerous. And if you must have a hot dog, cheesesteak, or Italian ice, they have those, too.

Accommodations

The **Holiday Inn Hotel & Suites Front Royal Blue Ridge Shadows** (111 Hospitality Dr., 540/631-3050, www.ihg.com, $152-185) is adjacent to the Blue Ridge Shadows Golf Club. There are 124 rooms in this seven-story hotel where you'll have free Wi-Fi, a 24-hour fitness center, and a heated indoor pool.

There's a **Hampton Inn** (9800 Winchester Rd., 540/635-1882, www.hamptoninn3.hilton.com, $149-182) in Front Royal. On weekday mornings, you'll have a free hot breakfast or to-go breakfast bags, and every day you'll have free Wi-Fi, access to a pool and sundeck, and a fitness center. The hotel is located about four miles out of town.

Lackawanna Bed & Breakfast (236 Riverside Dr., 540/636-7945, $174-184) is situated on two acres of beautiful property between the North and South Forks of the Shenandoah River. There are only a trio of rooms here, one being a suite, but the place is elegant and comfortable, and somehow manages to make you forget that Washington DC is only 60 miles east of here.

Woodward House on Manor Grade (413 S. Royal Ave., 540/635-7010 or 800/635-7011, www.acountryhome.com, $110-225) has seven guest rooms (each with a private bath) and a private cottage. Every day there's a homey breakfast ranging from hot or cold cereals to omelets to French toast. Guests can also enjoy complimentary beer or wine at the on-site pub. The view from here is lovely as the house sits on top of a hill overlooking the valley.

Campers should head to **Shenandoah River State Park** (350 Daughter of Stars Dr., Bentonville, 540/622-6840, www.dcr.virginia.gov, campsites $24-41, cabins $98-175, lodge $434), nine miles southwest of Front Royal. It has a number of tent sites, cabins, and a lodge.

Information and Services

The **Front Royal/Warren County Visitor Center** (414 E. Main St., 800/338-2576, www.frontroyalva.com, 9am-5pm daily) is located in the restored train station in the town park.

For emergencies, go to **Warren Memorial Hospital** (1000 Shenandoah Ave., Front Royal, 540/536-8000, www.valleyhealthlink.com).

Shenandoah National Park

Well over one million people visit **Shenandoah National Park** (540/999-3500, www.nps.gov/shen) each year. This 200,000-acre park is only 75 miles west of Washington DC and is a popular escape for those living in the DC metro area and the densely populated areas of Virginia, Maryland, and Pennsylvania.

This is a prime park for hiking. More than 500 miles of trails, many of which are accessible from Skyline Drive, wind through lush forests and across long ridgelines. On these hikes you'll find more than a dozen waterfalls and wildflowers, and be granted the opportunity to take a look at some of the park's wildlife. It's common to see white-tailed deer and black bears, but bald eagles, coyotes, and even timber rattlesnakes are also spotted throughout the park with regularity. Remnants of former homesites are visible in crumbling walls and chimneys and mossy cemeteries hidden in the underbrush. A 101-mile segment of the **Appalachian Trail** (AT) threads its way down Skyline Drive, making it ideal for short hikes as it crosses and recrosses the road. Many loop trails include part of the AT.

Visiting the Park
Getting There and Around
Washington DC is 75 miles to the east; I-66 carries you right to Front Royal, where you'll find the northern entrance to Shenandoah National Park. Only 10 miles to the west, I-81 cuts a northward diagonal path along the Blue Ridge Mountains toward Pennsylvania to the north.

The 105-mile vista-to-vista ridge-top **Skyline Drive** carries you through Shenandoah National Park from Front Royal to Rockfish Gap, just outside of Waynesboro, where the drive continues via the Blue Ridge Parkway. Along the route, 75 overlooks offer views of the Shenandoah Valley to the west and the Piedmont of Virginia to the east. The drive is lovely in any season but most colorful in the fall. Spring buds and wildflowers and jewel-green summer mountains are other seasonal attractions.

The park itself is divided into three sections, designated by roads bisecting Skyline Drive. The **Northern District** stretches from Front Royal (US-340, MP 0) to Thornton Gap (US-211, MP 31.5). The **Central District** continues south to Swift Run Gap (US-33, MP 62.7). Rockfish Gap (I-64, US-250, MP 104.6) marks the southern boundary of the **Southern District.**

Along the length of Skyline Drive, everything is referred to by milepost. The milepost markers make it easy to orient yourself in the park and give you a simple measure from place to place. Milepost 0 is at Front Royal, at the northern end of Skyline Drive. Milepost 104.6 is at Rockfish Gap at the southern end. It takes around three hours to drive from end to end.

Entrances
There are entrance stations at four points along Skyline Drive:

- **Front Royal** (MP 0)

- **Thornton Gap** (MP 31.5)

- **Swift Run Gap** (MP 62.7)

- **Rockfish Gap** (MP 104.6)

At each of these entrances, you can pay your fees and pick up a short informational guide to the park. Rangers stationed at the entrances are happy to answer questions and give directions or suggestions, but be aware of the traffic behind you and try to be courteous to your fellow park visitors.

Park Passes, Permits, and Regulations

A **pass** (good for seven consecutive days) costs $25 per vehicle, $20 per motorcycle, or $10 per pedestrian or bicyclist. Annual passes, which include the pass holder and three adults, cost $50 and are good for one year.

Pets are allowed on most trails, but only on leashes; ask at the visitors centers about which trails are off-limits. **Bicycles** are only allowed on Skyline Drive and other paved areas.

Backcountry camping permits are required, but are free and are available from entrance stations, park headquarters, and visitors centers. You may also download a backcountry camping permit application from www.nps.gov/shen and send it to Shenandoah National Park for advance trip planning. **Appalachian Trail permits** (for long-distance AT hikers) are available by self-registration on the trail near Shenandoah National Park entry points.

Anglers will want to familiarize themselves with Shenandoah National Park **fishing regulations** (available at www.nps.gov/shen) and obtain a **fishing license** from the state of Virginia. Licenses are available at sporting goods retailers across the state and online through the Virginia Department of Game and Inland Fisheries (www.dgif.virginia.gov, $8-47).

Visitors Centers

Shenandoah National Park has two

Top to bottom: road through Shenandoah National Park; trail in Shenandoah; the Shenandoah Mountains.

visitors centers: the **Dickey Ridge Visitor Center** (MP 4.6; 9am-5pm daily early Apr.-mid-Nov.) and the **Harry F. Byrd, Sr. Visitor Center** (MP 51; 9am-5pm daily late Mar.-Nov.; 9am-5pm Sat.-Sun. Dec.-mid-Mar.). Each visitors center has trail maps, along with topographical maps and detailed maps of the entire park. Various trail guides are available at the bookstore in the park visitors centers.

The **Park Headquarters** (540/999-3500, www.nps.gov/shen, 9am-5pm Mon.-Fri.) is four miles east of Luray on US-211.

Seasons
The most popular time to visit Shenandoah National Park and cruise along Skyline Drive is autumn, when the leaves turn and the broad, green valley views of summer turn to a riot of color. This can mean long lines at entrance stations and slow traffic along Skyline, so expect a lot of leaf-peeping companions, especially on weekends. Inclement weather can close the road any time of year, and spring and summer storms can bring heavy rain, lightning, fog, and hail to the area. During deer-hunting season (mid-Nov.-early Jan.), Skyline is closed at night to give the deer a little break.

The park is open year-round, though in winter, many sections of Skyline Drive and most of the amenities are closed (check the website or call for closures). During winter, many people hike in or drive a short way up Skyline to take in the snowy views.

Food and Accommodations
Unlike many national parks, Shenandoah offers two full-service dining rooms: one inside Skyland Resort and one inside Big Meadows Lodge.

If a full-service, sit-down meal isn't what you had in mind, you can stop by one of three Wayside Food Stops: the Elkwallow Wayside, Big Meadows Wayside, and Loft Mountain Wayside.

Camping
Backcountry camping is free, though you do need a permit (available online, by mail, or at visitors centers and entrance stations). In addition to backcountry campsites, there are four campgrounds in Shenandoah National Park. Three of the campsites accept **reservations** (877/444-6777, www.recreation.gov); Lewis Mountain Campground is first come, first served.

- **Matthews Arm Campground** (MP 22.1, 540/999-3132, $15, groups $50)

- **Big Meadows Campground** (MP 51.2, 540/999-3500, ext. 3231, $20, groups $45)

- **Lewis Mountain Campground** (MP 57.5, $15)

- **Loft Mountain Campground** (MP 79.5, $15, groups $35-50)

These are open spring through fall, but are closed in winter. All of the campgrounds have showers and potable water. Each of the campgrounds has tent sites, and all but Lewis Mountain Campground have space for RVs (note, though, there are no water hookups, although there are dump stations).

Lodges and Cabins
There are two lodges and a set of cabins in Shenandoah National Park:

- **Skyland Resort** (MP 41.7 and 42.5, $145-305)

- **Big Meadows Lodge** (MP 51.2, $125-206)

- **Lewis Mountain Cabins** (MP 57.5, $138)

These are all operated by DNC Parks & Resorts; **reservations** (877/847-1919, www.goshenandoah.com) can be made for all lodges and cabins. None of these accommodations are luxurious by any stretch. They are built instead to facilitate the enjoyment of the park, so the beds will be passable and the shower hot, but don't expect plush robes and after-dinner cordials.

Information and Services

Camping supplies are available at four places in the park: the Elkwallow Wayside, Big Meadows Wayside, Lewis Mountain Cabins and Campstore, and Loft Mountain Wayside.

Inside the park, gasoline is only available at the Big Meadows Wayside (MP 51.2).

In addition to the visitors centers, you can also ask the helpful folks at any of the accommodations for information, or visit the official site for the park (www.nps. gov/shen) or the official site for the lodging and food vendor for the park (www. goshenandoah.com). The **Shenandoah Valley Travel Association** (www.visits-kylinedrive.org) has more information on Skyline and the park.

If you need medical assistance, there are a few hospitals nearby. **Warren Memorial Hospital** (1000 Shenandoah Ave., Front Royal, 540/636-0300, www. valleyhealthlink.com) serves Front Royal and is convenient to the northern section of the park. In Luray, **Page Memorial Hospital** (200 Memorial Dr., Luray, 540/743-4561, www.valley-healthlink.com), a 25-bed hospital, can provide emergency care if you need it. At the southern end of Skyline Drive, **Augusta Health** (78 Medical Center Dr., Fisherville, 800/932-0262, www.augusta-health.com) can treat most any problem that may arise. In a true emergency, dial 911 and report your situation and location along Skyline Drive.

Northern District
Dickey Ridge Visitor Center (MP 4.6)

This is the first stop for most people as they travel south along Skyline Drive.

There's a very nice view, as well as the usual accoutrements of a visitors center: restrooms, racks full of informational brochures, and a gift shop. What sets it apart are the pleasant park rangers. It's evident that they love Shenandoah National Park and are excited to help you have a great visit. Take 10 minutes to watch the video (it starts on request rather than on a timer).

Fox Hollow Trail

Distance: 1.2-mile loop
Duration: 0.5-1 hour
Elevation gain: 300 feet
Difficulty: easy
Trailhead: across Skyline Drive from the Dickey Ridge Visitor Center, MP 4.6

Park at the Dickey Ridge Visitor Center and cross Skyline Drive to the trailhead. Turn left and begin to descend slightly. You'll pass a cement post at 0.15 miles, turn left and follow the blue-blazed trail for 0.2 mile along a pleasant forest walk. At 0.3 mile you'll reach a second concrete post and you'll turn right here to join Fox Hollow Trail and continue on past piles of rocks left over from clearing the forest and preparing agricultural fields.

A 0.5 mile in, you'll pass the Fox Farm Cemetery; take a few minutes to check it out. As you continue along, you'll pass a spring and an ornamental mill wheel. The trail crosses old farmland here, so keep an eye out for deer. The trail begins to rise after you pass the cemetery, but it's a gradual climb. Continue on, noting the rock piles and rock fences to either side. If you notice the path, it's wide, well graded, and relatively smooth. That's because it's an old road that once connected the farms here with Front Royal, a few miles north.

Gooney Run Overlook (MP 6)

Looking out from the Gooney Run Overlook, you can see Gooney Run, the stream that drains Browntown Valley. Several turns of the Shenandoah River are visible here as well, as are Signal Knob

Shenandoah National Park, Northern District

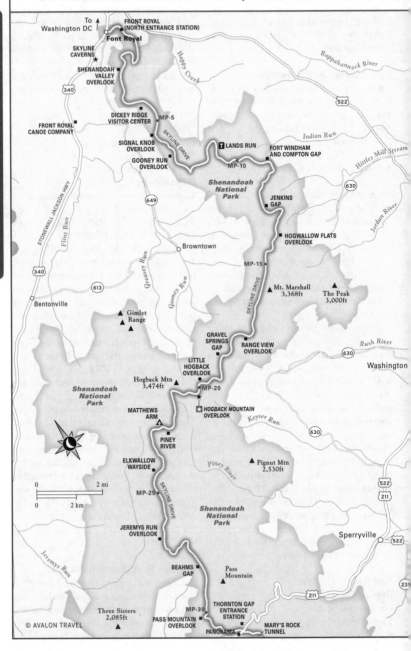

and Dickey Ridge. The original name of Gooney Run was Sugar Tree Creek, but Lord Fairfax was hunting here with his favorite dog, Gooney, and the dog had the misfortune to drown. Fairfax honored the hound by renaming the creek.

Lands Run (MP 9.2)

A short wooded stroll on the Lands Run Falls Trail is perfect for those pressed for time but who want to see one of the park's waterfalls.

Lands Run Falls Trail

Distance: 1.2 miles out and back
Duration: 0.5-1 hour
Elevation gain: 300 feet
Difficulty: easy
Trailhead: Lands Run parking area, MP 9.2

This short, pleasant hike leads down an old road to views of a small but pretty waterfall. Follow the fire road from Lands Run parking area as it descends immediately. At 0.6 mile in, you'll see a stream coming down the mountain from your left before passing through a culvert under the road. Look to the right and you'll see the falls. If you take a short spur trail, you can get some very good views. Retrace your steps back up the fire road to the parking area.

Fort Windham Rocks and Compton Gap (MP 10.4)

Carson Mountain (2,580 ft.) is unremarkable except for the summit, Fort Windham Rocks. Geologists say the rocks are 600-800 million years old and are examples of the Catoctin lava formations. Rock climbers will tell you that they're great for easy to moderate top-rope climbs if you feel like packing gear in, or perfect for bouldering if you're going in a little lighter.

Fort Windham Rocks Trail

Distance: 0.8 mile out and back
Duration: 30-45 minutes
Elevation gain: negligible
Difficulty: easy

Trailhead: fire road at Compton Gap, MP 10.4

From the parking area, follow the fire road—which is also part of the Appalachian Trail—to a four-way intersection. Turn left onto Dickey Ridge Trail (which will lead you to the Dickey Ridge Visitor Center). The path ascends quite gently, then, as it levels, you'll see the Fort Windham Rocks to your right. There's a short spur that leads into the rocks, where you should linger a bit, scramble around on the outcrop, and check out the rocks before retracing your steps to the parking lot.

Range View Overlook (MP 17.1)

Just a few miles south of Shenandoah National Park's Front Royal entrance, you'll get the chance to step out of the car and stretch your legs. Here, Range View Overlook opens up to provide big views of the Blue Ridge and the valley to the east, which was once home to the Great Wagon Road, the principal route taken south and west by settlers centuries ago. Looking down the long line of mountains, you'll see Stony Man Mountain to the south. This is a great spot for views of color-changing leaves in the fall.

★ Hogback Mountain Overlook (MP 20.8)

Truly one of the top views in the park, the Hogback Mountain Overlook provides a great look at Hogback Mountain, but the best part is the shimmering view of the Shenandoah River as it snakes through the landscape. The largest overlook area in Shenandoah National Park, this is a popular stop.

Matthews Arm Campground (MP 22.1)

One of the largest campgrounds in the park, **Matthews Arm Campground** (540/999-3132, reservations at 877/444-6777 or www.recreation.gov, $15, groups $50) has nearly 200 tent and RV sites. This campground is wooded and shady, making for a nice break from summer

heat and a great view right outside your door in autumn. Matthews Arm is near **Overall Run Falls** (a taxing hike), which has the highest drop of all the falls in the park.

Elkwallow Wayside (MP 24.1)

At **Elkwallow Wayside** (9am-6pm daily mid-Apr.-early Nov.), you can pick up something to snack on or cook from a limited grocery store, or order takeout from a small menu.

◆ US-211: Whiteoak Canyon, Old Rag, and Luray Caverns (MP 31.5)

From Skyline Drive, take **US-211 East** to Whiteoak Canyon and Old Rag, or **US-211 West** to Luray Caverns.

Whiteoak Canyon Trail

Distance: 5.8 miles out and back
Duration: 3-4 hours
Elevation gain: 1,700 feet
Difficulty: moderate to strenuous
Trailhead: parking area near Cedar Run
Directions: At MP 31.5, take US-211 east to Sperryville; turn south on US-522 for 0.8 mile; turn right onto VA-231 and go 9.5 miles to Route 643; follow Route 643 south for 10 miles; turn right onto Route 600 for 3.6 miles to the place where the road fords Cedar Run. The trailhead is in the parking area.

Finding the trailhead is the most daunting part of this hike, aside from its distance, but the reward is worth the effort as it takes you to a secluded canyon where you can get up close and personal with a half-dozen waterfalls. Going in, this hike is all uphill, so keep that in mind as you get on the trail. It means that coming back you just have to coast downhill.

Starting from that near-secret trailhead, cross Cedar Run via a footbridge. Immediately you'll see a cement post marking the junction with Cedar Run Trail. Stay on Whiteoak Canyon Trail. At 0.7 mile, continue on, bearing right. The ascent can be steep and could require

---

Top to bottom: Luray Caverns; Old Rag Mountain Trail; Dark Hollow Falls.

SHENANDOAH NATIONAL PARK

you to scramble around a few large rocks. At 1.5 miles, a cement post marks the first of the falls. Continue along for the next 1.4 miles to see the rest of the falls here. Take your time, dip your feet in the pool beneath at least one waterfall, take some pictures, and maybe eat a little lunch. It's a pleasant spot to linger. When it's time to go back, follow the trail back out by retracing your steps.

Old Rag Mountain Trail

Distance: 8.8-mile loop
Duration: 7-8 hours
Elevation gain: 2,380 feet
Difficulty: strenuous
Trailhead: Nethers, Virginia, at the Shenandoah National Park border along Route 600
Directions: Though the peak lies inside the park, the trailhead is outside the park, near the community of Nethers. Exit Skyline Drive at Thornton Gap (MP 31.5) and follow US-211 east to US-522 south in Sperryville. Follow the signs to VA-231/F. T. Valley Road south and stay on this road for 7.8 miles. Turn right onto VA-601/Peola Mills Road and continue along 601 until it turns into VA-707/Nethers Road. Just over a mile from Nethers, you'll reach the trailhead to Old Rag Mountain. An entrance permit to Shenandoah National Park is required; if you didn't pay at the entrance station, there's a self-serve station here.

Hiking Old Rag Mountain is a rite of passage for many visitors to Shenandoah National Park and offers some great views. It's harsh and rocky, and exposure near the summit is total, so if there's the chance of bad weather (especially lightning), keep an eye on the sky. Before you go, visit www.nps.gov/shen and watch the video about safety on Old Rag Mountain.

Prepare for a full, strenuous day by bringing a map, good shoes, at least two liters of water per person, an emergency kit, food, and your trekking poles. Park near the trailhead and walk up Nethers Road about 0.8 mile to the proper trailhead. The blue-blazed trail climbs steadily for 0.75 miles, growing much steeper as you climb the ridge. In another 0.5 mile, you'll reach the top of the ridge and emerge onto the rocks.

This is where the scramble begins. As you climb over granite boulders, you'll have some wide Piedmont views or closer views of Weakley Hollow and the Blue Ridge Mountains.

As you climb, you'll be convinced, several times, that you've reached the summit. There are a number of false summits along the trail; you'll know you've reached one when you see a higher peak ahead. The real summit is marked with a concrete post. Check out the view from here, walk over to the second summit on a 200-yard or so side trail, and get a look at the true peak. While you're there, look for "buzzard baths," potholes in the rock where water gathers.

You can return the way you came, a trip of 2.8 miles (making 5.6 miles total), but you'll have to climb through that boulder field again. The **Saddle Trail** is a longer route—4.4 miles—that's all downhill with nothing to climb over; it's the preferred option if you have the time. For the Saddle Trail, turn right when you reach Ridge Trail from the summit. Descend along the ridge for 0.4 mile to a marker post at Old Rag Saddle. Ahead, Byrds Nest Shelter No. 1 (day use only) is in sight. Turn right and descend for 1.1 miles to the Old Rag Shelter and spring. Continue along the fire road. At 0.4 mile beyond the shelter, you'll reach a double junction. Turn right onto Weakley Hollow fire road, which goes 2.6 miles back to your starting point.

★ Luray Caverns

Along the northern reaches of the Blue Ridge Mountains, the hills are full of holes, and caverns abound. **Luray Caverns** (MP 31.5 to US-211 West, 101 Cave Hill Rd., Luray, 540/743-6551, www.luraycaverns.com, open 9am daily with tours departing every 20 minutes, final tour times vary by season: 6pm Apr.-June 14, 7pm June 15-Labor Day, 7pm day after Labor Day-Oct., 4pm and 5pm Sat.-Sun. Nov.-Mar., $27 adults, $23 seniors, $15 ages 6-12, free ages 5 and under) are the cream of the crop. This cavern system has been wowing visitors since it was first discovered in 1878, though as their tourist literature likes to say, the spectacle was four million centuries in the making. Paved walkways lead through massive cavern "rooms" filled with stalagmites, stalactites, and columns of pillars where they sometimes join. Along the way you'll see chambers as tall as 10-story buildings and tiny stalagmites, no bigger than a nipple on a baby's bottle, which formed before the founding of our nation.

There's too much to see on the tour to describe here, but the **Stalacpipe Organ** is definitely worth mentioning. It's considered the largest musical instrument in the world, and seeing as it's made of stalactites covering some 3.5 acres, who's to argue? The organ produces symphonic sounds when the stalactites are tapped by rubber-tipped mallets. It took 36 years to perfect the organ, but visitors can hear it played on every tour. It sounds like something straight out of *Chiller Theatre*. If that's not creepy enough, how about this: Shortly after the caves were discovered, human bone fragments were found embedded in a stalagmite. That story's both creepy and amazing when you consider how slowly stalagmites grow.

Your general admission ticket covers the cavern tour and admission to the **Car and Carriage Caravan Museum** (which has restored modes of transportation from 1725 to 1941) and the **Luray Valley Museum** (interpreting Shenandoah Valley culture as far back as pre-contact Native Americans). The **Garden Maze** and the **Rope Adventure Park** are extra ($8 adults, $6 ages 6-12 per attraction).

Central District
Mary's Rock Tunnel and Trail (MP 32)

Mary's Rock is solid granite and sits astride the Skyline Drive route, making a tunnel the easiest way over, around, or through. At only 12.66 feet, Mary's Rock Tunnel is a little tight, so be aware if you're driving an RV, camping trailer, or horse trailer. The 670-foot-long tunnel was cut through Mary's Rock in 1932. No one is quite sure how Mary's Rock got its name, though it's thought to have originated with Francis Thornton who, according to one story, married a woman named Mary and brought her to this rock to show her the lands they'd own together; according to another story, Thornton's daughter Mary paid a visit to the rock and returned home with a black bear cub.

★ Mary's Rock Trail
Distance: 2.6 miles out and back
Duration: 2-3 hours
Elevation gain: 820 feet
Difficulty: moderate
Trailhead: Meadow Spring Trailhead, MP 33.5
Directions: Park at the Meadow Spring parking area and walk 50 feet or so along Skyline Drive to access Meadow Spring Trailhead.

The hike to the top of Mary's Rock is well worth it for the 360-degree views of Shenandoah National Park. There are a couple of ways to reach Mary's Rock; this route has less elevation gain by around 400 feet and is nearly a mile shorter than the alternative. Immediately the trail ascends, then levels and ascends again. You'll pass the remains of a huge stone chimney, all that remains of a Potomac Appalachian Trail Club cabin built in the 1930s (it burned down in 1946), at 0.4 mile in. Keep climbing through this typical hardwood forest. You'll reach the Appalachian Trail and a cement signpost at 0.6 mile in. Turn right here and follow the Appalachian Trail as it ascends, then descends. You'll reach a second post in another 0.6 mile. Turn left onto the spur trail that will lead you to the summit of Mary's Rock.

Pinnacles Overlook (MP 35.5)

From Pinnacles Overlook, you have a great view of Old Rag Mountain. In fall, when the colors sweep down either side of the valley and end with the bulk of Old

Shenandoah National Park, Central District

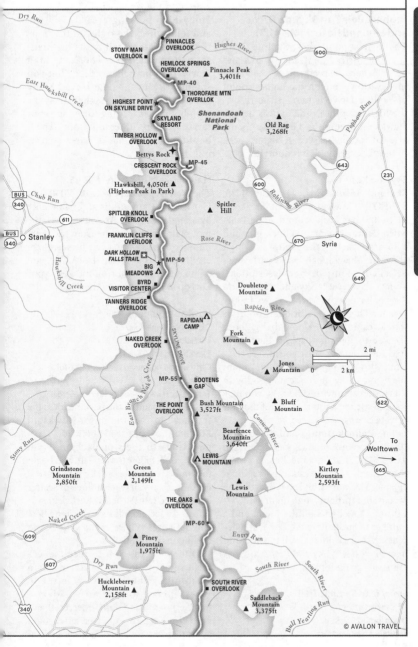

© AVALON TRAVEL

Rag, it's quite a sight, but it's a nice spot in any season.

Highest Point on Skyline Drive and Skyland Resort (MP 41.7)

The highest point along Skyline Drive is at the northern entrance to Skyland Resort where the road reaches 3,680 feet in elevation. Though the highest point of Skyline Drive is here at the resort, the highest point in the park is nearby Hawksbill Mountain. Less than a mile away by trail is the second-highest peak in the park, Stony Man Mountain.

Skyland Resort

Skyland Resort (MP 41.7 and 42.5, 877/847-1919, www.goshenandoah.com, $145-305) has been around since 1888, when George Freeman Pollock Jr. found a 16-acre tract in the mountains high above the Shenandoah Valley with views he called "beauty beyond description." Today, his retreat is Skyland Resort, and it does have some unreal views in any season. There are traditional rooms as well as cabins here. Know that eight of the cabins have multiple rooms, each sold individually, so if you're not traveling with a group large enough to rent the whole thing or you're no good with sharing a cabin with strangers, you may want to stick to a room or one of the four private cabins.

The **Pollock Dining Room** (7:30am-10:30am, noon-2:30pm, and 5:30pm-9pm daily, $11-25) at Skyland Resort serves three meals a day of seasonal regional cuisine. Meals are simple but hearty. The **Mountain Taproom** (2pm-10pm daily, $7-14) has a few items on the menu and a number of specialty cocktails and a decent selection of domestic, imported, and microbrew beers. Skyland Resort also has grab-and-go options.

Stony Man Summit Trail

Distance: 1.4 miles out and back
Duration: 1-2 hours
Elevation gain: 350 feet

Difficulty: easy
Trailhead: Stony Man parking area at Skyland Resort

Hop onto the Appalachian Trail at the Stony Man parking area in Skyland and follow it to the right. At 0.4 mile, the Appalachian Trail crests the highest point in the park. The Stony Man Horse Trail branches off left, but you should stick to the blue-blazed Stony Man Trail. At 0.5 mile in, the trail splits, with both sides leading to the summit, forming a loop. Either fork works. You'll be at the summit in less than a quarter mile from here.

Hawksbill Mountain (MP 45.6)

The **highest peak in the park,** 4,050-foot Hawksbill Mountain, is accessible only by a moderate hike. As you'd guess, the mountain drew its name from the great number of hawks that can be seen here circling on the thermals. While you climb, and once you summit, keep your eyes open for raptors on the wing.

Hawksbill Summit Trail

Distance: 2.8-mile loop
Duration: 2-3 hours
Elevation gain: 800 feet
Difficulty: moderate to strenuous (due to elevation gain)
Trailhead: Hawksbill Gap parking lot, MP 45.6

At the north end of the parking lot is the trailhead to the summit of Hawksbill Mountain. A spur trail about 100 yards long leads to the Appalachian Trail, which you'll follow to your left, and begin to climb. The trail is rocky for the first 0.4 mile, then you reach a slope of scatter rock (called talus), then a short clear section and a second talus slope. Along here you have great views of the valleys and mountains around.

One mile in, you'll reach a cement signpost noting the Appalachian Trail mileage and arrows pointing to Hawksbill and to Fishers Gap. Make a hard left onto the Salamander Trail and keep climbing. In a quarter mile, you'll come to a very rocky point, so be careful of your steps. As you approach the top, you'll join a fire road, making the rest of the route very easy. The summit is at 1.9 miles, so you're close.

On the summit, you'll find the Byrds Nest, a shelter built for former U.S. Senator and Virginia Governor Harry F. Byrd Sr. There's no water and no camping here. The summit is a few yards away.

The summit view is commanding. In every direction, mountains fade into the distance. To your north is Stony Man, Brown Mountain is to the west, Graves Mountain to the south, and Skyline Drive just below you. If you're lucky, you'll see the endangered peregrine falcon, the fastest bird in the nation, which can dive at speeds up to 120 miles per hour.

To return, retrace your steps to the shelter and turn left on the fire road to a cement post directing you to the Lower Hawksbill Trail. Turn left and head back to the parking area. Be careful going down; it's rocky, steep in places, and taxing.

Dark Hollow Falls (MP 50.7)
★ Dark Hollow Falls Trail
Distance: 1.4 miles out and back
Duration: 1.5-2 hours
Elevation gain: 440 feet
Difficulty: moderate to strenuous
Trailhead: Dark Hollow Falls Trailhead at MP 50.7

Dark Hollow Falls is one of the most popular waterfall hikes in Shenandoah National Park, and for good reason: the short hike and excellent view. Moss and ferns cling to the cliff around the falls, and at the base, there are several great opportunities for photographers to shoot leaf-littered rocks and small cascades, especially in autumn.

This short hike takes you to one of the most popular and easily accessible waterfalls. Take "easily accessible" with a grain of salt, though, as the trail is all downhill on the way to the 70-foot Dark Hollow Falls and a 440-foot elevation gain on the way back up. It's a thigh-burner, for sure.

From the parking area, the trail descends and follows Hog-camp Branch. You'll reach your first overlook of Dark Hollow Falls at 0.6 mile. Continue on the trail to the base of the falls at 0.7 mile. Climb back up to get to your car.

Along the way, you'll notice a rail to help you with your footing and keep you on the path. Don't be foolish and go past the rail and fences, which not only prevent trail erosion but also keep you safe.

Byrd Visitor Center (MP 51)
The **Harry F. Byrd, Sr. Visitor Center** (9am-5pm daily late Mar.-Nov.; 9am-5pm Sat.-Sun. Dec.-late Mar.) has the usual visitors center facilities—restrooms, information desk, videos—as well as a great exhibit telling the story of the establishment and development of Shenandoah National Park.

Story of the Forest Trail
Distance: 1.8-mile loop
Duration: 1-1.5 hours
Elevation gain: 300 feet
Difficulty: easy
Trailhead: across from the north entrance to the Byrd Visitor Center at MP 51

The Story of the Forest Trail is an easy loop and generally a good place to see wildlife, so it's good for children or to use as a leg-stretching break from a day in the car. The trail is wide and transitions from gravel to forest floor to paved. You pass over Hog Branch at 0.2 mile in, then meet up with a horse trail at 0.4 mile. At 0.8 mile, you'll reach the Big Meadows Campground. Turn left here and follow the paved bike/walking path back to the visitors center.

Big Meadows (MP 51)
Big Meadows is home to the largest open meadow in Shenandoah National Park, a lodge, a campground, and a full-service dining room. There's also a long, but fairly leisurely (save a few spots), hike leading to one of the highest waterfalls in the park. For excellent wildlife viewing, observe the fields shortly after dawn and

before dusk when the deer herds appear to graze. If you choose to hike at these times, be quiet and go slow. You'll be surprised at how much wildlife you can see.

Big Meadows Campground (MP 51.2, 877/444-6777, www.recreation.gov, $20, groups $45) has more than 220 tent and RV sites. At **Big Meadows Wayside** (MP 51.2, 9am-5:30pm Sun.-Thurs. and 8am-7pm Fri.-Sat. Apr.-Nov.), you can get groceries, a meal, camping supplies, and gasoline.

Big Meadows Lodge

Big Meadows Lodge (MP 51.2, 877/847-1919 or 877/247-9261, www.goshenandoah.com, $125-206) was built in 1939 of native stone and chestnut wood paneling. It's a beautiful property and listed on the National Register of Historic Places. Accommodations here range from lodge rooms to small, rustic cabins. The lodge is near the really large meadow that lends Big Meadows its name.

At Big Meadows Lodge, you can dine in the **Spottswood Dining Room** (MP 51.2, 7:30am-10am, noon-2pm, and 5:30pm-9pm daily, $7-28) or get a picnic-to-go box lunch to take with you (place your order at the front desk or at the hostess stand). Entrées here include smoked pork ribs, prime rib, roast turkey, and pan-seared trout. At the **New Market Taproom** (2pm-11pm daily, $8-13) you can get a little food and a number of cocktails, wines by the glass, and beer, and there's often musical entertainment.

Lewis Spring Falls Trail

Distance: 3.3-mile loop
Duration: 3-3.5 hours
Elevation gain: 1,000 feet
Difficulty: moderate
Trailhead: Big Meadows Campground, MP 51.2

Starting from the amphitheater behind the picnic area, take the Appalachian Trail to the left. At 0.1 mile, follow the blue-blazed Lewis Spring Falls Trail to the right. The trail is very well maintained, though it's rocky, requiring

approaching Big Meadows on Skyline Drive

caution and some good boots. For about a mile, you'll descend into a hollow. When the trail levels out, you'll hear the waterfalls. At one mile, a short ascent delivers you to a nice open view of the mountains to the west. To your left is an observation point just down the trail. Cross a stream and continue along until you reach Lewis Spring Falls. The fourth-highest in the park at 81 feet, the falls are more a cascade than a proper waterfall, but they're beautiful nonetheless.

From the overlook, backtrack to the blue-blazed trail and head uphill. You'll parallel a creek on your left and ascend via a set of switchbacks. At 1.9 miles you'll reach a cement marker. Follow Lewis Spring Fire Road for 70 or 80 yards, then turn left onto the Appalachian Trail. Follow the path uphill to the lodge and campground.

Rapidan Camp (MP 52.8)
A moderate to difficult hike from Milam Gap will take you to a waterfall and the

retreat of President Hoover; this is the only way to get to this perfect presidential mountain getaway. Hoover had three requirements for his retreat: It had to be within 100 miles of Washington DC; it had to be located on a trout stream; and it had to be at least 2,500 feet above sea level. This spot met all three criteria, and at one time there were 13 cabins and structures that served him and his guests during these working getaways. Today only 3 of the original 13 remain.

Rapidan Camp Trail
Distance: 4 miles out and back
Duration: 2.5-3 hours
Elevation gain: 850 feet
Difficulty: moderate to strenuous
Trailhead: Milam Gap parking lot, MP 52.8

Cross Skyline Drive to the trailhead. You'll follow the Appalachian Trail a short way until it joins Mill Prong Trail. Turn left onto Mill Prong Trail, descending as you parallel the stream (where fishing is allowed, provided you catch and release, using only single-hook, artificial lures). At 1.5 miles, you pass Big Rock Falls and continue downhill where you'll cross Mill Prong. Two miles in, cross the bridge and climb up to Rapidan Camp. The camp's namesake river is just a few paces away. Retrace your steps back uphill to the parking area.

Bearfence Mountain (MP 56.4)
From the top of 3,640-foot Bearfence Mountain, you'll get a commanding, 360-degree view of Shenandoah National Park. The view takes in several notable peaks—Massanutten Mountain to the west, and Bluff Mountain and Fork Mountain to the east, to name a few—and is from one of the best park mountaintops.

Bearfence Mountain Trail
Distance: 1.2-mile loop
Duration: 1-1.5 hours
Elevation gain: 380 feet
Difficulty: moderate to strenuous

Trailhead: across Skyline Drive from the Bearfence Mountain parking area, MP 56.4

This hike requires some real rock scrambling, but no technical gear or real technical experience, just common sense, a little upper-body strength, and the ability to determine when it's time to pack it in and turn back for the trailhead. Cross Skyline Drive from the parking area and set foot on the trail. It climbs uphill quickly and then at 0.1 mile, the blue-blazed trail crosses the Appalachian Trail. Bearfence Mountain Trail immediately gets rocky, and you'll begin to make your way through huge boulders only a few hundred yards from the parking area. Look closely and you'll notice that many of the boulders have a greenish hue. They're called greenstone, and it has taken millions of years for their color to show thanks to fractures and fissures in the rocks.

The boulder field is only a couple hundred yards long, though it feels longer. At 0.4 mile, you'll reach the summit, as evidenced by the view: You can see everything from here.

There are two ways back, though one is a little shorter. You can return to the parking lot by the way you arrived, a shorter route of only 0.8 mile; or you can continue toward the Appalachian Trail by turning right from the summit. From here you'll intersect with the Appalachian Trail 0.5 mile farther on, then follow the trail north to the parking lot.

Lewis Mountain (MP 57.5)

At Lewis Mountain, you'll find some first-come, first-served camping; some cute, rustic cabins; and a camp store to serve your minor grocery needs. **Lewis Mountain Campground** (877/444-6777, www.recreation.gov, daily mid-Mar.-late Nov., $15) is the smallest campground in the park, with only 31 sites. You won't find any RVs or reservations here, so if you want to camp at Lewis Mountain, show up early. **Lewis Mountain Cabins** (877/247-9261, www.goshenandoah.com,

$138) are cozy and quaint. How quaint? There's no phone signal to be had or wireless Internet access to speak of, but each cabin does have electricity, a private bathroom, linens, and an outdoor grill. To top all this off, the **Lewis Mountain Campstore** (540/999-2255, 9am-6pm Sun.-Thurs., 9am-7pm Fri.-Sat. mid-Mar.-late Nov.) carries a limited selection of groceries, a few retail gift items, and a small selection of alcohol, so everything you need for a night or two at the campground or cabins.

⬥ US-340 West: Grand Caverns (MP 62.7)

Grand Caverns (5 Grand Caverns Dr., Grottoes, 540/249-5705 or 888/430-2283, www.grandcaverns.com, 9am-5pm daily Apr.-Oct., 10am-4pm daily Nov.-Mar., $20 adults, $18 seniors, $11 children) is the oldest continually operating show cave in the nation, seeing its first paying visitors in 1806. It was discovered in 1804 by Bernard Weyer as he sought to retrieve one of his traps. Weyer spent the next two years exploring and mapping the cave before opening it to the public. During the Civil War, Union and Confederate soldiers visited the cave (though on separate occasions), and some 230 of the visiting soldiers signed their names on the cave walls.

On a guided tour of the cave, you'll pass through nine "rooms." The largest is Cathedral Hall, which is 50 feet tall at its highest and 280 feet long. Other rooms of note include the Grand Ball Room, where many candlelit balls and dances were held; the Lily Room, which has a huge formation that resembles a calla lily; and the Chapel, which has formations resembling a pulpit, organ, and chandelier, and was the site of many church services and still hosts weddings.

Tours take about 70 minutes. Wear comfortable, closed-toe shoes and a jacket as it's a constant 54°F in the caverns.

To reach Grand Caverns, you have a couple of options. From Skyline Drive, exit onto US-340/US-33 (also called the Spotswood Trail) at Swift Run Gap (MP 62.7) and travel west to Elkton, Virginia, then turn south on US-340 to Grottoes. This route is 23 miles long and takes approximately 30 minutes. Another option is to follow US-340 north from Waynesboro to Grottoes, a trip of 15 miles, taking approximately 25 minutes.

Southern District
South River Falls (MP 62.8)
These 83-foot waterfalls are the third largest in Shenandoah National Park, and you can only see them on a hike along the South River.

South River Falls Trail
Distance: 4.4 miles out and back
Duration: 2-3 hours
Elevation gain: 800 feet
Difficulty: moderate to strenuous
Trailhead: South River Picnic Area, MP 62.8

To the right of the drinking fountain at the South River Picnic Area, you'll find the trailhead to South River Falls. The trail descends 0.1 mile until it meets the Appalachian Trail, marked by a cement post. Follow the blue blazes and descend a series of gradual switchbacks. At times the trail here is rocky, but generally it's wide and smooth.

You'll pass by several creeks as they flow out of the mountain to join with South River. At 0.75 miles, you'll encounter a creek to your left that's almost entirely hidden by the rocks, although you can hear it. The South River begins to parallel the trail around here.

Another stream joins the South River, then, suddenly, the river plunges into a deep grotto. There's no real view of the falls from here, but there's a good overlook at 1.3 miles. Some may choose to return to the trailhead from here (making a 2.6-mile hike), and to do so, simply go back the way you came. I recommend continuing on the longer 4.4-mile hike.

To make the 4.4-mile trail, continue along and join up with an old road at 1.5

miles. Stay on the South River Falls Trail, which descends and then turns back toward the falls and a cement post at 2.1 miles. According to the post, the park's boundary is nearby, and there's a short spur trail to the base of the falls 0.1 mile away. Take the spur trail to the large pool at the base of South River Falls. Take off your shoes and socks and go for a wade; it's refreshing, and you'll find that it will help with the climb back to the top.

Brown Mountain Overlook (MP 76.9)
Traveling the Skyline Drive to Blue Ridge Parkway route from the north, this is the first Brown Mountain you'll encounter, but not the last. At least two more (including the North Carolina iteration where many have seen the strange Brown Mountain Lights appear in the dark of night) await on your journey south. Shenandoah National Park's Brown Mountain Overlook is excellent. The ridges descend to the valley floor in stacked waves, and at their head is a mountain, which in autumn is ablaze with color, save the spots where rocky protrusions show through the trees.

Loft Mountain (MP 79.5)
At the **Loft Mountain Wayside** (MP 79.5, 540/999-2255, 9am-6pm daily mid-Apr.-early Nov.), you can grab a bite to eat from a snack counter, pick up some grocery-type supplies, and add to your arsenal of camping and hiking equipment. You can also take a nearly three-mile trail to the summit of Loft Mountain and take in some remarkable views of the valleys and mountains surrounding the peak.

Loft Mountain Loop Trail
Distance: 2.7-mile loop
Duration: 2 hours
Elevation gain: 600 feet
Difficulty: easy
Trailhead: Loft Mountain Wayside parking lot, MP 79.5

This easy trail is family-friendly and

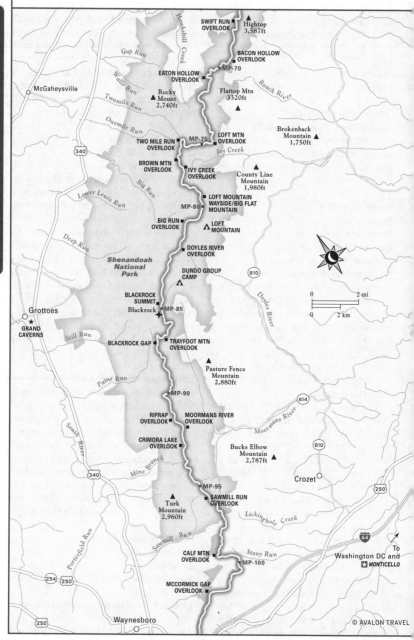

Shenandoah National Park, Southern District

canine-compatible, making it a popular leg-stretching hike. Walk north on Skyline Drive 150 or so yards from the wayside parking lot. You'll pass the Patterson Ridge Trail trailhead on the left, but continue on to the first dirt road and head to the Ivy Creek Hut. At 0.6 mile, a cement post marks the junction with the Appalachian Trail. Turn right and follow the white blazes through the forest.

Approaching the summit of Loft Mountain, you'll notice the trees grow thinner and the undergrowth, particularly the blackberry bushes, grow thicker. The trail will level off as it follows the ridge top around one mile in. At 1.1 miles, you'll reach an overlook on the left side that gives you a nice panoramic view of the Piedmont to the east. Continue along the trail until you reach the next cement post at 1.4 miles. Turn right on Frazier Discovery Trail (note: dogs are not allowed on Frazier, so if you brought the pooch, simply turn around and head back to the car) and make your way back to the Loft Mountain Wayside and your car. Prepare yourself for some monster views along Frazier Discovery Trail as a number of rock outcroppings afford you awesome vantage points.

Big Flat Mountain (MP 79.5)

The second-highest peak in the Southern District of Shenandoah National Park, Big Flat Mountain is just that: big and flat. On top, at the largest, most level spot, is **Loft Mountain Campground** (MP 79.5, information 434/823-4675, reservations 877/444-6777, www.recreation.gov, $15, groups $35-50), with more than 200 campsites for tents and RVs. The campground took its name from nearby Loft Mountain as the Park Service felt "Big Flat" Campground was not nearly so appealing.

Big Run Overlook (MP 81.2)

By this point in your journey along Skyline Drive, you know that fantastic views are everywhere, and Big Run Overlook is no exception. There's no picnic area, but this is still a great spot to pull off and take a look at the crenellated mountains. Big Run is an important watershed for this part of Virginia; here, one inch of rain equates to something along the lines of 200 million gallons of water feeding streams, wells, and the aquifer.

Blackrock Summit (MP 84.8)

Not only is this a beautiful spot to stop and take in the scenery, it's also got an interesting history. During the Revolutionary War, Virginia Governor Thomas Jefferson was concerned about the state archives and the Great Seal of Virginia. He gave them to a friend for safekeeping. That friend hid them in a cave at Blackrock Mountain until the end of the war.

Blackrock Summit Trail

Distance: 1-mile loop
Duration: 30-45 minutes
Elevation gain: 180 feet
Difficulty: easy
Trailhead: Blackrock parking lot, MP 84.8

This is an easy hike for families as it is just over 0.5 mile to the summit, and reaching the summit involves a short, rocky scramble through a boulder field, making hikers with less experience feel like they've accomplished a minor feat of mountaineering prowess.

Near the sign that describes the mountain's geography, step onto Trayfoot Mountain Trail and ascend rather steeply for 0.1 mile until you reach the Appalachian Trail. Turn left on the Appalachian Trail and follow the white-blazed, nearly level path 0.4 mile to where the trail ends just before the summit. To reach the summit, there's a short scramble through a boulder field to a great panoramic view of the valley below. Be careful on the boulders; the footing can be tricky. Also, hikers have reported seeing rattlesnakes sunning themselves here, so keep an eye and an ear open for them.

Riprap Overlook (MP 90)
Riprap Hollow Trail
Distance: 9.8-mile loop
Duration: 6-7 hours
Elevation gain: 2,300 feet
Difficulty: strenuous
Trailhead: Riprap Overlook, MP 90

One of the best loop hikes in the Southern District of Shenandoah National Park, Riprap Hollow Trail will lead you to some great views and awesome swimming holes in a spring-fed stream. Walk 50 yards along the blue-blazed trail from the Riprap parking area to where it intersects with the white-blazed Appalachian Trail. Turn right and head uphill 0.4 mile to the intersection with Riprap Hollow Trail.

Turn left at Riprap Hollow Trail and descend into a hollow on the ridge before a short climb leading you to the first vista at 0.7 mile. In another 0.3 mile, you'll reach Chimney Rock and a fantastic view. Linger here a moment before descending into Cold Springs Hollow. In 1.7 miles you'll reach a stream that cuts through a small gorge and leads to a 20-foot waterfall.

Continue past the waterfall another quarter mile to a large swimming hole. Just past this is a trail across the stream leading to an old shelter. After a side trip to the shelter, continue along the blue-blazed Riprap Hollow Trail next to the stream for 0.7 mile until it intersects with Wildcat Ridge Trail.

At Wildcat Ridge, turn left, cross the stream, and make your way through a small gorge. In 0.6 mile you'll reach a steep section and a set of switchbacks. Follow the trail for two miles to a four-way intersection with the Appalachian Trail. Turn left on the Appalachian Trail and hike back the final 2.8 miles to the Riprap parking area.

Crimora Lake Overlook (MP 92.6)
This is one of the top views along Skyline Drive primarily because of beautiful Crimora Lake forming the centerpiece of the view. Framed by Turk Mountain and Rocks Mountain, the lake is an absolute jewel. Crimora Lake is not a natural one; it's a relic of the valley's mining days. The mines here extracted more manganese than anywhere else in the United States, and at one time were among the largest manganese mines in the world.

Calf Mountain Overlook (MP 96.9)
From an elevation of 2,485 feet, the Calf Mountain Overlook provides some dizzying views. As you round the bend here, the road seems to continue right out into the air, but it really just makes a tight turn. The overlook is a long one, with near-360-degree views. To the south you can see Bear Den Mountain, while to the north you can see the Shenandoah Valley, the course of Sawmill Run, and a handful of named peaks. Calf Mountain is right behind you, and if you want to hike to the summit, the trailhead is just three miles down Skyline Drive.

Calf Mountain Trail
Distance: 2 miles out and back
Duration: 1-1.5 hours
Elevation gain: 525 feet
Difficulty: moderate
Trailhead: Beagle Gap parking area, MP 99.5 (3 miles south of Calf Mountain Overlook, MP 96.9)

Don't expect a view from the summit as it is treed in, but it's a pleasing, easy hike with chances to see wildflowers and berry bushes along the way. From the parking area, pass through the wire fence and begin to ascend through a broad meadow. As you enter the woods, the trail will become steeper, though it levels out again quite quickly and takes you through the remnants of an apple orchard (some of the trees still bear fruit).

At one mile in, you'll find a cairn (stack of stones) on the trail. Nearby, embedded in some rock, is a USGS marker noting the summit of Calf Mountain. If you choose to continue on to the Calf Mountain Shelter, a spur trail (blue-blazed) nearby leads down a 0.2-mile path to the shelter.

Waynesboro

Known early on as Teasville, Waynesboro sits at the point where the Appalachian Trail, Skyline Drive, and Blue Ridge Parkway meet. This town of 22,000 takes advantage of this confluence and welcomes guests in, offering up a number of surprisingly good local restaurants and even more national chains. Outfitters for outdoor adventures, from fly-fishing to river tubing, call Waynesboro home and cater to Appalachian Trail hikers. In the hills above town, you'll find some lovely inns and grand vistas of the Shenandoah River Valley.

Getting There

If time is of the essence, you can reach Waynesboro from DC in just three hours; this 164-mile route follows I-66 west to I-81 south to I-64 east. If you prefer to take Skyline Drive through Shenandoah National Park, it's a five-hour drive of 179 miles following I-66 west from DC to Front Royal, Virginia, then south along Skyline Drive to its southern end, where you're just five minutes west of Waynesboro.

Sights

The **Waynesboro Heritage Museum** (420 W. Main St., 540/943-3943, www.waynesboroheritagefoundation.com, 10am-4pm Thurs.-Sat., free) shows the history of this town from its 1797 inception to the present day. Permanent and rotating exhibit galleries allow conservators to highlight both major historical events and focus on the families, people, and smaller events that shaped this town.

There are 40 (and counting) wineries, breweries, and cider works within 30 miles of Waynesboro, making for a tasty day trip. Some of the nearest are **Barren Ridge Vineyards** (984 Barren Ridge Rd., Fisherville, 540/248-3300, www.barrenridgevineyards.com, 11am-6pm Mon.-Wed., 11am-sunset Thurs.-Sat., 1pm-6pm Sun.), six miles away in Fisherville; **Afton Mountain Vineyards** (234 Vineyard Ln., Afton, 540/456-8667, www.aftonmountainvineyards.com, 11am-5:30pm daily), eight miles away in Afton; and **Blue Mountain Brewery** (9519 Critzers Shop Rd., Afton, 540/456-8020, www.bluemountainbrewery.com, 11am-10pm Mon.-Sat., 11am-9pm Sun.), nine miles away in Afton. Tastings are $5-10 at each of these venues.

Entertainment
Nightlife
Seven Arrows Brewing Company (2508 Jefferson Hwy. 1, 540/221-6968, www.sevenarrowsbrewing.com, 11am-9pm Mon., 11am-10pm Wed.-Fri., noon-11pm Sat., noon-9pm Sun.) keeps a wide range of brews on tap and in cans. From their own take on pilsners and American wheat beer to lambics and kombucha, they keep it flowing. If you're there and need a bite to go with your brew, they share a space with **Nobos** (540/471-8435, $3-14), which serves standard bar food and a few upscale dishes.

Heritage on Main Street (309 W. Main St., 540/946-6166, www.heritageonmainstreet.com, 11am-midnight Sun.-Thurs., 11am-1am Fri.-Sat., free live music 7pm Wed., 9pm Sat.) is open late every night of the week. This downtown sports bar serves a full menu of bar food. The wings are especially good, as is the burger (they have 22 types of burgers). And there are 22 taps pouring some of the best beer and cider around; they carry both local and national craft beer and cider, and a handful of domestics. This is the spot to stop in to catch a fight or a ballgame, or to see a band.

Shopping
Rockfish Gap Outfitters (1461 W. Main St., 540/943-1461, www.rockfishgapoutfitters.com, 10am-6pm Mon.-Sat.,

noon-5pm Sun.) has everything you'll need to mount a successful expedition along the Blue Ridge Parkway or Skyline Drive, including all of the hikes, picnics, waterfalls, and roadside stops you'll include on your journey. You'll find clothing and gear from Patagonia, ExOfficio, Merrell, Outdoor Research, and a host of other top-rated outdoor brands. The shop is a popular stop for Appalachian Trail thru-hikers and segment hikers. At Rockfish Gap, you can get the skinny on the best hikes, river floats, and mountain biking trails (as well as those great local fishing holes) from outdoor enthusiasts who call the area home and know the top spots.

Stitch Amour (112 S. Wayne Ave., 540/942-9022, www.stitchamour.com, 11am-5pm Tues.-Wed., 11am-6pm Fri., 10am-4pm Sat.) has just about everything a knitting enthusiast could want: exciting natural yarns in pima cotton, alpaca wool, and wool/silk blends, patterns, knitting needles and crochet hooks, and finished goods. They also host knitting and sewing classes.

At the **Shenandoah Valley Art Center (SVAC)** (126 S. Wayne Dr., 540/949-7662, www.svacart.com, 10am-4pm Tues.-Sat.), you'll find a collection of galleries where art from SVAC members is displayed alongside high-quality shows by individual artists, group exhibits, and juried exhibitions. They have a gift shop where you'll find the typical art gallery gifts: jewelry, glass art, and pottery. The gift shop also showcases a selection of one SVAC artist's work.

Sports and Recreation

Shenandoah River Adventures (415 Long Ave., Shenandoah, 38 miles north of Waynesboro, 888/309-7222, www.shenandoahriveradventures.com, tubes $20, canoes and kayaks $30-55) has kayaks, canoes, and tubes you can rent and take out onto the Shenandoah River. If you feel more adventurous, they offer full-day canoe and kayak trips ($40-65)

countryside near Waynesboro

and multiday trips ($55/kayak first two days, $15/day thereafter; $85/canoe first two days, $25/day thereafter). You'll find a number of Appalachian Trail hikers giving their feet a little break and "Aquablazing" part of the monumental trail. Aquablazing is when hikers come off the trail and canoe or kayak from one spot to another; here it's generally done along the Shenandoah River since it runs parallel to the Appalachian Trail as it passes through Shenandoah National Park.

In addition to selling outdoors gear, **Rockfish Gap Outfitters** (1461 E. Main St., 540/943-1461, www.rockfishgapout-fitters.com, 10am-6pm Mon.-Sat., noon-5pm Sun., single kayaks and paddleboards $35, double kayaks $60) rents kayaks and stand-up paddleboards by the day. They also provide tips on the best places to get on the water.

South River Fly Shop (323 W. Main St., 540/942-5566, www.southriverflyshop.com, 9am-6pm Mon.-Fri., 9am-5pm Sat., noon-4pm Sun.) is run by two young men who have been fishing in mountain waters their entire lives. They know their flies, they know what gear is built to last, and they know where to go to put you on the fish. In their shop, they carry a selection of fly-tying materials and tools, rods and reels, clothing, boots and waders, and just about anything else you could need to spend a day on the water. They also offer a **guide service** that takes you out on the South River to fish for trout ($195 half day for 1-2 people, $295 full day); a full-day float trip for smallmouth bass and trout along the Shenandoah River ($400), the James River ($400), and the Jackson River ($450); and full-day trips into Shenandoah National Park ($325).

Food

Stella, Bella, & Lucy's (327 W. Main St., 540/949-5111, www.stellabellalucy.com, 9am-10:30am and 11am-2:30pm Mon.-Sat., $7-9) was named for a trio of dogs beloved by the restaurant's proprietors, but the food is anything but table scraps. Serving both breakfast and lunch, they keep it simple with smaller menus of very well-executed food. For lunch, try the pineapple boat (chicken or turkey salad on a wedge of fresh pineapple and a bed of lettuce) or the stuffed tomato; if you need something more filling, then try The Granny, a corned beef sandwich with homemade pimento cheese.

Scotto's Italian Restaurant and Pizzeria (1412 W. Broad St., 540/942-8715, www.scottos.net, 11am-9:30pm Mon.-Thurs., 11am-10:30pm Fri.-Sat., 11:30am-9:30pm Sun., $7-24) is a local favorite for all things pasta and pizza. Pies come in both deep-dish Sicilian style and hand tossed, and you can build your own or let them guide you with one of their specialty pies. The Pizza à la Scotto's (white sauce, ham, spinach, and mozzarella) is quite good.

The atmosphere at **The Fishin' Pig** (117 Apple Tree Ln., 540/943-3474, www.fishinpig.com, 11:30am-11pm Tues.-Thurs.,

11:30am-midnight Fri.-Sat., 11:30am-8pm Sun., $7-25) should be enough to draw you in. After all, who doesn't want to be around fun people having a good time? But if that's not enough, the smell of the smokehouse should do the trick. This restaurant serves a bit of Virginia barbecue, tacos, shrimp by the pound, and a range of Southern sides.

The Green Leaf Grill (415 W. Main St., 540/949-4416, www.thegreenleafgrill. com, 11am-9pm Tues.-Thurs. and Sun., 11am-10pm Fri.-Sat., $10-20) has a very good beer selection, stone-oven pizzas, and a menu filled with dishes that reflect a variety of influences. There's lasagna, crawfish étouffée, coconut curry, steaks, burgers, and fish tacos. They do an impressive job with all of it.

Accommodations

At the Belle Hearth Bed & Breakfast (320 S. Wayne Ave., 540/943-1910, www. bellehearth.com, $120-165), expect a candlelit breakfast at a table set with china and actual silver silverware. They've won a number of awards and accolades for their breakfast, which always includes some outstanding biscuits, fresh seasonal fruits and herbs, and a rotating array of quiches and breakfast casseroles. The house is Victorian in style, which sometimes means overdecorated, but not so at Belle Hearth; it's Victorian for certain, but tastefully so.

The ★ Iris Inn (191 Chinquapin Dr., 540/943-1991, www.irisinn.com, $229-339) looks out over the valley from a 12-acre Blue Ridge mountaintop. Built in 1991 to be an inn, the property includes the six-room inn, a half-dozen cabins, and three cottages. Every room has fabulous views and is decorated in a contemporary style that combines the mountaintop/cabin/nature feel of the inn with tasteful design. The common areas are beautiful: high ceilings, wood and stone accents, and abundant natural light.

There are also several chain hotels

in Waynesboro. The Best Western Plus Waynesboro Inn & Suites Conference Center (109 Apple Tree Ln., 540/942-1100, www.bwwaynesboro.com, $135-200) is a 75-room, 19-suite, pet-friendly hotel with free continental breakfast and a heated indoor saltwater pool, and it's right off I-64, making it easy to spot and even easier to get to. The Residence Inn Waynesboro (44 Windigrove Rd., 540/943-7426, www.residenceinn.marriott.com, $149-229) has 90 suites, free Internet, and spacious suites in addition to a continental breakfast.

Information and Services

Visitors to Waynesboro will find information and tools to help them plan a trip through the Waynesboro Department of Tourism (301 W. Main St., 540/942-6512, www.visitwaynesboro.net, 8am-5pm Mon.-Fri.), or they can visit the Rockfish Gap Tourist Information Center (130 Afton Circle, Afton, 540/943-5187, 9am-5pm daily). There's more information available through Waynesboro Downtown Development, Inc. (301 W. Main St., 540/942-6705, www.waynesborodowntown.org).

For police assistance, contact the Waynesboro Police Department (250 S. Wayne Ave., 540/942-6675, www. waynesboro.va.us), the Waynesboro City Sheriff (250 S. Wayne Ave., 540/942-6639, www.waynesboro.va.us), or the Augusta County Sheriff's Department (127 Lee Hwy., Verona, 540/245-5333, www.co.augusta.va.us).

Augusta Health (78 Medical Center Dr., Fisherville, 800/932-0262, www.augustahealth.com), in Fisherville, is the nearest local hospital.

Charlottesville

Established in 1762 along an important trade route, Charlottesville is a beautiful town of 45,000. It's home to the University of Virginia, an interesting array of restaurants and shops, and a deep field of historic and artistic figures, most notably, a pair of U.S. presidents, Thomas Jefferson and James Monroe. (James Madison, another U.S. president, lived one county over.) Jefferson's home, Monticello, draws nearly 500,000 visitors a year and is the most popular tourist destination in the area. Other recognizable Charlottesville figures include Edgar Allan Poe, who went to UVA for a semester; John Grisham; Dave Matthews and several bandmates; Corey Harris; NFL veteran Howie Long and son Chris Long; and actor Rob Lowe.

One of the most charming parts of the city is the Downtown Mall on West Main Street. This long, tree-shaded, statue-adorned pedestrian area is lined with shops, restaurants, and vendors, and capped by a movie theater and ice rink at one end, and the Charlottesville Pavilion at the other. The grounds of the University of Virginia are the very picture of a university campus, and the student population helps keep the town fresh and on trend.

Getting There

Both Skyline Drive and the Blue Ridge Parkway are only 24 miles west of Charlottesville, and I-81 is only 12 miles farther.

I-64 runs right by downtown Charlottesville. Richmond is 70 miles to the east along I-64; I-95 passes through Richmond, connecting that city and the I-64 corridor to a larger range of big cities on the East Coast. To the west, Beckley, West Virginia, is 186 miles away; there, I-77 and I-79 connect to a number of other destinations along the mid-Atlantic.

Charlottesville is served by **Charlottesville Albemarle Airport** (100 Bowen Loop, Charlottesville, 434/973-8342, www.gocho.com). Airlines flying to and from here include Delta, American Airlines, and United Airlines. At the **Charlottesville Amtrak station** (CVS, 810

W. Main St., 434/296-4559 or 800/872-7245, www.amtrak.com, 6am-9:30pm daily), the Cardinal/Hoosier State, Crescent, and Northeast Regional Lines pass through daily. The **Charlottesville Greyhound station** (310 W. Main St., 434/295-5131, www.greyhound.com, 8am-10pm daily) is just a few blocks from the Amtrak station.

Charlottesville Area Transit (1545 Avon St. Ext., 434/970-3649, www.charlottesville.org, schedules vary, one-way from $0.75), or CAT, has 11 routes and a free trolley serving the University of Virginia and downtown.

Sights
University of Virginia
The **University of Virginia** (434/924-0311, www.virginia.edu) is consistently among the top-rated state universities in the nation. Thomas Jefferson founded the university, which opened in March 1825 with a mere 123 students. For the first year of operations, Jefferson was heavily involved in the university, but he died on July 4, 1826. Today, UVA adds more than 20,000 students to the population of Charlottesville during the school year.

The main grounds (you never call UVA's campus a campus; it's uncouth) are on the west side of Charlottesville. A focal point on UVA's grounds is Thomas Jefferson's Academical Village. Rather than use that clumsy and odd-sounding name, most just call it "the Lawn." The Lawn reflects Jefferson's idea that at university, daily life should be infused with learning. To further that end, he designed 10 pavilions, each focused on a different subject. These pavilions had faculty living quarters upstairs, classrooms downstairs, and were attached to several rows of student housing. Today, only a select group of students and faculty live on the Lawn and in the Pavilions.

At one end of the Lawn, Jefferson had constructed a Rotunda to serve as a library, rather than building a chapel, as you'd find on most university campuses

THE SHENANDOAH VALLEY

Charlottesville

© AVALON TRAVEL

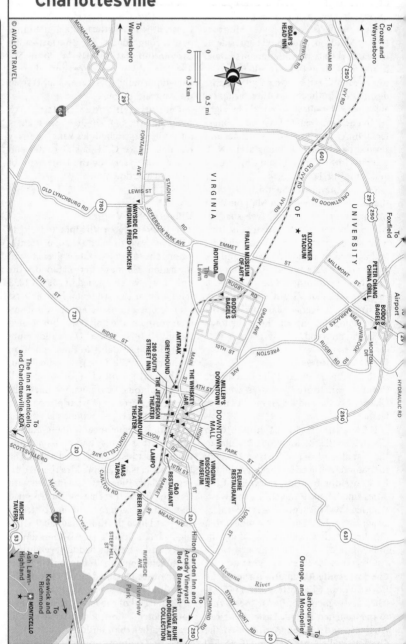

To Crozet and Waynesboro

To Waynesboro

BOAR'S HEAD INN

MONACAN TRAIL

BERWICK RD

EDNAM RD

250

IVY RD

29

64

0   0.5 mi
0   0.5 km

601

OLD IVY RD

29 250

CRESTWOOD DR

U N I V E R S I T Y

To Foxfield

To Airport

29

FONTAINE AVE

V I R G I N I A

IVY RD

OLD LYNCHBURG RD

780

LEWIS ST

STADIUM RD

JEFFERSON PARK AVE

WAYSIDE OLE VIRGINIA FRIED CHICKEN

EMMET ST

FRALIN MUSEUM OF ART ★

KLOCKNER STADIUM ★

MILLMONT ST

PETER CHANG CHINA GRILL

BODO'S BAGELS ▼

BARRACKS RD

RUGBY RD

MORTON DR

MEADOWBROOK RD

O F

250

HYDRAULIC RD

631

ROTUNDA ★

The Lawn

RUGBY RD

GRADY AVE

BODO'S BAGELS ▼

PRESTON AVE

10TH ST

MILLER'S DOWNTOWN ▼

5TH ST

731

RIDGE ST

AMTRAK ■

GREYHOUND ■

200 SOUTH STREET INN

THE JEFFERSON THEATER

THE PARAMOUNT THEATER

MAIN ST

THE WHISKEY JAR ▼

4TH ST

DOWNTOWN MALL

VIRGINIA DISCOVERY MUSEUM

FLEURIE RESTAURANT ▼

PARK ST

HIGH ST

LONG ST

The Inn at Monticello and Charlottesville KOA

SCOTTSVILLE RD

MONTICELLO AVE

20

AVON ST

MAS TAPAS ▼

LAMPO ▼

10TH ST

C&O RESTAURANT ▼

BEER RUN ▼

CARLTON RD

MARKET ST

MEADE AVE

20

Hilton Garden Inn and Arcady Vineyard Bed & Breakfast

To Orange, and Montpelier

MICHIE TAVERN ▼

64

53

Moores Creek

To Ash Lawn-Highland

Keswick and Richmond

★ MONTICELLO

STEEP HILL ST

RIVERSIDE AVE

Riverview Park

To Barboursville,

RICHMOND RD

STONY POINT RD

20

250

Rivanna River

KLUGE RUHE ABORIGINAL ART COLLECTION ■

in that day. The Rotunda is a replica of the Pantheon and is quite picturesque. **Tours** (434/924-7969, 10am, 11am, and 2pm daily during the academic year, free) are available; call for more information.

Fralin Museum of Art

The University of Virginia's **Fralin Museum of Art** (Thomas H. Bayly Building, 155 Rugby Rd., 434/924-3592, www.uvafralinartmuseum.virginia.edu, 10am-5pm Tues.-Wed. and Fri.-Sat., 10am-7pm Thurs., noon-5pm Sun., free) has a collection of more than 13,000 artifacts including 15th- to 20th-century European and American paintings and sculpture, Asian art, photography, and American figurative art. They continually bring in temporary exhibits and have an interesting collection of Greek and Roman coinage.

Kluge-Ruhe Aboriginal Art Collection

The **Kluge-Ruhe Aboriginal Art Collection** (400 Worrell Dr., 434/244-0234, www.kluge-ruhe.org, 10am-4pm Tues.-Sat., 1pm-5pm Sun., free) is the only museum in the United States fully dedicated to the artwork of Australian Aboriginal peoples. The collection is a fascinating array of sculptures; paintings and drawings on canvas, paper, and eucalyptus bark; carvings; musical instruments; and more. The museum is located three miles east of UVA.

Virginia Discovery Museum

The **Virginia Discovery Museum** (524 E. Main St., 434/977-1025, www.vadm.org, 9:30am-5pm Mon.-Sat., $8) is a kid-oriented museum at the east end of the Downtown Mall. Small by comparison to other children's museums, this is still a great resource for travelers with little ones in tow, especially on rainy days. Exhibits are of the bright, hands-on variety that you'd expect, and they have a beehive you can peek in on and an exhibit called *A-Mazing Airways,* in which puffs of air push balls and scarves through a complicated and twisted series of clear pipes.

★ Monticello

Thomas Jefferson's stunning mountaintop home, **Monticello** (931 Thomas Jefferson Pkwy., 434/984-9800, www.monticello.org, 8:30am-6pm daily, $28 adults, $16 children ages 12-18, $9 ages 5-11, free 4 and under), is just four miles southeast of Charlottesville. This is one of the most beautiful and historic sites in the region. The 5,000-acre plantation was the home of Jefferson, the third president, author of the Declaration of Independence, and founder of the University of Virginia. Oh, and as if that wasn't enough, he designed his home.

Jefferson began building Monticello when he was just 26, shortly after inheriting the land from his father. For the rest of his life, he lived here, expanding his home and experimenting with different crops and agricultural methods. Though it doesn't look the part, the Italian Renaissance architecture-inspired home was intended to be a functioning plantation house.

Touring the home takes a little more than 30 minutes. The home itself is notable for its interesting design choices, including the columns ringing the house and the octagonal dome that tops it. Inside, two large rooms, the entrance hall and a parlor/music room, anchor the interior, which measures some 11,000 square feet. Jefferson used the entrance hall to display items of scientific import or curiosity and the parlor/music room for spending what little idle time he had. The dome room is, unfortunately, off limits, but the floors are painted grass green and the octagonal walls "Mars yellow."

Be sure to spend time exploring the picturesque gardens and outbuildings, which include slave quarters and structures typical for a plantation home in those days. Historic Mulberry Row, once the area of the estate where many slaves and indentured servants worked and lived, is quite nice, lined as it is with mulberry trees.

There are several tour options available in addition to the standard house tour. Options include a Behind the Scenes Tour ($45) that takes you upstairs; the Revolutionary Garden Tour ($45), which allows guests to participate in seasonal gardening activities; and private tours (starting at $600 for four guests). Other tours, like the Slavery at Monticello and Garden and Grounds Tours, are free and don't require reservations.

There were two vineyards at Monticello, which Jefferson and his workers struggled to keep growing as a result of pests and disease that ravaged European rootstock (a problem not solved until much later with the invention of modern pesticides and grafting and hybridizing techniques). Jefferson experimented with many other grapes and did make wine using native grapes, though the poor quality of the fruit made for a poor-quality wine; nonetheless, Jefferson was committed to the idea of American-grown grapes and American-produced wines. Because of this, he's often called America's "first distinguished viticulturist."

Indeed, he was important to the industry, important enough for the **Monticello Wine Trail** (www.monticellowinetrail.com) and the wineries on the trail to draw inspiration for his vision of American winemaking. There are more than 30 wineries on the Monticello Wine Trail, including **Jefferson Vineyards** (1353 Thomas Jefferson Pkwy., 434/977-3042, www.jeffersonvineyards.com, tasting room 11am-6pm daily, tastings $12-20), on a site adjacent to Monticello where Thomas Jefferson and Italian Filippo Mazzei decided to first establish a vineyard. Tastings include a souvenir glass.

Carter Mountain Apple Orchard

You can pick your own apples and peaches (depending on the season,

Thomas Jefferson designed many of the University of Virginia's campus buildings.

of course) at **Carter Mountain Apple Orchard** (1435 Carters Mountain Trail, 434/977-1833, www.chilesfamilyorchard. com, hours vary by season and day, daily mid-Apr.-Nov., Sat.-Sun. Dec. 5-21). This is apple country, and toward the end of August, the trees are heavy with ripening apples that you can pick yourself or buy by the bag or basket. The orchard is beautiful, ripe apples or no, and they kick off spring with an Easter Egg Hunt, celebrate the arrival of apple blossoms with a Spring Fling Festival in May, and host the Ol' Fashioned Peach Festival in July.

Wineries and Vineyards

Established by Dave Matthews in 2000, **Blenheim Vineyards** (31 Blenheim Farm, 434/293-5366, www.blenheimvineyards. com, tastings 11am-5:30pm daily, $7) is just a short drive southeast of the city. Between their two vineyards, they grow chardonnay, cabernet franc, cabernet sauvignon, petit verdot, and viognier. The tasting room features a long

section of glass flooring that looks down into the barrel and tank room below; it's pretty cool.

First Colony Winery (1650 Harris Creek Rd., 434/979-7105, www.firstcolonywinery.com, tastings 10am-6pm Mon.-Fri., 11am-6pm Sat.-Sun., tours upon request Sat.-Sun.) started small, with only 4.5 acres of merlot and cabernet sauvignon planted, then expanded to a 6.5-acre vineyard growing chardonnay, petit verdot, cabernet franc, and vidal blanc. There are plans to keep expanding until they have 20 or more acres "under vine." As it stands now, though, the grounds are beautiful and ripe with picnic spots, and the tasting room is quite lovely.

At **Keswick Vineyards** (1575 Keswick Winery Dr., 434/244-3341, www.keswickvineyards.com, 10am-5pm Sun.-Thurs., 10am-8pm Fri., 10am-6pm Sat., tastings $6-10), they produce small lots of wine, employing a minimalist approach to growing their grapes that comes down to this: The focus is on growing the best fruit possible. They have a number of international award winners, with more than 60 silver medals and nearly 50 gold medals to their credit. Keswick is proud of the fact that they don't import any grapes into their vineyard, using only estate-grown fruit to make their wine.

Pippin Hill Farm and Vineyard (5022 Plank Rd., North Garden, Virginia, 20 minutes from Charlottesville, 434/202-8063, www.pippinhillfarm.com, tastings 11am-5pm Tues.-Fri. and Sun., 11am-4:30pm Sat., $10-13) is among the area's primo wedding locations, and one look at the facilities and vineyards and it's easy to see why. The kitchen here puts out fabulous food you can pair with wine for a tasting or a full meal. One notable thing about Pippin Hill is that they employ a sustainable viticulture program to produce their high-quality grapes.

If you want a day of touring vineyards, check out **Blue Ridge Wine Excursions** (434/531-5802, www.blueridgewineexcursions.com); they know the wines and vineyards and will put together a tour that you'll love.

Entertainment and Events
Nightlife
Beer and Breweries
Beer Run (156 Carlton Rd., 434/984-2337, www.beerrun.com, 8am-10pm Mon., 8am-11pm Tues.-Thurs., 8am-midnight Fri.-Sat., 11am-10pm Sun.) is one of the best beer bars in town. They have an extensive draft and bottle list, and a crazy good bottle shop on the premises. If you get hungry, they have a pretty big menu.

In Crozet, **Fardowners** (5773 The Square, Crozet, 434/823-1300, www.fardowners.com, 11am-midnight Mon.-Thurs., 11am-1:30am Fri.-Sat., 10am-midnight Sun.) has a great neighborhood feel and a tight little beer list and set of cocktails like you'd expect at the bar around the corner. They emphasize the local breweries, so it's a good spot to stop and sample some of the area suds. They also serve a pub-grub menu, and their burgers, especially the Fardowners Burger (on a pretzel bun) are very good.

You can tour area breweries that are on the **Brew Ridge Trail** (434/263-7015, www.brewridgetrail.com). The trail leads through Nelson and Albemarle counties on a pleasant and scenic drive, then into Charlottesville. Stops along the Brew Ridge Trail include:

- **Blue Mountain Barrel House** (495 Cooperative Way, Arrington, 434/263-4002, www.bluemountainbarrel.com, 11am-6pm Mon.-Thurs., 11am-8pm Fri.-Sun., open later in summer)

- **Blue Mountain Brewery** (9519 Critzers Shop Rd., Afton, 540/456-8020, www.bluemountainbrewery.com, 11am-10pm Mon.-Sat., 11am-9pm Sun.)

- **South Street Brewery** (106 W. South St., Charlottesville, 434/293-6550, www.southstreetbrewery.com, 11am-1am daily)

- **Starr Hill Brewing Company** (5391 Three Notched Rd., Crozet, 434/823-5671, www.starrhill.com, 1pm-8pm Wed.-Thurs., noon-8pm Fri., 11am-8pm Sat., noon-6pm. Sun.)

- **Wild Wolf Brewing Company** (2461 Rockfish Valley Hwy., Nellysford, 434/361-0088, www.wildwolfbeer.com, 11:30am-last call Mon.-Fri., 11am-last call Sat.-Sun.)

Live Music
Charlottesville's music scene is very vibrant, as you'd expect in a town with a college that numbers more than 20,000 students. The most well known of the local talent is Dave Matthews. He and several of his bandmates attended UVA. While they were here, Dave was a bartender at **Miller's Downtown** (109 W. Main St., 434/971-8511, www.millers-downtown.com, 11am-2am daily). This restaurant and bar is on the Downtown Mall and it stays open late, serves a full menu until closing time, and always has a full schedule of bands from jazz to rock.

Many believe the **Jefferson Theatre** (101 E. Main St., 434/425-4980 or 800/594-8499, www.jeffersontheatre.com) to be the best theater in town, though much of that debate is colored by music preference. Superlatives aside, the Jefferson Theatre was opened in 1912, showing silent movies and vaudeville acts, and seeing performers like Houdini and The Three Stooges grace the stage. Today, it has a state-of-the-art sound and light system and hosts bluegrass, heavy metal, hip-hop, electronic, jam, and rock acts.

Performing Arts
The **Paramount Theatre** (215 E. Main St., 434/979-1333, www.theparamount.net, box office 10am-2pm Mon.-Fri.) opened in 1931 and quickly became a landmark, flourishing during the Great Depression. It closed in 1974 and sat empty for more than three decades before reopening in

2004. Now restored to its former glory, the Paramount shows classic movies, hosts plays and opera performances, brings in lecturers and comics, and even airs cult classics like *The Rocky Horror Picture Show*.

Festivals and Events

In mid-April, the city holds its largest festival, the **Dogwood Festival** (434/218-5656, www.charlottesvilledogwoodfestival.org). Dates vary each year, but the festival lasts two weeks; includes a carnival, fireworks, that indulgent festival food, and a parade; and is the perfect way to welcome spring. The carnival is held in McIntire Park (off US-250 between US-29 and McIntire Rd.). Other events take place across the city.

Throughout August, suds-lovers across the state celebrate **Virginia Craft Beer Month** (www.virginia.org) with tasting events, fetes, and festivals. Charlottesville is home to the **Virginia Craft Brewers Fest** (www.vacraftbrewfest.com, $50-90), held in mid-August. Nearly every brewery in the state—that's close to 100—attends and pours its standard and specialty brews.

October is officially **Virginia Wine Month** (www.virginiawine.org), and all month, visitors pack the wineries in Charlottesville and other spots across the state to take in the fall leaves and find a new favorite vintage. Around Charlottesville, there are around 30 vineyards you can visit for Wine Month festivities or check out any other day of the year.

In November, the **Virginia Film Festival** (multiple venues, 434/982-5277, www.virginiafilmfestival.org) brings in some 100 films and the same number of guest artists during this three-day film bonanza. In addition to nearly around-the-clock screenings, there are lectures and panel discussions covering all aspects of the film process or examining topics pertinent to film history. The festival was founded in 1987 and shows no sign of stopping anytime soon.

Shopping

On the **Downtown Mall** (www.downtowncharlottesville.net), you'll find more than 120 shops (and 30 restaurants, many of them with outdoor seating) in the historic buildings on and around Old Main Street. Now a pedestrian area, the Mall is the perfect stop for those looking to shop, browse, or simply people-watch.

Bittersweet Clothing and Accessories (106 E. Main St., 434/977-5977, www.shopbittersweet.com, 10am-7pm Mon.-Thurs., 10am-8pm Fri.-Sat., noon-5pm Sun.) is a boutique catering to women who want to wear something a little different. It's not avant-garde fashion or haute couture at its hautest, but it is very fashionable and thoughtfully stocked. The owner makes it a point to work with small designers and buy in smaller quantities as a way to ensure both quality and the true one-of-a-kind sense of the clothing and accessories here.

If you find yourself ill prepared for some of the hikes coming up in your journey, visit **Great Outdoor Provision Company** (1125 Emmet St. N., 434/995-5669, www.greatoutdoorprovision.com, 10am-9pm Mon.-Fri., 9am-6pm Sat., noon-6pm Sun.). Great Outdoor carries a full line of hiking, camping, fishing, snow sports, and adventure travel gear, including brands like Patagonia, Mountain Hardwear, Columbia, The North Face, Prana, and Smartwool.

Though it's not a used bookshop, **New Dominion Bookshop** (404 E. Main St., 434/295-2552, www.newdominionbookshop.com, 9:30am-5:30pm Mon.-Thurs. and Sat., 9:30am-8pm Fri., 1pm-5pm Sun.) is a great one. The oldest independent bookseller in Virginia, New Dominion hosts readings and literary events, and has a broad selection of genres on their shelves. Browse a bit; if you don't see what you like, ask one of the staff; they're fellow bibliophiles and will be happy to help.

Sports and Recreation

Mountain bikers of a certain skill level should ride the five-mile single-track trail at **Walnut Creek Park** (4250 Walnut Creek Park Rd., North Garden, 434/296-5844, 7am-dark daily, $3-4.50 adults, $2-3 children, ages 3 and under free). The loop is challenging, so beginner bikers beware, but intermediate and experienced bikers, strap on those helmets. The trail flows through a hardwood forest around a 23-acre lake on a twisty, tight, and sometimes technical route. For those beginner to intermediate bikers who don't want to take on this ride, there are 15 miles of trails in this 480-acre park, which gives you plenty of space to sharpen your skills. There's also an 18-hole **disc golf** course here.

The 104-acre **Beaver Creek Lake** (4365 Beaver Creek Rd., 434/296-5844, 6am-10pm daily) is well stocked with largemouth bass, sunfish, and channel catfish. If you have your Virginia fishing license, see what you can catch.

Try something a little different with **Blue Ridge Ballooning** (434/589-6213, www.blueridgeballoon.com, from $250). You'll have a view of the countryside that you can get no other way than by hot-air balloon. Packages include sunrise and sunset flights, picnic flights, hot-air balloon weddings, and private flights. In late September and through October, it's best to make reservations well in advance so you'll have a spot and the best leaf-peeping vantage of your life.

There are no professional sports teams in Charlottesville, so the focus falls to the **Virginia Cavaliers** (434/924-8821 or 800/542-8821, www.virginiasports.com) and the 23 varsity sports at University of Virginia. Football is played at **Scott Stadium,** basketball at the **John Paul Jones Arena,** soccer and lacrosse at **Klöckner Stadium,** and other sports at various on- and off-campus venues.

The **Charlottesville Derby Dames** (www.charlottesvillederbydames.com) are a roller derby team and member of the Women's Flat Track Derby Association. If you've never seen roller derby, do yourself a favor and take in a bout (yes, it's a bout, like boxing or MMA, not a game like football or golf). Watch these athletes as they speed around the track and clobber each other at every turn.

Food
Fine Dining

★ **Mas Tapas** (904 Monticello Rd., 434/979-0990, www.mastapas.com, 5:30pm-2am Mon.-Sat., $4-30) creates beautiful tapas dishes using ingredients sourced from local and regional farms and has become known as one of the best restaurants in town. Their menu of Spanish and Mediterranean small plates is enormous, with over 100 items. Dishes range from a simple plate of Padrón peppers and olive oil to stone crab claws in an orange, garlic, and smoked paprika sauce. Reservations are recommended.

At ★ **Fleurie Restaurant** (108 3rd St. NE, 434/971-7800, www.fleurierestaurant.com, 5:30pm-9pm Mon.-Thurs., 5:30pm-10pm Fri.-Sat., $10-38) they serve a trio of menus: à la carte ($10-38), pretheater (served before 6:30pm most days, $36 for three courses), and a tasting menu ($79 for six courses, $55-85 wine pairing). Each is distinct but showcases the techniques, local ingredients, and flair for French food the restaurant is known for.

Expect a menu full of creative, French-influenced, American dishes at ★ **C&O Restaurant** (515 E. Water St., 434/971-7044, www.candorestaurant.com, 5pm-1am daily, $12-37). The restaurant has six distinct dining areas, from a barnwood-paneled bar to a cozy brick patio to a mezzanine warmed on cool nights by a wood-burning stove. In each of these spaces, the elegant dishes are equally at home. The menu is meat heavy, with limited choices for vegetarians. The roast chicken with black truffle butter, local mushrooms, and potato gnocchi; and the steak chinoise—beef tenderloin with gruyère-thyme potatoes and a tamari-ginger pan sauce—are some dishes you'll talk about for a long time.

The Whiskey Jar (227 W. Main St., 434/202-1549, www.thewhiskeyjarcville.com, 11am-2:30pm and 5pm-midnight Mon.-Tues., 11am-midnight Wed., 11am-2am Thurs.-Sat., 10am-2:30pm Sun., $5-28) has a broad selection of Scotch, rye, Irish whiskey, and bourbon, but be prepared for a meal that's Southern to the core with a fine-dining twist. The fried organic chicken with collards and chicken gravy (which goes well with a Bowman Brothers bourbon and ginger ale) is a great example: succulent chicken from a local Mennonite farmer, collards like the chef's grandmothers made, and the perfect chicken gravy. The chef owns a farm himself and uses his own fresh produce.

Local Favorites

Bodo's Bagels (1418 Emmet St., 434/977-9598, 6:30am-8pm Mon.-Fri., 7am-8pm Sat., 7:30am-4pm Sun., www.bodosbagels.com, $1-5) has three locations around town serving the best bagels you'll find in Charlottesville. These New York-style "water bagels" are quite popular, so expect a line if you get there at a busy time. They have two other locations in town, at 505 Preston Avenue and 1609 University Avenue.

Every self-respecting Southern city has at least one legendary fried chicken joint: **Wayside Ole' Virginia Fried Chicken** (2203 Jefferson Park Ave., 434/977-5000, www.waysidechicken.com, 9am-9pm Mon.-Thurs., 9am-9:30pm Fri.-Sat., $1.50-9) is Charlottesville's. The food here is dirt cheap and you can get chicken by the piece, meal, or bucket. They also

Top to bottom: the Downtown Mall in Charlottesville; Wayside Ole' Virginia Fried Chicken, a must-stop for Southern food lovers; Fleurie Restaurant.

serve burgers and sandwiches, but why bother when there's delicious fried chicken to be had?

Asian

Peter Chang China Grill (2162 Barracks Rd., 434/244-9818, www.peterchang-charlottesville.com, 11am-10pm daily, $8-20) is an unbelievable Szechuan Chinese restaurant headed up by chef Peter Chang. Chang moved to the United States to work as the chef in the Chinese Embassy and has since worked in a number of kitchens before opening his own place. Rightfully nicknamed the "Master of Peppers," Chang has a loyal and legion fan base. One bite and you'll join the converted.

Italian and Pizza

Dr. Ho's Humble Pie (4916 Plank Rd., North Garden, 434/245-0000, www.drhoshumblepie.com, 11:30am-9pm daily, $9-22) is a short drive from downtown, and totally worth it. The pizza here is killer, with creative toppings (eggs, arugula, crayfish tails) and creative names (Jack London, Buddha, Buff Orpington). You'll also find burgers, Philly cheesesteaks, lasagna, and other hearty items.

The dishes at **Lampo** (205 Monticello Rd., 434/244-3226, www.lampopizza.com, 11am-2:30pm and 5pm-midnight Mon.-Sat., $3-14) make it a serious contender for best Neapolitan pizzeria in Charlottesville. With a small but selective menu, Lampo's kitchen is high quality and creative, with salads like the Cavolo Nero (Tuscan kale, candied almonds, pickled mustard seeds, parsnip, and apple cider vinaigrette), pizzas like the Abruzzo (local beef and pork meatballs, *fior di latte*, San Marzano tomatoes, pecorino, and fresh basil), and a great selection of charcuterie.

Accommodations
$150-200

At ★ **200 South Street Inn** (200 W. South St., 434/979-0200, www.southstreetinn.

com, $145-355) you'll find 24 guest rooms and suites in an unbeatable location: two blocks from the Downtown Mall, one mile from the University of Virginia, and a four-mile drive to Monticello. The inn combines two houses. The larger of the two was built in 1856 for Thomas Jefferson Werenbaker, son of a close friend to Thomas Jefferson, and transformed from home to girls' finishing school to boardinghouse to its current role as inn. The smaller house was built in 1890 and became part of the inn during the 1980s. Each room has a private bath, and many rooms have whirlpool tubs. Though the rooms may lack some conveniences found in chain hotels, these aren't missed; the attentiveness of the innkeepers makes sure of that. There's a continental breakfast in the morning and cookies, wine, and cheese in the afternoon.

Over $200

Consistently rated as the top B&B in Charlottesville, the **Foxfield Inn** (2280 Garth Rd., 434/923-8892 or 866/369-3536, www.foxfield-inn.com, $190-310) is known to pamper guests and provide a place to escape the rush of daily life. There are five rooms here, so it's small, but each room offers you enough space to feel at home. Breakfast is of the three-course gourmet variety, and the four deluxe rooms have fireplaces, two-person whirlpool tubs, and large, walk-in showers.

★ **Arcady Vineyard Bed & Breakfast** (1495 Milton Rd., 434/872-9475 or 888/842-7273, www.innarcadyvineyard.com, $250-325) was started by a couple with decades of experience in the hotel, restaurant, and wine industries. Each room is large and comfortable, and several packages complement the excellent accommodations. Packages include a picnic for two ($80), massages ($100), and the "Sweetheart Celebration" ($100 in addition to the cost of the room; includes bottle of sparkling wine, custom jewelry, luxury room), perfect for that romantic getaway in Virginia's wine region. Wine tours can also be arranged through **Taste of Monticello** (424/960-0820, www.monticelloappellation.com, $145-165 per person).

At the **Boar's Head Inn** (200 Ednam Dr., 434/296-2181 or 844/611-8066, www.boarsheadinn.com, $250-655), the official hotel of the University of Virginia, expect nothing but the best. The 175 guest rooms and suites are furnished and decorated with antique pieces but still outfitted with all the modern conveniences you would require for your stay. You'll find the luxury experience in the private balcony and the spa-like bathroom in your room, and if that's not enough, the restaurants (there are four) will treat you to a fabulous dining experience.

Rooms at the **Hilton Garden Inn Charlottesville** (1793 Richmond Rd., 434/979-4442, www.hiltongardeninn3.hilton.com, $139-280) are what you'd expect from this well-known chain: comfortable, clean, and reasonably priced. Located on the east side of town, the hotel is about four miles from UVA and three miles from the downtown historic area and downtown shopping and dining.

Information and Services

Charlottesville and Albemarle County Tourism (www.visitcharlottesville.org) has a rich online listing of activities, accommodations, restaurants, and resources to help you plan a trip; you can also call or stop in at the **Downtown Visitors Center** (610 E. Main St., 434/293-6789, 9am-5pm daily) for in-person help with questions. The **Downtown Business Association of Charlottesville** (434/295-9073, www.downtowncharlottesville.net) also maintains a robust listing of downtown businesses and services, as well as information on parking and other logistics.

If you need police assistance, there are several agencies that can help. The **Charlottesville Police Department** (610 E. Main St., 434/970-3280, www.charlottesville.org), the **Virginia State Police** (900 Natural Resources Dr., 434/293-3223, www.vsp.state.va.us), **Albemarle County Police Department** (1600 5th St., Suite D, 434/296-5807, www.albemarle.org), and **Albemarle County Sheriff's Office** (411 E. High St., 434/972-4001, www.albemarleso.org) are all here to serve.

Charlottesville's **Martha Jefferson Hospital** (500 Martha Jefferson Dr., 800/633-6353 or 434/654-7000, www.marthajefferson.org) and the University of Virginia's **University Hospital** (1215 Lee St., 434/924-3627, www.uvahealth.com) have ample facilities and access to specialists.

Virginia
Blue Ridge

Rockfish Gap marks Mile 0 of the Blue Ridge Parkway. For the next 217 miles, the road follows the gentle swales and curves of Virginia's Blue Ridge Mountains.

Waynesboro

George Washington National Forest

White Sulphur Springs

I-64

WEST VIRGINIA

Blue Ridge Parkway National Park

200 ml / 322 km
4 hrs

NATURAL BRIDGE

81

Bedford

Lynchburg

NATIONAL D-DAY MEMORIAL

Jefferson National Forest

MCAFEE KNOB

O.WINSTON LINK MUSEUM

ROANOKE

Blacksburg

ROANOKE STAR

FRIDAY NIGHT JAMBOREE

Floyd

VIRGINIA

I-77

CHATEAU MORRISETTE WINERY

Galax

BLUE RIDGE MUSIC CENTER

Virginia Blue Ridge – North

Virginia Blue Ridge – South

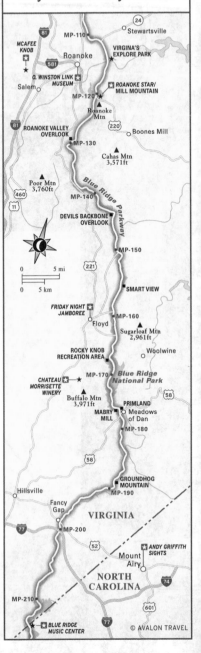

© AVALON TRAVEL

Highlights

★ **Natural Bridge:** This 215-foot-tall natural limestone span is one of the oldest tourist destinations in the United States (page 109).

★ **National D-Day Memorial:** The young men of Bedford paid the highest price when Allied troops invaded Nazi-controlled France in a bid to turn the tide of WWII. This hilltop memorial tells the story of D-Day and the Allied victory (page 115).

★ **O. Winston Link Museum:** Famous for his photography of the final days of Norfolk & Western's steam trains, Link is memorialized in Roanoke in a former rail station where many of his best photos are on display (page 124).

★ **McAfee Knob:** One of the most photographed spots on the Appalachian Trail is a short drive and pleasant hike from Roanoke. From this stone outcropping, the Blue Ridge Mountains look like they go on forever (page 128).

★ **Roanoke Star:** This 88.5-foot-tall neon star started as a Christmas tradition and is now Roanoke's most famous landmark. The views from its observation platform are unrivaled (page 135).

★ **Friday Night Jamboree:** In the eclectic mountain town of Floyd, seventh-generation farmers and new-age artists meet every week for bluegrass music and mountain dancing (page 138).

★ **Chateau Morrisette Winery:** Virginia has many mountaintop wineries, but no other has the stunning Blue Ridge views you'll find here (page 143).

★ **Andy Griffith Sights:** The inspiration for fictional Mayberry will make you feel like you're on the set of *The Andy Griffith Show* (page 146).

★ **Blue Ridge Music Center:** Catch a free concert and learn about musicians who hail from the mountains of North Carolina and Virginia at a museum that straddles the state line (page 152).

The first stretch of the Parkway is characterized by a pleasant patchwork of pastures, meadows, and hayfields, river crossings, more than a few lakes, and overlooks that take in wide valleys. Thick, mid-elevation hardwood forests grow all along the mountainsides, creating a lush green blanket in spring and summer and a bright patchwork in fall. A huge variety of wildflowers grows alongside the road.

For some ways, the Appalachian Trail (AT) parallels the Blue Ridge Parkway, either closely or on the next ridgeline over. For AT hikers, the long, nearly flat ridges of Virginia's mountains provide a well-earned break on their trek along the crest of the mountain chain. You'll find similar features on your drive. There are curves—what mountain road is missing curves?—and you will climb a mountain or two, but this part of the Parkway is the easiest to drive.

Blue Ridge Parkway planners elected to chase the wandering ridgelines of the mountains along the Virginia stretch of the route, often giving travelers spectacular views to the east and west without having to rely on so many overlooks. There are overlooks, though, and when you stop at one, the sight is often breathtaking. Many look across wide, flat-bottomed river valleys that were the interstate highways of their day, carrying settlers from New York to Alabama. Looking out from the highest vantage, Sharp Top in the Peaks of Otter, you'll gaze across valleys and up the slopes of the mountains some miles distant, the heads of their companions peeking over their shoulders. Gaps—passes through the mountains, connecting east with west—appear periodically. These spots, used by Native Americans and European settlers alike to cross these hills more easily, are blessed with the most panoramic of views.

Planning Your Time

You could spend anywhere from two days to a week exploring this region. If hikes aren't your thing, then the trip is shorter (2-4 days), as the easiest hikes don't take long to get you to some outstanding spots, and the sights, cities, and towns here will draw you in for a night or at least a daylong side trip. Hikers and thorough sightseers will want closer to a week, as some of the best hikes are half-day treks (or more), cities like Roanoke deserve at least two days to explore, and Floyd has a Friday-night-only happening that you simply must experience.

Planning ahead is key on this leg of the journey. The Parkway is open year-round, although few facilities outside Peaks of Otter are open beyond May-October. There are few restaurants along the Parkway and only a handful of places to rest your head, and if you're traveling during peak times (read: an autumn trip to take in some incredible fall colors), you may be in for a wait or be left with no place to stay. Make hotel or campground reservations in advance. Many of the best places can book up nearly a year out for late September and all of October (peak leaf-peeping months). Roanoke, the largest city in the region, has the widest selection of accommodations.

Driving Considerations

The Blue Ridge Parkway through Virginia is the easiest stretch along the route. Along this part of the Parkway, the weather is generally mild, though winter ice and snow can (and often do) close the Parkway. Perhaps the largest travel factor to take into account is traffic. During peak color season—late September through October—the Parkway gets crowded, things slow down, roadways are lined with leaf peepers and photographers, and the overlooks are filled to

Best Restaurants

★ **Town Kitchen & Provisions, Bedford:** Nosh on classic, casual American fare on the ground floor of a historic home (page 119).

★ **River and Rail Restaurant, Roanoke:** Modern Southern cuisine, a strong bar program, and a laid-back atmosphere make this a must for dining (page 130).

★ **Lucky, Roanoke:** Pair your duck-leg confit with a cocktail here. The drinks are among the best in Roanoke (page 131).

★ **The Historic Pine Tavern Restaurant, Floyd:** Dine on classic country dishes in a place packed with locals (page 140).

★ **Mabry Mill Restaurant, Meadows of Dan:** There's a good reason the pancakes here are famous (page 145).

★ **The Snappy Lunch, Mount Airy:** Feel like you've stepped into Mayberry at this café in Andy Griffith's hometown. It was even mentioned on his classic TV show (page 151).

capacity. That said, it's a marvelous time to visit; you just have to be alert to traffic and pedestrians and patient with your travels.

Getting There

If you're following the route prescribed in this guide, you'll join the Blue Ridge Parkway at **Rockfish Gap,** near Waynesboro and Charlottesville, as soon as you leave Skyline Drive and Shenandoah National Park. Following the Parkway south from here, you'll cover **217 miles,** a little less than half the distance of the whole route. At Milepost 216.9, the Parkway crosses the **North Carolina state line,** but not before passing close by the town of Galax, Virginia, and Mount Airy, North Carolina.

Car

Getting on and off the Blue Ridge Parkway isn't difficult on this segment. From **Richmond,** Virginia, drive west on I-64 for 93 miles (90 minutes) to reach the Parkway entrance. From **Charlottesville,** Virginia, drive west on I-64 for 25 miles (30 minutes).

Roanoke, the largest city in the region, is a good starting point. To get to Roanoke from **Greensboro,** North

Carolina, drive north on US-220 for 100 miles (two hours).

There are a number of other points you can use to enter the Blue Ridge Parkway, as many highways intersect with this part of the route.

Fueling Up

These are the most convenient spots to fuel up along this route:

- **MP 0,** US-250 less than one mile west

- **MP 45.6,** US-60 less than five miles west

- **MP 63.7,** US-501 less than two miles south

- **MP 90.9,** VA-43 less than five miles north

- **MP 106,** US-460 less than four miles west

- **MP 112.2,** VA-24 less than two miles east or west

- **MP 121.4,** US-220 less than five miles north

- **MP 177.7,** US-58 less than one mile east

Best Accommodations

★ **Sherando Lake Recreation Area Campground, Lyndhurst:** Kick back in a campsite with easy access to miles of hiking trails and a swimming beach (page 104).

★ **Peaks of Otter Lodge, Bedford:** Bed down in an excellent location right on the Parkway (page 114).

★ **Vanquility Acres Inn, Bedford:** Cabins and B&B-style rooms on a 10-acre farm give a taste of country life (page 119).

★ **Black Lantern Inn, Roanoke:** This green-certified inn offers jetted hydro-massage tubs as well as complimentary golf clubs and bicycles (page 131).

★ **Hotel Roanoke, Roanoke:** View historic murals painted by the Civilian Conservation Corps in the lobby of this luxe, yet affordable, hotel (page 132).

★ **Ambrosia Farm Bed & Breakfast, Floyd:** Unwind at this farmhouse retreat, nestled into hills and pastures (page 141).

★ **Primland, Meadows of Dan:** Enjoy incredible views and activities galore, from horseback riding to stargazing (page 145).

- **MP 199.4,** US-52 less than one mile north

- **MP 215.8,** VA-89 less than eight miles north

Air

The two major airports in the region are in Charlottesville and Roanoke. **Charlottesville Albemarle Airport** (CHO, 100 Bowen Loop, Charlottesville, 434/973-8342, www.gocho.com) is served by Delta, American Airlines, United Airlines, and US Airways, with flights arriving daily from cities all across the Eastern Seaboard and Midwest. Airlines flying out of the **Roanoke-Blacksburg Regional Airport** (ROA, 5202 Aviation Dr. NW, Roanoke, 540/362-1999, www. flyroa.com) include Allegiant Air, American Airlines, Delta Airlines, United Airlines, and US Airways.

The **Richmond International Airport** (RIC, 1 Richard E. Byrd Terminal Dr., Richmond, 804/226-3000, www.flyrichmond.com) is only about 90 minutes east of Rockfish Gap and Milepost 0 of the Blue Ridge Parkway along I-64.

Train and Bus

At the **Charlottesville Amtrak station** (CVS, 810 W. Main St., 434/296-4559 or 800/872-7245, www.amtrak.com, 6am-9:30pm daily), the Cardinal/Hoosier State, Crescent, and Northeast Regional lines pass through daily.

Roanoke's **Amtrak Station** (RNK, 101 Norfolk Ave., 800/872-7245, www. amtrak.com) opened in fall 2017 and serves passengers on the Crescent and Northeast Regional lines.

Both Charlottesville and Roanoke have Greyhound stations near downtown where it is easy to get to accommodations or a car rental agency. The **Charlottesville Greyhound station** (310 W. Main St., 434/295-5131, www.greyhound.com, 8am-10pm daily) is just a few blocks from the Amtrak station. The **Roanoke Greyhound station** (26 Salem Ave. SW, 540/343-5436, www. greyhound.com, 5:15am-6:15am and 9am-5pm Mon.-Fri., 9am-10am and 1pm-5pm Sat.-Sun.) is very convenient to downtown.

Rockfish Gap (MP 0.0)

At only 1,909 feet high, Rockfish Gap offered wildlife, then Native Americans, then colonists and settlers, and now endless interstate traffic—including you—an easy place to pass through these mountains. It's a rather ho-hum start to the epic Blue Ridge Parkway; there's little more than a sign here announcing the Parkway and another sign with the speed limit.

Two miles down is the first excellent stop of the Blue Ridge Parkway: At the **Rockfish Valley Overlook (MP 2)**, you'll be at around 2,100 feet of elevation, which gives a good vantage point over the surrounding land. The rolling valley and the Rockfish River below and the mountain peaks in the distance make this a prime spot for photos, especially in morning or evening light.

Humpback Rocks (MP 5.9)

The first visitors center you come to on the Blue Ridge Parkway is at Milepost 5.9, the **Humpback Rocks Visitor Center** (MP 5.9, 540/377-2377, 10am-5pm daily May-Nov.). At the visitors center, you'll find maps and pamphlets about many of the on- and off-Parkway attractions nearby, as well as restrooms. There are two short hikes here: one to a farm and homestead made up of relocated buildings and structures on Parkway land, which have been assembled here as a whole farm; the other to the namesake Humpback Rocks.

The self-guided Mountain Farm Trail leads through a reconstructed 19th-century farmstead, with exhibits on life in the rural Blue Ridge. Across the road, a steep, two-mile trail climbs to the jagged top of Humpback Rocks (3,080 ft.) for a 360-degree view of the mountains. Past Devil's Knob (3,851 ft.) is a turnoff to VA-664 east toward Wintergreen Resort.

Mountain Farm Trail

Distance: 0.5 mile out and back
Duration: 20 minutes
Elevation gain: negligible
Difficulty: easy
Trailhead: Humpback Rocks Visitor Center parking area at MP 5.9

Less of a hike and more of a stroll, this trail takes you through an 1890s mountain farm. Grab a brochure about the trail at the visitors center and follow the paved trail to a gravel path that leads through the farm. Along the way, you'll pass a cabin, a weasel-proof chicken house, a collection of farm tools, a garden, a barn and a pigpen, and the springhouse. All along the way, you'll have a view of Humpback Rocks.

Humpback Rocks Trail

Distance: 2 miles out and back
Duration: 90 minutes
Elevation gain: 750 feet
Difficulty: moderate to strenuous
Trailhead: Humpback Gap parking area at MP 6 (or cross the Parkway from the end of the Mountain Farm Trail)

A short hike, but one that is at times steep and rocky, this is more than a leg-stretching hike but less than a monumental undertaking. The sight of Humpback Rocks and the views from the pinnacle make the effort worth it.

Starting from the Humpback Gap parking area, follow the blue-blazed trail to the left of the kiosk. The trail ascends steeply, but it's in good condition. At the trail intersection at 0.5 mile, stay straight on the blue-blazed trail. The next 0.4 mile is tough—rocky with a few sets of wooden and rock steps in the hardest parts—but you're almost there. At the next intersection, bear left on a spur trail to the rocks (it's obvious). From your perch on the rocks, the view is simply spectacular. This is an especially good spot for a sunrise expedition as the sight of the countryside coming alive is quite remarkable.

Wintergreen Resort (MP 13.7)

Just off the Parkway at Reed's Gap, **Wintergreen Resort** (39 Mountain Inn Loop, Roseland, 434/325-2200, www.wintergreenresort.com, year-round) has plenty of accommodations, from two-person studios, lodges, and condos ($155-265) to two- to six-bedroom homes (requiring a two-night stay, $289-880) and lodges ideal for very large groups ($799-1,590). To get here, leave the Parkway at Milepost 13.7, then take VA-664 one mile to the resort entrance (on your left). Many environmentalists, Parkway advocates, and supporters of the Appalachian Trail weren't too happy when private land adjacent to the Parkway was turned into Wintergreen Resort. Though it gets a bad rap with some land-use advocates, the resort is known for its preservation program and on-property trail system. The whole resort is 11,000 acres, with more than 6,000 acres permanently dedicated to forest preservation and over 30 miles of trails lacing the mountainsides.

Activities include hiking the extensive network of trails that includes part of the old Appalachian Trail (hiking guides $3), fly-fishing guide services, archery, ziplining, a minigolf course, mountain biking, and too many more activities to list. The resort also has a huge snow-tubing park and the odd thrill of summer tubing (it's down a track, not on snow), and 26 ski and snowboard trails, including a terrain park. There are two golf courses at Wintergreen: **Devil's Knob Golf Course** (par 70, 6,712 yards, $49-119, depending on season), the highest course in Virginia; and **Stoney Creek Golf Course** (par 72, 7,158 yards, $39-79, depending on season).

There are several dining options available at Wintergreen, though they are for resort guests and members. If you're staying here, try **The Edge** (434/325-8080, 11am-10pm Sun.-Thurs., 11am-midnight Fri.-Sat., $9-25), serving pub food and a fun late-night menu; **The Copper Mine Bistro** (434/325-8090, 7am-11am and 5:30pm-9pm Mon.-Sat., 7am-11am Sun., $10-35), where you can grab breakfast and a fun Mediterranean-inspired dinner; and **Devils Grill** (434/325-8100, 11:30am-4pm and 5:30pm-9:30pm Mon.-Sat., 11:30am-4pm and 5pm-9pm Sun., $10-38), serving lunch and a hearty dinner with dishes like pasta Bolognese, steaks, and fish.

Sherando Lake (MP 13.7)

Just off the Parkway is **Sherando Lake Recreation Area** (96 Sherando Lake Rd., Lyndhurst, 540/291-2188, www.fs.usda.gov, 6am-sunset daily, $8/vehicle day-use fee). To get here, turn west on VA-664 at Reed's Gap (MP 13.7). Follow VA-664 for 2.6 miles, then take your first left; 2 miles in, turn right and you'll be at the recreation area.

Built by the Civilian Conservation Corps in the 1930s as a recreation area and flood-control measure, the distinctive features of the area are the lakes. The 25-acre lower lake has a sandy swimming beach and is open for boating; the 7-acre upper lake is known for trout, bass, and bluegill fishing. A 37-site campground, ★ **Sherando Lake Recreation Area Campground** (96 Sherando Lake Rd., Lyndhurst, 877/444-6777, www.recreation.gov, $20), rings the lakes, and there are miles of hiking trails in the surrounding George Washington and Thomas Jefferson National Forests. It's picturesque, well appointed, and rich with activities perfect for kids and Parkway explorers; combine this with its location and you have the makings of a great campground.

Recreation
Hiking
Pick up a trail map at the campground

and take a look at what hikes might appeal to you. Most everyone will at least want to take the mile-long **Lakeside Trail,** which circles Sherando Lake. You can add to that the short, but steep, 0.75-mile **Cliff Trail.** Both of these hikes will put you in prime position for some great photos of the lake, especially when fall colors are in full blush.

Most of the longer hikes here are full-day affairs. This shorter one gives you a view of the lake and a taste of ridge-top hiking:

Blue Loop Trail
Distance: 3-mile loop
Duration: 2 hours
Elevation gain: 950 feet
Difficulty: moderate with strenuous sections
Trailhead: Sherando Lake Recreation Area Campground

Begin climbing out of the campground on a moderate incline as you follow one arm of the mountain up to the ridge top proper. Sections of the trail are rocky, so watch your footing. Also keep an eye out for poison ivy, which you can see in a few places. For the most part, the trail is narrow, but there is no exposure to heights or steep drop-offs to speak of. At just over 0.5 mile into the hike, you'll come to a rocky overlook (possibly the site of a small landslide) where there's a great view of the larger of the two lakes.

Continue on the trail another quarter mile to the ridge, where Blue Loop Trail meets Torry Ridge Trail. Turn right and follow the ridgeline about a mile before turning right again down Blue Loop Trail. Along the ridge, it's very flat and easy to make good time, but pace yourself as the water you brought is all the water you'll have on the hike. Once you turn right back onto Blue Loop, it's about 0.5 mile to a Forest Service Road (FDR 91). From the road, it's another 0.5 mile back to the campground.

Mountain Biking
Mountain biking enthusiasts know

Sherando as the home of one of the burliest trails in this part of the state. Head up the steep, rocky **Blue Loop Trail** past the lake toward the park entrance—you'll end up carrying your bike, trust me—to the yellow-blazed **Torry Ridge Trail,** 1,000 feet above. Go down the ridgeline, carrying your bike yet again through a nasty rock garden, then head down the blue-blazed **Slacks Trail** to the orange-blazed **White Rock Trail** back to the lake. The whole thing is an 11-mile loop, and all the carrying makes the ride down that much sweeter.

Crabtree Falls (MP 27.2)

Where North Carolina and Great Smoky Mountains National Park to the south are rife with waterfalls, there are few that impress in Virginia, but when you find one like Crabtree Falls, it really impresses. Crabtree Falls descends down a set of five cascades, the first of which you can see after an easy, 10-minute hike from the trailhead. Called the highest waterfall "in Eastern America," the "highest in Virginia," and the "highest in the Virginia Blue Ridge," it's a tough call to say which is true, though through some crafty manipulation of the numbers, they all could be. At the very least, it's the highest waterfall in the Virginia Blue Ridge, falling and cascading a total distance of 1,200 feet. This isn't the only Crabtree Falls you'll encounter on the Blue Ridge Parkway; the other is in North Carolina (at MP 339.5).

Crabtree Falls Trail
Distance: 3.4 miles out and back
Duration: 2-2.5 hours
Elevation gain: 1,500 feet
Difficulty: strenuous
Trailhead: To reach the trailhead of Virginia's Crabtree Falls, exit the Parkway at MP 27.2 and head east on VA-56 for 6.6 miles. The parking area is on the right side of the road.

You're in for a climb as the trail gains

1,500 feet in only 1.7 miles. Start your climb by crossing the Tye River, then follow the trail a quarter mile to the first overlook. At 0.4 mile, you'll come to another platform and a great view of a 70-foot cascade. The next good view is at 0.7 mile, where you'll be able to look back downstream and get a feel for the elevation here. From this point, the falls become steeper and more impressive.

At 0.9 mile, the creek falls over a smooth, nearly vertical rock face, but as impressive as it is, it's not the best. At 1.5 miles, you'll come to the base of the upper and most impressive falls. As the water falls, it splits, taking multiple paths down the face, making for some very interesting photos. The trail continues beside the falls for another 0.2 mile, taking you to the top. The view from here is bad; you're too close to the action to gain any real perspective. Take the footbridge across the creek and follow a short side trail to another observation platform. Though the view of the falls from here is scant at best, you will be able to get a great look at the valley and gorge you just ascended.

The trail continues on another 1.2 miles to VA-826 (a four-wheel-drive-only road) and a second trailhead there. You're more than welcome to explore the forest here, but to get back to the trailhead, go back down the path and take a second look at Crabtree Falls on the way down.

Whetstone Ridge (MP 29)

Whetstone Ridge was so named because early settlers found the fine-grained stone along this ridge ideal for sharpening stones. You'll find flush toilets and little else here aside from a trailhead to the long Whetstone Ridge Trail.

Whetstone Ridge Trail

Distance: 23.6 miles out and back
Duration: 2 days, 8-9 hours total
Elevation gain: 1,700 feet

Difficulty: strenuous
Trailhead: MP 29 at the end of the parking area

This hike is quite pleasant other than the distance. Much of the trail follows the original route of the Appalachian Trail (dating back to the 1930s). In summer, there are no views to speak of as the greenery completely hems you in. In fall and winter, the views are expansive in every direction. Bring plenty of water (especially if you plan to camp), as there are no reliable water sources along the trail.

The hike is straightforward—ascend the ridgeline via a few switchbacks and follow the combination forest service road and trail. At four miles in, you'll reach a small **campsite.** At 5.7 miles, you'll begin a rocky descent that's steep at times. Ascend at six miles, just as steeply. At 7.3 miles, you'll come to one of the only summertime views of the distant countryside. When you reach the knob at 8.2 miles, you'll have a good view of the Parkway as it winds along the crest of the Blue Ridge Mountains. At 9.2 miles, a side road cuts away, down the mountain: Stay on the ridge. You'll leave the road at 9.5 miles and begin a long descent along a pretty narrow path. Continue on this route until you reach VA-603 in 2.3 miles.

The trail is open to hikers, **bicyclists,** and **horseback riders.** Trail etiquette states that horses have the right of way; hikers yield to horses; bicyclists yield to horses and hikers. This trail is maintained by the U.S. Forest Service, but Park Service regulations prohibit bikes on their trails (unless marked otherwise), so please walk your bike in the first 0.25 miles to the clearly marked boundary with Forest Service land. Horse folks and bicyclists can do this trail in one day. The same is not so true for hikers. Camping is permitted, making this hike doable in two long segments or three shorter ones. It is best to either camp or arrange for another car to pick you up at the VA-603 trailhead.

Yankee Horse Ridge (MP 34.4)

I love an odd place name, and Yankee Horse Ridge fits the bill. The story goes that during the Civil War, a hard-riding Union soldier drove his horse to exhaustion here. When the horse fell and couldn't get up, he did the only humane thing: put it down. The story is likely true as these mountains, ridges, and passes saw considerable activity during the Civil War. This stop is notable for two reasons: a pleasant little hike and waterfall, and a chance to see the remnants of a century-old logging operation.

Yankee Horse Overlook Trail

Distance: 0.2-mile loop
Duration: 20 minutes
Elevation gain: negligible
Difficulty: easy
Trailhead: MP 34.4 at the end of the parking area

Many like to think that the Blue Ridge Parkway passes through virgin forest and untouched lands, but the reality is that Native Americans and European settlers built homes and raised families here for hundreds of years before industrialists found the mineral- and timber-rich mountains and used them to their ends. This path follows a section of the Irish Creek Railway, a narrow-gauge railroad that carried more than 100-million board feet of lumber off the mountain and to mills below.

The trail starts with a short set of steps that lead to a reconstructed portion of the railroad laid on its original bed. Turn right onto the tracks and cross a bridge over Wigwam Creek. In a moment, the trail will turn left, up the hill, but you should continue along the tracks and railroad bed for a little way more. It's interesting to see how the forest reclaims the railroad, yet the railroad stays clearly visible once you know what to look for. Retrace your steps to the turn and head uphill. You'll find a pair of bridges across Wigwam Creek where you can take a gander at the 30-foot Wigwam Falls before continuing around this little loop and back to the parking area.

Bluff Mountain (MP 53.1)

If you needed evidence of the gentleness of Virginia's Blue Ridge Mountains, your evidence can be found here, at Bluff Mountain. Engineers only built 1 tunnel on the whole 217 miles of Virginia's Blue Ridge Parkway and 25 tunnels in North Carolina. The Bluff Mountain Tunnel is that lone Virginia subterranean crossing. It's 630 feet long and 13 feet tall (some sources claim 13 feet, 7 inches, but if you're concerned about tunnel height, it's best to err on the side of caution).

Otter Creek (MP 60.8)

There are several overlooks providing glimpses of Otter Creek as it makes its way to a parallel track with the Parkway. Otter Creek descends from 1,100 feet down to 650 feet, the lowest point on the Parkway, at the James River a few miles distant. Starting at Milepost 57.6, then again at Mileposts 58.2, 59.7, 60.4, 60.8, 61.4, 62.5, 63.1, and finally 63.2, you can catch glimpses of Otter Creek. One of the best views is at Milepost 60.4 at The Riffles Overlook, where Otter Creek drops over a 20-foot cascade.

At Milepost 60.8, you'll find the **Otter Creek Campground** (877/444-6777, www.recreation.gov, May-Oct., $16-19), with 42 tent and 26 RV sites, and Otter Creek Trail.

Otter Creek Trail

Distance: 6.8 miles out and back
Duration: 3-3.5 hours
Elevation gain: 200 feet
Difficulty: easy to moderate
Trailhead: Otter Creek Campground

Aside from one steep ascent/descent, this

is a languid walk beside a very pleasant creek. Cross Otter Creek via a set of concrete stepping-stones immediately after starting the trail. You'll reach a Parkway overpass at 0.3 mile and a nice look at the creek at 0.4 mile (in the creek are some inviting large, flat rocks, perfect for sunbathing and navel gazing). At 0.6 mile, you'll reach some steps to Terrapin Hill Overlook, a short trail with an elevation gain of nearly 800 feet. A stone culvert and concrete tunnel take you under the Parkway and VA-130 just before you cross Otter Creek and pass beneath a fern-laden cliff. The trail begins to ascend a little more steeply at 1 mile, becoming a little tougher at 1.2 miles.

When you reach the 1.4-mile mark, take a moment to check out the small cave just off the trail. Then begin the short, steep descent and return to Otter Creek. You'll soon pass the Lower Otter Creek Overlook (MP 62.5) and continue downstream. Cross Otter Creek again by boulder-hopping at 2 miles in, and continue until you meet with Otter Lake Loop Trail, 2.4 miles into your trip.

Walk the banks of the lake, then cross over Otter Creek at the dam and turn right (turn left and you'll loop the lake, which you can do on the return trip or as a separate hike). At 3 miles into the hike, you'll have excellent views of the creek and see some deep pools that you may want to dip your feet into. At 3.4 miles, you'll arrive at the **James River Visitor Center** (no phone, 10am-5pm Wed.-Sun.), where you can rest, check out the displays, ride back to the campground (if you are traveling with companions and you've arranged your own shuttle ahead of time) or retrace your steps back to base camp.

Otter Lake Loop Trail
Distance: 1-mile loop
Duration: 20 minutes

Top to bottom: rocky trail near Wintergreen Resort; Otter Creek Trail; Natural Bridge.

Elevation gain: 100 feet
Difficulty: easy to moderate
Trailhead: Otter Lake Overlook at MP 63.1

The trail starts at the dam where you'll cross the stream via a set of concrete stepping-stones, then ascend some stone steps. Follow the trail 0.3 mile to a bench where a short trail leads down to another lake view. On the main trail, you'll ascend gradually to the high point above the lake. At 0.4 mile, there's another bench and the trail descends. Cross a little creek and pass through a small wetland where the creek feeds the lake, then cross over Little Otter Creek at 0.5 mile. After you cross Little Otter, you'll come to the ruins of an old cabin. Take a moment to check it out and see how early settlers here built their homes to last quite some time.

Soon after the cabin, you'll come to a marked junction with Otter Creek Trail. Cross the bridges and head back to the parking area along the edge of the Parkway.

James River Overlook (MP 63.2)

The Parkway hits its lowest point—649.4 feet—where it crosses the James River at Milepost 63.2. Just beyond, at Milepost 63.6, are the **James River Visitor Center** (10am-5pm Wed.-Sun.), a picnic area, and a couple of trails: the **Trail of Trees Self-Guiding Trail** and **James River Self-Guiding Trail,** both of which are 0.4 mile long and pretty easy. The Trail of Trees is a loop that details the relationships between 40 or so plants and trees common to the region. The James River Trail is quite interesting as it leads to a system of canals and locks built to use the James River for shipping. It's a nice walk beside the river.

★ US-501 West: Natural Bridge

(MP 63.7)

One of Virginia's most impressive sights stands tall just 16 miles from the Blue Ridge Parkway. Exiting the Parkway at Milepost 63.7 and following US-501 west will take you right to **Natural Bridge** (6477 S. Lee Hwy., 540/291-1326, www. dcr.virginia.gov, 8am-dusk daily, $8 adults, $6 children ages 6-12, free ages 5 and under), a jaw-dropping 215-foot-tall limestone span. Thomas Jefferson, one-time owner of Natural Bridge, said it was "so beautiful in archaeology, so elevated, so light, and springing as it were up to Heaven, [that] the rapture of the spectator is really indescribable." Which is to say, a visit to this natural wonder will leave you speechless.

According to native legend, the "Bridge of God" materialized to help a band of Monocan Indians who were fleeing from raiding Shawnee and Powhatans. In 1749, British Lord Fairfax hired Colonel Peter Jefferson (father of six-year-old Thomas, a son destined to become president) to survey the land around today's US-11. One young assistant carved his initials on the stone wall; the faint "GW" is still visible, making George Washington the only president to have officially defaced a Virginia landmark. In 1773, Thomas Jefferson gained title to the bridge and 157 surrounding acres from King George III for 20 shillings (that's about $140 in today's money). Near the base, he built a two-room log cabin (one for him, one for guests) and installed a "sentiment" book in which prominent visitors could record their impressions. During the Revolutionary War, soldiers made bullets by pouring molten lead from the bridge into the creek below and mined saltpeter from nearby caves for gunpowder.

Today, all visits to Natural Bridge start at the main ticket building, which encloses a gargantuan gift shop, an indoor pool, a miniature golf course, an ATM, and a post office. Walk downhill or take a shuttle bus to the beginning of the trail, where a café (open seasonally) offers light fare in an open patio alongside the creek. Children's voices echo up the deep, wooded gorge, where you'll get your first glimpse of the sheer size of the thing. At 50-150 feet wide and 90 feet long, it's massive, but surprisingly graceful for 36,000 tons of stone. The trail continues along the creek. It's a pleasant walk when it's not too crowded. You'll encounter an old saltpeter mine, picnic areas, and the Lace Waterfalls past an open space where Easter sunrise services have been held since 1947.

Other Sights

It's said that the ghost of a woman haunts the **Natural Bridge Caverns** (15 Appledore Ln., 540/291-2482, www.naturalbridgeva. com, 9am-4pm daily mid-Mar.-late Mar., 9am-5pm daily Apr.-Nov., 9am-4pm Fri.-Sun. Dec.-mid-Mar., $18 adults, $12 children ages 6-12, free ages 5 and under), the deepest cave (37 stories) on the East Coast. Guided tours to spots including the Wishing Well Room, Colossal Dome Room, and Mirror Lake leave every half hour. Be aware that it's a hike to the bottom—a series of staircases, actually, and you have to take them back up.

Natural Bridge Zoo (5784 S. Lee Hwy., 540/291-2420, www.naturalbridgezoo. com, 9am-6pm daily Mar.-late May, 9am-6pm Mon.-Fri., 9am-7pm Sat.-Sun. late May-Aug., 9am-5pm Mon.-Fri., 9am-6pm Sat.-Sun. Sept.-late Oct., 9am-5pm daily late Oct.-late Nov., 9am-4pm daily late Nov.-early Dec., $12 adults, $10 seniors 65 and older, $8 children ages 3-12, free ages 2 and under), on US-11 South, harbors the usual: giraffes, camels, bears, and monkeys, along with rare and endangered species such as a white tiger born in 1997. It also boasts the largest petting zoo in the state.

If you haven't had your critter fix by

canoeing along the James River north of Roanoke

now, stop by the **Virginia Safari Park** (229 Safari Ln., 540/291-3205, www.virginiasafaripark.com, 9am-5pm daily mid-Mar.-late Mar. and Nov., 9am-5:30pm Mon.-Fri., 9am-6:30pm Sat.-Sun. Apr.-May and Sept., 9am-6:30pm daily June-Aug., 9am-5:30pm daily Oct., $20 adults, $19 seniors, $13 children ages 2-12, free ages 1 and under), a 180-acre drive-through zoo. A three-mile road takes you past bison, zebras, antelope, and ostriches roaming free (more or less). There's also a petting zoo, an aviary, and a primate house. Kids love the giraffe feeding station. Buy buckets of feed, giraffe grain, or lettuce (which giraffes love, evidently) and take a peek at these exotic animals up close.

Accommodations

The **Natural Bridge Hotel** (15 Appledore Ln., 540/291-2121, www.naturalbridgeva.com, $71-150) is comfortable and environmentally responsible. The hotel uses a number of sustainable products and practices across the entire property, proving that green can equal comfortable and luxurious. There are around 115 rooms, including several suites. Four restaurants serve cuisine from fine dining to pub standards.

Apple Orchard Mountain (MP 76.5)

Looking at these mountainsides, it's easy to imagine that the sparse trees and lower understory were either groomed to look this way or were planted, as the name suggests, as an apple orchard. After all, there are plenty of orchards in this part of Virginia. In fact, weather conditions have pruned the trees over time, peeling them back again and again, giving the mountainside the appearance of a cultivated orchard. Considering that Apple Orchard Mountain, at 3,950 feet, is the highest peak along Virginia's stretch of the Blue Ridge Parkway, it makes sense that it's a prime target for the wind, ice, and snow that gave the mountain its peculiar appearance and name. The "orchard" isn't the only odd sight here: The thing that looks like a giant golf ball on top of the mountain is a huge radar array that was used during the Cold War for defense purposes. Today, the FAA uses it to monitor air traffic.

Apple Orchard Falls Trail

Distance: 2.4 miles out and back
Duration: 1.5-2 hours
Elevation gain: 1,000 feet
Difficulty: moderate to strenuous
Trailhead: Sunset Field Overlook at MP 78.4
Directions: To reach the trailhead, drive south along the Parkway to MP 78.4.

This hike drops off the Parkway for a very pleasant 1.2-mile hike to Apple Orchard Falls and a return trip that will have your thighs burning as you gain 1,000 feet in elevation.

Head past the trail sign and cross the Appalachian Trail to enter the Jefferson

National Forest (camping is allowed within the national forest) just 0.2 mile into the hike. There's a series of switchbacks that will be a mild nuisance on the way down, but you'll love them on the return trip. At 0.6 mile, you'll come upon a roadway, then at 0.8 mile a wider roadway and Cornelius Creek Trail to the left. Continue straight for Apple Orchard Falls.

At one mile, the path begins to parallel the creek. Soon after, the trail descends steeply beneath a large rock outcropping and a rhododendron thicket. Once you cross the creek via a footbridge, the trail will ascend just as quickly, leading you immediately to Apple Orchard Falls.

Apple Orchard Falls drops some 150 feet over a rock face. The stone is lichen covered, fern riddled, and looks like the sort of place fairies would live. Walk around a bit and take in the waterfall, which looks quite different from different perspectives. When you've looked to your heart's content, reverse your path and head down from the falls, then immediately (and steadily) head back up the mountain to the parking area at Sunset Field Overlook.

Peaks of Otter (MP 85.9)

After dipping to its lowest point and climbing to the highest peak in Virginia, the Blue Ridge Parkway winds its way to the **Peaks of Otter Recreation Area** (MPs 83.1-85.9). Indeed there are two peaks: Flat Top, a lumpy mountain nearly indistinguishable from the others around it, and the conical Sharp Top, the shorter, more iconic, and more easily identifiable of the two. Sharp Top was believed by many to be the highest peak in Virginia for a long time (but it's actually Mount Rogers in the southwestern corner of the state), and in 1852, believing this was the case, state officials offered a chunk of stone from Sharp Top for inclusion in the Washington Monument.

It was embedded into the obelisk with the inscription: "From Otter's summit, Virginia's Loftiest peak, To crown a monument, To Virginia's noblest son."

Archaeological evidence suggests that Native Americans hunted elk in these valleys and on these mountainsides at least 8,000 years ago, and it's no doubt Sharp Top cut quite the sight then as now. In more recent history, the valley was visited by Algonquian, Cherokee, Iroquois, and Sioux tribes hunting buffalo, elk, deer, and bear. European settlers knew of the area long before beginning to clear land here in 1766, and the first permanent settlers began to arrive soon after the end of the Revolutionary War. In the late 1830s or early 1840s, an ordinary (another name for tavern) opened, and by 1860, it was a popular spot for wealthy vacationers from flatter regions of the state. Polly Wood's Ordinary still stands today between the Peaks of Otter Picnic Area and Abbott Lake. When the Park Service acquired land for the Blue Ridge Parkway in the 1930s, a community of 20 families lived here, including the Johnson family, for whom the Johnson Farm Trail is named. A church and school stood where the Peaks of Otter Lodge stands today.

Just down the Parkway from the Peaks of Otter Lodge is the **Peaks of Otter Visitor Center** (MP 86 at junction with VA-43, 85919 Blue Ridge Pkwy., Bedford, 540/586-4496, 10am-5pm daily). In addition to restrooms, there are a few displays on the history, flora, and fauna of the region. Three trails—**Harkening Hill Trail, Johnson Farm Trail,** and **Elk Run Trail**—make loops from here and range from easy to strenuous.

You can climb the marvelous peaks of both Sharp Top and Flat Top. There is also a **shuttle** (hourly 10am-4pm Sat.-Sun. early May-late May, Wed.-Sun. late May-Sept., daily Oct., one-way $6 adults, $4 children ages 12 and under, round-trip $10 adults, $6 children ages 12 and under) to a point near the summit of Sharp Top, and you can get tickets from the Country

Store in the lodge. The shuttle departs from the store. There's no bus to the top of the longer, but easier, Flat Top.

Flat Top Trail

Distance: 9 miles out and back
Duration: 6-6.5 hours
Elevation gain: 1,400 feet
Difficulty: moderate to strenuous
Trailhead: Flat Top Mountain Overlook parking area at MP 83.5

This hike goes from the Flat Top Mountain Overlook at Milepost 83.5 to the Peaks of Otter Picnic Area. If you have two cars, it's a great shuttle hike of 4.5 miles. Otherwise, you can hike to the picnic area and return, making a nine-mile trip; or turn back at the summit for a hike just under six miles.

The first 0.3 mile is a steady ascent along a ridgeline, but once you cross through the small gap, the trail gradually becomes steeper until, at 0.6 mile, you begin a set of switchbacks that carry you to mile 1.3. Along the way, you'll pass through mountain laurel and rhododendron and enter a small, rocky field.

At mile 1.5, you'll reach a bench and a new series of switchbacks. This is even steeper and rockier than the last section. At two miles in, you'll reach a second bench and a quarter mile on, an intersection with Cross Rock Trail. Drop briefly into a small gap at mile 2.7, then begin climbing through some impressive boulders. You'll reach the 4,001-foot summit at mile 2.8. From here, you'll have spectacular views of the Piedmont to the east, Sharp Top to the south, and Harkening Hill to the west.

Here you have two choices: press on to the picnic area or reverse course back to the trailhead. If you reverse course, take your time picking through the boulder field. If you press on, at mile 3, the view opens and you have a nice look at Sharp Top. At mile 3.4, you'll cross a ridgeline, then a second one at mile 3.6. At mile 4, you'll swing around onto the southeast face of the mountain and descend a series of laurel-lined switchbacks. The trail eases as you near the Peaks of Otter Picnic Area at mile 4.5.

Sharp Top Trail

Distance: 3 miles out and back
Duration: 2.5-3 hours
Elevation gain: 1,500 feet
Difficulty: strenuous
Trailhead: near MP 86, across the road from the Peaks of Otter Visitor Center

This hike is a lung-busting, thigh-burning workout, so take your time. In many places the trail is rocky, and you could twist an ankle if you misstep or are wearing improper footwear. But at the top, your effort pays off with unheralded views. You can hike before dawn to the summit in time for sunrise (be sure you have a strong headlamp with fresh batteries). It's windy and a good six degrees cooler on the summit, so you may want to pack an extra layer.

From the trailhead, begin your ascent and cross the bus road at 0.2 mile (pedestrians aren't allowed on the bus road, so don't think of hiking it up or back). The trail is steep in places and very rocky in others, but it's pretty straightforward. When you reach the 1.2-mile mark, a spur trail to your right will take you to Buzzards Roost, a lesser peak on the mountain, but one with good views. Immediately after passing the spur to Buzzards Roost, the trail turns much steeper and there are handrails bolted into the rock in places. As you approach the summit, which is made of giant, house-sized boulders, you'll meet one more path, which branches off to the left to the shuttle stop. Just below the summit is a stone shelter that exists in case of inclement weather (which can come up fast, so keep your eyes peeled). Head up another set of stone stairs to the summit, where you'll be treated to 360-degree views. You can see the lodge, Abbott Lake, the Parkway snaking off to the north and south, the lights of Bedford, and the bulk of Flat Top. To go back, simply reverse course, or head to the bus stop to catch a ride, provided you bought a ticket.

Accommodations

The ★ **Peaks of Otter Lodge** (85554 Blue Ridge Pkwy., Bedford, 540/586-1081 or 866/387-9905, www.peaksofotter.com, year-round with limited openings Dec.-Mar., from $154) is a must-stay on the Parkway, especially during leaf season. The food at the lodge's **restaurant** (7:30am-10:30am, 11:30am-3:30pm, and 4:30pm-9pm daily, $3-25) is all right, but the view of Abbott Lake and Sharp Top rising above as it's reflected in the lake's waters is quite striking. Get to your meal a little early to grab a window seat for an unobstructed view. On Friday nights, a seafood buffet and carving station ($28 adults, $15 children) is popular. In addition to the restaurant, there's a grab-and-go case and coffee shop (8am-4:30pm Mon.-Fri., 7am-4:30pm Sat.-Sun., $8), a gift shop (9am-8pm daily), and

lounge (4pm-9pm Mon.-Fri., 2pm-9pm Sat.-Sun.).

The **Peaks of Otter Campground** (10454 Peaks Rd., Bedford, 540/586-7321, reservations 877/444-6777, www.recreation.gov, May-late Oct., $20) has 140 sites for tents and RVs (there are no electric hookups). Campsites are shady and generally cool, and the Peaks of Otter Lodge is a short walk away.

❖ VA-43 South: Bedford (MP 86)

The first time I saw Bedford, established as the town of Liberty in 1782, I was hooked. The people are welcoming, the town center is a throwback to that idealized Main Street of old, and the mountain setting is beautiful. It's small, but Bedford lacks that cloistered feel that some small towns exude. Locals are open and kind, and most visitors leave with fond memories and a desire to return. Given its

The Peaks of Otter Lodge recalls classic motels from the golden age of road trips.

proximity to the Peaks of Otter and the Blue Ridge Parkway, it's a fantastic waypoint if you'd rather stay in a B&B than a lodge or campground on the Parkway, and there are enough good restaurants in town to make any meal one to remember. While in town, take a little time to learn some of the history and culture of Bedford by paying a visit to the National D-Day Memorial or Thomas Jefferson's other Virginia home—Poplar Forest.

VA-43 meets the Parkway at the Peaks of Otter, and Bedford is 11 miles to the southeast. At Milepost 106, US-460 will also take you to Bedford (21 miles east).

Sights
★ National D-Day Memorial
Bedford's **National D-Day Memorial** (3 Overlord Circle, 866/935-0700, 10am-5pm daily Mar.-Nov., 10am-5pm Tues.-Sun. Dec.-Feb., $10 adults, $6 students and children ages 6-18, $19 combo ticket with Poplar Forest) honors the men who fought and lost their lives in the

Normandy Invasion of World War II. The memorial stands on an 88-acre hilltop overlooking Bedford and is designed to be toured in chronological order, first telling of the planning and preparation for Operation Overlord (commonly known as D-Day), then leading through the storming of the beachheads at Normandy, and the eventual victory of Allied Forces. Informational placards and sculptures represent the generals, admirals, and commanders who made victory possible. The most moving element is the quartet of sculptures on the pool and simulated Normandy beach. *Through the Surf, Death on Shore, Across the Beach,* and *Scaling the Wall* show soldiers in various poses—rushing through the water onto the shore with rifle held high overhead; fallen on the sand; rushing across the beach; scaling the cliffs above—and tell the story of that day's events. A large stone arch at the top of the memorial signifies the end of the war in Europe.

As you enter the memorial from the gift shop, you'll find *Homage,* a statue honoring the Bedford Boys, a group of young men from Bedford. The Bedford Boys were part of the 29th Infantry Division, 116th Infantry Regiment, Company A, which assaulted Omaha Beach on D-Day. That morning, 31 men from Bedford loaded into landing craft to be part of the first wave of attackers. One landing craft struck an obstacle, keeping five of the Bedford Boys out of immediate action. Of the 26 who reached the beach, 16 were killed and 4 were wounded within minutes. Three were unaccounted for and later presumed killed in action. On D-Day, Bedford suffered the worst loss, per capita, of any community in the United States. When Congress approved plans for the National D-Day Memorial, Bedford was the natural choice.

Touring the memorial on your own is fine, but the **guided tours** (free), which are often led by veterans, offer a glimpse into the stories and symbolism that went into the overall design of the memorial and its individual elements, including those life-size statues on the "beach."

Thomas Jefferson's Poplar Forest

In 1773, Thomas Jefferson inherited a 4,812-acre working tobacco farm from his father-in-law, providing the future president with a welcome source of income. In 1806, he laid the foundation there for a house he would come to cherish. "When finished," he said, "it will be the best dwelling house in the state, except that of Monticello; perhaps preferable to that, as more proportioned to the faculties of a private citizen." **Poplar Forest** (1542 Bateman Bridge Rd., Forest, 434/525-1806, www.poplarforest.org, 10am-5pm daily Mar. 15-Dec., last tour leaves at 4:05pm, $16 adults, $14 seniors and military, $8 students and youth 12-18, $4 children ages 6-11, free ages 5 and under, $19 combo ticket with National D-Day Memorial) served as a year-round retreat from that other "curiosity of the neighborhood," which had already become a magnet for visitors. Eventually Jefferson was making the three-day ride from his official residence three or four times a year and staying at Poplar Forest up to two months at a time.

Poplar Forest was sold in 1828, two years after Jefferson's death. A nonprofit organization began restoration in the early 1990s. The exterior has been completely restored, but work continues inside and on the wing of service rooms. The sparsely furnished interior emphasizes the structure's simple, classical lines. Guided tours are included with admission. In the Hands-On History pavilion (open in midsummer), kids can learn colonial-era skills, like writing with a copy of Jefferson's polygraph and using a drop spindle.

A winding gravel drive leads to the north portico. The entire house forms a perfect octagon, a shape also used in the two brick privies on the opposite side.

Similarities to Monticello appear in the three-piece windows that fill the parlor with light, and alcove beds, one of which has been reproduced here. Twin earth mounds on either side of the house were formed from soil excavated from the wine cellar and sunken lawn and were once planted with aspens and weeping willows.

To reach Poplar Forest, take VA-811 from US-221 or US-460, then turn onto VA-661 (Bateman Bridge Rd.) and follow the signs.

Apple Orchards

This is apple country, and there are plenty of orchards to visit around Bedford. **Gross' Orchard** (6817 Wheats Valley Rd., 540/586-2436, www.grossorchards.com, 8am-6pm Mon.-Sat., free) has been family owned and operated since the late 1800s, so these folks know their apples. Located at the foot of the Peaks of Otter, the orchard grows peaches and several types of apples. Peaches are available in summer, from mid-June to mid-September, and the first of the fall apples come in around the first of September, with different types ripening throughout the season. In the store, you can buy an assortment of jams, jellies, butters, and other homemade treats.

Johnson's Orchard (2122 Sheep Creek Rd., 540/586-3707, www.peaksofotter-winery.com, noon-5pm Sat.-Sun. Jan.-Mar., noon-5pm daily Apr.-Dec., free) is another longtime family-owned orchard, dating back to the late 1800s as well, but the family's farming life in these mountains predates the farm by another century. On the 200 or so acres of the orchard, they have close to 200 varieties of apples on 7,500 trees, including the Gold Nugget, an apple they developed on site. Grab a basket and go pick your own or simply buy some from the store, but do take a few minutes to wander out into the orchard for the views of neat rows of trees and the surrounding mountains.

Bedford Wine Trail

There are six wineries within a short drive of Bedford, and the **Bedford Wine Trail** (http://thebedfordwinetrail.com) leads across some beautiful countryside as you learn a bit about Virginia's wine. Pick up a trail map at the **Bedford Welcome Center** (816 Burks Hill Rd., 540/587-5681 or 877/447-3257, www.visitbedford.com, 9am-5pm daily) and have it stamped at all six wineries, then return it to the welcome center for a free gift.

Stops on the trail include **Hickory Hill Vineyards** (1722 Hickory Cove Ln., Moneta, 540/296-1393, www.smlwine.com, noon-5pm Wed.-Sun.), **LeoGrande Vineyards and Winery** (1343 Wingfield Dr., Goode, 540/586-4066, 11am-6pm Fri.-Sun.), **Ramulose Ridge Vineyards** (3061 Hendricks Store Rd., Moneta, 540/314-2696, 1pm-6pm daily), **Seven Doors Winery** (5800 Johnson Mountain Rd., Huddleston, 540/589-9530, www.sevendoorswinery.com), **White Rock Vineyards** (2117 Bruno Dr., Goodview, 540/890-3359 or 540/798-0323, www.whiterockwines.com, noon-5pm Thurs.-Mon.), and **Peaks of Otter Winery** (2122 Sheep Creek Rd., Bedford, 540/586-3707, www.peaksofotterwinery.com, noon-5pm Sat.-Sun. Jan.-Mar., noon-5pm daily Apr.-Dec.). Tasting fees range from complimentary to $10.

Entertainment and Events

Bedford is a small town, so if you want to watch a sporting event or have a late-night beer, your choices are limited. One of the only spots to head to is **Clam Diggers** (109 S. Bridge St., 540/587-6727, www.idigtheclam.com, 5pm-9 pm Wed.-Thurs., 5pm-11pm Thurs.-Sat., $6-25). The attraction is their full bar and small but decent selection of draft beer. They also serve an assortment of seafood dishes, including steamed shrimp, crab, and clams.

Top to bottom: National D-Day Memorial; an apple at one of the orchards near Bedford; eclectic Town Kitchen & Provisions in Bedford.

Bedford has received several iterations of the "Main Street U.S.A." designation, and **Centerfest** (540/586-2148, www.centertownbedford.com, typically the fourth Sat. in Sept., free) is one of the reasons why. This one-day gathering has been occurring every year for more than three decades and regularly draws crowds in excess of 10,000 to Bedford's Main Street. Among the things you'll find at Centerfest are arts and crafts booths, pony rides and similar activities for kids, and, of course, fair food.

Shopping

The **Bedford Country Store** (115 N. Bridge St., 540/586-2222) sells a little bit of everything: antiques; garage-sale-worthy junk; handcrafted pieces of art and crafts; and a selection of local meat, produce, and dairy. It also has a deli and ice cream counter. It's an interesting little spot, though it's less country store than the name leads you to believe.

In the nearby town of Moneta, the **Diamond Hill General Store** (1017 Diamond Hill Rd., Moneta, 540/297-9309, www.diamondhillgeneralstore.info, 7am-8pm Mon.-Thurs., 7am-9pm Fri., 9am-9pm Sat., 9am-8pm Sun.) sells gifts, wine, gas, bait and fishing tackle, and groceries, and has a deli, ice cream counter, and garden center. It's the oldest operating business around Smith Mountain Lake, and the original part of the store dates back to 1857.

Peddler Antiques (1165 Burnbridge Rd., Forest, 434/525-6030, 11am-4pm Mon., 11am-5pm Tues.-Fri., 10am-5pm Sat., 1pm-5pm Sun.) is near Thomas Jefferson's Poplar Forest and is one of the oldest antiques shops in the region. Located in a brick schoolhouse, it has a nice assortment of furniture, jewelry, vintage accessories, fine china, and books. If you're in the area, it's worth the stop.

Sports and Recreation
Golf

The rolling hills around the lower elevations here are ideal for mountain golf. At **Ivy Hill Golf Club** (1148 Ivy Hill Dr., Forest, 434/525-2680, www.ivyhillgc.com, 18 holes, par 72, 4,811-7,107 yards, $23-45, rates vary by season) in Forest, 14 miles east from Bedford on US-221, the course is both fun and challenging. Water in play on four holes offers an additional challenge as you account for the slight grade and elevation changes.

Also in Forest is **London Downs Golf Club** (1400 New London Rd., Forest, 434/525-4653, www.londondowns.com, 18 holes, par 72, 4,965-6,938 yards, $20-39, rates vary by season), another nice club where you'll find wide, forgiving fairways that often favor long hitters.

Smith Mountain Lake State Park

The 20,600-acre, 40-mile-long Smith Mountain Lake has more than 500 miles of shoreline and more opportunities to fish, camp, swim, canoe, and kayak than you have time for in one visit. A great way to get a feel for the second-largest freshwater lake in Virginia is by visiting **Smith Mountain Lake State Park** (1235 State Park Rd., Huddleston, 540/297-6066, www.dcr.virginia.gov/state-parks, 8:15am-dusk daily, parking $5-10). **Cabins** as well as tent and RV **camping** are available (800/933-7275, www.reserveamerica.com, $20-125). Two public **beaches** on the lake are open from Memorial Day through Labor Day and are guarded during operating hours.

If you're interested in **fishing,** many charters are available, and the Smith Mountain Lake website (www.visitsmithmountainlake.com) has a comprehensive list and detailed information on acquiring a Virginia fishing license (if your guide doesn't take care of that for you). One of the more intriguing guides is Captain Bert with **Captain Bert's Fishing Charters and Waterfront Lodging** (540/721-5788, www.captainbert.com, $325 two people half day, $500 two people full day, extra $25 pp for additional anglers). Captain Bert is none other than

Daniel Berthiaume, former NHL goalie, and today he searches Smith Mountain Lake for another record fish. The lake already holds the record for a lake-caught striped bass at 49.4 pounds.

Boat rentals are available at several places. One of the easiest to get to is **Bridgewater Marina's State Park Rentals** (1235 State Park Rd., Huddleston, 540/297-3642, www.bwmarina.com, 10am-6pm daily Memorial Day-Labor Day) at the park marina. You can rent a pontoon ($240/day), a ski boat ($350/day), or a Wave Runner ($295/day), as well as water skis, tubes, wakeboards, and kneeboards.

Food

★ **Town Kitchen & Provisions** (309 N. Bridge St., 540/586-0321, www.townkitchenprovisions.com, 11am-7pm Tues.-Fri., 11am-3pm Sat., noon-3pm Sun., $6-11) serves a small but creative menu of sandwiches (including an excellent bahn mi and the Woody, their spin on a Reuben), salads, and frittatas; has an excellent little bottle shop with carefully curated wine and beer sections; and carries a nice assortment of local cheeses and other foodstuffs. Everything from the rotating selection of daily soups to the sides and mountainous sandwiches is top notch. The restaurant is on the first floor of a historic home, so interior seating is limited to a series of tables for two in the wide hallway and in the back, but there's seating outside that's perfect for groups. I recommend eating outside, weather permitting.

Folks Country Restaurant (1619 Forest Rd., 540/589-9041, 6am-2pm Mon.-Sat., 7am-2pm Sun., $5) serves home-style grub—biscuits, hotcakes, burgers, and sandwiches—every day of the week. You can get breakfast all day, and, if you're daring or just interested in trying some authentic country food, order the pork brains and eggs. Pork brains are something like soft tofu: they scramble up nicely and take on the flavors of whatever

is around. The hardest thing about eating them is wrapping your head around what's on your fork, but they are tasty.

Happycoffee (104 N. Bridge St., 540/707-9256, www.behappycoffee.com, 6am-10pm Mon.-Thurs., 6am-11pm Fri., 8am-11pm Sat., 8am-9pm Sun., $2-13) is a cheerful little place in downtown serving caffeine-loaded drinks and a small menu of pastries, bagels, quesadillas, and breakfast items. Coffee is sourced from select growers and roasted in Lynchburg, just a few miles away.

Get your barbecue and beer fix at **Beale's Beer** (510 Grove St., 540/583-5113, www.bealesbeer.com, 4pm-9pm Wed.-Thurs., 4pm-10pm Fri., noon-10pm Sat., noon-7pm Sun., $4-22). The barbecue spans styles and you can get chopped pork, sliced brisket, smoked turkey, Texas-style hot links, and some great variations on barbecued sandwiches. Their flagship beer, a Helles lager, is a good match with anything on the menu. Their other brews include several lagers, a selection of IPAs, and even some fruit-forward beers.

Bedford Social Club (124 S. Bridge St., 540/586-9454, www.bedfordsocialclub.com, 5pm-late Wed.-Sat., $19-27) has a little bit of everything and a scene that's hot with locals. The barbecued pork chops, grilled New York strip, and seared scallops get great reviews. On a weekend night, it's a great spot to be seen.

Accommodations

While you're in Bedford, you might as well go for the whole country experience. **Reba Farm Inn** (1099 Reba Farm Ln., 540/583-1906, www.rebafarminn.com, $105-115) is located on an amazing piece of country property that you can explore on foot or horseback. Trail rides are available through Saddle Soar Equitainment, owned by the inn's proprietors. Amenities include a pool, outdoor whirlpool tub, game room, and a range of trail rides.

★ **Vanquility Acres Inn** (105 Angus

Ter., 540/587-9113 or 540/761-3652, www.vanquilityacresinn.com, $75-225) has both B&B-style rooms and cabins on their 10-acre farm. The rooms are large, and the cabins perfect for groups. Every morning, they serve a full country breakfast on the back deck or in the dining room. Amenities include an outdoor fireplace, hot tub, massive deck, and a covered patio. Unlike many B&Bs of the "country" ilk, this one is very tastefully decorated, with enough flourishes to get the "country" across without drowning you in it.

Information and Services

The **Bedford Welcome Center** (816 Burks Hill Rd., 540/587-5681 or 877/447-3257, www.visitbedford.com, 9am-5pm daily) contains the typical racks of brochures advertising area attractions, restaurants, and accommodations, but this welcome center also contains a number of display cases representing the local cultural attractions. An architectural model of the National D-Day Memorial and two cases of memorabilia from WWII give you a taste of what the memorial has to offer, and from the back deck, you can see the victory arch and memorial on top of the hill; artifacts on loan from the Bedford Museum tease the stories they have to tell there; and other cases are filled with local art, crafts, and artisanal items, many of which are available in the small gift shop or area stores. The most helpful thing here is the staff, most of whom are lifelong residents with a deep and abiding love for this small town and what it has to offer. You can also purchase tickets to the D-Day Memorial here. The welcome center's website provides plenty of information on the town of Bedford, the National D-Day Memorial, the Peaks of Otter, and the countryside around this part of the Parkway.

Centra Bedford Memorial Hospital (1613 Oakwood St., 540/586-2441, www.centrahealth.com) offers 24-hour emergency services at their 50-bed facility in town.

If you need police services, look to the **Bedford Police Department** (215 E. Main St., 540/587-6011, www.bedfordva.gov) or **Bedford County Sheriff** (1345 Falling Creek Rd., 540/586-4800, www.bedfordcountysheriff.org).

Purgatory Overlook (MP 92.1)

Near Purgatory Overlook, a carriage road once wound through the mountains and valleys on a track so rough, passengers felt they'd been sentenced to Purgatory. Fortunately, the Blue Ridge Parkway is more like a bit of heaven than that. Less than 0.5 mile down the road, at the Sharp Top Parking Area (MP 92.5), you'll have a fantastic view of Sharp Top. This is a great spot to photograph the iconic mountain, so have your camera ready.

Great Valley Overlook (MP 99.6)

Looking west from the Blue Ridge Parkway, you'll notice that the valley is wide, flat-bottomed, and nearly arrow-straight. Today, I-81 travels this route from Pennsylvania down to Tennessee, but for hundreds of years it's been a highway of sorts. Called the Great Valley, this essentially unbroken path runs from New York to Alabama, bordered by the Blue Ridge on the east and the Allegheny Mountains on the west. There's evidence of it being used as a war path, a trading route, and a hunting path for Native Americans. German and Scots-Irish pioneers from Pennsylvania followed this route as they migrated into the wilds of the new continent and settled here and there along the way. Plus, it's a pretty great valley to look at.

N&W Railroad
Overlook (MP 106.9)

The Norfolk and Western Railroad played a very significant role in the development of the city of Roanoke, just a few miles from here. In 1852, the first rails were laid on a track running from Lynchburg (near Bedford) to Bristol, Tennessee. The view here is among the best on the Parkway. Green pastures on rolling hills dotted with farmhouses, the easy slope of the Blue Ridge Mountains, and that incredible expanse of sky overhead make this a place to linger.

Roanoke

Roanoke, the largest city in southwestern Virginia, sits in the Roanoke River Valley beneath the peaks of the Blue Ridge, and adjacent to the Great Valley. The metro area—which includes Roanoke and the nearby cities of Salem and Vinton—has a population of more than 300,000. Aided by accolades like being named one of the Top 50 Cities for Expansion and Relocation, a Five Star Community (for quality of life), and one of the 100 Best Places for Business Development, and helped by the city's proximity to the major corridor that is I-81, Roanoke is on a track for continual growth.

As the cultural, medical, and transportation center for the region, Roanoke can rightfully be called the "Capital of the Blue Ridge." Vibrant neighborhoods throughout the city each have their own flair, and you'll find that residents of these neighborhoods, in particular the hip Grandin Village, are especially proud of where they live. This lends the whole city a pride in the place, a pride that is well deserved. Downtown, the City Market Building, a historic market dating back to the city's earliest days, and Market Square Plaza, with its long row of permanent farmers market stalls, provide a focal point for visitors and residents alike, as a number of the top restaurants and shops are within shouting distance of one another.

Roanoke is known by two other names, Magic City and The Star City. Magic City came about due to its unprecedented growth following the arrival of the N&W. The Star City was earned in 1949, when downtown merchants installed a giant star on nearby Mill Mountain as a Christmas decoration.

Getting There and Around
Car
At Milepost 106, US-460 will take you to Roanoke (nine miles southwest). From Milepost 112.2, you're only five miles from Roanoke. From Milepost 121.4, the Parkway meets US-220, putting Roanoke only five miles north. Salem, a suburb of Roanoke, is only 12 miles west and accessible easily from any of these points as well.

With I-81 running right by the city, Roanoke is easy to reach. Two major North Carolina cities are within striking distance of Roanoke. From Raleigh and the RDU International Airport, it's a trip of 159 miles to the north to reach Roanoke. Charlotte and Charlotte Douglas International Airport lie only 200 miles south along I-77.

Air
The largest airport in southwestern Virginia is the **Roanoke-Blacksburg Regional Airport** (ROA, 5202 Aviation Dr. NW, Roanoke, 540/362-1999, www.flyroa.com). Airlines serving this airport include Allegiant Air, American Airlines, Delta Airlines, and United Airlines.

It's just a short cab ride to downtown; **Yellow Cab** (540/345-7711, www.yellowcabroanoke.com) is one option. There are several car rental agencies with locations in the airport, including **Avis** (540/366-2436, www.avis.com), **Budget** (540/265-7328, www.budget.com), **Enterprise** (540/563-8055, www.enterprise.com),

VIRGINIA BLUE RIDGE

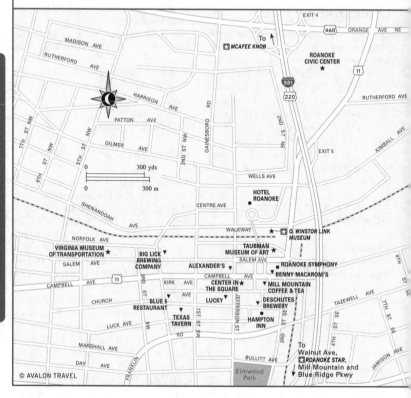

Downtown Roanoke

and **Hertz** (540/366-3421 or 800/654-3131, www.hertz.com).

Train and Bus

The **Amtrak Station** (101 Norfolk Ave., 800/872-7245, www.amtrak.com), extending Amtrak passenger service from Roanoke to Washington DC and beyond, opened in fall 2017. The station is served by the Crescent and Northeast Regional lines.

If you take a bus to Roanoke, the **Greyhound Bus terminal** (26 Salem Ave. SW, 540/343-5436, www.greyhound.com, 5:15am-6:15am and 9am-5pm Mon.-Fri., 9am-10am and 1pm-5pm Sat.-Sun.) is convenient to downtown, just a couple

of blocks away from the City Market Building and Market Square.

Valley Metro (1108 Campbell Ave. SE, 540/982-2222 or 800/388-7005, www.valleymetro.com, $1.50 one-way, weekly unlimited pass $14) provides bus service across Roanoke and to nearby Salem. The Star Line, a free trolley, will take you on a downtown route that's convenient to many shops and restaurants.

Sights
Market Square

In 1882, 25 area "Hucksters" (an antiquated term for vendors) received licenses to open for business in stalls, booths, and in the open air in the **Historic Roanoke City Market** (market 24 hours daily;

vendors 8am-5pm Mon.-Sat., 10am-4pm Sun.) in the heart of downtown Roanoke. Today, it's the oldest continuously operating open-air market in Virginia and one of the oldest such markets in the nation. And judging by weekend crowds and the bustling street and stalls any time, any day of the week, it's only grown in popularity. As Roanoke has evolved into a friendly, surprisingly cosmopolitan city, Market Square has served as a sort of anchor to the downtown renaissance.

Permanent awnings shade vendors and sidewalk shoppers. You can find the usual locally grown fruits and vegetables here, as well as eggs, flowers, cheese and other dairy products, and live plants. The market's oldest continuous vendor—Martin's Plant Farm—has been selling here since 1904. The market stalls only close two days a year: Christmas and New Year's. During growing season, many farmers are planting, picking, and preparing for the market on Sunday-Monday, so selection may be limited. On Saturdays in April-September you'll find live music and a few activities for kids in the market 11am-2:30pm.

City Market Building

Across Campbell Avenue from Market Square is the **City Market Building** (32 Market Sq. SE, 540/986-5992, www.citymarketbuilding.com, 10am-7pm Mon.-Tues., 10am-9pm Wed.-Sat., 11am-3pm Sun.). It's been quite some time since the City Market Building has been the site of livestock auctions or the home of butcher shops, fishmongers, and wholesale produce, but the spirit of the place survives. The City Market Building now houses a half-dozen restaurants, an interior food court, public restrooms, and ample outdoor seating.

Across the street, on the corner of Salem Avenue and Market Street, is an interesting cast-iron fountain. Since 1898, the **Dog Mouth Fountain** (so named because of the dog head on the fountain) has offered cool, clean drinking water to

human and beast alike. As with all good things, there's a legend that goes with it. It is said that if you drink from this fountain, you'll always feel the need to return.

Center in the Square

Center in the Square (1 Market Sq. SE, 540/342-5700, www.centerinthesquare. org, 10am-5pm Mon.-Sat., 1pm-5pm Sun., individual museum hours vary) opened in 1982 as a hub for Roanoke's cultural offerings, a place where various arts groups and museums could have permanent homes in a central location. After a $7.5-million renovation of the building once home to the W. E. McGuire's Farmers' Supply Co., five arts and science organizations moved in. On opening weekend, 40,000 visitors flooded through the doors, and it's been a success ever since. Purchase a **Center Pass** ($21 adults, $16 children ages 4-17, free under 4) or a **Center Pass with Roanoke Pinball Museum** ($25 adults, $20 youth ages 9-17, $15 children 4-8, free under 4) ticket if you plan on visiting everything here.

In the lobby, there's a trio of aquariums, one showing Roanoke River aquatic life, one with area turtles, and another that's a living coral reef. The **Mill Mountain Theatre** (540/342-5740, www.millmountain.org, performance times and prices vary), which puts on plays, concerts, and dance recitals throughout the year, is also in the lobby. You can find out a little more about what each museum offers and purchase tickets at the box office before taking the stairs or elevator to your museum of choice. Before you leave, be sure to head up to the sixth floor and go out onto the roof; the views are quite nice.

On the second floor, the **Harrison Museum of African American Culture** (540/857-4395, www.harrisonmuseum. com, 10am-5pm Tues.-Sat., 1pm-5pm Sun., $7 adults, $4.75 ages 5-17, free ages 4 and under) celebrates the art, history, and culture of African Americans in the Roanoke River Valley. The **Don & Barbara**

Smith Children's Museum, Kids Square (540/342-5724, www.kidssquare.org, 10am-5pm Tues.-Sat., 1pm-5pm Sun., $8) has 15,000 square feet devoted to places for kids to socialize, learn, and play. Play areas include a theater with costumes, lights, and props; a "sandbox" filled with rubber pellets; treehouses, rope bridges, and climbing walls; a grocery store, vet's office, and bank; and a sensory cove.

Take a fun break and check out the **Roanoke Pinball Museum** (11am-5pm Tues.-Thurs., 11am-8pm Fri., 10am-8pm Sat., 1pm-6pm Sun., $12.40 ages 9 and up, $6.78 ages 6-8, free ages 5 and under with adult ticket). Here, more than 50 pinball machines produced from 1932 to 2016 are waiting for you to step up and start playing.

The fourth and fifth floors are taken up by the **Science Museum of Western Virginia** (540/342-5710, www.smwv.org, 10am-5pm Mon.-Sat., 1pm-5pm Sun., $15 adults, $13.50 seniors, military, students, and children ages 6-17, $7.50 ages 2-5, free under 2). This is a great museum for kids, with tons of interactive exhibits such as a living river touch tank and a butterfly garden.

★ O. Winston Link Museum

The **O. Winston Link Museum** (101 Shenandoah Ave., 540/982-5465, www.roanokehistory.org, 10am-5pm Tues.-Sat., $6 adults, $5.50 seniors, military, and students, $5 ages 3-12, free ages 2 and under) displays the work of Brooklyn photographer Winston Link, who captured the end of the steam locomotive era. Depicting exclusively the N&W Railroad (the last major rail line to operate exclusively on steam engines) in Virginia, West Virginia, Maryland, and North Carolina in the 1950s, the dramatic photographs, almost all of which are black and white, bring the beauty and power of steam engines to life. Contrast the photographs of steam trains roaring past drive-in theaters with ones where they make their way around long, gentle

Roanoke is a charming blend of old and new.

curves in the mountains. In the latter photos, the landscape is as much the focus as the trains. It's a small museum, but it contains hundreds of photos as well as a few films.

At the same location, the **History Museum of Western Virginia** presents a full picture of Roanoke's history under one roof. Permanent exhibits tell the story of the Roanoke River Valley dating back thousands of years up to the present. Special exhibits include pieces of Roanoke memorabilia, Appalachian musical instruments, and other tidbits from the valley's past.

Other Museums

From the O. Winston Link Museum, a pedestrian bridge leads across the tracks to the Market Square and the Center in the Square areas. On the opposite side, a path leads to the **Virginia Museum of Transportation** (303 Norfolk Ave. SW, 540/342-5670, www.vmt.org, 10am-5pm Mon.-Sat., 1pm-5pm Sun., $10 adults, $8

BEST BET ARTS

seniors and children ages 3-18), which serves as a monument to the many methods of simply getting from one place to another. Inside the restored freight station three blocks west of Market Square are an O-scale model railroad, a gift shop, and a gorgeous collection of antique autos, including a 1934 Ford V-8 Model A Sedan and a 1950 Studebaker Landcruiser, the latter more spaceship than car. Dozens of train engines and cars, a few of which are open to visitors, fill the lot out back. Steam engines, diesel locomotives, post office cars, and a classic caboose cover virtually the entire history of rail travel.

The **Taubman Museum of Art** (110 Salem Ave. SE, 540/342-5760, www. taubmanmuseum.org, 10am-5pm Wed.-Sat., noon-5pm Sun., free, guided tours $8) is in a beautiful contemporary building that is sometimes the subject of ire from community members who do not like the design. Permanent exhibits include fine examples of folk art, as well as galleries of works by contemporary artists and American art from 1820 through the recent past. The museum is open until 9pm the third Thursday and first Friday of the month.

Entertainment
Nightlife
Bars and Nightclubs

Blue 5 (312 2nd St. SW, 540/904-5338, www.blue5restaurant.com, 11:30am-11pm Mon.-Tues., 11:30am-midnight Wed.-Thurs., 11:30am-1am Fri., 4pm-1am Sat.) has outstanding beer choices, hosts a fun lineup of live music, and serves an excellent menu ($8-34) of full meals and shareable appetizers. It's a one-stop spot with a broad selection of beers from multiple breweries.

At **Stellina** (104 Kirk Ave. SW, 540/400-7315, 5pm-late Mon.-Sat.), a speakeasy secreted away inside the Italian eatery Fortunato, expect to find some of the best cocktails in the city. The drinks here are on par with those at the fine-dining restaurant Lucky, which is no coincidence since they're sister establishments.

Corned Beef & Co. (107 S. Jefferson St., 540/342-5534, www.cornedbeefandco.com, 11am-midnight Mon.-Tues., 11am-2am Wed.-Sat., $8-25) is a fun spot to hit at night that also serves lunch and dinner. It's a lively place thanks to karaoke, DJs, a billiards room with nine tables, shuffleboard, and even the occasional standup comic.

Breweries

Roanoke is catching on to the craft beer scene at an incredible pace. New breweries and craft-beer-centered bars seem to open monthly.

Parkway Brewing Company (739 Kessler Mill Rd., Salem, 540/404-9810, www.parkwaybrewing.com, 2pm-8pm Sun.-Mon., noon-8:30pm Wed.-Sat.) is my favorite. Their Raven's Roost Baltic Porter is on its way to becoming my favorite porter. Parkway always has something going on, like live music, food trucks, Lego building contests, and tarot readings. You may catch a belly dancer or a burlesque show (Parkway is generally kid-friendly, but leave Junior at home for this one), or get sucked into a one-night cornhole tournament.

In 2017, Portland, Oregon, powerhouse **Deschutes Brewery** (315 Market St. SE, 540/259-5204, www.deschutesbrewery.com, 1pm-9pm daily) opened a taproom in Roanoke, with plans for a full-scale brewery in the area by 2021. With some two-dozen taps of Deschutes' killer beers—west coast IPAs, porters, wheats, excellent seasonal brews, and more—expect to find some new favorite pints to have in the Star City.

Big Lick Brewing Company (135 Salem Ave., www.biglickbrewingco.com, 5pm-9pm Thurs., 4pm-9pm Fri., 1pm-9pm Sat.) takes its name from the moniker Roanoke held long before it was a proper town. Their beer spans the spectrum from the usual IPAs (from very hoppy to reasonably hoppy) to stouts and porters, red ales, and wheat ales.

Performing Arts

Fans of opera, ballet, and symphony productions will be happy to know that Roanoke has all three. **Opera Roanoke** (540/982-2742, www.operaroanoke.org) puts on nearly a dozen performances a year, from full operas to Opera 101 lectures to short concerts, at venues across the region. **Roanoke City Ballet** (540/345-6099, www.roanokeballet.org) puts on performances at a number of venues throughout Roanoke. You can hear the **Roanoke Symphony** (128 E. Campbell Ave., 540/343-9127, www.rso.com) at a number of performances during the year at venues large and small. Past performances include works by major classical composers and themed holiday performances, as well as interesting arrangements of contemporary musicians like Billy Joel and Procol Harum. If you want to attend a concert by major touring acts, the **Berglund Center** (710 Williamson Rd., 540/853-2241, www.theberglundcenter.com) hosts dozens of concerts every year.

An outstanding example of the possibilities of regional theater, the **Mill Mountain Theatre** (540/342-5740, www.millmountain.org) shows original works, classics, and children's plays at Center in the Square.

Shopping

One definite stop in Roanoke, whether you're a shopper or not, is **Black Dog Salvage** (902 13th St. SW, 540/343-6200, www.blackdogsalvage.com, 9am-5pm Mon.-Sat., noon-5pm Sun.). This shop is a wonderland of reclaimed and salvaged architectural pieces, antiques, and decorative items. There are some crazy treasures to be found here, like a bin of mannequin parts, numbered nails used by railroad workers, old signs, and a dynamite plunger more at home in a cartoon than in real life. There are also all sorts of things in their expansive yard, and if you're looking for something specific, ask; they may just be able to find it for you. They have a second **salvage warehouse and yard** (629 Ashlawn St. SW, 9am-5pm Thurs.-Sat. or by appointment) where you'll find bins of bowling pins, slabs of marble, church pews, and massive stained-glass windows.

Eli's Provisions (209 Market St. SE, 540/982-2164, www.elisroanoke.com, 10am-8pm Mon.-Thurs., 10am-9pm Fri., 9am-9pm Sat., 11am-6pm Sun.) specializes in Virginia-made foodstuffs. If you want beer, wine, cheese, ham, preserves, peanuts, or anything else edible that's made, grown, fermented, or aged in Virginia, they've got it.

Since you're traveling along the Blue Ridge Parkway, it's safe to assume you'll be doing a hike or two. If you find that you need something—new socks, a water bottle, a daypack, a quick-dry shirt— **Walkabout Outfitter** (301 Market St. SE, 540/777-2727, www.walkaboutoutfitter. com, 10am-5:30pm Mon.-Sat., 11am-4pm Sun.) carries a small selection of camping and hiking goods as well as clothing and accessories you can use on the trail.

Roanoke Natural Foods Co-Op (1 Market Sq., 540/904-2733, www.roanokenaturalfoods.com, 10am-7pm Sun.-Mon., 9am-7pm Tues.-Sat.) is the largest cooperatively owned natural foods grocery in Virginia. The store carries a well-curated selection of organic, natural, and good-for-you items in their location on Market Square. At their second location in Grandin Village (1319 Grandin Rd., 540/343-5652, 8am-9pm daily), they have a full grocery store stocked with the highest-quality products they can find.

Also in Grandin Village is **Too Many Books** (1504 Grandin Rd. SW, 540/985-6469, www.toomanybooksroanoke.com, 10am-5:30pm Mon.-Sat., 1pm-5pm Sun.),

Top to bottom: Roanoke's Center in the Square; farmers market bounty; Black Dog Salvage, a great place to pick up a one-of-a-kind souvenir.

a used, rare, and out-of-print bookshop. For book nerds and the other folks who love the smell of those old pages, this is an awesome bookstore where you can plunder for hours. They have two stories of books, from the strange to the top sellers.

Chocolatepaper (308 Market St. SE, Suite 3, 540/342-6061, www.chocolate-paperroanoke.com, 10am-6pm Mon.-Fri., 9am-6pm Sat., noon-5pm Sun.) has a selection of gifts, Virginia goodies, chocolates and candies, and books. It's a fun shop, and you'll find some great gifts inside, but if you're a chocolate lover, schedule a tasting to sample a half-dozen chocolates and wines in a fun afternoon.

The Market Gallery (23 Salem Ave., 540/342-1177, www.marketgalleryroa-noke.com, 10am-5:30pm Tues.-Thurs. and Sat., 10am-9pm Fri.) is an artist-member cooperative gallery. Close to 30 regional artists exhibit their work here. Paintings, drawings, prints, photographs, sculpture, and other diverse art forms are represented, and just about everything is for sale, so when you see something you like, take it home with you.

Sports and Recreation

From urban greenways to the Appalachian Trail to water sports to caves, there's an awful lot to do outdoors in and around Roanoke. For trip ideas, outfitter details, and a crazy comprehensive catalog of things to do and see, check out the website for **Roanoke Outside** (www.roanokeoutside.com).

★ McAfee Knob

The Appalachian Trail extends nearly 2,200 miles on its way from Georgia to Maine. In Virginia, it passes near Roanoke and Salem. Just a few miles from a trailhead in the mountains above Salem, you'll find one of the most iconic overlook spots on the trail: **McAfee Knob.** Even if you don't know the name, you've seen the pictures: a hiker, maybe two, standing on a rock ledge seemingly suspended in midair, the valley below and mountains behind.

McAfee Knob Trail

Distance: 7 miles out and back
Duration: 3.5-4 hours
Elevation gain: 1,750 feet
Difficulty: moderate
Trailhead: 6 miles from I-81 exit 141 on VA-311 North
Directions: Finding the trailhead can be tricky. From Roanoke, get on I-81 South and take exit 141 for Salem. Turn left onto VA-419/Electric Road and go 0.4 mile to the next traffic light and turn right onto VA-311 North. Take VA-311 5.6 miles to the top of the mountain. The trailhead is on the left. Be careful as you park and pull out; it's nearly a blind curve.

This is a great hike for novices, and the views at the end are incredible. The distance is the toughest thing as the trail is easy and the ascent pretty gradual. In all, it's a good way to get a feel for hiking on a well-made, well-maintained trail. You don't need high-end hiking boots; boots are best, but comfy shoes with a beefy sole will suffice.

The trail to McAfee Knob begins across VA-311. An informational kiosk awaits around a quarter mile into the hike; here you can get a little more info on the trail ahead. Moving on, you'll cross a series of wooden walkways before you reach the John Springs Shelter about 0.8 mile in. Take a break, drink some water, and continue on. There are another five walkways between the John Springs Shelter and the Catawba Mountain Shelter, which you'll come to in 1.4 miles. Just before you reach the shelter, you'll pass a spring where you can refill water bottles (provided that you have something to use to treat the water).

The Appalachian Trail crosses a fire road, then goes through a right of way for a high-tension power line. About 0.3 mile beyond the power line is one of the first good overlooks, giving you a view of the Catawba Valley. A half mile on, you'll come to the short spur trail leading to McAfee Knob.

The view from McAfee Knob is about

270 degrees. To the west, you're looking at Catawba Valley and North Mountain; this is a spectacular view as the Allegheny Mountains ripple away into the distance. To the east is the Roanoke Valley. To the north you can see Tinker Cliffs, and to the northeast, you can see Sharp Top poking into the sky. To return, retrace your steps.

Greenways and Blueways

Roanoke has an outstanding set of **urban trails** and **greenways** spread throughout the city. There are greenway trails in Salem and in Vinton, and plans to eventually connect the three towns via a contiguous multiuse trail. The greenway system (several parts of which are former railroad beds) takes you on pleasant paths between neighborhoods, from downtown to the Star on Mill Mountain, along the Roanoke River, and into parts of the city you don't see or pay attention to when zipping past in a car. Maps are available in the **visitors center** (101 Shenandoah Ave. NE, 9am-5pm daily) and at www.roanokevalley.org. **UnderDog Bikes** (1113 Piedmont St. SE, Roanoke, 540/204-4276, www.underdogbikesva.com, 10am-6pm Mon. and Wed.-Fri., 10am-5pm Sat., 10am-4pm Sun.) is right on the greenway, making picking up or dropping off a bike easy as can be. They have rental bikes ($12/hour or $30/24 hours), tandem bikes ($20/hour or $50/24 hours), kids' trailers ($9/hour or $20/24 hours), and trail-a-bikes ($9/hour or $20/24 hours).

What the greenway is to terrestrial travel, the **blueway** is to aquatic travel. The **Roanoke River Blueway** (www.roanokeriverblueway.org) is a 45-mile water trail that runs from East Montgomery County Park, through Roanoke, Salem, and Vinton, and on to Smith Mountain Lake. The Roanoke River is a great spot for sports like waterskiing and wakeboarding, as well as calmer endeavors like fishing, tubing, and wading. You can canoe, kayak, stand-up paddleboard, and generally splash around all along the river. Unfortunately, canoes, kayaks, and stand-up paddleboards are difficult to come by in Roanoke, with the nearest outfitter a 20-minute drive away.

Caves

If you can't find enough to do outside exploring the mountains, how about going inside? There are caves all up and down the Blue Ridge Mountains, and near Roanoke, you have a couple of easy options. At **Dixie Caverns** (5753 W. Main St., Salem, 540/380-2085, www.dixiecaverns.com, 9:30am-5pm Mon.-Fri., 9:30am-6pm Sat.-Sun., $14 adults, $6 ages 5-12, free under 5), take a 45-minute guided tour of this cave system, discovered by a dog (and then two farm boys) in 1920. They also have a **rock shop** (9am-6pm daily), where you can buy all sorts of minerals, gems, and semiprecious stones and stone art pieces, as well as a **campground** ($12/person for tents, $34/RV hookups).

Guided tours of a cave that's well lit, packed with handholds, and filled with visitors is one thing; donning some coveralls, a helmet, and a headlamp is another type of cave exploration entirely. **Wilderness Adventure at Eagle Landing** (11176 Peaceful Valley Rd., New Castle, 540/864-6792, www.wilderness-adventure.com) is a teen adventure camp, but they periodically run caving trips for small groups and families. Call for a schedule.

Spectator Sports

Salem is home to the **Salem Red Sox** (540/389-3333, www.salemsox.com, tickets $8-14), a Class A farm team for the Boston Red Sox. They play home games at **LewisGale Field** (1004 Texas St., Salem) and tickets are cheap. With full concessions—that means hot dogs, those wonderfully salty soft pretzels, beer, and wine—and an enthusiastic home crowd, taking in a game here is just about the perfect way to spend a summer evening.

Food

Part recreation, part meal on the run, **Discover Roanoke Food Tours** (540/309-1781, www.roanokefoodtours.com, from $52 adults, from $34 children ages 8-12, from $20 ages 7 and under) is a great way to get a look at the city, learn a little of its more interesting stories, and find some great places to eat. They hit 5-6 restaurants for a bite and often a sip of something good. Tours include the Downtown Food and Cultural Tour, the Sunday Brunch Food Tour, and the Roanoke Craft Beer Tour. Your guides know their city and know a thing or two about food, so don't be shy about asking what you're seeing, smelling, or tasting.

Bakeries and Cafés

Mill Mountain Coffee & Tea (117 Campbell Ave. SE, 540/342-9404, www.millmountaincoffee.com, 6:30am-11pm Mon.-Thurs., 6:30am-midnight Fri., 7am-midnight Sat., 8am-9pm Sun., $4-8) is your typical coffee shop serving a variety of drinks and baked goods alongside a small selection of sandwiches and salads. This place is notable for its good coffee and its status as a late-night hangout. It's the place to get your late-night cup of coffee or just unwind for a few minutes before heading home.

Scratch Biscuit Company (1820 Memorial Ave., 540/855-0882, 6am-1pm Mon.-Fri., 7am-2am Sat., $2-8) makes biscuits from scratch, and they're crazy good. The menu is simple: $2-, $3-, and $4-biscuits, each with extra toppings like butter, mustard, country ham, smoked tofu, brisket, or a fried green tomato. They have a few other things like grits, pancakes, and cinnamon rolls, but always get a biscuit.

American

Texas Tavern (114 W. Church Ave., 540/342-4825, www.texastavern-inc.com, 24 hours daily, $4), also known as "Roanoke's Millionaires Club," was established in 1930 and has been serving up burgers, breakfast, and their famous chile (yup, that's how they've spelled it for more than 20 million bowls) in the heart of downtown ever since. It's an out-of-place building—squat white brick with one door and a window that looks in over the tiny cooktop—with only 10 seats, all at the counter. Specialties include that chile, as well as the Cheesy Western, a cheeseburger topped with a fried egg, relish, pickles, and onions.

★ **River and Rail Restaurant** (2201 Crystal Springs Ave. SW, 540/400-6830, www.riverandrailrestaurant.com, 11am-2pm and 5pm-10pm Tues.-Sat., 11am-2pm Sun., $12-28) works closely with a network of farmers, ranchers, and fishers from the Roanoke Valley and the region to put the best of the area's bounty on every plate. On the menu you'll find exceptional seafood and pork dishes, a killer charcuterie board (including some of the best pickles anywhere), oysters on the half shell, and cornbread served with charred onion butter. The wine list has a lovely selection by the bottle and glass, but the cocktails are stupendous. Expect to find creative drinks that deliver on flavor and booze.

Italian and Pizza

Benny Marconi's (120 E. Campbell Ave., 540/400-8818, www.bennysva.com, 11am-midnight Sun.-Thurs., 11am-3am Fri.-Sat., $4-35) sells one thing: pizza. Okay, two things if you count the beer, and three things if you count the fact you can buy a slice or a pie. The pies are massive—28-inch beasts—so the slices are equally massive, equal to a pair of normal slices. Pies come in five toppings—cheese, pepperoni, sausage, and two monthly specials—and there's a pizza-eating challenge if you're into culinary competitions. Order a Benny's Challenge Pizza ($40), eat the whole eight-pound monster in an hour or less, and you get $500 (and heartburn).

Fine Dining

A meal at downtown's cool and fun ★ **Lucky** (18 Kirk Ave. SW, 540/982-1249, www.eatatlucky.com, 5pm-9pm Mon.-Wed., 5pm-10pm Thurs.-Sat., bar open until late, $16-40) is one you'll tell your friends about. Just about everything is sourced from Virginia or neighboring states. Go for the fried chicken, boiled peanuts, or pork shoulder. The cocktails are, hands down, the best in Roanoke. They've been known to smoke glasses and liquors, freeze freshly juiced fruits and vegetables into giant ice cubes, and put new twists on classic drinks. And if that's not enough, they have prosecco on draft.

The menu at **The Blue Apron Restaurant and Red Rooster Bar** (210 E. Main St., Salem, 540/375-0055, www.blueapronredrooster.com, 11:30am-2:30pm and 5pm-close Tues.-Sat., $8-34) in Salem is built around small, shareable plates. Most everything can be sized up to become an individual entrée, but the only way to eat here is to order at least two small plates per person and share them. Chef Scott Switzer changes the menu seasonally, so there's always something new to try. The steak frites are always a winner, and the herb-marinated pan-roasted chicken will make you rethink the idea that chicken is boring. Anything the kitchen does with fish, order it. The wine list and cocktail menu pair well with the food, rounding out the whole experience.

Ask locals for a date-night spot and they'll invariably recommend **Table 50** (309 Market St., 540/904-2350, www.table50roanoke.com, 5pm-10pm Mon.-Sat., 5pm-9pm Sun., bar 4pm-late nightly, $14-35) with enthusiasm. It's a classic steakhouse kind of place: dark booths, a lush interior, and rich, meaty dishes on every plate. Any steak will satisfy, but so will the crab cakes, the duck duo, the lamb, or any of the pastas or sides.

City Market

The **City Market Building** (32 Market Sq. SE, 540/986-5992, www.citymarketbuilding.com) has around a half-dozen restaurants in it. **Wall Street Tavern** (540/342-9555, www.wallstreettavernva.com, 11am-10pm Sun.-Tues., 11am-11pm Wed.-Thurs., 11am-midnight Fri.-Sat., bar open later, $9-21) is a fun American restaurant and lunch counter with a nice-sized outdoor area and a menu that includes sandwiches, wraps, steak, pasta, and seafood dishes, plus a great drinks menu. **Doner Kebab** (540/904-2244, 11am-7pm Mon.-Thurs., 11am-9pm Fri.-Sat., $5-12) is a Mediterranean restaurant with an American touch at lunchtime prices. Think hummus and kebabs, but also burgers and a good Philly cheesesteak. **Fork in the Market** (540/400-0644, www.marketfork.com, 11am-10pm Mon.-Wed., 11am-11pm Thurs.-Sat., 11am-9pm Sun., $5-18) serves giant burgers, a crazy array of hot dogs and sausages, and pizzas topped with everything from the expected to mac and cheese. Fork in the Market also has two sister restaurants, Fork in the Alley and Fork in the City, and a food truck called Fork in the Road.

Accommodations
Under $100

In Salem, **Baymont Inn and Suites** (179 Sheraton Dr., Salem, 540/795-2114, www.wyndhamhotels.com, $79-120) is convenient to I-81, only a 15-minute drive into downtown Roanoke, and budget friendly. There are several two-room suites and a pool. Given that you can get into a room for right at $100 with tax, it's hard to pass up.

$100-150

★ **Black Lantern Inn** (1226 Franklin Rd. SW, 540/206-3441, www.blacklanterninn.com, $125-190) has three rooms, each one well appointed with a private bath with jetted thermal massage tub, complimentary bicycles and golf clubs, king-size bed with super-soft linens, and "pillows galore." A variety of drinks and refreshments are available. Breakfast offerings accommodate anyone from gourmet to vegan. The inn is Virginia Green certified, and there's a nice view of the Roanoke Star on Mill Mountain. For stays in October, there's a two-night minimum.

Rooms at **Brugh's Inn of Salem** (1226 Lynchburg Turnpike, Salem, 540/312-9138, www.brughsinn.com, $109-145) all have gas log fireplaces, queen-size beds, and free Wi-Fi. If you're cost-conscious, you can skip the full breakfast for a pretty nice continental spread and save a few dollars (but spring for the breakfast; you're on vacation). The rooms are nicely decorated and spacious enough to spread out in for a few days. There is a screened porch, which is a great spot to start the day with a cup of coffee or tea, and a great place to end it with a glass of wine.

The **King George Inn** (315 King George Ave., 575/675-4034, www.kinggeorgeinnbandb.com, $140-155) is walkable to downtown Roanoke, but that's not the only reason to stay here. Four large,

TV-free rooms with private baths, a gourmet breakfast every morning, and a gift basket with soaps made especially for the inn should help persuade you. It's a beautiful home and it's beautifully cared for. Decorations are tasteful and appropriate, the colors throughout are calming, and the overall decor is quite relaxing.

$150-200

One of the most luxurious accommodations in town, ★ **Hotel Roanoke** (110 Shenandoah Ave., 540/985-5900, www.hotelroanoke.com, $149-374) is surprisingly affordable. Part hotel, part conference center, Hotel Roanoke has a beautiful lobby, thanks to the fine woodworking, a half-dozen Great Depression-era murals, and stunning chandeliers. The hotel, which originally contained fewer than three-dozen rooms, was built in 1882 by the Norfolk and Western Railroad to accommodate visitors and executives carried here by the new railroad. Two dining rooms—**The Regency**

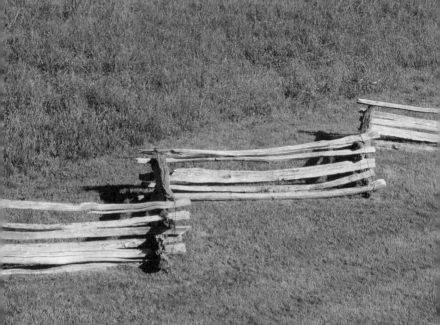

Fences like this one are built using traditional designs and methods.

Room ($21-43) and **The Pine Room** ($8-15)—serve guests and visitors. You must try the peanut soup at The Regency Room (the recipe is about as old as the hotel), and don't even think of skipping dessert.

Hampton Inn & Suites Roanoke Downtown (27 Church Ave. SE, 540/400-6000, www.hamptoninn3.hilton.com, $159-179) is one of the newest hotels in Roanoke and is in an excellent location near Center in the Square and the market there, the Market House, downtown shopping and restaurants, and a city park.

Camping

Surprisingly, there is one campground nearby. **Dixie Caverns** (5753 W. Main St., Salem, 540/380-2085, www.dixiecaverns.com, $12/person for tents, $34/RV) in Salem has around 60 campsites for tents and RVs, plus there's a cool cave to check out.

Information and Services

Your first stop for travel information should be this guide, but your second stop should be the **Roanoke Valley Convention and Visitors Bureau** (540/342-6025 or 800/635-5535, www.visitroanokeva.com); their website is chock-full of information and itineraries. The staff at the **Roanoke Valley Visitor Information Center** (101 Shenandoah Ave. NE, 540/342-6025 or 800/635-5535, 9am-5pm daily) will give you those locals-only tips that put you at the best restaurants, in the best shops, and out experiencing the city the way locals do.

Police can be contacted at the **Roanoke City Police Department** (348 Campbell Ave. SW, 540/853-2212, www.roanokeva.gov) and the **Roanoke County Police Department** (5925 Cove Rd., 540/562-3265, www.roanokecountyva.gov).

Carilion Roanoke Memorial Hospital (1906 Bellview Ave. SE, Roanoke, 540/981-7000, www.carilionclinic.org) is one of the biggest in Virginia.

Virginia's Explore Park (MP 115)

At Blue Ridge Parkway Milepost 115, you'll find **Virginia's Explore Park** (MP 115, 540/427-1800, www.explorepark.org, dawn-dusk daily, free), an 1,100-acre park with 14 miles of walking and mountain biking trails, a picnic area, and plenty to explore, all open to the public at no charge. There's a **Blue Ridge Parkway Visitor Center** (540/427-1800, 9am-6pm daily May-Oct.) here with a gift shop; two exhibit galleries detailing the history of the Parkway and the settling of the region around Roanoke, the highlight of which is a giant relief map/model of the Parkway; and a short film about the Parkway, which is worth the watch if you haven't seen it at any of the other visitors centers.

You'll also find two other buildings, the Arthur Taubman Center and

Virginia's Heritage Music Trail

In the hills and hollers of the Blue Ridge are stories that beg to be told. Thanks to **The Crooked Road** (276/492-2409, www.myswva.org/tcr), we're learning the stories of the people whose musical talent created bluegrass and country music, two genres that have influenced musicians for nearly a century.

The Crooked Road is a 333-mile-long driving trail stretching from Rocky Mount to Breaks Interstate Park at the Virginia-Kentucky border, connecting visitors with southwestern Virginia's incredibly rich musical history. The road connects nine major music venues and 60 or so affiliated venues and festivals, crossing 19 counties, four cities, 50 towns, and one state line. Along the way, you can stop for a concert or impromptu jam session; learn some of the history here at any of 26 waysides, where you can also hear recordings of musicians and songs important to the area; or attend one of the many music festivals and gatherings that celebrate these deep musical roots.

All along The Crooked Road, you'll hear names like the Carter Family (June Carter Cash, wife of Johnny Cash, was a second-generation Carter Family singer), "Tennessee" Ernie Ford, Dr. Ralph Stanley, the Mullins Family Singers, and the Stoneman Family. Each of these individuals or family troupes plucked their guitar, bass, and banjo strings and sent out musical vibrations that touched future musicians like Hank Williams, Bob Dylan, The Rolling Stones, Ray Charles, Nirvana, Grateful Dead, Willie Nelson, Steve Earle, and Ryan Adams.

The Floyd Country Store is one of the stops on The Crooked Road Music Trail, so it's easy to begin exploring some musical history from here. The Crooked Road is not an official byway in the manner of the Blue Ridge Parkway or Skyline Drive, but rather a recommended route along country roads. You can easily hit three highlights of The Crooked Road along the Parkway by visiting **Floyd, Galax,** and the **Blue Ridge Music Center,** each of which lies along or near the Parkway.

Mountain Union Church, beside the visitors center, but these are generally only open for recreational programs and activities, or for private events. There are a few other reconstructed buildings throughout the park, each of which tells some part of the story of settling here. Among these structures are a grist mill, Kemp's Ford School House, and a frontier fort.

If you're interested in hiking, pick up a trail map at the visitors center and go for a stroll in the woods. The trails are generally in good condition, though some of the mountain biking trails can get sketchy in spots. Speaking of mountain biking, nine miles of the trails here are International Mountain Biking Association sanctioned.

Old Salem Turnpike Trail

Distance: 1.36-mile loop, with options to extend the hike

Duration: 1 hour

Elevation gain: 300 feet

Difficulty: easy to moderate

Trailhead: beside the Blue Ridge Parkway Visitor Center

This easy hike takes you around the central point of Explore Park and down to the banks of the Roanoke River. Departing from the trailhead behind the Parkway Visitor Center and Taubman Center, the path wanders a relatively flat track for a little more than a quarter mile before a side trail leads to Palmer's Pond, a small forest pond that can be quite pretty. If you decide to head out to the pond, the trip is 0.8 mile out and back.

Continuing on, the trail reaches the River Walk and Roanoke River about a half mile in. Follow the banks and you'll find a trio of spur trails leading to a small network that weaves its way through the historic area. If you choose to explore here, you can add a half mile (and a half hour) or more to the walk. Around a mile in, you'll reach a second connector with the River Walk, and the Old Salem Turnpike Trail will turn right and lead you back up to the trailhead.

Mill Mountain and the Roanoke Star (MP 120)

Standing between Roanoke and the Blue Ridge Parkway is a single peak: Mill Mountain. The Roanoke Star, the city's most famous landmark, stands just below its summit.

Sights
★ **Roanoke Star**
In 1949, the Roanoke Merchants Association decided to announce the start of the Christmas season with a fantastically big decoration: a giant star to crown Mill Mountain and shine over downtown. They raised $28,000 for the construction and installation, and throughout the summer, Roanoke Iron & Bridge Works built the structure for the star and its supports. Once satisfied with the design, they drove it to the chosen site just below the summit of Mill Mountain. The 88.5-foot tall **Roanoke Star** was set in place, outlined with more than 2,000 feet of neon tubing, and wired for electricity. On November 23, 1949, Thanksgiving Eve, the switch was thrown and the star blazed with light. Visible from 60 miles away, it was quite the sight then as now. Though the Merchants Association intended it as a holiday decoration, it was so popular that the city left it on year-round. The star was lit white for a long time; then, in 1976, to celebrate the Bicentennial, the design was changed to include a red and blue star.

The views of the city and valley from the observation platform at the Roanoke Star are unrivaled. A trolley ran up here around 1910, but it was soon shut down as folks preferred the drive up winding Walnut Avenue. To drive to the star, simply follow Walnut Avenue up the mountain and follow the signs. You can also walk or bike there by taking the Mill Mountain Greenway to the Discovery Center and parking area, where two hiking trails—the long and the short versions of the **Star Trail**—lead to the star and a tremendous overlook.

Mill Mountain Zoo
The **Mill Mountain Zoo** (Mill Mountain Park, 540/343-3241, www.exemplum.com/mmzoo, 10am-5pm daily, last tickets sold at 4pm, $9 adults, $7 ages 3-11, free age 2 and under) has 175 animals representing 90 species, and among those numbers, 21 are listed as vulnerable species. You can see a red wolf, snow leopard, and red panda here. There's a ZooChoo Train ($2) that circles the zoo; zookeeper talks; and fun activities like Breakfast with the Animals (every third Sat., $15 adults, $11 children, reservations required) and Zoo Boo (regular admission costs only), a daylong, trick-or-treating, costume-contest Halloween-themed zoo bonanza.

Hiking
There are several walking and hiking trails on Mill Mountain. The **Star Trail** leads to the Roanoke Star, but others connect to neighborhoods in Roanoke. Parents with little hikers in tow may want to pay a visit to **Crystal Spring Trail** (trailhead at the end of Ivy St.; get there from the Parkway by turning onto Mill Mountain Pkwy. at MP 120.5, continuing along the J P Fishburn Pkwy. and Walnut Ave. SE, then turning left on Ivy St.), a 1.2-mile out-and-back hike that's about as easy as it gets. The good thing about this trail is that it's an easy way to get kids excited to hike. Surrounded as you are by the forest here, there's the sense that

you're somewhere wild, not three blocks from civilization.

Star Trail (Long)

Distance: 2.8 miles out and back
Duration: 1.5-2 hours
Elevation gain: 900 feet
Difficulty: moderate
Trailhead: on Walnut Avenue about 1 mile from Ivy Street
Directions: To reach the trailhead, exit the Blue Ridge Parkway at the Mill Mountain Parkway (MP 120.5); continue along to the J P Fishburn Parkway and then Walnut Avenue SE; turn left onto Ivy Street and the trailhead is at the end of the street.

There's an easier way to reach the Roanoke Star, but this route lets you earn the view and takes you through a dense forest filled with woodpeckers.

From the parking area, cross the street and head up a short set of stone steps. Immediately you'll be faced with six or eight fairly long switchbacks as you ascend. The switchbacks keep the trail at a nice, accessible grade and provide plenty of spots for benches where you can sit and soak up the noise of the forest. Continue along the trail until you reach the top, just under 1.5 miles into the hike. There, you'll find a junction with a gravel road and some brochures with trail maps. Turn left and you'll be in a paved parking area; turn right, you'll meet up with a paved path at the Roanoke Star and the overlook.

Star Trail (Short)

Distance: 0.4 mile out and back
Duration: 15 minutes
Elevation gain: 50 feet
Difficulty: moderate
Trailhead: parking area at the summit of Mill Mountain

Park in the paved parking area at the summit of Mill Mountain, then follow the gravel path and you'll be at the Roanoke Star in no time flat.

the Roanoke Star

Roanoke Mountain
(MP 120.4)

The scenic four-mile, one-way Roanoke Mountain Loop Road makes its way around Roanoke Mountain. Along the way there are seven overlooks that provide really good views of Roanoke, the Roanoke Valley, and Mill Mountain. At the top, there's a short spur road to a parking area where you'll find a trail that takes you to the summit.

Roanoke Mountain Summit Trail

Distance: 0.3-mile loop
Duration: 10 minutes
Elevation gain: 60 feet
Difficulty: easy to moderate
Trailhead: parking area on Roanoke Mountain Loop Road

This pretty little hike affords you a few good landscape shots and gives you a good place to watch the sun set. Begin at

the set of stone steps at the far end of the parking lot and descend. You'll immediately ascend a second set of stone steps and come to the summit. Wintertime is when the views are best, though it's quite pretty in summer when the mountain laurel is blooming. Continue on the trail and ascend again to the parking lot.

Roanoke Valley Overlook (MP 129.6)

Take one last look at Roanoke and the Roanoke Valley from this overlook, perched at 2,100 feet.

Devils Backbone Overlook (MP 143.9)

You'll find a lot of references to the Devil, Hell, and Purgatory in exceptionally rocky spots like Devils Backbone. I guess if I had to pick my way through rocky fields and outcroppings while on a wagon loaded with all my earthly possessions, I'd come up with a similar name for these places. As you look out here, Devils Backbone is the steep point jutting out between the overlook and Pine Spur.

Smart View (MP 154.1)

The **Smart View Overlook** (MP 154.1) gives you a great look at a beautiful valley. The **Smart View Recreation Area** (MP 154.4), a 500-acre recreation area at 2,503 feet, has 42 or so picnic tables, a restroom, and drinking water. A loop trail at the recreation area wanders the ridge and can be broken down into a couple of shorter hikes, though the longer one is recommended. As for the name, it's an antiquated way of saying "good view." In the case of Smart View, the smart part applies to the pastoral beauty of the long view here.

Floyd

© AVALON TRAVEL

Smart View Loop Trail

Distance: 3-mile loop
Duration: 1.5-2 hours
Elevation gain: 150 feet
Difficulty: easy to moderate
Trailhead: parking area at Smart View, across from the picnic area

Squeeze through the fence and cross an open meadow to enter the woods. At 0.2 mile, you'll meet a side trail to the picnic area, but ignore it (unless you're hungry) and continue on. At 0.4 mile, you'll reach another trail, which leads to the Smart View Overlook (MP 154.1); bear right. Here, the trail descends through ferns and switchbacks until it crosses the creek. After crossing, you'll ascend through a rhododendron thicket. From this point south, the rhododendron thickets are a constant companion as the Parkway continues to gain elevation.

At 0.7 mile in, you'll reach a set of steep rock steps, then at 1 mile you'll find that the restrooms are just to your right; keep going. In a few hundred yards, there's a second trail to the picnic area; rather than go that way, descend on the path to the left. The Trails family cabin at mile 1.2 was built in the 1890s. It's an attractive structure (if you're into the whole rustic thing), and between it and the

views of Virginia's Piedmont to the east, you can spend a few minutes taking photos here. Cross a small creek via a stone bridge, then ascend a small knob. A path to the right will lead back to the parking lot where the hike began if you need to shorten it.

Continuing down the trail from the knob, you'll have more great Piedmont views, then descend into a little pine grove. From here, the trail carries you right back to the parking area.

⚐ VA-8 North: Floyd (MP 165.2)

Floyd is a rare place where you'll find hippie holdouts, fifth-generation Floyd County families, retired college professors, and yurt-dwelling, alpaca-owning neo-hippies living side by side, and they all get along. Somehow the mix of old and new, mainstay and counterculture, contemporary art and long-held traditions works. It must be the music.

On Friday nights (well, on most nights, really, but especially on Friday nights), the streets of this small town echo with the high lonesome sound of bluegrass and old-time bands. In the Floyd Country Store, a hundred feet slap out a rhythm to the music as cloggers, flatfooters, and mountain dancers keep time. On the dance floor are homemakers and teachers, farmers and preachers, children and grandparents, newcomers and old-timers, all in this place to hear the music and share in a moment. This encapsulates the town. It's a place that people want to share and keep visiting every chance they get.

The town of Floyd is accessible via VA-8 at Milepost 165.2. Floyd is six miles north.

★ Friday Night Jamboree

There's only one stoplight in downtown Floyd, so it's easy to find the **Floyd Country Store** (206 S. Locust St.,

540/745-4563, www.floydcountrystore.com, 10am-5pm Mon.-Thurs., 10am-10:30pm Fri., 10am-6pm Sat., 11am-5:30pm Sun.), the heart of this town. In 1910, a business called Farmer's Supply opened here, and the building has been in continuous use ever since. It changed hands more than a few times, and in the 1990s, the decision was made to close the store for one evening a week, for the now legendary **Friday Night Jamboree** (6:30pm Fri., $5). There's also a **café** ($3.50-8) if you get hungry after dancing the night away at the Jamboree.

Through the week, you can get everything from overalls to penny candy to books on home remedies to a pair of hand-knit alpaca socks at the Floyd Country Store, but all that changes for the Friday Night Jamboree. Racks and shelves are cleared out, pushed to the side to make room for a dozen rows of folding chairs and a good-sized dance floor. The crowds build on the street. Musicians tune banjos and mandolins, and play runs on their fiddles and guitars on sidewalks, in parking lots, and doorways. Spontaneous songs build as one musician joins another. Then, promptly at 6:30pm, the music starts inside and the Jamboree is on.

The Jamboree celebrates the best of traditional Appalachian music, with acts ranging from country (real country, not the pop, Top-40 radio country) to bluegrass to old time. "Granny's Rules" apply here, and that means "no smoking, no drinking alcohol, no bad language, and no conduct unbecoming to a lady or gentleman." Don't be shy, work your way up front and get a seat where you can see the dancers, and, if the spirit so moves you, join in. Local bands, as well as regional and national touring acts, perform here, so you'll hear top talent every week.

There are two other musical programs

Top to bottom: musician at the Friday Night Jamboree in Floyd; Mabry Mill; Oddf3llows, Floyd.

at the Floyd Country Store, both also aimed at preserving the music of these hills. On Saturdays, they have **American Afternoon** (noon-1:30pm Sat.), followed by an Americana-themed open mic. On Sundays, there's an **open jam** (1:30pm-6pm Sun.) led by local old-time and bluegrass bands (old-time bands get the first and third Sundays, bluegrass the second and fourth).

FloydFest

For five days in July, **FloydFest** (894 Rock Castle Gorge Rd., 888/823-3787, www. floydfest.com, tickets $100-300) descends on the town, bringing with it an eclectic crowd hungry to hear music from a wide range of musical acts. Past performers include David Grisman, Los Lobos, Lauryn Hill, Lettuce, Thievery Corporation, and other acts from bluegrass to jam bands and everything in between. It's kid-friendly (but no dogs), you can camp (and even glamp), and with certain tickets, you can come and go as you please (and as traffic allows).

Shopping

Floyd Center for the Arts (220 Parkway Ln. S., 540/745-2784, www.jacksonville-ecenter.org, 10am-5pm Mon.-Sat., noon-5pm Sun.) is an old farm complex that has been transformed into a center for art, mountain music, theater, dance, crafts, and rural heritage. It's half a mile south of town on VA-8, with a gallery and gift shop on the premises.

Bookstores and coffee shops go together like, well, bookstores and coffee shops. When you need a caffeine fix in Floyd, head to **Black Water Loft & Notebooks** (117 S. Locust St., 540/745-5638, 7am-5pm Mon.-Fri., 8am-5pm Sat.). You'll find some outstanding locally roasted coffee and a selection of children's books, books by local authors, art and craft supplies, and, of course, local music.

New Mountain Mercantile (114 S. Locust St., 540/745-4278, 11am-5pm

Mon.-Thurs. and Sat., 11am-6pm Fri.) sells locally made art, jewelry, clothing, and home and garden accessories. You can pick up handmade aromatherapy products as well as soaps, candles, and crystals in this funky little shop. Next door is the **Republic of Floyd Emporium** (114-B S. Locust St., 540/745-2898, www. republicoffloyd.com, 11am-6pm Mon., Wed.-Thurs., and Sat., 11am-8pm Fri., 11am-5pm Sun.), a store featuring microbrews and imported beer; snack foods; a good wine selection; and all sorts of hats, shirts, prints, and collectibles designed by Floyd artists.

Food

Oddf3llows (110 N. Locust St., 540/745-3463, 11am-9pm Wed.-Sat., 10:20am-8pm Sun., $11-25) features eclectic food, a welcoming atmosphere, and fun people. The menu runs the gamut from steaks and seafood to a few vegetarian dishes. You can order a mushroom-smothered rib eye, tuna spiced with cinnamon and chili, a great burger, or some shrimp and grits that will make your mouth water. Their wine and beer selection is very good. From time to time, there's live music in the dining room. There's also a bar upstairs called **Oddbar** (4pm-9pm Thurs.-Sat.).

Two miles north of town, ★ **The Historic Pine Tavern Restaurant** (585 Floyd Hwy. N., 540/745-4482, www. thepinetavern.com, 4:30pm-9pm Fri., noon-9:30pm Sat., 11am-8pm Sun., $14) offers family-style meals on shared platters. Meals include heaping platters of fried chicken, roast beef, and country ham; and bowls overflowing with mashed potatoes, dumplings, green beans, pinto beans, coleslaw, and buttermilk biscuits. Oh, and you get dessert, too. Come hungry.

Dogtown Roadhouse (302 S. Locust St., 540/745-6836, www.dogtownroadhouse.com, 5pm-10pm Thurs., 5pm-midnight Fri., noon-midnight Sat., noon-10pm Sun., $5-15) offers up some

Searching for Fairy Stones

Fairy stones are small, red-brown cruciform stones found in and around **Fairy Stone State Park.** People collect them, make jewelry out of them, and generally wonder at these strange little stones, which, according to mountain lore, ward off illness, accidents, and haints (that's mountain talk for witches).

The legend behind the stones goes like this: Hundreds of years before Pocahontas' father, Chief Powhatan, reigned over the tribes of Virginia, fairies lived near the springs in the mountains, spending their days with naiads and nymphs. One day, an elfin messenger from far away arrived bearing the news of the death of Jesus Christ. Upon hearing of his good works, suffering, and crucifixion, the fairies wept. Because they were magical creatures, their tears were imbued with this same magic. When the tears struck the ground, they crystallized into crosses. Today, we find the remnants of their tears—fairy stones.

The scientific truth is that these stones, called staurolite, are composed of silica, iron, and aluminum, which together crystallize at 60- or 90-degree angles to form crosses both perfect and imperfect. To find out where to locate them, talk to park rangers; at different times, they've held fairy stone hunts and necklace-making workshops. Or just ask the next fairy you see.

fabulous wood-fired pizzas as well as a great beer selection. There are only six pizzas on the menu; fortunately, they're all delicious.

Accommodations

Two cabins built from hand-hewn logs and a 200-year-old log farmhouse make up ★ **Ambrosia Farm Bed & Breakfast** (271 Cox Store Rd., 540/745-6363, www. ambrosiafarm.net, $90-135). The innkeepers—she has her MFA in ceramic sculpture and he's an engineer focused on energy efficiency—have done a lot to make the accommodations feel like escapes. And their work pays off. Surrounded by pastures and hills, the farm is truly a retreat. Each of the rooms is comfortable, and breakfast focuses on the farm philosophy of using what's in season, easily available, and of the highest quality.

Stay in a yurt—a great, round, tent-like structure—with **Floyd Yurt Lodging** (540/505-4586, www.floydyurtlodging. com, $119). Yurts are portable, circular tents built on collapsible frames traditionally used by nomads in far-flung places like Siberia and Mongolia. It's spacious, comfortable, fun, and unusual.

Information and Services

The **Floyd County Chamber of Commerce** (109 E. Main St., 540/745-4407 or 540/239-8509, www.visitfloydva.com, 10am-5pm Mon.-Thurs., 10am-7pm Fri., 10am-3pm Sat., 11am-3pm Sun.) happily supplies information on the area. The website has a few good details for visitors.

⊕ VA-8 South: Fairy Stone State Park (MP 165.2)

At Milepost 165.2, the Parkway crosses over VA-8. From here, it's only 23 miles southeast to **Fairy Stone State Park** (967 Fairystone Lake Dr., Stuart, 276/930-2424, www.dcr.virginia.gov, 8am-10pm daily, parking $5). From VA-8, turn onto VA-57 to get into the park. This is one of the six original state parks in Virginia, and the largest one to boot. At 4,639 acres, there is plenty to explore at Fairy Stone, from more than 15 miles of hiking trails to a 168-acre lake, where you can fish, swim, or go boating. You can also seek out some of the namesake fairy stones for yourself.

There's also a **campground** (800/933-7275, www.reserveamerica.com, $20 group camping, $30 RVs) and **cabins** ($102). With 25 one- and two-bedroom cabins, one lodge, 50 tent and RV sites, and six group campsites, it's not difficult to find a place to spend the night, though reservations are recommended.

Rocky Knob Recreation Area (MP 167)

The **Rocky Knob Recreation Area** consists of more than 4,000 acres of backcountry that bulges out from the Blue Ridge Parkway, encompassing Rock Castle Gorge. This narrow, deep, impressive valley is breathtakingly beautiful, and the hikes will have you panting, too. The high-elevation meadows, deep coves, and craggy peaks, combined with the drastic elevation changes and abundant streams, create an area where the plant life is among the most diverse along the Parkway.

As inhospitable as these mountains may seem, at one time around 70 families lived in the immediate area. They scratched family farms out of the mountainsides, built sawmills and gristmills, and raised kids and livestock in this beautiful and rugged place.

While you're at Rocky Knob, it's worthwhile to get out on the trails and take a look at the mountains up close and personal.

The **Rocky Knob Campground** (877/444-6777, www.recreation.gov, May-Oct., $20) has more than 80 tent sites and close to 30 RV sites. It's a popular stop, especially during summer and fall, so call ahead for reservations.

Rock Castle Gorge Trail

Distance: 10.6-mile circuit
Duration: 7-8 hours
Elevation gain: 1,050 feet
Difficulty: strenuous
Trailhead: Rocky Knob Campground

With steep, narrow descents and grueling ascents, this is not a trail to be taken lightly. From the Rocky Knob Campground, cross the Parkway and pass through the fence. Turn left and head into the woods. Switchbacks start at 0.3 mile in, and here you'll cross Little Rock Castle Creek, thick with rhododendrons. Keep descending until you reach an old road at 0.5 mile. Follow the road another half mile to where a bench lets you rest before descending to an area that looks as if it were settled long ago.

At 1.5 miles, you'll reach another ridge. Descend again. The trail is steep here and will stay this way until you reach a draw at 2.3 miles in, where it still descends, but a bit more easily. You'll reach some pools in Little Rock Castle Creek at 2.5 miles in. Here, the valley opens up a good bit. Continue on the trail until you reach a fire road at 3 miles. Turn right. In a quarter mile, you'll reach a **backcountry camping** area, the site of a Civilian Conservation Corps work camp from the late 1930s. Stay on the road until it begins to swing away from the creek and skirt the lower part of the mountain. Cross a bridge at 4.25 miles in and make your way to the White House, once the home of a wealthy community member, at the 4.5-mile mark. The property is still privately owned, so take nothing but photos.

After you leave the White House, cross the creek a couple of times and begin ascending through more rhododendron thickets. Five miles in, you'll see a few small waterfalls, cascades, and rills. A tall rock face that's dry except during spring rains, at which time it turns into a lovely waterfall, will greet you at 5.4 miles. In a quarter mile, the trail will leave the road and you'll turn right. The road continues on to some now-defunct cabins a little over a mile distant.

There's a mess of boulders called Bare Rocks at mile 5.8. Though it may be tempting to stick your head into the small caves and clefts found here, don't.

They are perfect spots for copperheads, rattlesnakes, and other woodland creatures. The ascent turns steep at mile 6.2, then lessens a bit once you reach a set of switchbacks after a dense rhododendron and mountain laurel thicket. At mile 7.1, you'll arrive at Grassy Knoll. For the next quarter mile or so, you'll be on lovely pasture land, then, at mile 7.5, a cell phone tower will give you a jarring reminder of our intrusion into nature.

Keep on the trail and emerge from the woods into an absolutely stunning meadow around mile 7.6. The 360-degree views here are exactly what you've been working toward all day. After a half mile, you'll reenter the woods and come out again into another beautiful meadow.

At mile 9, you'll pass Rock Castle Gorge Overlook at Milepost 168.7, then begin to ascend Rocky Knob. Take the right-hand trail at 9.4 miles in, then make your way to the ridgeline leading to Rocky Knob. There's a shelter where Earl Shaffer, the first Appalachian Trail thru-hiker, stayed when this was part of the Appalachian Trail. At the 10-mile mark, you'll reach a trail leading to the picnic area in just over 0.5 mile; you can go this way and cut the trail short if you like. If not, keep climbing, cross another knob, then walk through a fence and into a final pasture. You'll go through a small orchard, then parallel the Parkway before arriving back where you started.

Shorter hikes are also possible here. From the picnic area at Rocky Knob, it's possible to do 1.1-, 2.3-, and 2.6-mile hikes that provide some of the same views as the 10.6-mile Rock Castle Gorge Trail, taking you through some of those meadows described at the end of the gorge trail.

★ Chateau Morrisette Winery (MP 171.5)

At Milepost 171.5, head west on Black Ridge Road to Winery Road, where you'll find **Chateau Morrisette Winery** (291 Winery Rd. SW, Floyd, 540/593-3647, www.thedogs.com, 10am-5pm Mon.-Thurs., 10am-6pm Fri.-Sat., 11am-5pm Sun.), a popular spot for locals and visitors, especially for their Sunday brunch. The mountaintop winery is composed of 13 acres of vines, an amazing 32,365-square-foot timber-frame tasting room made from salvaged timbers, and a great set of outdoor spaces for parties big and small. During fall, the views of the Blue Ridge are particularly excellent.

Chateau Morrisette is one of six Virginia wineries started prior to 1980, making it one of the oldest wineries in the state. Though grape production began on the property in the early 1970s, it wasn't until 1978 that Chateau Morrisette Winery came about. Then, winemaker and owner David Morrisette, a graduate of Mississippi State University's inaugural Viticulture and Enology program, ripped out the vines his father had planted, planted his own, and became the first official winemaker for Chateau Morrisette Winery. A mere 2,000 gallons of wine were produced in their first vintage in 1982; today, the winery produces well over 60,000 cases annually.

Visitors to the winery can take part in **tastings and tours** (11am, 1pm, and 3pm Mon.-Thurs.; 11am, 1pm, 3pm, and 5pm Fri. and Sat.; noon, 2pm, and 4pm Sun.). Tastings come in two flavors: the standard 10-wine tasting and a winery tour ($8), or the Elite Wine Tasting ($30) with 10 bottles of the current vintage and possibly barrel tastings or the pouring of a reserve wine. The Elite Tasting includes an in-depth talk about terroir, grape varieties, and Virginia wine as a whole. You'll also discuss pairing ideas and leave with a keepsake glass. Reservations are required for the Elite Wine Tasting but not for the standard tasting or for tours.

Sample some of their fine wine with fine food at the on-site **restaurant** (11am-2pm Wed.-Thurs., 11am-9pm Fri.-Sat., 11am-3pm Sun. Apr.-Nov.; 11am-4pm

Thurs. and Sun., 11am-8pm Fri.-Sat. Jan.-Mar.; $13-30). Lunch and dinner are good, with internationally influenced Southern fare, but the brunch ($7-22) sticks a little closer to home with a smaller menu that's Southern through and through. Reservations are highly recommended. The **HUT** (noon-4pm Sun. June-Oct., $3-8) serves picnic fare and welcomes a variety of musicians to perform in the Sunday Sounds concert series.

Mabry Mill (MP 176.1)

Called by many "the most picturesque spot on the Blue Ridge Parkway," Mabry Mill is among the top five places to photograph in any season, making it a sure-stop on your journey. The mill sits just off the road, fed by a series of flumes and chutes that channel the water from a nearby stream to the waterwheel, which turns the gristmill and sawmill inside.

The water empties into a little pond in front of the building. The pond is almost always still, though sometimes the surface is rippled by wind or the ducks that live here, so it reflects the sky, mill, and trees, making for a postcard-perfect shot. In the fall, when the trees are lit with color, it's quite striking.

The Mabry family settled in the area around 1782 when they received a land grant one county over. Ed Mabry was born here in 1867, spent a little time away, then moved back with his wife, Lizzy. He built the mill in 1903 to provide blacksmithing and wheelwright services to the community. Soon he was operating a sawmill here, then a gristmill.

A half-mile trail takes you through the grounds, where you'll learn about mountain industries, starting with the water-powered sawmill and **gristmill** (where you can buy cornmeal, buckwheat, and other meals ground on-site, demonstrations 9am-4pm daily May-Nov.), passing by a lumber-drying rack and log cart, and

view from Chateau Morrisette Winery

the family cabin. You then pass a moonshine still before seeing the sorghum mill and blacksmith shop. By the blacksmith, you can take the path back to your car or wander back to where one of the flumes directing water to the mill starts; either way, you'll be off the trail in no time.

The ★ **Mabry Mill Restaurant** (266 Mabry Mill Rd. SE, 276/952-2947, www.mabrymillrestaurant.com, 7:30am-6pm daily late Apr.-early Nov., $4-10) is famous for their pancakes, which come in buckwheat, cornmeal, sweet potato, and plain old pancake. You must order a stack. Breakfast is served all day, and it's the good, hearty country fare you'd expect. Lunch and dinner include meat loaf, pulled pork, chicken potpie, roast turkey, a burger, and a half-dozen sandwiches.

Primland (MP 177.7)

Perched on 12,000 acres in the Blue Ridge Mountains not far from the Parkway,

★ **Primland** (2000 Busted Rock Rd., Meadows of Dan, 866/960-7746, www.primland.com, $304-1,200) is more than a resort: it's an escape into luxury that most of us will only know a few times in our lives. The main lodge has rooms and suites, cottages line the fairways of the resort's golf course, and there are mountain homes suitable for large gatherings. Most fantastic of all are the tree houses, which sit high on the ridge overlooking the Dan River Gorge, the Roaring Creek Gorge, or the confluence of Roaring Creek and the Dan. From their decks, the view is stupendous. The interior of the tree houses (and all the rooms, cottages, and houses, for that matter) is sheer elegance. Everything is comfortable and plush, designed to help you forget the outside world for a while.

You can do just about anything you want at Primland. Activities include an ATV trail-riding program, birding outings, fly-fishing, horseback riding, mountain biking, sporting clays and other sports, a spa, and an acclaimed stargazing program. There's one of the prettiest disc golf courses you could ever play, and a real golf course that's the height of mountain course design.

Dining is exceptional. The dining room, **elements,** serves breakfast (7am-11am daily, $6-16) and dinner (6pm-9pm daily, $30-45), as well as a Chef's Table tasting menu ($150). The **19th Pub** (11am-11pm daily, $12-29) serves lunch and dinner in a less-formal atmosphere. There's also **Stables Saloon,** a buffet ($35 adults, $15 children) open seasonally for breakfast and periodically for events.

Groundhog Mountain (MP 188.1)

The tower (which looks like a tall tobacco barn) atop Groundhog Mountain is one of the loveliest sights on the Parkway. The grassy knob; the hand-hewn, primitively constructed fence; and the breadth of the

GROUNDHOG MOUNTAIN

sky above all add up to a beautiful scene. There is a picnic area and a comfort station with restrooms, so you can linger if you want to watch the sun go down (or come up, if you're an early riser). Views from here are sweeping, to say the least. You can see the Dan River Valley and the mountains easing into Piedmont as well as Pilot Mountain's odd, quartzite peak jutting upward.

Down the road at Orchard Gap (MP 194), you'll see a series of cabins on the top of a bald ridge just off the Parkway. These are the **Lonesome Pine Cabins** (64 Lonesome Cabin Ln., Fancy Gap, 888/799-9214 or 276/398-3332, www. lonesomepinecabins.net, $95-135), and it's quiet and starry here, making for a nice one-nighter in this area.

Fancy Gap (MP 199.5)

The Blue Ridge Parkway skirts the southern edge of Fancy Gap, and US-52 crosses its path here. Just a couple of minutes off the Parkway you'll find pretty much all Fancy Gap has to offer—a handful of shops, restaurants, hotels, and gas stations. US-52 will take you south to Mount Airy, North Carolina, and I-77 is just four minutes from the Parkway, making access easy from the north or south.

Fancy Gap was originally known as Foggy Camp, but the name changed sometime in the 1800s. Rumor has it that young Ira Blair Coltrane, who would become a self-taught engineer and a colonel in the Confederate army, was helping his grandfather drive a wagon up a steep and rutted road. He looked around, saw a better route up the mountain across the valley, and said that it would make a "Fancy Road."

Fancy Gap has a quartet of eateries as well as a few fast food chains. **The Gap Deli at the Parkway** (7975 Fancy Gap Hwy., 276/728-3881, www.thegap-deli.com, 11am-7pm Mon.-Fri., 10am-7pm Sat.-Sun., $5-8) serves sandwiches,

salads, soups, and some killer peanut butter pie in a lovely setting with indoor and some outdoor seating. **Gearhead Diner** (7145 Chances Creek Rd., 276/728-2773, 8am-7pm Wed.-Fri., 7am-7pm Sat., 7am-6pm Sun., $4-12) makes a mean burger but also serves up the usual diner fare for breakfast, lunch, and dinner. **Lakeview Restaurant** (7830 Fancy Gap Hwy., 276/728-7841, 7am-9pm Mon.-Sat., 7am-2:30pm Sun., $8) is where the locals go for breakfast. The fried chicken is spot on.

⚐ US-52 South: Mount Airy (MP 199.5)

In downtown Mount Airy, you'll notice 1960s police squad cars, business names that may seem oddly familiar, and cardboard cutouts of Barney Fife peering out from shop windows. Mount Airy is the hometown of Andy Griffith and a mecca for fans of *The Andy Griffith Show*. People who grew up in small towns in the Carolinas (and probably elsewhere, too) recognize their families and neighbors in the fictional residents of Mayberry. The show's inspired writing and acting are a deep well of nostalgia, and its fans are legion.

Getting There and Around

You can reach Mount Airy from the Blue Ridge Parkway by turning south on US-52 at Fancy Gap (MP 199.5), a 14-mile journey; by taking I-77/74 south to NC-89 west, a trip of 24 mostly interstate miles; or by taking a curvy back road that will let you catch a glimpse of life on the slopes of the Blue Ridge Mountains. To take the back road, VA-679/NC-1717, turn onto Orchard Gap Road at Milepost 194, then stay straight on Wards Gap Road, which will lead you into town over the course of a 14-mile, 30-minute journey.

Sights
★ **Andy Griffith Sights**
You can't leave Mount Airy without

Mount Airy

paying a visit to the sites that honor favorite son Andy Griffith. It isn't open for tours, but you can rent **Andy's boyhood home** (711 E. Haymore St., 336/789-5999, $175/night) on Haymore Street if you care to spend the night. The **Andy Griffith Museum** (218 Rockford St., 336/786-7998, www.andygriffithmuseum.com, 9am-5pm Mon.-Fri., 11am-4pm Sat., 1:30pm-4:30pm Sun., $3, $5 with audio guide) features hundreds of pieces of memorabilia from Griffith's long career

in television, movies, and music, including scripts and props from his still-running eponymous TV show. Outside the museum and the attached **Andy Griffith Playhouse** (www.surryarts.org, show times and ticket prices vary) stands a lifelike statue of Andy and Opie with fishing poles in tow that looks like it was grabbed right out of *The Andy Griffith Show* opening credits.

If you can't get enough of Andy and Barney, hop into a Mayberry squad car

to tour all the major sights in town. **Mayberry Squad Car Tours** (625 S. Main St., 336/789-6743, www.tourmayberry. com) leave from "Wally's Service Station" and cost "$35 for a carload." And if that's not enough, stop by **Floyd's City Barber Shop** (129 N. Main St., 336/786-2346, 7am-5pm Mon.-Wed. and Fri., 7am-3pm Sat.) for a haircut. You won't find Floyd the barber in there, but you will find some friendly folks in an old-fashioned barbershop. If you're in the mood for a trim, you may just sit in the same seat as Andy Griffith, who received many a haircut here during his Mount Airy days.

The Merry-Go-Round Show

Teamed up with WPAQ 740 AM, the Surry Arts Council hosts *The Merry-Go-Round* (Earle Theater, 142 N. Main St., 336/786-2222, www.surryarts.org, 11am-1:30pm Sat., $5), the country's third-longest-running live bluegrass and old-time music radio show. Come to the Earle Theater for the show, or show up as early as 9am toting an instrument if you'd like to join in the pre-show jam session. It's one of the state's great small-town treats.

Festivals and Events

A local institution that has a great deal to do with the vitality of Mount Airy's musical traditions is the **Bluegrass and Old-Time Fiddlers Convention** (691 W. Lebanon St., 336/345-7388, www.mtairy-fiddlersconvention.com), held every year since 1972 during the first full weekend in June at Veterans Memorial Park. Thousands of people come to the festival from around the world to play old-time and bluegrass music with their friends and compete in what is a very prestigious competition in this genre. The heart of the action takes place at the hundreds of individual campsites that spring up all over the park, in informal jam sessions

Top to bottom: The Snappy Lunch in Mount Airy; the lookout tower on Groundhog Mountain; storefronts in Mount Airy.

Welcome to Mayberry

"People started saying that Mayberry was based on Mount Airy. It sure sounds like it, doesn't it?"

Andy Griffith

Surely the bucolic town of Mount Airy was the inspiration for Mayberry. Comedian and actor Andy Griffith grew up here, drawing inspiration for his stand-up comedy, hit television show, and just about every character he ever played during his long career from its landscape and people. Like its fictional counterpart, Mount Airy is filled with friendly folks, and something in the air here just feels like yesteryear.

Griffith got his break in 1953 when a recording of one of his stand-up routines, a story called "What It Was, Was Football," sold more than 800,000 copies and

landed him a spot on *The Ed Sullivan Show* the next year. The premise is pretty simple: A country preacher, naive to all but his little world, happens upon a college football game. Having never heard of nor seen football, he's a bit confused. Griffith describes the game and field ("a purty little green cow pasture") like this:

Somebody had took and drawed white lines all over it and drove posts in it and I don't know what all. And I looked down there and I seen five or six convicts a-runnin' up and down and a-blowing whistles…I looked down and I seen 30 or 40 men come a-running out of one end of a great big outhouse down there. And everybody where I was a-sittin' got up and hollered.

among old and new friends. It's some of the best old-time music to be heard anywhere.

The Surry Arts Council hosts the citywide **Mayberry Days** (www.mayberrydays.org), an annual fall festival featuring a barbecue cook-off, concerts, and appearances by cast members of *The Andy Griffith Show*. During Mayberry Days, members of TAGSRWC, an acronym for *The Andy Griffith Show* Rerun Watchers Club, gather with other fans, some of the remaining cast members, and impersonators of Mayberry characters. They come to town and have a big-eyed time getting haircuts at Floyd's City Barber Shop, riding in squad cars, and arresting each other. TAGSRWC boasts hundreds of chapters whose names reference the series, such as "Her First Husband Got Runned Over by a Team of Hogs" (Texas) and "Anxiety Magnifies Fearsome Objects" (Alabama).

Sports and Recreation
Golf

A rare golf course among the pastures and hayfields is the beautiful **Cross Creek Country Club** (1129 Greenhill Rd., 336/789-5131, www.crosscreekcc.com, 18 holes, par 72, greens fees $40 daily, 9 holes $20, includes cart) in Mount Airy. Course conditions are always fantastic, and the course presents quandaries to golfers of all levels.

If you want a fun little par-3 course, head to **Hardy's Custom Golf** (2003 W. Pine St., 336/789-7888, www.hardrockgolf.net, 18 holes, par 54, greens fees $8, with cart $10, 9 holes $5, with cart $8). The course is lighted for play day or night. There's also mini golf (36 holes, $2.50) as well as foot golf (18 holes, walking $10 all day, 18 holes $8, 9 holes $5; with cart $20 all day, 18 holes $10, 9 holes $8), a combo of soccer and golf.

Kayaking and Canoeing

Yadkin River Adventures (104 Old Rockford Rd., Rockford, North Carolina, 336/374-5318, www.yadkinriveradventures.com, canoe trips $65/2 hours, $75/4 hours, and $85/6 hours; kayak trips $40/2 hours, $50/4 hours, $60/6 hours) in Rockford offers rentals of canoes, kayaks, and sit-on-tops, along with shuttle service for full- and half-day paddling adventures. The Class I Yadkin River is great for paddlers of all ages and experience levels, and it has beautiful views of Pilot Mountain.

Parks

Pilot Mountain State Park (1792 Pilot Knob Park Rd., Pinnacle, North Carolina, 336/325-2355, www.ncparks.gov) is a beautiful place for **hiking, swimming, rock climbing, rappelling** (in designated areas), **canoeing** on the Yadkin River, and **camping** ($10-23, $15 seniors) at one of the 49 designated tent and trailer sites. Each site has a tent pad, a picnic table, and a grill, as well as access to drinking water and hot showers. There are a dozen trails here, ranging in length from 0.1 mile (from parking lot to overlook) to 4.3 miles (circling the mountain) to 6.6 miles (connecting the two sections of the park). Pilot Mountain, the park's namesake 1,400-foot-tall rocky protrusion, is a startling sight that reminds some of a

UHF knob on an old television set, the kind you may have used to watch *The Andy Griffith Show*. Pilot Mountain is so named because it's a prominent and obvious landmark; it appears in *The Andy Griffith Show* as Mount Pilot.

The 400-foot rock faces that extend for two miles are the most striking feature of **Hanging Rock State Park** (1790 Hanging Rock Park Rd., Danbury, North Carolina, 336/593-8480, www.ncparks. gov, 7am-7pm daily Dec.-Feb., 7am-9pm daily Mar.-Apr. and Oct., 7am-10pm daily May-Sept., 7am-8pm daily Nov.), about 40 minutes outside Mount Airy. If you've exhausted the routes on Pilot Mountain (doubtful), this is a great place for **rock climbing** and **rappelling** (a permit and registration with park staff are required; climbers must also finish and exit the park by closing time). You can also **hike** to waterfalls and beautiful overlooks, and **swim** in a nearby lake. Hanging Rock State Park has 73 tent and trailer **campsites** ($10-22), one of which

The sun burns off the morning mist near Fancy Gap.

is **wheelchair-accessible.** Each site has a tent pad, a picnic table, a grill, access to drinking water, and access to a washhouse (mid-Mar.-Nov.) with hot showers and laundry sinks. There are also two-bedroom, four-bed vacation **cabins** ($88 daily Dec.-mid-Mar., $100 mid-Mar.-mid-June and Sept.-Nov., $520 weekly mid-June-Aug.) for rent. Reserve campsites or cabins at least a month in advance with the park office.

Food
While you're in Mount Airy, you have to eat at ★ **The Snappy Lunch** (125 N. Main St., 336/786-4931, www.thesnappylunch. com, 5:45am-1:45pm Mon.-Wed. and Fri., 5:45am.-1:15pm Thurs. and Sat., $1-5), a diner whose claims to fame include mentions on *The Andy Griffith Show* and a "World Famous Pork Chop Sandwich," which is notoriously sloppy, delicious, and cheap. Eating here is like stepping back in time. The Snappy Lunch has been in the community since 1923.

The Copper Pot Restaurant (123 Scenic Outlet Ln., Ste. 4, 336/352-4108, www. copperpotrestaurant.com, 7am-9pm Mon.-Sat., $10) is a down-home restaurant specializing in dishes of the "meat and two" or "meat and three" variety. It's country cooking all the way, so prepare for fried okra, pinto beans, and inexpensive food.

If you need a cup of coffee, **Brady's Coffee Company** (717 W. Independence Blvd., www.bradyscoffeecompany.com, 7:30am-5pm Mon.-Fri., 9:30am-3pm Sat., $2-7) is the place for you. The selection is small, so expect to find the usual drinks—lattes, cappuccinos, drip coffee—and not so many of the complicated ones you find elsewhere.

Accommodations
In Mount Airy, **Quality Inn** (2136 Rockford St., 336/789-2000, www. qualityinn.com, from $75), **Holiday Inn Express** (1320 Ems Dr., 336/719-1731, www.hiexpress.com, from $120), and **Hampton Inn** (2029 Rockford St., 336/789-5999, www.hamptoninn3.hilton. com, from $129) are good options.

Pilot Knob Inn Bed and Breakfast (361 New Pilot Knob Ln., Pinnacle, North Carolina, 336/325-2502, www. pilotknobinn.com, $159-249) in Pinnacle is an unusual B&B in that guests can stay in suites in the main lodge or in one of several restored century-old tobacco barns on the property. Each one-bedroom barn-turned-cabin is well equipped with modern conveniences, including two-person hot tubs and stone wood-burning fireplaces. Children and pets are not allowed, but horses can occupy a stall on the property for an additional $50 per night.

Information and Services
Find out more of what Mount Airy has to offer by stopping by the **Mount Airy Visitors Center** (200 N. Main St., 800/948-0949 or 336/786-6116, www. visitmayberry.com, 8:30am-5:30pm

Mon.-Fri., 10am-5pm Sat., 1pm-4pm Sun.).

There is a hospital in town, **Northern Hospital of Surry County** (830 Rockford St., 336/719-7000, www.northernhospital.com). If you require the police, contact the **Mount Airy Police Department** (150 Rockford St., 336/786-3535, www.mountairy.org).

Sugarloaf Mountain
(MP 203.9)

From the Piedmont Overlook at Milepost 203.9, you have a grand view of the Piedmont of Virginia and North Carolina rolling away from you. To the southwest, beside I-77, is Sugarloaf Mountain, which gets its name from the distinctively loafy roundness of its peak.

★ Blue Ridge Music Center (MP 213)

The **Blue Ridge Music Center** (700 Foothills Rd., Galax, 276/236-5309, www.blueridgemusiccenter.org, 10am-5pm daily May-Oct., free) is a museum dedicated to the roots music of the hills in this part of North Carolina and Virginia. Video and audio displays help tell the story of the development of old-time and bluegrass music and show how this distinct sound has influenced other genres throughout the years. As you tour the music center, you'll see fantastic antique and contemporary examples of banjos, fiddles, guitars, and dobros. **Midday Mountain Music concerts** (noon-4pm daily, free) give area musicians opportunities to play for a crowd, and regular **evening concerts** ($10) by more established acts draw crowds from all over.

High Meadow Trail
Distance: 2.8 miles out and back
Duration: 1.5 hours
Elevation gain: 100 feet

Difficulty: moderate
Trailhead: Blue Ridge Music Center parking area

From the handicapped parking area of the music center parking lot, descend along a service road. Very soon you'll go down some steps and cross a stream via a footbridge. You'll cross another bridge at 0.25 miles, but in the meantime enjoy the walk in these piney woods.

The Fisher Peak Trail joins our trail at 0.35 miles. Keep to the right to stay on the High Meadow Trail. A half mile in, there's a little rock face and a bench where you can rest. From here, you can hear concerts from the music center if someone's playing. Enter the meadow at 0.6 mile, then weave in and out of the woods and meadow for the next 0.4 mile. At 1 mile, the Fisher Peak Trail goes off to the left. Bear right and begin a gradual descent until you reach Foothills Road at 1.4 miles.

To return, you can retrace your steps or go along the Fisher Peak Loop Trail, a trek that's just a little longer than your return trip. If you want to go this way, there's a short spur trail to the peak, but besides that, Fisher Peak Trail joins the High Meadow Trail 0.35 miles from the parking lot, at which point you'll turn right and return to your car.

◈ VA-89 North: Galax (MP 215)

Music has played an important part in most cultures' development, and the Scots-Irish settlers who established communities in these mountains were no different. They brought with them fiddles, mandolins, and bagpipes, and they would have been happy to learn that today, music from these instruments (from fiddles and mandolins, mostly) echoes off the hillsides around Galax. Galax calls itself "The World Capital of Old-Time Mountain Music." The number of people who play an instrument, sing, square dance, clog, flatfoot, or mountain dance

Galax

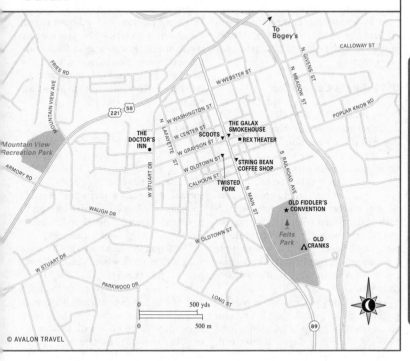

is astonishing. That's one of the reasons Galax has hosted the Old Fiddler's Convention every August since 1935. The **City of Galax Visitor's Center** (111 E. Grayson St., 276/238-8130, www.visitgalax.com, 9am-5pm Mon.-Thurs., 9am-7pm Fri., 9am-4pm Sat.) has information on the Old Fiddler's Convention and more.

Galax is just seven miles north of the Parkway at Milepost 215 via VA-89.

Music and Events

No music-loving mountain town is complete without a jam session or two. In Galax, you can come together with other fans and bluegrass, country, and old-time musicians at **Stringbean Coffee Shop** (215 S. Main St., 276/236-0567) for a musical gathering starting at 6:30pm on Tuesday nights. In nearby Independence,

there's a **jam session** (6:30pm-9pm Wed.) at the **Historic 1908 Courthouse** (107 E. Main St., Independence). And on Saturdays, the **Blue Ridge Music Center** has a **concert series** (4pm-6pm Sat., free).

Every Friday, WBRF 98.1 FM and the Galax Downtown Association sponsor *Blue Ridge Backroads* (8pm-10pm Fri.), one of the few remaining live bluegrass radio shows in the country. It's held at the historic **Rex Theater** (113 E. Grayson St., 276/236-0329, www.rextheatergalax.com), which also hosts live bluegrass and country bands. Ticket prices vary for concerts, but to attend a recording of *Blue Ridge Backroads,* tickets are $5 and available at the door only.

In mid-July, Galax hosts hordes of barbecue lovers during the two-day **Virginia State Barbecue Championship** (276/236-2184, www.smokeonthemountainva.

com). There's a $10,000 purse for the event, which is a qualifier for the World Food Championships. This is no backyard barbecue; pro teams come from all over the nation to compete for big money and the chance to qualify for more contests.

Old Fiddler's Convention

The annual six-day **Old Fiddler's Convention** (276/236-8541, www.oldfiddlersconvention.com, early Aug., $6-12/day, $40 full convention, camping $80) defines the character of Galax. Tens of thousands of musicians, mountain dancers, and music lovers descend on this town to play in impromptu groups in the campground and on the streets, meet up with seldom-seen friends, trade instruments, and swap stories of conventions past. Don't be surprised to see multiple generations of a family who've been coming every year since the convention was started in 1935.

The Old Fiddler's Convention is about getting together and playing, but it's also about friendly competition and a little showing off. Every day of the festival, musicians, bands, and dancers compete onstage. Young musicians can compete to see who is the best fiddler (old-time and bluegrass), mandolin player, clawhammer and bluegrass banjo picker, guitar player, and band. The competition is stiff, but it gets stiffer in other divisions. Old-time and bluegrass bands compete for a $775 top prize. Small cash prizes also go out to fiddlers, to autoharp, guitar, mandolin, dulcimer, dobro, and players of both clawhammer and bluegrass banjo styles. The best folk song, the best flatfoot dance, and the best all-around performer also go home with a little folding money in their pockets.

They're strict about their music here, and competition rules say things like: "to qualify, a band must consist of at least a banjo, a fiddle, and a guitar," "no bluegrass banjo style picking to be in old-time band. No old-time banjo style picking to

be in bluegrass band," and "dulcimer competition is for lap dulcimer only." If you're not attuned to the differences between bluegrass and old-time music, clawhammer versus bluegrass banjo styles, or exactly what a lap dulcimer may be, don't worry. You'll be surrounded by folks who will be more than happy to get into deep discussions explaining the finer points of these two genres.

Food

Twisted Fork (110 W. Oldtown St., 276/238-3313, www.twistedforkva.com, 11am-3pm and 5pm-9pm Tues.-Sat., $9-15) serves a menu of fresh pasta, Italian entrées, and sandwiches from a team that cooked at the lauded Primland Resort in nearby Meadows of Dan. Here, the food is simple and exceptionally executed.

The Galax Smokehouse (101 N. Main St., 276/236-1000, www.thegalaxsmokehouse.com, 11am-9pm Mon.-Sat., 11am-3pm Sun., $6-20) is, according to locals, one of the best restaurants in Galax. Specializing in barbecue, they serve pork spareribs, boneless rib tips, pulled pork barbecue, Texas-style beef brisket, smoked chicken, burgers, and all the barbecue sides you'd expect. Their sauce comes in seven varieties ranging from hot and spicy Texas style to sweet Tennessee sauce to the vinegar-based eastern North Carolina style.

It's worth eating at **Scoots** (104 N. Main St., 276/236-2006, 7am-9pm Mon.-Sat., $2-9) if for no other reason than the name. The sandwich-heavy menu includes a monster burger (topped with onion rings, among other things) and a double hamburger, grilled pimento cheese, a flounder sandwich, and corn dogs. There are also a few plates, like the seafood trio, a flounder dinner, and something called the Pig Wing Dinner.

Accommodations

The Doctor's Inn (406 W. Stuart Dr., 276/238-9998, www.thedoctorsinnvirginia.com, $149) was built in 1913 and is listed on both the Virginia Landmark Register and the National Register of Historic Places. The six rooms here can accommodate just about any party, from a couple on a romantic getaway to a girls' weekend in the mountains to someone passing through solo. Breakfast ranges from lighter fare like oatmeal or yogurt with granola to more filling meals like biscuits, sausage casseroles, and country ham.

Fiddler's Roost Bed & Breakfast Cabins (485 Fishers Peak Rd., 276/236-1212, www.fiddlersroostcabins.com, $120-300) consists of six private log cabins. Cabins include a three-bed, two-bath unit with a wraparound porch and hot tub, ideal for groups of six; other cabins are perfect for a pair of travelers. You may think that with separate accommodations you won't be getting breakfast, but you're wrong; the innkeepers deliver a full gourmet breakfast right to your door every morning of your stay.

Old Cranks RV Park and Campground (407 Railroad Ave., 276/728-6798, www.oldcranksrvpark.com, RV sites $33, tent sites $15) offers RV and tent camping near the site of the Old Fiddler's Convention and less than a mile from downtown Galax. There's also an ice cream shop and motorcar museum here. And the name doesn't come from a cranky owner—it refers back to the old cranks you had to use to start your car on the earliest models.

North Carolina High Country

The Blue Ridge Mountains grow rugged here. The landscape visitors encounter through much of Virginia is paltry in comparison to the grade, elevation, and vistas of North Carolina's High Country.

North Carolina High Country

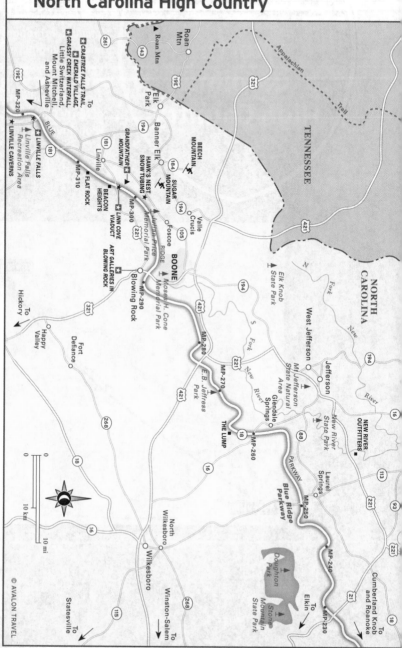

© AVALON TRAVEL

Highlights

★ **Art Galleries in Blowing Rock:** Galleries celebrating the region's beauty line Main Street in this small town (page 184).

★ **Linn Cove Viaduct:** One of the most iconic spots on the Parkway, this curved, elevated roadway is as beautiful as it is fun to drive (page 190).

★ **Grandfather Mountain:** Walk across the Mile High Swinging Bridge and take in views that are spectacular any time of year (page 191).

★ **Linville Falls:** One of the most photographed places in North Carolina, these falls tumble 90 feet over steep cliffs into Linville Gorge. Five trails lead to overlooks for spectacular views of the falls (page 194).

★ **Emerald Village:** Mine for gems and pan for gold at this group of once-active mines nestled in the mountains (page 198).

★ **Grassy Creek Waterfall:** It's a quick and easy hike to this mossy waterfall and cascade just off the Parkway (page 198).

★ **Crabtree Falls Trail:** Hike to this 70-foot cascade that spills delicately down a rock face. In spring, it's surrounded by wildflowers (page 199).

I n 1752, a settler crested a ridge in North Carolina's High Country and remarked, "We saw mountains to the right, to the left, before and behind us, rising like great waves in a storm." He wouldn't be surprised to learn that this section of North Carolina remained untamed for another century and a half.

Eventually, wagons gave way to automobiles and improved roads. Then the Blue Ridge Parkway opened, and the area opened to travelers. Though access improved and visitors have flocked here since the day the Parkway opened, the Blue Ridge Parkway was far from complete until the 1980s. Then, the final piece of the roadway, the Linn Cove Viaduct, was finished, tying together Great Smoky Mountains and Shenandoah National Parks.

This is a land of stories, and a good portion of the folklore to come out of Appalachia in the last century or so was collected and recorded here. It stretches back further, however. Here, a young Confederate veteran called Tom Dooley was memorialized in song after committing a gristly crime. Here, too, is where moonshiners plied their trade from colonial days to the present.

Stands of virgin forest blanket a few mountainsides here, though most have been logged, but not in some time, and to the untrained eye there is little difference. It's not all backwoods and back roads, though. Villages and towns like Blowing Rock, Elkin, West Jefferson, and Little Switzerland are charming, hospitable, and surprisingly artistic. Those interested in folk arts and crafts will find the Penland School of Crafts as well as Blowing Rock and its galleries of particular interest. Getting into certain corners of the region can still be challenging, but that just adds to the beauty.

Planning Your Time

Plan for at least three days here for a good overview, but five days to thoroughly experience the hikes, historic sites, waterfalls, peaks, and parks. This area offers several levels of accommodations, so you can rough it in beautiful campgrounds, stay in luxury lodges and inns, or somewhere in between. Your best bet for chain hotels is Boone, but if you're looking for a more rural, B&B experience, a handful of places in and around West Jefferson have beautiful countryside and river views, and Blowing Rock is filled with inns and B&Bs. Farther down the Parkway, in the town of Little Switzerland, you'll find some lovely places to stay as well. These cities are also the best (and the only) places to get a bite to eat along this leg of the trip.

Most visitors come in October for fall foliage, or midsummer for the cooler temperatures at these high elevations. At these times, B&Bs and inns fill fast, and it can be tough to come by a table at prime dining hours in the best restaurants. There are many seasonal businesses, so in winter and early spring, your selection of places to eat and shop may be limited. That said, business is booming at several ski resorts around Boone.

Driving Considerations

Traveling via the Parkway presents difficulties in the deepest part of winter, when ice, snow, and unpredictable weather cause periodic road closures. It's advisable to check real-time closures and road advisories on the National Park Service website (www.nps.gov/blri). In early spring, the Parkway should be open in this region, though as you get into the highest elevations of this leg—around Grandfather Mountain and Linn Cove Viaduct—and approach Asheville, you'll find more closures.

Best Restaurants

★ **Cobo Sushi Bistro and Bar, Boone:** Traditional and innovative sushi rolls make this a must stop (page 180).

★ **Lost Province Brewing Co., Boone:** Head here for wood-fired pizza, great beer, and a lively scene every night (page 180).

★ **Storie Street Grille, Blowing Rock:** Burgers and sandwiches make lunchtime a treat—and the entrées will have you coming back for dinner (page 185).

★ **The Best Cellar, Blowing Rock:** You don't need a special occasion to dine at one of the top restaurants in Blowing Rock, just an appetite and a love of good wine (page 185).

Getting There

This drive begins near where the Blue Ridge Parkway crosses from Virginia into North Carolina, at **Cumberland Knob** (MP 217.5), and ends **147 miles** later at **Craggy Gardens** (MP 364.6), just before Asheville. It's possible to drive from one end of this segment to another in about four hours.

The nearest **major travel hubs** to this region are Raleigh and Charlotte, North Carolina.

There are no train or bus services along this leg of the Parkway.

Car

From **Raleigh,** North Carolina, it's a three-hour, 165-mile drive to Cumberland Knob along I-40 West and I-74 West. About halfway through, you'll pass directly through **Greensboro.**

Charlotte, North Carolina, is only a shade over two hours from Cumberland Knob on the 105-mile drive via I-77 North.

I-77 crosses the Blue Ridge Parkway in Virginia, just over the Virginia-North Carolina state line. **I-40** intersects the Parkway just outside of Asheville, to the southwest. The two main routes used to access this region of North Carolina are US-321 and US-421.

Fueling Up

Take note of the following places where you can fuel up and grab a snack. Not only are they the most convenient, they're the only reliable places to gas up:

- **MP 229.7,** US-21 less than eight miles west

- **MP 248.1,** NC-18 less than three miles west

- **MP 261.2,** NC-16 less than 12 miles west

- **MP 291.8,** US-321 less than two miles north or south

- **MP 312,** NC-181 less than three miles north

- **MP 330.9,** NC-226 less than three miles north

Air

From Boone, **Charlotte Douglas International Airport** (CLT, 5501 Josh Birmingham Pkwy., Charlotte, 704/359-4013, www.cltairport.com) is two hours south, and **Raleigh-Durham International Airport** (RDU, 2400 John Brantley Blvd., Morrisville, 919/840-2123, www.rdu.com) is three hours east.

Best Accommodations

★ **River House Country Inn and Restaurant, Grassy Creek:** Relax in luxurious digs on the banks of the North Fork of the New River (page 173).

★ **New River State Park, Laurel Springs:** You'll appreciate amenities like showers and grills at these campsites, some of which can be accessed only by canoe (page 173).

★ **The New Public House & Hotel, Blowing Rock:** The combination of comfy rooms, an outstanding

restaurant, and a charming neighborhood make this a relaxing getaway (page 186).

★ **Westglow Resort and Spa, Blowing Rock:** Taking in views of Grandfather Mountain from your private deck is the definition of High Country luxury (page 186).

★ **Switzerland Inn, Little Switzerland:** Stunning views await at themed accommodations like the Heidi or Alpine Suites (page 198).

Cumberland Knob (MP 217.5)

The Blue Ridge Parkway crosses into North Carolina at Milepost 216.9, and less than a mile away is Cumberland Knob, the place where construction began on this jewel of a roadway on September 11, 1935. At the Cumberland Knob Recreation Area, you'll find a comfort and information station with restrooms, and 1,000 acres to explore via a pair of hikes, one very easy, one more strenuous.

Cumberland Knob Trail

Distance: 0.6 mile out and back
Duration: 30 minutes
Elevation gain: 100 feet
Difficulty: easy
Trailhead: Woodland Trail sign to the right of the information station at Cumberland Knob, far right trail

This easy hike leads to a fabulous stone picnic shelter at the top of Cumberland Knob. As you approach the Woodland Trail sign, you'll see two paved trails that go to the right. Take the one farthest to the right, which passes by a small cemetery. The path leads right to the stone shelter and a view that's unremarkable.

Once you're there, simply reverse course and head back to the trailhead. Due to the length of the trail and the lack of a memorable vista, you'll get the most out of this "hike" if you go at a brisk pace and use it to stretch out.

Gully Creek Trail

Distance: 2.5-mile loop
Duration: 1.5-2 hours
Elevation gain: 830 feet
Difficulty: strenuous
Trailhead: Woodland Trail sign behind the information station at Cumberland Knob, trail to the left

The Gully Creek Trail begins on the ridge, then dips into Gully Creek before making a short but strenuous climb back to the parking area, with an option for an additional climb to the peak of the unremarkable Cumberland Knob.

Soon after setting foot on the trail, you'll begin to descend through thickets of mountain laurel and rhododendron via a series of switchbacks. After a short way, you'll follow Gully Creek, which you'll cross several times in the next half mile. There are a few nice small waterfalls and cascades here. At 1.2 miles in, you'll begin to ascend on switchbacks that are blanketed in ferns. After a quarter mile of ferns, you'll reenter the rhododendron and mountain laurel thickets, which you'll be with for much of the trail back.

At 2.2 miles, you'll reach an intersection. To the left, a 0.2-mile trail leads to Cumberland Knob and the picnic shelter there. If you go that way, you can return to the parking area via a 0.4-mile Cumberland Knob Trail or you can double back to Gully Creek. As Cumberland Knob doesn't offer much by way of views, bear right and stick to Gully Creek Trail. At 2.4 miles, the summit trail joins yours for the final 0.1 mile to the parking area.

US-21 South: Roaring Gap to Elkin (MP 229)

At Milepost 229, the Blue Ridge Parkway crosses over US-21. Following US-21 South, you'll reach the unincorporated village of Roaring Gap in 4 miles, and the town of Elkin 22 miles off the Parkway. There is beautiful country in Roaring Gap, but not much else. Elkin, however, sits on the northwestern edge of North Carolina's Yadkin Valley Wine Country, a 1.4-million-acre wine region. As a town that calls itself "The Best Small Town in America" (and it is a good one), it's friendly and hospitable, so you can find a great meal or a comfy bed, though the selections may be limited.

Wineries

There are a handful of wineries within easy driving distance of Elkin, though the Yadkin Valley as a whole has more than three dozen wineries spread across North Carolina's first designated American Viticultural Area. My favorite is **McRitchie Winery & Ciderworks** (315 Thurmond P.O. Rd., Thurmond, 336/874-3003, www.mcritchiewine.com, 10am-5pm Wed.-Sat., 1pm-5pm Sun.), which makes a pair of great red blends—Arcturus and Ring of Fire—as well as sweet and dry hard sparkling cider.

Grassy Creek Vineyard and Winery (235 Chatham Cottage Circle, State Road, 336/835-2458, www.grassycreekvineyard.com, 11am-6pm Thurs.-Sat., 1pm-5pm Sun., tasting $5) produces wine in a variety of French styles with grapes grown here and at their sister vineyard in a town nearby. **Jones von Drehle Vineyards & Winery** (964 Old Railroad Grade Rd., Thurmond, 336/874-2800, www.jonesvondrehle.com, 11am-6pm Wed.-Sat., noon-5pm Sun., tasting $10), one of the newest wineries in the region, is gaining more fans daily with their rosé and their better red and white vintages. **Elkin Creek Vineyards** (318 Elkin Creek Mill Rd., Elkin, 336/526-5119, www.elkincreekvineyard.com, 11am-5pm Thurs.-Sun., tasting $6-7) planted their first vines in 2001 and bottled their first vintage just four years later, and today they're one of the more popular stops in the area. In downtown Elkin, **Brushy Mountain Winery** (125 W. Main St., Elkin, 336/835-1313, www.brushymountainwine.com, 1pm-5pm Thurs. and Sun., noon-8pm Fri.-Sat., tasting $6-12) uses grapes from around the Yadkin Valley to make a number of notable blends; combine tasty wine with a downtown tasting room, and you have a must-stop, must-sip winery.

Carolina Heritage Vineyard and Winery (170 Heritage Vines Way, Elkin, 336/366-3301, www.carolinaheritagevineyards.com, 1pm-6pm Sat.-Sun.) is North Carolina's first solar-powered winery and first USDA Certified Organic Vineyard. They have 35 acres, just three miles east of Elkin, where you can stop in for a tour, a talk on organic farming techniques, and, of course, a glass of wine. Most of their wines are blends, though their chambourcin and traminette are solid, single-grape bottles. They also have a wine made from the native muscadine grape, a grape that is often too sweet for my taste, but one they handle well.

Food and Accommodations
Roaring Gap

In Roaring Gap, you can stay at **High**

Meadows Inn (10498 US-21, 336/363-2221, www.highmeadowsinnnc.com, $75) and dine at the attached restaurant, **Nikola's** (336/363-6060, $11-20), serving a variety of pasta dishes and steaks as well as a small seafood selection.

Elkin

In downtown Elkin, **Southern on Main** (102 E. Main St., 336/258-2144, www.southernonmain.com, 11am-9pm Tues.-Thurs., 11am-10pm Fri.-Sat., $6-23) dishes up Southern favorites as small plates and full-sized entrées. Fried green tomatoes, blackened catfish, shrimp and grits, mountain trout, pimento cheese, fried okra, steaks, and salads are all there for your dining enjoyment.

Angry Troll Brewing @ 222 (222 E. Main St., 336/526-0067, www.angry-trollbrewing.com, 5pm-midnight Thurs., 11:30am-late Fri.-Mon., taproom 5pm-8pm Fri., noon-8pm Sat., $7-22) serves wood-fired pizzas, wings, salads, and chicken sandwiches, and a very good selection of house-brewed beer.

Just south of the Blue Ridge Parkway at Milepost 227 is the **Glade Valley Bed and Breakfast** (330 Shaw Ln., Glade Valley, 336/657-8811 or 800/538-3508, www.gladevalley.com, $130-179). Glade Valley B&B has six bedrooms and a private cabin built to look like a classic frontier cabin. This bed-and-breakfast sits on 29 acres of mountainside with miles of walking trails and tremendous views, making it a relaxing place to rest for a night or two. In addition to breakfast, they provide guests with complimentary bottled water.

If you want to make an event of the region's wineries, you'll need a place to sleep off the day's adventures. At **Frog Holler Cabins** (564 E. Walker Rd., 336/526-2661, www.froghollercabins.com, $135-145), you can stay in a well-appointed cabin with a fireplace and a hot tub overlooking Big Elkin Creek. Three cabins—The Cottage, Hawks Nest, and Mill House—are around 400 square feet

each and suitable for a couple; Deer Run is a bit bigger and sleeps four. There's plenty of peace and quiet, and they're within 30 minutes of more than two-dozen vineyards and wineries. On the property are miles of hiking trails and a fishing pond, but one of the big draws is the fact that you can park and take a guided tour ($60) of wineries. With their driver, everyone in your party can enjoy the wine tasting.

You can also stay at two vineyards: **Elkin Creek Vineyards** (318 Elkin Creek Mill Rd., Elkin, 336/526-5119, www.elkincreekvineyard.com, $129-159) and **Grassy Creek Vineyard and Winery** (235 Chatham Cottage Circle, State Road, 336/835-2458, www.grassycreekvineyard.com, $150-700).

Stone Mountain State Park (MP 229)

You can't see the namesake Stone Mountain upon entering **Stone Mountain State Park** (3042 Frank Pkwy., Roaring Gap, 336/957-8185, www.ncparks.gov, 7am-6pm daily Nov.-Feb., 7am-8pm daily Mar.-Apr. and Sept.-Oct., 7am-9pm daily May-Aug.), but when you do, you'll remember it. Just a few miles south of the Parkway along US-21, this 14,000-acre park's most prominent feature is the 600-foot granite dome that is Stone Mountain. The 25-square-mile pluton (an upthrust of igneous rock) is fun to hike but difficult to see from the park. For the best views, get back on the Blue Ridge Parkway and head to the **Stone Mountain Overlook** (MP 232.5).

Sights

Stone Mountain State Park was established in 1969 and named a National Natural Landmark in 1975. In the years before it was a park, the lands around were settled by the typical mix of Europeans who make up much of the Appalachian ancestry—English,

Irish, Scots-Irish, and German, with a few French families thrown in for good measure. They shaped churches, farms, log homes, and all they needed to create a community out of these woods; three sites around the park show different aspects of life for the early European inhabitants here. The **Mountain Culture Exhibit** in the park office provides some historical context to these bold families who settled here. The **Hutchison Homestead** was built in the mid-1800s and is representative of a typical homestead for the region; it includes a log cabin, barn, outbuildings, and even a blacksmith shop. Finally, the **Garden Creek Baptist Church,** built in 1897, is one of the few original churches in the county that stand in nearly original form, having undergone no remodeling or major repairs during its long life.

Hiking

There are a number of hiking trails in the park, ranging from easy forest strolls to the challenging Stone Mountain Loop Trail that takes you to the top of the impressive granite dome.

Stone Mountain Loop Trail

Distance: 4.5-mile loop
Duration: 3-3.5 hours
Elevation gain: 500 feet
Difficulty: strenuous
Trailhead: Upper Trailhead parking lot
Directions: Exit the Parkway at MP 229 and follow US-21 south and turn onto Oklahoma Road/Old Gap Road/Stone Mountain Road. Once in the park, follow the road to the trailhead across from the Stone Mountain State Park campground.

This hike is a killer, especially during late summer when the granite gets so hot that you feel like you're baking as you cross the wide stone face. Fall (specifically, mid-October) is when the views are best and the weather is ideal for this hike.

Start on a short spur trail that leads to a sign marking the trail. Follow the trail to the left and head to Stone Mountain Falls, a 200-foot waterfall. A set of nearly

300 very steep stairs leads to the bottom of the falls.

Continue on the trail to a pair of side trails leading to Lower and Middle Falls Trails. Unless you are a big waterfall fan, you can skip these (save your energy for the uphill portion of the hike as the spur trail is about 0.5 mile). About 1.7 miles into the hike, you'll notice the trees beginning to thin, and Stone Mountain begins to show a little granite. Just down the trail from here is the Hutchison Homestead, which is a good spot to catch your breath. The parking area for the lower trailhead is nearby. That trail is a more direct approach to the summit, but you should go for the loop because the whole hike is worthwhile, not just the main attraction.

Soon after you leave the homestead, the trail gets steep enough that there are a few cables along the way to help you climb. Don't stray far from the trail—it's marked with orange dots—as the granite can be slick. From the summit, you'll have a good view of the mountains. Look to the northwest and west: You may see the Blue Ridge Parkway cutting across the opposite hills. To complete the trail, simply follow the markings off the summit, back into the trees, and back to the spur trail that leads to the trailhead.

Cedar Rock Trail

Distance: 1 mile out and back
Duration: 30 minutes
Elevation gain: 250 feet
Difficulty: moderate
Trailhead: Lower Trailhead parking lot near the Hutchison Homestead

Some say this hike is easy, others say moderate, but it's relatively easy except for a couple of short, steep spots that may make you winded on the way up and give your quads a workout on the way back. Depart from the Lower Trailhead parking area where you'll also find the Wolf Rock and Black Jack Ridge Trailheads. Follow the sign and the round red blazes. From the trailhead, you'll take the Stone

Mountain Loop past the Hutchison Homestead, then turn right. When the trail forks, Cedar Rock stays to the right and you'll ascend to the small summit. Along the way, and especially at the top, you'll have some good views of Stone Mountain.

Camping

There are several camping options in **Stone Mountain State Park** (reservations: www.northcarolinastateparks.reserveamerica.com or www.ncparks.gov, $15-52). The Family Campground A and C Loops consist of 47 nonelectric campsites, while the B Loop has 41 sites with both electrical and water hookups; both of these sites are close to a washhouse with hot showers and drinking water, and there is an RV dump station available. There are four group campsites ($52/day), each suitable for up to 25 people; these sites are also convenient to the washhouse and water facilities. For those interested in a little backcountry camping, there are six primitive sites ($5-23/day).

Doughton Park (MP 238.5)

The open bluegrass meadows of Doughton Park are some of the best places for wildlife viewing in North Carolina's High Country. At just over 7,000 acres, Doughton Park is simply crawling with white-tailed deer, which forage the fields by the dozens in the early morning and shortly before sunset. Keen-eyed observers may catch a glimpse of a bobcat, red fox, bear, or even coyote at the edge of the woods or crossing a path ahead in the distance.

One of the more interesting points of Doughton Park is the fact that it looks much like these meadows and balds would have looked in the early 1900s when mountain farmers carved pastures and gardens out of the forest. Of course, today the National Park Service

Local stone was used to make the bridges on the Blue Ridge Parkway.

periodically mows the fields, doing the job of livestock with modern machinery, but it paints an interesting picture of how life here got along in the early 20th century.

Views here are huge. To the south and east, the National Park Service owns much of the land, so it remains lovely and uninhabited. To the northwest, there are clusters of houses that some feel detract from the scenery, but they only serve to provide some much-needed scale on these ridgelines, and reaffirm why people have felt drawn to these mountains for hundreds of years. If you look east, you'll see the granite face of Stone Mountain not too far away.

Sights

Just off the Parkway at Milepost 238.5 stands the **Brinegar Cabin,** one of the relics showing human habitation along the ridge tops of the Blue Ridge Mountains. Originally part of a 125-acre farm purchased in 1876 (for the princely sum of

$200), this cabin was the home of the bachelor Martin Brinegar for two years until he took for his wife the 16-year-old Carolina. On this farm, they raised four children as well as crops of food to sustain them through the year. Martin made shoes and acted as a justice of the peace and a notary public. When he died in 1925, Carolina became sole owner of the farm. In 1935, when the Blue Ridge Parkway made plans to come through their farm, she sold it to the state of North Carolina for inclusion in Parkway lands. As was common at the time, the National Park Service granted her lifetime rights to the cabin, which would have allowed her to live on the property for as long as she wanted (with a few restrictions on hunting, wood gathering, and the like). Shortly after the park was established, she left the farm, saying the traffic had made her mountaintop home too "noisy" a place to live.

Today, you can peek in the windows of the small cabin, learn about farming techniques that the Brinegars would have used at the garden maintained by the park, and check out their springhouse (where the spring still flows). On weekends in peak seasons, a park ranger gives presentations about the garden and about other aspects of daily life here.

Recreation

There are **ranger-led programs** on the flora, fauna, and folkways of the mountains and farms nearby (check the schedule at the Doughton Park office at MP 241.1, 336/372-1947) and also **fishing** for rainbow and brook trout in the Basin Cove Creek complex (MPs 238-244). You'll need a valid North Carolina or Virginia fishing permit as of the time of this writing, but check with the folks at the visitors center for current regulations.

Hiking

Thirty miles of trails crisscross Doughton Park, and hiking is what lures many visitors out of their cars here. A number of

trails lead through the park, the shortest of which is **Wildcat Rocks Overlook,** a five-minute, 0.1-mile, leg-stretching loop that will take you from the defunct Bluffs Lodge to an overlook where you can see the minuscule **Caudill Cabin** and the expanse of Basin Cove Creek. In this tiny, one-room cabin, Martin and Jamie Caudill raised 14 children, a tremendous family until you consider that Martin's father, who lived just down the hill (his cabin is no longer standing), had 22 children.

Of the other hikes in Doughton Park, Fodder Stack Trail is short and sweet, and the others grow longer and more strenuous as you climb the peaks and explore waterfalls.

Fodder Stack Trail

Distance: 1 mile out and back
Duration: 45 minutes
Elevation gain: 40 feet
Difficulty: easy to moderate
Trailhead: far end of the Bluffs Lodge upper parking area (MP 241.1) on the southeast side of the Parkway

Unobstructed views to the east make this hike popular for early risers staying at the campgrounds in Doughton Park. From the Bluffs Lodge upper parking area, follow the marked trail down a short, steep section, then along an easy path to the end, where the stone outcropping known as Fodder Stack stands. Along the way, you'll see a range of wildflowers depending on the time of year.

Bluff Mountain Trail

Distance: 15 miles out and back
Duration: 8-9 hours
Elevation gain: 400 feet
Difficulty: moderate
Trailhead: Brinegar Cabin Overlook parking area, MP 238.9

The toughest thing about this hike is the

Top to bottom: Brinegar Cabin in Doughton Park; grapes growing in the Yadkin Valley; informative sign about Tom Dula at the foot of the Lump.

distance, which is especially tough to handle when it's hot. Most of the trail is pretty easy, and some folks call this "the best walking" on the Parkway.

Start at the trail sign at the end of the Brinegar Cabin parking area and ascend. A quarter mile in, you'll reach an intersection with the Cedar Ridge Trail (to the left); keep to the right and continue on Bluff Mountain Trail. The path widens and you'll enter a field shortly after the trail intersection, then, a mile in, you'll walk through the RV portion of the campground. At 1.3 miles, you'll cross the Parkway and come to the main part of the campground and a trail-map poster. Keep going and head into the hardwood forest and rhododendron tunnels.

Two miles into the hike, you'll come to another field, followed by another crossing of the Parkway. At 2.7 miles, you'll reach the (unfortunately) closed Doughton Park Coffee Shop at Milepost 241.1. Keep going up the steps at the far end of the parking lot to cross the Parkway again and head into the woods.

A little over four miles in, you'll intersect with Bluff Ridge Trail (to the left); stay right to reach Bluff Mountain. Immediately after the intersection are a cliff and a set of switchbacks. Here is one of the best views of the Parkway.

For the next mile or so, you'll parallel the Blue Ridge Parkway. At mile 4.7, you'll reach the Alligator Back Overlook (MP 242.4), then the Bluff Mountain Overlook (MP 243.4) at 5.8 miles. There's an old road at mile 6.3; don't follow it. Stay left for the pathway below the roadbed. Soon, you'll cross Grassy Gap Fire Road and another large meadow. From here, it's an easy walk to the end of the trail. Flat Rock Ridge Trail intersects your trail at mile 7.4. At mile 7.5, you're at the end.

Cedar Ridge Trail
Distance: 9 miles out and back
Duration: 5-6 hours
Elevation gain: 2,100 feet

Difficulty: moderate to strenuous
Trailhead: Brinegar Cabin Overlook parking area, MP 238.9

Starting from the Brinegar Cabin Overlook parking lot, you'll ascend the Bluff Mountain Trail for a quarter mile, then turn left through the fence stile to continue along Cedar Ridge Trail. Soon after you split off from the Bluff Mountain Trail, you'll enter a rhododendron tunnel and a series of switchbacks. The trail will narrow and ascend a little over the next mile, until you begin to walk along a ridgeline. A set of switchbacks at 1.8 miles will take you up, then down a steeper section. At 2.3 miles, you'll be descending again.

The mountain laurel becomes abundant at 3.5 miles. Continue along this trail until you reach Grassy Gap Fire Road. From here, you can turn around or head up Basin Creek Trail to see a few waterfalls and Caudill Cabin.

Basin Creek Trail
Distance: 5.6 miles out and back
Duration: 3-3.5 hours
Elevation gain: 1,200 feet
Difficulty: moderate to strenuous
Trailhead: Cedar Ridge Trail and Grassy Gap Fire Road
Directions: From the Brinegar Cabin Overlook parking area, hike the 4.5-mile Cedar Ridge Trail to the Basin Creek Trailhead.

As you ascend alongside Basin Creek, keep in mind that the prolific Caudill family called this cove home. Along the way, you'll spy a few signs of their existence, but you'll end the hike at Caudill Cabin (which you can see from Wildcat Rocks Overlook).

Begin the trail at the intersection of Cedar Ridge Trail and Grassy Gap Fire Road. Walk a quarter mile up the fire road to Basin Creek Trail to your right. The trail is lined with rhododendrons, and there are a number of deep pools in the creek. Anglers love to visit this area as the streams are rife with trout. As you continue up the trail, you'll pass several more pools, some of which may just be the perfect place to cool off in warmer weather.

At 0.6 mile and 1.9 miles, you'll pass the remnants of old chimneys. You'll find some pretty cascades and small waterfalls around a mile in. At 1.3 miles, though, there's one of two 30-foot waterfalls that's quite nice to admire. Cross the stream several times as you climb on through pastures and then through steeper grazing lands. At 2.4 miles, you'll cross Basin Creek and see the second 30-foot falls. Soon you'll arrive at the Caudill Cabin, where you'll take a breather and retrace your steps back to Grassy Gap Fire Road, then back along Cedar Ridge Trail to the trailhead at Brinegar Cabin.

Accommodations

Accommodations are limited to tent and RV camping.

Camping

At Milepost 239.2, there is a **campground** (336/372-8877, www.recreation.gov for reservations, May-Oct., all sites $20/night) with 110 campsites, 25 trailer/RV sites, four restrooms, and a fire circle where many folks like to gather. Campsites are well maintained and pleasant.

Sally Mae's on the Parkway (MP 259)

Formerly Northwest Trading Post, **Sally Mae's on the Parkway** (414 Trading Post Rd., Glendale Springs, 336/982-2543, www.sallymaesgifts.com, 9am-5pm daily Apr. 15-Nov. 15) is a great version of the "old country store" right on the Parkway. It's worth a stop to stretch your legs and grab a sandwich (around $7); it's one of the few places to get something more than a snack along the whole Parkway. Take a long look at the handcrafted art, jewelry, and food items they carry.

There is a great little hike just down the road from here. At Milepost 260.3, you'll find the Jumpinoff Rocks parking area and small picnic area. From there, you have a pretty flat, one-mile hike to a rock observation deck with expansive views. Given that most folks will drive right by, it's a great place to take some fall foliage shots.

◆ NC-163 West: West Jefferson (MP 261)

Just 11 miles from Milepost 261 on NC-163 West is the charming small town of West Jefferson, a good launching point to explore this corner of the North Carolina High Country. From here, New River State Park is only 12 miles away, and the quaint little community of Todd is only 16 miles to the southwest.

West Jefferson, Jefferson, and Todd are in Ashe County, which is where the North and South Forks of the New River join to create the second-oldest river in the world, the New. The New flows through North Carolina, Virginia, then West Virginia, where it joins other rivers on the way to the Ohio River. In West Virginia, the New River is known for whitewater rafting and an impressive single-span arch bridge. Here, though, the river is wide, gentle, and slow, and you're more likely to wade it while casting a fly rod or float it in an inner tube than brave rapids in a raft or kayak.

Ashe County is also the center of two of North Carolina's more interesting industries: Christmas trees (Fraser firs, mostly) and cheese. North Carolina is the second-largest producer of Christmas trees in the United States; the industry brings in more than $100 million annually. The cheese here is also quite good.

West Jefferson is a surprisingly artsy town. There are 15 (at my last count) murals adorning buildings downtown, creating a lovely walking tour that gives you a look at how local artists have interpreted their history and surroundings. You'll also spot these strange concrete squares, once utilitarian (they were the bases of long-gone streetlights), now painted in whimsical forest scenes.

NC-194, which runs through West Jefferson and is connected to Jefferson by US-221, roughly parallels the Parkway. It's a beautiful drive in and of itself, leading by red barns and countless tree farms with orderly rows of Fraser firs. Many of these barns are decorated with vivid color-block paintings that resemble old-fashioned quilts. They're part of the **Quilt Trails of Western North Carolina** (www. quilttrailswnc.org), an ongoing art project. There are two dozen in the vicinity of West Jefferson, and even more in other parts of North Carolina.

Festivals and Events

The center of the arts community is the **Ashe County Arts Council** (303 School Ave., 336/846-2787, www.ashecountyarts. org, 9am-5pm Mon.-Fri., 10am-4pm Sat. Apr.-Dec.). They have a gallery showing a rotating series of exhibitions by local artists and art collectives working in any medium imaginable, and they help put on musical events and plays in the community. The Arts Council is also heavily involved in the **West Jefferson Arts District Gallery Crawl** (second Fri. of the month June-Oct.), with a final **Christmas Crawl** taking place in early December.

There are plenty of goings-on in West Jefferson. On Friday nights May-August, the **Backstreet Park Concert Series** (5:30pm-7pm on the third, fourth and fifth Fri., free) brings in family-friendly musical entertainment in the form of traditional, old-time, and bluegrass musicians. Every July 3 and 4, they have the **Christmas in July Festival** (www. christmasinjulyinfo.ipage.com), with music, a street fair, a farmers market, Civil War reenactors, activities for kids, and a pretty sizable crowd. September brings the **On The Same Page Literary Festival** (www.onthesamepagefestival. org), the **Olde Time Antiques Fair** (www.

oldetimeantiquesfair.com), and **Art on the Mountain** (www.ashecountyarts.org).

Shopping

Devoted entirely to photography, **CatchLight Gallery** (118 N. Jefferson Ave., 336/846-1551, www.catchlightgallery.net, 11am-5pm Mon. and Thurs.-Sat., 11am-4pm Sun.) shows the beauty in the sweeping views and intimate details of North Carolina's mountains. You'll often find artists in the gallery bringing in new photos or talking to the owner. **Originals Only Gallery** (3-B N. Jefferson Ave., 336/846-1636, www.originalsonlygallery. com, 10am-5pm Tues.-Sat.) has works by only a few Ashe County artists, but the works they carry—paintings, pottery, and furniture—are excellent.

Sports and Recreation

There are two undeniable natural features in West Jefferson that beg to be explored: Mount Jefferson (visible from the Mount Jefferson Overlook at Parkway MP 267) and the New River.

Mount Jefferson State Natural Area

Just outside of town is the **Mount Jefferson State Natural Area** (1481 Mt. Jefferson State Park Rd., 336/246-9653, www.ncparks.gov, 8am-sunset daily). The two main activities here are **picnicking** and **hiking.** A winding road dotted with scenic overlooks takes you close to the summit of the 4,683-foot Mount Jefferson, and from there you can reach the summit after a short 0.3-mile hike. From the **Summit Trail,** you can join up with the strenuous **Rhododendron Trail** (1.1 miles), which circles the summit ridge and passes through innumerable rhododendron thickets. From Rhododendron Trail, you can hike out to Luther Rock, an odd exposed piece of the black volcanic rock that makes up this massif. There's also **Lost Province Trail,** a 0.75-mile loop off Rhododendron Trail that passes through a lovely hardwood forest. Each of these trails is accessible from the Summit trailhead in the parking lot and is well marked, making it quite easy to do a little hiking. If you do anything, though, be sure to hit the summit; from here, you can see a number of the Christmas tree farms in the county, the New River (on a clear day), and the interesting shape of the mountains and river valley.

New River State Park
New River State Park (358 New River State Park Rd., Laurel Springs, 12 miles from West Jefferson, 336/982-2587, www.ncparks.gov, 7am-7pm daily Dec.-Feb., 7am-9pm daily Mar.-Apr. and Oct., 7am-10pm daily May-Sept., 7am-8pm daily Nov.) is 2,200 acres of hills, meadows, and river northeast of West Jefferson. This is a great park for **canoeing** and **kayaking** (there are no rentals available in the park, so bring your own or contact the park office for a current list of outfitters). Bass **fishing** is quite good on the North and South Forks of the New River, while trout fishing is best along the feeder streams and smaller, faster tributaries. You will need a North Carolina fishing license (available at the Walmart in West Jefferson or online at www.ncwildlife.org/licensing, $20-36) and should heed fishing regulations as established by the North Carolina Wildlife Resources Commission (www.ncwildlife.org/fishing). In addition to fishing, there are six miles of trails spread throughout the park. The best hikes are canoe-access only, so be sure to hop in a boat and head to the Alleghany Access for the **Farm House Loop Trail** and **Riverview Trail;** they're both filled with beautiful views of the river and park environs.

Outfitters
In Todd, 13 miles southwest of West Jefferson, **RiverGirl Outfitters** (4041 Todd Railroad Grade Rd., Todd, 336/877-3099, www.rivergirlfishing.com, 8am-5pm daily Apr.-Nov., by reservation Dec.-Mar., call for availability) offers fishing lessons ($50), guided fly-fishing trips (from $175), kayak and canoe rentals (from $35), tubing trips on the New River (from $15), and bike rentals ($35/day). Kelly, the RiverGirl herself, changed careers from fisheries biologist to river guide and angler, and has ingrained herself into the community of Todd, drawing in thousands of visitors every year for fishing, tubing, and other river activities. Before you leave, take your picture with Petunia, a huge potbellied pig.

New River Outfitters (10725 US-221 N., Jefferson, 800/982-9109, www.canoethenew.com, 8:30am-6pm daily, call for off-season availability, from $15) gets you on the water for a short, 3.5-mile paddle or an overnight adventure. They also have tubing trips, a popular way to pass an afternoon here. Located just nine miles north of Jefferson, they're close enough to the Parkway for an impulse tubing session.

Food
Over the last few years, North Carolina has experienced a brewery boom, but West Jefferson only has one brewpub—**Boondocks Brewing Tap Room & Restaurant** (108 S. Jefferson Ave., 336/246-5222, www.boondocks-brewing.com, 11am-9pm Sun.-Thurs., 11am-11:30pm Fri.-Sat. Apr.-Dec.; 11:30am-8pm Sun.-Thurs., 11:30am-10:30pm Fri.-Sat. Jan.-Mar., $6-32). Boondocks serves their own beer—they have a Kolsch, IPAs, a stout, a saison, and other seasonal creations—and a number of other North Carolina brews, in addition to a handful of domestics and imports. On their menu, you'll find steaks, quiche, flatbread pizza, burgers, and other expected pub fare.

Black Jack's Pub & Grill (18 N. Jefferson Ave., 336/246-3295, 11am-9:30pm Sun.-Wed., 11am-10pm Thurs.-Fri., 10am-10pm Sat., $6-10) is known for two things: fantastic burgers and wings galore (seriously, you can get an order of 30). If you're not in the mood for either of those, try the Philly Jack, a tasty take on the Philly cheesesteak. This is a sports bar, so expect larger crowds on game days and fight nights.

For a sit-down meal, try **The Hotel Tavern** (5 W. Main St., 336/846-2121, www.thehoteltavern.com, 11:30am-9pm Tues.-Thurs., 11:30am-10pm Fri.-Sat., 11am-2pm Sun., $9-32), where you'll find a mix of higher-end entrées like short ribs, steaks, and seafood, as well as pizza, burgers, and bar nosh. When the weather is good, you'll often find a band playing on the outdoor patio. Of late, Sunday brunch has been popular here.

Though it's not a restaurant, **Ashe County Cheese** (106 E. Main St., 336/246-2501 or 800/445-1378, www.ashecountycheese.com, 8:30am-5pm Mon.-Sat.) is worth a visit. They've been making cheese here since 1930, and you can watch the process or just pick up some cheese, butter, fudge, or other homespun food in their store. You can purchase any number of styles of cheese, all made here in North Carolina's Blue Ridge Mountains, at specialty shops and grocers at stops all along the Parkway.

You have one more option in Todd, the **Todd Mercantile** (3899 Todd Railroad Grade Rd., Todd, 336/877-5401, www.toddmercantile.com, 10am-5pm Mon.-Thurs., 9:30am-5pm Fri.-Sat., 9:30am-4pm Sun.). They have a bakery here, so don't come looking for a full meal, but the cinnamon rolls are legendary; grab a couple for the road.

Accommodations

There are a few B&Bs and cabin rentals in and around West Jefferson, as well as options for camping.

Buffalo Tavern Bed and Breakfast (958 W. Buffalo Rd., 877/615-9678, www.buffalotavern.com, $109-169) is a four-bedroom B&B built in 1872. This beautiful home is situated just outside of West Jefferson, surrounded by Bluff, Buck, and Three Top Mountains. Though it was a tavern in its early days, now it's a tastefully decorated, comfortable spot to rest your head for a night or two.

★ **River House Country Inn and Restaurant** (1896 Old Field Creek Rd., Grassy Creek, 336/982-2109, www.riverhousenc.com, $120-225) has close to a dozen rooms and cabins spread out across a farm along the banks of the North Fork of the New River. The property and rooms are stunning. Whether you go for a cozy room in the Caretaker's Cottage, the Chicken House (which is much more romantic than it sounds), or the Carriage House, your accommodations will be outstanding. They also have a great restaurant on site, serving prix-fixe ($45) and à la carte menus ($20-36) filled with fine-dining delights. If you're looking for a luxurious stopover in this area, River House is it.

In Deep Creek, south of West Jefferson, is **Fall Creek Cabins** (1105 Fall Creek Rd., Purlear, 336/877-3131, www.fallcreekcabins.com, $205-230), a 78-acre private retreat with eight two-story cabins and a trout stream running right through the property. It's beautiful and private, and close to the Parkway. Exit at Milepost 276 and you're just a few minutes away.

Camping

The best camping in the area is at ★ **New River State Park** (358 New River State Park Rd., Laurel Springs, 12 miles from West Jefferson, 336/982-2587, www.ncparks.gov), where you'll find canoe-access-only campsites ($10/day), two-dozen canoe-in/walk-in sites ($20/day), a pair of improved group campsites ($58/day, maximum of 35 people), a primitive group site ($10-42), and 20 drive-to campsites for tents and RVs ($15-28). The improved campsites, especially the tent/RV sites, are very nice, with water, restroom, and shower facilities available and picnic tables and grills at each site.

The Lump (MP 264.4)

The Lump, despite its lackluster name, is a must stop. The name is well earned as this tall, grassy knoll rises oddly from the hillside around, forming a sort of lump of earth that you can wander at your leisure. A sign telling an abbreviated version of the story of Tom Dula (pronounced Dooley, yes, the Tom Dooley of folk-song infamy) stands at the foot of the Lump. A short trail up the side of the small, round, treeless Lump leads to some spectacular views of the Yadkin Valley and the transition from Blue Ridge Mountains to North Carolina's Piedmont region.

E. B. Jeffress Park (MP 272)

When the creators of the Blue Ridge Parkway were first discussing the project, the idea of a toll road came up. One of the men who led the fight for keeping it free of charge was E. B. Jeffress, onetime chairman of the North Carolina State Highway and Public Works Commission. At this park named in his honor, you'll find some picnic tables, restrooms, and a great little hike to Cascade Falls.

Cascade Falls Trail

Distance: 1-mile loop
Duration: 30 minutes
Elevation gain: 175 feet
Difficulty: moderate
Trailhead: E. B. Jeffress Park, opposite the picnic area

Thanks to some signage from the Park Service, this trail gives you a good idea of the ecological diversity you'll find all along the Parkway. Twenty plaques tell about the environment here, and on a trail this short, they pack in a lot of information.

Keep right where the trail splits, just a few dozen paces into the hike, and begin to descend through some lovely wildflowers. At 0.1 mile in, there's a bench.

Christmas trees line the hills in neat rows near West Jefferson.

Then at 0.3 mile you'll cross Falls Creek. Bear right here, and you'll quickly find yourself at the upper viewing platform at the cascades' top. The lower viewing platform is nearby and gives you a closer look at the falls. Once you've seen your fill, retrace your steps to the trail junction and bear right again. Ascend up the trail and take one more right turn, and you're back at the start of the trail. The falls are best in the spring, after a rain, or in the late fall and early winter, when they're bearded with ice.

Tomkins Knob Trail

Distance: 1.2 miles out and back
Duration: 1 hour
Elevation gain: negligible
Difficulty: easy
Trailhead: E. B. Jeffress Park, at the back of the picnic area

Starting from the picnic area at E. B. Jeffress Park, follow the trailhead into the woods, where you'll soon enter a stand of pine trees. You'll climb a little through sassafras trees and wildflowers until you reach the Cool Spring Baptist Church. It's not what you'd expect—steeple and white clapboard—but a rather rustic structure. This is because the congregation usually met inside during inclement weather; the rest of the time they met outside, surrounded by the glory of nature. Soon after the church, you'll find Jesse Brown's Cabin, and almost immediately the Tomkins Knob parking lot at Milepost 272.5. Reverse course and head back to the start.

US-321 North: Boone (MP 291.9)

Boone is the quintessential western North Carolina city, a blend of old and new, where proponents of homesteading and holistic living find a congenial habitat in the culture of rural Appalachia. It's also a college town, home to Appalachian State University and some 18,000 students, lending the city an invigorating, youthful verve. Boone continues to grow as more people discover how amenable this part of the state is for year-round living.

Daniel Boone and his family inspired the name for the town. Local legend and historical evidence say Boone camped here several times on trips to explore the region and blaze his trail west into Tennessee and Kentucky. His nephews, Jesse and Jonathan Boone, were founders of the first church in town, Three Forks Baptist, which still stands today. *Horn in the West*, an outdoor drama running since 1952, tells the story of Daniel Boone and an interesting slice of the region's history.

Getting There and Around

Boone is easily accessible from the Blue Ridge Parkway. At Milepost 276.4, the Blue Ridge Parkway crosses over US-421, which you can take 11 miles west to Boone. At Milepost 291.9, you can access

MerleFest

It began as a small folk festival in 1988, but **MerleFest** (www.merlefest.org, late Apr., $40 per day, multiday packages $135-260), held annually in North Wilkesboro, 22 miles southeast of the Parkway, has grown into one of the premier roots-music events in the country. It was founded in honor of Merle Watson, the son of legendary guitarist Doc Watson. Merle, also a guitarist, died unexpectedly in 1985 in a tractor accident, cutting short an influential career. Doc Watson, who grew up in the nearby community of Deep Gap (MP 276.4), was the festival's ceremonial host until his death in 2012.

Although his absence is deeply felt by musicians and fans alike, MerleFest is as strong and successful as ever, speaking to his lasting legacy in bluegrass, roots, and Appalachian music. MerleFest draws thousands of visitors every year for many of the top-name performers in folk, country, and bluegrass music. Recent headliners have included Steep Canyon Rangers, Chatham County Line, Sam Bush, Jim Avett, The Avett Brothers (Jim's sons), and Tift Merritt. With multiple stages and dozens of artists, there's a great deal of musical variety to sample.

Boone via US-321. Both of these highways connect Boone to the larger world. Along US-321, Hickory and I-40 are just over an hour south, and along US-421, Boone is 52 miles west of I-77. Winston-Salem is 90 minutes east (along US-421), Charlotte two hours south (via US-321 and US-74), and Asheville two hours southwest (via US-221 and I-40).

Sights

The mountains of North Carolina are loaded with artists and art lovers. At Appalachian State University, the **Turchin Center for the Visual Arts** (432 W. King St., 828/262-3017, www.tcva.org, 10am-6pm Tues.-Thurs. and Sat., noon-8pm Fri., free) provides access to the arts to the community and visitors in Boone. The Kay Borowski Sculpture Garden displays contemporary sculpture outdoors, while six indoor galleries exhibit the Turchin's permanent collection as well as traveling exhibitions. Throughout the year, photography and drawing competitions grace gallery walls.

In the heart of downtown Boone, the **Jones House Community and Cultural Center** (604 W. King St., 828/268-6280, www.joneshouse.org, noon-5pm Tues.-Fri., concert and event prices vary), a beautiful home built in 1908, serves as a gallery for community artists, a meeting place for area groups, and a center for Independence Day and Christmas celebrations. Outdoor summer concerts and indoor fall concerts bring in string bands, bluegrass and roots country musicians, and other mountain music acts.

Entertainment
Nightlife

Appalachian Mountain Brewery (163 Boone Creek Dr., 828/263-1111, http://amb.beer, noon-10pm Sun.-Mon., noon-11pm Tues.-Sat.) is a microbrewery that's popular with beer connoisseurs and the college crowd. They brew about three dozen beers (and a cider), some of which are seasonal. Though many love their IPAs, their dark beers—Belgian Dark Strong, Oatmeal Stout, Porter, Imperial Stout, Schwartz Bier, and the like—are quite good. On any given night, some college band will set up in the corner of the main room and play for the evening. Outside, there's a giant set of Jenga blocks to play with. And if you're hungry, the brewery also owns **Farm to Flame** (www.f2flame.com, at the brewery 1pm-9pm Sun.-Mon., 1pm-10pm Tues.-Thurs., noon-10pm Fri., 3pm-10pm Sat., $6-12), a pizza food truck. There's a sizable

Boone

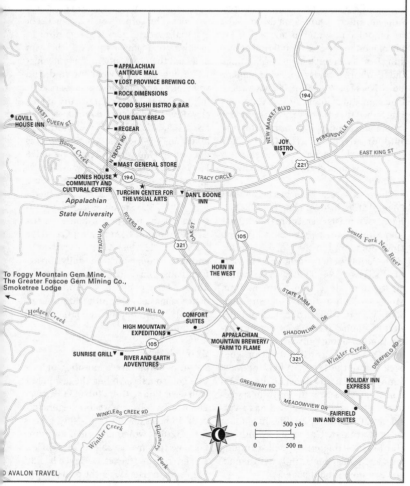

APPALACHIAN ANTIQUE MALL
LOST PROVINCE BREWING CO.
ROCK DIMENSIONS
COBO SUSHI BISTRO & BAR
OUR DAILY BREAD
REGEAR
LOVILL HOUSE INN
WEST QUEEN ST
Boone Creek
N DEPOT RD
MAST GENERAL STORE
JONES HOUSE COMMUNITY AND CULTURAL CENTER
Appalachian State University
TURCHIN CENTER FOR THE VISUAL ARTS
DAN'L BOONE INN
TRACY CIRCLE
NEW MARKET BLVD
PERKINSVILLE DR
JOY BISTRO
EAST KING ST
194
221
RIVERS ST
STADIUM DR
OAK ST
105
321
South Fork New River
To Foggy Mountain Gem Mine, The Greater Foscoe Gem Mining Co., Smoketree Lodge
Hodges Creek
POPLAR HILL DR
HORN IN THE WEST
COMFORT SUITES
HIGH MOUNTAIN EXPEDITIONS
105
SUNRISE GRILL
RIVER AND EARTH ADVENTURES
APPALACHIAN MOUNTAIN BREWERY/ FARM TO FLAME
STATE FARM RD
SHADOWLINE
321
Winkler Creek
DEERFIELD RD
GREENWAY RD
HOLIDAY INN EXPRESS
MEADOWVIEW DR
FAIRFIELD INN AND SUITES
WINKLERS CREEK RD
Winkler Creek
Flannery Fork
0   500 yds
0   500 m
© AVALON TRAVEL

wood-fired pizza oven onboard, and it takes about 90 seconds for them to cook a pie.

Theater

One thing worth checking out in the summer is **Horn in the West** (828/264-2120, www.horninthewest.com, 8pm Tues.-Sun. late June-mid-Aug., adults $25-45, students 13 and up $17-32, children ages 12 and under $13-32), the outdoor drama telling part of Daniel Boone's story. *Horn* is part of a long history of outdoor dramas in North Carolina, its most notable sister productions being *Unto These Hills* (written by the same playwright) in Cherokee and *The Lost Colony* in the Outer Banks.

Shopping

Several antiques shops in Boone make the downtown a great place for browsing.

Appalachian Antique Mall (631 W. King St., 828/268-9988, 10am-5pm Mon.-Thurs., 10am-6pm Fri.-Sat., 11am-5pm Sun. summer; 10am-5pm Mon.-Sat., noon-5pm Sun. winter) is one of the best and biggest in the area. You'll find everything from farm implements to paintings and furniture from far and wide. **Regear** (967 Rivers St., 828/386-6100, www.regearnc.com, 10am-6pm Mon.-Sat., noon-5pm Sun.), an outdoor gear consignment shop, makes equipping yourself for any outdoor adventure affordable. They carry everything from hats and shirts to tents and winter gear, and even kayaks and bikes.

There are several branches of the **Mast General Store** (630 W. King St., 828/262-0000, www.mastgeneralstore.com, 10am-6pm Mon.-Thurs., 10am-8pm Fri.-Sat., 11am-6pm Sun.) in the North Carolina High Country, but the original is in Valle Crucis (Hwy. 194, 828/963-6511, www.mastgeneralstore.com, 7am-6:30pm Mon.-Sat., noon-6pm Sun. summer, hours vary in winter), about 20 minutes west of Boone. It has been a visitor attraction for about 30 years, but its history as a community institution goes back before the 1880s. When the Mast family owned it, the store had the reputation of carrying everything "from cradles to caskets," and today it still has a varied inventory, with specialties in outdoor wear (Carhartt, Columbia, Mountain Hardware, Patagonia, Teva), camping gear, and more penny candy than a modern-day store should have.

Sports and Recreation

There's plenty to do in Boone. If Appalachian State University has a sporting event, you can catch a home game and root for the Mountaineers; if not, it's not difficult to find something to do.

Gem Mining

Many people don't know that North Carolina is rich in gems and gold. Around Boone and the more heavily visited places in the mountains, you'll find businesses that offer gem "mining." You don't need a pick and a shovel, just a keen eye and a few bucks. To "mine," you buy a bucket of material, graded and priced according to the likelihood of it having a valuable gem in it, and then sort, sift, and pan it yourself. You get to keep what you find, and you really can come across some beautiful specimens, some even worthy of jewelry. **River and Earth Adventures** (1655 Hwy. 105, 828/355-9797, www.raftcavehike.com, $15-100) offers gem mining, as does **Foggy Mountain Gem Mine** (4416 Hwy. 105, 828/263-4367, www.foggymountaingems.com, 9am-5pm Sat.-Sun. and Tues., 10am-5pm Mon. and Wed.-Fri., $30-325), where you can get gemstones cut and polished in-house. At **The Greater Foscoe Gem Mining Co.** (8998 Hwy. 105, 828/963-5928, www.foscoeminingco.com, 9am-5pm daily spring-fall, 10am-4pm daily winter, $16-212), 24 kinds of gemstones can be found, and the owner, a master goldsmith and stonecutter, will cut and polish the larger gems you find.

Golf

Around Boone are a number of private golf courses. Among the few public courses is **Boone Golf Club** (433 Fairway Dr., 828/264-8760, www.boonegolfclub.com, 18 holes, par 71, Apr.-Nov., greens fees $32-63), which has wide, forgiving fairways that are playable for all skill levels and from any tee set. Designed by Ellis Maples in the late 1950s, the course is picturesque and enjoyable to play.

Hiking, Rafting, and Cave Trips

Down the road from the Mast General Store in Valle Crucis, **River and Earth Adventures** (1655 Hwy. 105, 828/355-9797, www.raftcavehike.com) leads all sorts of exciting trips on the water, in the woods, and in the area's deep caves. Rafting expeditions ($45-100 adults, $55-75 children) ride the French Broad River (Class III-IV) and Watauga River (Class

II-III), or, for big white water, try the Watauga Gorge Ex-Stream Whitewater trip ($125, 4-person minimum), which gives you more than five miles of Class III, IV, and V rapids. This trip runs spring-fall, using rafts during high water and inflatable kayaks during low water. Participants must be at least 18 years old. Cave trips (daily year-round, $75 pp) meet at the company's Elizabethton, Tennessee, outpost, about an hour away, for a day's spelunking in Worley's Cave. Guided hiking trips are available ($45) that include all-day kids-only hikes with adult guides to free up parents who'd like a day on their own. If you're looking to hike or go rock climbing or bouldering, they offer guide services; inquire about routes and rates.

High Mountain Expeditions (1380 Hwy. 105 S., Banner Elk, 828/266-7238, www.highmountainexpeditions.com) has several locations across the North Carolina High Country and leads rafting trips on the Watauga River (Class I-III, $65 adults, $55 children), the much more challenging Nolichucky River (Class III-IV, $85), and Wilson Creek (Class II-V, $120). They also lead caving expeditions ($75) for adults and children, for which no experience is necessary, and offer tubing ($20) for a good time on the flat water.

Rock Climbing
Rock Dimensions (139 Depot St., 828/265-3544, www.rockdimensions.com, from $65) is a guide service that leads rock climbs at gorgeous locations throughout western North Carolina and parts of Tennessee and Virginia. Guides teach proper multi-pitch, top-rope anchoring, and rappelling techniques, and they lead caving expeditions ($340 for 4 people, $75 pp for groups of 5-10 people).

Winter Sports
The Banner Elk area has some of the state's best ski slopes. **Sugar Mountain** (1009 Sugar Mountain Dr., Sugar Mountain, 828/898-4521 or 800/784-2768, www.skisugar.com, lift tickets $20-72 adults, $17-49 children, rentals $17-32 adults, $9-22 children) is North Carolina's largest winter resort, with 115 acres of ski slopes and 20 trails. In addition to skiing, activities on the 5,300-foot-high mountain include snow tubing, skating, snowshoeing, and, in summer, the Showdown at Sugar National Mountain Bike Series. They offer lessons in skiing and snowboarding for adults and children.

Ski Beech Mountain Resort (1007 Beech Mountain Pkwy., Beech Mountain, 800/438-2093, www.beechmountainresort.com, lift tickets $20-65, rentals $10-40) peaks 300 feet higher than Sugar Mountain and has 15 slopes and 10 lifts, as well as skating and snowboarding areas. In summer, they shift focus to mountain biking and disc golf, with a beautiful disc course as well as challenging downhill biking trails that range from beginner-friendly to expert.

Hawksnest Snow Tubing (2058 Skyland Dr., Seven Devils, 828/963-6561, www.hawksnesttubing.com, 1.5 hours $27-34, zip-lining $80-90) is on a 4,800-foot mountain in Seven Devils. It has 12 slopes dedicated to the family-friendly art of tubing, making it one of the largest snow-tubing parks on the East Coast. Throughout the year, you can experience the thrill of zip-lining on more than four miles of zip lines, including two longer than 2,000 feet, at speeds up to 50 mph.

Food
Boone is a college town with dining that suits both students and their visiting parents. That means three things must be done well: pizza, breakfast, and moderately priced bistro or steakhouse fare. This town delivers on all counts.

Sunrise Grill (1675 Hwy. 105, 828/262-5400, www.sunrisegrillboone.com, 6:30am-2pm Mon.-Fri., 7am-3pm Sat.-Sun., around $9) is widely considered the best breakfast place in Boone. It's a regular bacon-and-eggs sort of place with some interesting omelets, tasty grits, and hot coffee, but everything is done well and the staff are friendly.

★ **Cobo Sushi Bistro and Bar** (161 Howard St., 828/386-1201, www.cobosushi.com, 5pm-10pm Mon.-Thurs., 5pm-11pm Fri., 5pm-1am Sat., $8-35) serves really good sushi in downtown Boone. The menu is heavy with nontraditional rolls but also includes a selection of nigiri, sashimi, and traditional maki. If you're a sushi purist, there are only a few of the fried rolls on the menu, but there are plenty of surprising flavor combinations.

Joy Bistro (115 New Market Centre, 828/265-0500, www.joybistroboone.com, 5:30pm-8:30pm Tues., 11:30am-2pm and 5:30pm-8:30pm Wed.-Thurs., 11:30am-2pm and 5:30pm-9pm Fri., 5:30pm-9pm Sat., 11:30am-2pm and 5:30pm-7:30pm Sun., $12-35) is Southern-French cuisine—not from the south of France but rather a fusion of French techniques and Southern flavors. You'll find a lot of ingredients from local and regional food producers; the baby beet salad, for instance, uses beets from a local farmer, and the ravioli is made fresh by a local pasta maker. Standards like the filet mignon (served with Boursin cheese mashed potatoes and finished with a roasted garlic and chive compound butter) are fantastic, and dishes like the scallops au poivre or lamb loin chop deliver big flavor.

The **Gamekeeper Restaurant and Bar** (3005 Shull's Mill Rd., 828/963-7400, www.gamekeeper-nc.com, bar from 5pm daily, dinner from 5pm Wed.-Sun., $28-59) is tucked away between Boone and Blowing Rock at the Yonahlossee Resort. This restaurant has built and maintained a reputation for high-quality meals using exotic meats. It's common to see ostrich, venison, bison, boar, and the like on the frequently changing menu. Don't skip dessert or the seemingly endless wine list ($20-215 per bottle).

The menu at **Our Daily Bread** (627 W. King St., 828/264-0173, www. ourdailybreadodb.com, 11am-9pm Mon.-Sat., noon-6pm Sun., under $10) includes no fewer than 30 specialty sandwiches, from their best-selling Jamaican Turkey Sub to the Fruity Chicken Sammy—chicken salad with shredded apples, red grapes, and walnuts on a fresh croissant. Try the tempeh Reuben, a daring mixture of flavors that features marinated tempeh, sauerkraut, swiss cheese, and mustard on rye. It sounds outrageous, but it works. Our Daily Bread also makes a variety of fresh soups and meat and veggie chilies every day.

The **Dan'l Boone Inn** (130 Hardin St., 828/264-8657, http://danlbooneinn.com, hours vary, dinner $19 adults, $12 ages 11-12, $10 ages 8-10, $8 ages 5-7, $6 ages 3-4, free ages 2 and under; breakfast $12 adults, $9 ages 11-12, $8 ages 8-10, $7 ages 5-7, $5 ages 3-4, free ages 2 and under) serves old-time country food family style. Despite the complicated pricing system, the food is straightforwardly good. At breakfast, feast on country ham and red-eye gravy, stewed apples, and grits; at dinner, there's fried chicken, country-style steak, ham biscuits, and lots of vegetable sides.

For the classic combo of pizza and beer, ★ **Lost Province Brewing Co.** (130 N. Depot St., 828/265-3506, www.lostprovince.com, 11:30am-10pm Mon.-Wed., 11:30am-11pm Thurs.-Sun., noon-9pm Sun., $9-17) has plenty of both. Their wood-fired pizza oven puts out pies from the traditional (their margherita is nearly perfect) to the creative (think pear, country ham, goat cheese; or buffalo chicken and gorgonzola), plus there are sandwiches and salads and wood-fired pretzels. They keep about a dozen beers on tap, and varieties include pilsners, IPAs, stouts, and even a grits-based light beer.

Accommodations

The **Lovill House Inn** (404 Old Bristol Rd., 828/264-4204, www.lovillhouseinn.com, $149-219) is close to the Appalachian State University campus, and it was in the parlor of this 1875 farmhouse that the papers were drawn up that led to the founding of the university. The inn sits on 11 evergreen-shaded acres and is a lovely place to relax and read.

The **Smoketree Lodge** (11914 Hwy. 105 S., 800/422-1880, www.smoketree-lodge. com, $74-139) is another good choice; it's a large hotel with basic but comfortable guest rooms and efficiencies, a large rustic lobby, a nice indoor pool, and saunas.

Parkway Cabins (599 Bamboo Heights, 828/262-5024 or 828/964-3560, www. parkwaycabins.com, $160-220) is just 5 minutes from downtown Boone and 10 minutes from Blowing Rock; it sits at 4,000 feet in elevation, providing a panoramic view of Grandfather Mountain, Beech Mountain, Seven Devils, and other peaks. Most of the cabins sleep four or more, making them perfect for mountain excursions with a group. At **Blue Ridge Vacation Cabins** (828/963-2393, www. blueridgevacationcabins.com), you'll find plenty of cabins and accommodations in and around Boone; it's a one-stop shop.

Among area chain motels, some good bets are **Fairfield Inn and Suites** (2060 Blowing Rock Rd., 828/268-0677, www. marriott.com, from $151), **Comfort Suites** (1184 Hwy. 105, 828/268-0099, www. choicehotels.com, from $110), **Holiday Inn Express** (1943 Blowing Rock Rd./US-321 S., 828/264-2451, www.ihg.com, from $90), and **Quality Inn & Suites University** (840 E. King St., 480/719-3016, www. choicehotels.com, from $73).

Information and Services
You can find all sorts of visitor information at the official site of the **Watauga County Tourism Development Authority** (www.exploreboone.com). You can also stop by the **High Country Host Visitor Center** (6370 US-321 S., 828/264-1299 or 800/438-7500, 9am-5pm Mon.-Sat., 9am-3pm Sun.). The **Blue Ridge National Heritage Area** (www.blueridgeheritage. com) has a great deal of traveler resources available online, covering not just Boone

and the High Country, but the extent of North Carolina's Blue Ridge Mountains.

Watauga Medical Center (336 Deerfield Rd., 828/262-4100, www.apprhs.org) is a 117-bed complex with primary and specialty care.

Blowing Rock (MP 291.9)

Blowing Rock, named for a nearby geological oddity, is an old resort town filled with beautiful homes that once belonged to wealthy early-20th-century industrialists. It's a small town, but the surprising array of restaurants, cafés, and galleries make it pleasant to stroll, window-shop, and sit to enjoy an ice cream. Blowing Rock also provides easy access to Moses Cone Manor and other notable landmarks.

Aside from the Blowing Rock itself, the best thing to see in Blowing Rock is downtown. Main Street is lined with shops, galleries, and restaurants, and it's a good spot for people-watching most of the year (winter excluded). The vibe here is very relaxed, so you won't find much by way of active entertainment; for that, you'll need to venture out onto the Parkway or into nearby Boone.

Blowing Rock is 15 minutes away from Boone, south along US-321. You can also access Blowing Rock from US-221 and the Blue Ridge Parkway at Milepost 291.9.

Sights
The **Blowing Rock** (434 The Rock Rd., 828/295-7111, www.theblowingrock.com, hours vary, generally 9am-5pm Thurs.-Mon. Jan.-Mar., 8:30am-7pm daily Apr.-Oct., 9am-5pm daily Nov.-Dec., $7 adults, $6 seniors and military, $2 children ages 4-11, free ages 3 and under) is a strange rock outcropping purported by *Ripley's Believe It or Not* to be the only place in the world where snow falls upward. Indeed, light objects (think handkerchiefs, leaves, hats) thrown off Blowing Rock do tend to come floating back up. Note that it's

The Legend of Blowing Rock

Adding to its otherworldly draw, there's a Native American legend associated with Blowing Rock. The story goes that a Chickasaw chieftain, fearful of the admiration his beautiful daughter was receiving, journeyed far to Blowing Rock, where he hoped to hide her away in the woods and keep her safe and pure. One day, the maiden spied a Cherokee warrior wandering in the valley below. Smitten by his looks, she shot an arrow in his direction, hoping he would seek her out. It worked. He found her arrow, tracked her down, and soon appeared at her home, courting her with songs of his land. They became lovers, and one day, a strange reddening sky brought the pair to the Blowing Rock. He took it as a sign that he was to return to his people in their coming time of trouble; to her it spelled the end of their love. She begged him not to go, but he was torn between staying loyal to his duties and following his heart; in his desperation, he leaped from their perch into the gorge below. The young maiden prayed for him to be spared death, but it didn't work. Still, she remained at the site, praying for his return, and one day the sky reddened and the now-famous winds of the John's River Gorge shifted, blowing her lover back into her world and her arms. Since that day, a perpetual wind has blown up onto the rock from the valley below.

prohibited for visitors to actually throw any objects off the rock, to prevent the valley from filling with litter.

The **Blowing Rock Art and History Museum** (159 Chestnut St., 828/295-9099, http://blowingrockmuseum.org, 10am-5pm Tues.-Sat., noon-4pm Sun., $7 adults, $6 seniors, $4 students and children, free for children under age 5 and military) opened in 2011 after more than a decade of work. In addition to rotating exhibits of fine art from private collections, gallery shows by local and regional artists, and traveling exhibitions, BRAHM also has galleries with rotating exhibits displaying artifacts of historical value to the area. It's small, but the art displayed is carefully curated and excellent. It's easy to spend a couple of hours admiring the collections.

Between Blowing Rock and Boone, **Tweetsie Railroad** (300 Tweetsie Railroad Rd., 828/264-9061 or 800/526-5740, http://tweetsie.com, 9am-6pm Fri.-Sun. mid-Apr.-late May and late Aug.-Nov., 9am-6pm daily late May-mid-Aug., Ghost Train 7:30pm Fri. late Sept.-early Nov., 5pm-10pm Fri.-Sat. late Nov.-Dec., $45 adults, $30 children ages 3-12, free under age 3) is a veritable gold mine for kids who are into trains. There are opportunities to pan for gold and gems in one section of the park; a Country Fair-themed area, a Western store and Cowboy Cantina in another; and the Tweetsie Junction area, where you'll find a saloon, a blacksmith, and an antique photo parlor. And, of course, the train: The Tweetsie Railroad's steam engines, number 12 or *Tweetsie,* and number 190, *Yukon Queen,* encircle the amusement park on a narrow-gauge track as part of a Wild West show featuring a frontier outpost and Indian attacks. The railroad isn't all fun and games; it's also partly a history lesson, as the *Tweetsie* was an actual working train in the early part of the 20th century, until washed-out tracks and the advent of reliable automobiles and roads rendered it obsolete.

One little oddity in Blowing Rock is **Mystery Hill** (129 Mystery Hill Ln., 828/264-2794, www.mysteryhill-nc.com, 9am-8pm daily June-Aug., 9am-5pm daily Sept.-May, adults $9, seniors $8, children ages 5-12 $7, children ages 4 and under free.). Like Mystery Hills in other states featuring some gravitational anomaly, this one is fun, but only to a point for grown-ups. It's best for kids, which is fine, because it's fun to watch them try to figure out the mystery of Mystery Hill.

Adjacent to Mystery Hill is **Doc's Rocks Gem Mines** (111 Mystery Hill Ln., 828/264-4499, www.docsrocks.net, 9:30am-5pm daily, $12-55). As at other gem mines, here you'll buy a bucket of ore that they source from a variety of mines across the Blue Ridge, and then you pan and sift through it for gems and fossils. As you make your way through your bucket, they will help you identify the stones you find. You can find all sorts of things, from a variety of fossils to gems like rubies and emeralds.

Entertainment
Festivals and Events

Blowing Rock may be a small town, but you won't want for things to do. You won't find a free concert or wine tasting every night of the week, but the events and activities that go on here are put on well and are well attended.

The biggest event to hit Blowing Rock kicks off in spring and brings thousands of foodies into town. **SAVOR Blowing Rock** (various locations, 828/295-7851, www.savorblowingrock.com), formerly the Blue Ridge Wine & Food Festival, takes place during early May. The tastings, classes, dinners, and events take place at hotels, inns, bars, and restaurants all around town. The Grand Tasting Tent is home to a tasting event with some of the top restaurants and wineries in the area, as well as the Grand Wine Tasting. Generally running from Thursday through Sunday, it's four days of great food and drink, and many of the locals and visitors at the festival are ready to cut loose and celebrate the passing of winter and arrival of spring.

From May through mid-October, the **Blowing Rock Farmers Market** (4pm-6pm Thurs.) takes over Park Avenue,

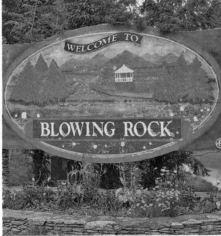

Top to bottom: Jones House Community and Cultural Center; welcome to Blowing Rock; The New Public House & Hotel.

bringing all sorts of baked goods, artisanal cheeses, and the usual bounty of fruits and veggies. The **Music on the Lawn** (5:30pm-8:30pm Fri. May-Oct.) series has made **The Inn at Ragged Gardens** (203 Sunset Dr., 828/295-9703, www. ragged-gardens.com) a hot spot every Friday night. They have a cash bar and serve a limited menu, so get there early, find a place for your blanket, and order a bite to eat.

Shopping
★ Art Galleries
Along Blowing Rock's Main Street, you'll have your pick of galleries. Park at the Blowing Rock Art and History Museum (159 Chestnut St.), which also happens to be the location of the visitors center, and gallery hop your way down Main Street.

Reinert Fine Art (1153 Main St., 828/414-9580, www.reinertfineart.com, 9am-5pm daily) showcases art by contemporary artists, including the gallery's namesake, Rick Reinert. Besides Reinert's bold, colorful paintings, you'll find works by Neil Patterson, Christopher Zhang, and Zhiwei Tu.

At **Traditions Pottery** (1155 Main St., 828/295-6128, www.traditionspottery. com, 10am-6pm Sun.-Thurs., 9am-7pm Fri.-Sat.) fifth- and sixth-generation potters have their own works and wares on display alongside pottery and ceramics from other local artists.

Other Shops
There's more than a fair share of antiques stores, boutiques, and gift shops on Main Street. If you're in the market for antiques, it's hard to beat **Windwood Antiques** (1157 Main St., 828/295-9260) and **Carriage Trade Living** (1079 Main St., 828/295-3110), both on Main Street. **Blowing Rock Estate Jewelry & Antiques** (167 Sunset Dr., 828/295-4500) has a large and constantly changing selection of fine estate jewelry; with its precious gems and heirloom pieces, this is the spot to look for a piece of stunning jewelry from past ages.

At **Gaines Kiker Silversmith** (132 Morris St., 828/295-3992, www. gaineskikersilversmith.com, 11am-5pm Tues.-Sat.), the silver jewelry is exquisite. Gaines Kiker finds inspiration for the shapes and curves of his jewelry in the mountains around him, and his work displays a simplicity and elegance that's difficult to master.

Celeste's (1132 Main St., #1, 828/295-3481, www.celestesinteriors.com, 10am-5pm Sun.-Thurs., 10:30am-5:30pm Fri.-Sat.), a boutique offering a range of lifestyle, fashion, and home goods, was chosen as one of *Southern Living Magazine*'s "Favorite Stores," and for good reason. The selections range from whimsical to funky, but all with a touch of Southern class.

If it's a souvenir T-shirt you're looking for, try **Sunset Tee's & Hattery** (1117 Main St., 828/295-9326, 9am-6pm Sun.-Thurs., 9am-8pm Fri.-Sat.). They have loads of gift items from tacky to fridge-worthy, and the selection of hats is huge. In the back of the store, hats from poker visors to baseball caps to leather stovepipe hats to bowlers and derbys are for purchase.

Barking Rock (1179 Main St., 828/295-8883, 11am-5pm Mon.-Fri., 10:30am-5pm Sat., 1pm-5pm Sun.) has what you need for the canine member of your family. Inside, you'll find dog treats, cool collars and leashes, toys galore, and even sweaters. They also carry a few equestrian items as well.

Recreation
Sky Valley Zip Tours (634 Sky Ranch Rd., Blowing Rock, 855/475-9947, www.sky-valleyziptours.com, $84) operates one of the best zip lines I've been on. Their signature zip, Big Mamma, is massive—more than 1,600 feet long and nearly 300 feet high—but one of the wildest parts of this zip-line tour is the Leap of Faith between lines five and six, where you hook into a self-belay device and step off the

edge of a 40-foot cliff. It's fun and the staff knows how to make zipping comfortable for novices and exciting for veterans.

VX3 Trail Rides (828/963-0260, www.vx3trailrides.com, rides departing at 10am and 2pm daily, $200) offers horseback-riding outings with Tim Vines, a trail guide with decades in the saddle. Groups are small, typically a maximum of four riders, unless it's one family or group, and you need reservations at least a day in advance.

Food

The Speckled Trout (922 Main St., 828/295-9819, www.thespeckledtrout.com, 11am-10pm Sun.-Wed., 11am-11pm Thurs.-Sat., kitchen closed 3pm-5pm daily, $8-25) does an outstanding job cooking trout in many forms—pan seared, cracker-meal crusted, even smoked—but the other dishes on their short, excellent menu are Southern to the core yet creative. Think deviled eggs with a splash of hot sauce, venison sliders, pickled watermelon salad, chicken brined in Cheerwine then fried, and rich chicken 'n' dumplings. They have an outstanding beer and wine list here, and an equally great bottle shop.

★ **Storie Street Grille** (1167 Main St., 828/295-7075, www.storiestreetgrille.com, 11am-3pm and 5pm-9pm Wed.-Sat. early Dec.-Mar., 11am-3pm and 5pm-9pm Mon.-Sat. Apr.-early Dec., $9-28) has a long lunch menu of sandwiches and main-course salads. Try the Storie Street Burger for one of the best burgers in town, or the caprese sandwich for something meat-free. At dinner, don't miss the trout, horseradish salmon, or the mushroom ravioli.

Bistro Roca and Antlers Bar (143 Wonderland Trail, 828/295-4008, http://bistroroca.com, 11am-3pm and 5pm-10pm Wed.-Mon., bar 11am-midnight Wed.-Mon., $10-30) serves hearty and creative dishes like lobster mac-and-cheese, their take on coq au vin (made

with riesling instead of red wine), and a pork rib eye with goat-cheese "butter" and a peach *gastrique*. An interesting note is that the Antlers Bar has been open since 1932, making it the oldest continuously serving bar in the state.

Southern Comforts (840 Main St., 828/295-7114, 7am-2pm daily, $5-12) is an all-day breakfast place that's inexpensive and tasty. Flapjacks, fried eggs, and biscuits and gravy are breakfast staples, but don't turn down their cheesesteak, chicken and dumplings, or the fried oysters. On Friday and Saturday nights, they do a seafood feast.

★ **The Best Cellar** (203 Sunset Dr., 828/295-3466, www.ragged-gardens.com, 5pm-late daily, $19-44), located inside The Inn at Ragged Gardens, is a longtime Blowing Rock occasion place. The seafood-heavy menu shows a good range of flavors, techniques, and influences, with dishes like North Carolina black grouper, locally sourced mountain trout, sea scallops over shiitake mushrooms and spinach, and crab cakes. There's also steak, lamb, and a roasted half duckling. On the wine list, you'll find more than a dozen excellent by-the-glass options and pages of bottles that span the globe.

Foggy Rock Eatery & Pub (8180 Valley Blvd., 828/295-7262, www.foggy-rock.com, 11:30am-9:30pm daily, $7-17) is a sports bar with upgraded food. Seafood graces their menu, with dishes like Appalachian Fish 'n' Chips (fried catfish and waffle fries) and Trout Trout Trout (a trio of trout), and they have a good selection of sandwiches, burgers, and Philly cheesesteaks.

Roots Restaurant (7179 Valley Blvd., 828/414-9508, www.roots-restaurant.com, 5pm-late Mon.-Sat., $13-35) has a great menu filled with rich and creative takes on some classic dishes. The chicken and dumplings are made in the traditional Southern style, but drizzled with truffle oil. The rib eye is rubbed with a hops-infused seasoning. The meatloaf is stuffed with blue cheese. Everything they serve has some sort of tie back to simple country food, but it's all prepared with a bent toward fine dining.

Since you're in North Carolina, you might as well have some barbecue. **Woodlands Barbecue Restaurant** (8304 Valley Blvd., 828/295-3651, www.woodlandsbbq.com, 11am-9pm Sun.-Thurs., 11am-10pm Fri.-Sat., $3-27) serves a variety of styles and sauces representing 'cue from North Carolina and beyond. Their chopped pork is excellent, but their brisket and chopped chicken are surprise hits, as is the smoked turkey. You can also get ribs, tacos, and some outstanding sides and desserts.

Accommodations
$100-150
Blowing Rock Inn (788 US-321 Business, 828/295-7921, www.blowingrockinn. com, Apr.-early Dec., $104-130, villas $165-250) has the feel of an old motor court, with rooms wrapped around a lawn and parking area, but it's been upgraded to modern standards. Just a short walk or even shorter drive to downtown, Blowing Rock Inn is both quiet and conveniently located. The inn provides free Wi-Fi, and you can add all sorts of packages to your room or villa, including a wine basket, cake, and flowers.

Another good value is the **Cliff Dwellers Inn** (116 Lakeview Trail, 828/295-3098, www.cliffdwellers.com, from $130), with clean, simple guest rooms and a beautiful lakefront view. They're less than a mile from the Blue Ridge Parkway and just a short distance from downtown Blowing Rock, making this a choice spot for the budget conscious.

$150-200
The Inn at Ragged Gardens (203 Sunset Dr., 828/295-9703, www.ragged-gardens. com, from $145) is a stone-walled and chestnut-paneled manor, a handsome and stylish turn-of-the-20th-century vacation home. The plush guest rooms

feature goose-down bedding, fireplaces, and, in most rooms, balconies and whirlpool tubs. A sister property to the Inn at Ragged Gardens, the **Blowing Rock Ale House and Inn** (152 Sunset Dr., 828/414-9254, www.blowingrockalehouseandinn. com, $175-195) is an eight-room bed-and-breakfast and full pub. It has been in operation as a B&B since the late 1940s, once heralded as a fancy place to stay because most guest rooms had private baths. Today, the addition of the restaurant and tavern **Blowing Rock Brewing Co.** (828/414-9600, http://blowingrockbrewing.com, 11:30am-9pm Mon.-Tues. and Thurs., 11:30am-10pm Fri.-Sat., noon-9pm Sun., $14) has helped keep this long-running institution going in a new era.

★ **The New Public House & Hotel** (239 Sunset Dr., 828/295-3487, www.thenewpublichouse.com, $175-250) has seven luxurious rooms and a cottage, all with roomy showers, fantastic linens, and breakfast at the delicious restaurant included. That **restaurant** (8am-11am and 4:30pm-9:30pm Mon.-Fri., 8am-3pm and 4:30pm-9:30pm Sat., 8am-3pm Sun., $12-26) is excellent, with many seating options (the porch and yard are choice spots in good weather). The menu goes beyond typical B&B fare, and the kitchen does an outstanding job on each dish, so a meal here is a must, whether it's a bison flank steak or blackened catfish for dinner, crawfish enchiladas for lunch, or an order of biscuits and gravy for breakfast.

Over $200
The lavish 1916 Greek Revival mansion of painter Elliot Daingerfield is now home to the ★ **Westglow Resort and Spa** (224 Westglow Crescent, 828/295-4463 or 800/562-0807, www.westglow.com, from $400, spa packages from $225). In addition to the cushy guest rooms, many of which have whirlpool tubs, private decks, and views of Grandfather Mountain, the menu of spa treatments and health services befits the elegance of

the surroundings. All kinds of massages and body therapies are available, as well as fitness classes, cooking and makeup lessons, and a variety of seminars in emotional well-being. Taking advantage of the spa's wonderful location, visitors can also sign up for hiking, cycling, snowshoeing, and camping trips.

Information and Services

You'll find all the information you need about Blowing Rock at the **visitors center** inside the Blowing Rock Art and History Museum (159 Chestnut St., 828/295-4636 or 877/750-4636, www.blowingrock.com).

The nearest hospital is the **Watauga Medical Center** (336 Deerfield Rd., Boone, 828/262-4100, www.apprhs.org).

Moses H. Cone Memorial Park (MP 294)

The **Moses Cone Manor** (MP 294, 828/295-7938, 9am-5pm daily Mar. 15-Nov. 30, free), more commonly called Flat Top Manor, is a wonderfully crafted house, a huge white, ornate mountain palace built in 1901 that was the country home of North Carolina textile baron Moses Cone. He became a leading philanthropist, and as you drive around the state, especially in the northern Piedmont, you'll notice his name on quite a few institutions. Today, the manor is the centerpiece of the Moses H. Cone Memorial Park. Appropriately, it is home to one of the **Southern Highland Craft Guild** (828/295-7938, www.southernhighlandguild.org, 9am-5pm daily mid-Mar.-Nov.) stores, a place to buy beautiful textiles, pottery, jewelry, furniture, and dolls handmade by some of the best craftspeople of the Appalachian Mountains. There are also extensive hiking and riding trails on the estate.

Hiking

The 3,500-acre Moses H. Cone Memorial Park is one of the Parkway's largest developed areas set up for public recreation. There are 25 miles of trails for hiking and horseback riding, a 16-acre trout lake, and a 22-acre bass lake on the property. You can pick up a map of the trails at the manor house and Bass Lake Entrance (on US-221). The trails here are largely old carriage roads, so they're wide, well maintained, and pretty gentle.

Flat Top Road Trail

Distance: 5.6 miles out and back
Duration: 3-3.5 hours
Elevation gain: 600 feet
Difficulty: moderate
Trailhead: Moses Cone Manor parking area at the far end (away from the house)

This out-and-back hike will take you to the summit of Flat Top, where you'll have an unobstructed view of mountains in every direction. From the top of this 4,558-foot peak, you'll understand what drew the Cone family here.

As soon as you start the trail, which is really a carriage road, you'll cross under the Parkway via a tunnel and emerge onto the north side. Follow the trail into the meadow until you reach a fork; the left trail leads to Rich Mountain Road, so bear right and leave the meadow behind. Just under a mile in, you'll see a spur trail on your left leading to the Cone family graves.

The trail will cross another meadow, then turn back into the woods. At two miles in, the trail takes a couple of tight turns, then makes its way to the summit. On the summit, there's a tower you can climb if it's open. The climb up is breezy and can be a little disconcerting, but the views pay off. To get back, simply retrace your steps.

Rich Mountain Trail

Distance: 5.2 miles out and back
Duration: 3-3.5 hours
Elevation gain: 510 feet

Difficulty: moderate

Trailhead: Moses Cone Manor parking area at the far end (away from the house)

Rich Mountain is known by another name by some in these parts: Nowhere Mountain. While it is in the middle of nowhere (at least it was ages ago), it's definitely somewhere to be. In the winter, you'll find many people cross-country skiing or snowshoeing to the summit.

The trail begins by crossing under the Parkway into the meadow on the north side. Here the trail splits, with Rich Mountain going to the left and Flat Top bearing right. Follow the trail to the left and cross the wide meadow before entering the forest. Before you reach the notable corkscrew path to the summit, there's little of note save the scenery, though you do pass through several rhododendron tunnels and thickets, and at the right times of year, this path can be packed with wildflowers.

Rich Mountain Trail's most notable feature is the corkscrew path (a double corkscrew, actually) to the top of the 4,370-foot peak. As the path begins the ever-tightening turns, you'll see the view from all possible angles. Take a break at the top before returning to the trailhead. Before you go, take a look at the trees here. Many are stunted, windblown, and damaged by ice and snow. Many of the mountains around here are high enough to get frequent snow and ice throughout the year, so be aware of weather reports if you're hiking late in the season, during winter, or early spring.

Bass Lake Trail

Distance: 0.8-mile loop

Duration: 30 minutes

Elevation gain: none

Difficulty: easy

Trailhead: Bass Lake entrance on US-221, one mile south of Parkway MP 294.6

This easy loop hike around Bass Lake gives you some absolutely stunning views of Moses Cone Manor in any season, but it's especially beautiful when autumn leaves are in full blaze or winter's snow blankets everything around. From the parking area, take either trail; they both circle the lake and will both take you right back here.

Julian Price Memorial Park (MP 297.1)

Julian Price Memorial Park (828/936-5911, www.recreation.gov) abuts Moses H. Cone Memorial Park, but unlike Cone, which was a family home and estate, Price was set aside as a retreat for the employees of Julian Price's insurance company. Price's death in 1946 put those plans on hold, and the land was deeded to his company. His company, with the approval of his family, turned the land over to the National Park Service for inclusion in the Blue Ridge Parkway, so, in a roundabout way, Price's wish that this beautiful mountain land be used and enjoyed by his employees came to be. Today, there's a 47-acre pond, created by the damming of Boone Fork; as well as a large amphitheater; more than 100 picnic sites; camping; and the 13.5-mile Tanawha Trail, which parallels the Parkway and skirts the lower edges of Grandfather Mountain.

There are 197 **campsites** (828/936-5911, www.recreation.gov, mid-May-late Oct., $20) at Julian Price Memorial Park, with spaces for tents and RVs. Canoeing on the lake is also a possible activity here.

Price Lake Trail

Distance: 2.5-mile loop

Duration: 2-2.5 hours

Elevation gain: none

Difficulty: easy to moderate

Trailhead: Price Lake Overlook at MP 296.7 or Boone Fork Overlook at MP 297.2

If you want to get a great look at Price Lake and check out the campground (if you're not already staying there), this loop hike will give you what you're looking for.

Since this trail is a loop, you can start

from either trailhead and go in either direction. Much of what you'll see on the hike will be dominated by the lake. Along the west side of the lake, near the Price Lake Overlook, you'll have fantastic views of Grandfather Mountain, no matter the season. There are plenty of benches along the trail, so taking a moment to rest or soak in the view is no problem. As you circle the lake, you'll see the typical wildflowers, rhododendrons, and mountain laurel that blanket the mountainsides here.

If you depart from the Boone Fork Overlook, the first half-mile or so of the hike is a good one for those in **wheelchairs** as part of the trail crosses over a marshy area on a long boardwalk.

Green Knob Trail

Distance: 2.1-mile loop
Duration: 2-2.5 hours
Elevation gain: 460 feet
Difficulty: easy to moderate
Trailhead: Sims Pond Overlook at MP 295.7

Immediately after you leave the trailhead, you'll cross the bridge across the spillway and the dam forming the small but picturesque Sims Pond. The path turns left along the shore, then climbs gradually through a stand of hemlock trees. For a long while, you'll hike beside Sims Creek, but about a half mile in, the sound of the stream will periodically be drowned out by the sound of cars passing over on the viaduct above. As you continue on the trail, the gorge around you will narrow and climb, and you will make several crossings of the stream. At 0.6 mile in, you'll be in for some great scenery along the trail at the Sims Creek Viaduct Overlook (MP 295.3).

After the overlook, the trail steepens and crosses a number of side streams. At the one-mile mark you'll enter a meadow. There are a dozen or so concrete pillars guiding you across the grassy expanse

and pointing you to the trail as it reenters the woods a quarter mile on.

The trail doesn't touch the summit of Green Knob, but rather stays below it a couple hundred feet. At 1.4 miles, you're as close to the summit as you'll ever be, so if you want to climb up to check it off your list, now's the time. Otherwise, take in the view of Grandfather Mountain and continue on. From here, the trail descends through the woods back to the trailhead.

Tanawha Trail to Rough Ridge

Distance: 1.6 miles out and back
Duration: 1-1.5 hours
Elevation gain: 550 feet
Difficulty: moderate to strenuous
Trailhead: Wilson Creek Overlook at MP 303.6

The Tanawha Trail is a trail-building masterpiece that cost $750,000 and required helicopters to place bridges during construction. The whole trail is 13.5 miles and stretches from Price Lake to Beacon Heights, just below Grandfather Mountain. One of the best sections of the Tanawha Trail is to Rough Ridge from the Wilson Creek Overlook.

Starting at Wilson Creek, pass under the Parkway and meet with the Tanawha Trail; here you'll turn right and cross Little Wilson Creek. The trail descends for the next 0.1 mile, then reaches a long, gradual climb through a boulder field interspersed with tall trees and beautiful wildflowers.

Shortly after climbing through a small pine grove, you'll reach stone steps that will carry you to the top of Rough Ridge, where the views, especially in fall, are smashing. From here, retrace your steps to the trailhead.

If you'd like to extend the hike, push on through to the Rough Ridge parking area and walk back along the side of the Parkway (about 0.8 mile), making this a 2.4-mile hike.

★ Linn Cove Viaduct

(MP 304.4)

One of the most iconic spots along the Blue Ridge Parkway, the Linn Cove Viaduct is a bridge-like structure hanging from the side of the mountain in a dizzying S-curve. At nearly 1,300 feet long, this amazing feat of engineering makes you feel like you might just fly off into space if you lose focus. A pair of viewing areas about 0.25 miles from either end of the viaduct give you the chance to stretch your legs and snap a few pictures of this amazing part of the road.

Grandfather Mountain looming above offers great photo opportunities, as does the road itself when it ducks back into one deep cove and emerges on the side of the mountain opposite, snaking away into the trees. The sight of this winding concrete and asphalt peeking out from the trees and following the contours of the mountains is enough to take your breath away.

The story of the viaduct is a long one, but one well told at the **Linn Cove Viaduct Visitor Center** (828/298-0398, 10am-5pm daily Apr.-Nov.) at Milepost 304.4. It was the last piece of the Parkway to be completed, and upon its completion on September 11, 1987, 52 years after construction began on this jewel of a road, the route from the Shenandoah Valley to the Great Smoky Mountains was whole. What caused the delay? One reason was the route. Hugh Morton, the owner of Grandfather Mountain, wasn't fond of the proposed site of the Parkway, which would have climbed much higher up the side of Grandfather Mountain. After the Parkway route was settled at a lower elevation, Morton donated land to the National Park Service, and all that was left to do was the engineering.

Linn Cove Viaduct Trail

Distance: 1 mile out and back

Linn Cove Viaduct

Duration: 30 minutes
Elevation gain: 60 feet
Difficulty: easy to moderate
Trailhead: Linn Cove parking area at the visitors center

The first 0.15 mile of the trail is paved, making it ideal for **wheelchairs.** At the turnaround, you'll have great views of the underside of the viaduct.

Pushing farther along the trail, in 0.5 mile, you'll reach a postcard view of the viaduct, which you can achieve by taking a short spur trail to the top of a rocky outcrop. It really is a phenomenal view and worth taking a few minutes to climb onto this rocky perch for the shot.

★ Grandfather Mountain (MP 305)

Grandfather Mountain (2 miles north of Linville, 2050 Blowing Rock Hwy./US-221, 828/733-4337, http://grandfather. com, 8am-7pm daily summer, 9am-6pm daily spring and fall, 9am-5pm daily winter, weather permitting, $20 adults, $18 over age 60, $9 ages 4-12, free under age 4), at a lofty 5,964 feet, is not the highest mountain in North Carolina, but it is one of the most beautiful. The highest peak in the Blue Ridge Mountains (the only peak higher, Mount Mitchell, is in the Black Mountains), Grandfather is a United Nations-designated biosphere reserve. Privately owned for decades though open to the public, Grandfather Mountain has remained a great expanse of deep forests and wildlife with many hiking trails. The main attraction is the summit and the **Mile High Swinging Bridge.** It is indeed a mile high, and it swings a little in the breeze, but it should be called the "Singing Bridge" because of the somewhat unnerving sound of the constant wind through the steel cables holding it in place. The view from Grandfather Mountain is stunning, and the peak is easily accessible via the scenic road that traces the skyward mile. From the parking lot just below the summit, you can access a number of trails (open during park hours only) that lead to nearby peaks, under the crest of Grandfather, and along nearby ridgelines.

Though the Mile High Swinging Bridge is a mile above sea level, it's not that far above the gap it crosses from the gift shop to a sub-peak of Grandfather Mountain. Even so, with the giant views all around and the dizzying distance to the valley floor below, some visitors find themselves more than a little nervous when it comes time to cross the bridge. If you find that the bridge is a little much for you, don't sweat it; just take in the impressive view from the parking lot and spend some time at the other attractions on Grandfather Mountain. The **Wildlife Habitats** are always popular. Here, large enclosures provide a place for white-tailed deer, eagles, river otters, black bear, and cougars to live. Daily feedings draw the animals out of their secret places in each enclosure and bring them into view.

Hiking

Aside from the view, many come to Grandfather Mountain for the hiking. There are a few short hikes along the drive to the top, and more hikes that will test your stamina and mettle as you climb to the true summit of Grandfather Mountain. At the Grandfather Mountain Picnic Area, the 0.4-mile **Woods Walk** trail leads you on an easy walk through the forest on the lower flanks of the mountain; it's gentle on the youngest and oldest visitors. Near the Mile High Swinging Bridge, park in the Trails parking area and hike the **Bridge Trail,** another 0.4-mile winding trail that takes you under the bridge. There's one more, easier hike of note, but the rest are significantly tougher.

Black Rock Nature Trail

Distance: 2 miles out and back
Duration: 1.5-2 hours
Elevation gain: 400 feet
Difficulty: moderate

Trailhead: Trails parking area
Directions: Exit the Parkway at MP 305 and follow US-221 north one mile to the entrance to Grandfather Mountain. Follow the road up Grandfather Mountain to the Trails parking area three turns below the summit.

This is a straightforward hike that leads through a forest of rhododendron, galax, Fraser fir, and red spruce, down a gentle grade to a short loop where you'll have views of Grandmother Mountain, Beacon Heights, and, of course, the Blue Ridge Parkway. Along the way, a number of interpretive signs provide information on the route and environment. The trail is rocky, though not too bad, but that gentle grade that led you to the end of the trail will seem a little steeper on the way back up.

Grandfather Trail

Distance: 4.8 miles out and back
Duration: 6-7 hours
Elevation gain: 1,800 feet (with several 700-800 foot ascents and descents)

Grandfather Mountain, one of North Carolina's iconic destinations

Difficulty: strenuous

Trailhead: Parking area at the top of Grandfather Mountain

This unusual hike traverses the finest sub-alpine/alpine environments in the South. Though many believe the promontory at the end of the Mile High Swinging Bridge is the peak of Grandfather Mountain, it's not; but this trail will take you to the next three highest points on the mountain: MacRae Peak (5,845 ft.), Attic Window Peak (5,949 ft.), and Calloway Peak (5,964 ft.). This trail is marked with blue diamonds (it was blue blazes, and in places the ghosts of these marks may be visible).

The trail is relentless, beginning with a short, steep switchback ascent. This section is a good taste of the rest of the hike and may help you decide whether to continue. At a quarter mile in, you'll reach a spot called The Patio that has great views of MacRae Peak ahead. Shortly after passing the 0.5-mile mark, you'll come to the first of several cables that have been

bolted into the rock faces to provide safety handholds. You don't need any special gear; just hang on. Continuing on the trail, you'll climb a half-dozen ladders (which can make you feel a bit exposed at times). After climbing the final ladder, you'll be on a narrow ledge that leads to the summit ridge. Wind through the forest to a 20-foot ladder that takes you to the top.

When you've had your fill of the view, climb back down and head to Attic Window Peak. You'll encounter a pair of interesting spots before reaching Attic Window: The Subway and The Chute. The Subway is a jumbled stretch of massive boulders. The Chute is a steep, narrow climb up the side of Attic Window Peak. Be sure of your hand and foot placement as you climb The Chute. From here, the trail continues along the edge of the cliff until you pass over a significant rock outcropping and descend back into the woods.

Soon after descending into the woods, Profile Trail meets Grandfather Trail at Calloway Gap. As you climb to Calloway Peak, there are several steep sections, but nothing too bad considering what you've done so far. The view from the top isn't much, but you've made it to the highest point on Grandfather Mountain. To get back, retrace your steps and be careful on those ascents and descents.

Beacon Heights (MP 305.2)

Beacon Heights sits on the edge of Grandfather Mountain, affording you a fabulous view of the slope and one of the peaks of Grandfather as the Parkway sweeps around the massif. The Grandfather Mountain view is from the parking area, but a spectacular, sweeping view of the lands south of the Parkway can be had at the actual Beacon Heights—a rocky escarpment up a short trail.

Beacon Heights Trail

Distance: 0.2 mile out and back
Duration: 30 minutes
Elevation gain: 300 feet
Difficulty: moderate
Trailhead: Beacon Heights parking area at MP 305.2

This trail is short and often in a state of disrepair, making for some rocky footing nearly the whole way. The reward, though, is the excellent view sweeping from the southeast to the northeast as the trail emerges onto a rocky bluff.

Flat Rock (MP 308.3)

A short walk from the Parkway is a rather large, flat slab of stone aptly named Flat Rock. From here, you have a great view of Grandfather Mountain and the Linville Valley.

Flat Rock Loop Trail

Distance: 0.7-mile loop
Duration: 30 minutes
Elevation gain: 100 feet
Difficulty: easy
Trailhead: Flat Rock parking area at MP 308.3

Somehow trail designers managed to build one here that appeals to both experienced hikers and Parkway drivers. If you want, this trail can be either a quick walk to a nice view or a longer woodland stroll if you take your time to read the interpretive signage along the way, then stop for a picnic. Either way, this path through a rhododendron-filled hardwood forest is a pleasant one.

From the parking area, a short trail connects you to the loop. At the loop, turn left and take the trail around to a pair of viewpoints, the first being Flat Rock, a massive slab of quartzite, and the second providing a great vantage of Grandfather Mountain. Continue along the trail until you descend and return to the trail from the parking lot.

Linville Gorge (MP 316.3)

The deepest gorge in the United States, **Linville Gorge** is located near Blue Ridge Parkway Milepost 316.3 in a 12,000-acre federally designated wilderness area. It's genuine wilderness, and some of the hollers in this preserve are so remote that they still shelter virgin forests—a rarity even in these wild mountains. The National Park Service operates the **Linville Falls Campground** (MP 316.3, 828/765-2681, www.linvillefalls.com, $20) near the spectacular Linville Falls. Tent and RV sites are interspersed, and water and flush toilets are available May-October.

★ Linville Falls

Linville Falls (MP 316.3) is one of the most-photographed places in North Carolina, a spectacular series of cataracts that fall crashing into Linville Gorge. It can be seen from several short trails that depart from the **Linville Falls Visitor Center** (MP 316.3, 828/765-1045, 10am-5pm daily late Apr.-Nov.), including the recommended **Linville Falls Trail.**

Recreation
Linville Falls Trail

Distance: 2 miles out and back
Duration: 1-1.5 hours
Elevation gain: 300 feet
Difficulty: easy to moderate
Trailhead: Linville Falls Visitor Center

There are three overlooks providing the best views of Linville Falls and the Linville Gorge from the west side. This trail will lead you to all three. For the most part, this trail is easy, though if you're speed hiking it, the steep parts can be a little challenging, and there is a section of the trail that's often wet; for those reasons, it's a moderate rather than easy hike.

From the visitors center, cross the bridge over the Linville River and along a parallel path. A little less than 0.5 mile in, you'll come to an intersection with a sign directing you to turn left for Upper Falls and right for the other views. Turn left and take the short spur trail to an overlook at the falls. Here, the drop is small—only 15 feet—but the pool below is huge, and you can feel the power of the water rushing toward the bigger drop just downstream.

Rejoin the main trail and follow it for another 0.1 mile, then turn left again to descend some steep, often wet, steps to Chimney View, where you'll have a great look at the whole falls. Many people find this to be their "picture postcard" view, and it's good, but I prefer the vista at Erwin's View. To get there, head back up the steps and climb into the piney woods. The trail dead-ends at Erwin's View, where a set of steps and platforms leads to views of the gorge from several spots and then a massive view of the gorge, river, and falls that truly shows the size of this place. When you're done, head back.

Rock Climbing

Linville Gorge has some great climbing spots, including Table Rock, parts of which are popular with beginning climbers and other parts of which should only be attempted by experts. Other extremely strenuous options are the Hawksbill cliff face and Sitting Bear rock pillar. Speak to the folks at the visitors center or at **Fox Mountain Guides** (3228 Asheville Hwy., Pisgah Forest, 888/284-8433, www.foxmountainguides.com), a Hendersonville-area service that leads climbs in the gorge, to determine which of Linville Gorge's many climbing faces would be best suited to your skill level.

Top to bottom: on the trail to Linville Falls; the entrance to Linville Caverns; Linville Falls.

✦US-221 South: Linville Caverns
(MP 317.4)

A complete visit to the Blue Ridge Mountains includes more than looking at their outsides: **Linville Caverns** (US-221, between Linville and Marion, south of MP 317, 800/419-0540, www.linvillecaverns.com, 9am-4:30pm daily Mar. and Nov., 9am-5pm daily Apr.-May and Labor Day-Oct., 9am-6pm daily June-Labor Day, 9am-4:30pm Sat.-Sun. Dec.-Feb., $8.50 adults, $7.50 seniors 62 and older, $6.50 ages 5-12) is one of the venerable underground attractions of the Southern mountains. The natural limestone caverns feature all sorts of strange rock formations, underground trout streams, and, of course, a gift shop. Don't worry if you're mildly claustrophobic; the caverns are much bigger than you might think.

Chestoa View (MP 320.8)

It's easy to miss one of the best views on the Parkway at Chestoa View, but if you slow down at Milepost 320 (heading south) or Milepost 321 (heading north), you'll spy a sign pointing to the parking area here. Grab a spot and take a short walk (less than 0.25 mile) to the viewing area, a rock-walled promontory looking over the **Linville Gorge.** In spring and summer it's a grand view, but in fall the colors are nothing short of marvelous, making it one of the must-stops overlooks for leaf peepers. From here you can see Grandfather Mountain and Table Rock, and, when the leaves are finally down, the Linville River far below.

McKinney Gap (MP 327.5)

McKinney Gap is the lowest pass through the Blue Ridge Mountains for a hundred miles. Long before European settlers pushed this far west, Cherokee people used this gap as a hunting and trading route. The first permanent European settler here was Charlie "Cove" McKinney, who settled down in the 1790s with his family. And what a family it was; he had four wives and 48 children. Many of the McKinneys are buried on the mountain.

In the late 1800s, McKinney Gap caught the eye of the railroads that sought easy passage across the mountains. By 1908, the Clinchfield Railroad opened. Four thousand workers built 18 tunnels and 13 miles of track on, through, and around the hills nearby. The railroads renamed McKinney Altapass. A resort sprang up, as did two hotels and a golf course adjacent to the railroad station. In a few years, Clinchfield ceased passenger service and the resort began to fail. The end came finally when a highway was built through a nearby pass.

During the building of the railroad, Clinchfield planted hundreds of acres with apple trees. The geography here—hills facing southeast, the land largely free of frost, cold air at night but warm in the day, good sun exposure—made it perfect for apples. The **Orchard at Altapass** (MP 328.3, 1025 Orchard Rd., Spruce Pine, 828/765-9531, www.altapassorchard.org, 10am-5pm Wed.-Sun.) was born. In its best years, it produced 125,000 bushels of apples. Today, though, apples are just part of the story. From May to October, they have all sorts of programs—from dancing to music to educational opportunities—all centered around the nature, history, and culture of this part of the Appalachian Mountains.

Museum of North Carolina Minerals (MP 331)

The mountains around here are absolutely packed with minerals and gems; in fact, they're some of the richest in the nation. The **Museum of North Carolina Minerals** (214 Parkway Maintenance Rd., Spruce Pine, at MP 331 and NC-226, 828/765-2761, 9am-5pm daily, free) displays more than 300 types of minerals and gems found in the vicinity. You can also view interactive displays on mining and exhibits outlining the geological processes that put rubies, emeralds, and other precious and semi-precious gems in the ground here.

NC-226 West: Penland School of Crafts (MP 331)

In the 1920s, Lucy Morgan, a teacher at a local Episcopal school, and her brother embarked on a mission to help the women of the North Carolina mountains gain some hand in their own economic well-being. Equipping several households in the Penland area with looms, they touched off a local cottage industry in weaving, which quickly centralized and grew into the Penland School, a center for craft instruction and production. Several "folk schools" sprouted in the southern Appalachians in that era, most of them the projects of idealistic Northerners wanting to aid benighted mountaineers. The Penland School, however, is one of the few such institutions that was truly home-grown, as Miss Lucy was herself a child of the rural Carolina highlands. Today, the **Penland School of Crafts** (off Penland Rd., Penland, 828/765-2359, www.penland.org) is an arts instruction center of international renown. More

than 1,000 people, from beginners to professionals, enroll in Penland's one-, two-, and eight-week courses every year to learn about crafts in many different media. Tours of the workshops (Tues. and Thurs. Apr.-Dec., reservations required) are available, and the school operates a beautiful shop, the **Penland Gallery** (Conley Ridge Rd., 828/765-6211, www.penland.org, 10am-5pm Tues.-Sat., noon-5pm Sun. Mar.-Dec.), where visitors can purchase works by many of the school's instructors and students.

Little Switzerland (MP 334)

Little Switzerland earned its name thanks to the views of the surrounding mountains and deep valleys, which are reminiscent, many say, of the foothills of the Swiss Alps. The mountains around here have been mined for years— millennia, if some archaeological findings are correct. Mica, that shiny stone, is found here in abundance, and there's evidence to suggest that Native Americans mined for it here some 2,000 years ago. Desoto is thought to have visited the area around 1540, searching for gold and silver but finding mica instead. Mica was mined here during the Civil War and Reconstruction. In 1895, emerald mining began. Soon Tiffany's and the American Gem & Pear Company had a large mine here. That mine is abandoned today, but gem hunters and rock hounds still find their way inside to see what they can find. And for good reason: In addition to mica and emeralds, mines nearby have produced aquamarines, beryl, garnets, kyanite, and smoky quartz.

History

Little Switzerland was founded in 1910 by Heriot Clarkson, a North Carolina Supreme Court judge and powerful member of the state's Democratic Party. Clarkson held some despicable beliefs that informed the creation of this town, which he saw as a "whites only" village. To this day, there are (thankfully unenforceable) laws on the town's books stating that African Americans cannot own property here.

Clarkson's influence also affected Blue Ridge Parkway construction. Proposed routes had the Parkway detouring to Tennessee near Linville, though some continued along the present-day route. After the route through North Carolina was settled, Clarkson, one of the largest landholders in town, was appalled at the acreage that the National Park Service was seeking. He hired several lawyers and fought for a higher price for his land, getting $575 per acre, nearly 10 times the average paid for land elsewhere. His demands also included an interchange at the Switzerland Inn and a very narrow right of way. Fortunately, Little Switzerland has shaken off the avarice and ill-informed biases of its founders and embraces both the Blue Ridge Parkway and anyone who chooses to travel any part of its length.

Sights
★ Emerald Village

Emerald Village (331 McKinney Mine Rd., Spruce Pine, 800/765-6463, www.emeraldvillage.com, 10am-4pm daily mid-Mar.-Apr., 9am-5pm daily May and Sept.-Oct., 9am-6pm Memorial Day-Labor Day), a can't-miss collection of gem mines and historical attractions, shows the story of Little Switzerland's long mining history. Emerald Village has seven mines to explore, the **North Carolina Mining Museum** (a self-guided underground mine tour, $8 adults, $7 seniors, $6 students), and gem mining (from $10), gold panning ($10-500), and dig-your-own emeralds ($20). The very unusual Black Light Mine Tour is held on select Saturdays ($15 adults, $10 students). This tour is wild, as the minerals shine with otherworldly light under the black light.

★ Grassy Creek Waterfall

An easy hike leads to the pretty **Grassy Creek Waterfall** (trailhead on Grassy Creek Falls Rd., off Chestnut Grove Church Rd. after it passes under the Parkway). Park before the "No Parking Beyond This Point" sign and follow the road on foot about 0.6 mile, then turn at the sign another 0.3 mile to the 30-foot falls. It's mossy and lush, and when there's been rain, the thin sheets of water flowing over the falls are quite lovely.

Food and Accommodations

The ★ **Switzerland Inn** (86 High Ridge Rd., 828/765-2153 or 800/654-4026, www.switzerlandinn.com, $139-299) opened in 1910 and still serves travelers today with accommodations ranging from The Diamondback Motorcycle Lodge (a collection of eight rooms and a central living area catering to motorcyclists) to the luxurious Heidi and Alpine Suites. There are two restaurants on site, the **Fowl Play Pub** (hours vary by season, entrées around $12) and the **Chalet Restaurant** (serving breakfast, lunch, and dinner year-round, hours vary by season, breakfast and lunch under $15, dinner around $18), that dish up some tasty food from pub grub to more refined fine-dining dishes. This inn is simply stunning, so if you want to stay at a place with fabulous views, make reservations early.

Big Lynn Lodge (10860 NC-226A, 828/654-5232, www.biglynnlodge.com, $105-160) is another fixture in the Little Switzerland lodging community. It started in the early 1900s with a collection of cabins on a dahlia farm and has grown into a 42-room lodge. Prices include breakfast and dinner, and it really is a charming little spot to stay.

You can stay and eat at the **Skyline Village Inn & Cavern Tavern** (122 NC-226A, 828/765-9394, www.skylinevillage-inn.com, $80-120). They have 16 rooms and each one is extremely affordable, though in need of some updating. One of the coolest things about this spot is the

Cavern Tavern, a restaurant exclusive to hotel guests. It seems that in the 1940s, a cave under the parking lot was the perfect place for a moonshine still. Today there's no illegal moonshine, though there is a good selection of craft beer. They serve breakfast ($6.50) and dinner (under $12), and both menus are what you'd expect from a mom-and-pop place like this: easy-to-prepare comfort food.

The **Switzerland Café** (9440 NC-226A, 828/765-5289, www.switzerland-cafe.com, 10am-4pm daily Mar.-Nov., under $12) is a combination restaurant and general store, so you can pick up everything from a barbecue sandwich to a souvenir T-shirt. Most of their food is smokehouse inspired, and their trout is surprisingly good.

Crabtree Falls (MP 339.5)

Crabtree Meadows Recreation Area is a small recreation area—only 253 acres—but it's quite scenic. One of the best waterfalls on the Parkway is here, as is a great **camping** area (877/444-6777, www.recreation.gov, $19). The camping area has close to 100 total tent and RV sites. The highlight, though, is the 70-foot Crabtree Falls, easily accessible via a 2.5-mile trail.

★ Crabtree Falls Trail

Distance: 2.5-mile loop
Duration: 1.5-2 hours
Elevation gain: 480 feet
Difficulty: moderate
Trailhead: Crabtree Meadows Campground at MP 339.5

At the parking area, you'll find a trailhead sign and a short spur trail leading to the loop. Once at the loop, turn right and wind your way into a shady cove, down some steep stone steps. You'll cross a bridge that's dry most of the time, but can be wet and slick if the falls are raging or if it has rained recently. When you cross the bridge, you'll find that the trail

has become a bit rougher, and you can hear the falls not far off.

The trail goes through several switchbacks, rock steps, and damp areas before you reach the falls. At the base of the 70-foot falls, there's a bridge with benches, a great spot to sit and look. These falls are particularly photogenic, thanks in no small part to the strange little "island" below the falls. Take shots from the left or right for foolproof angles.

Continuing on the loop, just beyond the falls is the hardest part of the hike—a 200-foot elevation gain in less than a quarter mile. Climb up and catch your breath at the bench on top before heading out. The next section is a long set of stairs that lead to the ridge above.

Follow the ridge for a little way until you arrive at a rocky outcrop with a handrail. You can see the falls from here, barely, but to do so, you have to lean out past the rail, so don't bother. Continue along the trail and begin to descend, crossing a couple of streams as you do. Soon you'll see a trail and sign at an intersection. This leads to the campground, so continue on down the trail and you'll soon find the place where the trail from the parking area met the loop.

Mount Mitchell State Park (MP 355.3)

At 6,684 feet, **Mount Mitchell** (accessible from MP 355.3, near Burnsville, 828/675-4611, www.ncparks.gov) is the highest mountain east of South Dakota. It is the pinnacle of the Black Mountain range, a 15-mile-long J-shaped ridge that was formerly considered one mountain. Now that the various peaks are designated as separate mountains, 6 of them are among the 10 highest in the eastern United States. Elisha Mitchell, for whom the mountain is named, is buried at the summit. He was one of North Carolina's first great scholars, a geologist and botanist who taught at the University of

North Carolina in Chapel Hill. His skill as a scientist is demonstrated by his 1830s calculation of the height of the peak that now bears his name; using the technology of the day, he estimated the height within 12 feet of today's measurement. In the 1850s, he became embroiled in a controversy when Senator Thomas Clingman, one of his former students, disputed the calculation. On a return trip to remeasure Mount Mitchell, Elisha Mitchell fell from the top of a waterfall (now Mitchell Falls) and drowned in the water below. The rivalry recalls the climactic moment when Sherlock Holmes and his nemesis, Dr. Moriarty, fall to their deaths from the top of a waterfall—although in this case, Senator Clingman went on to live another 40 years. He also has a mountain named for him, Clingmans Dome, a mere 41 feet shorter, which glares up at Mount Mitchell from the Tennessee state line.

The best view of the mountain is at Milepost 350. **Mount Mitchell State Park** (MP 355.3, 2388 NC-128, 828/675-4611, www.ncparks.gov, 7am-8pm daily Mar.-Apr., 7am-10pm daily May-Aug., 7am-9pm daily Sept.-Oct., 7am-6pm daily Nov.-Feb.) is not only a place to get an amazing panoramic view—up to 85 miles in clear weather—it also has an education center, a gift shop, and nine **campsites** (877/722-6762, late May-late Oct., $15-23). There is also a **restaurant** (828/675-1024, 10am-9pm daily May-Aug., 10am-8pm daily Sept.-Oct., $15), which is unremarkable to all but hungry hikers.

Mount Mitchell Summit Trail

Distance: 0.3 mile out and back
Duration: 20 minutes
Elevation gain: 40 feet
Difficulty: easy
Trailhead: upper parking lot just below the summit

You can take NC-128 right to the top of Mount Mitchell, some 6,684-feet above sea level, and this hike puts you in the parking lot and leaves you with a very short hike to the observation tower. Park in the lot, then walk up the ramp. It's that easy. If you're able, the better option is to spend the day hiking all the way to the top on the Mount Mitchell Trail. Whichever way you decide to get here, the views are fantastic from the highest peak east of the Mississippi.

Mount Mitchell Trail

Distance: 12 miles out and back
Duration: 6-7 hours
Elevation gain: 3,700 feet
Difficulty: strenuous
Trailhead: Black Mountain Campground off Forest Road 472
Directions: Finding the trailhead is the trickiest part of the hike. Turn off the Parkway at MP 344 and head west on NC-80. Go 2.2 miles and turn left onto Forest Road 472. In 3 miles you'll reach the Black Mountain Campground and the trailhead.

The trail, which is blazed with blue marks, skirts a small nature trail (a loop, if you're interested) and crosses a few streams as it climbs. At 1.5 miles, you'll come to a junction with Higgins Bald Trail; stay right on the Mount Mitchell Trail. You'll cross Setrock Creek at 2.5 miles, then meet up with the Higgins Bald Trail again at 2.7 miles. Continue along the trail and meet up with the Buncombe Horse Range Trail, where you'll turn left up a rocky climb. Near the summit, you'll join with Balsam Nature Trail. Keep climbing until you reach the top of the observation tower.

On the return trip, take a right on the white-blazed Higgins Bald Trail. The detour is short—only 0.3 mile—and the bald is beautiful, as is the waterfall you'll find there. Continue down Mount Mitchell Trail until you arrive back at your car.

Craggy Gardens
(MP 364.6)

Craggy Gardens is one of the most appropriately named spots on the Parkway. The principal features here are the rocky crags studded with rhododendrons, mountain ash, wildflowers, and other rare plants. As with much of Appalachia, this area was settled by Scots and Scots-Irish, and the rugged rocks along the peak reminded them of the craggy mountains back home.

The **Craggy Gardens Visitor Center** (MP 364.6, 10am-5pm daily Memorial Day-Oct.) has information on the flora and fauna of this part of the park, and the folks there can answer just about any question you throw at them. There's a picnic area here, as well as a pair of worthwhile hikes.

Craggy Pinnacle Trail

Distance: 1.4 miles out and back
Duration: 45 minutes-1 hour
Elevation gain: 250 feet
Difficulty: moderate
Trailhead: Craggy Dome parking area at MP 364, north of the visitors center

This is the view you're looking for. The whole of the Parkway is filled with great views, but this is one of the best. As you climb up, the view opens up to give you a 360-degree look at the country around. On a clear day, you can see a dozen notable peaks, maybe more. This trail is easy enough for young hikers; just watch them when you get to the top,

which is somewhat exposed and could be dangerous.

Follow the trail to a junction at 0.3 mile. To the left is a vista that looks over the visitors center, but if you stay straight on the trail, you'll go right to the top for that stunning view you were hiking to see. To return, simply turn around and head back to the car.

Craggy Gardens Trail

Distance: 1.6 miles out and back
Duration: 1 hour
Elevation gain: 150 feet
Difficulty: moderate
Trailhead: Craggy Gardens Visitor Center

The trail begins on the south side of the Craggy Gardens Visitor Center, climbing through one of the most perfectly shaped rhododendron tunnels you'll ever see. Benches and signs naming the plants line the trail. As you leave the woods, you'll reach Craggy Flats and a picnic shelter built in the 1930s by Civilian Conservation Corps workers. From here, there's a short side trail that leads to a stone observation platform. If you continue on this trail, you'll reach the Craggy Gardens Picnic Area in about a half mile. To get back to the car, simply reverse your path and head back down that marvelous rhododendron tunnel.

Asheville and the Southern Blue Ridge

The final leg of the Blue Ridge Parkway is its most rugged and twisty section, but all those curves are worth it. Time and again you're rewarded with stunning vistas—some of which are all the more breathtaking due to the lack of guardrails.

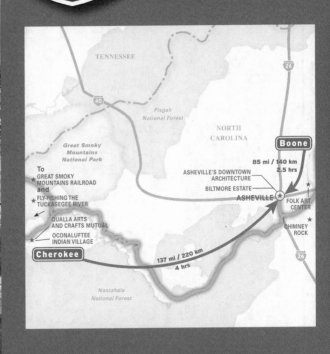

TENNESSEE

Pisgah National Forest

Great Smoky Mountains National Park

NORTH CAROLINA

Boone

85 mi / 140 km
2.5 hrs

ASHEVILLE'S DOWNTOWN ARCHITECTURE

BILTMORE ESTATE

ASHEVILLE

FOLK ART CENTER

To
GREAT SMOKY MOUNTAINS RAILROAD and
FLY-FISHING THE TUCKASEGEE RIVER

QUALLA ARTS AND CRAFTS MUTUAL

OCONALUFTEE INDIAN VILLAGE

CHIMNEY ROCK

Cherokee

137 mi / 220 km
4 hrs

Nantahala National Forest

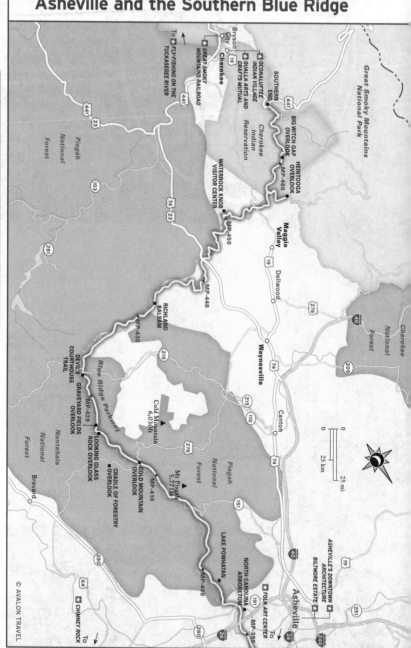

Asheville and the Southern Blue Ridge

To ★ FLY-FISHING ON THE TUCKASEGEE RIVER

★ GREAT SMOKY MOUNTAINS RAILROAD

Bryson City

★ Cherokee

★ OCONALUFTEE INDIAN VILLAGE
★ QUALLA ARTS AND CRAFTS MUTUAL

Cherokee Indian Reservation

Great Smoky Mountains National Park

SOUTHERN END

BIG WITCH GAP OVERLOOK

HEINTOOGA OVERLOOK

MP-460

WATERROCK KNOB VISITOR CENTER

MP-450

Maggie Valley

Dellwood

Pisgah National Forest

RICHLAND BALSAM

MP-440

MP-430

Waynesville

Canton

DEVIL'S COURTHOUSE TRAIL

GRAVEYARD FIELDS OVERLOOK

MP-420

Blue Ridge Parkway

Cold Mountain 6,030ft

ROCK OVERLOOK

LOOKING GLASS OVERLOOK

CRADLE OF FORESTRY OVERLOOK

COLD MOUNTAIN OVERLOOK

MP-410

Mt Pisgah 5,721ft

Pisgah National Forest

Nantahala National Forest

Brevard

MP-400

LAKE POWHATAN

NORTH CAROLINA ARBORETUM

Cherokee National Forest

ASHEVILLE'S DOWNTOWN ARCHITECTURE

BILTMORE ESTATE

FOLK ART CENTER

MP-390

Asheville

To ★ CHIMNEY ROCK

© AVALON TRAVEL

0   25 mi
0   25 km

Highlights

★ **Folk Art Center:** Part gallery, part store, the Folk Art Center displays works like woven baskets and wood carvings by master craftspeople from the southern Appalachians (page 209).

★ **Asheville's Downtown Architecture:** Downtown Asheville is packed with art deco and Beaux-Arts masterpieces (page 212).

★ **Biltmore Estate:** Asheville's most popular attraction is not only an awe-inspiring palace and symbol of the Gilded Age, it's also a collection of great little restaurants, shops, and a popular winery, all in a beautiful riverside setting (page 213).

★ **Chimney Rock:** A natural tower of stone growing out of a mountainside like a rhino's horn, Chimney Rock is the centerpiece of a large park with amazing hiking trails and rock-climbing routes (page 234).

★ **Qualla Arts and Crafts Mutual:** Ancient craft traditions thrive among Cherokee artists in western North Carolina. At the Qualla Mutual, visitors can discover and purchase the work of today's masters (page 261).

★ **Oconaluftee Indian Village:** This living history site leads visitors through a recreated Cherokee village where you can see traditional dances, arts, and crafts performed and made by tribe members (page 261).

★ **Great Smoky Mountains Railroad:** See the Blue Ridge in its deepest summer green or a blaze of autumn color on a rail tour departing from the historic depot in Bryson City (page 265).

★ **Fly-Fishing the Tuckasegee River:** Several outfitters can hook anglers up for a great day on the river, which conveniently flows right through Bryson City (page 266).

Asheville, the largest city in this region but small by many standards, may surprise you with its cosmopolitan flair. Having recently garnered international attention for its award-winning restaurants and breweries, Asheville's food scene has bolstered the city's reputation as an artistic, musical town. The Biltmore Estate, a palatial home built by George Vanderbilt, shows how the wealthy lived in the late 19th and early 20th centuries. The Folk Art Center just outside Asheville showcases traditional southern Appalachian folk art alongside contemporary works.

As the Blue Ridge Parkway wriggles toward Cherokee, you'll pass trailheads and wildflower-filled meadows. Go ahead and stop if you can't resist the lure of a hike. While you're exploring towns like Brevard in Transylvania County, detour into waterfall country, where more than 250 cascades lie within a few miles of one another, just a few minutes from the Parkway.

At the southern end of the Parkway in the town of Cherokee, the ancestral home of the Eastern Band of the Cherokee Nation, you'll encounter a mix of tribal traditions, yesteryear kitsch, and modern luxury. Signs are in English as well as Tsalagi, the Cherokee language, and you're likely to hear Cherokee greetings like *Osiyo* (OH-si-yo) on the street.

Here too are elk, a species recently reintroduced to the region, and the unimaginable biodiversity of the deep mountains. Trout-filled streams run out of the hills and form rivers where whitewater rafters and kayakers challenge nature, and the Great Smoky Mountains Railroad provides unforgettable tours of the landscape. All across this region, you'll find folks who are proud of their heritage and their land. And with this beautiful bounty right outside their doors, how can you help but join them?

Planning Your Time

Plan to spend at least four days in this region. Asheville is a food mecca and Cherokee is so rich in history and culture that you should spend at least a day in each. Both make good overnight stops. Add another day for hiking, camping, or checking out the waterfalls just off the Parkway, and one last day to do what you love. Get a taste for the nightlife in Asheville or visit Harrah's casino or some Cherokee cultural activities before exploring Great Smoky Mountains National Park.

Summer is always a popular time to hit mountain towns on this end of the Blue Ridge Parkway. The elevation and breezes that cross the mountaintops and sweep down coves bring cooler temperatures than you'll find in flatter, lower climes. Pack a light jacket or a long-sleeved shirt, as nighttime temperatures can be a bit too cool for summer garb.

The southern end of the Blue Ridge Parkway is beautiful year-round, but many restaurants, attractions, and accommodations (particularly B&Bs) are seasonal. Check ahead if you're traveling in early spring, late fall, or winter. Of the places that remain open during these times, many operate with limited hours. That said, larger towns like Asheville and, to some extent, Cherokee can see an increase in the number of visitors as weather turns colder. Smaller towns feel the effects of the seasons more strongly.

Driving Considerations

Traveling this stretch of the Parkway can be difficult at certain times of year as weather conditions—snow, ice, extreme fog—can cause road closures. During winter and the earliest and latest parts of spring and fall, it's advisable to check real-time maps of road closures and

Best Restaurants

★ **Buxton Hall Barbecue, Asheville:** Head here for whole hog barbecue and gourmet sides from a James Beard Award nominee (page 227).

★ **Biscuit Head, Asheville:** Tear into awesome biscuits topped with crazy delicious items like fried green tomatoes, sriracha honey, bacon jam, and house-made marmalade (page 227).

★ **Rhubarb, Asheville:** Chef John Fleer and his crew put on a show here that redefines "farm to table" (page 228).

★ **The Admiral, Asheville:** Inside this low-slung cinderblock building are adventurous chefs who aren't afraid to try something new (page 228).

★ **Cucina 24, Asheville:** Innovative Italian is the mainstay at one of Asheville's favorite restaurants, but the wine and cocktail lists will impress as well (page 228).

★ **En la Calle, Asheville:** Contemporary Latin street food meets Asheville's farm-to-table obsession (page 229).

★ **Cúrate, Asheville:** Sample Spanish tapas from one of the most brilliant chefs in North Carolina (page 229).

★ **Hobnob Restaurant, Brevard:** This eatery has a reputation as one of the best restaurants in Brevard (page 247).

★ **The Square Root, Brevard:** Whether you dine on the patio or inside, the food's always seasonal and inventive (page 247).

★ **Frogs Leap Public House, Waynesville:** Southern standards and American classics grace the menu here (page 254).

advisories on the National Park Service website (www.nps.gov/blri).

Getting There

This drive begins northeast of **Asheville** and ends **120 miles** southwest in **Bryson City**, a quaint town on a beautiful river in the Smoky Mountains. You can easily drive this route in an afternoon. Another convenient starting point is **Cherokee**, site of the southern terminus of the Blue Ridge Parkway, only 10 miles from Bryson City.

The nearest **major travel hubs** to this region are Charlotte, North Carolina, and Johnson City, Tennessee.

Car

Asheville lies at the crossroads of **I-40,** North Carolina's primary east-west highway, and **I-26,** a roughly north-south artery through the Southern Highlands. The Blue Ridge Parkway passes by just a few miles from downtown as it moves west-southwest toward Cherokee.

To reach Asheville from **Charlotte,** North Carolina, drive north on US-321 then west on I-40 for 130 miles (two hours). For a slightly more picturesque route, take US-74 west, then I-26 north for 124 miles (two hours, 10 minutes).

To get to Asheville from **Johnson City,** Tennessee, take I-26 south for 60 miles (one hour).

From **Spartanburg,** South Carolina, Asheville is a 70-mile (75-minute) drive north on I-26. To get to Cherokee from **Alcoa,** Tennessee, drive southeast on US-321 then US-441 for 70 miles (two hours).

Fueling Up

These are the most convenient spots to fuel up along this route:

• **MP 382.5,** US-70 less than two miles east or west

Best Accommodations

★ **Sourwood Inn, Asheville:** Tucked high in the hills just outside Asheville, this picturesque inn offers exquisite views and comfy beds (page 230).

★ **ASIA Bed and Breakfast Spa, Asheville:** This small B&B serves one of the best breakfasts in town and has an on-site spa, making for a relaxing stay (page 231).

★ **Grove Park Inn Resort & Spa, Asheville:** Relax in a renowned spa and some truly amazing guest rooms (page 231).

★ **Sunset Motel, Brevard:** This affordable and classic motel is just kitschy enough and the owners and staff are a fun bunch (page 248).

★ **Balsam Mountain Inn, Balsam:** One look at the mountains from the huge porches and you'll know why this inn has been a popular spot since 1908 (page 255).

★ **Harrah's Cherokee Casino Resort, Cherokee:** A fabulous spa, several quality restaurants, comfortable rooms, and a casino set Harrah's apart (page 264).

★ **Panther Creek Cabins, outside Cherokee:** These rustic, comfortable cabins are nestled in the hills away from the bright strip of downtown (page 264).

★ **Folkestone Inn, Bryson City:** Fresh European pastries daily are just one of the charms at this 1920s farmhouse turned inn (page 268).

- **MP 384.7,** US-74A less than three miles south

- **MP 388.8,** US-25 less than one mile south, less than three miles north

- **MP 393.6,** NC-191 less than three miles north

- **MP 411.8,** US-276 less than 10 miles north

- **MP 443.1,** US-74/23 less than three miles east

- **MP 455.7,** US-19 less than three miles east

- **MP 469.1,** US-441 less than one mile south

Air

Asheville is served by **Asheville Regional Airport** (AVL, 61 Terminal Dr., Fletcher, 828/684-2226, www.flyavl. com). The next-closest airport in North Carolina is the **Charlotte Douglas International Airport** (CLT, 5501 Josh Birmingham Pkwy., 704/359-4013, www.cltairport.com), two hours away. Charlotte Douglas is the 10th-largest hub in the United States, with nonstop flights to and from more than 125 destinations worldwide.

In South Carolina, only 80 minutes south of Asheville, is the **Greenville-Spartanburg International Airport** (GSP, 2000 GSP Dr., Greer, South Carolina, 864/877-7426, www.gspairport.com). Airlines serving Greenville-Spartanburg include Allegiant, American Airlines, Delta, Southwest, and United.

The closest airports to Cherokee are the Asheville Regional Airport and the **McGhee Tyson Airport** (TYS, 2055 Alcoa Hwy., Alcoa, Tennessee, 865/342-3000, www.tys.org) in Alcoa, Tennessee, just south of Knoxville, about two hours northwest of Cherokee. Airlines serving McGhee Tyson include Allegiant, American Airlines American Eagle, Delta, United, and Frontier.

Seasons of Color

As you plan your trip, think of the seasons. **Spring wildflowers** begin to appear in late March, peaking in mid- to late-April. Azaleas, mountain laurel, and rhododendrons put on the best show during summer, blooming first in lower elevations, then creeping up the mountains. Flame azalea is a funny plant, peaking in different areas as the microclimates here dictate; they're ablaze with color between April and July. Mountain laurel overlaps some with blooms in May and June, and rhododendrons shows their color in June and July.

Fall colors appear in the opposite order, with the mountaintops the first to show autumn's arrival in early October. The colors bleed down until mid- to late-October and early November, when trees from the foot to the crest of the mountains are alight with color. Summer heat can throw the schedule for springtime blooms and fall colors off a bit, as can rainfall levels. Call the Great Smoky Mountains National Park or check with regional websites to find out how the leaf season is progressing.

Bus and Train
There is a **Greyhound station** (2 Tunnel Rd., 828/253-8451, www.greyhound.com) in Asheville. There is no direct bus or rail service to Cherokee.

★ Folk Art Center
(MP 382)

The **Folk Art Center** (828/298-7928, www.southernhighlandguild.com, 9am-5pm daily, free) is home to the Southern Highland Craft Guild and is one of the most popular stops on this part of the Blue Ridge Parkway. The guild was established in 1930 to preserve the traditional crafts and techniques found in nine states that comprise the southern Appalachians.

There are around 30,000 square feet of space at the Folk Art Center, including three galleries, an auditorium, a research craft library, a small Blue Ridge Parkway information booth, and the Allanstand Craft Shop, the oldest continuously operating craft shop in the United States. Started in 1897 by a Presbyterian missionary, Allanstand is your chance to take home a beautiful piece from some talented Appalachian craftsperson. Though the galleries only take up a portion of the building's footprint, they're exceptional.

Since the 1990s, the Folk Art Center has displayed and sold fine folk art. The center has become quite discerning, so only the best pieces are on display or for sale.

There is a permanent collection of some 2,400 pieces of art and assorted artifacts, mainly focused on the decorative arts of the southern Appalachians, on display year-round. Pieces include hand-stitched quilts in traditional patterns like double wedding ring and log cabin; delicate lace; intricate needlework tapestries; pine needle, river rush, and willow baskets; musical instruments; clay pots and vessels; and even toys, every one made from natural materials. If you find yourself wondering, "How'd they make that?" stick around and ask an artist. Every day, one or more members of the guild is on hand to demonstrate their craft at the entrance to the Folk Art Center. They may be whittling away at a chunk of wood with their pocketknife, spinning wool into yarn or weaving, or tying brooms. No matter what they're doing, they're happy to talk to you and explain their process and the history of their craft.

Folk Art Center ADA Trail
Distance: 0.4-mile loop
Duration: 10-15 minutes
Elevation gain: 50 feet
Difficulty: easy

Trailhead: Folk Art Center parking area, MP 382

This fully **wheelchair-accessible** pathway starts at the front of the Folk Art Center parking lot, follows the **Mountains-to-Sea Trail** for a short bit, and loops around to put you back where you started. Along the way, interpretive signs note a number of trees, particularly those trees used in making traditional crafts like the ones inside the Folk Art Center.

As you leave the parking lot, join with the Mountains-to-Sea Trail until you come to an intersection; keep to the right. Follow the trail another 0.1 mile, where the Mountains-to-Sea Trail separates. You'll stay on the main trail, which narrows a bit not far from here. A quarter mile in, you'll get to another trail intersection; this leads to another area of the parking lot, but to get back to the starting point, stay left and continue on another 0.2 mile.

Asheville (MP 382.5)

Asheville is filled with a lively assortment of chefs, artists, musicians, dancers, and other creative sorts whose collective efforts have earned the city the moniker "Paris of the South." Though it sounds trite, it's true; this progressive city has made itself open to change and outside influence while retaining a strong grasp on its roots.

Situated around the confluences of the Swannanoa (swan-uh-NO-uh) and French Broad Rivers and a mountain stagecoach road, Asheville served as a trading post and regional center in its early days. Commerce found its way here throughout the 18th and 19th centuries. When rail lines began to bring vacationers to Asheville in the late 1800s, the town was discovered by the rich. The mild summer climate and fresh mountain air helped turn Asheville into a summer retreat for wealthy industrialists, among them George Vanderbilt, who

built his mountain home, the Biltmore, just south of downtown.

The mountains around Asheville are thick with centuries-old folk art and music. Events like the thoroughly modern Moog Fest, which pays homage to the godfather of electronic music, Robert Moog, are part of the reason Asheville's music scene is so lively, but much of the credit goes to the tireless buskers you'll see around town, picking banjos and playing spoons, washtub basses, and even theremins. Galleries and studios around town display folk carving and weavings as well as contemporary works. A number of entrenched arts organizations like the **Southern Highland Craft Guild** (www.southernhighlandguild.org) help preserve traditional arts, while places like the River Arts District and a number of small guilds, groups, and galleries support contemporary artists.

All of this makes Asheville feel like a counterculture center. Elements of Haight-Ashbury circa-1968 mix with Woodstock, the Grand Ole Opry, Andy Warhol's Factory, and a beatnik vibe, but with better food, to create an electric atmosphere.

Getting There and Around
Car
From Charlotte, take I-85 South and I-26 West, or take slightly more picturesque US-74 West. Either way, the trip is about 125 miles (two hours, 10 minutes). From Knoxville, Asheville is 115 miles (about two hours) east on the quickest route (I-40); or you can take the scenic route through the national park and Cherokee, adding a few more miles and an hour of drive time.

Air
Asheville Regional Airport (AVL, 61 Terminal Dr., Fletcher, 828/684-2226, www.flyavl.com) is 20 minutes south of the city on I-26. **ART** (www.ashevillenc.gov, $1), Asheville's public bus system, connects the airport with downtown

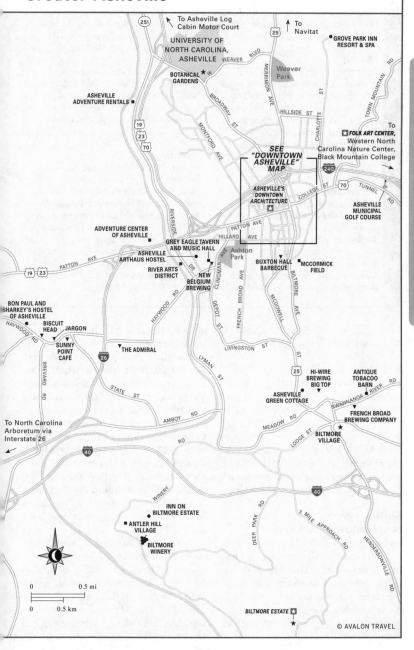

Greater Asheville

One Day in Asheville

Only have one day to devote to Asheville? Here are the city's must-see, must-do, and must-eat attractions.

Morning

Start the day with some great breakfast grub from **Biscuit Head** in West Asheville. Spend the morning **exploring boutiques and galleries** downtown like those in the **Grove Arcade** and **Woolworth Walk,** taking time to stroll by examples of Asheville's notable **architecture,** including the First Baptist Church and the Jackson Building.

Afternoon

At lunchtime, linger downtown for the **Eating Asheville** food tour, which begins at the Grove Arcade. **Buxton Hall Barbecue,** on the South Slope just a few blocks from downtown, and **Cúrate,** in the heart of downtown, are other good lunch options. After lunch, get a new perspective on the city by boarding the

LaZoom Comedy Tour bus, floating down the French Broad River with **Zen Tubing,** or zip-lining over the forests north of Asheville with **Navitat.**

Alternatively, spend the afternoon at the **Biltmore Estate,** a three-mile drive from downtown. Enjoy lunch at the **Stable Café,** but make sure to leave at least three hours to tour the house and gardens before they close at 4:30pm (3:30pm in winter).

Evening

Head back downtown for the evening, kicking the night off with beers from **Hi-Wire** or **Burial Beer.** When you're ready for dinner, try **The Admiral** for inventive American cuisine or **Chai Pani** for Indian. Walk dinner off with a stroll—a number of buskers will entertain you. Grab a nightcap at **Nightbell** or a chocolate at **French Broad Chocolates.** If you're in town on a Friday, check out the drum circle at **Pritchard Park.**

Asheville. A taxi from the airport to downtown will run around $45.

Bus

There is a **Greyhound station** (2 Tunnel Rd., 828/253-8451, www.greyhound.com) in Asheville. Asheville's extensive public bus system, **ART** (www.ashevillenc.gov, 5:30am-10:30pm Mon.-Sat., 8am-6pm Sun., $1, $0.50 seniors), connects most major points in the metropolitan area, including the airport, with downtown. See the website for routes and schedules.

Sights
★ Downtown Architecture

As beautiful as Asheville's natural environment may be, the striking architecture is just as attractive. The Montford neighborhood, a contemporary of the Biltmore, is a mixture of ornate Queen Anne houses and craftsman-style bungalows. The Grove Park Inn, a huge luxury hotel, was built in 1913 and is decked

out with rustic architectural devices intended to make vacationing New Yorkers and wealthy people feel like they were roughing it. In downtown Asheville is a large concentration of art deco buildings on the scale of Miami Beach. Significant structures dating to the boom before the Great Depression include the **Buncombe County Courthouse** (60 Court Plaza), built 1927-1929, the 1925 **First Baptist Church** (Oak St. and Woodfin St.), the **S&W Cafeteria** (56 Patton Ave.), and the **Public Service Building** (89-93 Patton Ave.), both built in 1929, and the **Grove Arcade** (1 Page Ave.) which was built 1926-1929.

The **Jackson Building** (22 S. Pack Sq.), built 1923-1924, is a fine example of neo-Gothic architecture with a disturbing backstory. According to legend, on the day of the stock market crash in 1929 that started the Great Depression, one of the wealthiest men in Asheville lost it all and leaped to his death from the building.

Downtown Asheville

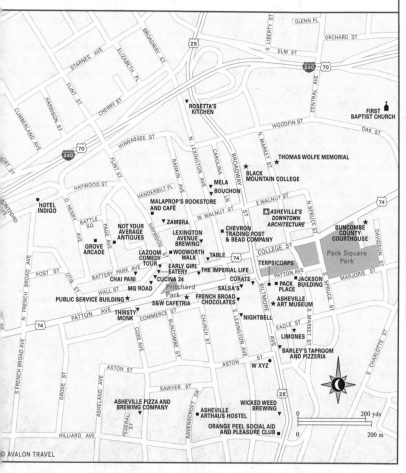

GLENN PL
S LIBERTY ST
ORCHARD ST
S ELM ST
GLENN PL
STARNES AVE
BROADWAY ST
ELIZABETH PL
25
240 70
CENTRAL AVE
FLINT ST
CHERRY ST
WOODFIN ST
OAK ST
FIRST BAPTIST CHURCH
HARRISON AVE
CUMBERLAND AVE
ROSETTA'S KITCHEN
PORT ST
70
HIAWASSEE ST
240
FLINT ST
N LEXINGTON AVE
CAROLINA LN
BROADWAY
N MARKET ST
THOMAS WOLFE MEMORIAL
HAYWOOD ST
RANKIN AVE
N SPRUCE ST
74
MELA
BOUCHON
BLACK MOUNTAIN COLLEGE
HOTEL INDIGO
O HENRY AVE
BATTLE SQ
VANDERBILT PL
MALAPROP'S BOOKSTORE AND CAFÉ
E WALNUT ST
ASHEVILLE'S DOWNTOWN ARCHITECTURE
BUNCOMBE COUNTY COURTHOUSE
PAGE AVE
HAYWOOD ST
ZAMBRA
W WALNUT ST
CHEVRON TRADING POST & BEAD COMPANY
DAVIDSON ST
NOT YOUR AVERAGE ANTIQUES
LEXINGTON AVENUE BREWING
GROVE ARCADE
LAZOOM COMEDY TOUR
WODWORTH WALK
TABLE
74
COLLEGE ST
Pack Square Park
POST OT ST
N FRENCH BROAD AVE
BATTERY PARK AVE
EARLY GIRL EATERY
THE IMPERIAL LIFE
TERPSICORPS
MARJORIE ST
CHAI PANI
CUCINA 24
CURÀTE
PATTON AVE
S SPRUCE ST
MG ROAD
Pritchard Park
SALSA'S
PACK PLACE
JACKSON BUILDING
OTIS ST
PUBLIC SERVICE BUILDING
S&W CAFETRIA
FRENCH BROAD CHOCOLATES
BILTMORE AVE
ASHEVILLE ART MUSEUM
WALL ST
THIRSTY MONK
COMMERCE ST
74
PATTON AVE
NIGHTBELL
S MARKET ST
S CHARLOTTE ST
N FRENCH BROAD AVE
COKE AVE
BUNCOMBE ST
S LEXINGTON AVE
CHURCH ST
EAGLE ST
LIMONES
ASTON ST
BARLEY'S TAPROOM AND PIZZERIA
GROVE ST
ASHELAND AVE
ASTON ST
ST
W XYZ
SAWYER ST
25
ASHEVILLE PIZZA AND BREWING COMPANY
RAVENSCROFT DR
WICKED WEED BREWING
0   200 yds
FEDERAL ST
ASHEVILLE ARTHAUS HOSTEL
0   200 m
HILLIARD AVE
ORANGE PEEL SOCIAL AID AND PLEASURE CLUB

© AVALON TRAVEL

Three or four (depending on who's telling the story) more of Asheville's wealthiest followed suit. What is known to be true is that there's a bull's-eye built into the sidewalk in front of the building as a morbid monument to the story.

★ Biltmore Estate

Much of downtown Asheville dates to the 1920s, but the architectural crown jewel, the **Biltmore Estate** (1 Approach Rd., 800/411-3812, www.biltmore.com,

8:30am-6:30pm daily, $55-65 adults, $27.50-32.50 children ages 10-16, free ages 9 and under, additional fees for activities), predates that by decades. It was built in the late 1800s for owner George Vanderbilt, grandson of Gilded Age tycoon Cornelius Vanderbilt. Like many of his wealthy Northern contemporaries, George Vanderbilt was first introduced to North Carolina when he traveled to Asheville for the mountain air and nearby hot springs. He found himself so awestruck by the land that he amassed a tract of land south of Asheville where he would build his "country home." He engaged celebrity architect Richard Morris Hunt to build the manor, and because the land and the views reminded them of the Loire Valley, they planned to build the home in the style of a 16th-century French château. Vanderbilt also hired the esteemed Frederick Law Olmsted, creator of New York City's Central Park, to design the landscape for the grounds, gardens, and surrounding forest, a project nine times the size of the New York project for which Olmsted is famous. The resulting Biltmore Estate was the largest privately owned home in the country at the time of its completion.

A three-mile-long approach road leads through manicured forests, revealing bits of the landscape and hiding the house until you are upon it, creating a sense of drama for arriving visitors. While the Biltmore Estate's original 125,000 acres are now greatly diminished—the estate comprises a little more than 8,000 acres today—it's easy to see just how big it was: If you stand on the South Terrace and look south and west, everything in view was once part of the estate. A large tract of the land was sold to the federal government and has become part of the Pisgah National Forest; what remains is immaculately manicured.

Construction of the home was done primarily between 1888 and 1895, though there were a number of projects that continued up through World War II (when part of the home was turned into a bunker to store part of the National Gallery of Art's collection). Many are astounded at how long it took to complete the home, but consider this: Approximately 5,000 tons of stone were used to build it, there are 65 fireplaces and more than 250 rooms, the square footage is equal to nearly four acres, and the Banquet Hall is large enough to fit a 35-foot Christmas tree. For its time, the Biltmore was a technological marvel, with electricity,

the Biltmore Estate

elevators, central heat, and hot water. In the basement, there's a heated pool, a gymnasium, and a bowling alley. But as astounding as the building itself may be, it's nothing compared to the art displayed here. There are paintings by Renoir, Whistler, and Sargent; a collection of European antiques including Napoleon's chess set; and room upon room of masterwork in tiling, woodworking and carving, masonry, and stone carving.

George Vanderbilt found the concept of a self-sustaining estate appealing, and he included in the estate a working farm with crops, herds of cattle, a dairy, and all the farmers and workers required for such an operation. The Asheville neighborhood known as **Biltmore Village** was part of this mountain empire. If Vanderbilt stepped onto his estate today, he'd be happy to find that his vision endures. A vineyard (not open to the public) produces grapes that are processed at the estate's winery; a livestock breeding program produces fine stock; and a farm supplies more than 70 percent of the seasonal and specialty vegetables for the estate's restaurants. Visitors can eat, shop, explore, and relax without leaving the grounds, and there's easily enough here to fill a weekend.

Today the **Biltmore Winery** in **Antler Hill Village** operates in the estate's former dairy, vestiges of which include the industrial-farm rafters in the tasting room and the tile floor (designed for easy cleanup). Daily tours and complimentary wine tastings allow visitors to sample some award-winning wines and see how they're made. More than 500,000 people visit the tasting room annually, so expect a wait if you're here in high season. Tastings include something on the order of 20 wines (don't worry; they're small pours). You can also experience the Premium Wine Tasting ($3/pour or three pours for $8, complimentary for Biltmore Wine Club Members) of Biltmore's reserve and sparkling wines; there are also daily tastings of bubbly wine ($18) and pairings of red wine and chocolate ($20).

Antler Hill Village is also home to **Cedric's,** a brewery named after a beloved family dog, as well as a small museum, a souvenir shop, and a green to relax on. **River Bend Farm** is a beautiful compound that was once the hub of the estate's farming operation but now stands as a showpiece for traditional period crafts like woodworking and blacksmithing.

The **Equestrian Center** gives lessons and provides the opportunity to ride more than 80 miles of equestrian trails, many with sweeping views of the estate and glimpses of the main house that will take your breath away. Other ways to tour the estate include carriage rides; paved bike trails and mountain bike trails; canoes, kayaks, and rafts (the French Broad River bisects the estate); Segways; and, of course, on foot. You can even challenge your driving skills at the **Land Rover Experience Driving School.**

Most of the house is open to visitors on self-guided tours, while other

sections—like the roof and some servants' areas—are accessible on behind-the-scenes tours. Admission cost for the Biltmore Estate varies by season and includes the house, gardens, and winery; activities such as horseback riding, rafting, and behind-the-scenes tours cost extra. Special events such as the Christmas Candlelight Tour (Nov.-Dec.) also have additional fees. Parking is free, and a complimentary shuttle takes you from parking lots to the house.

Botanical Gardens at Asheville

The **Botanical Gardens at Asheville** (151 W. T. Weaver Blvd., adjacent to UNC-Asheville campus, 828/252-5190, www.ashevillebotanicalgardens.org, dawn-dusk daily, by donation) is a 10-acre preserve for the region's increasingly threatened native plant species. Laid out in 1960 by landscape architect Doan Ogden, the gardens are an ecological haven. The many "rooms" are planted to reflect different environments of the mountains, including the Wildflower Trail, the Heath Cove, and the Fern and Moss Trail. Spring blooms peak in mid-April, but the gardens are an absolutely lovely and visually rich place to visit any time of year. Because of its serious mission of plant preservation, neither pets nor bicycles are allowed. Admission is free, but because the facility is entirely supported by donations, your contribution will have a real impact. There is also a **visitors center** and **gift shop** (noon-4pm daily Mar.; 10am-4pm Mon.-Sat., noon-4pm Sun. Apr.-Oct.; noon-4pm daily Nov.-early Dec.).

Western North Carolina Nature Center

Asheville, and western North Carolina generally, tend to be very ecologically conscious, as reflected in the **Western North Carolina Nature Center** (75 Gashes Creek Rd., 828/259-8092, www.wildwnc.org, 10am-5pm daily, $11 adults, $10 seniors ages 65 and up, $7 children ages 3-15, free ages 2 and under, discount for Asheville residents). On the grounds of an old zoo—don't worry; it's not depressing—wild animals that are unable to survive in the wild due to injury or having been raised as pets live in wooded habitats on public display. This is the place to see some of the mountains' rarest species: cougars, wolves, coyotes, bobcats, and even the elusive hellbender. What's a hellbender, you ask? Come to the nature center to find out.

Black Mountain College

Considering the history of Black Mountain College from a purely numerical standpoint, one might get the false impression that this little institution's brief, odd life was a flash in the pan. In its 23 years of operation, Black Mountain College had just 1,200 students, only 55 of whom actually completed their degrees. But between 1933 and 1956, the unconventional school demonstrated an innovative model of education and community life.

The educational program was almost devoid of structure. Students had no set course schedule or requirements; they lived and farmed with the faculty, and no sense of hierarchy was permitted to separate students and teachers. Most distinguished as a school of the arts, Black Mountain College hired Josef Albers as its first art director when the Bauhaus icon fled Nazi Germany. Willem de Kooning taught here for a time, as did Buckminster Fuller, who began his design of the geodesic dome while he was in residence. Albert Einstein and William Carlos Williams were among the roster of guest lecturers. I had the honor of working with and befriending poet Robert Creeley, one of the few people to get a degree here, and who taught here briefly before the school shut down in 1956, partly due to the prevailing anti-left climate of that decade.

The **Black Mountain College Museum and Arts Center** (56 Broadway,

828/350-8484, www.blackmountaincollege.org, 11am-5pm Wed.-Mon., free), an exhibition space and resource center devoted to the lauded college, is located in downtown Asheville. The downtown location keeps the spirit of the college alive by exposing more visitors to its historic and inspired-by-the-legacy contemporary works.

Entertainment and Events
Nightlife
Bars and Clubs
Sovereign Remedies (29 N. Market St., 828/919-9518, www.sovereignremedies.com, 4pm-2am Tues.-Thurs., 10am-3pm and 4pm-2am Fri.-Mon.) has quickly become a go-to for Asheville's cocktail lovers and those hankering for a small, delicious plate of food. Between the bartenders and some local foragers, Sovereign Remedies stays stocked with wild herbs, berries, fruit, and roots used to make cocktails or bitters, infuse or macerate various liquors, and create shrubs (drinking vinegars).

The Double Crown (375 Haywood Rd., 828/575-9060, www.thedoublecrown.com, 5pm-2am daily) has all the trappings of a dive bar but serves legitimately good cocktails. They have an exceptional bourbon list, and the requisite beer selection stretches far beyond that of a tiny neighborhood bar. In addition to drinks, The Double Crown always has something going on: DJs (spinning actual records), karaoke, and live musical acts ranging from rock and rockabilly to country, soul, and gospel. It's well worth a stop, whether to sample some top-shelf bourbon, a cocktail, or a bottle of suds.

And now for something completely different: a board-game café. **Well Played** (58 Wall St., 828/232-7375, www.wellplayedasheville.com, 2pm-10pm Mon.-Wed., 2pm-1am Thurs.-Fri., 11am-1am Sat., 11am-10pm Sun.) has more than 500 board games from classics to some that are just out of the wrapper, plus cheap beer, wine, coffee, and food. If you have

a hard time deciding on what to play, don't worry: Games masters can help you choose the right game.

The vibe at **Banks Ave.** (32 Banks Ave., 828/785-1458, www.32banksave.com, 4pm-2am Mon.-Fri., 2pm-2am Sat., 1pm-2am Sun.) is of the "I don't give a damn, I'm having fun" variety. Graffiti on the walls, a Nintendo 64, impromptu pizza parties and cookouts, and odd holiday parties (like the Dead Celebrity-themed Halloween costume contest) bear witness to the laid-back attitude. For a real taste of how freewheeling this bar can be, ask one of the bartenders about their former name, Public School, and why they changed it.

Nightbell (32 S. Lexington Ave., 828/575-0375, www.thenightbell.com, 5pm-late Tues.-Sun.) is the latest from Katie Button, a 2014 nominee for the James Beard Rising Star Chef of the Year Award and one of the finest chefs in Asheville. This speakeasy-esque bar serves sophisticated, imaginative cocktails and some mighty fine nosh.

Brewpubs and Taprooms
Asheville has earned the title of Beer City, USA, a handful of times since the title was first created in 2009. The beer scene here is off the hook. It seems like there's a brewery on every corner (or one planning to open there next month) and experimental brewers are introducing new styles, funky ingredients, and any little twist they can to get people talking. Loyal locals and pint hounds from all over frequent Asheville's bars, breweries, and pubs.

New Belgium Brewing (21 Craven St., 828/333-6900, www.newbelgium.com) opened a 500,000-barrel brewery in Asheville in 2016. This huge operation will be the company's East Coast brewing headquarters for the foreseeable future, and the community has welcomed them with open arms. The facility includes a giant brewery and the **AVL Liquid Center** (11am-8pm Mon.-Sat., noon-8pm Sun.),

more commonly known as a tasting room. Perched on a bluff overlooking the French Broad River, New Belgium hosts food trucks and events, drawing thirsty crowds. In the Liquid Center, they pour favorites like Fat Tire and Voodoo Ranger IPA, but also a nice slate of sours and special releases.

Hi-Wire Brewing (828/738-2448, www.hiwirebrewing.com) has a location on the **South Slope** (197 Hilliard Ave., 4pm-11pm Mon.-Thurs., 2pm-1am Fri., noon-1am Sat., 1pm-10pm Sun.) as well as a spot near Biltmore Village they call the **Big Top** (2 Huntsman Pl., 4pm-10pm Mon.-Thurs., 3pm-midnight Fri., noon-midnight Sat., 1pm-10pm Sun.; tours 5pm and 6pm Fri., hourly 2pm-5pm Sat., and 2pm and 3pm Sun.). They focus on lagers, pale ales, and IPAs, but their winter brew, the Strongman Coffee Milk Stout, is a local favorite. At the Big Top, **Foothills Local Meats** (2 Huntsman Pl., 828/216-2966, www.foothillslocalmeats.com, 4pm-9pm Mon.-Thurs., 11am-10pm Fri., noon-10pm Sat., $5-12) has a food truck where they serve burgers, an unbelievable Cuban sandwich, house-made hot dogs, tallow fries, and poutine.

Burial Beer Co. (40 Collier Ave., 828/475-2739, www.burialbeer.com, 2pm-10pm Mon.-Thurs., noon-10pm Fri.-Sun.) produces some of Asheville's most exciting beers from its brewery/taproom on the south side of town. With a dozen taps open at any given time, Burial is able to show off its creativity. You'll find a lot of saisons and farmhouse ales on tap, as well as dubbels and Belgian-style stouts, but there's no shortage of IPAs, pilsners, blonde ales and other crisp, golden brews to taste. If you're here and you're hungry, **Salt & Smoke** (5pm-10pm Tues.-Fri., noon-10pm Sat., noon-3pm Sun., $4-16) has set up their mobile kitchen in the

Top to bottom: Asheville's Jackson Building; the gardens on the Biltmore Estate; New Belgium Brewing, one of the largest breweries in Asheville.

patio area, where you can get mushroom toast, rabbit wings (like chicken wings but they're rabbit legs), sandwiches, *moules frites* (mussels and fries), and a great charcuterie board.

Located in an old warehouse in the River Arts District, **Wedge Brewing Company** (37 Paynes Way, Ste. 001, 828/505-2792, www.wedgebrewing. com, noon-10pm daily) has more than a dozen brews on tap, including pale ales, pilsners, and a Russian imperial stout flavored with raspberries. Their strong relationship with area food trucks makes this a great hangout for local beer and local grub with local beer enthusiasts any evening.

Catawba Brewing (32 Banks Ave., 828/552-3934, www.catawbabrewing. com, 2pm-10pm Mon.-Thurs., noon-11pm Fri.-Sat., noon-10pm Sun.) has an excellent taproom on Asheville's South Slope (right next to the phenomenal Buxton Hall Barbecue) where they pour White Zombie (a white ale), Hopness Monster (an IPA), Friki Tiki (a blood orange IPA), and a raft of special and seasonal brews.

To sample a variety of Asheville's great microbreweries, join a tour from **Asheville Brews Cruise** (828/545-5181, www.ashevillebrewscruise.com, from $60). The enthusiastic beer experts will shuttle you from brewery to brewery in the Brews Cruise van to sample some beer, learn about the growth of Asheville's beer scene, and gain some insight into the art and craft of brewing. On the tour, you'll visit **Asheville Pizza and Brewing Company** (675 Merrimon Ave., 828/254-1281, http://ashevillebrewing.com, 11am-midnight or later daily), where you can start off the evening with one of this pizzeria, microbrewery, and movie house's tasty beers and fortify yourself for the evening by filling up on good pizza. The **French Broad Brewing Company** (828/277-0222, www.frenchbroadbrewery.com, 1pm-8pm daily) is another popular local nightspot that has

grown up around a first-rate beer-making operation, where you can choose from a varied menu that includes signature pilsners, lagers, and ales while listening to some good live music. The third destination on the cruise is Asheville's first microbrewery, the **Highland Brewing Company** (12 Old Charlotte Hwy., Ste. H, 828/299-3370, www.highlandbrewing.com, tasting room 3pm-9pm Mon.-Thurs., noon-10pm Fri.-Sat., noon-6pm Sun, tours daily). They've been making beer and raking in awards for well over a decade, and on first sip you'll understand why they're one of the Southeast's favorite breweries.

Urban Orchard Cider Company (210 Haywood Rd., 828/774-5151, www.urbanorchardcider.com, 2pm-10pm Mon., 2pm-11pm Tues.-Thurs., noon-midnight Fri.-Sat., noon-10pm Sun.) is part of a new trend in craft booze: cider. Theirs is like no other cider you know, with offerings that include the Sidra Del Diablo cider with smoked habanero pepper, the Ginger Champagne cider with delicate bubbles and a ginger infusion, or the Saison, cider fermented with saison yeast.

Live Music

Great live music is the rule in Asheville—not just national touring acts, but regional and local bands that give the national acts stiff competition on any given night. Everywhere you turn, you'll find buskers on street corners, solo guitarists in cafés, or a bluegrass trio set up on a restaurant's deck; at **Pritchard Park** (at Patton Ave., Haywood St., and College St.), a huge drum circle forms every Friday night. There are also formal music venues where you can hear rock, jam bands, bluegrass, funk, blues, country, rockabilly, alt-country, mountain swing, old-time music, electronica, and too many other genres to name.

A favorite spot for live music is the **Orange Peel Social Aid and Pleasure Club** (101 Biltmore Ave., 828/398-1837, www.theorangepeel.net, noon-midnight or later daily). They're billed as "the nation's premier live music hall and concert venue," and they can back that up with some powerful acts taking the stage, including Bob Dylan, Smashing Pumpkins, Bruce Hornsby, Mickey Hart of Grateful Dead fame, Mike Gordon from Phish, Chvrches, Beastie Boys, Flaming Lips, and My Morning Jacket. The Orange Peel is a cool concert hall with a big dance floor, great sound, and great history.

One of the best venues in town for roots music and eclectic small bands is the **Grey Eagle Tavern and Music Hall** (185 Clingman Ave., 828/232-5800, www.thegreyeagle.com). It's a small space set up more like a listening room than a bar or club, meaning folks come to listen to the music and interact with the performer rather than grab a beer and hop to the next bar. While you're there, have a bite from **The Grey Eagle Taqueria** (828/271-7987, 11am-late daily, $3-12), where the menu is small but tasty.

Performing Arts
Ballet
Asheville's noteworthy ballet company, **Terpsicorps** (2 S. Pack Sq., 828/257-4530, http://terpsicorps.org) performs for two brief but brilliant runs in the summer. Terpsicorps takes advantage of what is normally a slow season for other companies and hires some of the country's best dancers for a short-term stint in Asheville. Summer productions usually have three-night runs, so tickets sell out fast.

Comedy
You may notice a giant purple bus zipping through the streets around Asheville, laughter and bubbles (yes, bubbles) coming from the windows. That's the **LaZoom Comedy Tour** (info and tickets at 14 Battery Park Ave., tickets and departures from 76 Biltmore Ave., 828/225-6932, www.lazoomtours.com, from $23, must be at least age 13), delivering tours big in history and hilarity. The tour guides are

outrageous—they're some of Asheville's weirdest (in a good way) people—and you'll learn a thing or two (some history, a joke you may or may not want to tell your mom). They also offer the Haunted Comedy Tour (departing from 92 Patton Ave., $21), which adds in a supernatural note and tales of some of Asheville's spectral denizens. The Band & Beer Bus Tour ($31) departs from Tasty Beverage (162 Coxe Ave.) to visit a trio of area breweries for samples and some live local music.

The Altamont Theatre (18 Church St., 828/782-3334, www.thealtamont.com, show times and ticket prices vary) calls itself "Asheville's Best Listening Room," and they may be right. They host a variety of musical acts (country, soul, jazz, bluegrass, instrumental progressive space rock—you name it), spoken-word performances, and comedians. Their comedy and improv shows are both smart and hilarious; comedian Cliff Cash, one of the funniest rising stars in the South, performs here on the regular. Since Asheville doesn't have a dedicated comedy club, The Altamont gladly fills that role.

Festivals and Events
Twice yearly, in late July and late October, the Southern Highland Craft Guild hosts the **Craft Fair of the Southern Highlands** (U.S. Cellular Center, 87 Haywood St., www.southernhighlandguild.org, 10am-6pm Thurs.-Sat., 10am-5pm Sun., $8 adults, under age 12 free). Since 1948, this event has brought much-deserved attention to the guild's more than 900 members, who live and work throughout the Appalachian Mountains. Hundreds of craftspeople participate in the event, selling all sorts of handmade items.

August's **Mountain Dance and Folk Festival** (828/258-6101, ext. 345, www.folkheritage.org, ticket prices vary) is the nation's longest-running folk festival, an event founded in the 1920s by musician and folklorist Bascom Lamar Lunsford to celebrate the heritage of his native Carolina mountains. Musicians and dancers from western North Carolina perform at the downtown Diana Wortham Theater at Pack Place for three nights each summer. Also downtown, many of the same artists can be heard on Saturday evening at the city's **Shindig on the Green concert series** (Martin Luther King Jr. Park, 50 Martin Luther King Jr. Dr., www.folkheritage.org, July-Aug.), which runs from July through August.

The biggest of Asheville's festivals and fairs (or at least the most anticipated), is the annual **Warren Haynes Christmas Jam** (www.xmasjam.com, mid-Dec.). Warren Haynes, longtime guitarist for The Allman Brothers Band, founding member of Government Mule, and Asheville native, invites a who's-who of musical acts to perform a benefit concert for Habitat for Humanity. The acts are generally biggies in the rock/jam world as well as bands on the rise. Buy tickets in advance, as the Christmas Jam tends to sell out quickly. In addition to the general admission tickets (around $70), there are VIP packages ($399-699) that allow access to a side-stage viewing area, pre-show shows, the Christmas Jam Friends & Family lounge and bar, a gift bag, and more.

Shopping
Shopping Centers and Districts
Grove Arcade

One of Asheville's shopping highlights is the 1929 **Grove Arcade** (1 Page Ave., 828/252-7799, www.grovearcade.com), a beautiful and storied piece of architecture that is now a chic shopping and dining destination in the heart of downtown. The expansive Tudor Revival building, ornately filigreed inside and out in ivory-glazed terra-cotta, was initially planned as the base of a 14-story building, a skyscraper by that day's standard.

There are some fantastic galleries and boutiques, including **Mountain Made** (828/350-0307, www.mtnmade.com, 10am-6pm Mon.-Sat., noon-5pm Sun.), a gallery celebrating contemporary art

created in and inspired by the mountains around Asheville. Another favorite is **Alexander & Lehnert** (828/254-2010, 10am-6pm Mon.-Sat.), which showcases the work of two talented jewelers with different styles—Lehnert takes an architectural approach to designs, and Alexander chooses organic forms as inspiration. Not all stores in the Grove Arcade sell fine art and jewelry: At **Asheville NC Home Crafts** (828/350-7556, www.asheville-homecrafts.com, 10am-6pm Mon.-Sat., noon-5pm Sun.) you can buy specialty yarn, patterns, hooks, and needles for all sorts of knitting, weaving, and crocheting projects, or you can buy a piece made by local artists. **Battery Park Book Exchange & Champagne Bar** (828/252-0020, 11am-9pm Sun.-Thurs., 11am-late Fri.-Sat.) has two things that go great together in a relaxed atmosphere: wine and books. Outside the Grove Arcade, a row of shaded stalls houses many great artisans selling everything from soap to miniature topiaries.

River Arts District
Along the Swannanoa River, many of Asheville's old warehouses and industrial buildings have been transformed into studio spaces, galleries, restaurants, and breweries in an area known as the **River Arts District** (828/552-4723, www.riverartsdistrict.com). More than 160 artists have working studios here, and twice a year, during the first weekend of June and November, nearly every artist in the district opens their studios to the public for a two-day **Studio Stroll.** On the second Saturday of each month, some of the studios (they rotate based on medium, so one month may be photography, the next clay, and so on) are open for **A Closer Look,** a day of artist demonstrations, classes, workshops, and creative activities.

Some studios are open daily, among them **Jonas Gerard Fine Art** (240 Clingman Ave., 828/350-7711, www.jonasgerard.com, 10am-6pm daily), where the namesake artist specializes in abstract art that uses vivid colors and unusual composition to draw the viewer in. He works across many media, so there's a lot to see. **Odyssee Center for Ceramic Arts** (236-238 Clingman Ave., 828/285-0210, www.odysseyclayworks.com, 10am-6pm daily) is full of sculptors and teachers. Part of their mission is to promote artistic appreciation and advancement of ceramic arts; they hold regular classes, workshops, and talks led by master ceramic artists.

At the 1910 **Cotton Mill Studios** (122 Riverside Dr., 718/414-9651, hours vary), several painters work alongside potters and jewelers. **Riverview Station** (191 Lyman St., 828/231-7120, http://riverviewartists.com, hours vary) is a circa 1896 building housing the studios of a wonderful array of jewelers, ceramicists, furniture designers, painters, and photographers. Another favorite gallery is **CURVE Studios & Garden** (6, 9, and 12 Riverside Dr., 828/388-3526, www.curvestudiosnc.com, most studios 11am-4pm daily). A fun, funky studio that has been around since before the River Arts District was a thing (it was once a punk-rock club called Squashpile), CURVE is home to encaustic painters, ceramic workers, jewelry designers, glass artists, fiber artists, and more. This is just a sampling of what's happening in the River Arts District; visit the website for detailed listings of the artists and their studios.

Antiques

For lovers of vintage, retro, and aged things, the **Antique Tobacco Barn** (75 Swannanoa River Rd., 828/252-7291, www.atbarn.com, 10am-6pm Mon.-Thurs., 9am-6pm Fri.-Sat., 1pm-6pm Sun. Mar.-Oct.; 10am-5pm Mon.-Sat., 1pm-5pm Sun. Nov.-Feb.) has more than 77,000 square feet of goodies to pick through. This perpetual winner of the *Mountain XPress* "Best Antiques Store in Western North Carolina" has toys, art, tools, furniture, radios, sporting equipment, folk art, farm relics, oddball

bric-a-brac, mid-century furniture, and all those great weird things you can only find in a collection this large. It takes a while to explore this humongous shop.

Along Swannanoa River Road is the **Biltmore Antiques District** (120 Swannanoa River Rd., www.biltmoreantiques.homestead.com), a small shopping district that's packed with an intriguing group of antiques shops. Some specialize in imports, others in lamps, European furniture, or fine jewelry. Exploring is always a good time because you never know what you'll find or where you'll find it.

Books, Toys, and Crafts

One of the social hubs of this city is **Malaprop's Bookstore and Café** (55 Haywood St., 828/254-6734, www.malaprops.com, 9am-9pm Mon.-Sat., 9am-7pm Sun.). This fun and progressive bookstore carries a deep selection of books that includes tomes by North Carolina authors and a particularly fine collection of regional authors. You'll find the requisite coffee bar and café with wireless Internet access, making it a good spot to hang out. It's bright and comfortable, and the staff are well versed in all sorts of literature, so they can help you find a local author you'll enjoy reading. People in all walks of Asheville life come to Malaprop's, so expect to see creative dressers, the tattooed, business types, artists, students, and grandparents.

A pair of great gem and crystal shops in Asheville fascinates me. Not only do they have some breathtaking minerals for sale, they also have fossils—fish, starfish, plants, even claws, teeth, and skulls. My favorite is **Cornerstone Minerals** (52 N. Lexington Ave., 828/225-3888, www.cornerstoneminerals.com, 11am-7pm Sun.-Mon., 11am-8pm Tues.-Thurs., 11am-9pm Fri.-Sat.). The other spot is **Enter the Earth** (1 Page Ave., #125, inside the Grove Arcade, 828/350-9222, www.entertheearth.com, 10am-6pm Mon.-Sat., 11am-5pm Sun.), where they have some very impressive fossils and a good selection of jewelry using many of the stones and gems sold in the store.

The **Mast General Store** (15 Biltmore Ave., 828/232-1883, www.mastgeneralstore.com, 10am-6pm Mon.-Wed., 10am-9pm Thurs.-Sat., noon-6pm Sun.) is an institution in western North Carolina and beyond. They call themselves a general store, but they mean it in a very contemporary way. Cast-iron cookware, penny candies, and Mast logo shirts and jackets sit alongside baskets and handmade crafts. A good selection of outdoor clothing and equipment can get you outfitted for some time in the woods, or you can fill up a bag with candy and eat it while you drive the Blue Ridge Parkway.

Dancing Bear Toys (518 Kenilworth Rd., 800/659-8697, www.dancingbeartoys.com, 10am-7pm Mon.-Sat., noon-5pm Sun.) is located among the motels and chain restaurants out on US-70 (Tunnel Rd.), but inside it has the ambience of a cozy village toy shop. Dancing Bear has toys for everyone from babies to silly grown-ups: a fabulous selection of Playmobil figures and accessories, Lego, Brio, and other favorite lines of European toys; beautiful stuffed animals of all sizes; all sorts of educational kits and games; and comical doodads.

Galleries

There are a number of galleries in downtown Asheville, and while most exhibit works from multiple artists, none can match the size of the **Woolworth Walk** (25 Haywood St., 828/254-9234, www.woolworthwalk.com, 11am-6pm Mon.-Thurs., 11am-7pm Fri., 10am-7pm Sat., 11am-5pm Sun., soda fountain closes one hour before the gallery), a two-story, 20,000-square-foot gallery featuring more than 160 local artists. Nearly every conceivable medium is represented, including digitally designed graphic prints, oil paintings, watercolors, jewelry, and woodworking. This gallery is a favorite not just because it has a soda fountain but

also because the work on display is affordable as well as stunning.

American Folk Art and Framing (64 Biltmore Ave., 828/281-2134, www.amerifolk.com, 10am-6pm Mon.-Sat., noon-5pm Sun.) does a wonderful job of displaying the work of contemporary Southern folk artists, including potters, painters, and woodcarvers, as well as helping the art-appreciating public learn more about local folk-art traditions and styles. They host six openings a year in the gallery, so work changes frequently, keeping the place bubbling with energy.

Sports and Recreation

Asheville is a "go out and do it" kind of town. It's not unusual to see mountain bikers, road riders, runners, hikers, flat-water kayakers, and their daredevil white-water-loving cousins all on the streets in town. A number of gear shops call Asheville home, and access to trails, rivers, and mountain roads are all right here. The **Asheville Tourists** (30 Buchanan Pl., 828/258-0428, www.milb.com), the Class A farm team of the Colorado Rockies, play here. They're the only spectator sport in town.

Biking

Take a tour of Asheville by bicycle. If you're thinking "It's too hilly; I'll never be able to climb that," **Electro Bike Tours** (departs from Weaver Park's Merrimon Ave. entrance, 828/450-8686, http://electrobiketours.com, tours 10am daily, $55) can provide you with pedal-assisted bikes that make the hills easier and the flats seem like nothing at all. Rather than relying on a throttle, like a moped or electric scooter, these ingenious bikes use their power to make pedaling easier; you still have to work, just not as hard, to get where you're going. Start with the hill to the Grove Park Inn, the first stop on a two-hour tour of Asheville's historic and cultural sites.

Golf

Golf in the mountains can be a challenge, with course layouts big on blind approaches and hard doglegs, but it pays off with beautiful views and long downhill shots that can make you feel like you hit it like a pro.

Play a round at the **Grove Park Inn Golf Club** (290 Macon Ave., 828/252-2711, www.groveparkinn.com, 18 holes, par 70, greens fees $65-140 peak season, $75-85 off-season, includes cart, discounts for juniors, late play, and off-season), where President Obama played a round during his 2010 stay. *Golf Digest* named this course one of the top 10 courses that are at least 100 years old, and it plays beautifully. This is a must-play course for serious golfers—not just because the views are spectacular but also because the course contains so much history.

The **Asheville Municipal Golf Course** (226 Fairway Dr., 828/298-1867, www.ashevillegc.com, 18 holes, par 72, greens fees $23-42, all greens fees include cart, tee-time reservation required) opened in 1927 and is one of the oldest in the western part of the state. This Donald Ross-designed course is nearly 6,500 yards long from the championship tees and features a good mix of forgiving and narrow fairways, par-5 fairways begging for a birdie, and par-3 fairways that will challenge your ball placement.

Hiking

Ready for mountain air? Join **Blue Ridge Hiking Co.** (828/713-5451, http://blueridgehikingco.com, $50-265) on a half-day, full-day, or overnight hike in the Pisgah National Forest. Founder Jennifer Pharr Davis has hiked more than 11,000 miles of long-distance trails and became the first woman to be the overall record holder for fastest through-hike of the Appalachian Trail: She hiked its 2,181 miles in 46.5 days. Don't worry: She and her guides don't go that fast on the trail; they like to slow down, enjoy the moment, and make sure everyone gets a look and feel for what they love about hiking.

Water Sports

Wai Mauna Asheville SUP Tours (tours depart from 159 Riverside Dr., 808/264-3005, www.waimaunaashevillesuptours.com, rentals from $40, tours $65) is a natural fit for Asheville (*wai mauna* is Hawaiian for "mountain waters"). Wai Mauna offers four tours: the Sunrise Dawn Patrol, a midmorning tour, a midday paddle, and the Sunset Session. Many SUP outfitters ignore the two most beautiful parts of the day—dawn and dusk—but these guys embrace them. On the Dawn Patrol tour, the river is often shrouded in fog, the birds are waking up, and the water is perfectly still; it's an ideal time to paddle. All tours depart from the River Arts District, and paddlers are shuttled to Hominy Creek, a few miles away; you then paddle downstream back to where you started.

The French Broad and Swannanoa Rivers offer a lot of opportunities to try your hand at stand-up paddleboarding. **Asheville Outdoor Center** (521 Amboy Rd., 828/232-1970, www.ashevilleoutdoorcenter.com) offers tours on kayaks ($38, $28 for youth under 18), tandem kayaks ($60), canoes ($60), and paddleboards ($65). If you want to take it easy, you can go tubing (half day $12, full day $18).

Tubing isn't a sport in so much as you simply recline in an inner tube and float from point A to point B, but it's a lot of fun. **Zen Tubing** (855/936-8823, 9:30am-7:30pm daily mid-May-early Sept., trips run 10am-3pm, $20 adults, minimum age 4, $5 cooler carrier, $5 for same-day second trip) sends their tubers on calm sections of the French Broad River. If you pick up a six-pack of your favorite beverage, book a cooler carrier tube ($5) to keep any snacks and beverages close at hand. Tube trips take a while, but you'll have plenty of company—the river is often mobbed by tubing enthusiasts. There are two locations: one in downtown Asheville (608 Riverside Dr.) and one in south Asheville (1648 Brevard Rd.).

Zip-Lining

For a different perspective on the Asheville area, head north for 30 minutes along I-26 West and spend the day at **Navitat** (242 Poverty Branch Rd., Barnardsville, 855/628-4828 or 828/626-3700, www.navitat.com, 8am-5pm daily), where you can streak through the forest canopy on a pair of zip line courses like an overgrown flying squirrel. The **Blue Ridge Experience** (from $89) has the tallest zip line; it's an incredible 350 feet high (they say "don't look down," but please do). The longest zip line is more than 3,600 feet—that's a long ride. Two rappels, a pair of sky bridges, and three short hikes provide interludes from all the zipping and flying, and there are plenty of opportunities for photos and action-camera videos. The **Moody Cove Adventure** ($99), a smaller course, has 10 zip lines up to 2,000 feet long, a pair of bridges, and two rappels. Combine the two courses ($169) into one giant day of adventure.

If you're tempted to zip line but want something a little less heart-pounding, try **The Adventure Center of Asheville** (1 Resort Dr., 877/247-5539, www.ashevilletreetopsadventurepark.com, 9am-5:30pm daily), which has a number of high-flying adventures. Their **Treetops Adventure Park** ($47) has 60 challenges (read: rope swings, sky bridges, cargo nets to climb, short zip lines, leaps from tall platforms) spread over five different adventure trails, allowing you to face the trail that presents you with the best challenges. The **Zipline Canopy Tour** ($59-86) has 11 zips, three sky bridges, and so many great views you'll forget about the zip lines. **Kid Zip** ($47) is a zip line course designed for kids ages 4-10. They also have the **KOLO Mountain Bike Park** ($19 adult full-day access, $14 youth full-day access) and something called the

QuickJump ($10 first jump, $5 additional jumps), where you can leap off a 65-foot tower and trust your harness to lower you safely to the ground.

Spas

After a day (or two) of playing hard in and around Asheville, you'll need to relax. The **Grove Park Inn Resort & Spa** (290 Macon Ave., 828/252-2711 or 800/438-5800, www.groveparkinn.com) has a spa known the world over, and there are several places where you can get a massage. **Shoji Spa & Lodge** (96 Avondale Heights, 828/299-0999, www.shojiretreats.com, 10am-8pm Sun.-Mon. and Wed.-Thurs., 10am-10pm Fri.-Sat., $41 one hour, $65 90 minutes, $90 two hours) does things a little differently. This Japanese-inspired spa has private outdoor hot tubs as well as coed hot tubs, saunas, and cold-plunge pools open to spa guests. The private hot tubs are big enough for groups of up to six, and each is perched on the side of the mountain, open on one side to give you a broad view of the mountain while staying out of sight of other guests. Shoji also offers massage treatments ($125-375).

Biltmore Estate

George Vanderbilt was drawn to Asheville by the mountain air and the glories of nature that surround the city. The **Biltmore Estate** (1 Approach Rd., 800/411-3812, www.biltmore.com) was once a huge estate of some 125,000 acres, almost every bit of it untamed. Landscape architect Frederick Law Olmsted groomed the forest around the house—the same forest you see today—but the rest was left a natural playground. Visitors can explore the forests, fields, trails, and waters of the Biltmore Estate and try their hand at sports and activities from the familiar (bicycling) to the exotic (the Land Rover Experience Driving School). The **Adventure Center** (800/411-3812, Antler Hill Village) can make reservations and point you in the right direction for any number of outdoor activities.

For starters, there are countless miles of bicycle trails on the **Biltmore Estate** (8:30am-6:30pm daily, $55-65 adults, $27.50-32.50 children ages 10-16, free under age 10). Bring your bike, or rent one in Antler Hill Village from the **Bike Barn** (single-speed beach cruiser $15 per hour, mountain and hybrid bikes half-day and full-day $30-60 adults, $20-40 children, $50 tandem bikes, home tour admission not included). Riding on paved roads is not allowed; they're too narrow to share with cars. Stick to the marked paths, which lead past prime photo spots and some of the most beautiful land on the estate.

Hiking on the Biltmore Estate can mean anything from walking 2.5 miles of mulched paths in the manicured gardens to exploring the hills, meadows, streams, and riverbank on more than 22 miles of trails. None of the trails are rugged, so all you need is water, your camera, and maybe a walking stick.

Segway tours come in four flavors: a basic tour ($50) on a paved trail to the lagoon below the house; an off-road tour ($75) to a vista of the house past the lagoon; the west-side tour ($100) to a seldom-seen side of the estate; and the advanced tour ($75), which follows the Deerpark Trail.

Equine enthusiasts can saddle up for an hour-long guided **horseback ride** ($60), a two-hour private trail ride ($160), or a private trail ride and picnic lunch ($230). Those who would rather sit back and relax can take one-hour carriage rides ($65), private carriage rides ($350 up to four guests), and wagon rides ($35).

Spend the day on the water with **guided raft trips** ($35 adults, $25 children ages 12 and under), a self-guided kayak trip ($25), or a guided **stand-up paddleboarding** trip ($50) on the French Broad River for a rare view of the estate. Novice anglers can sign up for a **fishing lesson** (from $125, kids' lessons available), but experienced anglers may opt for a **daylong wade trip** ($350 for two guests) or **drift boat trip** ($350 for two guests).

If you're feeling really adventurous, learn to **shoot sporting clays** ($175-225). After a few lessons, they'll have you knocking clay pigeons out of the sky. There's also a sporting clay course ($100) and a full-day shotgun sports clinic ($450).

The **Land Rover Driving Experience** gets you behind the wheel of a Land Rover with a lesson on off-road driving (one hour $275, two hours $425). After your lesson, hit the trail (two hours $425) or go out for a full day ($1,200) and master those off-road skills. You can also just ride along ($25) with an expert driver if you're nervous about getting behind the wheel.

Food

No matter what you're craving, Asheville has the eateries that both embrace the Southern traditions of its mountain home and explore well beyond its borders. This is a town that clearly loves its food, with 13 active farmers markets, more than 250 independent restaurants, and 21 microbreweries in a city of fewer than 100,000 residents. Farmers work with restaurants to provide the highest-quality produce and meats, and artisanal bakers and cheese makers supply their tasty foodstuffs to restaurants across the price spectrum.

For a sampling of the best of what Asheville has to offer the gastronome, take a walking tour with **Eating Asheville** (828/489-3266, http://eatingasheville.com, daily tour $54, High-Roller tour $69). Tours stop at six of Asheville's best farm-to-table restaurants for a taste of what they're cooking and provide two or three drink pairings. Held Thursday-Saturday, the High-Roller Tour visits seven of the top restaurants—with at least one James Beard Foundation-recognized restaurant—and includes four or five beverage pairings (wine, beer, and craft cocktails); for just a few bucks more, it's the way to go.

Barbecue

You can't make a trip to North Carolina and not have at least one meal of barbecue. The 'cue at ★ **Buxton Hall Barbecue** (32 Banks Ave., 828/232-7216, www.buxtonhall.com, 11:30am-3pm and 5:30pm-10pm daily, $5-16) defies North Carolina traditions in every delicious bite. Elliot Moss, chef, owner, and pitmaster, cooks whole hogs, the way it's done along the coast and in his home county in South Carolina, using a vinegary mop and serving it ready for you to sauce. The sides reveal Moss's culinary background, adding gourmet touches to green beans, potato salad, grits, and more. But if you really want to dig into his cooking history, go for the buttermilk fried chicken sandwich, inspired by his time at Chick-fil-A.

Breakfast and Brunch

West Asheville's ★ **Biscuit Head** (733 Haywood Rd., 828/333-5145, www.biscuitheads.com, 7am-2pm Mon.-Fri., 8am-3pm Sat.-Sun., $3-10) has one of the best breakfasts in the city, and, as with much of Asheville's food, it's a fun blend of traditional and innovative. They serve "cathead" biscuits—giant biscuits the size of a tomcat's head, along with a bevy of toppings like sriracha-infused honey, herbaceous butter, house-made jam, and more. Get a flight of gravy (no joke) or a biscuit with pulled pork, fried catfish, or brisket, or even a biscuit benedict.

Chocolate

French Broad Chocolates (10 S. Pack Sq., 828/252-4181, http://frenchbroadchocolates.com, 11am-11pm Sun.-Thurs., 11am-midnight Fri.-Sat.) isn't the typical tourist trap you find in mountain and beach

Top to bottom: biscuits and gravy; French Broad Chocolates; smoky ribs, the perfect example of Western NC barbecue.

towns. Instead, it's a bean-to-bar chocolatier making truly gourmet treats. Get here at the wrong time (read: after dinner or late night) and you'll wait in line to get your chocolate brownies, sipping chocolate, and ice cream. Look next door at **Chocolate + Milk** (11am-11pm Sun.-Thurs., 11am-midnight Fri.-Sat.), where you'll find French Broad's bars and toffee as well as ice cream galore. You can visit their **factory** (21 Buxton Ave., 828/505-4996, noon-6pm daily) to buy some chocolates, or come for a tour on Saturdays at 11am if you're curious as to how chocolate is made.

American

One of the best meals you'll eat in Asheville is at ★ **Rhubarb** (7 SW Pack Sq., 828/785-1503, www.rhubarbasheville.com, 3pm-9:30pm Mon., 11:30am-10:30pm Wed and Fri., 11:30am-9:30pm Thurs., 10:30am-10:30pm Sat., 10:30am-9:30pm Sun., $13-64), helmed by chef John Fleer. The menu is in constant flux based on seasonality, availability, and, as they say, "the whim of the chefs," but whatever you get is guaranteed to be stellar. Start with The House Cure, a plate of pickles and cured meats, then move on to something like the wood-roasted whole trout, the pork collar with collard greens, or a vegetarian dish like the seared squash. Their Sunday Supper—a fixed meal, family-style meal—has been a hit since the doors opened, so make a reservation.

Jargon Restaurant (715 Haywood Rd., 828/785-1761, www.jargonrestaurant.com, 5pm-10pm Mon.-Thurs., 5pm-2am Fri.-Sat., 10am-3pm and 5pm-10pm Sun., $7-18), another West Asheville restaurant, keeps broadening the town's culinary horizons with dishes like General Tso's quail, ramen, a chimichurri-slathered steak, and a late-night menu that features deep-fried deviled eggs, a stellar burger, and specialty drinks. But don't miss Blunch—that's what they call brunch—with dishes like fried green tomatoes, breakfast salad, and waffle sliders (smoked salmon on a waffle? Indeed).

Table (48 College St., 828/254-8980, http://tableasheville.com, 5:30pm-close Mon.-Tues., 11:30am-2:30pm and 5:30pm-close Wed.-Sat., 10:30am-2:30pm and 5:30pm-close Sun., $14-30) is upscale, interesting, innovative, and, above all else, delicious. They use ingredients like locally caught bass and mountain-raised pork and lamb, but you'll also find some unusual items, like sweetbreads or quail, on the menu. They're renowned for their charcuterie. Call for reservations and, if you're feeling bold, go with the chef's tasting menu, a selection of dishes that showcase the best this minuscule kitchen (you'll see it on your way in) has to offer.

★ **The Admiral** (400 Haywood Rd., 828/252-2541, www.theadmiralnc.com, 5pm-9:30pm daily, $11-34) has been a food destination since its opening in a humble cinderblock building in West Asheville. The always-interesting menu is loaded with fresh, local ingredients and outstanding seafood. Dishes like the beef tenderloin tartare, fried oysters, duck leg adobo, and blackened scallops stand out, but you can't go wrong with anything here.

Indian

Local favorite **Chai Pani** (22 Battery Park Ave., 828/254-4003, www.chaipani.net, 11:30am-3:30pm and 5pm-9:30pm Mon.-Thurs., 11:30am-3:30pm and 5:30pm-10pm Fri.-Sat., noon-3:30pm and 5pm-9:30pm Sun., $7-15) continues to win fans because of its cool atmosphere and great food. The restaurant's name means "tea and water," a phrase that refers to a snack or a small gift. This restaurant is inspired by Indian street-food vendors and serves casual and affordable specialties from all over India.

Italian

★ **Cucina 24** (24 Wall St., 828/254-6170, http://cucina24restaurant.com,

11am-2:30pm and 5:30pm-9pm Tues.-Thurs., 11am-2:30pm and 5pm-10pm Fri.-Sat., 5pm-10pm Sun., $10-26) is, as executive chef Brian Canipelli says, "not a fettuccine Alfredo-and-lasagna kind of place; we do cooking like it's done in Italy, but with North Carolina ingredients." That's a strong statement, but his food backs it up. The pizzas are creative, accessible, and just a bit decadent (microplaned black truffles over pizza, anyone?); the pastas are fresh, always elevated by interesting ingredients like sunchokes, trumpet mushrooms, pork cheeks, or smoked mackerel broth; and the charcuterie is made in-house. When eating in the dining room, go a little dressier, but it's okay to stay more casual when eating at the bar; a good rule of thumb is to look as good as the food.

Latin American

Limones (13 Eagle St., 828/252-2327, http://limonesrestaurant.com, 5pm-10pm Mon.-Sat., 10:30am-2:30pm and 5pm-10pm Sun., $12-22) is delicious. Chef Hugo Ramírez, a native of Mexico City, combines his background in Mexican and French-inspired Californian food to create dishes that are as flavorful as they are memorable. However, if you're trying to work your way through the menu of margaritas, tequilas, and mescals, your recollection of what you ate may grow a little fuzzy.

Next door to Limones is ★ **En la Calle** (15 Eagle St., 828/232-7012, www.enlacalleasheville.com, 5pm-11pm Mon.-Thurs., 5pm-midnight Fri.-Sat., $3-16), where the menu is all about upscale street food and playful cuisine. Think grilled street corn, lobster nachos, duck confit taquitos, empanadas, and hot dogs topped with pico de gallo, pickled jalapenos, and fries. They also serve fun cocktails, making this a hip spot for dinner and drinks.

Spanish

★ **Cúrate** (11 Biltmore Ave., 828/239-2946, www.heirloomhg.com, 11:30am-10:30pm Tues.-Thurs., 11:30am-11pm Fri.-Sat., 10am-10:30pm Sun., $5-20) serves a Spanish tapas-style menu, meaning you'll have your choice of dozens of small, delicious plates to order and share. Chef Katie Button brings her own culinary genius and her time cooking at legendary restaurant elBulli in Spain to bear in dishes that dazzle in their simplicity and depth of flavor. The *pulpo a la gallega* (octopus and paprika with potatoes), *butifarra con mongetes* (mild pork sausage with sautéed white beans), *cochinillo* (a quarter of a roast suckling pig), and *albóndigas* (meatballs in a rustic tomato sauce) are excellent dishes to share. While you're here, try their cider, as it's a good introduction to Spanish-style dry cider, and give their list of vermouths and sherries a look.

Biltmore Estate

There are no fewer than nine places to eat (plus snacks, ice cream, and coffee) on the **Biltmore Estate** (800/411-3812, www.biltmore.com, estate admission required to visit restaurants). The **Dining Room** (7am-11am and 5:30pm-9:30pm daily, reservations required, $22-95) is an elegant restaurant, led by chef David Ryba, featuring estate-raised Angus beef, mountain trout, Biltmore wines, and vegetables grown on estate gardens. The food is spectacular, and tables with a mountain view make the meal all that much better. Evening dress and reservations are recommended.

The **Bistro** (Antler Hill Village, adjacent to the winery, noon-9pm Sun.-Fri., 11:30am-9pm Sat., $11-30, lunch buffet $45, dinner buffet $55) has a well-rounded gourmet menu sourced from the Biltmore's own kitchen garden, locally raised heirloom crops, meat and seafood delicacies, and artisanal cheeses and breads.

The dining room of the **Deerpark Restaurant** (11am-2pm Fri.-Sat., 10am-2pm Sun., lunch buffet $20, Sun. brunch buffet $35) is a former barn designed by architect Richard Morris Hunt, now renovated to airy splendor with walls of windows. Expect hearty and homey meals based on Appalachian cuisine. Like the Deerpark, the **Stable Café** (11am-4pm daily, $13-30) was once livestock housing, and guests can sit in booths that were once horse stalls.

In the stable area near the house, both the **Bake Shop** (8:30am-5:30pm daily) and the **Ice Cream Parlor** (11am-6pm daily) serve fresh treats, and **The Courtyard Market** (noon-5:30pm daily) has hot dogs, salads, and snacks. The **Creamery** (11am-8pm Mon.-Thurs., 11am-9pm Fri., 10am-9pm Sat., 10am-8pm Sun.) is the place for sandwiches and hand-dipped ice cream in Antler Hill Village. **The Conservatory Café** (9am-6pm daily), adjacent to the gardens, has snacks and drinks. If you have a hankering for barbecue, a quick sandwich, some snacks, or a cold drink, the **Smokehouse** (noon-4pm Fri.-Sun.) in Antler Hill Village serves just what you need.

While you're in Antler Hill Village, check out **Cedric's Tavern** (11:30am-10pm Mon.-Fri., 11am-10pm Sat.-Sun., $17-30). Named for George Vanderbilt's beloved Saint Bernard (you can see his huge collar on display at the entrance), Cedric's pays homage to pubs and taverns found in Britain, with a Southern twist.

Accommodations

The **Asheville Bed & Breakfast Association** (www.ashevillebba.com) has a constantly growing membership of inns and B&Bs in the area, and they band together to promote getaways, tours, and seasonal packages. Check with them for any current specials.

Under $100

With so many neo-hippie types, college kids, dirtbags (it's not an insult; it's what rock climbers often call themselves), kayakers, hikers, and bikers coming through, it's no surprise to find a nice hostel nestled among the hotels and bed-and-breakfasts. At the **Asheville ArtHaus Hostel** (16 Ravenscroft Dr., 828/423-0256, http://avlhostel.com, $75, bungalow with private bath $150) you'll find only private guest rooms and even a private bungalow. Reservations are available up to five months in advance. At the hostel, you'll find free waffles, coffee, and tea at make-your-own stations; free Wi-Fi; and free parking. Downtown is within walking distance.

Bon Paul and Sharky's Hostel of Asheville (816 Haywood Rd., 828/775-3283, www.bonpaulandsharkys.com, $22-30, cash only) is a pleasant old white house with a porch and a porch swing, high-speed Internet access, and dorm-style bunks in women-only or coed shared rooms ($30) as well as camping ($22) in the yard. If you want a little more of a retreat, a private room with a TV and a queen bed ($78) and a cottage ($105) are available. Dogs can stay in the outdoor kennels or in private rooms.

$150-200

One of the most hospitable bed-and-breakfasts in Asheville is **Asheville Green Cottage** (25 St. Dunstans Circle, 828/707-6563 or 828/707-2919, www.ashevillegreencottage.com, $125-165 peak season, $95-135 off-season). This 1920s arts and crafts-style home is built of huge granite blocks and is simply decorated but cozy. Guest rooms are big enough, but breakfast is outstanding, and they can cater to special dietary needs. Asheville Green Cottage is a "healthy and green" bed-and-breakfast, meaning they are smoke-free and fragrance-free, and use natural products for cleaning. It's a great place to come home to after a day of exploring Asheville.

Just off the Blue Ridge Parkway north of Asheville is an inn that's a true retreat. The first time I saw the ★ **Sourwood Inn** (810 Elk Mountain Scenic Hwy., 828/255-0690, www.sourwoodinn.com, $155-205 inn rooms, $210 separate cabins), it charmed me so much that I made reservations for an anniversary weekend. The inn is situated on the end of a ridgeline, and the view is nearly 270 degrees from every balcony and bedroom window. There's no Wi-Fi or cell service, so you can truly unplug. There are a couple of miles of easy hiking trails, a pond, a bamboo grove, and some sculptures tucked in the woods nearby, but if you're feeling adventurous, there are options. The innkeeper's son-in-law happens to be a fly-fishing guide and an active hawker. Fishing and hawking packages are available. Call for directions—it's tricky to find.

Over $200

Hotel Indigo (151 Haywood St., 828/239-0239, www.ihg.com, $189-519) is shiny, modern, and steps away from downtown. The staff are attentive and courteous, and the concierges know the ins, outs, shortcuts, best restaurants and bars, and top townie things to see and do. As one of the tallest buildings in Asheville, the Indigo has spectacular mountain views from upper floors; keep that in mind when making a reservation.

★ **ASIA Bed and Breakfast Spa** (128 Hillside St., 828/255-0051, www.ashevillespa.com, $189-419) is one of my favorite places to stay in town. Every room has a big, comfortable bed and a two-person Jacuzzi tub; there's a sauna and cold shower, and a European steam shower; breakfast is a healthy, filling affair; and, most important, the rooms are private and quiet. ASIA keeps a group of massage therapists and aestheticians on call, so you can arrange for treatments of almost any kind on-site. Throughout the house, comfortable seating areas make it easy to find a spot for breakfast or tea, or to just read or talk; check out the tatami porch overlooking the Japanese garden at the front of the house.

If you've spent the day touring Biltmore House, viewing the incredible splendor in which a robber baron of the Gilded Age basked, it may be jarring to return to real life, unless you're Richard Branson or European royalty. You can soften the transition with a stay at the luxurious **Inn on Biltmore Estate** (866/336-1245, www.biltmore.com, $350-550, suites up to $2,250). It's everything you'd wish for from a hotel in this location. The suites are beautifully furnished and luxurious, the views are magnificent, and the lobby, dining room, and library have the deluxe coziness of a turn-of-the-20th-century lodge. On the other hand, if you do happen to be Richard Branson or Queen Elizabeth and simply need a mountain getaway, consider the inn's **Cottage on Biltmore Estate** (from $1,700). This historic two-room cottage was designed by Richard Howland Hunt, son of the mansion's designer, Richard Morris Hunt. Your own personal butler and chef come with the digs. In 2015, the Biltmore opened **Village Hotel on Biltmore Estate** ($269-469) in Antler Hill Village. The 209-room hotel is a testament to the ongoing and growing popularity of Biltmore.

AC Hotel by Marriott Asheville Downtown (10 Broadway, 828/258-2522, www.marriott.com, $166-410) has a prime location. Just a block off Pack Square, it's an easy walk to just about any restaurant, brewery, cocktail lounge, or music venue in town. Or you could just head up to the roof and get a drink or dinner at **Capella on 9 @ AC Lounge** (828/258-2522, ext. 5505, www.capellaon9.com, 4pm-midnight Mon.-Thurs., 2pm-1am Fri.-Sat., 2pm-11pm Sun., $8-30) for magnificent views of the mountains and downtown, and equally good cocktails and food.

Grove Park Inn Resort & Spa

The ★ **Grove Park Inn Resort & Spa** (290 Macon Ave., 828/252-2711 or 800/438-5800, www.groveparkinn.com, $349-942 peak season, $220-810 off-season, spa and golf packages available) is the sort of place Asheville residents bring their out-of-town houseguests when

Motor Courts

In days of yore, before budget hotels became the norm, the motor court or cottage court was the stay-over of choice for middle-class travelers. In one of the greatest road-trip movies ever, *It Happened One Night,* unmarried and feuding Clark Gable and Claudette Colbert build a "Wall of Jericho" between their beds with a rope and a blanket as a means to keep themselves in check while staying in a cottage court somewhere between Miami and New York. I like to think it was Asheville.

Today, these motor courts and cottage courts are relics of the past and few remain, but the mountains of North Carolina still contain a handful of fine examples. In the Asheville area at least two are still operating, providing travelers with retro accommodations. **Asheville Log Cabin Motor Court** (330 Weaverville Hwy., 828/645-6546, www.theashevillecabins.com, 2-night minimum stay weekends, $95-305, pets allowed for a fee), 6.2 miles north of downtown Asheville, has cable TV and wireless Internet access but no phones. Some rooms are air-conditioned, but that's not usually a necessity at this elevation. Another great cabin court is the **Pines Cottages** (346 Weaverville Hwy., 828/645-9661, http://ashevillepines.com, $109-330, $15 per pet, up to 2 pets allowed), only 6.3 miles north of Asheville. How could you resist staying at a place billed as "A nice place for nice people"?

giving them a grand tour of the city, simply to walk into the lobby to ooh and aah. The massive stone building—constructed by a crew of 400 who had only mule teams and a single steam shovel to aid them—was erected in 1912 and 1913. Eight U.S. presidents have stayed here, as has a glittering parade of early-20th-century big shots, among them Henry Ford, Thomas Edison, Eleanor Roosevelt, Harry Houdini, and F. Scott Fitzgerald.

Even if you're not staying here, it's worth the visit just to see the lobby and enormous fireplaces, and to take in the view while having a cocktail or dinner at one of the many on-site establishments: **Vue 1913** (5:30pm-9:30pm daily, $24-38) has well-done French and American dishes; **Edison craft ales + kitchen** (4pm-11pm Mon.-Thurs., 4pm-midnight Fri., 11am-midnight Sat., 11am-11pm Sun., $8-38) serves some high-quality bar food and craft beer; **Blue Ridge** (6:30am-10:30am Mon.-Thurs., 6:30am-10:30am and 5pm-9pm Fri.-Sat., 6:30am-10:30am and noon-2:30pm Sun., $17-44) calls itself a farm-to-table artisanal buffet; and the **Sunset Terrace** (11am-3pm and 5pm-10pm daily, $22-59) and **Sunset Terrace Cocktail Lounge** (11am-10pm daily, $7-18). Each venue has phenomenal views, allowing you to have dinner or a glass of wine while watching the sun set.

Being a guest at the Grove Park is quite an experience. In addition to the spectacle of the lodge, for an additional charge guests have access to its world-famous **spa** (access pass $85 for guests); nonguests may also purchase day passes (Mon.-Thurs., $110). The pass gives access to the lounges, pools, waterfall, steam room, inhalation room, and outdoor whirlpool tub. The indoor pool is a fantastic place, a subterranean stone room with vaulted skylights and tropical plants. For extra fees ($189-510, most $200-300), guests can choose from a long menu of spa treatments: massages, facials, manicures, aromatherapy, and body wraps.

Information and Services

The **Asheville Visitors Center** (36 Montford Ave., near I-240 exit 4C, 828/258-6129, 8:30am-5:30pm Mon.-Fri., 9am-5pm Sat.-Sun.) can set you up with all the maps, brochures, and recommendations you could need. Other sources are **Explore Asheville** (www.exploreasheville.com) and the **Asheville Area Chamber of Commerce** (www.ashevillechamber.org). The **Blue Ridge National Heritage Area** (www.blueridgeheritage.com) has a number of valuable trip-planning resources.

Mission Hospital (509 Biltmore Ave. and 428 Biltmore Ave., 828/213-1111, www.mission-health.org) in Asheville has two campuses and two emergency departments.

Blue Ridge Parkway Visitor Center (MP 384)

The **Blue Ridge Parkway Headquarters** (MP 384, 828/348-3400, www.nps.gov/blri) are working park offices and offer very little to visitors. For an overview of the Blue Ridge Parkway, a gift shop, and as much information as you can handle regarding what to do, where to go, and how to get there on the Parkway, try the **Blue Ridge Parkway Visitor Center** (828/298-5330, 9am-5pm daily, free). Here, a 22-foot-long interactive map, displays on the history and heritage of the Parkway, and a great video (it runs about 25 minutes and is worth the wait) give you a better idea about the Parkway, but the real help comes from the desk operated by the Blue Ridge National Heritage Area (www.blueridgeheritage.com). They have information on the numerous cultural sites and happenings along the Parkway, and can provide you with directions and ideas for stops and side trips.

This building is notable for being certified Leadership in Energy Efficient Design (LEED) Gold by the U.S. Green Building Council. Energy-saving features include active/passive heating and cooling, a living roof planted with sedum, and other features designed to reduce everything from water use to nighttime lighting. All of this is in keeping with the founding principles that guided the construction of the Blue Ridge Parkway. These principles said that the structures and buildings found in the park would have a natural look, blend in with their environments, and be generally kind to the earth nearby.

Visitor Center Loop Trail

Distance: 1.5-mile loop
Duration: 45 minutes
Elevation gain: 50 feet
Difficulty: easy to moderate
Trailhead: near the far end of the visitors center parking lot, near the bus and RV parking area

This popular trail was built by volunteers from the Carolina Mountain Club and Friends of the Blue Ridge Parkway to create a loop that incorporates part of the Mountains-to-Sea Trail. Not far in, you'll enter a bit of a clearing and begin to descend into the woods. Here, you'll find a rhododendron thicket and see that the ground is covered in English ivy. If you look closely (and you should), you'll see poison ivy leaves here and there. Be wary; poison ivy is everywhere on this hike. But the trail is well traveled, so if you stick to the path, you should be rash free.

As you near the half-mile mark, you'll need to cross the Blue Ridge Parkway. Be quick and be safe when you do. After crossing, you have a clear hike until you reach the 0.75-mile mark, when you reach the top of a small rise. Take a drink and a picture, and head on down the trail until you reach the fork where the Mountains-to-Sea Trail breaks off. This is 1.1 miles in, so you're close to the end. (If you continued on the Mountains-to-Sea Trail, in 2.5 miles you'd reach the Folk Art Center.) Continue on, pass under the Parkway via a stone culvert, and stroll back to the starting point.

★ US-Alt 74 East: Chimney Rock (MP 384.7)

Chimney Rock State Park (431 Main St., Chimney Rock, about 45 minutes from Asheville at MP 384.7 via US-Alt 74 E., 800/277-9611, www.chimneyrockpark. com, ticket plaza open 8:30am-5:30pm daily late Mar.-early Nov., 8:30am-4:30pm daily Nov., 10am-4:30pm Fri.-Tues. Dec.-late Mar., $15 adults, $7 children ages 5-15, ages 4 and under free) is just one of the many geological beauties you'll find along the Blue Ridge Parkway corridor. The 315-foot tower of stone that is Chimney Rock stands on the side of the mountain. To get to the top of the chimney, you can take a 26-story elevator ride, or hike the **Outcroppings Trail,** a 0.25-mile trail nicknamed "The Ultimate Stairmaster." No matter how you get there, the view is spectacular.

There are a number of additional dizzying views, like the **Opera Box,** to take in, as well as mountain-hugging trails, like the **Needle's Eye,** to hike in Chimney Rock State Park. The **Hickory Nut Falls Trail** takes you to the top of the 400-foot Hickory Nut Falls via a moderately difficult 0.75-mile trail. One of the most recognizable views is on the **Skyline-Cliff Trail** loop, a strenuous two-hour hike that will take you to some places you may recognize from the 1992 film *The Last of the Mohicans.* There are also kid-friendly trails. Bring your little ones along on the 0.6-mile **Woodland Walk,** where animal sculptures and "journal entries" from Grady the Groundhog wait to be discovered. A trail map covering the entire park is available on the park's website.

Chimney Rock is more than just

Top to bottom: Blue Ridge Parkway Visitor Center and Headquarters; Hickory Nut Falls in Chimney Rock State Park; autumn view off the Blue Ridge Parkway southwest of Asheville.

hiking trails. In November, Santa rappels down the tower in a pre-Christmas display of his chimney-navigating prowess, but year-round you'll find rock climbers in the park for bouldering, top-rope, and multi-pitch climbs. Want to try but don't know the terms? **Fox Mountain Guides** (888/284-8433, www.foxmountainguides.com, half-day lessons $215 for one climber, $145 each for two climbers) will gear you up and show you the ropes.

Nearby **Rumbling Bald Mountain** (Boys Camp Rd., Lake Lure) is part of Chimney Rock State Park, and climbers couldn't be happier. Here you'll find more than 1,500 bouldering "problems" to solve (solving it means traversing it successfully). Currently, only the south face is open to climbing and no commercial climbing guides are allowed to operate there.

Rumbling Bald and Chimney Rock are the sites of some strange phenomena over the centuries. In January 1947, Bald Mountain began giving off low rumbles that grew louder and louder as spring wore on. Then, just as the crocuses were showing their heads, the mountain gave a tremendous shake that shattered windows and knocked crockery off shelves all along the valley. A smoking, hissing crack opened in the side of the mountain, causing many to move away or find religion.

In the early 1800s, locals and visitors reported spectral sights on and above Chimney Rock. There they saw groups of people gathered on the rock pinnacle rise into the heavens and disappear. They also saw, on several occasions, two cavalry armies battling on winged horses in the air over the summit. At least that's how the stories go.

North Carolina Arboretum (MP 393)

The enormous **North Carolina Arboretum** (100 Frederick Law Olmsted Way, Asheville, 828/665-2492, www.ncarboretum.org, 8am-9pm daily Apr.-Oct., 8am-7pm daily Nov.-Mar., free, parking $14, RV parking $50) is considered by many to be one of the most beautiful arboretums in the country. The 434 natural and landscaped acres back into the Pisgah National Forest, just off the Blue Ridge Parkway. Major collections include the National Native Azalea Repository and the very special Bonsai Collection, where staff horticulturists care for over 200 bonsais, many of their own creation.

Bicycles and leashed dogs are permitted on many of the trails. Walking areas range from easy to fairly rugged, but with 10 miles of trails to choose from, it's no problem finding one that suits your skill level. **Guided tours** (1pm Tues. and Sat.) give you more on the history of the arboretum and its plants, as well as the natural history of the region. These two-mile walk and talk tours go on rain or shine, so dress for the weather. The arboretum also has a very nice café, the **Savory Thyme Café** (11am-4pm Tues.-Sat., noon-4pm Sun., $6-10) and gift shop, **Connections Gallery** (11am-4pm daily).

Lake Powhatan (MP 393)

At Milepost 393, the Blue Ridge Parkway crosses over the French Broad River. Exit here, at Brevard Road/NC-191, and you're not far from the **Lake Powhatan Recreational Area and Campground**, the **Bent Creek Experimental Forest**, the **Shut-in Trail**, and **Zen Tubing**. Stop and hike or bike the day away, then go for a relaxing float on the river before retiring to your campsite.

Lake Powhatan Recreational Area

Lake Powhatan Recreational Area and Campground (375 Wesley Branch Rd., Asheville, 877/444-6777 for reservations, 828/667-0391 for local information, www.recreation.gov, daily Apr.-Nov.,

Day Trip to Carl Sandburg's Home

In 1945, American poet Carl Sandburg moved his family to the picturesque mountains of North Carolina. He wasn't seeking inspiration for his writing; he was simply seeking the best place for his wife to raise her herd of prize-winning Chikaming goats. At the 264-acre Connemara Farm, he found both.

This is where Sandburg wrote around one-third of his body of work; received his second Pulitzer Prize, the International United Poets Laureate award, and the Presidential Medal of Freedom; and passed away at the age of 89. Today, you can experience the solitude and muse this poet, journalist, storyteller, folk singer, and goat raiser found at the **Carl Sandburg Home National Historic Site** (81 Carl Sandburg Ln., Flat Rock, parking area at 1800 Little River Rd. across from the Flat Rock Playhouse, 828/693-4178, www.nps.gov/carl, 9am-5pm daily, house tour $5 adults, $3 seniors ages 62 and over, free for ages 15 and under).

Tour the house and see more than 65,000 artifacts, including more than 12,000 books and the desk and office where Sandburg worked. The farm still operates a small dairy and the National Park Service raises goats like the ones Mrs. Sandburg raised; you can find their milk in specialty stores in Flat Rock.

Connemara and the Carl Sandburg site are crowded in fall, as the more than five miles of hiking trails that crisscross the farm come alive with leaf peepers. It's worth the stop in any season, however, as spring and summer wildflowers and winter's snow complement Sandburg's literary legacy.

Reaching Connemara and the Carl Sandburg site is easy from both Asheville and the Blue Ridge Parkway. From Asheville, head south out of town on McDowell Street/US-25; at Biltmore Forest, merge onto Hendersonville Street/US-25 and continue along this road. Merge on US-74/I-26 East and follow the signs to Flat Rock and the historic site. From the Blue Ridge Parkway, exit at Milepost 388.8 and turn south on Hendersonville Road and follow the same route. Expect a drive of around 45 minutes and 27 miles from downtown Asheville; 30 minutes and 22 miles from the Blue Ridge Parkway.

campsites $22 single campsite, $44 double, RV hookups campsite fee plus $3 water and sewer, $6 electric, $9 combined; dump station $10-50, day use $2 pp) is surrounded by the 6,000-acre Bent Creek Experimental Forest and miles of **mountain biking** and **hiking** trails. There are 97 **campsites** here, each with a picnic table, tent pad, and fire ring; a bathhouse outfitted with hot showers and flush toilets; and a lifeguard-protected beach and swimming lake. Downtown Asheville is just 10 minutes away, so if you're hungry for something you didn't cook yourself, if you're here for a concert, or if you just want to go out on the town, it's not far. Quiet hours begin at 10pm nightly, at which time the gates are closed and locked. If you plan on being out after the gates are closed, be sure to let someone know and you can make accommodations to get back in.

Bent Creek Experimental Forest

Surrounding Lake Powhatan is the **Bent Creek Experimental Forest** (1577 Brevard Rd., Asheville, 828/667-5261, www.srs.fs.usda.gov/bentcreek). You may be wondering what exactly an experimental forest is. Well, it's a designated forest that's part of ongoing research on silvicultural practices that help in the development of new forest management practices. Bent Creek is the oldest federal experimental forest east of the Mississippi, and the research done here has helped sustain or rehabilitate hundreds of thousands of acres of forest in the United States alone.

As cool as an experimental forest is,

the thing that draws most visitors here are the **hiking** and **mountain biking** trails, many of which allow **horseback riders** as well. Before you set off on any trail, note if it allows your chosen mode of exploration. And remember to bring water, your camera, bug spray, and, if you can, a bag for any litter you find on the trail.

Hiking
Homestead Trail

Distance: 1 mile one-way
Duration: 30 minutes
Elevation gain: 30 feet
Difficulty: easy
Trailhead: near the campsites on the shore of Lake Powhatan

The Homestead Trail takes you along the shores of Lake Powhatan, past the dam, and then downstream beside Bent Creek. It's a flat, easy hike, despite a couple of footbridges and wet patches, and offers several opportunities for great photos of the lake, especially in the fall.

Small Creek Trail

Distance: 0.5 mile one-way
Duration: 15 minutes
Elevation gain: 150 feet
Difficulty: easy to moderate
Trailhead: on the Homestead Trail

On the Homestead Trail, when you pass the beach and cross Small Creek, the trail splits. Stay left for Homestead, but go right to explore the Small Creek Trail and connect to Deerfield Loop. Though Small Creek is short, it does gain a little elevation as it rises through rhododendron and mountain laurel thickets.

Deerfield Loop Trail

Distance: 0.8-mile loop
Duration: 25 minutes
Elevation gain: 250 feet
Difficulty: easy to moderate
Trailhead: off Small Creek Trail or near the start of Homestead Trail

This short loop can be made longer by combining parts of Homestead and Small Creek Trails, but on its own, it's a quick workout with a couple of steep spots (not too steep; they'll just slow you down). There is a portion where the trail ducks into a mountain cove, traversing a steep slope and a slippery spring or seep as it does so. Just use a little caution in spots where it's wet or steep and you'll do just fine.

Pine Tree Loop Trail

Distance: 2-mile loop
Duration: 1 hour
Elevation gain: 200 feet
Difficulty: easy to moderate
Trailhead: near Wesley Branch Road after it crosses Bent Creek but before it reaches Lake Powhatan

This two-mile loop takes you up the hill above Bent Creek through a mixed forest of hardwoods and the rhododendron that grows everywhere here. As you climb, you'll cross one of Bent Creek's feeder streams before gaining a little more elevation and then passing by the origins of this stream about halfway up the mountain. As you return, you'll find a couple of places where the trees open up, especially in spring and fall, to reveal the valley you're in. For the last leg of this trail, you join with Deerfield Loop until you get back to Lake Powhatan.

Lower Sidehill Trail

Distance: 3.5 miles one-way
Duration: 1.5-2 hours
Elevation gain: 400 feet
Difficulty: moderate
Trailhead: near Boyd Branch Trailhead parking area on Bent Creek Gap Road
Directions: Bent Creek Gap Road is the continuation of Wesley Branch Road. As you leave the campground at Lake Powhatan, turn left after you cross Ledford Branch at the place where you meet Wesley Branch Road. This will put you on Bent Creek Gap Road; the trailhead is just over one mile away.

The Lower Sidehill Trail is hilly, but not too difficult. It follows a number of old roads—logging and forestry roads, most likely—as it climbs smaller hills on the north end before hitting a steeper section on the south end. Along the way, it passes through a range of forest types, from hardwoods to dry oak and pine to moist hemlock and other cove-found hardwoods like sycamore. Of course, you'll see more of the mountain laurel and rhododendron that love this area. This trail feels pretty remote, even though you're never far from a road or either end of the trail.

Once you reach the south end of the trail, you can reverse direction or walk back along Bent Creek Gap Road, a pleasant, flat stroll through the woods alongside the namesake creek.

Shut-In Trail

Shut-In Trail is an old one, dating back to around 1890 when George Vanderbilt, of the Biltmore Estate, established this trail to link his hunting lodge at Buck Springs, just below the summit of Mount Pisgah, to his estate. When the Blue Ridge Parkway came through, parts of the trail were lost, but the pieces that remain follow the original track. The trail earns its name from the "tunnels" the path forms through the dense rhododendron and mountain laurel thickets, giving it a close, shut-in feeling.

You can use this trail as a long-distance hike, but considering there's no overnight camping along the Parkway, it would be brutal. At 16.3 miles with around 3,000 feet of elevation gain, to tackle the whole trail in one go is a feat best left to ultra-hikers and long-distance trail runners. Here, the trail is broken down into more easily hiked sections, using the access points to Shut-In Trail along the Blue Ridge Parkway as convenient shuttle points and starting areas:

French Broad River to Walnut Cove Overlook

Distance: 3.1 miles one-way
Duration: 2-2.5 hours
Elevation gain: 800 feet
Difficulty: moderate to strenuous
Trailhead: just off the exit at MP 393.6

Directions: There is a very small parking area on the exit ramp, but you may want to park at the Bent Creek River and Picnic Park, a few hundred yards south on NC-191 from the Parkway ramp. There, a short trail (only a few hundred feet long) takes you to the Shut-In Trail.

This first segment of the Shut-In Trail isn't as shut in by the rhododendron thickets as the rest of the trail, and, in fact, the forest here is quite open. The Mountains-to-Sea Trail follows the Shut-In Trail all the way to Mount Pisgah, so you may encounter some thru-hikers.

About a quarter mile into the Shut-In Trail, you'll find your first "tunnel" through the mountain laurel. When you emerge, it's time to ascend, and quick. The trail is steep here, but manageable as it climbs to an old road. In the late fall, winter, and early spring, you can see the river from here. The road continues to climb, then gradually descends into a hardwood forest. At just over a mile in, you'll encounter a second road; bear left and follow this road up to another road (at 1.6 miles in) and descend to mile 1.8, where you'll turn onto yet another road that parallels the Blue Ridge Parkway.

Two miles in, you'll encounter your last left turn, and immediately the road will begin a series of switchbacks as it climbs the mountain. Be wary of poison ivy here as it tends to be prolific. As you descend from these heights, you'll find the road and trail are broad and tree-lined, giving the sense of a lush, manicured forest. Continue through these woods until you reach the Blue Ridge Parkway at 3.1 miles in. A right turn on the Parkway takes you to Milepost 396.4 and the Walnut Cove Overlook.

Walnut Cove Overlook to Sleepy Gap Overlook

Distance: 1.8 miles one-way
Duration: 1.25-1.5 hours
Elevation gain: 200 feet
Difficulty: moderate
Trailhead: MP 396.4 at the Walnut Cove Overlook

You're past the roads on this part of the

Shut-In Trail. Here, the trail is, well, more trail-like, so take a little more care with how and where you step. For the first 0.75 miles, be wary of the poison ivy, which grows quite heartily here. At 1.25 miles in, you'll come to an intersection. This is the Grassy Knob Trail, connecting the Shut-In Trail to part of the Bent Creek trail system. Keep to the left and continue on to cross a small creek—it may be dry in summer months—then another even smaller water feature before you enter the final tunnel of mountain laurel. On the other side, you're not far from the Sleepy Gap Overlook at Milepost 397.3.

Sleepy Gap Overlook to Chestnut Cove Overlook

Distance: 0.9 mile one-way
Duration: 45-60 minutes
Elevation gain: 600 feet
Difficulty: moderate to strenuous
Trailhead: MP 397.3 at the Sleepy Gap Overlook

Here, you'll find that the hardwoods are enormous, taking on proportions that may surprise you. This short trail has a steep ascent and descent around 0.6 mile in, but the end point—Chestnut Cove Overlook at Milepost 398.3—isn't far.

Chestnut Cove Overlook to Bent Creek Gap

Distance: 2.8 miles one-way
Duration: 1.5-1.75 hours
Elevation gain: 200 feet
Difficulty: strenuous
Trailhead: MP 398.3 at the Chestnut Cove Overlook

Starting from Chestnut Cove Overlook, you may be wondering where the chestnut trees are. You'll be hard pressed to find one as a blight that was accidentally introduced here from Asia destroyed the trees by the end of the 1930s. Chestnuts made up around 25 percent of the trees in many areas, and it's hard to imagine the richness of these woods if they'd lived.

Here, the Shut-In Trail earns its name. The thickets of mountain laurel and rhododendron form tunnels and passageways for much of the trail as it

descends into Chestnut Cove. The effect is one of isolation. Though you're close to the Parkway and not far from civilization, the sounds of the forest overtake the intermittent road sounds and you feel very remote.

For the first 1.5 miles, give or take, you'll find yourself on a slow, gradual descent that takes you in and out of the "tunnels" and patches of hardwood forest. At 1.1 miles in, you'll encounter a woods road; stay to the left and cross a creek at 1.4 miles, then it's back into the "tunnels" for the long ascent out. You'll cross two more streams, at 2 and 2.4 miles, and continue on through the rhododendron tunnels. As you near the 2.8-mile mark, you'll find Forest Service Road 479 and Bent Creek Gap. Blue Ridge Parkway Milepost 400.3 is just to the left.

Bent Creek Gap to Big Ridge Overlook

Distance: 4 miles one-way
Duration: 2.5-2.75 hours
Elevation gain: 700 feet
Difficulty: strenuous
Trailhead: MP 400.3 Bent Creek Gap

This section combines three smaller, more strenuous sections of the Shut-In Trail. The first goes from Bent Creek Gap to the Beaver Dam Gap Overlook at Milepost 401.7, and it gives a truly wide view of the countryside.

The trail ascends from Forest Service Road 479 near the Bent Creek Experimental Forest sign; a short way in—about 250 feet—you'll turn onto an old road. A half mile in, you'll pass a spring with some cold and tasty water, but if you're there at the end of an especially dry or hot summer, you'll be out of luck. Continue climbing until you summit Ferrin Knob, where you have a great view to the northeast. At 1.5 miles in, you'll find yourself in the midst of a wildflower-choked gap. Enjoy it for a moment before descending to the Beaver Dam Gap Overlook at Milepost 401.7.

From here to the Stoney Bald Overlook is only 0.9 mile, but it's a tough stretch.

The trail sticks close to the Parkway, but rises and falls quite steeply. Expect about 300 feet of elevation gain and loss as you crest knobs and ridges. A quarter mile in, be mindful of the poison ivy, but pay some attention to the exquisite craftsmanship that went into the rock cribbing stabilizing the hillside along the trail as you crest a high point. Descend to a low point where you'll find violets and other wildflowers and ascend again. Once you reach the ridgeline at 0.7 mile in, you'll descend the final 0.2 mile through switchbacks lined with buttercups and orchids to the Stoney Bald Overlook at Milepost 402.6.

On the final leg of this segment, the trail is more of the same: a couple of steep sections and some wildflowers. You'll ascend immediately on this trail and continue to climb for 0.4 mile until you reach the top of a knoll and descend. At 0.7 mile, you'll cross the Blue Ridge Parkway (be careful) and continue through until you reach the Big Ridge Overlook at Milepost 403.6.

Big Ridge Overlook to the Mount Pisgah Trailhead

Distance: 4.2 miles one-way
Duration: 2.75-3 hours
Elevation gain: 1,100 feet
Difficulty: moderate to strenuous
Trailhead: Big Ridge Overlook at MP 403.6

The final leg of the Shut-In Trail is made up of three segments. The first two are easier than the last, but the payoff is worth the effort. Keep in mind, though, that you can stop at any of the overlooks to shorten your hike if you're running low on daylight.

From the Big Ridge Overlook to Mills River Valley-Elk Pasture Gap is a pretty easy 1.1 miles. The first half of the trail is mostly flat, but 0.5 mile in you begin a steady, and increasing, ascent. Along the way, you'll pass assorted wildflowers and even blueberries (if they're in season, try

Big Ridge Overlook has the big views visitors are looking for.

a few). A narrow ridgeline awaits at 0.8 mile in.

Like the last segment, this next one features one short but steep ascent; the rest of the elevation gain is hardly noticeable. A little more than a quarter mile in, you'll pass a spring where you can refill your water bottle. Closer to the end of the section, you'll find some great trail-building work in the rock walls supporting the trail. Imagine hauling the stone to build that wall on your back. The trail just got a little easier, didn't it? Take a break at Mills River Valley-Elk Pasture Gap at Milepost 404.5; the toughest section is ahead.

If you're itching to get to Mount Pisgah, skip a couple of sections and jump right to Elk Pasture Gap. Here, at the Mills River Valley-Elk Pasture Gap (MP 404.5), you're at an elevation of about 4,200 feet. You'll climb to around 5,000 in under two miles, so get ready. Is it worth it? You bet. The views of Mount Pisgah and other peaks and valleys are worth framing (especially in fall), and there are a couple of berry patches along the way.

You'll start climbing immediately once you leave Mills River Valley-Elk Pasture Gap. Climb steadily for 0.35 miles, where you reach the top of a knob, and then descend to a wide, flat gap. Next, there's another steep ascent at 0.7 mile, with a break at 0.8 mile for a photo op of Mills River Valley to the east. Continue climbing until you begin to level out near the large patch of wild berries. The next 0.2 mile is relatively level, but then you climb again, and hard. As the elevation changes, so does the vegetation. The plants are smaller and scrubbier here than they were just a few hundred feet below. When you reach the ridgeline at 1.5 miles, you'll be rewarded with a view to the east and Mount Pisgah above and to your right. Climb a small knob (with the scantest of views from the top) and descend into a thicket of mountain laurel and hike on another 0.3 mile to the Mount Pisgah Trailhead parking area at Milepost 407.6. This is the proverbial end of the Shut-In Trail.

Water Sports

How about floating down the French Broad River, feet in the water, relaxing on an inner tube? **Zen Tubing** (1648 Brevard Rd., Asheville, 855/936-8823, 9:30am-7:30pm daily mid-May-early Sept., trips run between 10am and 3pm, $20 adults, minimum age 4, $5 cooler carrier, $5 for same-day second trip) does just that. With single and double inner tubes and even cooler-carrier inner tubes available, it's BYOB if you choose to imbibe (no glass and be responsible with your empties). It's easy to get a group out on the water for a 1.5- to 3.5-hour float. Once you pay and go over some safety basics, Zen Tubing shuttles you to their put-in a few miles away. There, you back down some steps into the river and flop onto your tube. The river around here is rapid-less, so there's little to worry about other than sunburn.

Mount Pisgah (MP 408.6)

At one time, Mount Pisgah was owned by the Vanderbilts, and their estate stretched from the Biltmore Estate, some 16 miles distant in Asheville, to this 5,721-foot summit. The mountain and the land between here and the Biltmore were used as a private hunting retreat. Accessing Mount Pisgah is easy from the Blue Ridge Parkway. At Milepost 408.6, you'll find the **Mount Pisgah Campground** and, across the Parkway, the **Pisgah Inn.**

Hiking

A network of trails and connectors circle Mount Pisgah. The two below are highly recommended.

Mount Pisgah Summit Trail

Distance: 2.6 miles round-trip
Duration: 2-2.5 hours
Elevation gain: 750 feet
Difficulty: moderate to strenuous
Trailhead: Mount Pisgah Trailhead (MP 407.7)

The view from the summit of Mount Pisgah is well worth the effort you'll put into getting up here. It can be strenuous, especially if you're not in the best shape, but it can be hiked if you take your time. Note that the elevation gain is about 200 feet in the first half of the hike and a little more than 500 in the second half. At times, this trail is steep.

You'll start the hike on Little Pisgah Mountain, where you'll eventually crest a ridge between Little Pisgah and Mount Pisgah. This is where it gets more difficult and many people turn back. Ahead, the trail follows the ridgeline and becomes a bit steeper before it cuts away from the ridge onto a very steep section with several difficult step-ups and rocky sections that are a little nerve-wracking if you're not an experienced hiker. This is the steepest section, so if you can do this, you've pretty much summited.

After this steep section, you'll enter a mountain laurel tunnel that's long and rocky. The trail turns, switches back, and follows a new ridge to the summit as it passes through an impressive stand of beech trees.

Once on top, you'll see the transmission tower for WLOS-TV and an observation deck. Though the deck is nice, it and the giant metal tower pull you out of the nature moment and into the modern world, but the view from here is spectacular. To the west, you'll see the Shining Rock Wilderness and Cold Mountain (at the northern end) and, on clear days, the Great Smoky Mountains in the distance. To the north are Asheville, the Craggy Mountains, Mount Mitchell, and, if you're keen-eyed, the Biltmore Estate.

Buck Spring Trail

Distance: 6 miles one-way
Duration: 4 hours
Elevation gain: 500 feet
Difficulty: easy to moderate
Trailhead: behind the Pisgah Inn

This trail runs from the Pisgah Inn down the mountain to US-276, making for a long 12-mile out-and-back, and the back part, that's all uphill. Keep that in mind as you're planning how far to go and how much water to bring with you.

Some folks have called this an ideal walking path or the perfect hike. After a short section of moderately steep trail, things even out and the grade becomes so gradual, you won't notice that you're descending. Don't expect mountain vistas on this hike; it's all downhill and never really pops out to a bald or clearing with any kind of view. It does, however, have more than a dozen stream crossings, meaning the little waterfalls, pools, and cascades you'll see, many ringed with rich beds of ferns, moss, and wildflowers, which more than make up for the lost view.

Hike the trail as far as you want, but

remember that it is all uphill on the way back, so it will take a little longer and tax you a little more. Still, most everyone should be able to enjoy a nice long, peaceful hike in the woods on this trail.

Food and Accommodations

Despite the shortcomings of the accommodations, the **Pisgah Inn Restaurant** (MP 408.6, 828/235-8228, www.pisgahinn.com, 7:30am-10:30am, 11:30am-4pm, and 5pm-9pm daily Apr.-Oct., $4-27) dishes up some tasty grub. Breakfast ranges from light to hearty, depending on what you want and what you're up to that day; lunch ranges from salads to barbecue to burgers; and dinner runs the gamut from steaks and mountain trout to chicken pot pie and the Pisgah Pasta—garlic and white wine cream sauce, fresh tomatoes, mushrooms, and spinach over pasta, served plain or with chicken or shrimp.

Up on the Blue Ridge Parkway above Waynesville and quite close to Asheville is the fantastic **Pisgah Inn** (MP 408.6, 828/235-8228, www.pisgahinn.com, Apr.-Oct., $160-275), which is much like Skyland and Big Meadows on Virginia's Skyline Drive, with motel-style accommodations surrounding an old lodge with a large family-style dining room and a Parkway gift shop. The inn is on a nearly 5,000-foot-high mountaintop, so the view is sensational. Trails lead from the inn to short, pretty strolls and challenging daylong hikes. The on-site restaurant has a mesmerizing view and an appetizing and varied menu of both country cooking and upscale meals. The guest rooms are simple but comfortable, each with its own balcony and rocking chairs overlooking the valley. Rooms have a TV but no telephone. The Pisgah is a perfect spot for resting, reading, and porch-sitting, but it's quite kitschy; I hope someone helps restore it to its potential.

The **Mount Pisgah Campground** (MP 408, Canton, reservations 877/444-6777, local information 828/648-2644, www.

recreation.gov, early May-late Oct., campsites $20) has more than 60 tent-only and RV campsites. Note that although there are some modern amenities like flush toilets and drinking water, there is no electricity, water, or sewer hookups for RVs. Also, take caution with food storage and disposal as black bears frequent the area.

Cold Mountain Overlook (MP 412)

Cold Mountain is a massif everyone in these parts has known about for years, but one that was popularized in the outside world by Charles Frazier's 1997 novel and the 2003 Academy Award-winning film, *Cold Mountain*. Frazier set his historical novel in the land of his kin, and based characters on his ancestors, but one of the largest, most looming characters is certainly the mountain and the land around it. View the famed mountain from the Cold Mountain Overlook at Milepost 411.8 or, even better, from Milepost 412.2. Pull off at the Wagon Gap Road parking area (you may recognize Wagon Gap from the book) and walk north along the Parkway a short distance for a fantastic view of the mountain. When you look at it, you may say, "It didn't look like this in the movie." That's because the film was shot in Romania, not western North Carolina.

The 6,030-foot Cold Mountain has a well-earned name. This section of the Parkway is closed for much of the winter and often well into spring. According to Blue Ridge Parkway sources, most closures are from November through March and sometimes well into April. Be sure to check the closure map (www.nps.gov/blri/; click Road Closures).

For another great look at Cold Mountain, you can hike to the top of Mount Pisgah via the Mount Pisgah Summit Trail. And you can do more than just admire Cold Mountain from a distance—you can climb it. There's no direct access to the trail from the Parkway, but you can reach it from the Art Loeb Trail.

✿ US-276 South: Pisgah Ranger District and Brevard (MP 412)

Wending through the mountain roads between Waynesville and Brevard, and easily accessible from the Blue Ridge Parkway at Milepost 412, US-276 carries you right into the **Shining Rock Wilderness,** a part of the larger **Pisgah National Forest.** Is it worth the drive? You bet. As part of the 79-mile **Forest Heritage Scenic Byway** (a loop that twice crosses the Parkway as it circles the Pisgah National Forest), it's simply spectacular. Continue down the Scenic Byway to reach the town of Brevard, just 18.5 miles off the Parkway. From the Parkway, it will take you around 30 minutes of driving along this beautiful, waterfall-laced road to reach downtown Brevard. Simply follow US-276 South to US-64 West and you're there.

Before you turn off the Blue Ridge Parkway and onto the Forest Heritage Scenic Byway, stop at Milepost 411 at the **Cradle of Forestry Overlook.** Here you can see **Looking Glass Rock,** a smooth, bald bit of near-white rock that's quite distinct as it shines through the surrounding green. In the fall, it's a sight, especially when the trees are in their full blaze of color.

Pisgah Ranger District
Sights
Pisgah Ranger Station
Just south of the Blue Ridge Parkway and north of Brevard in the town of Pisgah Forest is the **Pisgah Ranger Station** (1600 Pisgah Hwy., 828/877-3265, www.fs.usda.gov, 9am-5pm daily mid-Apr.-early Nov., 9am-4:30pm Mon.-Fri. early Nov.-mid-Apr.) of the Pisgah National Forest. The forest covers 500,000 acres, which is a large swath of western North Carolina, but this 157,000-acre ranger district has many of the forest's favorite attractions. A good topographic map of the ranger district is available from National Geographic (www.natgeomaps.com/ti_780). In the ranger district are more than 275 miles of hiking trails and several campgrounds; the most easily accessible is **Davidson River Campground** (828/877-3265, reservations 800/444-6777 or www.recreation.gov, year-round, $22-44), which is 1.5 miles from the Brevard entrance. It has showers and toilets.

Cradle of Forestry
If you have kids with you, make your first stop off the Parkway the **Cradle of Forestry** (11250 Pisgah Hwy., 828/877-3130, www.cradleofforestry.com, 9am-5pm daily mid-Apr.-early Nov., $5 adults, free for children ages 15 and under), a museum and activity complex commemorating the rise of the forestry profession in the United States, which originated here at a turn-of-the-20th-century training school in the forests once owned by George Washington Vanderbilt, master of Biltmore. Plow days and living history days throughout the year give an interesting glimpse into this region's old-time methods of farming and frontier living. Self-guided trails lead through the woods to many interesting locations of this campus of America's first school of forestry. Most of what's here is geared toward little ones.

Sliding Rock
Not to be confused with Shining Rock, **Sliding Rock** (off US-276, 7.2 miles from the Parkway, 828/885-7625) is an easily accessible waterfall and swimming spot with a parking lot ($2 fee), bathhouse, and lifeguards (10am-6pm daily Memorial Day-Labor Day). You can actually ride down the 60-foot waterfall, a smooth rock face (not so smooth that you shouldn't wear sturdy britches) over which 11,000 gallons of water rush every

minute into the chilly swimming hole below. How chilly? It's a breathtaking 55°F in the summer. Given its proximity to the Cradle of Forestry—it's just four miles south—it's worth a stop with a car full of kids, especially if they are adventurous and outdoorsy.

Looking Glass Falls
This is the land of waterfalls, and here's a chance to see a beaut. The 60-foot **Looking Glass Falls** (off US-276, 9.3 miles from the Parkway) plunges over a granite face into a deep, and cold, swimming hole. Looking Glass Falls is both kid-friendly and **wheelchair accessible** (at least to the upper overlook); that and its proximity to the Blue Ridge Parkway make it the perfect quickie waterfall. There are a number of beautiful waterfalls in North Carolina, and this is the best. The proportions of the falls and the lush vegetation around it are reminiscent of Oahu's Waimea Falls.

Hiking
Looking Glass Rock Trail
Distance: 6.2 miles round-trip
Duration: 4 hours
Elevation gain: 1,650 feet
Difficulty: moderate to strenuous
Trailhead: on Forest Road 475, just south of Looking Glass Falls
Directions: Just down the road from Looking Glass Falls, heading toward Brevard, you'll pass National Forest Road 475 on your right. Turn here. In less than a half mile, you'll find the Looking Glass Rock trailhead.
This is a great out-and-back hike. There's only one trail at the trailhead, and it goes straight to the top, making this a fairly easy trail to follow. The elevation gain will test your legs as you ascend and as you descend. Bring plenty of water and a snack, and dress appropriately for the weather.

The trail opens beside a small stream. Cross it and ascend through a hemlock forest. After crossing the creek, you'll top a small ridge and head into a cove on the other side. Here you'll find a larger stream with a few pretty, but small, cascades. Continue climbing.

Soon after you find the second stream, you'll encounter the first of many switchbacks. Notice that the forest has grown sparser and the view has opened up. As you climb higher, the trees will get shorter, with one notable exception that we'll get to in a moment. Soon the switchbacks will shorten, becoming tighter and more frequent as you climb up a small ridge.

When you're about a mile in, you'll reach a left-hand switchback with a large, magnificent Carolina hemlock at the tip. Behind the tree, the view opens up a bit more, revealing cliffs on the north face of the mountain. Be extremely careful if you go around the hemlock to ogle the cliffs; there's a sheer, very dangerous, 30-foot drop right behind the tree.

As you start to ascend again, you'll find that the cliffs you saw from the hemlock switchback form a sort of ring around the mountain. The trail gets steeper and rockier. This route is just about the only way up this mountain, save scaling the near vertical cliffs. The next set of switchbacks leads through this steep slope covered with Carolina hemlocks. These are different from the hemlock at the start of the trail. In fact, the Carolina hemlock is only found in a small area around the Blue Ridge and Smoky Mountains in five states. Soon, though, these trees will all be dead due to an insect infestation.

After passing a campsite at the midway point of the hike, you'll enter an area where rhododendrons and mountain laurel are more dominant. As the trail moves off the edge of the ridge you're following, you'll find a helipad painted with a large "H." It seems out of place, but even stranger is the carved signature Max Wilson left on the rock here, accompanied by the two dates he climbed to this rock in the 1930s and 1950s. The final push to the top of the mountain is steep and rocky, so watch your footing.

The round, flat summit is rather

anticlimactic. For the real reason you came up here, walk a few more yards and pop out of the oak and rhododendron forest onto the top of the cliffs. The view is among the best in the area, but be careful—the surface can be slick.

Brevard

Brevard is the pleasant seat of the improbably named Transylvania County (it's not creepy, but beautiful in a very gothic forest sort of way). As you might expect, Halloween is a big deal in this town. Brevard is also known for sheltering a population of rather startling and odd-looking white squirrels. The local legend about their origin goes that their ancestors escaped from an overturned circus truck in Florida in 1940 and made their way to Brevard as pets. More likely, say researchers, is that they came from an exotic pet breeder in Florida, and were acquired by a Brevard area family. In any case, the white squirrels escaped into the wild of Transylvania County, and you'll probably see their descendants in the area when you visit.

Entertainment and Events

The **Brevard Music Center** (349 Andante Ln., 828/862-2100, www.brevardmusic. org) has attracted the highest-caliber young musicians for more than 70 years for intensive summer-long classical music instruction. Throughout the summer, Brevard Music Center students, as well as visiting soloists of international fame, put on a world-class concert series, performing works from Tchaikovsky to Gilbert and Sullivan.

Shopping

A center for a very different sort of music is **Southern Comfort Music** (16 W. Main St., 828/884-3575, www.celestialmtnmusic.com, 10am-5:30pm Mon.-Fri., 10am-4pm Sat.). Among more usual musical items, this nice little shop carries two lines of locally made instruments: Cedar Mountain Banjos, of the open-backed,

Looking Glass Rock

old-time variety, are beautifully crafted and ring clear and pretty, while local builder Lyle Reedy hand-makes fiddles from a variety of fine woods. Reedy's instruments have a deep, biting sound loved by fiddlers. Musicians and woodworkers alike will enjoy a stop at this Main Street shop.

Brevard is also home to a number of artists, and if you're here for a quick bite and then it's back to the Parkway, take the time to stick your head in **Number 7 Fine Arts and Crafts Cooperative** (12 E. Main St., 828/883-2294, 10am-6pm Mon.-Sat., 1pm-4pm Sun.). This gallery has featured works by a diverse group of around 25 Transylvania County artists for more than 15 years. Many of the works are inspired by and created in the midst of the phenomenal local landscape.

Food

The Falls Landing Eatery (18 E. Main St., 828/884-2835, www.thefallslanding. com, 11:30am-3pm Mon., 11:30am-3pm and 5pm-9pm Tues.-Sat., $13-27) is a spot popular among locals. They specialize in seafood (foreshadowed by the rainbow trout on their sign), and their North Carolina trout sautéed in lemon butter and bourbon is particularly good. Don't discount their burgers, steaks, or lamb chops, though, because they deliver on flavor and value.

★ **Hobnob Restaurant** (192 W. Main St., 828/966-4662, www.hobnobrestaurant.com, 11:30am-2:30pm and 5pm-9pm Mon.-Sat., 11am-2:30pm and 5pm-9pm Sun., $7-32) is one of the best places to eat in Brevard because the food is good and interesting. Fried oysters and sweet chili aioli, salad topped with smoked local trout, Southern fried tofu, duck with pumpkin salad, and beer-braised pork keep the menu interesting but accessible. Vegetarians will find a wide selection of dishes here.

One of the top restaurants in Brevard is ★ **The Square Root** (33 Times Arcade Alley, 828/884-6171, www.squarerootrestaurant.com, 11am-9pm Sun.-Mon. and Wed.-Thurs., 11am-10pm Fri.-Sat., $9-26). Inside, the exposed brick walls create a warm room where the food is more like delicious art. A covered patio makes alfresco dining possible for much of the year. Something as simple as a burger and onion rings comes out as a tower of food, and fine dinner entrées, like the five-spice tuna or the rack of lamb, are almost too pretty to eat.

For a quick bite or a shake, malt, or ice cream soda, check out **Rocky's Grill & Soda Shop** (50 S. Broad St., 828/877-5375, www.ddbullwinkels.com, 10am-7pm Mon.-Thurs., 10am-8pm Fri.-Sat., 11am-6pm Sun., $8). This place has been around since 1942, and the nostalgic counter with its line of chrome stools takes you back to the heyday of this soda fountain. Enjoy a malt, milkshake, ice cream soda, root beer float, and even an egg cream (try one if you've never had one). It's a must stop, especially as a reward after a morning hike or bike ride.

Accommodations

Slip back in time at the ★ **Sunset Motel** (523 S. Broad St., 828/884-9106, www.the-sunsetmotel.com, $85-120). This kitschy motel is a throwback to the days of the classic roadside motel experience: it's cheap, comfortable, and has chairs right outside your door so you can visit with your neighbors (and it has the best modern convenience—free Wi-Fi). The staff is exceedingly friendly and ready to help with suggestions for places to eat and things to do. You can add on tickets to the Brevard Music Center, waterfall tours, and more when you book your room, so it's super-convenient. Note for film buffs: Robert Mitchum stayed here when he was filming *Thunder Road*.

The **Campbell House Bed and Breakfast** (243 W. Main St., 800/553-2853, www.campbellhousebrevard.com, from $159) has five rooms that feature queen beds and private baths; none are suites, but all are spacious. Though other accommodations in town are bicycle-friendly, Campbell House is the home of bicycle enthusiasts. One of the innkeepers is an avid bicyclist and uses Brevard as a base from which to ride.

Walkable to anything you want to do in downtown Brevard, **Red House Inn** (266 W. Probart St., 828/884-9349, www.brevardbedandbreakfast.com, $160-300) was once a general store but now has a mix of guest rooms and outlying guest cottages. Cute and contemporary, it's a fine place to spend a weekend or longer.

Camping

Davidson River Campground (Davidson River Circle, reservations 800/444-6777, local information 828/862-5960, www.recreation.gov, open year-round, sites $22-44) is just outside Brevard in the Shining Rock Wilderness Area. There are around 160 sites, some with river frontage, and all have access to hot showers and flush toilets; each site comes equipped with a picnic table, fire ring, and grill. It's the most convenient campground for exploring the hiking and fishing in the area, as well as checking out the waterfalls here.

Ash Grove Mountain Cabins and Camping (749 East Fork Rd., 828/885-7216, www.ash-grove.com, open year-round, tents and RVs $27-44, cabins $115-165) occupies 14 mountaintop acres just 10 minutes outside of Brevard. This retreat is open year-round, unlike others in the area, so you can experience all four seasons in this lovely spot. The cabins are quaint and cozy, and the tent and RV sites are well maintained. Common areas include a bonfire pit, a few lawn games, and a tiny waterfall.

Just 12.5 miles south of downtown Brevard, **Black Forest Family Camping Resort** (280 Summer Rd., Cedar Mountain, 828/884-2267, www.black-forestcampground.com, Mar. 15-Nov., limited facilities in winter, tent sites $31-34, RV sites $36-39, RV with full hookup $38-45, cabin $54-57, travel trailers $91-94) has 100 campsites that are level and, more important, shaded. Nearby, you'll find hiking, fishing, rock climbing, and mountain biking; on-site, you'll find a playground complete with horseshoe pits, a large heated swimming pool, and a video arcade. There's also free Wi-Fi.

Dupont State Forest

Transylvania County is known as the "Land of Waterfalls," and with more than 250 in the area, the moniker is well earned. About 10 miles south of Brevard, **Dupont State Forest** (US-276, 828/877-6527, www.dupontforest.com) has more than 90 miles of hiking trails crisscrossing its 10,000 acres. Some of Transylvania County's most beautiful waterfalls are located within the forest and are accessible on foot via moderate or strenuous forest trails or, with special permits and advance reservation for people with disabilities, by vehicle. Visitors should use caution, wear bright-colored clothing, and leave that bearskin cape at home from September through

December, when hikers share the woods with hunters.

Looking Glass Rock Overlook (MP 417)

Here, you'll have an impressive view of Looking Glass Rock, a mountain that's mostly bare rock that shines in the sun kind of like a looking glass.

Skinny Dip Falls Trail

Distance: 0.8 mile round-trip
Duration: 45 minutes
Elevation gain: 210 feet
Difficulty: moderate to strenuous
Trailhead: MP 417, across the Parkway from the Looking Glass Rock Overlook

This is a short hike with a tantalizing name, and if you're here during the right time of year and there's no one around, you can make sure that name was well earned with your own au naturel swimming session at the base of the falls. If you do decide to dip more than a toe in the water, know that it's cold.

Start the hike by crossing the Parkway and ascending through a forest of oak, maple, and birch trees. Climb a set of steps and cross the Mountains-to-Sea Trail onto an old roadbed. Take this all the way to the falls. There are only a few spots where the trail gets rough with wet areas, eroded bits, and the typical rocks and roots, but other than that, the trail's about as easy as you'll find around here.

Cross a couple of bridges and go down another steep set of steps and you're here. The Yellowstone Prong runs right by, and the three-tiered falls, with each tier around 10 feet high, plunges down the cliffs. This is your chance to strip, dip, then drip dry on one of the small beaches or flat rocks.

Graveyard Fields Overlook (MP 418.8)

The East Fork Overlook at Milepost 418.3 gives you a great look back over the Shining Rock Wilderness. Look until you've had your fill and head down the road a half mile to Milepost 418.8 at the Graveyard Fields Loop Trail.

Graveyard Fields takes its name not from a literal graveyard, though if you've been vigilant, at several places along the Parkway you'll have seen little country churches and fence-ringed graveyards alongside them, but rather from the stumps left standing after decades of logging and a couple of raging forest fires. After the last, name-giving fire in 1942, the charred stumps looked like tombstones, hence the name.

Graveyard Fields Loop Trail

Distance: 2.2 miles round-trip
Duration: 1.5 hours
Elevation gain: 300 feet
Difficulty: easy to moderate
Trailhead: MP 418.8

The Graveyard Fields Loop Trail is easy and picturesque, and spur trails lead to two waterfalls, so during peak times (read: wildflower season and autumn), you may find parking at the trailhead difficult.

The trail begins on a paved trail through a mountain laurel and rhododendron thicket. Soon, the paving ends and the trail begins in earnest, crossing a small creek and then a rock outcropping with a small cave. This part of the trail is prone to eroding, so watch your step. Cross the river on the footbridge ahead and turn right on a short spur trail to the first waterfall, Yellowstone Falls, also called **Lower Falls.** Notice that the rock behind the falls is golden in the right light, giving the falls its name. As you retrace your steps back to the footbridge, grab a handful of wild blueberries if they're in season.

Don't cross the bridge or your hike will be far too short. Instead, continue following the river upstream. Here, you're in the area known as Graveyard Fields. It's a wide expanse, dotted with wildflowers and berry bushes (wild blueberries, gooseberries, and blackberries), and is very pretty when the light is right.

Stay on this trail until you reach an intersection about 1.4 miles in. If you follow the trail to the right, you'll be on a path that's about 0.75 miles long, unmaintained, and steep. What's at the end? Upper Falls, an impressive sight and one worth seeing, but only if you're up to the task of following a potentially difficult trail. If you do head to Upper Falls, it will add a little time to your hike as you must go up and then back down this steep section of trail.

The left-hand path at this intersection loops back to the trailhead, crossing the river, part of which you'll need to boulder-hop or wade. Continue on the trail. When you reach a long log bridge over a marshy area, you're almost back to the start.

Devil's Courthouse
(MP 422.4)

According to Cherokee legend, this spot was the home of a giant spirit with slanted eyes named Judaculla. He's something like the Cherokee version of Sasquatch, so be sure to snap a picture if you find him holding court on this distinct rocky outcropping. Whether he's here or not, this little hike is well worth the effort.

Devil's Courthouse Trail
Distance: 0.9 mile round-trip
Duration: 45 minutes
Elevation gain: 150 feet
Difficulty: moderate to strenuous
Trailhead: MP 422.4

About half of this trail is paved; the other half is steep. After you pass through the spruce-fir forest, you'll pop out onto the

Lower Falls is one of the waterfalls you'll see at Graveyard Fields.

gnarly rock outcropping that is Devil's Courthouse. It's a great place to watch for hawks and eagles riding the thermals in the valley below. It's also a great vantage point in general, providing a 360-degree view of the land around. Markers in the rock help you identify landmarks. Stay inside the designated area, though; if you don't, you risk a 200-foot sheer drop off the Courthouse.

US-215 North: Cold Mountain (MP 423.2)

Cold Mountain may not be the tallest (though it is more than 6,000 feet high) in the Blue Ridge, but its name is the most recognizable, thanks to Charles Frazier, novelist and native to western North Carolina. His novel, *Cold Mountain,* and the subsequent film adaptation, takes place here during the Civil War (and is based somewhat on his family history) and made the mountain known to those

outside the region. You can view Cold Mountain from the Parkway (back at MP 411, 412, and many others) and from the summit of Mount Pisgah, but you can't drive to it. To reach the summit, or even its lower slopes, you'll have to hike in. It's tough but beautiful, and since this is one of the highest peaks in the area, the views are well worth the effort.

Cold Mountain Summit Hike via the Art Loeb Trail

Distance: 10.6 mile round-trip
Duration: 6-7 hours
Elevation gain: 2,800 feet
Difficulty: strenuous
Trailhead: Daniel Boone Scout Camp
Directions: Take the exit at Parkway MP 423.2 and follow NC-215 North for 13 miles. Turn right onto Little East Fork Road. Go 3.8 miles to the Daniel Boone Scout Camp. After you pass the last building, the trailhead is on the left.

Getting to the trailhead for the Cold Mountain Summit Hike seems like a hike in and of itself, but once you set foot on the trail, all of that disappears. Bring plenty of water, weather-appropriate clothing (including something a little warmer for near the summit), something to eat (you'll be out here all day), a light, and a map.

Leaving the trailhead behind, you'll ascend via a series of switchbacks 1.1 miles to a ridgeline (and the first campsite if you're overnighting it). Two miles in, you'll cross Sorrell Creek (and see another campsite). As the trail continues to rise, you'll pass through some rich land. Keep your eyes out for wildflowers, especially the trillium. At 3.8 miles in, turn left at Deep Gap, where you'll find another campsite. From here, you're only 1.5 miles from the summit. The primo **campsite** is near the summit, but be aware it's chilly up here, even in the summer when temperatures can dip into the 50s at night.

The summit of Cold Mountain is tree-covered and viewless, but make a stop there anyway so you can say you summited. If you backtrack 10 or 12 yards down the trail, you'll see a small spur trail that leads to a rock ledge. Here's where you'll find your million-dollar view: a 180-degree panorama to the south.

The summit trail is not marked, but it is well traveled and pretty obvious. But any time you go into the woods for a hike, especially an unmarked one, bring a detailed topographic map with you. You'll be able to find maps at any of the outdoor outfitters in Asheville and at many of the gift shops you spot along the Blue Ridge Parkway.

Richland Balsam Overlook (MP 431.4)

The last dozen miles of the Parkway have been the highest on the route, and you're about to reach the apex. At 6,047 feet, Richland Balsam is the **highest point on the Parkway.** At the Haywood-Jackson Overlook at Milepost 431 (6,020 feet), you get views to the south and west where long lines of mountains march off into the blue distance, and, on the closer hills, spruce-fir dominated mountainsides are so thick with the dark green conifers that they seem black.

Richland Balsam Self-Guiding Trail

Distance: 1.4-mile loop
Duration: 1.25 hours
Elevation gain: 270 feet
Difficulty: moderate
Trailhead: MP 431

The summit to Richland Balsam is at 6,292 feet, so you have a little climb ahead of you. Begin your hike on a short section of paved trail at the end of the parking area. Continue along until you reach the loop trail intersection. Stay right and begin a steeper ascent. Along the way, you'll pass several benches where you can rest or snap a picture or two, but the

best opportunities for photos are near the summit.

A little over a half mile in, you'll reach the summit. Stop, look around, take a deep breath of fir-scented air, and begin your descent. A mile in, you'll reach a break in the trees that gives you a glimpse of the land to the east. Push on through the tunnel formed by evergreen boughs, and when you reach the bench, take a long look at the excellent view here. Follow the trail back to the intersection, bear right, and you're back at the parking lot.

◆ US-74 East: Waynesville (MP 443.1)

Waynesville, just west of Asheville and east of Cherokee, is the very definition of the word quaint. Writers have compared it to a Norman Rockwell painting with its storybook Main Street, busy with shops and lined with brick sidewalks and iron lampposts. This is an artistic little community where the art and craft galleries and studios are seemingly endless. In nearby Cullowhee, Western Carolina University is one of the mountain region's leading academic institutions, as well as the location of the Mountain Heritage Center museum and Mountain Heritage Day festival.

Waynesville is easy to reach from the Blue Ridge Parkway. From Milepost 423.4, follow US-276 north for 30 minutes right into town. From Milepost 443.1, turn onto US-74 East/US-23 North and zoom into Waynesville from the west in about 10 minutes.

Sights

One interesting stop in Waynesville is the **Museum of North Carolina Handicrafts** (49 Shelton St., 828/452-1551, www.sheltonhouse.org, 11am-4pm Tues.-Sat. May-Oct., $6 adults, $5 students, free children ages 5 and under). Consisting of a farmhouse, barn, and gardens, the museum

Waynesville

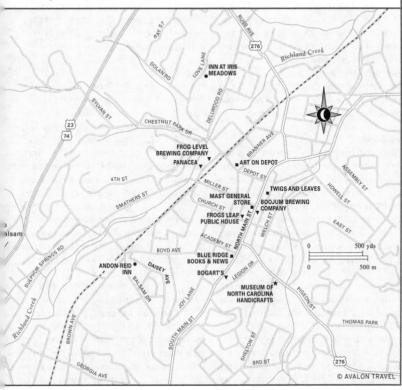

opened in 1980 and shows off the work of Native American and North Carolina heritage artists. This means mountain musical instruments, ceremonial items and crafts from Native American tribes, basketry, wood carvings, quilts, and even antique farm tools. Tours of the museum are guided, so you'll hear plenty of stories to go with the items you see.

Shopping
Books and Specialty Items
Blue Ridge Books & News (152 S. Main St., 828/456-6000, www.blueridge-booksnc.com, 9am-6pm daily) is a nice bookstore specializing in regional-interest titles and good coffee. A number of prominent Southern authors come through here to read and sign books; check the shop's schedule online to see whose book tour is coming through town, and ask about signed copies while you're there.

One of the several locations of **Mast General Store** (63 N. Main St., 828/452-2101, www.mastgeneralstore.com, 10am-6pm Mon.-Sat., noon-6pm Sun.) is here in Waynesville. While the stores are perhaps best known among vacationers for making children clamor for the candy kept in big wooden barrels, they have an even larger selection of merchandise for adults, including camping gear, such as top-brand tents, cookware, and maps and outdoors-oriented upscale clothing and shoes by Columbia, Teva, Patagonia, and Mountain Hardwear.

Think of **Mountain Favors** (98 N. Main St., 828/734-4281, www.mountainfavors.com, 10am-5:30pm Mon.-Sat.) as a depot of mountain-made crafts, gourmet goods, pottery, and woodworking gifts. For just a few bucks, you'll have a lovely memento of your time in the mountains and, if you're lucky, the artist whose goods you bought will be there.

Galleries

Waynesville's galleries are many and varied, although the overarching aesthetic is one of studio art with inspiration in the environment and folk arts. **Twigs and Leaves** (98 N. Main St., 828/456-1940, www.twigsandleaves.com, 10am-5:30pm Mon.-Sat., 1pm-4pm Sun., Sun. hours vary seasonally) carries splendid art furniture that is both fanciful and functional, pottery of many hand-thrown and hand-built varieties, jewelry, paintings, fabric hangings, mobiles, and many other beautiful and unusual items inspired by nature.

Art on Depot (250 Depot St., 828/246-0218, www.artondepotgallery.com, 10am-6pm Wed. and Fri., 10am-5pm Sat.-Tues. and Thurs.) is a working pottery studio and gallery where local and regional artists exhibit and sell their work. Artistic creations for sale include decorative and functional pottery by the resident potter and many of her contemporaries, as well as paintings, jewelry, sculpture, and a few pieces by area fiber artists.

Studio Thirty Three (822 Balsam Ridge Rd., 828/452-4264, www.studio33jewelry.com, by appointment) carries the work of a very small and select group of fine jewelers from western North Carolina. Their retail and custom inventory consists of spectacular handcrafted pieces in a variety of styles and an array of precious stones and metals. This is a must-see gallery if you have a special occasion coming up. The gallery describes its stock as ranging in price from "$65 to $16,000," and most items cost upward of $2,000. Even if you're not about to mark a major life event or spend that kind of money just for fun, it's worth stopping in to gaze at all that sparkle.

Food

Waynesville's ★ **Frogs Leap Public House** (44 Church St., 828/456-1930, http://frogsleappublichouse.com, 5pm-9pm Tues.-Thurs., 5pm-10pm Fri.-Sat. mid-May-Oct., 5pm-9pm Fri.-Sat. Nov.-mid-May, brunch served 11am-3pm Easter-late Oct., $8-29) serves an interesting menu that's quite sophisticated, yet not afraid of its Southern roots. Dishes like the wood-grilled sirloin tip in a bourbon-shallot demi-glace or the spicy Korean pork belly sliders show an adventurous spirit that diners appreciate, not just because it's ambitious, but because it's excellent.

If you're just passing through town and need a jolt of good strong coffee, visit **Panacea Coffee** (66 Commerce St., 828/452-6200, http://panaceacoffee.com, 7am-5pm Mon.-Fri., 8am-5pm Sat., 10am-3pm Sun., $5-11) in the funky Frog Level neighborhood downhill from downtown. The proprietors give back to their community, and trade fairly with the communities that supply their coffee. They stock beans, blends, and brews from all around the world.

The ever-popular **Bogart's** (303 S. Main St., 828/452-1313, www.bogartswaynesville.com, 11am-9pm Sun.-Thurs., 11am-10pm Fri.-Sat., $8-24) is locally famous for its filet mignon, though their local trout also has a good reputation. The menu is huge but very steak-house; vegetarians will have a tough time, although a few dishes, like the chipotle black bean burger and the grilled portobello salad, provide options.

Beer lovers, take note: Waynesville has several good breweries. **Boojum Brewing Company** (50 N. Main St., 828/246-0350, www.boojumbrewing.com,

11:30am-10pm Mon. and Wed.-Thurs., 11:30am-midnight Fri.-Sat., 11:30am-9pm Sun.) takes their name from a gem-stealing mountain man. They brew beer in a variety of Belgian, German, and American styles. Their brown ale, porter, and slate of IPAs are quite good. At **Frog Level Brewing** (56 Commerce St., 828/454-5664, www.froglevelbrewing.com, 2pm-9pm Mon.-Thurs., 2pm-10pm Fri., noon-10pm Sat., 2pm-7pm Sun.), they make six brews, including an IPA, a porter, a rye ale, and a peaty scotch ale.

Accommodations

Waynesville has quite a selection of luxury inns. The **Andon-Reid Inn** (92 Daisey Ave., 800/293-6190 or 828/452-3089, www.andonreidinn.com, $135-225, no children or pets) is a handsome turn-of-the-20th-century house close to downtown with five tranquil guest rooms, each with its own fireplace. The sumptuous breakfast menu might include sweet-potato pecan pancakes and pork tenderloin, homemade corn bread with honey butter, or the intriguing baked lemon eggs. With advance notice, they can cater to special dietary needs.

In the community of Balsam, seven miles southwest from Waynesville, the ★ **Balsam Mountain Inn** (68 Seven Springs Dr., Balsam, 800/224-9498, www.balsammountaininn.net, $100-230, no pets) has stood watch for a century in a haunting location—an imposing old wooden hotel with huge double porches overlooking a rather spooky little railroad platform and the beautiful ridges of Jackson and Haywood Counties beyond. The interior has barely changed since it was opened in 1908, paneled in white horizontal beadboard throughout and with 10-foot-wide hallways said to have been designed to accommodate steamer trunks. The one telephone is at the front desk, and there are no TVs, so plan to go hiking or to sit on the porch before dining in the downstairs restaurant, and then curl up and read in the library. There is, incongruously, fast Wi-Fi. Among the inn's reported ghosts is a woman in a blue dress, said to originate in room 205 but to come and go elsewhere on the second floor. This inn has a few rough edges, but the atmosphere can be found nowhere else.

For absolute tip-top luxury, try **The Swag** (2300 Swag Rd., 800/789-7672 or 828/926-0430, www.theswag.com, $500-875). Superb guest rooms and cabins of rustic wood and stone each have a steam shower, and several have saunas, wet bars, and cathedral ceilings. The menu is decidedly country and upscale, two things you wouldn't think go together, but they do, and quite nicely. The inn is at 5,000 feet elevation in a stunning location at the very edge of Great Smoky Mountains National Park.

Information and Services

The **Haywood County Tourism Development Authority** (1110 Soco Rd., Maggie Valley, 800/334-9036, http://visitncsmokies.com, 9am-5pm Mon.-Sat.) has a wealth of information about visiting Waynesville and surrounding towns. **MedWest Haywood** (262 Leroy George Dr., Clyde, 828/456-7311, www.myhaywoodregional.com), accessible from the Lake Junaluska exit off US-23/US-74, is the region's hospital.

Waterrock Knob Visitor Center (MP 451.2)

The **Waterrock Knob Visitor Center** (828/298-0398, 10am-5pm daily May-Sept.) is a small affair. A tiny gift shop, restrooms with pit toilets but no running water, and a parking area with a fabulous view of the sunset of the Smokies round out what you'll find here. There is a trail that takes you out to Waterrock Knob, a picturesque spot drawing its name from a cool stream where hunters would come to fill waterskins or canteens. It's a beautiful hike that I highly recommend.

Waterrock Knob Trail

Distance: 1.2 miles round-trip
Duration: 1 hour
Elevation gain: 600 feet
Difficulty: strenuous
Trailhead: MP 451.2 at the Waterrock Knob Visitor Center

This trail is short but surprisingly strenuous as it's all uphill (until you come back, and then it's all downhill, which is even worse). While many visitors will take the quarter-mile paved trail to a platform with a great view of its own, for the best vista, keep climbing.

As you follow the trail beyond the platform, the paving falls away, and the path turns into a typical dirt trail. The view keeps opening up the farther you go. You'll pass through huckleberry brambles, as well as blackberries and blueberries (ripe in late summer), and picture-perfect rock outcroppings.

In a few spots, you may have to scramble over some rocks for the best views or pictures, and so long as you're careful, it's worth it. At the summit, you'll find a bench where you can rest your legs and soak in the scenery.

Follow the trail a few steps more and you'll come to another rock outcropping where you'll have views of Clingmans Dome (6,643 ft.), Mount LeConte (6,593 ft.), and Mount Guyot (6,621 ft.), the highest peaks in Great Smoky Mountains National Park to your west.

US-19 North: Maggie Valley (MP 455.7)

Maggie Valley is a vacation town from the bygone era of long family road trips in wood-paneled station wagons. Coming down the mountain toward Maggie Valley, you'll pass an overlook that, on a morning when the mountains around Soco Gap are looped with fog, is surely one of the most beautiful vistas in the state. Only four miles east of the Blue Ridge Parkway at Milepost 455.7 via US-19 North, it's an easy spot to reach for a refuel for you or your vehicle.

Sights and Entertainment

In a state with countless attractions for automotive enthusiasts, Maggie Valley's **Wheels Through Time Museum** (62 Vintage Ln., 828/926-6266, www.wheelsthroughtime.com, 9am-5pm Thurs.-Mon. Apr.-late Nov., $15 adults, $12 seniors, $7 children ages 6-14, free ages 5 and under) stands out as one of the most fun. A dazzling collection of nearly 300 vintage motorcycles and a fair number of cars are on display, including rarities like a 1908 Indian, a 1914 Harley-Davidson, military motorcycles from both world wars, and some gorgeous postwar bikes. This collection, which dates mostly to before 1950, is maintained in working order—almost every one of the bikes is revved up from time to time, and the museum's founder has been known to take a spin on one of the treasures.

Sports and Recreation

Hiking

Near Maggie Valley, the mountains become rough. Located on the valley floor, Maggie Valley is surprisingly short on trails, and what trails there are are quite strenuous. There's the 2.6-mile stroll around **Lake Junaluska,** but other than that, the majority of the trails are found at the crest of the mountains, along the Blue Ridge Parkway. To the east of Maggie Valley, the mountains are a little more forgiving and there are many trails of various intensities and lengths. In the immediate area, you'll have to take the Heintooga Spur Road, a connector road between the Parkway and Great Smoky Mountains National Park, to a mile-high campground, picnic area with unparalleled views, and the **Flat Creek Trail.** On Heintooga Spur Road, you'll pass into Great Smoky Mountains National Park proper and be treated to no fewer than five stunning overlooks, the best of which is the Mile High Overlook, offering a

Maggie Valley

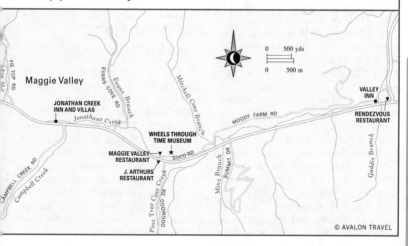

© AVALON TRAVEL

glimpse of Clingmans Dome, Mount LeConte, Mount Kephart, and Mount Guyot.

Flat Creek Trail

Distance: 5 miles round-trip
Duration: 3 hours
Elevation gain: 250 feet
Difficulty: moderate
Trailhead: Heintooga Ridge picnic area off Heintooga Spur Road, accessible at MP 458.2

Though named the Flat Creek Trail, you will find a waterfall—the 200-foot Flat Creek Falls, a beautiful but difficult-to-see waterfall—along the path. The main trail is easy, with little elevation gain or loss until you turn off onto the short spur trail that takes you to the falls. The falls trail is steep and slick, so be careful if you decide to explore in this area.

Heavy logging at the turn of the 20th century opened the forest up and allowed a thick swath of grass to grow here. Today, much of the grass remains, and the forest seems to rise from it like an island in a sea of green. It's a strange sight.

Skiing and Winter Sports

Maggie Valley's **Cataloochee Ski Area**

(1080 Ski Lodge Rd., off US-19, 800/768-0285, snow conditions 800/768-3588, www.cataloochee.com, lift tickets $32-65 adults, $20-40 children ages 12 and younger; rentals under $30) has slopes geared to every level of skier and snowboarder. Classes and private lessons are taught for all ages.

Cataloochee's sister snow-sports area, **Tube World** (US-19, next to Cataloochee Ski Area, 800/768-0285, www.cataloochee.com, $25, must be over 42 inches tall, mid-Dec.-mid-Mar.) caters to the non-skiing snow lover. Here you can zip down the mountain on inner tubes, and there's a "Wee Bowl" area for children (call ahead, $5). It's a fun time and it gets packed, so plan ahead and consider making a reservation.

Food and Accommodations

Rendezvous Restaurant (70 Soco Rd., 828/962-0201, 11:30am-9pm Mon.-Wed., 11:30am-10pm Thurs., 11:30am-11pm Fri., 7:30am-11pm Sat., 7:30am-8pm Sun., $8-20) serves a menu that has a little bit of something for everyone. Pizza and calzones, burgers, fish sandwiches, cheesesteaks, fried chicken, steaks, and ribs are just some of what they serve.

J. Arthurs Restaurant (2843 Soco Rd., 828/926-1817, www.jarthurs. com, 4:30pm-9pm Tues.-Thurs., noon-2:30pm and 4:30pm-9pm Fri.-Sun., $15-25) is a popular spot for steaks, which are the house specialty; they've been serving them up since 1986. The restaurant also has a variety of seafood and pasta dishes, but there are few vegetarian options.

A Maggie Valley dining institution that's been around since 1952 is **Maggie Valley Restaurant** (2804 Soco Rd., 828/926-0425, www.maggievalleyrestaurant.net, 7am-9pm daily May-Oct., $4-12). Expect comfort-food classics—meatloaf, meatloaf sandwiches, something called a chuck wagon, pork chops, biscuit sandwiches, grits, bottomless coffee, and even buttermilk—along with one of the best pieces of fresh fried trout you'll find in these mountains.

The main drag through Maggie Valley (Soco Rd./US-19) is lined with motels, including some of the familiar national chains. Among the pleasant independent motels are **The Valley Inn** (236 Soco Rd., 800/948-6880, www.thevalleyinn.com, from $85 in-season, from $39 off-season) and **Jonathan Creek Inn and Villas** (4324 Soco Rd., 828/926-1232 or 800/577-7812, www.jonathancreekinn.com, $109-155), which has creekside rooms with screened-in porches and a few cabins with Jacuzzi tubs.

Soco Gap (MP 455.7)

When you reach the 4,570-foot Soco Gap, you're on the edge of the Qualla Boundary and Cherokee country. The overlook here is less of an overlook and more of a parking area until the National Park Service clears a few trees. Don't worry about views, though. As you round some of the big sweeping turns on the descent toward Cherokee and the end of the

Blue Ridge Parkway, you'll have plenty more views to take in.

Big Witch Gap Overlook (MP 461.9)

Like Devil's Courthouse, this spot is intriguing, with the potential to see the namesake Big Witch, the anglicized name of a famous Cherokee medicine man who lived in these parts for more than 90 years. Here, at the Big Witch Gap Overlook, you have an excellent view of the Great Smoky Mountains. If you're here at the right time of day or year, you'll see why they call them the Great Smoky Mountains, as fog and mist rise like tendrils of smoke from what seems like every cove and hollow in these hills.

Southern End (MP 469.1)

Congratulations, you made it to the end of the Blue Ridge Parkway. At Milepost 469.1, you'll intersect US-441 just a mile or so from Cherokee to the south and east, and Great Smoky Mountains National Park to the north and west. This is the time to pull off, get out of the car, and snap a selfie in front of the Blue Ridge Parkway sign at the southern end of the route. After that, it's on to Cherokee for a meal, a massage, and some blackjack.

⬦ US-441 South: Cherokee

The town of Cherokee is a study in juxtapositions: the cultural traditions of the Cherokee people, the region's natural beauty, a 24-hour casino, and community-wide preparation for the future. Cherokee is the seat of government of the Eastern Band of the Cherokee, who have lived in these mountains for centuries. Today, their traditional arts and crafts, government, and cultural heritage are very much alive. The Qualla (KWA-lah) Boundary is not a reservation but is rather a large tract of land owned and governed by the Cherokee people. Institutions like the Museum of the Cherokee Indian and the Qualla Arts and Crafts Mutual provide a solid base for the Eastern Band's cultural life. As you drive around, take a look at the road signs. Below each English road name is that same name in Cherokee, a beautiful script created by Sequoyah, a 19th-century Cherokee silversmith. This language was once nearly extinct, and few Cherokee people speak it fluently, but it is now being taught to the community's youth, and there is a Cherokee language immersion school on the Qualla Boundary.

The main street in Cherokee is a classic cheesy tourist district where you'll find "Indian" souvenirs—factory-made moccasins, plastic tomahawks, peace pipes, and faux bearskins. In a retro way, this part of Cherokee, with its predictable trinket shops and fudgeries, is charming; check out the garish 1950s motel signs with comic-book Indians outlined in neon. Aside from the town's proximity to Great Smoky Mountains National Park (which is just two miles from Cherokee along heavily traveled Newfound Gap Road), the biggest draw here is Harrah's Cherokee Casino, one of the largest casino hotels in the state. Take all that you see—the casino, the tacky tourist shops, and the stereotyping signs—with a grain of salt, as they don't represent the true nature of the Cherokee people and their long history.

Getting There

Cherokee is located on a pretty, winding section of US-19 between Maggie Valley and Bryson City, 2.5 miles south of the southern terminus of the Blue Ridge Parkway. From the Blue Ridge Parkway, a six-minute drive south along US-441 will take you right to the cultural center of Cherokee.

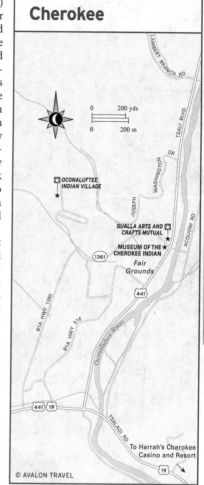

Cherokee

© AVALON TRAVEL

Sights
Museum of the Cherokee Indian

The **Museum of the Cherokee Indian** (589 Tsali Blvd., 828/497-3481, www.cherokeemuseum.org, 9am-7pm Mon.-Sat., 9am-5pm Sun. Memorial Day-Labor Day, 9am-5pm daily Labor Day-Memorial Day, $10 adults, $6 children ages 6-12, free ages 5 and under) was founded in 1948 and was originally housed in a log cabin. Today, it is a well-regarded modern museum and locus of community

culture. In the exhibits that trace the long history of the Cherokee people, you may notice the disconcertingly realistic mannequins. Local community members volunteered to be models for these mannequins, allowing casts to be made of their faces and bodies so that the figures would not reflect an outsider's notion of what Native Americans should look like; the mannequins depict real people. The Museum of the Cherokee Indian traces the tribe's history from the Paleo-Indian people of the Pleistocene epoch, when the ancestral Cherokees were hunter-gatherers, through the ancient days of Cherokee civilization, and into contact with European settlers.

A great deal of this exhibit focuses on the 18th and 19th centuries, when a series of tragedies befell the Cherokee as a result of the invasion of their homeland. It was also a time of great cultural advancement, including Sequoyah's development of the script to write the Cherokee language. The forced relocation of Native Americans called the Trail of Tears began near here, along the North Carolina-Georgia border, in the early 19th century. A small contingent of Cherokees remained in the Smokies at the time of the Trail of Tears, successfully eluding, and then negotiating with, the U.S. military, who were trying to force most of the Native Americans in the Southeast to move to Oklahoma. Those who stayed out in the woods, along with a few others who were able to return from Oklahoma, are the ancestors of today's Eastern Band, and their history is truly remarkable.

The best parts of the museum are the stories, legends, and myths described on placards throughout the museum. There's the story of a boy who became a bear and convinced his entire clan to become bears also. There's one about Spearfinger, a frightening creature that some say still

Top to bottom: Museum of the Cherokee Indian; kayaks at the Nantahala Outdoor Center; Tuckasegee River.

lives in these woods. And there are tales about Selu, the corn mother, and Kanati, the lucky hunter. Cherokee member and contemporary writer Marilou Awiakta has written widely about Selu, tying the past and present together with taut lines of thought that challenge our views on culture and technology.

★ Qualla Arts and Crafts Mutual

Across the street from the Cherokee museum is the **Qualla Arts and Crafts Mutual** (564 Tsali Blvd., 828/497-3103, http://quallaartsandcrafts.com, 8am-7pm Mon.-Sat., 8am-5pm Sun. June-mid Aug., 8am-4:30pm Mon.-Sat., 9am-5pm Sun. Sept.-Dec. and Mar.-May, 8am-4:30pm Mon.-Sat. Jan.-Feb.), a community arts co-op where local artists sell their work. The gallery's high standards and the community's thousands of years of artistry make for a collection of very special pottery, baskets, masks, and other traditional art. As hard as it is to survive as an artist in a place like New York City, artists in rural areas such as this have an exponentially more difficult time supporting themselves through the sale of their art while maintaining the integrity of their vision and creativity. The Qualla co-op does a great service to this community in providing a year-round market for the work of traditional Cherokee artists, whose stewardship of and innovation in the arts are so important. The double-woven baskets are especially beautiful, as are the carvings of the masks representing each of the seven clans of the Cherokee people (the Bird, Deer, Longhair, Blue, Wolf, Paint, and Wild Potato).

★ Oconaluftee Indian Village

Oconaluftee Indian Village (218 Drama Rd., 828/497-2111, http://visitcherokeenc. com, 10am-4pm Mon.-Sat. May-mid-Oct, $19 adults, $11 children, free ages 5 and under) is a recreated Cherokee village tucked into the hills above the town. Here, you'll see how the tribe lived in the 18th century. Tour guides in period costumes lead groups on walking lectures with stops at stations where you can see Cherokee cultural, artistic, and daily-life activities performed as authentically as possible. (Tours depart every 15 minutes 10am-4pm.) From cooking demos to flint knapping (for arrowheads and spear points) and clay work, you'll get a look at how the Cherokee lived centuries ago. The highlight of the tour is the ritual dance demonstration showing a half dozen dances and explaining their cultural significance.

Harrah's Cherokee Casino

The Eastern Band of the Cherokee operates **Harrah's Cherokee Casino Resort** (777 Casino Dr., 828/497-7777, www. caesars.com/harrahs-cherokee, 24 hours daily). This full-bore Vegas-style casino has more than 3,800 digital games and slot machines along with around 150 table games, such as baccarat, blackjack, roulette, and a poker-only room. Inside the casino complex is a 3,000-seat concert venue where acts like Alicia Keys and the Black Crowes have performed, as well as a huge buffet and a grab-and-go food court next to the casino floor. Unlike in the rest of the state, smoking is allowed on the casino floor, though certain areas have been designated as nonsmoking. If you're a nonsmoker, it may take some patience. Inside the hotel portion of the casino are a restaurant, a Starbucks, and the **Mandara Spa,** which offers salon and spa services such as massages and facials.

Entertainment and Events

Of the several outdoor dramas for which North Carolina is known, among the longest running is Cherokee's *Unto These Hills* (Mountainside Theater, 688 Drama Rd., adjacent to Oconaluftee Indian Village, 866/554-4557, www.visitcherokeenc.com, 8pm Mon.-Sat. June-Aug. 15, $20-23 adults, $10-13 children ages 6-12, free under age 6). For more than 60 summers, Cherokee actors have told the story of their nation's history from

Qualla Boundary: The Story of the Cherokee

The Cherokee believe that the mountains of western North Carolina have been part of their homeland dating back to at least the last Ice Age (some 11,000 years ago). By the time Spanish soldiers encountered the Cherokee in the 1540s, the tribe controlled around 140,000 square miles across the southern United States, living in log cabins in towns and villages throughout their territory. They farmed corn, squash, and beans (known as "The Three Sisters"); hunted elk, deer, and bear; and prospered in peace times and warred with other tribes periodically.

During the first two centuries of earnest European contact, the Cherokee were peaceful and hospitable with the colonists they encountered. Through the course of those 200 years, strings of broken treaties and concessions by the Cherokee had shrunk their once-vast empire dramatically. When President Andrew Jackson insisted that all Indians in the Southeast be moved west of the Mississippi, the real trouble began.

As Jackson's forced march and relocation of the Cherokee and other tribes, known as the **Trail of Tears,** pressed on, a small group of Cherokee avoided relocation by becoming North Carolina citizens, and a band of resistance fighters stayed behind near present-day Cherokee, hiding in the hills, hollows, and caves high in the mountains. These holdouts would become the core of the **Eastern Band of Cherokee Indians.** Unable to own any land, the Cherokee turned to an adopted tribe member to purchase and hold land in his name. He did so, and in 1870, the Cherokee formed a corporation and took control of their land, which they called the Qualla Boundary.

Today, the Eastern Band of the Cherokee Indians has nearly 15,000 members (their counterparts in Oklahoma number 10 times as many), many of whom live within the 82-square-mile Qualla Boundary. Tribe members are fiercely proud of their heritage, traditions, stories, and language. An afternoon spent at the **Museum of the Cherokee Indian,** the **Qualla Arts and Crafts Mutual,** and the **Oconaluftee Indian Village,** and an evening at a showing of *Unto These Hills,* will give you a more complete understanding of their history.

ancient times through the Trail of Tears. Every seat in the house is a good seat at the Mountainside Theater, and the play is certainly enlightening. If you're gun-shy or easily startled, be warned: There is some cannon fire and gunfire in the play.

Hear stories, learn dances, and interact with Cherokee storytellers at the **Cherokee Bonfire** (Oconaluftee Islands Park, Tsalagi Rd. and Tsali Blvd., intersection of US-19 and US-441, 800/438-1601, www.visitcherokeenc.com, 7pm-9pm Fri.-Sat. May-Oct., free). Bring your bathing suit and some water shoes to the bonfire; afterward, you may want to go for a wade or a quick dip in the Oconaluftee River, which is wide, rocky, and fun.

Sports and Recreation
Fishing

Cherokee has more than 30 miles of streams, rivers, and creeks ideal for fishing. Add to that the fact that the Eastern Band owns and operates a fish hatchery that releases around 250,000 trout into these waters every year and you have the perfect mix for fantastic fishing. Unlike in the rest of North Carolina, you don't need a North Carolina fishing license; you need a **tribal fishing permit** (www.fishcherokee.com, 1 day $10, 2 days $17, 3 days $27, 5 days $47), sold at a number of outlets in Cherokee. You'll find brook, brown, golden, and rainbow trout, and it's fly-rod-only, so you have to have your cast down pat if you want to bring in a big one. There are both catch-and-release and catch-and-keep waters in the Qualla

Boundary. If you want to fish outside the boundary, where several streams and the Oconaluftee River have great fishing, you need a North Carolina or Tennessee fishing permit. Tennessee permits are only valid inside Great Smoky Mountains National Park boundaries in North Carolina.

Golf

The **Sequoyah National Golf Club** (79 Cahons Rd., Whittier, 828/497-3000, www.sequoyahnational.com, 18 holes, par 72, greens fees from $55), five miles south of Cherokee in Whittier, is a stunning mountain golf course. Making the most of the contours and elevation, the course offers tee boxes with breathtaking views of the fairways and the Smoky Mountains. The course record is 62, an impressive feat on a normal course, but here it's something else. Holes like number 12, a par 5 that plays uphill the whole way, present the usual par-5 difficulties combined with steep elevation gain, and number 15, a par 4 that entices golfers to play over aggressively and drop a ball short of the fairway and into the woods, test a golfer's club knowledge and course IQ. This is a tough course for first-timers because so many of the holes have blind approaches, doglegs, or both, but it's enjoyable enough.

Water Sports

For fun on the water, try **Smoky Mountain Tubing** (1847 Tsali Blvd., 828/497-4545, http://cherokeetubeandraft.com, 10am-6pm daily Memorial Day-Labor Day weekend, weather permitting, $10). They do only one thing: rent tubes on which you'll drift down the river and splash your friends. Smoky Mountain Tubing has mountains of tubes, so rent one and float down the Oconaluftee River for two or three hours. They have a fleet of shuttle buses to pick you up a few miles downstream.

Food

The arrival and expansion of **Harrah's Cherokee Casino** (777 Casino Dr., 828/497-7777, www.caesars.com/harrahs-cherokee) brought with it a bevy of restaurants. **Ruth's Chris Steak House** (828/497-8577, 5pm-10pm Mon.-Thurs., 5pm-11pm Fri.-Sat., 4pm-9pm Sun., $60) is here and, like its other locations, serves a variety of steaks and chops, a handful of seafood dishes, and more than 220 wines.

Brio Tuscan Grille (828/497-8233, 11:30am-10pm Sun.-Thurs., 11:30am-11pm Fri.-Sat., lounge opens 10:30am daily, $25-40) at Harrah's is a fine Italian restaurant specializing in dishes from northern Italy. This isn't a spaghetti-and-meatballs kind of place; it's more refined, with dishes like lasagna Bolognese *al forno,* lobster and shrimp ravioli with crab *insalata,* Tuscan grilled pork chops, and *bistecca alla Fiorentina.* The ambience is nice, the wine list is nicer, and the food is great.

What's a casino without a buffet? Anyone can find something that satisfies at **Chef's Stage Buffet** (4:30pm-10pm Mon. and Thurs., 4:30pm-11pm Fri.-Sat., 1pm-10pm Sun., $26), where four chefs run four distinct micro-restaurants. There's everything here: Asian dishes, Latin, Italian, seafood, Southern, barbecue, a salad bar you could land an airplane on, and desserts for days. A second buffet option is the **Selu Garden Café** (7am-2:30pm daily, $15), which offers up a hearty breakfast every day, an à la carte lunch ($15-58), a slightly more upscale brunch on weekends (11:30am-2:30pm Sat.-Sun.), and a bottomless soup and salad bar.

Just outside of the town of Cherokee is **Granny's Kitchen** (1098 Paint Town Rd., 828/497-5010, www.grannyskitchencherokee.com, 11am-8pm Tues.-Sun. mid-Mar.-late Mar.; 11am-8pm Tues.-Thurs., 7am-8pm Fri.-Sun. Apr.-May, Sept., and Nov.; 7am-8pm Tues.-Sun. June-Aug. and Oct.; $12), a country-buffet restaurant where you can get some of the best fried chicken in North Carolina. You won't find Granny here; Granny is actually a man who likes to joke, "no one wants to eat at grandpa's, so I became granny."

Accommodations

Cherokee has many motels, including a **Holiday Inn** (376 Paint Town Rd., 828/497-3113, www.ihg.com, from $115) and an **Econo Lodge** (20 River Rd./US-19, 828/497-4575, www.choicehotels.com, from $72).

★ **Harrah's Cherokee Casino Resort** (777 Casino Dr., 828/497-7777, www. caesars.com/harrahs-cherokee, $130-510) is without a doubt the best place to stay in Cherokee. The rooms are spacious, comfortable, and well kept; there's the casino and a number of dining options an elevator ride away; and the spa provides an added layer of amenities you don't find at other hotels in town. From the higher floors, the view of the mountains is spectacular.

There's something about visiting a place and living where the residents live, and ★ **Panther Creek Cabins** (Wrights Creek Rd., 828/497-2461, www.panther-creekresort.com, cabins $79-340) gives you that chance with your choice of 10 cabins, ranging from private two-person affairs to larger lodges that could easily sleep you and seven others in four beds. These quaint cabins are quiet, just outside of downtown Cherokee, and comfortable.

Information and Services

The **Cherokee Welcome Center** (498 Tsali Blvd., 800/438-1601, www.visitcherokeenc.com, hours vary) can help you with tickets, directions, and things to do and see.

◈ US-19 South: Bryson City

To look at the mountains here, you'd think that the defining feature in this part of North Carolina would be the

Great Smoky Mountains Railroad

surrounding peaks, but that is only half right. This is a land dominated by water. Smoke-thick fog crowds valleys in the predawn hours. The peaks stand ringed in clouds. Moss, ferns, and dense forests crowd the edge of rivers and streams. All of it—the mountains, the mist, the ferns, the fog—makes it feel like you've stepped into a fairy tale when you're in the **Nantahala Gorge.** According to Cherokee stories, a formidable witch called Spearfinger lived here, as did a monstrous snake and even an inchworm so large it could span the gorge. Spearfinger and her cohorts haven't been seen in years, and the Nantahala River runs through the narrow gorge, attracting white-water enthusiasts to the rapids.

To reach Bryson City from Cherokee or the Blue Ridge Parkway, take US-19 south. Bryson City is 20 minutes from Cherokee.

★ Great Smoky Mountains Railroad

The **Great Smoky Mountains Railroad** (45 Mitchell St., 800/872-4681, www.gsmr. com, from $50 adults, from $29 children) is one of the best and most fun ways to see the Smokies. On historic trains, the GSMR carries sightseers on excursions, from two to several hours long, through some of the most beautiful scenery in the region. The half-day trips between Dillsboro and Bryson City (with a layover at each end for shopping and dining) follow the banks of the Tuckasegee River, while 4.5-hour round-trips from Bryson City follow the Little Tennessee and Nantahala Rivers deep into the Nantahala Gorge. Many other excursions are offered, including gourmet dining and wine- and beer-tasting trips, Thomas the Tank Engine and Little Engine That Could themed trips for kids, and runs to and from river-rafting outfitters.

Sports and Recreation
Nantahala River Gorge

The stunningly beautiful Nantahala River Gorge lies just outside Bryson City in the Nantahala National Forest. Nantahala is said to mean "land of the noonday sun," and there are indeed parts of this gorge where the sheer rock walls above the river are so steep that sunlight only hits the water at the noon hour. Eight miles of the Nantahala River flow through the gorge over Class II-III rapids. The nearby Ocoee River is also a favorite of rafters, and the Cheoah River, when there are controlled water releases, has some of the South's most famous and difficult Class III-IV runs.

Outfitters and Tours

The Nantahala River Gorge supports scores of river guide companies, many clustered along US-19 West. Because some of these rapids can be quite dangerous, be sure to call ahead and speak to a guide if you have any doubts as to your readiness. If you are rafting with

ASHEVILLE AND THE SOUTHERN BLUE RIDGE

Fly-Fishing in the Foothills

As you travel west of Asheville, deeper into the foothills of the Smoky Mountains, you're entering fly-fishing country. The streams here are crystal clear, cool all year, and teeming with trout. Jackson County is the home of the first and only fly-fishing trail in the nation. The **Western North Carolina Fly Fishing Trail** (www.flyfishingtrail.com) includes 15 spots on some of the best trout streams in the Smokies, where you can catch rainbow, brook, and brown trout, even the occasional golden trout. Though the many mountain communities that are near the trail's streams are a short drive from the Parkway, they're still convenient if you feel the need to fish. Complimentary **maps** are available at www.flyfishingtrail.com, www.mountainlovers.com, and https://greatsmokiesfishing.com.

For an "urban" fishing experience, try the **Tuckasegee River** as it passes through Dillsboro, 17 miles to the east of Bryson City. You can park and fish at a number of places between Dillsboro Park and the Best Western River Escape Inn,

and you run a good chance of catching a large rainbow or brown trout.

The **Lower Tuckasegee River,** running from Bakers Creek Bridge to Whittier along US-19/US-74, is around 10 miles of excellent fishing for rainbow and brown trout as well as smallmouth bass. About 15 miles east of Bryson City, you'll find some excellent fishing on streams beside the stretch of highway between Whittier and Dillsboro.

Fly Fishing Trail co-founder Alex Bell, who knows the waters of western North Carolina intimately, operates **AB's Fly Fishing Guide Service** (828/226-3833, www.abfish.org, half-day wading trips $150 for one person, $225 for two people, $300 for three people; full-day with lunch, $225 for one person, $300 for two people, and $375 for three people; full-day float trips with lunch, $350 one or two people). AB's supplies tackle and waders if you need them, as well as extensive lessons in proper casting, water reading, and fly selection, but you're responsible for securing your own North Carolina fishing license and trout stamp.

children, check the company's weight and age restrictions beforehand.

Endless River Adventures (14157 US-19 W., near Bryson City, 800/224-7238, www.endlessriveradventures.com, from $20) has white-water and flat-water kayaking instruction, rentals, and guided trips on the Nantahala, Ocoee, and Cheoah Rivers. They'll be able to suggest a run suited to your skill level. **Carolina Outfitters** (715 US-19, Topton, 800/468-7238, www.carolinaoutfitters.com, from $27) has several package outings that combine river trips with horseback riding, bicycling, panning for gems, and riding on the Great Smoky Mountains Railroad. **Wildwater Rafting** (10345 US-19 W., 12 miles west of Bryson City, 828/488-2384, www.wildwaterrafting.com, from $40) offers river guide services and zip-line canopy tours

(828/488-8899, from $66 for adults and $50 for children).

You can explore the mountains around Bryson City with the **Nantahala Outdoor Center** (13077 US-19 W., Bryson City, 828/785-5082, www.noc.com, 9am-5pm daily, from $30), which offers a variety of adventure options that include white-water rafting, stand-up paddleboarding on the flat-water sections of the river, hiking, mountain biking, and zip-lining. Half-day, full-day, and overnight trips are possible, and excursions like the Rapid Transit combine a relaxing morning train ride with an afternoon rafting trip.

★ Fly-Fishing the Tuckasegee River

The Smoky Mountains, especially the eastern grade of the Smokies, are laced with streams perfect for fly-fishing.

Anglers from all over come here to float, wade, camp, fish, hone their fly-tying craft, and learn the finer points of fly-fishing. The Tuckasegee River flows right through downtown Bryson City, and many of its feeder streams and creeks are ideal spots to throw a line.

Fontana Guide Service (3336 Balltown Rd., Bryson City, 828/736-2318, www.fontanaguides.com, $200-500 full-day trips, price depends on group size) has a number of options depending on season, interest, and skill level, including options to fish in the national park. In addition to fly-fishing excursions, they also offer kayak fishing, bass and lake fishing, and night fishing in select spots.

Fly Fishing the Smokies (Bryson City, 828/488-7665, www.flyfishingthesmokies.net) has a number of guides and options for a day or more of fishing. Wade the streams with them for two hours (one person $120, two people $150), a half day (one person $160, two people $180), or a full day (one person $220, two people $260). Try a float trip (half day $225 per boat, full day $325 per boat) or go backcountry camping and fly-fishing in Great Smoky Mountains National Park ($500-850 pp). They also go bass fishing on nearby Fontana Lake (half day $275, full day $400).

Top fishing guide **Steve Claxton's Smoky Mountain Adventures** (Bryson City, 828/736-7501, http://steveclaxton.com) specializes in leaving civilization behind in favor of camping, catching wild mountain trout, and getting a true taste of the wilderness. Four-day, three-night camping and fly fishing trips are $575-675 per person. They also offer daylong fishing trips (one person $225, two people $275, three people $325) and half-day excursions (one person $150, two people $200, three people $250).

Nantahala Fly Fishing Co. (Robbinsville, 828/479-8850 or 866/910-1013, www.flyfishnorthcarolina.com, guided trips and private lessons half day $150 one angler, $75 per additional person, full day $300 one or two anglers, $75 per additional person) provides guided trips for fly-rod fishing. If you've never held one of these odd fishing rods in your hand, they also provide a fly-fishing school ($300 for two days) and private instruction. Best of all, they have a "No Fish, No Pay" guarantee.

Food

The Bistro at The Everett Hotel (24 Everett St., 828/488-1934, www.theeveretthotel.com, 4:30pm-9pm Mon.-Thurs., 4:30pm-9:30pm Fri., 8:30am-3pm and 4:30pm-9:30pm Sat., 8:30am-3pm Sun., $9-36) serves excellent meals, using local and seasonal ingredients to create updated takes on familiar dishes or regional specialties. The trout cakes (or any preparation of locally sourced trout) are outstanding, as is any venison dish, but you can't go wrong with a burger either. Guests at The Everett Hotel can also enjoy complimentary breakfast (Mon.-Fri.) or brunch (Sat.-Sun.), and brunch is open to the public on weekends.

The Appalachian Trail passes only a few feet from **River's End Restaurant** (13077 US-19 W., 828/488-7172, www.noc.com, 8am-8pm Sun.-Fri., 8am-9pm Sat., $6-20) at the Nantahala Outdoor Center. Given its proximity to the trail (really a footbridge over the river, but on the trail nonetheless) and to the center's rafting, paddling, hiking nexus, it's a popular spot for outdoorsy sorts. The menu reflects this with dishes like the Sherpa bowls (rice, veggies, and optional meat) that are packed with protein, calories, and carbs to fuel you through a day on the trail.

Just across the footbridge from River's End Restaurant is another restaurant from Nantahala Outdoor Center, **Big Wesser's BBQ & Brew** (828/488-7174, www.noc.com, 11am-6pm Sun.-Thurs., 11am-10pm Fri.-Sat, $8-14). Barbecue platters and sandwiches, live music on weekends, and an open-air bar on the banks of the river make it a perfect place for hikers, paddlers, and outdoors lovers.

For a hearty steak, check out **Jimmy Mac's Restaurant** (121 Main St., 828/488-4700, www.jimmymacsrestaurant.com, 11:30am-9pm Wed.-Thurs., 11:30am-9:30pm Fri.-Sat., noon-8pm Sun., $8-25). In addition to steak, they serve seafood and beef, elk, and buffalo burgers. Service is fantastic; let them know you're there for a special occasion and they'll treat you even better.

Accommodations

The ★ **Folkestone Inn** (101 Folkestone Rd., 828/488-2730 or 888/812-3385, www.folkestoneinn.com, $125-169) is one of the region's outstanding bed-and-breakfasts, a roomy 1920s farmhouse expanded and renovated into a charming and tranquil inn. Each room has a balcony or porch. Baked treats at breakfast include shortcake, kuchen, cobblers, and other delicacies. An 85-year-old hotel listed in the National Register of Historic Places, the **Fryemont Inn** (245 Fryemont St., 828/488-2159 or 800/845-4879, www.fryemontinn.com; mid-Apr.-late Nov. $125-310 with meals; late-Nov.-mid-Apr. $115-215 no meal service) has a cozy, rustic feel with chestnut-paneled guest rooms and an inviting lobby with an enormous stone fireplace.

The Everett Hotel (16 Everett St., 828/488-1976, www.theeveretthotel.com, $129-349) was once the Bryson City Bank, opening its doors in the early 1900s. Since 2015, this boutique hotel has been offering modern, luxurious rooms and chic social areas, making it a comfortable place visitors can call home.

Some river outfitters offer lodging, which can be a cheap way to pass the night if you don't mind roughing it. The **Rolling Thunder River Company** (10160 US-19 W., near Bryson City, 800/408-7238, www.rollingthunderriverco.com, no alcohol permitted) operates a large bunkhouse with beds ($10-12 pp per night) for its rafting customers. **Carolina**

the Nantahala River

Outfitters (715 US-19, Topton, 828/488-6345, www.carolinaoutfitters.com) has a number of accommodations available ($50-100), including two-room cabins, two-bedroom apartments, and three-bedroom cabins suitable for a large group. Many of the outfitters also offer camping on their properties.

Nantahala Outdoor Center (13077 US-19 W., 828/785-5082, www.noc.com) has more than just white-water rafting and guided hikes. You can stay here, too. Their **Dogwood Motel** ($70-170) is an eight-room lodge on the NOC campus. **Basecamp** (from $40) is the hub for Appalachian Trail hikers and offers hostel-style lodging. There are also **platform tents** (from $200) perfect for groups. The **deluxe cabins** ($200-600) sleep up to 22 and are packed with creature comforts.

Camping

Among the nicest camping options available in the Nantahala National Forest is **Standing Indian Campground** (90 Sloan Rd., Franklin, 877/444-6777, www.recreation.gov, Apr.-Nov., $16). Standing Indian has a nice diversity of campsites, from flat, grassy areas to cozy mountainside nooks. Drinking water, hot showers, flush toilets, and a phone are all available on-site, and leashed pets are permitted. At 3,400 feet in elevation, the campground is close to the Appalachian Trail.

Deep Creek Tube Center and Campground (1090 W. Deep Creek Rd., 828/488-6055, www.deepcreekcamping.com, early Apr.-Oct., camping $27-53, cabins $75-205) has more than 50 campsites and 18 cabins, as well as access to Deep Creek, where you can go tubing (tube rentals $5 per day). The creek runs right by many campsites. You can also go gem "mining" here, a great mountain tradition; they sell bags and buckets of gem-enriched dirt in the camp store. The best part is that the facility is within walking distance of Great Smoky Mountains National Park.

Great Smoky Mountains

The Smokies draw more than 10 million visitors annually. It's easy to see why: These mountains are laced with hiking trails, rivers, and waterfalls and populated with diverse wildlife—from rare salamanders to huge elk.

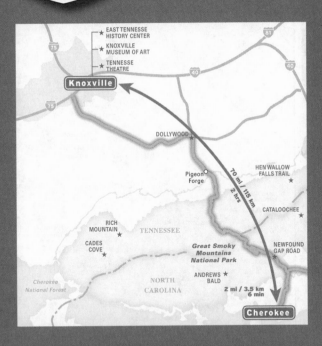

EAST TENNESSEE HISTORY CENTER

KNOXVILLE MUSEUM OF ART

TENNESSEE THEATRE

Knoxville

DOLLYWOOD

Pigeon Forge

HEN WALLOW FALLS TRAIL

CATALOOCHEE

70 mi / 115 km
2 hrs

RICH MOUNTAIN

TENNESSEE

CADES COVE

Great Smoky Mountains National Park

NEWFOUND GAP ROAD

ANDREWS BALD

Cherokee National Forest

NORTH CAROLINA

2 mi / 3.5 km
6 min

Cherokee

Great Smoky Mountains

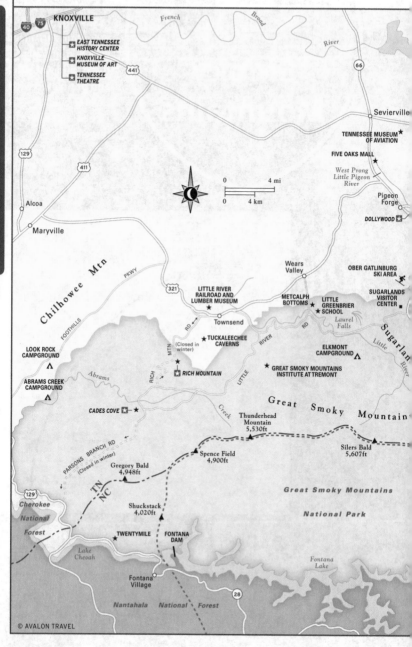

KNOXVILLE
- EAST TENNESSEE HISTORY CENTER
- KNOXVILLE MUSEUM OF ART
- TENNESSEE THEATRE

French Broad River

Sevierville

TENNESSEE MUSEUM OF AVIATION

FIVE OAKS MALL

West Prong Little Pigeon River

Pigeon Forge

DOLLYWOOD

Alcoa

Maryville

Chilhowee Mtn

PKWY

FOOTHILLS

Wears Valley

OBER GATLINBURG SKI AREA

LITTLE RIVER RAILROAD AND LUMBER MUSEUM

METCALPH BOTTOMS
LITTLE GREENBRIER SCHOOL

SUGARLANDS VISITOR CENTER

Townsend

Laurel Falls

Sugarlan

Little River

TUCKALEECHEE CAVERNS
(Closed in winter)

RICH MTN

ELKMONT CAMPGROUND

LOOK ROCK CAMPGROUND

RICH MOUNTAIN

GREAT SMOKY MOUNTAINS INSTITUTE AT TREMONT

ABRAMS CREEK CAMPGROUND

Abrams

RICH MTN

LITTLE RIVER

Great Smoky Mountain

Creek

CADES COVE

Thunderhead Mountain 5,530ft

PARSONS BRANCH RD (Closed in winter)

Spence Field 4,900ft

Silers Bald 5,607ft

Gregory Bald 4,948ft

Great Smoky Mountains

TN NC

Shuckstack 4,020ft

National Park

Cherokee National Forest

TWENTYMILE

FONTANA DAM

Lake Cheoah

Fontana Lake

Fontana Village

Nantahala National Forest

© AVALON TRAVEL

0   4 mi
0   4 km

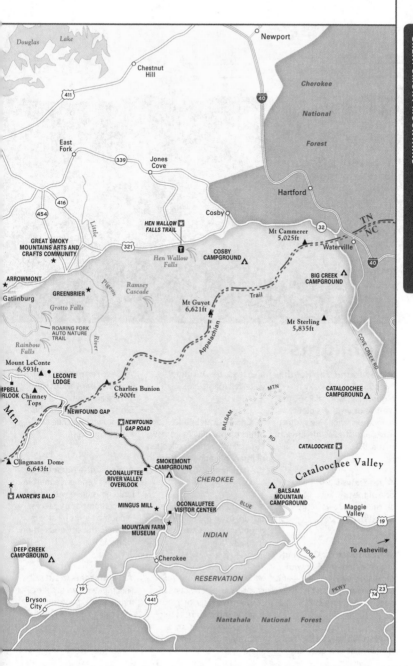

Douglas Lake

Newport

Chestnut Hill

Cherokee

411

National

Forest

East Fork

339

Jones Cove

416

Hartford

454

Cosby

TN
NC

GREAT SMOKY MOUNTAINS ARTS AND CRAFTS COMMUNITY

HEN WALLOW FALLS TRAIL

321

Mt Cammerer 5,025ft

32

Waterville

40

ARROWMONT

Hen Wallow Falls

COSBY CAMPGROUND

BIG CREEK CAMPGROUND

Gatlinburg

GREENBRIER

Pigeon

Ramsey Cascade

Trail

Grotto Falls

Little

Mt Guyot 6,621ft

Mt Sterling 5,835ft

ROARING FORK AUTO NATURE TRAIL

River

Appalachian

COVE CREEK RD

Rainbow Falls

Mount LeConte 6,593ft

LECONTE LODGE

Charlies Bunion 5,900ft

MTN

CATALOOCHEE CAMPGROUND

MPBELL RLOOK

Chimney Tops

NEWFOUND GAP

BALSAM

RD

Mtn

NEWFOUND GAP ROAD

CATALOOCHEE

Clingmans Dome 6,643ft

SMOKEMONT CAMPGROUND

Cataloochee Valley

ANDREWS BALD

OCONALUFTEE RIVER VALLEY OVERLOOK

CHEROKEE

BALSAM MOUNTAIN CAMPGROUND

Maggie Valley

MINGUS MILL

OCONALUFTEE VISITOR CENTER

BLUE

19

MOUNTAIN FARM MUSEUM

INDIAN

RIDGE

To Asheville

DEEP CREEK CAMPGROUND

Cherokee

RESERVATION

PKWY

23

Bryson City

19

441

74

Nantahala National Forest

Highlights

★ **Newfound Gap Road:** Bisecting Great Smoky Mountains National Park, the 33-mile drive offers plenty of long-distance views, short hikes, and streamside driving (page 283).

★ **Andrews Bald:** Hike to one of the prettiest high-altitude meadows in the Smokies (page 287).

★ **Cataloochee:** Camping in this secluded valley with Milky Way views is bliss—and driving through isn't half bad, either (page 292).

★ **Hen Wallow Falls Trail:** An easy out-and-back day hike leads to a beautiful waterfall (page 296).

★ **Cades Cove:** Cades Cove offers plenty of wildlife viewing and the largest collection of intact historic structures in the park (page 303).

★ **Rich Mountain:** Hike up, up, up in the hills for gorgeous views of Cades Cove (page 307).

★ **Dollywood:** Ride roller coasters and get a taste of southern Appalachian music, history, and culture at this theme park owned by a country music legend (page 317).

★ **East Tennessee History Center:** Learn about the history and culture of the Tennessee foothills at this downtown Knoxville landmark (page 324).

★ **Knoxville Museum of Art:** This Tennessee marble building is filled with impressive contemporary pieces, including works by artists native to the city and region (page 325).

★ **Tennessee Theatre:** This theater is an architectural marvel (page 326).

At the southern terminus of the Blue Ridge Parkway, you'll find the most-visited national park: Great Smoky Mountains National Park (GSMNP). The diversity of forest flora here remains unrivaled on the East Coast.

The 522,427-acre GSMNP straddles the North Carolina/Tennessee state line, and is just about equally split between the states. The slightly larger North Carolina side of the park is wilder and less developed than the Tennessee side, and in both places you can find spots so remote they have stood undisturbed by humans for untold lengths of time. You'll also find places like Cades Cove, a wide, secluded valley that welcomed some of the first pioneers to push west into Tennessee.

As you drive Newfound Gap Road from Cherokee, North Carolina, you'll climb high into the Smokies before descending into Tennessee and the touristy town of Gatlinburg, which is as quirky and cheeky as it is lovely. Dollywood, Dolly Parton's theme park, is here, and her hometown of Sevierville is just a few miles away.

Knoxville, the nearest proper city, is a half hour away. Knoxville has been named to a number of lists—Best Outdoor Towns to Live In and Southern Cities on the Rise, to name a couple—and it lives up to the hype. In 1982, the World's Fair visited, and the city has been on the upswing ever since. The food scene, kept busy by the population of young professionals and students from the University of Tennessee, is vibrant and growing, and the cultural offerings—museums, festivals, public art, and events—are rich. Here you'll find two lauded music venues, the Tennessee Theatre and the Bijou Theatre, and a field of local and touring musicians to rival Nashville.

Planning Your Time

Many visitors to Great Smoky Mountains National Park (GSMNP) only devote a day to the park. They drive Newfound Gap Road, take a short hike along the way, and circle Cades Cove before moving on. To do justice to the park and towns in the foothills of East Tennessee, give the area at least five days. Spend one day in the Cataloochee Valley. Spend another day savoring the sights of Newfound Gap Road, including Clingmans Dome and Cades Cove. Visit Dollywood and kitschy Gatlinburg and Pigeon Forge in a day, then spend two days in Knoxville.

Lodging is limited to camping within the park, unless you want to hike to the rustic LeConte Lodge, so your best bet for hotels, inns, cabins, and B&Bs is to look in Gatlinburg, Pigeon Forge, or Knoxville.

Seasons matter when visiting GSMNP and the Tennessee foothills towns. Fall is prime time, and the hiking trails can be crowded. If you seek another kind of fall color—the distinct orange of the University of Tennessee—you'll find Knoxville crowded and crazy on game day; you'll score tickets if you're lucky. In spring, the weather is mild and pleasant during the day and cool in the evenings. In summer, the park sees an uptick of visitors as those to the south flee to the cooler mountains and as vacationing families head to the park. Your best bet for missing the crowds is to be just ahead of them, visiting in early spring to midspring, in September and the first part of October, or in winter. Knoxville, however, is great to visit in any season.

Driving Considerations

In fall, Newfound Gap Road and Cades Cove can become clogged with traffic. In winter, the Blue Ridge Parkway closes due to ice and snow, and Newfound Gap

Best Restaurants

★ **Buckhorn Inn, Gatlinburg:** A four-course dinner at an elegant inn overlooking the Smokies makes for a memorable meal (page 314).

★ **Big Daddy's Pizzeria, Gatlinburg:** Big Daddy's pies, wood-fired in a brick oven, include classic combos as well as creative twists (page 314).

★ **Crockett's Breakfast Camp, Gatlinburg:** This spot offers filling breakfast options that won't empty your wallet (page 315).

★ **The Pottery House Café and Grill, Pigeon Forge:** Enjoy country and comfort food favorites in a popular shopping destination (page 322).

★ **Local Goat New American Restaurant, Pigeon Forge:** Local ingredients and fresh preparations give you another option in the Smokies (page 322).

★ **Dead End BBQ, Knoxville:** Fill up on barbecue, but save a little room for the ultra-rich banana pudding (page 330).

★ **Sweet P's Barbecue & Soul House, Knoxville:** Savor some excellent barbecue and equally excellent sides (page 331).

Road can be a nerve-wracking drive in the worst weather.

Getting There

This segment of your drive begins at the **southern terminus of the Blue Ridge Parkway,** just outside of Cherokee, North Carolina, and ends in **Knoxville,** Tennessee, **70 miles** to the northwest through Great Smoky Mountains National Park along US-441 and TN-71. It's easy to make the trip from one end to the other in an afternoon, though it may take a little longer in peak seasons.

The nearest **major travel hubs** to this region are Asheville, North Carolina, and Knoxville, Tennessee.

Car

To get to the southern entrance of the park from **Asheville,** North Carolina, drive 52 miles (1 hour, 10 minutes) west on I-40 and US-19 to reach the gateway town of Cherokee.

To get to the northern entrance of the park from **Knoxville,** Tennessee, take US-441 and then US-321 36 miles (one hour) southeast to the gateway town of **Gatlinburg.** Alternately, it's a 44-mile (one-hour) drive on I-40, TN-66,

Veterans Boulevard/TN-449, and US-321 to Gatlinburg from Knoxville.

Fueling Up

There are no gas stations along the southern end of the Blue Ridge Parkway or along Newfound Gap Road. You'll need to fuel up and buy snacks in Cherokee, North Carolina, or in Gatlinburg or Pigeon Forge, Tennessee, where you'll have your choice of filling stations.

Air

McGhee Tyson Airport (TYS, 2055 Alcoa Hwy., Alcoa, Tennessee, 865/342-3000, www.tys.org), the closest major travel hub to Knoxville and the southern end of the Blue Ridge Parkway, is about 12 miles south of Knoxville and is an easy drive into the city along the Alcoa Highway.

Asheville Regional Airport (AVL, 61 Terminal Dr., Fletcher, North Carolina, 828/684-2226, www.flyavl.com) is about 50 miles (1 hour, 10 minutes) from Cherokee, the southern gateway to the park. **Charlotte Douglas International Airport** (CLT, 5501 Josh Birmingham Pkwy., Charlotte, North Carolina, 704/359-4013, www.cltairport.com) is a 130-mile (2.5-hour) drive to Asheville.

Best Accommodations

★ **LeConte Lodge, GSMNP:** The only non-camping option in the park is a hike-in affair (page 288).

★ **Cataloochee Campground, GSMNP:** This secluded campsite inside the park is a prime spot to view elk (page 293).

★ **Mountain Laurel Chalets, Gatlinburg:** Bunk down in a private and cozy cabin that's great for groups and families (page 315).

★ **The Foxtrot Bed and Breakfast,**

Gatlinburg: Not many bed-and-breakfasts have a chef who whips up a gourmet breakfast, but this one does (page 316).

★ **Dollywood's DreamMore Resort, Pigeon Forge:** Family-friendly amenities and the perfect touch of Dolly's country charm meet at this resort (page 323).

★ **The Oliver Hotel, Knoxville:** Enjoy exceptional service and ultimate comfort (page 332).

GREAT SMOKY MOUNTAINS NATIONAL PARK

Bus

There is bus service to the **Knoxville Greyhound station** (100 E. Magnolia Ave., 865/525-9483, www.greyhound.com). **Knoxville Area Transit** (301 E. Church Ave., 865/215-7800, www.katbus.com, $1.50), or **KAT,** is a bus line running several routes throughout the city.

Great Smoky Mountains National Park

Great Smoky Mountains National Park (GSMNP, 865/436-1200, www.nps.gov/grsm) was the first—and the largest—of three National Park Service units established in the southern Appalachians. The park was founded in 1934, followed in 1935 by the Blue Ridge Parkway and in 1936 by Shenandoah National Park. These sister facilities include some 600 miles of contiguous roads and close to 800,000 acres of land, all of it acquired from private landholders, and all of it standing testament to the wild, rugged beauty of the Appalachian Mountains and the people who helped to tame these places.

Great Smoky Mountains National Park is the most-visited national park,

with visitor numbers approaching 11 million each year. In the 522,427-acre park, there are 850 miles of hiking trails, including 71 miles of the Appalachian Trail; 16 mountains over 6,000 feet; 2,100 miles of mountain streams and rivers; and an astoundingly diverse set of flora and fauna.

More than 17,000 species have been documented here, including more than 100 species of native trees, 1,500 flowering plant species, 200 species of birds, 66 types of mammals, 67 native species of fish, 39 varieties of reptiles, and 43 species of amphibians. And that's not even counting the mushrooms, mollusks, and millipedes. Researchers believe an additional 30,000-80,000 species may exist. No other area of a similar size in a similar climate can boast a higher number of species. A multitude of factors are believed to have contributed to this astounding number, including the wide elevation range (875-6,643 feet), which provides a large variance in temperature, as well as the fantastic growing conditions created by summer's high humidity and abundant rainfall (apart from mountains in the Pacific Northwest, these are the rainiest mountains in the country). Plus, as some of the oldest mountains in the world—it is believed they were formed

Great Smoky Mountains National Park

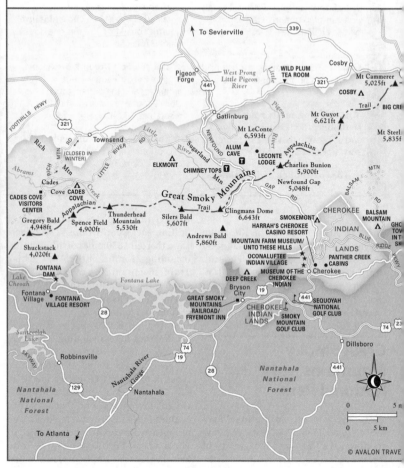

To Sevierville

To Atlanta

© AVALON TRAVE

some 200-300 million years ago—the Smokies have seen a number of dramatic climatic changes. During the last ice age (10,000 years ago), the glacial intrusion into the United States didn't reach the Smokies, making them a refuge for species of plants and animals displaced from homes farther north.

Visiting the Park
Getting There and Around
There are three main entrances to Great

Smoky Mountains National Park that access the busiest parts of the park. Each entrance is easily approached from a nearby gateway town:

- From **Cherokee, North Carolina,** drive two miles north along US-441 into the park.

- From **Gatlinburg, Tennessee,** follow US-441 south two miles into the park.

One Day in GSMNP

Morning

Enjoy breakfast at **Crockett's Breakfast Camp** in Gatlinburg, the first pancake house in Tennessee. Head out of town toward GSMNP and stop off at the **Sugarlands Visitor Center** to pick up maps, then continue on down Little River Road to **Cades Cove.** Easily the most popular auto tour in the park, Cades Cove has amazing scenery but even more amazing wildlife watching. Get there at the right time of day (early morning or near dusk) and you'll see herds of deer grazing the fields and black bears playing, eating, and napping in the remnants of former apple orchards. Hike to **Abrams Falls** and visit the nearby **Cable Grist Mill** to stretch your legs.

If you're in an SUV, truck, or some sort of high-clearance, off-road-appropriate vehicle, leave Cades Cove via **Rich Mountain Road,** a beautiful, eight-mile road that takes you up and over the mountains to Townsend (not far to the east of Gatlinburg). The views of Cades Cove are unparalleled, so have your camera ready.

Afternoon

Leave the park for lunch in Gatlinburg, then hit the **Roaring Fork Motor Nature Trail,** from which you can hike to four falls with relative ease. For a 2.6-mile round-trip hike, try **Grotto Falls Trail,** which leads through a lovely forest before you reach the 25-foot Grotto Falls. You can hike behind the falls, and if you're lucky, you may see pack llamas hauling supplies to LeConte Lodge. As you're leaving the Motor Nature Trail, stop at the **Thousand Drips Falls,** sometimes called Place of a Thousand Drips. It's literally just a few steps off the road and is an excellent cascade as it falls down the mossy rock face.

• From **Townsend, Tennessee,** take TN-73 three miles east into the park.

In addition to the main entrances, there are 17 other points to enter the park via automobile. The majority of these are gravel roads of varying states of maintenance and requiring varying degrees of driving confidence and skill, but if you're up for an adventure, you can find some beautiful corners of the park along these routes.

The 33-mile **Newfound Gap Road** (US-441) bisects the park from north to south. It's the most heavily traveled route in the park and provides a good introduction for first-time visitors.

Knoxville is 36 miles northwest of Great Smoky Mountains National Park along US-441 and TN-71.

Permits and Regulations

Great Smoky Mountains National Park is unusual in the national park system in that it has **no entrance fee,** so if you see a Friends of the Smokies donation box and you're so inclined (or so moved by what you see around you), toss a few bucks their way.

There are very few permits required for recreational activities within GSMNP. If you're an angler and you want to try your hand at fishing in the more than 2,100 miles of streams and rivers, you'll need to get a **fishing license** from either Tennessee or North Carolina, and then, depending on where you're fishing, you may need an additional permit from Gatlinburg or Cherokee. Permits are available for North Carolina at www.ncwildlife.org, and for Tennessee at www1.tn.wildlifelicense.com. To fish in Gatlinburg, pick up a license at the **Gatlinburg Welcome Center** (1011 Banner Rd., 865/277-8957, www.gatlinburg.com, 8:30am-7pm daily Apr.-Oct., 8:30am-5:30pm daily Nov.-Mar.), and keep in mind that there's no fishing on Thursdays; that's when the town stocks its streams. In Cherokee, you can pick up an Eastern Band Sport Fishing License, also called a Tribal Fishing Permit, online at www.ebcis.sovsportsnet.net; at the **Cherokee Welcome Center** (498 Tsali Blvd., 800/438-1601, www.visitcherokee-enc.com, hours vary); or at other businesses in Cherokee. You can also arrange for a fishing guide to lead you to the best spots; most guides provide licenses to their clients, so that option is hassle free. For complete regulations on accessible streams, permitted tackle, daily limits, and the like, visit www.nps.gov/grsm or the websites of Cherokee and Gatlinburg.

Hikers are not required to get permits or register with rangers, except when staying overnight in the backcountry. Those on multiday hikes or interested in backcountry **camping** can reserve (www.smokiespermits.nps.gov) tent sites and shelter space up to 30 days in advance of the trip. More information and trip-planning assistance are available through the **backcountry office** (865/436-1297, 8am-5pm daily, permits $4 pp/night). Hikers, campers, anglers, and equestrian enthusiasts are asked to follow Leave-No-Trace practices.

No dogs or other **pets** (other than service animals) are permitted on park trails, except the Gatlinburg Trail and Oconaluftee River Trail, though they are allowed in frontcountry campsites and picnic areas, so long as they remain on leash.

And, of course, don't feed, touch, or tease wildlife, and don't approach within 50 yards (150 feet) of elk or bears.

Visitors Centers

Begin your exploration of Great Smoky Mountains National Park with a stop at one of the park's four visitors centers. You'll find rangers who know the trail and road conditions as well as what's blooming where. You can also grab detailed maps and trail guides.

If you're entering Great Smoky Mountains National Park from the North Carolina side, **Oconaluftee Visitor Center** (1194 Newfound Gap Rd., Cherokee, North Carolina, 828/497-1904, www.nps.gov/grsm, 8am-4:30pm daily Dec.-Feb., 8am-5pm daily Mar. and Nov., 9am-6pm daily Apr.-Oct.), just 2 miles north of Cherokee on US-441/Newfound Gap Road, is the best place to begin your tour. You'll find public restrooms, snack machines, and a bookstore and shop operated by the Great Smoky Mountains Association (www.smokiesinformation.org). Adjacent is the **Mountain Farm Museum,** a collection of log structures including a farmhouse, barn, smokehouse, and other homestead structures; demonstrations of early farm life are held here regularly.

Along Newfound Gap Road is the turnoff to Clingmans Dome and the **Clingmans Dome Visitor Contact Station** (Clingmans Dome Rd., off Newfound Gap Rd., 25 miles from Cherokee, North Carolina, and 23 miles from Gatlinburg, Tennessee, 865/436-1200, www.nps.gov/grsm, 10am-6pm daily Apr.-June and Aug.-Oct., 10am-6:30pm daily July, 9:30am-5pm daily Nov.). Clingmans Dome is the highest peak in Great Smoky Mountains National Park and features a fantastic viewing platform. At the visitor contact station, you'll find information on the park, a bookstore operated by the Great Smoky Mountains Association, and restrooms.

The busiest information center in the park is also the first stop for visitors entering the park from Tennessee. **Sugarlands Visitor Center and Park Headquarters** (1420 Old TN-73 Scenic, Gatlinburg, Tennessee, 865/436-1200, www.nps.gov/grsm, 8am-4:30pm daily Dec.-Feb., 8am-5pm daily Mar. and Nov., 9am-6pm daily Apr.-May, 8am-7:30pm daily June-Aug., 8am-6:30pm daily Sept.-Oct.) is located just inside the park, only 2 miles from Gatlinburg. Here you'll find the usual visitors center information as well as a 20-minute film introducing you to the park. The **Backcountry Information Office** (865/436-1297, https://

Smoky Mountain Blooms and Foliage

You'll find the most abundant display of spring wildflower blooms in mid- to late April. Keep in mind that the dates for wildflower blooms and fall color displays are only guidelines. A number of factors contribute to peak timing of blooms and changing leaves. Check with park officials for the best times and places to experience the finest each season has to offer. At the highest elevations, **leaves begin to change** during the first two weeks of October, creeping down the mountains and ending in late October or early November.

* **Catawba rhododendron:** Grows at elevations above 3,500 feet; blooms in June.

* **Flame azalea:** This wild shrub blooms at lower elevations in April and May, at higher elevations through June and early July.

* **Mountain laurel:** Blooms from early May through June.

* **Rosebay rhododendron:** Blooms in lower elevations in June and July.

smokiespermits.nps.gov, 8am-5pm daily) is located at the Sugarlands Visitor Center. This is the place to get backcountry permits, as well as thru-hiker permits for the Appalachian Trail. Facilities include restrooms, snack machines, and a Great Smoky Mountains Association bookstore and shop.

In Cades Cove, about halfway around the ever-popular Loop Road, is the **Cades Cove Visitor Center** (Cades Cove Loop Rd., Townsend, Tennessee, 865/448-2472, 9am-4:30pm daily Dec.-Jan., 9am-5:30pm daily Feb. and Nov., 9am-6:30pm daily Mar. and Sept.-Oct., 9am-7pm daily Apr. and Aug., 9am-7:30pm daily May-July). Indoor and outdoor exhibits illustrate Southern mountain life and culture, and there are a number of historic structures to photograph and explore. You'll also find a Great Smoky Mountains Association bookstore (www.smokiesinformation.org) and shop, as well as restrooms, at the Cades Cove Visitor Center.

Seasons

The seasons have a major impact on visitation to GSMNP. Crowds arrive for the blooming of wildflowers in spring, and every autumn, GSMNP grows thick with visitors and even thicker with a blaze of red, yellow, and burgundy leaves on each mountainside. During fall, spots like Newfound Gap Road and Cades Cove can become absolutely lousy with cars (expect bumper-to-bumper as you loop Cades Cove), and the hiking trails crowded with picture-takers. If fall color is on your agenda, consider spending more time exploring the back roads, long hikes, and seldom-seen corners of the park in the extreme northern and southern ends.

Winter can be an excellent time to visit the park, especially if there's been a dusting of snow. With fewer crowds and with maintained roads like Cades Cove Loop and Newfound Gap Road, the mountains, trails, streams, and historic structures here can be a lonely, lovely sight.

Food and Supplies

Groceries and camping supplies are quite limited in GSMNP. Food is virtually nonexistent, so bring snacks. The **Sugarlands** and **Oconaluftee Visitor Centers** have a small selection of vending machine beverages and a few convenience items (batteries, memory cards), but little else. At the **Cades Cove Campground Store** (10035 Campground Dr., Townsend, Tennessee, 865/448-9034, www.cadescovetrading.com, 9am-5pm daily Mar.-May, 9am-9pm daily June-Aug. 15, 9am-5pm daily Aug. 16-Nov.), you can grab breakfast, a sandwich or wrap, pizza, and other snack bar items as well as a very limited selection of groceries and camping supplies. **Elkmont Campground Concessions** (434 Elkmont Rd., Gatlinburg, Tennessee, 865/430-5560, 4pm-8pm daily Mar. 8-May, 9am-9pm daily June-Aug. 15, 4pm-8pm daily Aug. 16-Oct., 4pm-6pm daily Nov.) has a handful of snack foods and beverages as well as firewood, ice, and a few camping items. That's it for food, so stock up in Gatlinburg, Cherokee, or whichever town you visit outside the park.

At **Fontana Village** (300 Woods Rd., Fontana Dam, North Carolina, 800/849-2258, www.fontanavillage.com), just outside GSMNP, there are two restaurants, a snack bar, ice cream shop, and general store. **Mountainview Restaurant** (828/498-2215, 7:30am-2:30pm and 5:30pm-8pm daily, $14-28) serves steaks, chicken, and a nice selection of fish that includes several preparations of trout. Reservations are recommended during weekends and in peak season. **Wildwood Grill** (828/498-2211, 11:30am-9pm daily Apr.-Oct., $8-19) serves pizza, burgers, and an array of fried appetizers. In the summer, concerts on the deck give visitors a little listening enjoyment to go with dinner.

Accommodations

As big as GSMNP may be, there are few places to stay within the boundaries, and all but one option are either campsites or backcountry shelters. The lone exception is **LeConte Lodge** (865/429-5704, www.lecontelodge.com, mid-Mar.-mid-Nov., adults $145, children ages 4-12 $85, includes breakfast and dinner), a collection of cabins and small lodges and a central dining room/lodge. It's only accessible by hiking in, so you have to be dedicated to stay there.

Other lodging in the park includes **frontcountry camping** in 10 developed campgrounds featuring restrooms with cold running water and flush toilets. These sites are at Abrams Creek, Balsam Mountain, Big Creek, Cades

Cove, Cataloochee, Cosby, Deep Creek, Elkmont, Look Rock, and Smokemont. Only Cades Cove, Cataloochee, Cosby, Elkmont, and Smokemont take **reservations** (877/444-6777, www.recreation.gov, $14-20); all others are first-come, first-served.

Backcountry camping includes more than a dozen shelters and around 100 campsites. They're sprinkled throughout the park at convenient intervals. To reserve a backcountry site, visit www.smokiespermits.nps.gov; you can call the GSMNP **backcountry office** (865/436-1297) for more information on your chosen campsite or for trail or campsite closings or warnings.

There are also seven **tent-only group campgrounds** (877/444-6777, www.recreation.gov, $26-65) at Big Creek, Cades Cove, Cataloochee, Cosby, Deep Creek, Elkmont, and Smokemont. Additionally, there are five **horse camps** (877/444-6777, www.recreation.gov, $20-25) at Anthony Creek, Big Creek, Cataloochee, Round Bottom, and Tow String.

Just outside the park, **Fontana Village** (300 Woods Rd., Fontana Dam, North Carolina, 828/498-2211 or 800/849-2258, www.fontanavillage.com, lodge $133-183, cabins $133-459, camping $20-45) offers a place to lay your head in your choice of accommodations: tent or RV camping, one- to three-bedroom cabins, and lodge rooms. There are 100 lodge rooms, 110 cabins, and 20 campsites. At the lodge, you'll find complimentary wireless Internet in the public areas; other amenities include an outdoor pool and lazy river, as well as a fitness center and small day spa.

Information and Services

The official website of **Great Smoky Mountains National Park** (www.nps.gov/grsm) has a good deal of the information you'll need to plan a trip. At the visitors centers in Sugarlands, Oconaluftee, Cades Cove, and Clingmans Dome, you'll

The Chimney Tops Wildfire

On November 23, 2016, a wildfire—later determined to be arson—was reported on Chimney Tops off Newfound Gap Road. Due to drought conditions and high winds, it spread quickly and affected lands inside and outside Great Smoky Mountains National Park. Inside the park, nearly 18,000 acres burned, causing the temporary closure of dozens of trails, roads, campsites, and facilities. Fortunately, the park suffered little permanent damage aside from the burned acreage. Outside the park, the towns of Gatlinburg and Pigeon Forge in Tennessee suffered devastating losses. All told, more than 2,400 homes, businesses, and other structures were destroyed; 175 people were injured; and 14 people lost their lives. Damages exceed $500 million and rebuilding efforts are ongoing.

Park officials moved quickly to prevent more loss within the park, closing trails and campgrounds during the fire and after. Cleanup and rebuilding efforts began almost immediately, and major repairs should be completed by the 2018 season. On several trails—Chimney Tops, Road Prong, Sugarland Mountain, Rough Creek, Twin Creeks, Baskins Creek, Bull Head, Rainbow Falls, Trillium Gap, and others in the vicinity of Chimney Tops and Roaring Fork Motor Nature Trail—and in a few campsites, visitors may experience some temporary closures as crews work to complete reclamation tasks.

Campers in frontcountry and backcountry sites should be aware of the seriousness and potential dangers of campfires. A stray spark could start another wildfire like this one, and an improperly extinguished fire could do the same. Even the most seasoned camper could make a mistake with tremendous consequences. Be mindful of the fire regulations when camping in the park and be attentive to your campfire if you have one. If you have questions on fire etiquette, ask a ranger or campground official, and adhere to Leave-No-Trace principles (www.LNT.org).

find additional information from helpful rangers and fellow travelers.

The nearest hospitals are **LeConte Medical Center** (742 Middle Creek Rd., Sevierville, Tennessee, 865/446-7000, www.lecontemedicalcenter.com), about 25 minutes from the west park entrance; **Blount Memorial Hospital** (907 E. Lamar Alexander Pkwy., Maryville, Tennessee, 865/983-7211, www.blountmemorial.org), an hour away from the west park entrance; and **Swain County Hospital** (45 Plateau St., Bryson City, North Carolina, 828/488-2155, www.myswaincommunity.com), a little less than 30 minutes from the eastern park entrance in Cherokee.

★ Newfound Gap Road

Easily the most heavily traveled route in the Smokies, Newfound Gap Road (US-441) connects Cherokee with Gatlinburg and sees thousands of visitors a day. Newfound Gap Road is the perfect introduction to Great Smoky Mountains National Park: Contour-hugging curves, overlooks with million-dollar views, easy hikes right off the roadway, and a 3,000-foot elevation change give you a great overview of these mountains and this spectacular park. During peak times in the summer and fall, it's not uncommon to encounter a traffic jam or two along this 33-mile scenic route, especially when bears are taking their time crossing the road.

Newfound Gap Road earned its name in 1872 when Swiss geographer Arnold Henry Guyot determined that a newly found gap was the lowest pass through the Great Smoky Mountains. Lower in elevation and easier to access than the former passage at Indian Gap, 1.5 miles away, the name Newfound Gap was soon used to refer to the entire route.

Oconaluftee Visitor Center and Mountain Farm Museum

As you begin your trip along Newfound Gap Road from the North Carolina side, your first stop will probably be the "Welcome to Great Smoky Mountains National Park" sign, but the **Oconaluftee Visitor Center** (1194 Newfound Gap Rd., Cherokee, North Carolina, 828/497-1904, www.nps.gov/grsm, 8am-4:30pm daily Dec.-Feb., 8am-5pm daily Mar. and Nov., 9am-6pm daily Apr.-Oct.), just 2 miles north of Cherokee on US-441/Newfound Gap Road, will likely be the second stop you make. You can pick up a park map, grab the schedule of ranger-led programs, and see exhibits on the people who called these hills home long before the park was in existence. The visitors center and adjacent comfort station are LEED Gold certified for their environmentally friendly design.

Next to the visitors center is **Mountain Farm Museum** (sunrise-sunset daily, free), which showcases some of the finest farm buildings in the park. Most date to the early 1900s and among them are a barn, apple house, and the Davis House, a log home built from chestnut wood and constructed before the American chestnut blight decimated the species. This collection of structures is original to the area and dates back to the turn of the 20th century. Though the barn is the only structure original to this site, the other buildings were moved here from inside and adjacent to the park and arranged much like the typical farm of the era would have been laid out. If you visit during peak times, you'll see costumed living-history interpreters demonstrating the day-to-day chores that would've occurred on this farm: preparing meals, sowing seeds, maintaining and harvesting the garden, taking care of the hogs, and the like.

Smokemont Campground (information 828/497-9270, reservations 877/444-6777, www.recreation.gov, year-round, $17-20) is just off Newfound Gap Road,

view from Newfound Gap Road

3.2 miles from the Oconaluftee Visitor Center. There are 142 total sites available between tent campsites and RV sites. It's located on the banks of the Oconaluftee River and thus can get quite buggy, so be prepared.

Oconaluftee River Trail

Distance: 3 miles round-trip
Duration: 45 minutes
Elevation gain: 70 feet
Difficulty: easy
Trailhead: Oconaluftee Visitor Center, or just outside of Cherokee on US-441

This trail by the Oconaluftee River runs 1.5 miles from the **visitors center** to the outskirts of Cherokee. Flat save for a bridge or two and a few gentle rises, the Oconaluftee River Trail is a lovely walk. In the spring the banks of the Oconaluftee are blanketed with wildflowers, and throughout the year you may see a herd of elk crossing the river at any number of places. Bring bug spray because it can get a bit buggy right by the river on a still day. This is a great option for walking or jogging, and is one of only two paths in Great Smoky Mountains National Park where you can walk your **dog** or ride your **bike.**

Deep Creek Valley Overlook

The **Deep Creek Valley Overlook,** 14 miles from the Oconaluftee Visitor Center (and 16 miles from Sugarlands Visitor Center if coming from the other direction), is one of the most popular overlooks in the park for good reason. From here you'll have a long view of the mountains, which roll away from you for as far as you can see.

Oconaluftee River Valley Overlook

Halfway through Newfound Gap Road is the **Oconaluftee River Valley Overlook,** a spot where you can spy the deep cut of the valley formed by the Oconaluftee River. This place is ideal for a picnic, so if you're hungry and you've brought your blanket and something to eat, spread out and relax for a few minutes.

Newfound Gap

One of the most-visited overlooks is at **Newfound Gap.** This is the highest elevation on Newfound Gap Road, at 5,048 feet, and though the views here are fantastic, the first thing you'll probably notice is the Rockefeller Memorial, a simple stone terrace that straddles the Tennessee/North Carolina state line and commemorates a $5 million gift made by the Rockefeller Foundation to acquire land for the park. In 1940, President Franklin D. Roosevelt dedicated the park from this site. Plan to spend a little time here, especially early in the morning or near sunset. At sunset, you can see the Smokies' namesake haze settling into the folds and wrinkles of the mountains, and in the early morning, the mountains emerge from a blue haze in a subtle display of color that's been the subject of many a postcard and computer screen background.

Appalachian Trail to Mount LeConte via The Boulevard

Distance: 15.9 miles round-trip
Duration: 7.5-9 hours
Elevation gain: 3,000 feet
Difficulty: strenuous
Trailhead: Appalachian Trail trailhead at the Newfound Gap Road Overlook
Directions: From the Sugarlands Visitor Center on Newfound Gap Road, drive 13 miles southeast along Newfound Gap Road to the Newfound Gap Overlook.

This is a tough hike. The trail largely follows the crest of the mountains, and thus rises and falls several times with some significant elevation gains and losses.

From the start, the trail climbs for two miles. You'll be on a steady incline, but there are views aplenty to give you a little boost. At 1.7 miles, just before the junction with **Sweat Heifer Creek Trail,** you'll have a good look at Mount LeConte to the north. At 2.8 miles, **The Boulevard** forks off to the left.

Continue along The Boulevard, ignoring the sign for the Jump-Off Trail (you can hike that one-mile trail on the return trip if you want). Soon you'll drop down to an elevation around 5,500 feet, after which the trail bounces back and forth between 5,500 and 6,000 feet until you begin to properly climb **Mount LeConte** and make your way to the lodge there and the 6,593-foot summit.

If you want to turn this into an overnighter by staying at the lodge or in the backcountry shelter, you'll need advance reservations (which can be difficult to come by). Otherwise, prepare for a long day on the trail.

Charlies Bunion Hike

Distance: 8.1 miles round-trip
Duration: 7-8.5 hours
Elevation gain: 1,700 feet
Difficulty: strenuous
Trailhead: Appalachian Trail trailhead at the Newfound Gap Road Overlook
Directions: From the Sugarlands Visitor Center on Newfound Gap Road, drive 13 miles southeast along Newfound Gap Road to the Newfound Gap Overlook.

Originally named Fodderstack, the rock formation of Charlies Bunion earned its new name when two men, Charlie Conner and Horace Kephart, were hiking here. According to legend, they stopped to rest at Fodderstack and Conner removed his boots and socks, revealing a bunion that Kephart felt resembled the rocks around them. Impressed, Kephart promised Charlie that he'd get the name of this place changed on official maps in honor of the bunion.

The first leg of this trail follows the **Appalachian Trail** and **The Boulevard** to **Mount LeConte.** The trail climbs for two miles. At 1.7 miles, you'll come to the junction with Sweat Heifer Creek Trail. At 2.8 miles, The Boulevard forks off to the left; continue straight to reach Charlies Bunion.

The **Icewater Spring Shelter,** aptly named for the cold spring that flows out of the mountain here (treat the water before you drink it), is just 0.25 mile from the junction and is a good spot to rest. From the spring, continue a little less than a mile to a short **spur trail** on your left that leads out to the rock outcrop known as **Charlies Bunion.**

Clingmans Dome

At 6,643 feet, **Clingmans Dome** is the third-highest mountain in the eastern United States and the highest in the Great Smoky Mountains. A flying saucer-like **observation tower** at the end of a long, steep walkway gives 360-degree views of the surrounding mountains, and on a clear day that view can be as far as 100 miles. More often, though, it's misty up here in the clouds, and Clingmans Dome receives so much precipitation that its woods are actually a coniferous rainforest. The road to the summit is closed December-March, but the observation tower remains open for those willing to make the hike. To get to Clingmans Dome, turn off Newfound Gap Road 0.1 mile south of Newfound Gap and then take **Clingmans Dome Road** (closed in winter), which leads 7 miles to the parking lot. The peak is near the center of the park, due north of Bryson City, North Carolina.

★ Andrews Bald

Distance: 3.5 miles round-trip
Duration: 3 hours
Elevation gain: 1,200 feet
Difficulty: moderate
Trailhead: Clingmans Dome parking area at the end of Clingmans Dome Road

The highest grassy bald in Great Smoky Mountains National Park, Andrews Bald is a beautiful sight at the end of a nearly 2-mile hike from Clingmans Dome. Balds are meadows found higher up on the mountains, and this one is absolutely lousy with flame azalea and rhododendron blooms in the summer. Note that Clingmans Dome Road is closed in the winter.

Before trail renovations, the Andrews Bald hike had some of the most rugged sections of rocky trails in the park. Thanks to the Trails Forever program, work crews fixed drainage issues, rebuilt parts of the trail, and even built a few stairways from native rocks and trees. Now the hike is easier and safer and leads to a spectacular view of the Smoky Mountains. A bonus: The hike is just long enough to discourage some potential hikers, but it's still short enough to be doable by everyone in your party.

The **Forney Ridge Trail** starts in a spruce-fir forest that was once beautiful, but is now unfortunately dead or dying. That's because the forest has been ravaged by a tiny bug—the balsam woolly adelgid—that devours Fraser firs. However, there is a certain beauty in the white bones of the tree trunks jutting up from the land. Don't worry, though; the views get considerably better in a short time. Around 1.6 miles into the hike,

Top to bottom: observation tower at Clingmans Dome; a typical cabin in the Great Smoky Mountains; LeConte Lodge.

you'll reach the edge of **Andrews Bald,** where the forest opens up into a fantastic panorama. In spring and summer, there is a proliferation of wildflowers, flame azaleas, and rhododendrons.

Mount LeConte

Just below the 6,593-foot peak of Mount LeConte is the only true lodging in Great Smoky Mountains National Park, the ★ **LeConte Lodge** (865/429-5704, www. lecontelodge.com, mid-Mar.-mid-Nov., adults $145, children ages 4-12 $85, includes lodging, breakfast, and dinner). Like the mountain's summit, the lodge is accessible only via the network of hiking trails that crisscross the park. And if the accessibility limitation isn't rustic enough for you, this collection of cabins has no running water or electricity. It does have views for days and the seclusion of the Smoky Mountains backcountry.

For the most part, the environs harken back to the lodge's 1934 opening. LeConte Lodge has no hot showers. In every cabin, there is a bucket for a sponge bath—which can be surprisingly refreshing after a hot day on the trail— that you can fill with warm water from the kitchen, though you need to supply your own washcloth and towel. There are a few flush toilets in a separate building, and the only lights, aside from headlamps and flashlights, are kerosene lanterns. Your room does come with two meals: dinner and breakfast. Both are served at the same time every day (6pm for dinner and 8am for breakfast), and feature food hearty enough to fuel another day on the trail.

The lodge doesn't lack for charm, but it does for comfort, so if you're the five-star-hotel, breakfast-in-bed type, this may not be the place for you. Catering to hikers who are happy to have a dry place to sleep and a bed that's comfier than their sleeping bag, it's short on luxury amenities, and rooms are, in truth, bunk beds in small, drafty cabins. But if you're a hiker or if you just love to have a completely different experience when you travel, this is a one-of-a-kind accommodation.

The **Roaring Fork Motor Nature Trail** (Mar.-Nov.) at the foot of Mount LeConte is the starting point for a trio of hiking trails that lead to LeConte Lodge. **Bull Head Trail** is a 6.8-mile trip from the trailhead to the lodge, as is **Rainbow Falls Trail.** (Bull Head and Rainbow Falls Trails share a trailhead at the designated parking area on the motor nature trail.) **Trillium Gap Trail,** the trail used by the lodge's pack llamas, passes by the beautiful Grotto Falls on its 6.7-mile route (the trailhead is at the Grotto Falls parking area on the Roaring Fork Motor Nature Trail). Each of these three trails requires a four-hour hike to reach the lodge from the trailhead.

Three other trails lead to Mount LeConte from various points in the park. **Alum Cave Trail** (5 miles one-way) enters from Newfound Gap Road; it's the shortest and easiest to access, but it's also the steepest.

Alternatively, **The Boulevard** connects the Appalachian Trail to LeConte Lodge (8 miles from Newfound Gap Overlook). The Boulevard is relatively easy, with little elevation change, but there's the issue of exposure on this trail—the rock path has more than a few dizzying drops right beside the trail. These drops, combined with The Boulevard coming in from the Appalachian Trail, deter most day- or overnight-hikers from its use. **Brushy Mountain Trail** (11.8 miles round-trip) leads to the summit from the Porters Creek Trailhead off Greenbrier Road (closed in winter). Despite the significant elevation change, this is a relatively easy trail.

Alum Cave Bluff to Mount LeConte Hike

Distance: 5 miles one-way
Duration: 3-3.5 hours
Elevation gain: 2,560 feet
Difficulty: moderate with strenuous sections
Trailhead: Alum Cave Trailhead
Directions: From the Sugarlands Visitor Center on

Newfound Gap Road, drive 8.7 miles southeast along Newfound Gap Road to the Alum Cave Trailhead.

As one of the most popular hikes in the park, this trail receives a lot of wear-and-tear. Fortunately, the park does periodic repairs to keep the trail in fantastic condition. Hikers will find sturdy handholds along the stone stairs and narrow, exposed sections at the upper end of the trail.

The trail starts off fairly gently as it climbs up to Arch Rock. **Alum Cave Creek** runs alongside the trail for a while, and here you'll have the chance to snap pictures of several cascades and beautiful rhododendron thickets (which bloom in late June and July). You'll reach **Arch Rock,** which is less arch and more natural tunnel, around 1.5 miles in.

Here the trail begins to climb more steeply. A set of stone steps leads out of Arch Rock, and the forest changes from hemlock and hardwood to spruce and fir trees. In another half mile, you'll reach **Inspiration Point,** where the view opens onto one of the mid-elevation balds.

When you reach **Alum Cave Bluff,** you're halfway to Mount LeConte. The rock formations aren't caves but rather deep overhangs that create an impressive shelter from the rain. The Smokies receive more than 85 inches of rain a year, yet the majority of the soil under the bluffs remains dry and dusty, an arid spot in one of the wettest forests in the nation.

Most hikers turn around at Alum Cave Bluff, but if you're pushing on to Mount LeConte, the path steepens and grows more challenging as you gain elevation. The trail narrows to a set of rock ledges where **steel cables** have been bolted into the mountain for use as a handhold. The drop may be precipitous, but the views are fantastic. Soon, the trail intersects with **Rainbow Falls Trail,** leading you to the summit of **Mount LeConte** in short order.

If you plan on hiking to Mount LeConte and back in a day or spending the night at the lodge, it's in your best interest to arrive early so you can get a parking space.

Chimney Tops

Chimney Tops takes its name from the twin knobs that rise from a ridge like chimneys. These rocky summits are rare in the Smokies, but that's not the draw; what brings people up this steep, challenging trail is the 360-degree view.

Chimney Tops Hike

Distance: 4 miles out and back
Duration: 3.5 hours
Elevation gain: 1,400 feet
Difficulty: strenuous
Trailhead: Chimney Tops trailhead on Newfound Gap Road

This popular hike leads to an outstanding view from its namesake pinnacles. The trail has suffered some severe storm damage in the past few years, and was closed intermittently until a Trails Forever team completed repairs, fixing drainage issues, installing or refreshing rock steps and staircases, and building elevated turnpikes, as well as other laborious methods to mitigate the impact from hikers and Mother Nature. The 2016 wildfires that ravaged the Smokies and surrounding towns were started on Chimney Tops, so this area will have extensive fire damage for years to come. Trails Forever crews and workers from the National Park Service rehabilitated the trail after the fires, along with constructing a new observation deck; the trail reopened in October 2017.

Chimney Tops is incredibly steep, gaining nearly 1,000 feet in the last mile. To reach the pinnacles, the actual Chimney Tops, requires a very steep scramble over bare rock, which can be dangerous—and it's easier to climb up than to come back down.

Many people explore the first few hundred yards of this trail because it's right off Newfound Gap Road. The cascades, pools, and boulders found along **Walker Camp Prong** are picturesque and good for wading and sunbathing. As you climb, you'll cross **Road Prong,** another stream, twice. Just after the second crossing, the trail splits, with one part following Road Prong and the other heading to Chimney Tops. Stay right and head to the chimneys.

After a brief ascent, the trail steepens significantly. Take a breather here before tackling this long, straight climb. The trail continues and narrows as you walk the ridgeline. Soon, you'll be at the foot of the **Chimney Tops,** and you'll see a sign from the National Park Service warning you to proceed at your own risk. Beyond this point, the trail is closed, as the 2016 fires rendered the peaks unsafe. The 2017-built observation deck just below Chimney Tops provides views of both Mount LeConte and the namesake pinnacles.

Campbell Overlook

The **Campbell Overlook** is only three miles from the Sugarlands Visitor Center, and it is home to one of the best views of Mount LeConte you'll find along the road. LeConte is an interesting mountain. At 6,593 feet, it's the third-highest peak in the Smokies, but it's the tallest mountain east of the Mississippi in that it rises more than a mile from the foot of the mountain to the summit.

Sugarlands Visitor Center

The **Sugarlands Visitor Center** (1420 Old TN-73 Scenic, Gatlinburg, Tennessee, 865/436-1200, www.nps.gov/grsm, 8am-4:30pm daily Dec.-Feb., 8am-5pm daily Mar. and Nov., 9am-6pm daily Apr.-May, 8am-7:30pm daily June-Aug., 8am-6:30pm daily Sept.-Oct.) is the most popular visitors center in the park due to its proximity to Gatlinburg. There's the usual visitors center stuff—maps, guidebooks, a few gift items, some snacks—and it's also the origination point for the 1.9-mile Gatlinburg Trail.

Gatlinburg Trail

Distance: 3.8 miles out and back
Duration: 2 hours
Elevation gain: 20 feet
Difficulty: easy
Trailhead: Sugarlands Visitor Center

This is one of only two trails in the park to allow **pets** and **bicycles** (the other is the Oconaluftee River Trail in Cherokee). More of a walk than a hike, the Gatlinburg Trail follows the **West Prong Little Pigeon River** and Newfound Gap Road for most of the trip. It's pretty and not especially challenging, but the optional walk to **Cataract Falls**—a few hundred yards up **Cove Mountain Trail,** which splits off the Gatlinburg Trail near the trailhead—can provide some photo opportunities and a pretty, easy-to-reach waterfall.

Eastern Smokies

The eastern side of Great Smoky Mountains National Park was settled before the western side, so there are plenty of coves and hollows with historic structures or the ruins of cabins, barns, and other buildings in the fields and woods and along creek banks and floodplains. There are also many herds of elk here, introduced since 2001 in an attempt to revive the species that once roamed these hills.

Balsam Mountain Road

Since most of the crowds who visit Great Smoky Mountains National Park use Newfound Gap Road exclusively, it's nice to find a route that's less traveled and possibly more beautiful. One such route is **Balsam Mountain Road** (May-Nov.), a lovely drive where you may be lucky to see 10 other cars.

Accessible only from the Blue Ridge Parkway near Soco Gap, the road traverses 14 miles of ridgeline. To reach Balsam Mountain Road, turn off the Parkway at Milepost 458 and follow Heintooga Ridge Road to the Heintooga Overlook and Picnic Area; here the road changes names to Balsam Mountain Road and turns to gravel.

As soon as it turns into Balsam Mountain Road, it becomes one-way, so you're committed to follow it to its end. This will take about 1.5 hours (if you don't stop to hike or take in the scenery), primarily because the gravel road forces you to slow down. It's narrow but well maintained, so you can drive most cars along the route. If you're in doubt of the road's condition or are concerned about your vehicle's clearance, check online (www.nps.gov/grsm) for road closures and advisories.

Balsam Mountain Road is an excellent place to see spring wildflowers, summer rhododendron, and fall leaves. At these times, traffic may pick up, but the idea of a gravel road discourages enough visitors to keep this road the one less traveled.

When you've driven about 13 miles along Balsam Mountain Road, it becomes two-way again. Here, it begins to follow Straight Fork, which will lead you right onto Straight Fork Road (closed in winter); this road cuts through the Qualla Boundary to Cherokee and US-441.

Deep Creek

Just south of Cherokee and just north of Bryson City, Deep Creek is a spot more popular with locals than tourists, but it's worth a stop. Deep Creek is relatively placid, aside from a couple of waterfalls a bit upstream. If you're not into wading or tubing, don't worry—this is a lovely place to picnic and hike or even camp away from the crowds found in some of the more popular spots in the park.

There are two nice waterfalls to see here. **Juney Whank Falls** is less than a half mile from the Deep Creek Campground, and it cuts an impressive figure as it drops a total of 90 feet in two stages. **Indian Creek Falls** is a stunning set of falls and cascades some 60 feet high, located a mile from the campground.

At the end of Deep Creek Road are the trailheads leading to the waterfalls. You'll also find the **Deep Creek Campground** (first come, first served for individual sites; reservations for group camping 877/444-6777, www.recreation.gov, Apr.-Oct., $17). There are nearly 100 campsites here, many of which fill up with locals. If you want to camp here, arrive early or reserve well in advance.

Outside the park, there's also the **Deep Creek Tube Center and Campground** (1090 W. Deep Creek Rd., Bryson City, North Carolina, 828/488-6055, www.deepcreekcamping.com, camping $27-53, cabins $75-205), a charming collection of tent and RV campsites and cabins for rent. As the name implies, they rent tubes for use on Deep Creek. Rentals ($6 for all-day use of your tube) are cheap, so you can play in the water as long as you like.

Juney Whank Falls Trail
Distance: 0.6-mile loop
Duration: 30 minutes
Elevation gain: 120 feet
Difficulty: moderate
Trailhead: parking area at the end of Deep Creek Road across from the campground

Juney Whank Falls supposedly got its name from Junaluska "Juney" Whank, a Cherokee person said to have been buried near the falls. The path here is pretty straightforward: It's short, at times steep, and at the end, a little slick. You'll walk across a log bridge to get a look at the tall, skinny falls, which actually descend in two stages. The first stage drops 40 feet to a stone outcropping, then flows beneath the log bridge to fall and cascade another 50 feet.

Indian Creek Falls Trail
Distance: 2 miles round-trip
Duration: 1 hour
Elevation gain: 160 feet
Difficulty: easy to moderate
Trailhead: parking area at the end of Deep Creek Road across from the campground

This easier but longer hike takes you past a smaller waterfall, Tom's Branch Falls,

The Return of Native Elk

Elk are native to the mountains of North Carolina and Tennessee, but overhunting decimated their population across the region. In North Carolina, the last elk was believed to have been killed in the late 1700s; in Tennessee, the mid-1800s. In 2001, the National Park Service reintroduced elk to the park by bringing 25 elk to Great Smoky Mountains National Park from Land Between the Lakes National Recreation Area in Kentucky. The next year, they brought in another 27 animals. Today, they believe somewhere between 150 and 200 elk live in the park.

The majority of the elk can be seen in the **Cataloochee Valley**, though a small herd lives near the **Oconaluftee Visitor Center** and **Smokemont Campground** and can be seen wading across the river and grazing in the fields and forest there.

Adult males, called bulls, weigh 600-700 pounds, while females, referred to as cows, weigh around 500 pounds. Some bulls have antlers that are five feet across. They're territorial, and bulls sometimes see humans as a threat and may charge. It's best to watch the elk from a safe distance. In Great Smoky Mountains National Park, it is illegal to approach elk within 50 yards (150 feet) or any distance that disturbs or displaces the animals.

At certain times of the year, you may see calves walking close by their mothers. Never approach or touch a calf. If an elk calf feels threatened and its mother is not nearby, its natural defense is to lie down and be still. It may look orphaned, but mom's within earshot, so back away slowly.

Elk are most active in the early morning and evening, much like deer. Also like that of deer, their diet is primarily grass, bark, leaves, and acorns. There are no natural predators of elk in the Smokies today, though sick, injured, and young elk are sometimes targets of opportunity for black bears, coyotes, or even the boldest of bobcats.

---

on your way to Indian Creek Falls. For about a mile, you'll follow a gently graded roadbed, and soon you'll arrive at the falls. Really, Indian Creek Falls is more of a steep, long, slick cascade of water than an actual waterfall, but it's quite serene.

Road to Nowhere

An odd place to visit is the so-called **Road to Nowhere.** Just south of the Deep Creek entrance outside Bryson City is a short stretch of highway leading north into Great Smoky Mountains National Park. Lonely, even spooky, the road is all that remains of a parkway planned to trace a path through the Smokies along Fontana Lake. Construction was started on the parkway before being abandoned. Today, the road stops quite abruptly about 6 miles inside the park, at a stone tunnel. Though hard feelings over the failed parkway have softened, many families still hold a grudge against government officials who vowed to build a road along the lake to provide access to old family cemeteries there.

Cars are prohibited from using the tunnel at the end of the Road to Nowhere, but visitors on foot are welcome to stroll right through. After you pass through the tunnel, there a hike waiting for you that clocks in at 36.5 miles. Fortunately, it follows the northern bank of Fontana Lake, giving you a little reward for the effort.

★ Cataloochee

Nestled in the folds of the mountains and encircled by 6,000-foot peaks, the Cataloochee Valley was settled in the early 1830s. This isolated valley on the northeastern edge of Great Smoky Mountains National Park was home to two communities—Big and Little Cataloochee—and more than 1,200 people in 1910. By the 1940s, all but a few were gone, having left the valley for hills and hollows nearby. Today, this is one of the more beautiful spots in the national park, and a few historic structures are all that remain of the communities that thrived here, save a few memories and stories written down.

Cataloochee Valley is not far from I-40, but it can be a little difficult to find because the signage directing you here is poor at best. From I-40, take exit 20 onto US-276. Take an immediate right onto Cove Creek Road. The condition of the road—it's alternately gravel and paved—and the narrow, winding route will make you doubt you made the right turn, but you did. Zigzag up this road for about 12 miles and suddenly it will open up into the wide, grassy expanse that is Cataloochee Valley. Before you begin your descent into the valley, stop at the overlook just past the intersection with Big Creek Road. From here, you can marvel at the valley sweeping away before you and the mountains rising up all around.

The valley is open to vehicular traffic from 8am to sunset, so keep that in mind if you're visiting without plans to camp. Though less visited than other areas, like Cades Cove on the western side of the park, Cataloochee sees its fair share of visitors. Most arrive in the evenings shortly before sunset to see the elk grazing in the fields. If you don't plan on camping and you'd rather avoid the crowds, as small as they may be, visit in midday and take a hike and see if you can find the elk in the woods; it's where they go to escape the heat.

The ★ **Cataloochee Campground** (Cataloochee Entrance Rd., information 828/497-9270, reservations 877/444-6777, www.recreation.gov, Apr.-Oct., $20, reservations required) has 27 tent and RV sites. There is also a horse camp with seven sites not far up the valley; down the valley there's a group campground with three sites and room for much larger parties. This highly recommended campsite is one of the most secluded you'll find in the frontcountry. The campground is located 3.1 miles along the entrance road.

Sights

There are four prominent structures still standing in Cataloochee Valley: two homes, a school, and a church. A few other structures and ruins, cemeteries, fences, and walls remain throughout the valley as well. The most prominent building is the **Palmer Chapel and Cemetery.** The chapel was built in 1898, and it's been some time since there's been a regular service here. Today, the chapel sees sporadic use, the most regular being the annual reunion of the descendants of some of the oldest Cataloochee families. Descendants of the Barnes, Bennett, Caldwell, Noland, and Palmer families gather here to eat, hold a short church service, and maintain the cemetery. Throughout the year, there are some great opportunities to capture the chapel in all sorts of lighting, weather, and seasonal conditions.

Across the road is the **Beech Grove School,** the last of three schools to serve the children of the valley. It's empty save for a few artifacts. Beech Grove School operated on a very different school schedule than we're familiar with: The only regular school sessions were held from November to January, sometimes February and rarely into March. This odd schedule was built around the seasons and freed children for planting and harvesting, as well as hunting and preserving food—staple activities for many living in the mountains.

Just up the road is the **Caldwell House.** We know from records that the owner, Hiram Caldwell, was prosperous, but you could tell that just by comparing this 1906 home with the other historic homes in the park, which are, by and large, log cabins. The Caldwell House is frame-built (similar to houses now), with paneling on the interior walls.

The final structure is the **Palmer House,** located off Big Creek Road, not far from the Cataloochee Ranger Station.

This was once a log home—two, actually, connected by a covered walkway called a dogtrot—but as the owners came into money in the early 1900s, they began making improvements and remodeling the home. They covered the exterior and interior with weatherboarding and began using fancy wallpaper in some rooms (scraps of the wallpaper are there today). When the son inherited the property, he remodeled it, adding rooms to the home and operating it as a boardinghouse. Renters were primarily anglers who came to fish in the three miles of stocked trout stream the family owned.

Boogerman Trail

Distance: 7.4-mile loop
Duration: 3.5-4 hours
Elevation gain: 1,050 feet
Difficulty: moderate
Trailhead: just past Cataloochee Campground

This trail isn't named for some fearsome and mythical creature from the woods; it's named for Robert "Boogerman" Palmer, the former owner of much of the land along this hike. Palmer is rumored to have earned his nickname in school, where he told his teacher that he wanted to be "the Boogerman" when he grew up. This trail is anything but fearsome, and in the summer you'll likely see a few other hikers; if it's solitude you're seeking, hit the trail during the shoulder seasons.

Start the hike by crossing **Palmer Creek.** Follow Caldwell Fork upstream for nearly a mile and you'll come to **Boogerman Trail.** Turn left onto the trail and begin a gentle climb. When you reach a lower ridgeline, the path levels out, then descends through a grove of pine trees before ascending again. Soon, the trail makes a steep ascent to another level ridge. This section features some of the largest trees, mostly poplars, that you'll see on this hike.

As you continue on this short ridgeline section, you'll encounter some signs of human settlement, the first of which is

The Palmer Chapel is one of many historic structures you'll find in Cataloochee.

a **stone wall.** Continue your descent and cross the stream you're following a few times, passing more rock walls along the way. If the wildflowers aren't too high, you may spot a large, strange piece of metal just off the trail. It's the remnant of some sort of homesteading equipment, perhaps a sluice gate for a water flume or maybe a piece from a sawmill. Whatever it is, it's alien here.

When you pass the decayed remains of a **cabin,** you're close to the junction with Caldwell Fork Trail. At **Caldwell Fork Trail,** turn right and cross Snake Branch (the stream you've been following) and, soon thereafter, Caldwell Fork. You'll cross Caldwell Fork several more times before reaching the junction with **Boogerman Trail** and the path back to the trailhead.

Big Creek

Big Creek is the site of a beautiful and seldom-visited frontcountry campground and has one of the best hikes for beginning day hikers and backpackers. The Big Creek Trail is more of an easy creekside walk than a hike, but it's long enough to make you feel accomplished when you're done.

For more of a challenge, turn Big Creek into a big overnighter by including a summit of Mount Sterling, or you can take on Mount Sterling from a couple of different routes, all accessible from this region.

Big Creek Trail

Distance: 10.6 miles round-trip
Duration: 5-6 hours
Elevation gain: 600 feet
Difficulty: easy
Trailhead: Big Creek Picnic Area off I-40 at the Waterville exit (exit 457)

Big Creek Trail follows an old motor road built by the Civilian Conservation Corps (CCC) in the 1930s, so it's smooth and wide with a very gentle grade for its entire length. The difficult part of this trail is the distance, so be sure to bring plenty of water and something to eat.

Roughly one mile in from the trailhead, you'll see **Rock House,** an impressive rock cliff that has sheltered more than a few loggers, Civilian Conservation Corps workers, hunters, and hikers from a rainstorm. Just beyond Rock House is **Midnight Hole,** where Big Creek flows through a narrow chute in the rock, then drops 6-7 feet into a deep, dark pool before flowing on.

Two miles in, you'll see **Mouse Creek Falls,** a 35-foot cascade that drops right into Big Creek. It's a fantastic spot to sit, relax, take some pictures, and enjoy the woods. It's also a great spot to turn around if you may not be up for the whole 10-mile trip.

Push on past Mouse Creek Falls and you'll come upon **Brakeshoe Spring.** In another 2.5 miles, you'll reach **Walnut Bottoms** and **Campsite 37.** This is one of the best campsites in the park if you're going to make this hike an overnighter.

CHAPEL
CHURCH

From here, it's time to retrace your steps back to the trailhead.

Cosby

For the first half of the 20th century, Cosby was known as the moonshine capital of the world. The national prohibition on liquor turned many locals to making their own. When scientists and workers began to come to Oak Ridge to work on secret military ventures like the Manhattan Project, they weren't accustomed to Tennessee's dry county laws, and the demand for moonshine skyrocketed. Today, there isn't much by way of moonshine production in town, and most of the visitors come here for the national park.

Cosby's present reputation is as a friendly town with one of the lesser-used park entrances. That's good for you, because when autumn leaves begin to change and the crowds pack Gatlinburg and clog the easy-to-access trails along Newfound Gap Road, you can head to Cosby. In town you'll find a few restaurants and a handful of cabin rentals, but the park is the real treasure.

Cosby Campground (471 Cosby Campground Rd. A, Cosby, Tennessee, 423/487-2683, www.recreation.gov, Apr.-Oct., $14) has 157 sites for tents and RVs. Despite being home to the park's third-largest campground, Cosby is known as the quietest of the park's gateways. There are a number of trails that originate from the campground.

★ Hen Wallow Falls Trail
Distance: 4.4 miles out and back
Duration: 3.5 hours
Elevation gain: 900 feet
Difficulty: moderate
Trailhead: Gabes Mountain Trailhead, across the road from the Cosby Campground picnic area

From the outset, **Gabes Mountain Trail** is a steady climb on a path that's at times rugged. Follow this trail until you see a sign for the **side trail** leading to the waterfall (2.1 miles into the hike). The 0.1-mile side trail is a little steep, but not problematically so.

Hen Wallow Falls tumbles 90 feet into a small pool below, where there are plenty of salamanders to see. The falls themselves are only 2 feet wide at the top but fan out to 20 feet at the bottom; during dry months, the falls are still pretty, but less wow-inducing. To get back to the trailhead, just retrace your steps.

Mount Cammerer Trail
Distance: 11.2 miles round-trip
Duration: 7-7.5 hours
Elevation gain: 2,740 feet
Difficulty: strenuous
Trailhead: Low Gap Trailhead, just beyond the Cosby Campground amphitheater area

To start, park in the group parking area and walk along the road to where it curves into the B Section of the campground. Just before **campsite 92,** you'll see a trailhead; follow it for a short distance until it crosses Cosby Creek, then turn right on **Low Gap Trail.** From here, the trail climbs a little less than 3 miles up the mountain via a series of winding switchbacks until you reach the Appalachian Trail.

Turn left to join the **Appalachian Trail** for 2.1 miles. The first mile of this trail is more level, so it gives you a chance to catch your breath or make up some time. You'll know when you reach the junction with the **Mount Cammerer Trail** because the Appalachian Trail descends to the right; you want to stay straight. The **summit** is 0.6 mile from where you leave the Appalachian Trail.

At the summit is a **stone fire tower** built in the 1930s and restored by volunteers throughout the years. The view from the deck here is awesome—it's one of the best in the park.

Roaring Fork Motor Nature Trail
One of the most beautiful drives in Great Smoky Mountains National Park is the **Roaring Fork Motor Nature Trail** (Mar.-Nov.). This one-way loop passes through

rhododendron thickets and dense hardwood forests as it follows the old roadbed of the Roaring Fork Community. To get here, turn onto Historic Nature Trail (Old Airport Road) at traffic light #8 in Gatlinburg and follow the signs. Before you reach the trail, you'll drive a short distance on Cherokee Orchard Road, which runs through what was an 800-acre commercial orchard in the 1920s and 1930s; shortly after the orchard, you'll be at the head of the trail and have the chance to purchase an inexpensive tour booklet from a roadside exhibit.

Unfortunately, Roaring Fork was one of the areas affected by the 2016 wildfires. Immediately after the fires, the area was closed, but trails here have since opened, with cosmetic changes being the biggest difference most visitors will find. Forest fires can dramatically change the shape of the forest, burning out underbrush and dead (or dying) trees, making room for wildflowers, brambles, and saplings, so expect the trails to be the same great hikes, but with a slightly different look.

The roadbed here was built by hand in the 1850s, which explains both its narrowness and serpentine route. Around 25 families lived here, and though it may look quaint and primitive to our eyes, a few of the homes had running water thanks to the system of troughs—some of which are still standing—that carried water right to the houses.

As the road climbs through the forest, roll down your windows and take in a few deep breaths of that fresh, cool mountain air. There is a pair of **overlooks**, though they're overgrown and in poor repair. When you stop, take in the silence. You'll soon find yourself surrounded by the sounds of nature: wind, birds calling, and streams rumbling and echoing through the forest.

Be sure to stop at the cabins still standing here. **Ogle Place,** a two-room

Top to bottom: Grotto Falls; typical bridge found in the national park; hiking in GSMNP.

cabin surrounded by rhododendrons; **Ephraim Bales Cabin,** which is smack in the middle of a boulder field; and **Alfred Regan Cabin,** which has an amazing trough system still in place, are all worth spending a few minutes exploring and photographing.

There are three waterfalls within hiking distance of the Motor Nature Trail: **Rainbow Falls** (the most popular of the hikes); **Grotto Falls;** and **Baskins Falls.** If you're not up for a hike, **Thousand Drips Falls** (sometimes called the Place of a Thousand Drips) is just off the road. In wet times, it's a great cascade plummeting down the mountain, and during drier times, it's much more tame but still serene.

Rainbow Falls Trail

Distance: 5.4 miles round-trip
Duration: 3.5-4 hours
Elevation gain: 1,700 feet
Difficulty: strenuous
Trailhead: Roaring Fork Motor Nature Trail, 3.3 miles from Gatlinburg traffic light #8, at the Rainbow Falls and Bull Head Trail parking area

This trail is strenuous due to how steep and rocky it is and how slick it can become in places where the trail nears the water and as you get closer to the falls. Note that Roaring Fork Motor Trail is closed in the winter.

As you leave the parking area, you'll cross **Trillium Gap Trail** and begin to climb alongside LeConte Creek. Follow the trail as it goes through a couple of switchbacks and then crosses the creek on a **log bridge.** Here, you'll enter a stretch where some impressive trees stand. Soon you'll cross LeConte Creek again. At this crossing, you can see **Rainbow Falls** above you. Continue up the trail to a spot just below the falls.

Here, LeConte Creek plunges 80 feet to the rocks below. During that plunge, the water becomes more of a heavy mist, giving us the name Rainbow Falls. Though you can get some good photographs from the trail, there are other interesting shots to be had from different angles around the falls. Be aware that if you scramble around the falls, the rocks are slick and you could slip and hurt yourself; with a 2.7-mile hike back to the car, who wants to do that? If you decide to explore the area around the falls, use caution and stay safe.

You may notice that the **Rainbow Falls Trail** continues on past the waterfall itself. It is possible to take this trail to the summit of Mount LeConte, but that is a strenuous, steep, full-day hike of close to 14 miles.

Grotto Falls Trail

Distance: 2.6 miles round-trip
Duration: 2-2.5 hours
Elevation gain: 585 feet
Difficulty: moderate
Trailhead: Roaring Fork Motor Nature Trail, about 2 miles into the trail, Grotto Falls parking area on the left

From the parking area, you'll follow a short, unnamed spur before joining **Trillium Gap Trail,** which leads to **Grotto Falls** before continuing to the top of **Mount LeConte.** As you hike, you'll notice the path is hard packed—that's because this trail is the resupply route for **LeConte Lodge,** so it sees traffic from the llama trains carrying supplies up to the lodge. If you're lucky, you'll see one of these trains.

The forest was once composed mostly of hemlock trees, but thanks to a nasty little bug—the hemlock woolly adelgid—many of these trees are dead or dying. Even though some of the trees are being ravaged, the forest is still thick, and it opens dramatically where the stream plunges 25 feet to form Grotto Falls.

The most intriguing part of Grotto Falls is the grotto. Trillium Gap Trail passes behind the falls thanks to a hefty rock overhang. It provides some interesting photographic opportunities that make it is one of the most popular waterfall hikes on this side of the park.

Baskins Falls Trail

Distance: 3.2 miles
Duration: 3 hours
Elevation gain: 950 feet
Difficulty: strenuous
Trailhead: Roaring Fork Motor Nature Trail, on the left near the Jim Bales Place

This 30-foot waterfall is like a little secret hidden along the popular **Roaring Fork Motor Nature Trail** (Mar.-Nov.). Seldom visited, it's almost a forgotten hike, meaning you can have the falls to yourself.

As soon as you start the hike, you'll pass a cemetery before making a climb up to a ridgeline. A steep descent from the ridge will take you to **Baskins Creek.** Cross the creek (be careful, especially in high water) and make the steep climb over another ridge. From here, you can see what's left of an old chimney standing in the woods. Just beyond a tiny, wildflower-filled meadow is the side path leading to the base of the falls. On the right side of this trail is an old **homesite,** followed by a steep descent down to the **falls.**

Many hikers turn around here and return to their car, but it is possible to continue along this trail another 1.5 miles and arrive near the entrance to the Roaring Fork Motor Nature Trail. If you do this, know that you will have a 3-mile walk along the road back to your car.

Western Smokies

The western Smokies are a bit wilder than the eastern Smokies. As pioneers moved in from the east, they first settled the coves and hollows there, then found passes through the Smokies and settled there. The mountains are tall and steep, and the valleys deep, and where there are coves and meadows, they're broad, rich-soiled places that, before the national park, were home to several small communities.

Fontana Lake Area

At the southern edge of Great Smoky Mountains National Park lies Fontana Lake, a 10,230-acre reservoir created in the 1940s as part of the Tennessee Valley Authority's (TVA) efforts to supply electricity to the various communities and government and industrial facilities in the region.

Fontana Dam

The 480-foot-tall, 2,365-foot-wide **Fontana Dam,** complete with three hydroelectric generators, was completed in 1944. It provided much-needed electricity to the factories churning out materials for World War II, including facilities in Oak Ridge, Tennessee, where research leading to the atomic bomb was conducted.

To build Fontana Dam, the Tennessee Valley Authority (TVA) purchased more than 1,000 tracts of land and relocated roughly 600 families comprising five communities. Those folks left behind homes, schools, churches, and barns, all of which were covered by the lake. This displacement of so many families and elimination of these small communities was part of the tradeoff that resulted in the modernization of the region via cheap, readily available electric power and the great number of jobs required to complete the project. The dam also provides much-needed flood control to a region that receives between 55 and 82 inches of rainfall each year. The TVA can regulate the depth of the lake by releasing water in anticipation of flood events, and the water level of Fontana Lake can vary by as much as 50 feet.

Fontana Dam is the highest concrete dam east of the Mississippi, and its impoundment provides great recreational opportunities. The Appalachian Trail crosses the dam itself, and thousands of boaters and anglers take to the lake each year. There are more than 238 miles of shoreline along Fontana Lake, and over 10,000 acres of water surface.

The exhibits at the **Fontana Dam Visitor Center** (Fontana Dam Rd., off NC-28 near the state line, www.tva.com,

9am-7pm daily Apr.-Aug., 9am-6pm daily Sept.-Oct., free) tell the story of the region and the construction of the dam. There's also a small gift shop, and a viewing platform overlooks the dam. Hikers take note: They sell backcountry camping permits (perfect for those long overnight trips along Lakeshore Trail) and have showers in the back.

Twentymile

One of the most remote sections of the park, Twentymile is on the southern end, just past Fontana Lake and Dam and alongside the smaller Cheoah Lake. Despite the name, Twentymile Trail only goes 5 miles into Great Smoky Mountains National Park, but you can make it into a 20-mile journey by combining it with other trails, or you can keep it to a manageable day hike of around 8 miles by doing a smaller loop. Though this part of the park is out of the way, Twentymile is a popular hike, so expect to see some fellow hikers, especially on weekends and through the week on beautiful days in summer and autumn. There is a trio of **backcountry campsites** (reservations: www.smokiespermits.nps. gov) at Twentymile Trail: campsites 13, 92, and 93.

Twentymile Loop Trail
Distance: 7.6-mile loop
Duration: 3.5-4 hours
Elevation gain: 1,200 feet
Difficulty: easy
Trailhead: Twentymile Ranger Station
Directions: Twentymile Ranger Station is six miles west from Fontana Dam on NC-28. Turn at the sign for Twentymile.

This hike is very easy, following a roadbed and a well-maintained trail along Twentymile Trail, Twentymile Loop Trail, and Wolf Ridge Trail. There are a number of stream crossings along this route, and though there are log bridges spanning Moore Springs Branch and Twentymile Creek, floods may wash them away. If you're there before repair

crews can fix the bridges, you may have to wade across.

From the trailhead, go 0.5 mile to where **Wolf Ridge Trail** branches off to the left. Follow Wolf Ridge Trail for 1.1 miles to **Twentymile Loop Trail.** Along Wolf Ridge, you'll cross Moore Springs Branch five times as you climb. Along the way, there are abundant wildflowers, including bloodroot, fire pink, and trilliums, and the opportunity to see bears, deer, and other wildlife.

After following Wolf Ridge just over a mile, you'll see Twentymile Loop Trail branching off to the right. Cross Moore Springs Branch and follow the trail 2.9 miles along an easy grade before descending to a crossing of Twentymile Creek and the junction with **Twentymile Trail.**

Turn right on Twentymile Trail to descend back along the creek and to the trailhead. From here, it's just over three miles back to your car.

Gregory Bald via Twentymile Trail
Distance: 15.7-mile loop
Duration: 9 hours (strenuous day hike or overnighter)
Elevation gain: 3,650 feet
Difficulty: strenuous
Trailhead: Twentymile Ranger Station
Directions: Twentymile Ranger Station is six miles west from Fontana Dam on NC-28. Turn at the sign for Twentymile.

This hike makes Twentymile live up to its name, even though it's a mere 15.7 miles. It's doable in a day, but it's a long, hard day, so camping for a night in the backcountry is recommended.

From the trailhead, follow **Twentymile Trail** for 0.5 mile until it intersects with **Wolf Ridge Trail.** Turn here and follow Wolf Ridge Trail 6.3 miles to **Gregory Bald Trail.** The grade of Wolf Ridge Trail is somewhat steep, but more than that, it's a relentless uphill climb all the way to where you crest the ridge before reaching **Parson Bald.** As you approach the ridge and Parson Bald, you'll find copious amounts of blueberry bushes, and, if the berries are in season, a fair number of bears enjoying blueberries. The same holds true at Parson Bald, just over the ridge. If you're on the trail in August, when the blueberries tend to ripen, be cautious.

When you reach Parson Bald, it's a short, easy walk to Sheep Pen Gap, where you'll find **Campsite 13** (reservations and information 865/436-1297, www.smokiespermits.nps.gov) and the end of Wolf Ridge Trail. Turn right on Gregory Bald Trail and climb just under a half mile to **Gregory Bald.** There are azaleas in great abundance, and during midsummer the bald is a riot of blooms. But even if you come when there's not a bloom to be found, the views make the hike worth it.

From here, keep heading east to **Rich Gap,** where you'll come upon a four-way trail junction. Follow **Long Hungry Ridge Trail** to the right, heading south. This trail is pretty flat for the first mile, then it begins to descend, and the descent becomes increasingly noticeable as you move down the trail. You'll find **Campsite 92** 3.4 miles from Rich Gap. Once you've reached the campsite, you've left the steepest part of the hike behind you.

Continue down Long Hungry Ridge Trail to the place where it meets Twentymile Trail, following Twentymile Creek 2.6 miles back to the junction with Wolf Ridge Trail. At this point, you're only 0.5 mile from the trailhead.

Elkmont

At the **Elkmont Campground,** only eight miles from Gatlinburg, drifts of male fireflies rise up from the grass to flash their mating signal, but they don't do so as individuals—they blink in coordinated ways that still baffle researchers. For a two-week window every summer (often **early to mid-July,** but it depends on a variety of factors), their nightly light show delights crowds. It starts slowly, with only a few of these insects showing off. Then more join in, and more, until they reach a crescendo. Slowly, they begin to synchronize until, at the peak, whole fields may flash all at once, giving you a sudden and startling blink of light and, just as sudden, darkness. Or they may flash in waves moving around the fields and hillsides. Or large groups may appear to flash their lights at one another and wait in the darkness for a response. Whatever the reason for their display, the synchronous fireflies are amazing little creatures. Nineteen species of fireflies live in Great Smoky Mountains National Park, but these are the only fireflies in the park to synchronize their flashing.

The synchronous fireflies may have been one of the reasons the Wonderland Park Hotel was built here in Elkmont. In 1908, the little logging town of Elkmont was born, and in 1912, the Wonderland Park Hotel was built. Cottages dotted the hillsides and bottoms. Once the park was established, cottage owners were granted lifetime leases on their property, and family members continued to renew the leases at 20-year intervals until the early 1990s. The Wonderland Park Hotel and the cottages were at one time slated for demolition, but the **Elkmont Historic District** is now listed in the National Register of Historic Places. The hotel collapsed in the early 2000s.

The **Elkmont Campground** (434 Elkmont Rd., Gatlinburg, Tennessee, 865/430-5560, www.recreation.gov, mid-Mar.-late Nov., $17-23) has 220 campsites, 55 of them along the Little River, with front-row seats to the firefly light show for those here at the right time. This is the largest of the campgrounds in Great Smoky Mountains National Park, and one of the most visited. In addition to the firefly show and the attraction of Little River, this site also serves as a good base for exploring the area.

Laurel Falls Trail
Distance: 2.5 miles round-trip
Duration: 1.5-2 hours

Elevation gain: 400 feet

Difficulty: easy to moderate

Trailhead: parking area 3.9 miles west of Sugarlands Visitor Center on Little River Road

As the shortest and possibly easiest waterfall hike in Great Smoky Mountains National Park, Laurel Falls is the most popular of such hikes. The trail is paved and the grade is gentle (after you get past a short, steep section at the start of the trail), and the falls are a little over 1.3 miles from the trailhead.

Prepare to be dazzled when you reach the falls. Laurel Falls drops 75 feet in a wide, picture-perfect cascade. It's a gorgeous spot to photograph, but you have to be there early in the day to get a shot of the falls without people in it.

Greenbrier Cove

Greenbrier Cove, like many other coves in the park, was once home to a mountain community. This area was settled in the early 1800s, and families farmed, trapped, and hunted the land until the establishment of the national park. This cove has an interesting footnote: Dolly Parton's ancestors, Benjamin C. and Margaret Parton, moved here in the 1850s, and their descendants left when the park was formed.

Greenbrier is stunning, especially in the spring. The cove is known as a wildflower hot spot, but don't underestimate the beauty of this place in any season.

Ramsey Cascades Trail

Distance: 8 miles round-trip

Duration: 5.5 hours

Elevation gain: 2,375 feet

Difficulty: strenuous

Trailhead: Ramsey Cascades Trailhead at the Greenbrier park entrance, six miles east of Gatlinburg off US-321

Ramsey Cascades is the tallest waterfall in Great Smoky Mountains National Park, spilling 100 feet in a series of steps

Top to bottom: Cable Grist Mill; summer in Gatlinburg; historic structure in Cades Cove.

before collecting in a pool at the base. As if that wasn't reason enough to undertake this hike, this section of the park is known as a wildflower paradise; a springtime visit is highly recommended.

The first portion of this trail is a continuation of the gravel road you took to the parking area. You'll soon cross **Little Laurel Branch** and almost immediately after, the Middle Prong of Little Pigeon River via a long **footbridge.** If you've timed your hike with the wildflower bloom, the next half mile will be a riot of color.

The hiking here is easy until you reach the 1.5-mile mark, where the Jeep trail you're on ends. To the left (north) is the **Greenbrier Pinnacle Trail,** a trail that's not maintained by the park; **Ramsey Cascades Trail** continues on through a thicket of rhododendrons.

Past this point, you find yourself on a trail where roots and rocks are more the norm, so watch your footing. Continue along this trail; it will turn steep, you'll cross the **Ramsey Prong** and a side stream, and you'll know you've arrived when you hear the waterfall. The final approach is rocky and slick, with a lot of scrambling, so use caution. When you've taken in all of the **Ramsey Cascades** you can handle, simply reverse your course to the trailhead.

Brushy Mountain to Mount LeConte Hike

Distance: 11.8 miles round-trip
Duration: 6-7 hours
Elevation gain: 3,000 feet
Difficulty: moderate
Trailhead: Porters Creek Trailhead on Greenbrier Road, six miles east of Gatlinburg off US-321
Directions: At traffic light #3 in Gatlinburg (junction of US-441 and US-321), travel east on US-321. Drive six miles, then turn right on Greenbrier Road (which becomes a gravel road soon). At the fork in the road 3.1 miles in, continue straight 1 mile to the Porters Creek Trailhead.

The first mile or so of this trail follows an old gravel road, the **Porters Creek Trail.** In the spring, trilliums are profuse here. You'll pass a **cemetery** and several stone walls and then cross a **footbridge** at a fork in the road. Turn left at the fork. You'll meet another fork 100 yards or so down the trail, at which you turn right onto **Brushy Mountain Trail.**

The trail continues for 4.5 miles, climbing some 2,500 feet as it does. At 5.5 miles, you'll meet **Trillium Gap Trail.** Go left on the Trillium Gap Trail and you'll reach **Mount LeConte.** Turn right and you can reach the summit of **Brushy Mountain** in 0.6 mile.

Foothills Parkway

It's not technically in the park, but the **Foothills Parkway** is a great scenic drive that gives you high-elevation views without the traffic on more popular routes in the park proper. The Foothills Parkway is reached via US-321, 5.5 miles from **Townsend.** The 17-mile road has plenty of places to pull off to picnic or take in the view. There's one short hike here at **Look Rock,** a 0.5-mile stroll to an observation tower.

★ Cades Cove

Easily the most popular auto tour loop in Great Smoky Mountains National Park, Cades Cove receives around two million visitors a year. They come for the scenery—a long, wide, grassy-bottomed valley surrounded by undulating mountains—to see the handful of preserved homesteads and historic structures, and because it's one of the park's best, and most reliable, spots to see wildlife.

The **Cades Cove Loop** is approximately 11 miles long, but in the summer and especially in the fall when the leaves are at their best, expect to spend two hours or more on this one-way road through the valley floor—and that's if you don't stop to photograph the wildlife or explore the historic structures. If you're the curious type or find the light is perfect for taking pictures, you can easily double the amount of time you spend here. When

Black Bears

Biologists estimate there are more than 1,500 black bears living in Great Smoky Mountains National Park, and if you know where and when to look, your chances of seeing one in the wild are quite good.

Though bears can be spotted throughout the park, one of the most reliable places to see them is **Cades Cove.** Here, in the early morning and as dusk settles, the bears are more active, prowling the forest's edge and even eating apples that have fallen from the trees.

As awesome as it is to see a bear, they can present a problem to park visitors, and we can present a problem to them. With the great number of visitors to Great Smoky Mountains National Park, many bears have grown accustomed to seeing people and have therefore lost their natural fear of humans, automobiles, and horses. As the bears grow more used to people, we decide to give them "treats" and lure them closer to our cars and our campsites with food. Bears that are too accustomed to people, especially bears that have been fed a few times, can grow bold, even borderline aggressive, searching campsites and open cars for food or even approaching open car windows or picnic tables.

Fortunately, serious incidents with black bears are rare, but they do occur. In 2000, a mother bear and her cub attacked and killed a camper near the Elkmont Campground. Every year, campsites and trails are closed due to bear activity and the potential for interaction between bears and visitors.

Park staff and volunteers do their best to educate visitors on proper human-bear interaction. Throughout the park, you'll see signs and placards advising you on how to properly store and dispose of food and reminding you not to approach bears. Remember that bears are wild animals and unpredictable, and keep these tips in mind:

- **Do not approach** within 50 yards or any distance that disturbs a bear, and do not allow a bear to approach you. For a good view, invest in a pair of binoculars.

- **Never feed bears.** It only gets them used to humans and causes them to think of us as a source of food.

- **Store food** in appropriate containers and in the proper places when camping. If you're not sure of the proper procedure, ask a ranger.

- **Dispose of garbage** in bear-proof receptacles.

- **Report** nuisance bear behavior or visitors breaking these rules to park officials.

In the unlikely event that **a bear approaches you,** stand tall, wave your arms, and make as much noise as possible. If you need to, throw sticks or rocks at the bear. In most cases, this will intimidate the bear and deter it from coming any closer. If the bear charges, don't run—they can sprint 30 miles per hour, so you don't stand a chance. Instead, keep making noise and back away slowly, never turning your back to the bear. Often, bears will make bluff charges, so this is likely what you're seeing. If a black bear actually makes contact, fight back with anything and everything available to you; with a loud-enough and fierce-enough fight, the bear may see you as too much to deal with and leave you alone.

you do stop, be sure to pull off the road and leave enough room for traffic to pass. One source of traffic jams in Cades Cove is visitors who stop in the middle of the road to ooh and aah at the wildlife and scenery.

The popularity of this drive is well deserved. In the hours around dawn and dusk, wildlife is especially active. Vast herds of white-tailed deer are the most common sight (I once tallied 50 in a field before I quit counting), but black bears are also frequently spotted. The bears like to cozy up to the apple trees that dot the cove, and you'll occasionally spot them and their cubs napping or eating in the branches.

You may notice that the fields look especially manicured. They are, to an extent. Far from being mown and maintained like a golf course, the fields in Cades Cove are allowed to run wild, but only so wild. The National Park Service maintains the fields and fences, mowing, repairing, and reseeding as necessary to keep the valley looking much like it did when settlers lived here.

To take this lovely-in-any-season drive, follow Little River Road west from the Sugarlands Visitor Center for 17.2 miles; there it will turn into Laurel Creek Road and lead you into Cades Cove in another 7.4 miles. You can also access Cades Cove by entering the park at Townsend on TN-73, then turning right on Laurel Creek Road, following it for 16 miles to the entrance to the cove. Cades Cove is closed to vehicular traffic every Saturday and Wednesday morning from May until late September. On those days, the loop is open exclusively to bicycle and foot traffic until 10am. The rest of the year, the road is open to motor vehicles from sunrise to sunset daily, weather permitting.

The **Cades Cove Campground** (10042 Campground Dr., Townsend, Tennessee, 877/444-6777, www.recreation.gov, $17-20) is a popular spot where you'll definitely want to reserve a campsite. This campground is open year-round, and though the occupancy is a little lower in the dead of winter, you'll still find a few intrepid visitors taking refuge from the cold in one of the 159 campsites here. Hikers, take note: There are several backcountry campsites off the trails in Cades Cove, making it a good base for overnight trips.

Sights

According to some historians, long before European settlers pushed west through the Smokies, the Cherokee Indians had hunting camps and possibly even a small settlement established in Cades Cove. In fact, the name Cades Cove is believed to have come from Chief Kade, a little-known Cherokee leader. By the early 1820s, the first Europeans were here, building cabins and barns and carving homesteads out of the forest. More settlers arrived, having heard of the rich, fertile bottomland in Cades Cove, and by 1850 nearly 700 people called the valley home. As the collection of cabins and homesteads grew into a community, buildings like churches and schools were constructed. Families lived here even after the National Park Service began purchasing land. The last remaining school in Cades Cove closed in 1944 and the post office in 1947.

Today, a number of historic structures remain standing along the valley floor. Among them is the most-photographed structure in the park, the **Methodist Church.** From time to time a wedding is held here, though it's more common for visitors to leave handwritten prayers on scraps of paper at the altar.

The **Cable Mill Area** is the busiest section of the loop. Here you can see the **Cable Grist Mill** in operation and even buy cornmeal or flour ground on-site. In addition to the mill and Methodist Church, the area contains two other churches, a few barns and log houses, and a number of smaller structures.

Halfway around the loop, you'll find the **Cades Cove Visitor Center** (Cades Cove Loop Rd., Townsend, Tennessee, 865/448-2472, 9am-4:30pm daily Dec.-Jan., 9am-5:30pm daily Feb. and Nov., 9am-6:30pm daily Mar. and Sept.-Oct., 9am-7pm daily Apr. and Aug., 9am-7:30pm daily May-July), which has a good bookstore and gift shop, and, most important, the only public restroom you'll find on the tour.

Abrams Falls Trail
Distance: 5 miles round-trip

Duration: 3 hours

Elevation gain: 350 feet

Difficulty: moderate

Trailhead: Turn right onto a gravel road 4.9 miles from the start of the Cades Cove Loop; at 0.4 mile in is a parking area and the trailhead.

Several trails lead off into the woods from this parking area, but it's obvious which route to take—the most well-worn trail you see. If you're in doubt, follow the group in front of you, as Abrams Falls is the destination for most hikers who set off from this lot. Only a few steps from the trailhead is a **kiosk** that will set you on the right path.

The trail is pretty straightforward—it follows **Abrams Creek** all the way to the waterfall. The only real elevation gains come when you thrice leave the creek to climb up and around a ridge, crossing a feeder stream in the process. The first stream you cross is Arbutus Branch, then Stony Branch, and then Wilson Branch, which is very close to the falls.

After you cross Wilson Branch on a **log bridge,** you'll follow the trail downstream, cross Wilson Branch once again, and arrive at the falls.

Abrams Falls is pretty, and in wet weather can be downright thunderous. Slick, mossy rocks make up the wall where the 20-foot waterfall, which has the largest volume of water of any waterfall in the park, tumbles into the pool below. Tempted as you may be to take a dip after a sweaty hike, don't do it; the currents are strong, and a few folks have drowned here.

Rocky Top and Thunderhead Mountains Trail

Distance: 13.9 miles round-trip

Duration: 7-8 hours

Elevation gain: 3,665 feet

Difficulty: strenuous

Trailhead: Anthony Creek Trailhead at the Cades Cove picnic area

Hiking to the famed Rocky Top is borderline brutal—you gain more than 3,500 feet in elevation, and on the trail's first few miles you share the path with horses, so it can get quite muddy and slippery. However, this exceptional hike is worth it. Time your hike for mid-June to see the rhododendrons and mountain laurel in full bloom.

Shortly after starting the **Anthony Creek Trail,** you'll reach Crib Trail Junction, then **Anthony Creek Horse Camp** (reservations required, 877/444-6777, www.recreation.gov, Apr.-early Nov., $20). Follow Anthony Creek Trail 3.5 miles to the **Bote Mountain Trail,** where hikers will turn right.

Climbing Bote Mountain Trail, you'll enter a long series of rhododendron "tunnels" and at 5.1 miles in, you'll reach **Spence Field** and the **Appalachian Trail.** Turn left and you'll get some stunning views of North Carolina and equally stunning views of hillsides and meadows covered in mountain laurel. Continue east along the Appalachian Trail to reach Rocky Top and Thunderhead Mountain.

Thunderhead Mountain is made up of three distinct summits. The first summit is **Rocky Top,** 1.2 miles from the Bote Mountain/Appalachian Trail junction and arguably the best view in the park. Next is the middle peak, sometimes called **Rocky Top Two,** just 0.3 mile beyond Rocky Top. Finally, another 0.3 mile on, is the unremarkable summit of **Thunderhead.** Many hikers turn around at Rocky Top, never summiting Thunderhead.

Parsons Branch Road

Parsons Branch Road (spring-fall) is a great drive. Take a right turn just beyond the Cades Cove Visitor Center parking area, and you'll find yourself on a 10-mile long, one-way gravel road leading to US-129 and Deals Gap on the extreme southwestern edge of the park. At times riddled with potholes and crossing 18 or so small streams along the way, the road is a slow one, taking around an hour to drive. If you're careful, the drive is doable in a sedan, but you may feel more comfortable in a vehicle with a little more clearance.

The road passes **Henry Whitehead Place,** an odd-looking pair of conjoined cabins with an interesting backstory. Henry Whitehead, a widower with three daughters, remarried Matilda Shields Gregory after she and her small child had been abandoned by her husband. During the crisis, the community rallied and built her the small cabin, which is in back of the main structure that Whitehead built after they married.

You'll cross the same stream several times before climbing to the crest of the drive. Here you'll find the trailhead for **Gregory Bald Trail.** This is the halfway mark of the road, and it is, as they say, all downhill from here.

★ Rich Mountain

Rich Mountain Road (Apr.-Nov.) is a photographer's dream. Running north from Cades Cove over Rich Mountain to **Tuckaleechee Cove** and **Townsend,** this **one-way gravel road** provides a few stunning views of Cades Cove and Tuckaleechee Cove. You're likely to see bears, deer, turkeys, and other wildlife along the way. The road is typically in good condition and isn't too challenging as far as backroads go, but I'd avoid tackling this drive in a low-clearance vehicle or your economy rental car; instead, go with a truck or SUV (no four-wheel drive necessary). Know that the road gets a little steep once it passes outside park boundaries, but it's nothing too hair-raising.

If you're stuck with a rental or you aren't confident in your off-road driving abilities, you can always enjoy similar views on the 8.5-mile Rich Mountain Loop hike, a great way to see Cades Cove without the high-season gridlock.

Rich Mountain Loop
Distance: 8.5-mile loop
Duration: 4-4.5 hours
Elevation gain: 1,740 feet

Difficulty: moderate
Trailhead: Park at the entrance gate to Cades Cove; the trail begins in the opposite parking lot.

The first part of this hike passes one of the meadows that make Cades Cove such a fabulous place. For 1.4 miles, you'll walk through the woods and along the edge of the meadow until you reach the **John Oliver Cabin.**

The trail continues behind the cabin and soon meets up with **Martha's Branch** and begins to climb. As you climb, you'll cross the branch a number of times. At mile 3, you'll find a place where you have a tight view of Cades Cove; don't sweat it, because better views are coming.

Continue 0.3 mile to **Indian Grave Gap Trail** and turn right. In 0.8 mile is **Campsite 5** (for backpackers) and the junction with Rich Mountain Trail. The saddle here has nice views.

Avoid the junction and follow Indian Grave Gap Trail 0.3 mile to a side trail. This path is only about 100 yards long and takes you to the highest point on Rich Mountain, **Cerulean Knob,** and the foundation of the former fire tower. Views are okay, but not fantastic. Get back to the main trail and continue east, where you'll find a much better view than on the top.

When you reach a power-line clearance, you're almost at **Scott Mountain Trail** and **Campsite 4.** From the junction of these trails, continue straight ahead on **Crooked Arm Ridge Trail** (it's what Indian Grave Gap Trail turns into). This trail is steep and rutted and littered with the evidence of horses, so watch your step—that horse evidence can be slippery.

This trail leads back to **Rich Mountain Loop Trail** 0.5 mile from the parking area.

Gatlinburg

On a typical Saturday night, when 40,000 people pack the restaurants and sidewalks of Gatlinburg, you would never know only about 4,000 people live here.

As the unofficial capital of the Smokies and gateway to the national park, it benefits greatly from the more than 10 million visitors drawn here for the views, the wildlife, the hikes, and the kitsch. Because if there's anything Gatlinburg has in abundance, it's kitsch.

Gatlinburg is unabashedly a tourist town, and owning up to that fact makes it all the more charming. On Parkway, the cheekily named main drag, there are T-shirt shops, candy stores and fudgeries, taffy pullers, more than one Ripley's attraction, novelties both racy (in that family-friendly, double-entendre way) and tame, knife shops, mini golf, ice cream parlors, restaurants, and more odd little art, craft, and gift shops than you can count. Don't let that deter you from staying (and even enjoying yourself) here. The Ripley's Aquarium is quite nice, and at Great Smoky Arts and Crafts Community and the Arrowcraft Shop, you'll find modern interpretations of traditional mountain arts that were handmade nearby.

Getting There and Around
Car
If you've followed the Blue Ridge Parkway to this point, you'll be coming into Gatlinburg along US-441 through GSMNP; on this route, one minute you're in the park, and the next revolution of the wheels you're in Gatlinburg.

For those arriving from the north or west, I-40 is the most convenient road into town. Exit the interstate at exit 407 and hop on US-66 South, a road that feeds into US-441 and will lead you into Gatlinburg. This is the easiest and most heavily traveled route into town from I-40. You can avoid the peak-season crowds by taking exit 435 near Knoxville (an hour away) and following US-321 south into Gatlinburg.

Coming in from the east on I-40, the best bet is to take exit 443 and drive along the beautiful Foothills Parkway to US-321 south and cruise right into town.

Parking
Finding parking in Gatlinburg can be quite tough. There are a number of public and private parking lots and garages where you can park your car if you're not staying at a hotel nearby. Parking rates vary, depending on public or private ownership. For affordability, it's often best to stick to the public parking garages at **Ripley's Aquarium of the Smokies** (88 River Rd., $1.75 first hour, $1 each hour after, or $6/day) and the **McMahan Parking Garage** (520 Parkway, at traffic light #3, $1.75 first hour, $1 each hour after, or $6/day).

Air
The **McGhee Tyson Airport** (TYS, 2055 Alcoa Hwy., Alcoa, 865/342-3000, www.tys.org), outside of Knoxville, is 42 miles from Gatlinburg. Head south to Maryville on US-129. Once you're in Maryville, take US-321 north to Pigeon Forge, then turn right and take US-441 into Gatlinburg.

Public Transportation
Gatlinburg has a great trolley system that can get you to and from every attraction in Gatlinburg and nearby Pigeon Forge, including Dollywood. The **Gatlinburg Trolley** (865/436-3897, www.gatlinburgtrolley.org, 10:30am-10pm daily Mar.-Apr., 8:30am-midnight daily May-Oct., 10:30am-6pm Sun.-Thurs., 10:30am-10pm Fri.-Sat. Nov.-Feb.) has more than 100 stops in Gatlinburg alone and will get you to where you need to go. Most routes cost $0.50 per ride; a few others cost $1-2. There's also a $2 day pass.

Sights
All of downtown Gatlinburg is a sight to behold. The mountains rise all around you, that namesake Smoky mist rising from them, and the street glitters and twinkles like a sort of vacationland Milky Way. One of the best ways to take it all in is from the **Space Needle** (115 Historic Nature Trail, 865/436-4629,

www.gatlinburgspaceneedle.com, 9am-midnight Sun.-Thurs., 9am-1am Fri.-Sat., adults $11, seniors and military $8, children ages 4-11 $6, free under 4). I know what you're thinking: "But the Space Needle is in Seattle." Yeah, it is; this is the other one. From the observation deck 407 feet above Gatlinburg, you have truly stellar views. For the best views, get to the top shortly before sundown and watch as the mountains darken and the strip of downtown comes alive with lights. At the foot of the tower, there's a two-level, 25,000-square-foot arcade with games galore, laser tag, a gift shop, snack bar, and restrooms.

The **Gatlinburg Sky Lift** (765 Parkway, 865/436-4307, www.gatlinburgskylift.com, 9am-9pm daily Apr.-May, 9am-11pm daily June-Aug., 9am-10pm daily Sept.-Oct., as posted Nov.-Mar., adults $16, military and children $14) is a ski lift that carries you 1,800 feet up the side of a mountain to a gift shop and snack bar. You have pretty views of Gatlinburg on the way up and back down, and even better views from the top, and nighttime tends to be the best time to ride the Sky Lift. The Sky Lift was built in the early 1950s and was the first chairlift in the region, seeing more than 100,000 visitors by its third season in operation. You'll find the lift in the heart of downtown; it's impossible to miss.

Moonshine is a high-octane corn liquor made in the hills, hollows, and coves all throughout and around GSMNP, especially in Gatlinburg. Today, moonshine is brewed legally and there are a few distilleries right in Gatlinburg, the best of which is **Sugarlands Distilling Company** (805 Parkway, 865/325-1355, www.sugarlandsdistilling.com, 10am-10pm Mon.-Thurs., 10am-10:30pm Fri.-Sat., noon-6:30pm Sun.). Sugarlands has their whole distilling process on display, and free tours are offered, but if you want to really get into it, the Blended Sampling Tour ($15) provides a tasting with a private tour and mixology class;

the Distiller Workshop ($40) is a hands-on experience that sends you home with a full jar; and Distiller for the Day ($250) guides you through the process from start to finish. There are sampling stations (with valid ID), a gift shop, and the chance to buy a quart or two. The Back Porch is their performance space, where musicians and storytellers come to sing songs and spin yarns; check to see who's there when you visit.

At the other end of downtown from Sugarlands is **Doc Collier Moonshine** (519 Parkway, 865/325-1468, https://doc-collier.co, 10am-11pm Mon.-Sat., 11am-7pm Sun.). Using the recipe of locally famous Doc Collier, his ancestors continue the tradition of making some of the finest 'shine in Tennessee and selling it to the thirsty public at their Gatlinburg storefront. According to the family, Doc's moonshine was in such high demand that he needed a better way to distribute it, so he bought a mercantile and sold straight goods to some customers and jars of white lightning to those in the know. In the store, you can see some great photos and even pieces of Doc's equipment while you sample some moonshine before grabbing a bottle and going on your way.

Ripley's Aquarium of the Smokies (traffic light #5, 88 River Rd., 865/430-8808, www.ripleyaquariums.com/gatlinburg, 9am-8pm Mon.-Thurs., 9am-10pm Fri.-Sun. Jan.-Feb.; 9am-9pm Mon.-Thurs., 9am-10pm Fri.-Sun. Mar.-Memorial Day and Labor Day-New Year's Day; 9am-10pm Mon.-Thurs., 9am-11pm Fri.-Sun. Memorial Day-Labor Day; adults $28, children $18) is one of countless Ripley's attractions in Gatlinburg and Pigeon Forge. The other attractions are skippable unless you have kids in tow, but the aquarium is another story. Ripley's Aquarium is the largest in the state, with more than 1.4 million gallons of water. Exhibits include the Touch a Ray Bay, where you can touch a stingray; the Penguin Playhouse, where tunnels lead you through the exhibit, putting

Wedding Fever

To say that Gatlinburg is a popular place to get married is a gross understatement. This tiny town is second in the nation only to Las Vegas in the number of weddings held each year. On average, around 20,000 couples tie the knot here (that's 55 ceremonies a day), and the number of witnesses and guests they bring push that number north of 600,000 people in town for weddings. Guess that explains why Gatlinburg is called the "wedding capital of the South."

What makes Gatlinburg such a hot spot for weddings, even celebrity weddings (Billy Ray Cyrus, Patty Loveless, and a few other names of note were married here)? It could be that Tennessee makes it easy.

No blood tests or waiting periods are required before getting married. It could be the abundance of wedding venues both natural and man-made. It could be the fact that there are plenty of romantic spots where one can retreat with their betrothed.

If being here has you in the mood for marriage, it's easy to find a place. In Gatlinburg alone, there are more than a dozen chapels and more officiants than you can count. You can find all the information you'll ever need for planning a Smoky Mountain wedding at the website of the **Smoky Mountain Wedding Association** (www.smwba.com).

you eye to eye with penguins as they do their thing; and Shark Lagoon, where a 340-foot-long glide path takes you under the lagoon where sand tiger and nurse sharks swim with sea turtles and moray eels.

Gatlinburg has a surprising artistic side. The artists and craftspeople here take their work very seriously. Many of them are carrying on mountain traditions, while others are finding new modes and media to express the inspiration they draw from the landscape here. Artists go to the **Arrowmont School of Arts and Crafts** (556 Parkway, 865/436-5860, www.arrowmont.org, 8:30am-5pm Mon.-Fri., 8:30am-4pm Sat, workshops $325-1,100) to hone their techniques. Founded in 1912 as a philanthropic project by the Pi Beta Phi women's fraternity, the Pi Beta Phi Settlement School sought to deliver basic education and health services to the children of the area. The schoolchildren brought the school staff homemade gifts—baskets, weavings, wood carvings—made by their parents. Recognizing the talent here, the school brought in a weaving teacher and began some vocational education. Then in 1926, the school opened the Arrowcraft

Shop, a market selling crafts and wares made by the people of the region. As this gained popularity, the idea of summer craft workshops came about. In 1945, 50 students attended the first of many summer workshops. Today the school holds weekend and one- and two-week workshops for adults every spring, summer, and fall. Classes include traditional and contemporary takes on weaving and fiber arts, pottery, metal and jewelry, painting, and drawing. Three galleries in the school display rotating and permanent exhibitions and are open year-round.

Entertainment and Events
Nightlife

One spot to grab a drink other than moonshine is **Smoky Mountain Brewery** (1004 Parkway, 865/436-4200, www.smoky-mtn-brewery.com, 11:30am-1am daily), a microbrewery with close to a dozen handcrafted beers brewed here or at one of the three nearby sister breweries. Mainstay beers include a light beer, red ale, pilsner, porter, and pale ale; they also brew seasonal and specialty beers, like the creamy Winter Warmer Ale and the Brown Trout Stout. Stop in and grab a hot pretzel (or some wings or a pizza) and a sampler flight of beers.

Performing Arts

There are a number of stage shows going on nightly throughout Gatlinburg. The **Iris Theatre** (115 Historic Nature Trail, 888/482-3330, www.iristheater.com, show times vary, tickets adults $28, military and seniors $20, children ages 4-11 $13) is home to a rotating slate of performers. Expect to see family-friendly comedy and magic shows, hypnotists, and the like. Shows go on most nights except Monday; check the schedule for times and current performers.

Then there's the **Sweet Fanny Adams Theatre** (461 Parkway, 865/436-4039, www.sweetfannyadams.com, box office open 10am-10pm on show days, tickets adults $27, seniors, military, and AAA $25, children under 12 $10), home to a musical comedy review and "outrageous humor and hilarious fun" since 1977. Shows vary by the theater season but typically include an improv showcase, a vaudeville-type revue, a holiday show, and other original musical comedies.

Festivals and Events

Throughout the year, several events draw attention to the things that make Gatlinburg the place it is. The **Spring Wildflower Pilgrimage** (865/974-0280, www.springwildflowerpilgrimage.org, adults $50-75, students $15, children under 12 free), usually during mid-April, is a five-day event with around 150 guided walks and presentations that celebrate the spring blooms, a photography contest, and more. From the end of September to early November, celebrate **Oktoberfest at Ober Gatlinburg** (865/436-5423, www.obergatlinburg.com) with a beer hall, sing-alongs, yodeling, and authentic German food. **Gatlinburg Winter Magic** (800/588-1817) is a 120-day celebration of all things winter and holiday. From early November through February, the city is a riot of

millions of LED bulbs strung up in trees and lining elaborate displays. There's a chili cook-off, carolers, a Christmas parade, and more.

Shopping

Gatlinburg's touristy side has a big personality, and there are plenty of shops selling T-shirts and the expected souvenirs. For something that truly speaks to the heritage of this place, you'll need to do a little looking around.

Great Smoky Arts and Crafts Community

Your first stop should be the **Great Smoky Arts and Crafts Community** (turn right at traffic light #3 and go three miles to Glades Rd., www.gatlinburgcrafts.com). Founded in 1937, it is among the largest (if not the largest) group of independent artisans in the United States. There are more than 100 shops, studios, and galleries along this eight-mile loop consisting of Glades Road, Buckhorn Road, and US-321. Look for the logo denoting membership in the community so you know that wares you're seeing and buying are from genuine local and regional artisans. One thing that sets this apart is the fact that you can interact with the artists in their studios and galleries. You can watch them work, ask questions, maybe even lend a hand (if asked). With 100 stops here, you can easily spend a day if you want to take a peek into each and every gallery, shop, and studio.

The shop artisans range from candlemakers to watercolor artists to photographers to leatherworkers to the creators of traditional mountain crafts. **Ogle's Broom Shop** (670 Glades Rd., 865/430-4402, www.oglesbroomshop.com) is one such traditional crafts shop, with third-generation broom makers. The owner carries on the tradition today, making brooms from broom straw and hand-carving canes and walking sticks.

Otto Preske, Artist in Wood (535 Buckhorn Rd., 865/436-5339, www.

ottopreskeartistinwood.com) is a superb wood-carver. He carves and turns Christmas ornaments, hiking staffs, fireplace mantels, religious carvings, and highly detailed figures and relief carvings. The work is stunning, and to watch him carve is simply amazing. Another woodworker is **Tim Weberding Woodworking** (600 Glades Rd., Unit 5, 865/430-8811, www.timweberding.com), where the eponymous owner, a fourth-generation woodworker, makes religious signs and placards, wooden baskets, ornaments, boxes, and more.

Throughout the community there are several basket weavers, but nothing like what you'll find at **Licklog Hollow Baskets** (1360 E. Parkway, 865/436-3823). Not only do they have the strangest name, the work here is superb. Whether you're buying for form or function, you'll find a basket that fits your style and probably your budget.

At **Woodland Tiles** (252 Buckhorn Rd., 865/640-0989, www.woodlandtiles-byvmarie.com), they create tiles and functional pottery pieces inspired by the leaves on the trees surrounding Gatlinburg. Custom glazes capture the jewel green of summer and the blazing colors of fall, and the sizes and shapes are spot on as the tiles mirror the leaves that inspired them.

The Village

In downtown Gatlinburg, you'll find **The Village Shops** (634 Parkway, 865/436-3995, www.thevillageshops.com, 10am-5pm daily Jan.-Feb., 10am-6pm daily Mar., 10am-8pm Sun.-Fri. and 10am-10pm Sat. Apr.-May and Nov., 10am-10pm June-Oct., hours vary Dec.), a collection of 27 shops centered around a courtyard in a Bavarian-style structure. Among the shops here is **Cartoons & Toys** (865/430-8666, www.cartoon-sandtoys.com), a kid-centric shop loaded with toys and games. They also sell wool socks, dress socks, and more, as long as it goes on your feet. **The Day Hiker**

(865/430-0970, www.thedayhiker.com) provides the basic gear you need to take day and short overnight hikes in GSMNP. **The Silver Tree** (865/430-3573) is a silver lover's paradise with plenty of silver jewelry and accessories to peruse. Last but not least is **The Donut Friar** (865/436-7306, www.the-donut-friar.com, from 5am daily), an amazing bakery making doughnuts, cinnamon bread, and other pastries. They sell coffee to go with your morning doughnut.

Other Shops

For a downright bizarre shop/museum (there is only one other place in the world like this, and it's in Spain), stop in at **The Salt and Pepper Shaker Museum** (561 Brookside Village Way, 865/430-5515, www.thesaltandpeppershakermuseum.com, 10am-2pm Mon.-Sat., noon-4pm Sun., on call during winter, $3). The name tells you what you'll find here, but it doesn't prepare you for the more than 20,000 salt and pepper shakers from around the world and the growing collection of pepper mills. The collection began on a lark, growing from one pepper mill into this massive assembly of the most banal of kitchen accessories. It's weird, so it's worth the cost of admission, especially when you can apply your admission fee to any gift shop purchase. Who doesn't want a salt and pepper set shaped like outhouses?

Recreation

There is no end to the outdoor recreation opportunities near Gatlinburg. At **Nantahala Outdoor Center Gatlinburg** (1138 Parkway, 865/277-8209, www.noc.com, 10am-9pm Tues.-Sat., 10am-7pm Sun.-Mon.), you'll find a huge retail store selling everything you'd ever need to gear up for an outdoor adventure. NOC is the region's leader in outdoor guide services, providing white-water rafting, float trips, and kayaking on several rivers across the region; guided hikes and fly-fishing trips; and more. Their trips vary by season, so check the website or ask someone at the store about current trips and activities.

Rafting in the Smokies (813 E. Parkway, 800/776-7238, www.raftingthesmokies.com, Tues.-Thurs. and Sat. Memorial Day-Labor Day) is another white-water rafting outfitter (trips from $35-42) in the area. Trips depend on the weather and water levels, so it's a good idea to call ahead or check online for current trips and reservations. Once you've gotten it nailed down, check in at the rafting outpost in Hartford and I-40, exit 447. They also have a zip line ($39), high ropes course ($33), and climbing wall ($20).

At **CLIMB works** (155 Branam Hollow Rd., 865/325-8116, www.climbworks.com, 9am-mid-afternoon daily, check for schedule) they brag that "your feet won't touch the ground for two and a half hours." And it's true, no matter whether you take their impressive zip-line canopy tour ($89), try sunset or night zip-line tours ($89), or ride their intermediate- to expert-level mountain biking trails ($59 with rental bike, $25 with own bike).

Ober Gatlinburg

Ober Gatlinburg (1001 Parkway, 865/436-5423, www.obergatlinburg.com, hours vary by activity, but generally 9:30am-9pm daily in spring, summer, and fall, 10am-7pm in winter, $4-12 or activity pass $22-33 adults, $19-28 children ages 5-11), the mountaintop resort that looks out over Gatlinburg, is a ski resort in winter and a mountain playground the rest of the year. There are eight ski and snowboard trails, and Ober Gatlinburg is equipped with plenty of snowmaking equipment to make up for what Mother Nature doesn't supply. Warm-weather activities include the awesome Alpine Slide, a sort of luge that follows one of the ski slopes down the hill; a pair of raft-based water slides; a maze; and year-round indoor ice skating. There's also a Wildlife Encounter where you can see many of the native species found in the area. If you're hungry, there are several places to grab a bite ranging from a slice of pizza to a steak.

The resort is a little dated and leans toward the campy end of the spectrum, and many people skip it if it's not ski season. Others think it's worth the little bit of time and money to ride the tram to the top of the hill and ride the Alpine Slide one more time.

Food

Dining in Gatlinburg, especially for foodies, can be tricky. In a town where, literally, millions of people pass through, you get a lot of restaurants that have stopped caring about repeat customers and seek only to provide a heaping plate of food and mediocre service at premium prices, knowing their diners will be in for one, maybe two meals during their visit. And there are plenty of major chains ready to take your dining dollars. That said, it is possible to find a good, even great, meal here.

Mama's Chicken Kitchen (1244 E. Parkway, 865/412-1333, www.mamaschickenkitchen.com, 11am-10pm daily, $8-25) might be a tongue twister of a name, but the fried chicken they serve is a delight the minute it hits your lips. Whether you get a plate or bucket, and whether you eat there or make a picnic of it (nothing like a cold fried chicken picnic in Cades Cove), you'll love every bite.

The **Smoky Mountain Trout House** (410 Parkway, 865/436-5416, www.gatlinburgtrouthouse.com, from 5pm daily, around $20) has a mesmerizing aquarium window teeming with rainbow trout. The menu is trout heavy: rainbow trout grilled, broiled, pan fried, seasoned with dill or parmesan; trout amandine; and smoked trout. There are a few items— prime rib, a rib-eye steak, country ham, chicken, catfish, and shrimp—that aren't trout on the menu. The food tastes better than the looks of the dining room would have you believe. This is a pretty good meal, especially if you like trout.

At ★ **Buckhorn Inn** (2140 Tudor Mountain Rd., 865/436-4668, www.buckhorninn.com, 7pm-late daily, $35) they serve a four-course prix-fixe meal nightly to inn guests and visitors. The food here makes creative use of regional ingredients, with dishes that at times span Southern, East Tennessee, and international cuisine pantheons. Expect to find dishes like pan-seared trout or tandoori salmon, flank steak, or pork tenderloin with soy-citrus sauce, all served with a soup, salad, and dessert.

Gatlinburg favorite **Alamo Steakhouse and Saloon** (705 E. Parkway, 865/436-9998, www.alamosteakhouse.com, 11am-10pm Sun.-Thurs., 11am-11pm Fri.-Sat., $14-31), which earns "Best Steak" accolades year after year, was lost during the 2016 wildfire but reopened in 2017. If you're not in the mood for steak, there are a number of pork, chicken, and seafood dishes. The service is generally very good, but, like all restaurants in a busy vacation town, can get bogged down in the high season.

Another longtime Gatlinburg eatery, **The Peddler Steakhouse** (820 River Rd., 865/436-5794, www.peddlergatlinburg.com, from 5pm Sun.-Fri., from 4:30pm Sat., $23-37), has a reputation for making a fantastic steak. The dining room overlooks the river, making it a nice spot to eat. The menu is steak heavy, but they also have shrimp, chicken, and trout, and every entrée comes with a pretty robust salad bar.

★ **Big Daddy's Pizzeria** (714 River Rd., 865/436-5455, www.bigdaddyspizzeria.net, 11am-10pm Sun.-Thurs., 11am-11pm Fri.-Sat., $9-23) has locations in Gatlinburg, Pigeon Forge, and Sevierville. Their claim to fame is a wood-fired brick oven and a creative flair in the creation of their pies. Get the tried and true pepperoni and cheese, or go wild with the Smoky Mountain Cheesesteak (with shaved prime rib, caramelized onions, gorgonzola cheese, and potato

Pancake Pantry, the oldest pancake house in Tennessee, still flips a mean flapjack.

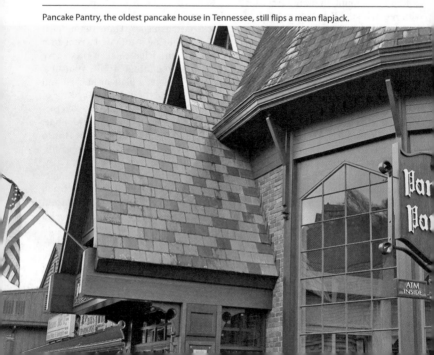

slices), The Herbivore (a veggie-packed delight), or one of their other signature pizzas. They also have salads, meatballs, and sandwiches prepared on house-made focaccia.

Gatlinburg has pancake houses in spades. The oldest pancake house in town opened in 1960, and it also happens to be the first of its kind in Tennessee. **Pancake Pantry** (628 Parkway, 865/436-4724, www.pancakepantry.com, 7am-4pm daily June-Oct., 7am-3pm daily Nov.-May, $6-10) still puts out a great spread of flapjacks. There are 24 varieties of pancakes and crepes, as well as a half-dozen waffles, omelets, and French toast. Breakfast is served all day, but if you feel like a burger or sandwich for lunch, they have a few of those too.

Near the entrance to the park, ★ **Crockett's Breakfast Camp** (1103 Parkway, 865/325-1403, www.crockettsbreakfastcamp.com, 7am-1pm daily, $2-15) serves, predictably, breakfast. A giant cast-iron skillet outside marks the restaurant but doesn't accurately predict how fun the menu is. Fried cinnamon rolls (think French toast plus cinnamon roll), the Waffle of Insane Greatness, and the Thick Aretha Frankensteins Pancakes (great pancakes, funny name), as well as biscuits and breakfast burritos, are only part of the menu.

Wild Plum Tea Room (555 Buckhorn Rd., 865/436-3808, www.wildplumtearoom.com, 11am-3pm Tues.-Sat., $10-19) is a lunch-only restaurant inspired by Austrian teahouses. They serve the Southern classic, tomato pie, but the real stars of the menu are the chef specials. The specials vary daily, but in the past have included lobster pie, a salmon burger, smoked salmon sandwiches, and yellowfin tuna.

Accommodations

Something about being in Gatlinburg makes me want to stay in a cabin. Fortunately, there are plenty of options whether you're traveling solo, as a pair, or with even the largest of groups. ★ **Mountain Laurel Chalets** (440 Ski Mountain Rd., 800/626-3431, www.mtnlaurelchalets.com, $139-239 2- to 4-person cabin, $179-409 6- to 10-person cabin, $309-1,100 10- to 24-person lodge) has several lodges and large houses sleeping anywhere from 10 to 24 people if you're traveling with your extended family, or smaller cabins that sleep a couple or small group on a getaway. The cabins are spread out over a huge property, so they're private in addition to being cozy. Some of the cabins, the last ones in line for a refresh, are dated, but others are quite nice inside, so check cabin descriptions online if this matters to you.

Located between Gatlinburg and Pigeon Forge, **Autumn Ridge** (505 Crest Rd., 865/436-4111, www.autumnridgerentals.com, Jan.-Mar. $105, Apr.-Dec. $115, Oct. and holidays $135) has five cabins, each with a two-night minimum and a view you'll come back for. King-size beds are the norm here, as are whirlpool tubs or hot tubs and wood-burning fireplaces (firewood provided). This is a romantic spot and a popular one for honeymoons, so make your reservation sooner rather than later.

Laurel Springs Lodge Bed and Breakfast (204 Hill St., 888/430-9211, www.laurelspringslodge.com, $130-175) is lovely, comfortable, and highly regarded. There are five rooms, all well decorated and comfortable, and a gourmet breakfast is served every morning. Downtown is a short walk away, but even though you're close, you're away from the buzz of Gatlinburg's main drag and can relax when you come back to your room.

★ **The Foxtrot Bed and Breakfast** (1520 Garrett Ln., 865/436-3033, www. thefoxtrot.com, $190-230) is a little different than most B&Bs in that an actual chef prepares breakfast. That's just one thing that sets it apart. The Foxtrot is high on the hill, well above the noise, traffic, and bustle of downtown Gatlinburg, making it a true retreat. There are several packages you can add to your room, like spa packages, honeymoon and anniversary packages, cooking schools, and more.

Camp LeConte Luxury Outdoor Resort (1739 E. Parkway, 865/205-0201, www. campleconte.com) has a variety of accommodations that include luxury tree houses (from $149), safari tents (from $89), retro campers (from $99), and RV (from $39) and tent (from $29) sites. The open-air tree houses offer views of Mount LeConte and can sleep up to four guests. The safari tents are tents on pads, similar to a "glamping" experience, while the cool retro campers are replica 1961 Shasta Airflytes. There's a pool and small general store on-site as well.

Throughout Gatlinburg, there are a number of chain hotels with prices ranging from budget to mid-range. **Courtyard by Marriott Gatlinburg** (315 Historic Nature Trail, 865/436-2008, www.marriott.com, $189-259) is in a good location for exploring Gatlinburg. The **Gatlinburg Inn** (755 Parkway, 865/259-7223, www.gatlinburginn.com, $197-299) sits one block back from the main drag and is within walking distance to most everything you want to do in Gatlinburg. Finally, the **Hilton Garden Inn** (635 River Rd., 865/436-0048, www. hiltongardeninn3.hilton.com, $179-220) is also walkable to downtown and has free parking.

Information and Services

There are two visitors centers in Gatlinburg, the **Gatlinburg Welcome Center** (1011 Banner Rd., 865/436-7318, www.gatlinburg.com, 8:30am-7pm daily Apr.-Oct., 8:30am-5:30pm daily Nov.-Mar.), and the **Aquarium Welcome Center** (88 River Rd., 9am-9pm daily).

LeConte Medical Center (742 Middle Creek Rd., Sevierville, 865/446-7000, www.lecontemedicalcenter.com) is the nearest hospital, just over 20 minutes away. The **Gatlinburg Police** (1230 E. Parkway, 865/436-5181) are available if the need arises.

Pigeon Forge and Sevierville

The most dominating presence in Pigeon Forge and Sevierville is Dolly Parton. Her namesake amusement park is in Pigeon Forge and she was born and raised in Sevierville, where a statue of Dolly stands in front of the courthouse. You'll see her face, hear her music, and maybe even meet one of her many cousins everywhere across these two towns.

These towns have grown a lot since Dolly was born, thanks largely to the popularity of the national park. More growth came in the 1970s when the amusement park that would become Dollywood opened its doors, and again in 1982 when nearby Knoxville hosted the World's Fair. But to keep more than 10 million annual visitors coming back year after year, Pigeon Forge and Sevierville had to become destinations unto themselves, and, for the most part, they've succeeded. Pigeon Forge has become one of the biggest "tourist traps" (which I say not with disdain, but with astonishment as the place is a wonderland of vacation delights) on the East Coast. Want to ride go-karts and go bungee jumping at 9pm on a Wednesday? No problem. Midnight mini golf? Got it. Roller coasters, neon signs, and fudge shops? Pigeon Forge has got you covered. But don't be fooled by all the neon, hotels, and attractions around; like Gatlinburg, Pigeon Forge is small, with fewer than 7,000 people living here full-time.

In the midst of this swirl of touristy flotsam is a surprising center for engaging with the community's culture: Dollywood. This amusement park has been around in some form or another since the 1960s, though in the early days it was kitsch over culture. As the park matured and expanded, so did its attention to the culture of mountain living. Today, the park is home to some great bluegrass and country shows and a good many shops and exhibits where Appalachian crafters showcase their skills and their wares.

Getting There and Around

The most traveled route to Pigeon Forge and Sevierville is I-40, carrying visitors in from the east and west. Exit 407 puts you on US-66 southeast, which leads into Sevierville and then feeds into US-441, taking you to Pigeon Forge. Most travelers will be going north on US-441, following the road from Great Smoky Mountains National Park and Gatlinburg.

It's surprising to see a well-organized public transit system in a town the size of Pigeon Forge, but the **Fun Time Trolley** (186 Old Mill Ave., 865/453-6444, www.pigeonforgetrolley.org, 8am-midnight daily Mar.-Oct., 10am-10pm daily Nov.-Dec., $0.50-0.75 or an all-day pass for $2.50) has more than 100 regular stops in Pigeon Forge, Sevierville, and Gatlinburg. Routes run on a regular schedule, as traffic allows, and stops include all of the high points in the area. Passes are available at Fun Time Trolley.

Sights
★ Dollywood

At **Dollywood** (2700 Dollywood Parks Blvd., Pigeon Forge, 800/365-5996, www.dollywood.com, Apr.-Dec., $55-68, parking $11, $16.25 RVs), you might just catch a glimpse of Dolly Parton walking through the park or performing for the crowds at the park's opening. Even if you don't see her, the park has plenty of rides, cultural stops, shows, and nature experiences to keep you busy.

Dollywood started in 1961, when Rebel Railroad, a small attraction with a steam train, general store, blacksmith shop, and saloon, opened. By 1977, the park had grown and changed hands more than once. Renamed Silver Dollar City, the park eventually caught the attention of Dolly Parton. She became a partner and lent the park her name. Since then, it's become Tennessee's most-visited tourist attraction (outside GSMNP) and is consistently named among the top theme parks in the world.

Dollywood has a great look: one part Appalachian village, one part small Southern town. There are tree-lined streets and paths, and several streams follow their courses through the park. You don't see the rides until you're right up on them because they're tucked away in the woods. One of the best-known spots in the park is **Showstreet,** where stages and theaters are always busy with musicians, square dances, and storytellers. There's also a bevy of master craftspeople practicing their Appalachian arts for all to see: blacksmiths, basket weavers, candlemakers, and woodworkers. On Showstreet, you may see some of Dolly's relatives playing and singing in shows throughout the year. Seasonal shows include a half-dozen Christmas concerts,

Harvest Celebration Southern Gospel, and more.

Also on Showstreet is a carriage, sled, and wagon shop called **Valley Carriage Works.** It takes orders from clients from around the world and builds beautiful, fully functional, historically accurate carriages. At the Museum of the Cherokee Indian in Cherokee, North Carolina, you can see a replica Cherokee wagon that they built to commemorate the 165th anniversary of the Trail of Tears.

Given that the park allows nature to be such a prominent feature in its design, it's no surprise to learn that Dollywood has partnered with the American Eagle Foundation and is authorized by the U.S. Fish and Wildlife Service and the Tennessee Wildlife Resources Agency to possess eagles and other birds for education, exhibition, rehabilitation, and breeding. The 30,000-square-foot **aviary** is home to the nation's largest group of non-releasable bald eagles (many of these birds have been injured and wouldn't survive if released into nature). Daily shows put visitors in close proximity to these incredible birds.

Dollywood has more than 40 rides and attractions that range from kid-friendly to thrilling. My favorites were the Blazing Fury, an indoor roller coaster where you're trying to outrun an out-of-control fire; Thunderhead, a great wooden coaster; and Daredevil Falls, an updated version of the log flume ride.

Plenty of snack stands and restaurants are located throughout the park.

Dollywood's Splash Country

Water parks abound in Pigeon Forge and Sevierville, but the best is **Dollywood's Splash Country** (2700 Dollywood Parks Blvd., Pigeon Forge, 800/365-5996, www. dollywood.com, May-Sept., $44-49, parking $11, $16.25 RVs). This water park has 30 waterslides, a lazy river, three water play areas for kids, a 7,500-square-foot leisure pool, and a 25,000-square-foot wave pool. There are also concessions

Sky Rider in Dollywood

and a gift shop, stroller rentals, and lockers to rent.

Dolly Parton Statue

Local artist Jim Gray sculpted a **statue** (125 Court Ave.) that shows Dolly with a wide smile and her guitar, as if she's ready to write a song at any moment. Stop by downtown Sevierville to take a picture with the statue, located on the courthouse lawn.

Tennessee Museum of Aviation

Head to the Gatlinburg Pigeon Forge Airport in Sevierville to brush up on your aviation history at the **Tennessee Museum of Aviation** (135 Air Museum Way, Sevierville, 866/286-8738, www. tnairmuseum.com, 10am-6pm Mon.-Sat., 1pm-6pm Sun., adults $12.75, seniors $9.75, children ages 6-12 $6.75). Housed in a 35,000-square-foot hangar are a number of exhibits and a dozen historic aircraft, including two airworthy P-47 Thunderbolts (that sometimes take to the air), a MiG-21, and F-86 Saberjet. But the best treat is when you visit the museum and one of the historic WWII aircraft is taking flight.

Titanic Pigeon Forge

One somewhat odd attraction is the *Titanic* **Pigeon Forge** (2134 Parkway, Pigeon Forge, 417/334-9500 or 800/381-7670, www.titanicpigeonforge.com, from 9am daily, adults $28.50, children ages 5-12 $11.59). This massive museum includes three decks and 20 galleries in its 30,000 square feet. The galleries feature artifacts salvaged from the sunken luxury ship. There are reproductions of the Marconi wireless room, a first-class suite, and a third-class cabin, as well as a full-scale reproduction of the grand staircase. Touring the ship takes about two hours.

WonderWorks

WonderWorks (100 Music Rd., Pigeon Forge, 865/868-1800, www.wonderworksonline.com, 9am-10pm daily, adults $28, children $19) is another weird one. From the outside, the building appears to be upside down, and inside there are more than 100 interactive exhibits. Some, like the Tesla Coil and the Earthquake Café, are strange and seem dangerous, while others challenge you to use your imagination to solve challenges or test your willpower. While it's definitely geared toward kids in the tween range, adults will find plenty to marvel at. There's also the **Wonders of Magic** ($19), a family-friendly show of illusions and magic tricks.

Entertainment

If you want to wet your whistle in Pigeon Forge, your options are exclusively bars in restaurants. The two best bars happen to be in Smoky Mountain Brewery and Mellow Mushroom at the Island in Pigeon Forge. **Smoky Mountain Brewery** (2530 Parkway, Ste. 15, Pigeon Forge, 865/868-1400, www.smoky-mtn-brewery.com, 11am-midnight Sun.-Thurs., 11am-1am Fri.-Sat.) brews every drop of

their draft beer in-house or at one of their three sister restaurants, and they serve up some good grub if you want something to munch on or are hungry enough for a full meal. **Mellow Mushroom** (131 Island Dr., #3101, Pigeon Forge, www.mellow-mushroom.com, 11am-midnight daily) specializes in the best national and regional craft beer and some very tasty pizza, subs, and salads. **Iron Boar Saloon** (104 Waldens Main St., Pigeon Forge, 865/429-7779, www.ironboarsaloon. com, 11am-late daily) has a bottom-shelf beer selection, but it's the only biker bar in town. Come here for the crowd and to hang out with other bikers and bike lovers. Plus, they have good tacos.

Dolly Parton's Dixie Stampede (3849 Parkway, Pigeon Forge, 877/782-6733, www.dixiestampede.com, daily, call for show times, adults $50-55, children $25-30) is one part dinner, one part show. (Fair warning: It's a Civil War-themed show that involves some glorification of the Confederacy.) The dinner's a four-course country feast, and the show is jam-packed with horseback stunts, comedy, pyrotechnics, and some downright strange sights to take in while you're eating in what is essentially a small arena.

The Smoky Mountain Opry (2046 Parkway, Pigeon Forge, 865/428-7469 or 800/768-1170, www.smokymtnopry. com, daily, show times vary, adults from $45, children from $20) is a variety show filled with singers and dancers, jugglers and aerial acrobats, magicians, comedians, and musicians; they even have a white lion for some reason. They also have a Christmas show that draws quite the crowd.

Shopping

There's no shortage of touristy shopping around here, but you can find specialty shops, galleries, and decent shopping if you know where to look.

Pigeon Forge earned part of its name from a forge set up in 1820 by Isaac Love. (The other part of its name came from the incredible number of passenger pigeons the early settlers found living along the banks of the Little Pigeon River.) A decade later, Love's son established a mill, which is now a National Historic Site that you can visit: The **Old Mill Square** (175 Old Mill Ave., Pigeon Forge, 865/428-0771, www.old-mill.com, hours vary by store) is a collection of shops and restaurants in a cute restored and recreated historic area. **The Old Mill General Store** (865/453-4628, 8am-9pm Mon.-Thurs., 8am-10pm Fri.-Sat., 8:30am-8pm Sun., hours vary off-season) has all sorts of country provisions, including fresh-ground grains milled next door at the Old Mill. **The Old Mill Farmhouse Kitchen** (865/428-2044, 9am-9pm Mon.-Thurs., 9am-10pm Fri.-Sat., 9am-8pm Sun., hours vary off-season) also sells a variety of provisions and ingredients that you need to cook your own country meal at home. They also have a nice pottery shop and gift baskets. You can get your fill of candy at **The Old Mill Candy Kitchen** (865/453-7516, 9am-9pm Mon.-Thurs., 9am-10pm Fri.-Sat., 9am-8pm Sun., hours vary off-season).

Three Bears General Store (2861 Parkway, Pigeon Forge, 800/867-2272, www.threebearsgeneralstore.com, 9am-9pm Sun.-Thurs., 9am-10pm Fri.-Sat.) has candy and fudge, corny gifts and T-shirts, jams and jellies, pocketknives, jewelry, Christmas decor, and just about anything else you might want to bring home.

At **The Apple Barn Cider Mill and General Store** (230 Apple Valley Rd., Sevierville, 800/421-4606, www.apple-barncidermill.com, 9am-7pm Mon.-Thurs., 9am-9pm Fri.-Sat., 9am-5:30pm Sun.), you can buy fresh cider, a bushel of just-picked apples, a pie hot from the oven, and more. At this great stop, you'll be on a working orchard with more than 4,000 trees, and you can watch the cider presses at work while you munch on an apple doughnut.

Tanger Outlets (1645 Parkway,

Sevierville, 865/453-1053, www.tanger-outlet.com, 9am-9pm Mon.-Sat., 10am-7pm Sun.) in Sevierville has dozens of shops including brand-name outlets like Coach, Levi's, Michael Kors, Polo Ralph Lauren, Samsonite, Vera Bradley, and Banana Republic.

Smoky Mountain Knifeworks (2320 Winfield Dunn Pkwy., Sevierville, 865/453-5871, www.smkw.com, 9am-9pm daily May-Dec., 9am-6pm Sun.-Thurs., 9am-8pm Fri.-Sat. Jan.-Apr.) has long held a reputation for quality pocketknives, hunting knives, and specialty blades. You can pick up a Swiss Army Knife here, a fishing or kitchen knife, even antique and collectors knives that can cost upward of $4,000.

Sports and Recreation

There is plenty to get into when you're in Pigeon Forge and Sevierville. Of course you can hike in the national park, but you can also white-water raft, ride a crazy alpine coaster, or even try skydiving, but with a twist.

You can try indoor skydiving at **Flyaway Indoor Skydiving** (3106 Parkway, Pigeon Forge, 877/293-0639, www.flyawayindoorskydiving.com, 10am-8pm daily, $34 first flight, $22 additional flight). Indoor skydiving is done in a vertical wind tunnel—think a silo with giant fans in the base—with an experienced skydiving instructor. After a brief ground school, you'll get dressed and be ready to fly. In the wind tunnel, it's disorienting the first time you leave your feet and assume the skydiving position because you're floating a few feet off the net where you were just standing. Relax, follow your instructor's directions, and enjoy the experience. If you're lucky, before or after your session, you'll get to see some experienced indoor skydivers perform amazing acrobatic tricks that look like something out of *The Matrix* as they whirl around the tunnel with precise control.

One of the most interesting outdoor activities is the **Smoky Mountain Alpine Coaster** (867 Wears Valley Rd., Pigeon Forge, 865/365-5000, www.smokymountainalpinecoaster.com, 10am-10pm Sun.-Thurs., 10am-midnight Fri.-Sat., adults $14, children ages 7-12 $11, ages 3-6 $4.50). This odd little quasi-roller coaster puts you in a track-mounted sled complete with an automatic speed control and manual brakes, and then sends you down a one-mile track, spiraling through tight turns and down a few steep(ish) drops.

At **Adventure Park Zip Lines** (1628 Parkway, Pigeon Forge, 865/453-8644, www.adventureziplinesofsevierville.com, 9am-4pm daily, $75) the zip routes range from a measly 450 feet to a long 2,000-foot ride. Their sister, **Legacy Mountain Zip Lines** (2431 Upper Middle Creek Rd., Sevierville, 888/869-0289, www.adventureziplinesofpigeonforge.com, 9am-4pm daily, $100) has 4.5 miles of zip lines, with some runs as long as 2,500 feet that will take you 450 feet into the air.

SpeedZone Fun Park (3315 S. River Rd., Pigeon Forge, 888/352-7507, www.speedzonefunpark.com, 10am-9pm daily, $10 one track, $20 three tracks) is one of many go-kart places in Pigeon Forge, but what sets this one apart is the quartet of tracks in one spot. The Slick Track is a fast, paved go-kart track where you drift around every turn. The Tennessee Twister is a curve-riddled wooden track. The Coaster Track has a steep downhill drop at the end for big speed. And the Kids Track is slower, easier, and lets little drivers get behind the wheel.

Though most of the golf you've seen has been of the mini variety, the **Gatlinburg Golf Course** (520 Dollywood Ln., Pigeon Forge, 800/231-4128, www.golf.gatlinburg.com, daily, call for hours and tee times, $30-60) offers you a full-size round on a beautiful course with some dramatic holes. The signature 12th hole, nicknamed "Sky Hi," is 194 yards long and has a 200-foot drop from the tee to the green, making it a puzzling hole for many golfers and a fun one for all. The pro shop here has everything you'll need to play a round, including a full-service restaurant so you can grab a bite and a beer after your round.

The Island in Pigeon Forge (131 Island Dr., 865/286-0119, www.islandpigeonforge.com, 10am-11pm Mon.-Thurs., 10am-midnight Fri.-Sat., 10am-10pm Sun.) is a tourist extravaganza. You'll find a half-dozen restaurants and as many snack shops, 35 or so stores selling everything from jerky to puzzles to gems, and rides galore. Rides and entertainment options include the 200-foot-tall Great Smoky Mountain Wheel, a mirror maze, and a huge arcade.

Food

At Old Mill, there's a quaint collection of shops and a pair of restaurants. **The Old Mill Restaurant** (164 Old Mill Ave., Pigeon Forge, 865/429-3463, www.old-mill.com, 8am-9pm daily, off-season hours vary, $13-23) is family-friendly and has a small selection for kids. The Pigeon River flows by right outside the dining room, and this is a bigger draw than the food, which is traditional country fare, though breakfast is pretty good.

★ **The Pottery House Café and Grill** (175 Old Mill Ave., Pigeon Forge, 865/453-6002, www.old-mill.com, 11am-9pm Mon.-Fri., 8am-9pm Sat.-Sun., $7-19) is known for its delicious quiche and outstanding desserts. They serve everything from steaks to fried chicken livers (served with Buffalo sauce and blue cheese dressing) and sandwiches. Rather than trout, which is served by many area eateries, they serve catfish here, which is just as good. If you like what you get for dessert, it's likely you can get a whole cake or pie to take home with you.

Poynor's Pommes Frites (131 The Island Dr., Ste. 3107, Pigeon Forge, 865/774-7744, 11am-10pm daily, $5-10) may not look like much from the outside, but the food is great. The specialty is the pommes frites (french fries). Done in a Belgian style (fried, cooled, then

fried again), they're crispy on the outside and fluffy inside, and served plain, with your choice of sauce, or even topped with cheese, bacon, onions, and jalapenos. You can't make a meal of french fries, so Poynor's serves a short menu of German bratwurst served on a German hard roll.

Mel's Diner (119 Wears Valley Rd., Pigeon Forge, 865/429-2184, www.mels-dinerpf.com, 7am-midnight daily, $6-10) serves up classic diner food with a side of 1950s flair. With tasty, relatively inexpensive dishes served at breakfast, lunch, and dinner (and even rare late-night dining), you can't go wrong here. The breakfast plates are quite hearty, and the burgers and sandwiches piled high with toppings, but save room for dessert and order a whopping six-scoop banana split or a more reasonable shake or malt.

All throughout the Smokies, pancake houses rule the breakfast world. A good option to get your fix of pancakes, French toast, waffles, and the like is **Sawyer's Farmhouse Restaurant** (2831 Parkway, 865/366-1090, www.sawyersbreakfast.com, 8am-2pm daily, $4-12). It's breakfast and lunch only, but that works because there are only so many times you can eat pancakes in a day.

For the best burger in town, go to ★ **Local Goat New American Restaurant** (2167 Parkway, 865/366-3035, www.localgoatpf.com, 11am-11pm Mon.-Thurs., 11am-midnight Fri.-Sat., 11am-10pm Sun., $8-26), where the beef is ground fresh and the buns are baked daily. This place is a rarity in Pigeon Forge and Gatlinburg: It's dedicated to staying as local as possible. That means 22 of their 24 draft beers are from regional brewers, and they make almost everything in-house.

Mama's Farmhouse (208 Pickel St., Pigeon Forge, 865/908-4646, www.mamasfarmhouse.com, 8am-9pm Sun.-Thurs., 8am-10pm Fri.-Sat, breakfast $13 adults, $6 children ages 6-12; lunch $17 adults, $8 children ages 6-12; dinner $20 adults, $9 children ages 6-12) is the place for a family-style Southern meal. Every meal is all you can eat, and once you put in your drink order, the food will arrive, and there's a whole lot of it. For dinner, you'll get three meats—fried chicken with meatloaf, turkey and stuffing, ham, country-fried steak, or turkey pot pie—and your choice of five sides, plus soup or salad, biscuits, and dessert. Try the peach butter on your biscuits; you can thank me later.

Accommodations

There are several chain hotels in Pigeon Forge and Sevierville, and for the most part, they're all the same. The **Courtyard Pigeon Forge** (120 Community Center Dr., 844/631-0595 or 865/366-3201, www.marriott.com, $109-269) is convenient to anything you'll want to do in Pigeon Forge.

Whispering Pines Condominiums (205 Ogle Dr., Pigeon Forge, 800/429-4361, www.whisperingpinescondos.com, $150-300) has a great location if you want a front-row seat on the action of Pigeon Forge, or you can opt for mountain views and unwind a little. The condos here are large, so they're ideal for families or small groups traveling together, especially if you don't want to break the bank.

The Inn at Christmas Place (119 Christmas Tree Ln., Pigeon Forge, 888/465-9644, www.innatchristmasplace.com, $150-329) is an outstanding place to stay. Given that the place is permanently festooned with Christmas decorations (they are somewhat subdued from January to October) and they play Christmas music on a constant loop, I was surprised at how great this property is. Impeccable landscaping; a robust breakfast; an indoor and outdoor pool, complete with a 95-foot waterslide; and a game room are only a few of the reasons this inn is such a find.

The Inn on the River (2492 Parkway, Pigeon Forge, 877/986-4243, www.myinnontheriver.com, $139-240) has 128 rooms, many with a fireplace, in configurations perfect for solo, duo, or family travelers. On the property, you'll find an outdoor pool, fire pit, covered patio seating, and a riverside walkway.

★ **Dollywood's DreamMore Resort** (2525 DreamMore Way, Pigeon Forge, 865/365-1900 or 800/365-5996, www.dollywood.com, from $189), inspired by Dolly's own family-filled front porch, gives guests that same experience. In addition to its 307 rooms, indoor and outdoor pools, restaurants, and views of the Smokies, there are storytelling stations, seasonal and holiday activities, and plenty of things for the kids to do. It's the first hotel on Dollywood property, and staying here has its privileges, like a complimentary shuttle to the park, early Saturday entry to Dollywood, and a complimentary TimeSaver pass, which gives you priority spots in line on 10 different rides and attractions.

Information and Services

The **Pigeon Forge Welcome Center** (1950 Parkway, 800/251-9100, www.mypigeonforge.com, 8:30am-5pm Mon.-Sat., 1pm-5pm Sun.) is located at traffic light #0 on Parkway. Here, and at the **Pigeon Forge Information Center** (3107 Parkway, 865/453-8574, 8:30am-5pm Mon.-Fri.), you can find all the information on the area and volunteers ready to help you plan your time here.

The folks at the **Sevierville Chamber of Commerce Visitors Center** (3099 Winfield Dunn Pkwy., 865/436-1291, www.visitsevierville.com, 8:30am-5:30pm Mon.-Sat., 9am-6pm Sun.) are ready to help with trip planning or simply pointing you in the right direction and helping you enjoy your vacation.

If you need a hospital, **LeConte Medical Center** (742 Middle Creek Rd., Sevierville, 865/446-7000, www.lecontemedicalcenter.com) is your best bet.

There are two police departments here: the **Sevier County Sheriff's Office** (106 W. Bruce St., 865/453-4668) and the **Pigeon**

Forge Police Department (225 Pine Mountain Rd., 865/453-9063).

Knoxville

Perhaps best known among college football fans, Knoxville is the biggest city in East Tennessee and a major travel hub granting access to Great Smoky Mountains National Park and, beyond that, the Blue Ridge Parkway. Unlike Nashville and Memphis, which have national reputations as music towns, Knoxville's comes from the University of Tennessee Volunteers athletics, but the city is also home to the historic Tennessee Theatre and the Bijou Theatre, and has a very lively music scene of its own.

In 1982, the World's Fair came along and ignited Knoxville's hometown pride, and many residents and business owners saw what Knoxville could become. By the early 2000s, downtown Knoxville resonated with business owners. Restaurants and shops opened in spruced-up buildings from yesteryear. Bars followed, and boutiques flourished. Soon, downtown had turned into what it is today—a fun cultural center for the city.

Getting There and Around
Car
Driving to Knoxville is easy. If you've followed the Blue Ridge Parkway through Great Smoky Mountains National Park, just stay on US-441, which runs right into downtown. Coming from the east or west via I-40, take exit 388 for Gay Street.

From Asheville, take I-40 West 116 miles (two hours) to Knoxville. From Charlotte, where you'll find a major airport, take US-74 West to I-40 West into Knoxville, a four-hour drive. Alternatively, take the same route but leave I-40 for US-19 into Cherokee, then take US-441/TN-71 through GSMNP and into Knoxville.

From the south, I-75 offers a direct route into Knoxville from Chattanooga, Tennessee (one hour and 45 minutes), and Atlanta, Georgia (three hours). Likewise, I-40 is a direct route from Nashville to Knoxville (two hours and 45 minutes). From the north, Knoxville is accessible via I-81.

Air
McGhee Tyson Airport (TYS, 2055 Alcoa Hwy., Alcoa, 865/342-3000, www.tys.org) is located 20 minutes south of Knoxville in Alcoa, Tennessee. You can get there on US-129. From I-40, take exit 386-B to US-129 South; it's 12 miles to the airport. Airlines serving McGhee Tyson include Allegiant, American Airlines, Delta, Frontier, and United.

If you need taxi service between the airport and Knoxville, **Discount Taxi** (865/755-5143), **Odyssey Airport Taxi** (865/577-6767), and **Knoxville Taxi** (865/691-1900) are just a few of the car services you can call.

Public Transportation
Once you're in town, there is plenty to walk to. **Knoxville Trolley Lines** (301 Church Ave., 865/215-7800, www.katbus.com, free), operated by Knoxville Area Transit, also run throughout downtown. Check online or call for current schedules and routes.

Sights
★ East Tennessee History Center
In the heart of downtown, there's a great little museum telling the story of more than 200 years of East Tennessee's history. The **East Tennessee History Center** (601 S. Gay St., 865/215-8830, www.easttnhistory.org, 9am-4pm Mon.-Fri., 10am-4pm Sat., 1pm-5pm Sun., adults $5, seniors $4, children ages 16 and under free, free admission on Sun.) has exhibits on the Cherokee, the local involvement in skirmishes and battles during the Civil War, notable slaves and former slaves from the region, the origins of country music, and many displays and scenes showing Knoxville throughout the

Knoxville

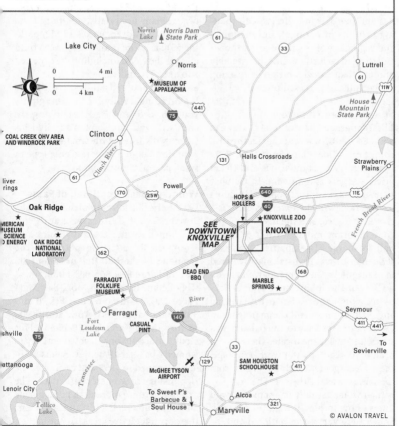

Lake City

Norris Lake

Norris Dam State Park

61

33

Norris

Luttrell

61

11W

★ MUSEUM OF APPALACHIA

House Mountain State Park

441

75

COAL CREEK OHV AREA AND WINDROCK PARK

Clinton

Halls Crossroads

131

Strawberry Plains

liver rings

61

170

25W

Powell

640

11E

French Broad River

Oak Ridge

HOPS & HOLLERS

40

MERICAN USEUM SCIENCE D ENERGY

OAK RIDGE NATIONAL LABORATORY

162

SEE "DOWNTOWN KNOXVILLE" MAP

★ Knoxville Zoo

KNOXVILLE

168

DEAD END BBQ

FARRAGUT FOLKLIFE MUSEUM ★

MARBLE SPRINGS ★

River

Seymour

shville

75

Fort Loudoun Lake

Farragut

CASUAL PINT

140

411

441

To Sevierville

attanooga

Tennessee

33

SAM HOUSTON SCHOOLHOUSE

411

Lenoir City

Tellico Lake

McGHEE TYSON AIRPORT

129

To Sweet P's Barbecue & Soul House

Alcoa

Maryville

321

© AVALON TRAVEL

0   4 mi

0   4 km

years. There are also displays on logging and mining, two vocations important to the region, as well as Oak Ridge National Laboratory, where important work in WWII's Manhattan Project went on.

The museum itself is great, but also take note of the wonderful neoclassical Italianate architecture of the building as you walk in. It's Knoxville's old Customs House, built in 1874. Since then, it has served several purposes—a courthouse, post office, TVA offices. Like many buildings around town, it's built with Tennessee marble.

★ Knoxville Museum of Art

The **Knoxville Museum of Art** (1050 Worlds Fair Park Dr., 865/525-6101, www.knoxart.org, 10am-5pm Tues.-Sat., 1pm-5pm Sun., free, donations accepted) is a three-story showcase of art and artists of East Tennessee. A huge exhibition, *Cycle of Life: Within the Power of Dreams and the Wonder of Infinity,* from renowned glass artist Richard Jolley, hangs on the walls and ceiling of the ground floor, and a colorful, impressive element of it—a nebula of colored glass orbs—can be seen as you walk through the museum doors. On the top level, two galleries show historical and contemporary works created by artists from or inspired by East Tennessee. The main level has another pair of galleries with rotating exhibits of national, international, and regional works; single-artist shows; and themed collections, like the assembly of more than a dozen pieces of amazing blown and cast glass sculptures.

★ Tennessee Theatre

The **Tennessee Theatre** (604 S. Gay St., 865/684-1200, www.tennesseetheatre.com, box office 10am-5pm Mon.-Fri., 10am-2pm Sat., show times and ticket prices vary) is magnificent. In October 1928, this fabulous space opened its doors to rave reviews. The exterior features a classic marquee, and the inside puts any contemporary movie theater or music hall to shame. The Spanish-Moorish-style interior was painstakingly restored to its original grandeur. Today, when you walk into the lobby, huge chandeliers twinkle high above. The ornate ceiling and walls complement the marble floor. Twin staircases lead to the balcony upstairs, and inside the theater, there's more ornate wood and plaster work. On stage, there's a gorgeous Wurlitzer organ from the same era as the theater. The best part is the theater actually has someone who knows how to play it, and play it well. Shows here vary from national and international musicians to plays and stage shows to a handful of films.

Sunsphere

When the World's Fair came in 1982, the city was transformed. The most dramatic transformation is a recognizable symbol of the city. The **Sunsphere** (810 Clinch Ave., 865/215-8160, www.worldsfairpark.org, 9am-10pm daily Apr.-Oct., 11am-6pm daily Nov.-Mar., free) is a 266-foot-tall tower topped by a huge golden ball. Inside the ball are private offices, a lounge, and a great observation deck that gives you a 360-degree view of Knoxville.

Knoxville Zoo

The **Knoxville Zoo** (3500 Knoxville Zoo Dr., 865/637-5331, www.knoxvillezoo.org, 9:30am-6pm daily, adults $20, seniors and children ages 2-12 $17, parking $5) has more than 900 animals from all over the world, including the expected zoo animals and some surprises. There are a number of red pandas here (the zoo is a breeding facility for them), a giraffe you can feed, and Budgie Landing, an enclosed aviary in Clayton Family Kids Cove that's filled with what seems like a million budgies (a parakeet, a type of small parrot) flying around.

Women's Basketball Hall of Fame

Given the basketball prowess of the University of Tennessee Lady Vols and famed former coach Pat Summitt, Knoxville is a fitting place for the **Women's Basketball Hall of Fame** (700 Hall of Fame Dr., 865/633-9000, www.wbhof.com, 10am-5pm Mon.-Sat. May-Labor Day, 11am-5pm Tues.-Fri., 10am-5pm Sat. Labor Day-Apr., adults $8, seniors and children ages 6-15 $6). This facility, the only one devoted entirely to women's basketball achievements at all levels, opened in 1999 and celebrates the rich history of women's basketball. The exhibits here are more than just a plaque and write-up on Hall of Fame members; there are interactive areas like the basketball court where you can practice passing and dribbling skills or shoot a few balls at baskets both contemporary and from the earliest days of the game. Other exhibits include displays honoring current NCAA national champions and a set of mannequins dressed in uniforms from over the years. There's also a gift shop where you can pick up basketballs autographed by Hall of Fame members. The building is hard to miss—one end has the world's largest basketball, which appears to be dropping into a net.

Tours

Haunted Knoxville Ghost Tours (36

Downtown Knoxville

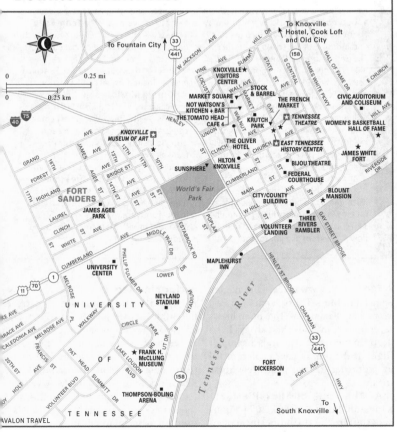

AVALON TRAVEL

Market Sq., 865/377-9677, www.
hauntedknoxville.net, adults $40, children ages 9-12 $35, tour dates and times
vary, reserve online) is more than just
a person walking around telling some
"scary" stories filled with local color;
these guides offer one of the leading historical and investigation-based
ghost tours. They've dug up some juicy,
and creepy, stories that reveal a hidden
side of this friendly city. And they continue to carry out investigations, bringing with them on every tour a host of
tools used to gather information on the
paranormal.

Entertainment and Events
Nightlife

Hops & Hollers (937 N. Central St.,
865/312-5733, www.hopsandhollers.
com, 2pm-midnight Mon.-Thurs., 2pm-
late Fri., 10am-late Sat., 11am-10pm Sun.)
is a fun little craft beer bar with 100 bottles and cans and 32 beers on draft. The
bartenders know their brews and can
make reliable recommendations (when in
doubt, ask for a tasting pour). Musicians
play here on a regular basis, and food
trucks stop by just about every night of
the week.

Casual Pint (421 Union Ave.,

Tennessee's Unsung Music Town

Knoxville gets short shrift when folks talk about Tennessee music. Ever eclipsed by Nashville and overlooked by bluegrass and mountain string band lovers for spots like Gatlinburg and Pigeon Forge, Knoxville is forgotten. But no more. The music scene in this hip Southern town is lively and growing livelier by the minute. Bands like The Black Lillies, with their mountain-influenced indie rock, and The Black Cadillacs, who take a more bluesy spin, have made a name for themselves nationally in recent years, playing at Bonnaroo and the Grand Ole Opry.

All across town, you'll find buskers playing on the street, bands tucked into restaurants and bars, and free concerts on the Market Square during summer. Jam sessions pop up, and band members flow freely from one impromptu band to another until they find the perfect fit. Two historic venues—The **Tennessee Theatre** (a stunning place to see a band) and the **Bijou Theatre**—host concerts with clockwork regularity.

Music festivals, like **Big Ears Festival** (www.bigearsfestival.com), **Smoky Mountain Music Fest** (www.smm-festival.com), and **Rhythm N Blooms Fest** (www.rhythmnbloomsfest.com), celebrate the sounds of the city and bring in visiting bands and music fans from all over.

Make it a point while you're in town to take in one of the daily free shows at **WDVX-FM,** where their noontime Blue Plate Special concert series brings in local and regional acts to play for a live radio broadcast in front of a studio audience.

865/951-2160, www.thecasualpint.com, 3pm-11pm Mon.-Thurs., 1pm-2am Fri., 11am-2am. Sat., noon-11pm Sun.) brews several beers in-house and always has a deep lineup on draft. Grab a sampler flight or the pint of your choice, or fill up a growler to take your brew home with you.

At **The EDGE of Knoxville** (7211 Kingston Pike, 865/602-2094, 5pm-3am daily), you'll find performances of almost any kind. Live music, drag shows, karaoke? They got it. Trivia, comedy, bar games? Got that, too. Toss in friendly people and good drinks, and it works.

Peter Kern Library (407 Union Ave., 865/521-0050, www.theoliverhotel.com, 4pm-1:30am Tues.-Fri., 11am-1:30am Sat.-Sun.), the bar in The Oliver Hotel, names their drinks after literary characters. The bar is modeled after a library: To read the menu, you have to crack open an old book. It's a cozy bar with boozy and flavorful cocktails—what's not to love?

Performing Arts

Along with the Tennessee Theatre, the **Bijou Theatre** (803 S. Gay St., 865-522-0832, www.knoxbijou.com, ticket prices vary) is one of Knoxville's most important venues for live musical performances. **The International** (940 Blackstock Ave., 865/200-5143, www.internationalknox.com, ticket prices and show times vary) brings in musical acts from heavy metal to rap and even hosts the occasional burlesque show.

Festivals and Events

Knoxville has several great events throughout the year, and two good ones are the **Big Ears Festival** (www.bigears-festival.com), a celebration of music and movies, and the **International Biscuit Festival** (865/238-5219, www.biscuitfest.com), an annual spring gathering of foodies, food writers, and biscuit enthusiasts. The Biscuit Festival is a strange one, but entertaining, and Big Ears can bring in some outstanding artists and musicians. Both events are worth seeing at least once.

Shopping

Market Square (800/727-8045, www.knoxvillemarketsquare.com) provides a central square (actually, a rectangle) around which people can gather. Just one block off Gay Street, this excellent little shopping and dining district is always busy. Summer concerts, buskers, and a small fountain for the kids to play in draw folks here, and the variety of people walking by and stores to peruse make it easy to kill time while waiting for your table to be ready. There are a half-dozen restaurants on the square, and close to a dozen shops, including the **Mast General Store** (865/546-1336, www.mastgeneralstore.com, 10am-6pm Mon.-Wed., 10am-9pm Thurs.-Fri., 9am-9pm Sat., noon-6pm Sun.), where you can buy everything from camping gear to home goods to penny candy; **Earth to Old City** (865/522-8270, www.earthtooldcity.com, 10am-9pm Sun.-Thurs., 10am-10pm Fri.-Sat.), which carries all sorts of odd and funky home decor, some of which may be more at home in a dorm room than your house; and **Bliss** (865/329-8868, www.shop-inbliss.com, 10am-9pm Mon.-Thurs., 10am-10pm Fri.-Sat., 11am-8pm Sun.), which sells home goods and lifestyle accessories. The **Market Square Farmer's Market** (11am-2pm Wed. and 9am-2pm Sat. May-Nov.) shows up in late spring, bringing with it dozens of farmers and craftspeople selling their wares, edible and otherwise.

Nothing Too Fancy (435 Union Ave., 865/951-2916, www.nothingtoofancy.com, 10am-9pm Mon.-Fri., 9am-9pm Sat., 11am-6pm Sun.) has some very cool T-shirts and other silk-screened goods designed by local artists. Reflecting the culture, in-jokes, and vibe of Knoxville in their work, the shirts are fun, even for those not in the know.

Nostalgia (5214 Homberg Dr., 865/584-0832, www.nostalgiamarket.com, 11am-6pm Mon.-Fri., 10am-6pm Sat., noon-5pm Sun.) calls itself a "vintique market," as they sell both vintage items and antiques. Portmanteau aside, it's a cool shop. Inside, you'll find mid-century modern furniture, vinyl records, vintage clothing, shabby chic furniture, and more, from around 30 vendors with well-stocked spaces.

Sports and Recreation

The star of Knoxville's recreational scene is **Ijams Nature Center** (2915 Island Home Ave., 865/577-4717, www.ijams.org, grounds 8am-dusk daily, visitors center 9am-5pm Mon.-Thurs., 9am-7pm Fri.-Sat., 11am-7pm Sun.). This 300-acre urban wilderness is laced with hiking and single-track mountain biking trails, and former quarries to explore on foot or even paddle around; it's also dog friendly. This vast, wild space is a strange thing so close to the city, but people love it. At any time of any day, there are walkers, hikers, trail runners, bikers, families, couples, and singles on the trails here. From Ijams Nature Center, you can connect with a larger, nearly contiguous loop some 40 miles long. Grab a map when you come in or download one and plan your route ahead of time, or you could just bring some water and your camera and wander.

World's Fair Park (www.worlds-fairpark.org) is the best city park in Knoxville. This 10-acre park has walking paths, a small lake, open grassy spaces, soccer fields, fountains, and a gorgeous stream running right down the middle. It's the home of the Sunsphere and Tennessee Amphitheatre, and at the north end of the park, past a fantastically large fountain, is a 4,200-square-foot playground. The playground and fountain get pretty crowded with kids, but there are other places you can go if you're traveling without a few of your own.

The **University of Tennessee Knoxville** (www.utk.edu) has a loyal (some say rabid) fan base. UT fields more than a dozen varsity-level teams including football (six national championships), men's and women's basketball (eight national championships for the women's team), soccer, rowing, volleyball, and more. If you want to cheer on the UT Volunteers (the Vols, if you want to sound like a local), tickets are available at www.AllVols.com (865/656-1200). Football season runs from September to late November, barring a bowl game appearance; basketball season goes from November to March; and tennis from September to April. Soccer and volleyball run from August to mid-November and swimming and diving go from September to late February. Men's basketball tickets range from $7-45, women's basketball from $10-20. Football tickets are both difficult to come by and pricey as most games sell out or come very close; some tickets fetch upwards of $1,000 a seat on resale markets (and resale markets may be the only tickets available to some games). The football team plays at **Neyland Stadium** (1235 Phillip Fulmer Way), basketball at **Thompson-Boling Arena** (1600 Phillip Fulmer Way), baseball at **Lindsey Nelson Stadium** (1511

Pat Summitt Dr.), and softball at **Sherri Parker Lee Stadium** (2323 Stephenson Dr.); more information on facilities and teams is available at www.utsports.com.

Food

Knoxville Food Tours (865/201-7270, www.knoxvillefoodtours.com, $99) shows off some of the best spots to drink and dine in downtown Knoxville. Tour dates are Friday and Saturday afternoons and evenings, but custom tours are available any day. The walk's not far—generally under a mile—and you get to find a place to have dinner, all while under the tutelage of a local foodie.

★ **Dead End BBQ** (3621 Sutherland Ave., 865/212-5655, www.deadendbbq. com, 11am-9pm Sun.-Thurs., 11am-10pm Fri.-Sat., $8-23) was started by a group of guys who would get together and make barbecue. Turns out they were onto something good. After their neighbors and wives praised them enough, they decided to enter a barbecue competition.

the Sunsphere looking over World's Fair Park in Knoxville

This obsession turned into a restaurant, and a good one at that. Everything they do here is top-notch, so unless the brisket or ribs or some other dish catches your eye, get the sampler plate. They have one dish you don't see very often—beef brisket burnt ends. Far from being burnt, these succulent little morsels are trimmings off the brisket, and they go down easy. The sauce here is fantastic, and the sides outstanding. Save room for dessert; their banana pudding is so rich and thick that it's more like cheesecake.

The burgers at **Nick & J's Cafe** (1526 Lovell Rd., 865/766-5453, www.nickandjscafe.com, 7am-4pm Mon.-Fri., 8am-2pm Sat., $2.50-11) may find a spot on your personal Top Five Burger list. If you're not a burger fan, something on the menu at this diner will find a place on your own "best of" list. Maybe it's the egg sandwich, the stack of buttermilk pancakes, or the breakfast bowl; could be the grilled Reuben or their all-veggie

pita. Whatever it is, it'll be good and you'll come back for more.

When a former rock musician opens a restaurant, you expect it to have a lot of personality, and ★ **Sweet P's Barbecue & Soul House** (3725 Maryville Pike, 865/247-7748, www.sweetpbbq.com, 11am-9pm Tues.-Thurs. and Sun., 11am-10pm Fri.-Sat., $4-22) delivers. Owner and pitmaster Chris Ford ate in every barbecue joint he could find while on tour with his band Gran Torino and began developing recipes long before he had the idea for a restaurant. The ribs and brisket make for some fine barbecue. The potato salad is good and the mac and cheese is done just right, but the coleslaw is out of this world.

The French Market (526 S. Gay St., 865/540-4372, www.thefrenchmarketknoxville.com, 9am-3pm Sun.-Mon., 9am-9pm Tues.-Thurs., 9am-10pm Fri., 9am-3pm and 4pm-10pm Sat., $3-12) has breakfast and lunch daily, and as the city's first authentic crepe restaurant, it's where you have to go if you're a fan of these French staples. Dinner is good too, with a nice array of dishes that will transport you to France with a bite.

At **The Tomato Head** (12 Market Sq., 865/637-4067, www.thetomatohead.com, 11am-9:30pm Mon.-Fri., 10am-10:30pm Sat., 10am-9pm Sun., brunch 10am-3pm Sat.-Sun., $5-34), sit outside, weather permitting, and watch the crowds on Market Square while you eat your pizza. The menu here features pizzas, sandwiches, burritos, and salads, but stick to the pizza—not because the other stuff is bad, but because the pizza is so good. You can build your own or get one already put together. Odd combos like fresh spinach and black bean, lamb sausage and sundried tomato, and smoked salmon and pesto actually go down quite easily.

Stock & Barrel (35 Market Sq., 865/766-2075, www.thestockandbarrel.com, 11am-late daily, $7-16) has an unparalleled bourbon selection, a list of burgers that are as tasty as they are creative,

and a line out the door. Even if you make a reservation, you'll wait for a seat, but it's worth it because once you get in, you won't want to leave. Get a flight of bourbon and whatever burger strikes your fancy, then settle in.

Café 4 (4 Market Sq., 865/544-4144, www.cafe4ms.com, 7am-9:30pm Mon.-Thurs., 7am-10:30pm Fri., 9am-10:30pm Sat., 9am-8:30pm Sun., $11-23) has more than just a great-looking menu for lunch and dinner. Their bakery makes macarons and other treats for breakfast or snacks; The Mezz—their cocktail lounge—shakes up some excellent drinks; and they've got space to hang out. The black bean burger is a solid choice, as is the Tomato Duet, a dish that combines fried green tomatoes and tomato jam to make a fine sandwich. If you want something heartier, go for the blackened fish and grits, meatloaf, or fried chicken.

Not Watson's Kitchen + Bar (15 Market Sq., 865/766-4848, www.notwatsons. com, 11am-10pm Mon.-Thurs., 11am-11pm Fri.-Sat., 11am-9pm Sun., $9-22), an eatery on Knoxville's Market Square, dishes up plates full of tasty favorites like fried green tomatoes, fish-and-chips, beef short ribs, blackened mahi-mahi, and chicken and waffles. Get a beer off their long list of drafts and bottles, then order something to eat while you watch the people on the Square.

Accommodations

★ **The Oliver Hotel** (407 Union Ave., 865/521-0050, www.theoliverhotel.com, $216-410) is an outstanding boutique hotel. The service is impeccable and the rooms amazing—everything is done to a luxurious, but not ostentatious, level. When you first find the hotel, you'll likely walk right past it as it blends in with the rest of the block almost seamlessly. Originally built in 1876 as a bakery,

Top to bottom: the historic Tennessee Theatre; Ijams Nature Center; Market Square, a great spot for shopping.

it was converted into a hotel for the World's Fair. There are 24 guest rooms with wet bars, coffee service, and fabulous bedding.

The Tennessean (531 Henley St., 844/413-0026 or 865/232-1800, www.thetennesseanhotel.com, $188-495) overlooks World's Fair Park and offers rooms that are truly luxurious. Whether you stay in an ordinary room or in the Governor's Suite ($3,000), you'll find sumptuous linens, tasteful decoration, and an attentive staff.

Home 2 Suites by Hilton Knoxville West (380 N. Peters Rd., 855/618-4702, www.home2suites3.hilton.com, $150-190) offers large rooms where you can spread out and stay affordably for a few days, making this a good selection for spending some time in Knoxville and exploring this part of the Smokies and the Tennessee mountains.

Hilton Knoxville (501 W. Church Ave., 865/523-2300, www3.hilton.com, $175-355) is only two blocks off Gay Street and has fantastic rooms. With on-site dining, a Starbucks right in the lobby, and parking next door, it's the best of the name-brand hotels you'll find.

There are a number of other chain hotels in town, including the **Hampton Inn Knoxville North** (5411 Pratt Rd., 865/689-1011, www.hamptoninn3.hilton.com, $139-170) and the **Country Inn & Suites Knoxville at Cedar Bluff** (9137 Cross Park Dr., 855/693-4500, www.countryinns.com, $95-180).

Information and Services

The **Knoxville Visitors Center** (301 S. Gay St., 865/523-7263 or 800/727-8045, www.visitknoxville.com, 8:30am-5pm Mon.-Fri., 9am-5pm Sat., noon-4pm Sun.) is what visitors centers should be. They have the expected rack of maps and helpful volunteers on hand to answer questions, but what sets them apart is the gift shop filled with locally made art and foodstuffs, a kids' corner, coffee, and a radio station. This is the only visitors center I know of where you can watch a free concert every day at lunch or listen to it as a live radio broadcast.

If you need medical care, there are more than a half-dozen clinics and hospitals in Knoxville. The **University of Tennessee Medical Center** (1924 Alcoa Hwy., 865/305-9000, www.utmedicalcenter.org) is a 581-bed teaching hospital, and **Fort Sanders Regional Medical Center** (1901 Clinch Ave., 865/541-1111, www.fsregional.com) is conveniently located downtown.

Essentials

Getting There

Air

While most visitors drive to the Blue Ridge Parkway, Shenandoah National Park and Skyline Drive, or Great Smoky Mountains National Park, it's convenient to fly into a nearby city, rent a car, and hit the road at any point along the route.

Washington DC

Three airports serve the Washington area. **Dulles International Airport** (IAD, 1 Saarinen Circle, Dulles, Virginia, 703/572-2700, www.flydulles.com) accommodates domestic and international travelers. Around three-dozen airlines serve Dulles, and if you're flying internationally, this airport is much closer to downtown than your other options.

Reagan National Airport (DCA, 2401 Smith Blvd., Arlington, Virginia, 703/417-8000, www.flyreagan.com) sees primarily domestic flights, though a few international flights come in. Airlines here include Air Canada, Delta, Frontier, Jet Blue, Southwest, United, and Virgin America.

In Baltimore, 35 miles to the northeast, the **Baltimore Washington International Airport** (BWI, 7050 Friendship Rd., Baltimore, 410/859-7111, www.bwiairport.com) sees a handful of international flights but serves mostly domestic airlines similar to those at Reagan National Airport. Depending on your departure city, Baltimore may be a cheaper flight into the region, but know that even though it's only 35 miles from DC, the traffic around Washington is notorious. It could be a costly cab ride or frustrating commute in your rental car if this is where you land.

Virginia

Charlottesville is served by **Charlottesville Albemarle Airport** (CHO, 100 Bowen Loop, Charlottesville, 434/973-8342, www.gocho.com). Airlines here include Delta, American Airlines, and United Airlines.

The largest airport in southwest Virginia is **Roanoke-Blacksburg Regional Airport** (ROA, 5202 Aviation Dr. NW, Roanoke, 540/362-1999, www.flyroa.com). Airlines serving this airport include Allegiant Air, American Airlines, Delta Airlines, and United Airlines.

Richmond International Airport (RIC, 1 Richard E. Byrd Terminal Dr., Richmond, 804/226-3000, www.flyrichmond.com) is only about 90 minutes east of Rockfish Gap and Milepost 0 of the Blue Ridge Parkway, and may be a viable option.

North Carolina

Asheville Regional Airport (AVL, 61 Terminal Dr., Fletcher, 828/684-2226, www.flyavl.com) is located south of the city in Fletcher. The next-closest airport in North Carolina is the **Charlotte Douglas International Airport** (CLT, 5501 Josh Birmingham Pkwy., Charlotte, 704/359-4013, www.cltairport.com), two hours away. Charlotte Douglas is the tenth-largest hub in the United States, with nonstop flights to and from more than 125 destinations worldwide.

Piedmont Triad International Airport (GSO, 1000 A. Ted Johnson Pkwy., Greensboro, 336/665-5666, www.flyfrompti.com), in Greensboro, is less than 90 minutes from the Blue Ridge Parkway and is served by Allegiant, American Airlines, American Eagle, Delta Airlines, Frontier Airlines, and United.

Farther to the east, **Raleigh-Durham International Airport** (RDU, 2400 John Brantley Blvd., Morrisville, 919/840-2123, www.rdu.com) sits between the cities of Durham and Raleigh. Eight airlines serve RDU, providing close to 400 nonstop flights to around 40 destinations daily. AirTran Airways, Southwest, Air Canada, American Airlines, Delta, Frontier Airlines, Jet Blue Airways, and United stop at RDU coming from domestic and international destinations. RDU is close to two hours from the Blue Ridge Parkway, but the volume of air traffic and the ease of reaching the Parkway make this a good choice when price-shopping flights.

South Carolina

Greenville-Spartanburg International Airport (GSP, 2000 GSP Dr., Greer, 864/877-7426, www.gspairport.com) is 80 minutes south of Asheville. Airlines serving Greenville-Spartanburg include Allegiant, American Airlines, Delta, Southwest, and United.

Tennessee

McGhee Tyson Airport (TYS, 2055 Alcoa Hwy., Alcoa, 865/342-3000, www.tys.org) in Alcoa is about two hours from Cherokee, and about 20 minutes south of Knoxville. Airlines serving McGhee Tyson include Allegiant, American Airlines American Eagle, Delta, Frontier, and United.

Bus

You can take a **Greyhound bus** (800/231-2222, www.greyhound.com) to every major city and most of the larger towns on or near the Blue Ridge Parkway. The most useful routes are those that take you to Washington DC's **Union Station** (WAS, 50 Massachusetts Ave. NE, 24 hours daily); the **Charlottesville Greyhound station** (310 W. Main St., 434/295-5131, www.greyhound.com, 8am-10pm daily); the **Roanoke Greyhound station** (26 Salem Ave. SW, 540/343-5436, midnight-2am and 9am-5pm daily); or the **Knoxville Greyhound**

station (100 E. Magnolia Ave., 865/525-9483, www.greyhound.com, 4:30am-1:30am daily), because they put you in places where it's easy to get started on the Parkway. At Washington DC's Union Station, a number of buses arrive daily from cities from across the country. Both the Charlottesville and Roanoke stations are downtown, where it's easy to get to your accommodations or to a rental car agency. The **Asheville Greyhound station** (2 Tunnel Rd., 828/253-8451, 7:30am-4:30pm and 8pm-10pm Mon.-Fri., 7:30am-9:30am, 2:30pm-4:30pm, and 8pm-10pm Sat.-Sun.) is another option, though the route does take a bit longer to get into town due to the station's location about a mile east of Asheville.

Train

Amtrak (800/872-7245, www.amtrak.com) service is dependable through this region. Amtrak pulls into Washington DC's **Union Station** (50 Massachusetts Ave. NE, 24 hours daily) with trains coming from and going to destinations all over the Eastern Seaboard. Amtrak services include the Acela Express, Northeast Regional, Silver Service/Palmetto, Cardinal/Hoosier State, Crescent, Vermonter, Capitol Limited, and Carolinian/Piedmont.

Amtrak also serves **Charlottesville** (CVS, 810 W. Main St., 434/296-4559, www.amtrak.com, 6am-9:30pm daily), where the Cardinal/Hoosier State, Crescent, and Northeast Regional Lines pass through daily.

The Amtrak station in **Roanoke** (101 Norfolk Ave., 800/872-7245, www.amtrak.com) opened in fall 2017 and serves passengers on the Crescent and Northeast Regional lines.

Major Highways

Two major interstates—**I-64** and **I-77**—intersect the Blue Ridge Parkway at the northern and southern ends, and **I-81** provides easy access as it runs diagonally up the western border of Virginia, parallel to the Parkway.

I-66 connects Washington DC with the beginning of Skyline Drive in northern Virginia. **I-64** passes by Shenandoah National Park and is the de facto dividing line between Skyline Drive and the Parkway, providing easy access to both at Rockfish Gap just outside Waynesboro. To the south, **I-77** crosses the Parkway at Fancy Gap, Virginia. **I-40** skirts the Parkway at several points in North Carolina and Great Smoky Mountains National Park in Tennessee. A number of smaller roads, from U.S. highways to state routes, offer access to the Parkway and parks at various points along the way. Cities like Charlottesville, Waynesboro, and Roanoke, Virginia, are just a few miles off the Parkway or Skyline Drive. In North Carolina, the Parkway goes right by Asheville and ends in Cherokee. In Tennessee, Knoxville (touched by both **I-40** and **I-75**) is the nearest city to Great Smoky Mountains National Park, though the towns of Gatlinburg and Pigeon Forge are nestled close to the park's borders.

Road Rules

Along the Blue Ridge Parkway, **mileposts** mark the way. Starting at the southern end of Shenandoah National Park with Milepost 0 at Rockfish Gap all the way through Milepost 469 in Cherokee, North Carolina, you'll pass stone markers along the side of the road. Overlooks, hikes, historic sites, and spots to stop and explore are referenced both by name and milepost. Skyline Drive through Shenandoah National Park is marked by mileposts as well.

Car Rental

Rental cars are available at every airport listed in this guide, and if you take a train to your departure point, you'll find rental agencies in or near the station. Since many bus and train stations

Bridges and Tunnels

The **viaducts, 168 bridges,** and **26 tunnels** are some of the most distinctive architectural elements you'll find along the Blue Ridge Parkway. The bridges make extensive use of native stone as a decorative and functional element (the stonework was used as the form for the concrete frames on each bridge). The same goes for the tunnels: Their faces are both decorative and structural and make the same use of native materials.

While the bridges are regular features for the length of the Parkway, the tunnels and the most striking of the viaducts (the Linn Cove Viaduct at Milepost 304.4) are a North Carolina thing. In North Carolina, the mountains grow sharper and steeper,

and at times it's easier to go through rather than around them. That's why of the 26 tunnels, only 1, the Bluff Mountain Tunnel at Milepost 53.1, is found in Virginia; the other 25 are found within a 130-mile stretch of the southern section in North Carolina.

For anyone traveling in cars or on motorcycles, the tunnels are little more than another pretty aspect of the roadway. But if you're hauling a **trailer** or driving an **RV,** you'll be more concerned with the tunnels' height and length. Visit www.nps.gov/blri/planyourvisit/tunnel-heights.htm for a list of the 26 tunnels, complete with mileposts, length, and height restrictions.

share a facility or are near one another, the same is true if you bus in. The major rental players—Hertz, National, and Enterprise, among others—will be readily available with their standard fleet of cars, but if you are looking for a specific vehicle (like a 4x4 or a convertible), check availability with the agencies and reserve your vehicle. Most of these vehicles will be available for one-way rental, allowing you to rent a car at one end and drive it to another, returning it there before you board a plane, or hop a bus or train back home. Before you embark on a long, one-way trip with a rental vehicle, be sure you can return it at the other end. Check with your car rental agency about additional fees for one-way rentals, as some charge hefty fees for this type of rental.

Driving Rules and Highway Safety

Foreign visitors who wish to drive should obtain an **International Driving Permit,** which is available from the nation that issued your driver's license. Drivers licensing rules vary from state to state. It's a good idea to familiarize yourself with driving rules in the states that you'll be visiting (you can do this at

www.usa.gov). Throughout the United States, drivers drive on the right side of the road, and distance and speed are measured in miles. Speedometers display both miles and kilometers; road signs display only miles.

On Skyline Drive, the **speed limit** is 35 miles per hour; it's 45 miles per hour along most of the Blue Ridge Parkway, though it does slow in areas; in Great Smoky Mountains National Park, the speed limit is 45 miles per hour as well. Please observe the posted speed limit. Maintaining the speed limit allows you time to stop or avoid wildlife, debris, or other hazards on the road surface, as well as pedestrians or other vehicles. Since long sections of all three segments of this route are unprotected—read: no guardrails to break up the view—obeying the speed limit has the added benefit of keeping you and your passengers safe from leaving the roadway on an unexpected downhill trip. Mind the posted speed limit on highways and interstates as well, especially in Virginia, where speeding violations can result in jail time.

One reason for the low speed limits along this scenic drive is to keep **wildlife** free from harm. You'll see a number of

Mind the Gaps

You'll encounter more **gaps** in the Blue Ridge Parkway than I can count, and if you're not from the mountains, this may be an unfamiliar term. Gaps, sometimes called passes, are simply low spots in the mountain chain. If you needed to get across the mountain, you'd look for these low spots for your crossing, as opposed to going up and over the high, steep, rocky places. Rockfish Gap, at Blue Ridge Parkway Milepost 0, is one such low spot. At only 1,909 feet high, it offered wildlife, then Native Americans, then colonists and settlers, and now endless interstate traffic an easy place to pass through these mountains.

woodland creatures on your drive, and as your route cuts through the forests where they live, you'll see many animals on or near the roadway. Be extra vigilant at dawn and dusk, when wildlife is most active. If you must stop on the road to allow an animal to cross, use your hazard flashers to alert other drivers, and try not to stop in blind curves or just over the crest of a hill where you'll be difficult to see.

Weather Considerations

From Skyline Drive through to Gatlinburg, Tennessee, the weather can slow and stop traffic or even shut down sections of the route under the most severe conditions. Generally, though, the weather is quite pleasant, and **winter** is the only time when there are widespread closures of Skyline Drive or the Blue Ridge Parkway. In both cases, the route is high and exposed, making it vulnerable to ice and snow; these conditions, combined with the expense of the equipment necessary for proper snow and ice removal, make wintertime closures inevitable. Newfound Gap Road through Great Smoky Mountains National Park is a public highway and is maintained throughout the year. It may still close if heavy snowfall is expected or is more than road crews can cope with, but closure is rare. More often, you'll be delayed as crews clear the road. Road conditions are available by contacting the **National Park Service** (828/298-0398, www.nps. gov/blri).

Spring generally brings a good amount of rain to the Blue Ridge Mountains. During the earliest months, and even toward the first part of April in the highest elevations, you can experience road closures if a spring snowstorm visits the high passes. The rest of the season, it may rain, but it doesn't impede traffic.

In **summer,** there is a chance of thunderstorms, and on rare occasions hail, along the route. Most likely, you'll encounter a rain shower or fog. The fog can be quite dense, so slowing down or even pulling off at a socked-in overlook is advisable.

In **autumn,** there are occasional rainstorms, and in the latest part of the season, the rare high-altitude snowstorm that dusts the tops of the mountains white. Traffic is generally not a consideration on the Blue Ridge Parkway or elsewhere along the route, but autumn sees the highest number of visitors to Skyline Drive, the Blue Ridge Parkway, and GSMNP, and leaf lookers often slow down well below the speed limit, causing some **congestion on the roadway.** Autumn color seekers also fill overlooks and line the sides of the road to snap pictures and take in the views, slowing traffic in these busy areas as drivers watch for pedestrians.

Road Etiquette

If this is your first visit to the South, you can start fitting in by simply waving. Many drivers along the Blue Ridge Parkway and Skyline Drive and in the Smokies will raise a finger or two from the steering wheel or proffer a little salute to passing drivers, as if to say, "Beautiful, ain't it?" and "Sure is" with the return wave. So give a little wave, nod, or two-fingered salute at your fellow travelers.

Standard etiquette applies—only use your bright headlights if there's no on-coming traffic, for example—but there are a few things to remember. You're on this road trip to relax, so loosen up, slow down, and lose yourself to the rambling speed of these mountaintop byways. There's no need for tailgating, horn honking, or agitation, and if you encounter this type of frustrated, rush-everywhere traveler, pull off at the next overlook while they move on down the road.

Parking

All along Skyline Drive, the Blue Ridge Parkway, and Great Smoky Mountains National Park, parking is limited to designated parking areas at overlooks and trailheads, though parking is permitted along the road shoulder, provided all four wheels are off the road surface and your vehicle doesn't impede traffic.

Fuel

Fuel is not readily available on the Blue Ridge Parkway, a slightly inconvenient byproduct of efforts to protect the Parkway from unintentional spills or leaks. The Blue Ridge Parkway Association (www.blueridgeparkway.org) provides an index of fuel availability by milepost, which is listed at the beginning of each applicable chapter in this guidebook. At major highway intersections and any place you meet a town or city, you'll find fuel close at hand.

In Shenandoah National Park, the one gas station is at the Big Meadows Wayside (MP 51.2), but you will find fuel at Front Royal, at the north end of the park, and in Waynesboro and all along the I-64 corridor on the south end of the park.

You won't find any fuel inside Great Smoky Mountains National Park, but you will find it in Cherokee and the other towns on the North Carolina side. Gas stations are plentiful on the Tennessee side once you leave the national park.

Maps

One of the best resources for exploring a new region is a good map. DeLorme's atlas and gazetteers are indispensable. The detail provided is enough to plan short day hikes or longer expeditions, and they point out everything from trailheads and boat launches to campgrounds, hunting and fishing spots, and back roads of all types. Look for the **North Carolina Atlas & Gazetteer** (Yarmouth, ME: DeLorme, 2012), the **Tennessee Atlas & Gazetteer** (Yarmouth, ME: DeLorme, 2014), and the **Virginia Atlas & Gazetteer** (Yarmouth, ME: DeLorme, 2009).

Motorcycles

Motorcyclists love the Blue Ridge Parkway for its views, mild temperature, and fun twists and turns. Helmets are required, and all other road regulations should be followed. During autumn, motorcyclists should exercise a little extra caution as wet leaves on the roadway can be quite slick. Many bike enthusiasts consider a trip through Great Smoky Mountains National Park a must, and the curves along Newfound Gap in particular provide thrills.

Bicycles

Of the three roads along this trip, the Blue Ridge Parkway is, hands down, the most popular for cyclists. This 469-mile ride through picturesque peaks provides challenges and thrills to cyclists in spring, summer, and fall. Elevations range from 600 feet to more than 6,000, so there's the challenge of long climbs and the reward of lazy downhills. The Parkway was originally intended for automobile traffic, so there are no bike lanes along the route. It's best to adopt a defensive mindset and assume that most drivers have no experience around cyclists. Always wear your helmet, be sure lights and reflectors are in good condition, and ride in single file.

The route is spread out, and there is almost nothing by way of bicycle-specific facilities, so prepare for the worst, bringing your tool kit, spare tubes, and anything else you'll need to perform a quick repair. The facilities that exist—campgrounds, visitors centers, and the like—do have potable water, though it isn't advisable to drink from streams without purification first.

Keep in mind that mountain bikes aren't permitted on Blue Ridge Parkway trails, but they are permitted in national forests, of which the Parkway abuts a number. Check for specific trails within each national forest.

Public Transportation
There's no public transportation that runs along Skyline Drive, the Blue Ridge Parkway, or through Great Smoky Mountains National Park. Only in cities along the way will you find any sort of public transportation infrastructure in place.

Travel Tips

Visas and Officialdom
Visitors from other countries must present a valid **passport** and **visa** issued by a U.S. consular official unless they are citizens of a country eligible for the Visa Waiver Program (such as Canada) in order to enter the United States. For more information on traveling to the United States from a foreign country, visit www.usa.gov.

Access for Travelers with Disabilities
The overwhelming majority of hikes in Shenandoah National Park, the Blue Ridge Parkway, and Great Smoky Mountains National Park are not accessible for travelers with disabilities, particularly those that impede mobility. Luckily, a huge number of attractions, accommodations, and restaurants are accessible.

Traveling with Children
There's no shortage of kid-friendly activities along Skyline Drive, the Blue Ridge Parkway, or in Great Smoky Mountains National Park. Along the route, there are kid-friendly hikes, Junior Ranger programs, animals galore, and visitors centers and gift shops where you can pick up a little something to keep the youngest traveler occupied while in transit. In the cities, you'll find children's museums, parks, zoos, and playgrounds.

Senior Travelers
Aside from stubble-faced and bearded bikers cruising the Parkway, one of the most common sights is the gray-haired couple tooling about in their Subaru, RV, or truck towing an RV. Many attractions, accommodations, and dining options have senior discounts, so flash that AARP card and save a few bucks. Overall, the route from Front Royal to the Smoky Mountains is a safe and leisurely one for seniors.

Gay and Lesbian Travelers
While the Blue Ridge Mountains doesn't have the same kind of atmosphere as San Francisco or Key West, LGBTQ travelers may be pleasantly surprised at how tolerant the region is, despite being rural and, in areas, part of the Bible belt. Washington DC and Knoxville, our travel bookends, have open and active gay cultures, and in larger cities along the way, including Charlottesville and Roanoke, Virginia, and Asheville, North Carolina, the culture is open and accepting. This isn't to say you won't encounter any problems, but generally, you'll find that locals hardly bat an eye.

Environmental Concerns
The parklands and forests along the route are preserved so future generations can enjoy nature in as pristine a state as

possible. That's why there's no gas available on the Blue Ridge Parkway. It also explains the constant reminders to adhere to **Leave No Trace** (www.LNT.org) principles. These principles are remarkably similar to the Boy Scouts of America teachings: Plan ahead and prepare, travel and camp on durable surfaces, dispose of waste properly, leave what you find, minimize campfire impacts, respect wildlife, and be considerate of other visitors. These easy rules can improve the outdoor experience for everyone.

If you pack something in, pack it out, and consider carrying a **trash bag** on trails to pick up after less responsible hikers. If each of us would make this a habit, we could clean up a lot of litter that clutters up our view and is detrimental to the environment.

Dogs are allowed on some trails throughout our route, though they must be on leash or under physical control at all times. If you have Fido out on the trail or let him use the grassy facilities at an overlook or wayside, be sure to pick up what he's putting down.

You'll pass several ponds and lakes as you travel from Virginia to Tennessee, but unless there's a designated **swimming** area, going for a dip isn't cool. There are exceptions, but those exceptions are noted near the potential swimming hole. When in doubt, ask before you dive in.

You'll spot lots of **wildlife** on your trip. Common animals include white-tailed deer, raccoons, opossums, turtles, bobcats, and even black bears. Coyotes are becoming a more frequent sight along the way, and in certain areas of the Smoky Mountains, you can even see the occasional elk. Many times, a herd of deer will be in a pasture off the Parkway. If you see a deer (or any other animal), and you want to get a photograph, keep a safe distance from the animal and don't offer it any food as this makes the animal grow accustomed to people and can have negative impacts on its health.

Health and Safety

For the most part, your trip should be unremarkable as far as health and safety are concerned, provided you're attentive to your situation and surroundings, but there are a few things you should know. Those going on long hikes would also be wise to familiarize themselves with the **10 essentials** (www.rei.com/learn/expert-advice/ten-essentials.html).

Emergencies

For emergencies anywhere in the United States, dial **911** on your phone for immediate assistance. In Virginia, dialing **#77** will connect you with the state police. In North Carolina, dialing *77 connects you to state police and *67 puts you in contact with the highway patrol. In Tennessee, dial *847 for police assistance. If you have to call, try to note your milepost as a reference point for any assistance that's headed your way.

Wilderness Safety

Hikers should beware of **ticks**, some of which can transmit Lyme disease. An insect repellent and some thorough body checks (use a partner for more fun) should keep you tick free after a jaunt through the woods. If you do get a bite or if you notice a red circular rash that's similar to a bull's-eye, consult a physician; Lyme disease can be life-threatening in the worst cases.

You'll encounter woodland insects including bees, wasps, yellow jackets, and hornets, so if you're allergic, be sure to have an **EpiPen** on hand. A number of **snakes,** including rattlesnakes and copperheads, live in these woods. Be alert and keep an ear open for that warning rattle, and if you unexpectedly smell cucumbers in the woods, you may be near a copperhead; in either case, back away slowly and detour around. **Spiders** can be a concern in places, namely woodpiles and some of the backcountry shelters.

Most are harmless, though the brown recluse is seen from time to time, but more commonly you'll see a black widow spider, easily identifiable by the red hourglass on the female's abdomen.

Along the trails and roadsides, you'll likely encounter **poison ivy, poison oak,** and **poison sumac,** all of which deliver an itchy blister when you come in contact with the oils they secrete. These oils are active for several months, so if you walk through a field of poison ivy, be sure to wash your pants, socks, and boots well, lest you inadvertently get poison ivy a month later. You may also come upon **stinging nettles,** which leave itchy welts akin to mosquito bites; these are harmless and generally go away quickly.

Information and Services

Money

If you're traveling to the United States from a foreign country, you'll need to exchange your currency at the airport or at a bank or currency exchange in your destination city as every attraction, restaurant, and lodging on the route accepts U.S. dollars only. **Credit cards** are widely accepted, but for moments when you need cash, there are plenty of **ATMs** along the route. Though ATMs are limited in Shenandoah National Park and along the Blue Ridge Parkway, you will find them at some visitors centers.

Communications
Internet Access

Nearly every hotel, B&B, inn, or lodge will have Wi-Fi, often for free. You won't find Wi-Fi at the lodgings in Shenandoah National Park or at most of the campgrounds along the Blue Ridge Parkway. With the exception of campgrounds, in most places where Wi-Fi is not available, you'll find a computer or business center you can use at your lodging. When you

have cell service, you will likely have a 3G or 4G connection, affording you Internet access on your phone.

Cell Phones

Around all of the cities and most of the towns, cell reception should be fine and free Wi-Fi abundant. From Washington DC to Front Royal, Virginia, you'll have excellent coverage. As you enter Shenandoah National Park, expect a quick drop-off in signal quality, but the signal should strengthen at a few overlooks. Around Waynesboro and Charlottesville, the signal returns, just in time to get on the Blue Ridge Parkway and enter a cell-signal wilderness (surrounded by actual wilderness).

Accommodations
Hotel and Motel Chains

The great thing about chain hotels is this: They're everywhere, and you always know what you're getting. They make it easy to travel on a budget and also to travel without reservations, as chains typically have a large number of rooms and, when full, can refer you to a sister-hotel in the area. I prefer inns, cottages, and B&Bs, but those may require advance reservations. Chain hotels come in a variety of budgets and amenity levels. All along the route, you'll find chain hotels and motels including Marriott, Holiday Inn, Hilton (in larger cities), Hampton Inn, Sleep Inn, and La Quinta.

Camping

Along the Blue Ridge Parkway and in both Shenandoah and Great Smoky Mountains National Parks, no unauthorized backcountry camping is allowed. Reserve a spot at a backcountry shelter or campground, or get a spot at a front-country campground. In national forests, like the Jefferson, Washington, and Pisgah National Forests, you can camp in the backcountry so long as you do so responsibly. This means no campfires. Due to the hazard of fire, campfires are generally only permitted in frontcountry campsites. If you are frontcountry camping, be aware that you can't bring in your own firewood; you'll need to purchase or gather it on-site. This is to prevent the spread of insect infestations, parasites, and diseases that may harm local plants.

Reservations

For much of the year, you should be able to travel without reservations, though even in the off-season, you may not be able to get into your first choice of campgrounds, lodges, hotels, or B&Bs. During peak seasons, namely October and late summer, you'll need reservations as visitors increase exponentially to see the autumn color show or squeeze in one more summer getaway. For some of the most popular campgrounds and lodging along the route, you will want to book months in advance.

Suggested Reading

Travel

Fussell, Fred, and Steve Kruger. *Blue Ridge Music Trails of North Carolina: A Guide to Music Sites, Artists, and Traditions of the Mountains and Foothills*. Chapel Hill, NC: University of North Carolina Press, 2013. A guide to destinations—festivals, restaurants, opries, church singings—in North Carolina, where authentic bluegrass, old-time, and sacred music rings through the hills and hollers. An accompanying CD gives you a chance to hear some tunes rather than just read about them.

Simmons, Nye. *Best of the Blue Ridge Parkway: The Ultimate Guide to the Parkway's Best Attractions*. Johnson City, TN: Mountain Trail Press, 2008. Beautiful photography of some of the most iconic and picturesque spots along the Parkway accompanied by write-ups of some of the highlights.

History and Culture

Hall, Karen J. *Building the Blue Ridge Parkway*. Charleston, SC: Arcadia Publishing, 2007. Narrative and archival photos combine to tell the story of the early days of the Blue Ridge Parkway including construction, folkways, and cultural tidbits.

Pegram, Tim. *The Blue Ridge Parkway by Foot: A Park Ranger's Memoir*. Jefferson, NC: McFarland & Company, 2007. A fascinating story of a former park ranger who decided to hike the Parkway—not the trails along the Parkway, but along the roadside, experiencing the 469-mile drive on foot.

Hiking

Adams, Kevin. *Hiking Great Smoky Mountains National Park*. Guilford, CT: Globe Pequot Press, 2013. An excellent hiking-only guide to trails and on-foot sights in Great Smoky Mountains National Park from FalconGuides.

Gildart, Bert, and Jane Gildart. *Hiking Shenandoah National Park*. Guilford, CT: Globe Pequot Press, 2011. Another FalconGuides look at trails and hikes in Shenandoah National Park.

Johnson, Randy. *Hiking the Blue Ridge Parkway: The Ultimate Travel Guide to America's Most Popular Scenic Roadway*. Guilford, CT: Globe Pequot Press, 2010. A thorough trail guide to the Blue Ridge Parkway from FalconGuides.

Internet Resources

General Tourism Information
Washington DC
Destination DC
www.washington.org
The official tourism site of Washington DC has itineraries, travel tips, calendars, and planning tools.

Arlington Convention and Visitors Service
www.stayarlington.com
Arlington, Virginia, is just across the Potomac River from DC and is an excellent place to stay. You'll find details on lodging and activities in Arlington but also information on a trip into Washington DC.

Virginia
Virginia Tourism Corporation
www.virginia.org
Trip ideas, lists and maps of festivals and fairs, itineraries, and other fantastic trip-planning tools are here.

North Carolina
North Carolina Division of Tourism
www.visitnc.com
This comprehensive guide contains trip itineraries in each region, including a dedicated section on the Blue Ridge Parkway. The site is rich with photos and videos, and the index of accommodations, attractions, and more is comprehensive.

Tennessee
Tennessee Department of Tourist Development
www.tnvacation.com
The official site of Tennessee's state tourism office is user-friendly, allowing you to narrow your focus on one region with just a couple of clicks. Resources for the Smokies and East Tennessee include interactive maps that provide a great overview of the region's offerings from natural sights to man-made attractions.

National Park Information
Blue Ridge Parkway
Blue Ridge Parkway
www.nps.gov/blri
Details the history of the park and provides real-time road maps that show detours, delays, and closures; downloadable maps that make hiking and planning a trip section-by-section easy; and

write-ups on the flora, fauna, and geographical features of the Parkway.

Virtual Blue Ridge
www.virtualblueridge.com
Information on the Blue Ridge Parkway including wildflower and fall color reports, road conditions and closures, and weather along the route. You'll also find a store with maps, books, and mementos.

Blue Ridge National Heritage Area
www.blueridgeheritage.com
Created in 2003 to recognize the unique character, culture, landscape, and beauty of the Blue Ridge, this organization promotes the history, folkways, arts and crafts, and exploration of the region.

Blue Ridge Parkway Association
www.blueridgeparkway.org
A nonprofit association of businesses and individuals promoting tourism along the Blue Ridge Parkway, from Virginia to Tennessee. Their website includes interactive maps; indexes to activities, sights, restaurants, hikes, and more along the Parkway; highlights of the route; real-time road reports; regional breakdowns; and other resources to help you plan a trip.

Great Smoky Mountains National Park
Great Smoky Mountains National Park
www.nps.gov/grsm
An extensive history of the park; details on the flora, fauna, and natural features in the park; and downloadable maps and contact information for rangers and park offices.

Friends of the Smokies
www.friendsofthesmokies.org
Friends of the Smokies works to raise funds for park initiatives, trail maintenance and improvement, and a variety of other needs. They accept donations of time and money, so if you had a good

time in the Smokies, consider lending them a hand or a few bucks.

Great Smoky Mountains Association
www.smokiesinformation.org
A nonprofit partner of Great Smoky Mountains National Park, the group operates retail stores in and benefiting the park; provides guidebooks, maps, logo-emblazoned clothing and gear, and other gifts; and helps with expenses associated in promoting the park.

Shenandoah National Park
Shenandoah National Park
www.nps.gov/shen
Information on trails and park activities as well as Skyline Drive, the flora and fauna, the history, and the landscape. Skyline Drive details include maps of the road and trails, contact information for various waysides and lodges, and links to secure in-park lodging.

Washington DC
National Mall and Memorial Parks
www.nps.gov/nama
Excellent historical, educational, and kids' resources for Washington DC's National Mall, along with maps of the Mall, contact information, and tips.

Outdoor Recreation
Appalachian Trail Conservancy
www.appalachiantrail.org
The Appalachian Trail Conservancy provides support to the Appalachian Trail, which parallels and even crosses the Blue Ridge Parkway in many places.

North Carolina State Parks
www.ncparks.gov
Since a number of state parks brush against the Blue Ridge Parkway in North Carolina, many travelers use their campgrounds and facilities as resources and

waypoints along their journey. Learn more about the facilities and amenities of Parkway-adjacent parks at the website of the North Carolina State Parks system.

North Carolina Wildlife Resources Commission
www.ncwildlife.org
Information on hunting, fishing, and boating in North Carolina, including easy-to-understand hunting and fishing regulations and online license procurement.

Tennessee Wildlife Resources Agency
www.state.tn.us/twra
Need-to-know information regarding hunting and fishing regulations and licenses.

Virginia Department of Game and Inland Fisheries
www.dgif.virginia.gov
The Virginia Department of Game and Inland Fisheries manages the state's wildlife to ensure that everyone—hunters, anglers, hikers, and nature lovers—can enjoy the state's outdoor offerings. They handle licensing and permits, so if you want to hunt or fish, they're the folks to see.

Virginia Outdoors
www.virginiaoutdoors.com
A comprehensive list of activities, outfitters, and resources for planning an outdoor getaway in any season.

Virginia State Parks
www.dcr.virginia.gov/state-parks
Information on parks, programs, lodging, and activities. This site can be a little difficult to navigate, but your patience is rewarded as just about any question you have can be answered with a little looking.

Index

A

Abrams Creek: 306
Abrams Falls: 279
Abrams Falls Trail: 305
accessibility: 341
accommodations: 343-344; *see also specific place*
AC Hotel by Marriott Asheville Downtown: 16, 231
African American history: Harrison Museum of African American Culture 123; Little Switzerland 197-198; Mount Vernon tours 46; National Museum of African American History and Culture 40
Afton Mountain Vineyards: 81
air travel: 9; general discussion 335-336; Asheville 208, 210; Charlottesville 85; Gatlinburg 308; Knoxville 324; North Carolina 161; Shenandoah Valley 30; Virginia 102
Alexandria: 47
Alfred Regan Cabin: 298
Alum Cave Bluff to Mount LeConte Hike: 13, 288
Alum Cave Creek: 289
Alum Cave Trail: 288
Ambrosia Farm Bed & Breakfast: 14, 102, 141
American Art Museum: 39
An American in Paris: 47
Andrews Bald: 13, 19, 274, 287
Andy Griffith Museum: 147
Andy Griffith Playhouse: 147
Andy Griffith sights: 99, 146-148
antiques: Asheville 222; Bedford 118; Blowing Rock 184; Boone 177; Front Royal 60; Olde Time Antiques Fair 171; Roanoke 126
Antler Hill Village: 215
Appalachian Trail: 8, 128, 286, 296, 306
Appalachian Trail to Mount LeConte via The Boulevard: 286
Apple Orchard Falls Trail: 111
Apple Orchard Mountain: 111-112
apple orchards: Bedford 116; Carter Mountain Apple Orchard 88-89; Orchard at Altapass 196
architecture: Asheville 205, 212; Biltmore Estate 213-214; Blue Ridge Parkway 338; Linn Cove Viaduct 190; Monticello 87; Moses Cone Manor 187; National Mall 33-42; Poplar Forest 116; Tennessee Theatre 326
Arch Rock: 289
Arlington House: 45
Arlington National Cemetery: 12, 27, 32, 44-46
Arrowmont School of Arts and Crafts: 310
art events/galleries: Arrowmont School of Arts and Crafts 310; Asheville 221, 223; Black Mountain College Museum and Arts Center 216-217; Blowing Rock 159, 184; Brevard 247; Centerfest 118; Floyd 140; Folk Art Center 209; Great Smoky Arts and Crafts Community 311; Jones House Community and Cultural Center 176; National Gallery of Art 37; Penland Gallery 197; Qualla Arts and Crafts Mutual 261; River Arts District 221; Roanoke 123; Shenandoah Valley Art Center (SVAC) 82; Smithsonian Institution 38-39; Taubman Museum of Art 125; Turchin Center for the Visual Arts 176; Waynesville 254; West Jefferson 170-171; *see also* museums
Art Loeb Trail: 251
Art on the Mountain: 171
Ashe County Arts Council: 171
Asheville: 16, 210-233
Asheville and the Southern Blue Ridge: 8, 203-269
Australian Aboriginal art: 87
auto museums: 256
autumn travel: 9, 209, 281, 339

B

B&Bs: 9; *see also specific place*
backpacking: Great Smoky Mountains National Park 280, 300; Rock Castle Gorge Trail 142; Whetstone Ridge Trail 106; wilderness safety 342
Backstreet Park Concert Series: 171
Bad Saint: 19, 29, 53
ballet: 48, 126, 220
Balsam Mountain Road: 290-291
Barren Ridge Vineyards: 81
Basin Creek Trail: 169
Baskins Creek: 299
Baskins Falls: 298
Baskins Falls Trail: 299
Bass Lake Trail: 188
Beacon Heights: 18, 193-194
Beacon Heights Trail: 194
Bearfence Mountain: 75
Bearfence Mountain Trail: 75
bears, black: 300-301, 304
Beaver Creek Lake: 92
Bedford: 13, 114-120
Bedford Wine Trail: 117
Beech Grove School: 293
beer, craft: Asheville 217-219; Biltmore Estate 215; Boone 176; Brew & Blues Festival 60; Brew Ridge Trail 90; Charlottesville 90; Gatlinburg 310; Roanoke 126; Virginia Craft Beer Month 91; Virginia Craft Brewers Fest 91; Waynesboro 81

INDEX

Belle Boyd Cottage: 59
Ben's Chili Bowl: 12, 29, 53
Bent Creek Experimental Forest: 236-237
Bent Creek Gap to Big Ridge Overlook: 241
Big Creek: 295
Big Creek Trail: 295
Big Ears Festival: 328
Big Flat Mountain: 79
Big Meadows: 20, 73
Big Meadows Campground: 17, 64, 74
Big Meadows Lodge: 12, 17, 74
Big Ridge Overlook to the Mount Pisgah
    Trailhead: 240
Big Run Overlook: 23, 79
Big Witch Gap Overlook: 16, 258
Bijou Theatre: 328
Bike and Roll: 32, 41
biking: Asheville 223; Biltmore Estate 226; Blue
    Ridge Parkway 340; National Mall 12, 32;
    Washington DC 51; see also mountain biking
Biltmore Estate: 9, 16, 205, 212, 213-214, 225, 229
Biltmore Village: 215
Biltmore Winery: 215
Birch & Barley: 19
bird-watching: 72
Biscuit Head: 16, 212, 227
Bishop Boutique: 47
black bears: 300-301, 304
Black Cat: 12, 48
Black Mountain College: 216
Black Rock Nature Trail: 192
Blackrock Summit: 17, 79
Blackrock Summit Trail: 79
Blenheim Vineyards: 89
Blowing Rock: 8, 14, 181-187
Blowing Rock Art and History Museum: 182
Bluegrass and Old-Time Fiddlers Convention:
    148
Blue Loop Trail: 105
Blue Mountain Barrel House: 90
Blue Mountain Brewery: 81, 90
Blue Ridge Backroads: 153
Blue Ridge Music Center: 14, 22, 99, 134, 152
Blue Ridge Parkway: general discussion 13,
    97-269; architecture 338; best views 18; fall
    foliage 23
Blue Ridge Parkway Visitor Center: 133, 233
Bluff Mountain: 107
Bluff Mountain Trail: 168
boating: Mount Vernon tours 46; Roanoke River
    129; Sherando Lake 104; Smith Mountain Lake
    State Park 119; Washington DC tours 43
Bodo's Bagels: 18, 93
Boogerman Trail: 294
Boone: 175-181

Boone, Daniel: 175
Bote Mountain Trail: 306
Boulevard, The: 286, 288
Boyd, Belle: 59
Brakeshoe Spring: 295
Brevard: 244-249
Brew & Blues Festival: 60
Brew Ridge Trail: 90
bridges of the Blue Ridge Parkway: 338
Brinegar Cabin: 167
Brown Mountain Overlook: 77
Brushy Mountain: 303
Brushy Mountain to Mount LeConte Hike: 303
Brushy Mountain Trail: 288
Brushy Mountain Winery: 163
Bryson City: 264-269
Buckhorn Inn: 16, 276, 313
Buck Spring Trail: 242
Bull Head Trail: 288
Buncombe County Courthouse: 212
Burial Beer: 212
bus travel: 30, 336; see also specific place
Buxton Hall Barbecue: 16, 207, 212, 227
Byrd Visitor Center: 73

C

C&O Restaurant: 12, 29, 92
Cable Grist Mill: 279, 305
Cades Cove: 16, 19, 20, 274, 279, 303
Cades Cove Visitor Center: 281
Caldwell Fork Trail: 295
Caldwell House: 293
Calf Mountain Overlook: 80
Calf Mountain Trail: 80
Campbell Overlook: 290
camping: general discussion 343-344; Brevard
    248; Cades Cove 305; Cataloochee 293; Cosby
    296; Crabtree Falls 199; Doughton Park 170;
    Great Smoky Mountains National Park 282,
    284, 291, 295, 301; Hanging Rock State Park
    150; Lake Powhatan Recreational Area 235-
    236; Linville Gorge 194; New River State Park
    173; Parson Bald 301; Peaks of Otter 114; Pilot
    Mountain State Park 150; Pisgah National
    Forest 244; reservations 9; Roanoke 133;
    Shenandoah National Park 64, 67, 76, 79;
    Sherando Lake 104; Smith Mountain Lake
    State Park 118; Stone Mountain State Park 166
canoeing/kayaking: Asheville 224; Mount Airy
    149; Nantahala River 266; Roanoke River
    129; Shenandoah River 82; South Fork of the
    Shenandoah 60; Yadkin River 150
Capital Pride: 50
Capitol Steps: 49
Carl Sandburg Home National Historic Site: 236

Carolina Heritage Vineyard and Winery: 163
car rental: 337
Carter Mountain Apple Orchard: 88-89
Cascade Falls Trail: 14, 174
casinos: 261
Cataloochee: 20, 274, 292
Cataloochee Campground: 22, 277, 292
Cataloochee Ski Area: 257
Cataloochee Valley: 292
Caudill Cabin: 168
caves: Boone 178-179; Grand Caverns 76; Linville
    Caverns 196; Luray Caverns 69-70; Natural
    Bridge Caverns 110; Roanoke 129; Skyline
    Caverns 59
Cedar Ridge Trail: 169
Cedar Rock Trail: 165
Cedric's: 215, 230
cell phone reception: 11, 343
Centerfest: 118
Center in the Square: 123
Center Pass with Roanoke Pinball Museum: 123
Central District, Shenandoah National Park: 62,
    70-77
Cerulean Knob: 307
Chai Pani: 212, 228
Charlies Bunion Hike: 286
Charlottesville: 12, 17, 29, 84-95
Charlottesville Derby Dames: 92
Chateau Morrisette: 14, 99, 143-144
Cherokee: 9, 16, 19, 258-264
Cherokee Welcome Center: 280
cherry blossom festival: 49
Chestnut Cove Overlook to Bent Creek Gap: 241
Chestoa View: 23, 196
children, traveling with: see family activities
Chimney Rock: 205, 234-235
Chimney Rock State Park: 234
Chimney Tops: 289
Chimney Tops Hike: 289
Chimney Tops Wildfire: 283
Christmas celebrations: Asheville 221; Gatlinburg
    Winter Magic 311; National Christmas Tree
    Lighting 50; Roanoke Star 135
churches: 165, 293, 305
cider, hard: 163
City Market Building: 123, 131
City of Galax Visitor's Center: 153
Civil War sights: Manassas Battlefield National
    Park 57-58; Warren Rifles Confederate
    Museum 59
classical music: 48, 126, 246
Cliff Trail: 105
Clingmans Dome: 19, 286
Clingmans Dome Road: 286
Clingmans Dome Visitor Contact Station: 280

Cold Mountain: 243, 251
Cold Mountain: 251-252
Cold Mountain Overlook: 243-244
Columbia Station: 12, 48
comedy: 49, 220
communications: 343
Compton Gap: 67
Cosby: 296
Crabtree Falls: 105-106, 199
Crabtree Falls Trail: 105
Cradle of Forestry Overlook: 244
crafts: Arrowmont School of Arts and Crafts
    310; Asheville 221, 222; Blowing Rock 184;
    Centerfest 118; Craft Fair of the Southern
    Highlands 220; Floyd 140; Folk Art Center 209;
    Great Smoky Arts and Crafts Community 311;
    Museum of North Carolina Handicrafts 252;
    musical instruments 246; Number 7 Fine Arts
    and Crafts Cooperative 247; Penland School
    of Crafts 197; Qualla Arts and Crafts Mutual
    261; Sally Mae's on the Parkway 170; Southern
    Highland Craft Guild 187; Virginia Wine and
    Craft Festival 60
Craggy Gardens: 16, 200-201
Craggy Gardens Trail: 13, 201
Craggy Pinnacle Trail: 201
Crimora Lake Overlook: 18, 23, 80
Crooked Arm Ridge Trail: 307
Crooked Road: 134
Crooked Road Music Trail: 22, 134
Crystal Spring Trail: 135
Cumberland Knob: 162-163
Cumberland Knob Trail: 162
Current Boutique: 47

D

dance: 220
Dark Hollow Falls: 12, 13, 17, 27, 73
Dark Hollow Falls Trail: 73
DAS Ethiopian Cuisine: 32, 54
D-Day Memorial: 115
Deep Creek: 291
Deep Creek Valley Overlook: 285
Deerfield Loop Trail: 239
Devils Backbone Overlook: 137
Devil's Courthouse: 16, 23, 250-251
Devil's Courthouse Trail: 250
Dickey Ridge Visitor Center: 65
disabilities, access for travelers with: 341
distilleries: 309
Dixie Caverns: 129
Doc's Rocks Gem Mines: 183
Dogwood Festival: 91
Dolly Parton's Dixie Stampede: 321
Dolly Parton Statue: 319

INDEX

Dollywood: 9, 16, 19, 22, 274, 317-318
Dollywood's Splash Country: 318-319
Don & Barbara Smith Children's Museum: 123-124
Doughton Park: 14, 166-170
driving tips: general discussion 11; Asheville and the Southern Blue Ridge 206; Great Smoky Mountains 274; North Carolina High Country 160; Shenandoah Valley 29; Virginia Blue Ridge 100-101
Duke's Grocery: 17, 53
Dupont State Forest: 248

E

Eastern Band of Cherokee Indians: 262
Eastern Smokies: 290-299
East Tennessee History Center: 19, 274, 324
Eating Asheville: 212
E. B. Jeffress Park: 174-175
elk: 292
Elkin: 14, 163-164
Elkin Creek Vineyards: 163
Elkmont: 20, 301
Elkmont Campground: 19
Elk Run Trail: 112
Elkwallow Wayside: 68
Emerald Village: 159, 198
emergencies: 342
environmental concerns: 341
Ephraim Bales Cabin: 298
etiquette, road: 339

F

fairs: 60
fairy stones: 141
Fairy Stone State Park: 141-142
fall foliage: 23; Cades Cove 303; Great Smoky Mountains National Park 281; Pinnacles Overlook 70; Southern Blue Ridge 209
fall travel: 9, 209, 281, 339
family activities: Crystal Spring Trail 135; Dollywood 317-318; Dollywood's Splash Country 318-319; Don & Barbara Smith Children's Museum, Kids Square 123-124; Grand Caverns 76; Great Smoky Mountains Railroad 265; Knoxville Zoo 326; Luray Caverns 70; Mill Mountain Zoo 135; Mystery Hill 182; National Mall 33-42; National Zoo 39; Natural Bridge Zoo 110; Pigeon Forge 323; Ripley's Aquarium of the Smokies 309; Roanoke Pinball Museum 124; Science Museum of Western Virginia 124; Skyline Caverns 59; Sugar Mountain 179; travel tips 341; Tweetsie Railroad 182; Virginia Discovery Museum 87; Virginia Safari Park 111; Western North Carolina Nature Center 216;

WonderWorks 319
Fancy Gap: 146
farmers markets: Asheville 226; Blowing Rock 183; Knoxville 329; Washington DC 50; West Jefferson 171
farms: 215
Festival of Leaves: 60
film festivals: 91
fireflies: 301
First Baptist Church: 212
First Colony Winery: 89
fishing: Beaver Creek Lake 92; Biltmore Estate 226; Cherokee 262; Doughton Park 167; Moses H. Cone Memorial Park 187; Nantahala Outdoor Center Gatlinburg 312; Shenandoah River 83; Smith Mountain Lake State Park 118; Tuckasegee River 205, 266-267; Western North Carolina Fly Fishing Trail 266; Wintergreen Resort 104
Fishin' Pig: 12, 83
Flat Creek Trail: 256
Flat Rock: 194
Flat Rock Loop Trail: 194
Flat Top Road Trail: 187
Flat Top Trail: 113
Fleurie Restaurant: 12, 29, 92
Floyd: 14, 134, 138-141
FloydFest: 22, 140
fly-fishing: 205, 266-267, 312
Fodder Stack Trail: 168
Folger Theater: 49
Folk Art Center: 16, 205, 209-210
Folk Art Center ADA Trail: 209
Fontana Dam: 299
Fontana Lake Area: 299
food events: Great Smoky Mountains Railroad 265; International Biscuit Festival 328; SAVOR Blowing Rock 183; Virginia State Barbecue Championship 153
Foothills Parkway: 303
Ford's Theatre: 49
Forest Heritage Scenic Byway: 244
Forney Ridge Trail: 287
Fort Windham Rocks: 67
Fort Windham Rocks Trail: 67
Fox Hollow Trail: 65
Fralin Museum of Art: 87
Freer Gallery of Art and the Arthur M. Sackler Gallery: 39
French Broad Chocolates: 212, 227
French Broad River to Walnut Cove Overlook: 240
The French Market: 19, 331
Friday Night Jamboree: 8, 14, 22, 99, 138-139
Front Royal: 12, 17, 58-62
fuel: 340

G

Gadsby's Tavern: 47
Galax: 134, 152-155
gaps of the Blue Ridge Parkway: 339
Garden Creek Baptist Church: 165
gardens: Botanical Gardens at Asheville 216; Monticello 87; Mount Vernon 46; North Carolina Arboretum 235
gasoline: 11, 340
Gatlinburg: 9, 16, 19, 307-316
Gatlinburg Sky Lift: 309
Gatlinburg Trail: 290
Gatlinburg Winter Magic: 311
gem mining: 178, 183, 266
gem museum: 197, 198
Georgetown: 51
George Washington National Forest: 60
ghost tours: 326
golf: Asheville 224; Bedford 118; Boone 178; Cherokee 263; Mount Airy 149; Pigeon Forge 323; Primland 145; Washington DC 52; Wintergreen Resort 104
Gooney Run Overlook: 65-67
Grand Caverns: 76
Grandfather Mountain: 8, 14, 20, 159, 191-193
Grandfather Trail: 192
Granny's Kitchen: 20, 263
Grassy Creek Vineyard and Winery: 163
Grassy Creek Waterfall: 159, 198
Graveyard Fields Loop Trail: 23, 249
Graveyard Fields Overlook: 249-250
Great Smoky Arts and Crafts Community: 311
Great Smoky Mountains: 16, 271-333; Gatlinburg 307-316; Great Smoky Mountains National Park 277-307; Knoxville 324-333; Pigeon Forge and Sevierville 316-324
Great Smoky Mountains National Park: 9, 13, 19, 277-307
Great Smoky Mountains Railroad: 20, 205, 265
Great Valley Overlook: 120
Greenbrier Cove: 301
Greenbrier Pinnacle Trail: 303
Green Knob Trail: 189
Green Leaf Grill: 17, 84
Gregory Bald Trail: 307
Gregory Bald via Twentymile Trail: 300
Griffith, Andy: 147, 149
Gross' Orchard: 116
Grotto Falls: 298
Grotto Falls Trail: 279, 298
Groundhog Mountain: 14, 18, 145-146
Grove Arcade: 212, 221
Gully Creek Trail: 162

H

Hanging Rock State Park: 150
Harkening Hill Trail: 112
Harrah's Cherokee Casino Resort: 16, 20, 208, 261, 264
Harrison Museum of African American Culture: 123
Harry F. Byrd, Sr. Visitor Center: 73
Hawksbill Mountain: 20, 72
Hawksbill Summit Trail: 72
Hawksnest Snow Tubing: 179
health: 342
Henry Hill Visitors Center: 57-58
Henry Whitehead Place: 307
Hen Wallow Falls Trail: 13, 274, 296
Hickory Hill Vineyards: 117
Hickory Nut Falls Trail: 234
Highest Point on Skyline Drive: 72
High Meadow Trail: 152
highway safety: 338
hiking: 72, 224; Apple Orchard Mountain 111; best bets 13; Biltmore Estate 226; Boone 178-179; Bryson City 266; Craggy Gardens 201; Cumberland Knob 162; Doughton Park 167-168; Dupont State Forest 248; E. B. Jeffress Park 174; Grandfather Mountain 191-193; Great Smoky Mountains National Park 277-307; Hanging Rock State Park 150; Ijams Nature Center 329; Julian Price Memorial Park 188-189; Lake Powhatan 237-241; Lake Powhatan Recreational Area 235-236; Linville Gorge 194; Maggie Valley 256; McAfee Knob 128; Mill Mountain 135; Moses H. Cone Memorial Park 187; Mount Jefferson State Natural Area 171; Mount Mitchell State Park 200; Mount Pisgah 242; Otter Creek 107; Peaks of Otter 112; Pilot Mountain State Park 150; Pisgah Ranger District 245; Roanoke Mountain 137; Rocky Knob Recreation Area 142; Shenandoah National Park 65-81; Sherando Lake 104-105; Smart View 137; Stone Mountain State Park 165; Virginia's Explore Park 133; Washington DC 52; Waterrock Knob Trail 256; Wintergreen Resort 104; Yankee Horse Ridge 107
Hill Country Barbecue: 12, 53
Historic Pine Tavern Restaurant: 14, 101, 140
Historic Roanoke City Market: 122-123
historic sights: Arlington National Cemetery 44-46; Big Meadows Lodge 74; Blackrock Summit 79; Cades Cove 305; Carl Sandburg Home National Historic Site 236; Cataloochee 293; Doughton Park 167; East Tennessee History Center 324; Henry Whitehead Place 307; Historic Roanoke City Market 122-123; Mabry Mill 144; Monticello 87; Motor Nature Trail

297; Mountain Farm Museum 284; National Mall 33-42; Stone Mountain State Park 165; Waynesboro Heritage Museum 81
History Museum of Western Virginia: 125
Hi-Wire: 212
Hogback Mountain Overlook: 18, 27, 67
Holocaust Memorial: 40
Homestead Trail: 239
Hoover, J. Edgar: 75
Horn in the West: 177
horseback riding: Biltmore Estate 215, 226; Blowing Rock 185; Front Royal 60; Moses H. Cone Memorial Park 187; Washington DC 52; Whetstone Ridge Trail 106
hot-air ballooning: 92
hotels: 9, 343
Humpback Rocks: 13, 103
Humpback Rocks Trail: 103
Humpback Rocks Visitor Center: 103
hunting: 249
Hutchison Homestead: 165

I
Icewater Spring Shelter: 286
Ijams Nature Center: 329
Independence Day: 50
Indian Creek Falls: 291
Indian Grave Gap Trail: 307
indoor skydiving: 323
I-95: 30
Inn on the River: 19
Inspiration Point: 289
International Biscuit Festival: 328
International Spy Museum: 42
Internet access: 343
Iris Inn: 12, 17, 30, 87
itineraries: Asheville 212; fall foliage 23; 14-day road trip 12-17; Great Smoky Mountains National Park 279; Knoxville 19-22; music of the Blue Ridge 22; Old Town Alexandria 47; Washington DC 17-19, 32

J
Jackson Building: 212
James River Overlook: 109
James River Self-Guiding Trail: 109
James River Visitor Center: 13, 23, 109
Jefferson Memorial: 36
Jefferson Theatre: 22, 90
Jefferson, Thomas: Jefferson Memorial 36; Monticello 87; Thomas Jefferson's Poplar Forest 116
Jefferson Vineyards: 88
John F. Kennedy Center for the Performing Arts: 48

John Oliver Cabin: 307
Johnson Farm Trail: 112
Johnson's Orchard: 116
Jones House Community and Cultural Center: 176
Jones von Drehle Vineyards & Winery: 163
Julian Price Memorial Park: 188-189
Juney Whank Falls: 291

K
kayaking: *see* canoeing/kayaking
Kennedy Center: 22, 32
Kennedy, John F.: 45
Kennedy, Robert: 45
Kennedy, Ted: 45
Keswick Vineyards: 89
Kluge-Ruhe Aboriginal Art Collection: 87
Knoxville: 9, 324-333
Knoxville Museum of Art: 274, 325
Knoxville Zoo: 326

L
Lake Junaluska: 256
Lake Powhatan: 235-242
Lake Powhatan Recreational Area: 235-236
Lakeside Trail: 105
Lands Run: 67
Lands Run Falls Trail: 65-67
Laurel Falls Trail: 301
LaZoom Comedy Tour: 212
Leave No Trace: 342
LeoGrande Vineyards and Winery: 117
Lewis Mountain: 76
Lewis Spring Falls Trail: 74-75
LGBTQ+ events: 50
LGBTQ+ travel tips: 341
Lincoln Memorial: 12, 17, 33
Link, Winston: 124
Linn Cove Viaduct: 8, 14, 159, 190-191
Linn Cove Viaduct Trail: 190
Linville Caverns: 196
Linville Falls: 14, 159, 194
Linville Falls Trail: 13, 194
Linville Gorge: 194-195
Little Laurel Branch: 303
Little Switzerland: 197-199
Local Goat New American Restaurant: 19, 276, 322
Loft Mountain: 77
Loft Mountain Loop Trail: 77
Looking Glass Rock: 244
Looking Glass Rock Overlook: 23, 249
Looking Glass Rock Trail: 245
Look Rock: 303
Lower Sidehill Trail: 239

Lower Tuckasegee River: 266
Lump, the: 174
Luray Caverns: 8, 12, 27, 68-70

M

Mabry Mill: 14, 18, 23, 144-145
Maggie Valley: 256-258
Mama's Chicken Kitchen: 16, 313
Manassas Battlefield National Park: 17, 27, 57-58
maps: 340
Market Square: 14, 22, 122
Martha's Branch: 307
Martin Luther King Jr. Memorial: 17, 37
Mary's Rock Trail: 13, 27, 70
Mary's Rock Tunnel and Trail: 70
Mas Tapas: 17, 29, 92
Matthews Arm Campground: 17, 67
Mayberry Days: 149
McAfee Knob: 99, 128
McAfee Knob Trail: 128
McKinney Gap: 196
McRitchie Winery & Ciderworks: 163
Memorial Amphitheater: 45
MerleFest: 22, 176
Merry-Go-Round Show: 148
Methodist Church: 305
Midnight Hole: 295
Mile High Swinging Bridge: 14, 191
mileposts: 11
Millennium Stage: 48
Mill Mountain: 135-137
Mill Mountain Theatre: 123
Mill Mountain Zoo: 135
mineral museum: 197, 198
mining: 198
Mint Condition: 47
money: 343
Monticello: 12, 17, 27, 87
Monticello Wine Trail: 17, 88
Moses H. Cone Memorial Park: 14, 187-188
motels: 343-344
motor courts: 232
motorcycles: 340
Motor Nature Trail: 298
mountain biking: Bryson City 266; Front Royal 60; Gatlinburg 313; Ijams Nature Center 329; Lake Powhatan Recreational Area 235-236; Sherando Lake 105; Virginia's Explore Park 133; Walnut Creek Park 92; Whetstone Ridge Trail 106; Wintergreen Resort 104
Mountain Culture Exhibit: 165
Mountain Farm Museum: 16, 280, 284
Mountain Farm Trail: 103
Mount Airy: 146-152
Mount Cammerer Trail: 296

Mount Jefferson State Natural Area: 171
Mount LeConte: 286, 288, 303
Mount Mitchell State Park: 199-200
Mount Mitchell Summit Trail: 200
Mount Mitchell Trail: 200
Mount Pisgah: 16, 242-243
Mount Pisgah Summit Trail: 242
Mount Vernon: 12, 19, 46, 47
Museum of North Carolina Minerals: 197
Museum of the Cherokee Indian: 19, 259-261, 262
museums: Andy Griffith Museum 147; Blowing Rock Art and History Museum 182; Fralin Museum of Art 87; International Spy Museum 42; Kluge-Ruhe Aboriginal Art Collection 87; Knoxville Museum of Art 325; Luray Caverns 70; Mountain Farm Museum 284; Museum of North Carolina Handicrafts 252; Museum of North Carolina Minerals 197; Museum of the Cherokee Indian 259-261; National Gallery of Art 37; National Portrait Gallery 42; Newseum 42; North Carolina Mining Museum 198; Phillips Collection 42; Roanoke 123; Smithsonian Institution 38-39; Tennessee Museum of Aviation 319; Titanic Pigeon Forge 319; Wheels Through Time Museum 256; see also art events/galleries
music: Asheville 219, 220-221; Bluegrass and Old-Time Fiddlers Convention 148; Blue Ridge Music Center 152; Brevard Music Center 246; Brew & Blues Festival 60; Charlottesville 90; FloydFest 140; Friday Night Jamboree 138-139; Galax 152, 153; heritage music trail 134; Jones House Community and Cultural Center 176; Knoxville 328; MerleFest 176; Old Fiddler's Convention 154; Smoky Mountain Opry 321; Washington DC 48; West Jefferson 171
Mystery Hill: 182

N

N&W Railroad Overlook: 121
Nantahala Gorge: 265
Nantahala Outdoor Center Gatlinburg: 312
Nantahala River Gorge: 265
Nasime: 47
National Air and Space Museum: 12, 32, 39-40
National Cherry Blossom Festival: 49
National D-Day Memorial: 14, 99, 115
National Gallery of Art: 37
National Mall: 32, 33-42
National Museum of African American History and Culture: 12, 27, 32, 40
National Museum of African Art: 39
National Museum of American History: 39
National Museum of Natural History: 12, 32, 39
national parks: Great Smoky Mountains National

INDEX

Park 9, 277-307; Shenandoah National Park 8, 62-81
National Portrait Gallery: 12, 39, 42
National Symphony Orchestra: 48
National Theatre: 49
National Zoo: 39
Native American sights: Blowing Rock 182; Cherokee 258-259; Cherokee history 262; Museum of the Cherokee Indian 259-261; National Museum of the American Indian 39; Natural Bridge 109; Oconaluftee Indian Village 261; Peaks of Otter 112
Natural Bridge: 99, 109-111
Natural Bridge Caverns: 110
Natural Bridge Zoo: 110
Navitat: 212, 225
Needle's Eye: 234
Newfound Gap: 285
Newfound Gap Road: 16, 19, 274, 279, 283-290
New Public House & Hotel: 14, 162, 186
New River State Park: 162, 172, 173
Newseum: 12, 42
Nightbell: 212
9:30 Club: 22, 48
North Carolina Arboretum: 235
North Carolina High Country: 8, 157-201, 336
North Carolina Mining Museum: 198
Northern District, Shenandoah National Park: 62, 65-70
Not Watson's Kitchen + Bar: 17, 332
Number 7 Fine Arts and Crafts Cooperative: 247

O

Ober Gatlinburg: 313
Oconaluftee Indian Village: 20, 205, 261, 262
Oconaluftee River Trail: 285
Oconaluftee River Valley Overlook: 285
Oconaluftee Visitor Center: 16, 284
Ogle Place: 297
Oktoberfest at Ober Gatlinburg: 311
Old Fiddler's Convention: 22, 154
Old Rag: 68-70
Old Rag Mountain Trail: 69
Old Salem Turnpike Trail: 134
Old Town Alexandria: 19, 47
Onassis, Jacqueline Kennedy: 45
opera: 48, 126
Orange Peel Social Aid and Pleasure Club: 22, 219
Orchard at Altapass: 23, 196
orchards: see apple orchards
Otter Creek: 107-109
Otter Creek Trail: 107
Otter Lake Loop Trail: 108
Outcroppings Trail: 234
O. Winston Link Museum: 99, 124

P

packing tips: 9
Palmer Chapel and Cemetery: 293
Palmer Creek: 294
Palmer House: 293
Pancake Pantry: 19, 315
Panther Creek Cabins: 20, 208, 264
parking: 340
parks: Charlottesville 92; Doughton Park 166; E. B. Jeffress Park 174-175; Julian Price Memorial Park 188; Moses H. Cone Memorial Park 187; Mount Airy 150; Mount Jefferson State Natural Area 171; Virginia's Explore Park 133; Washington DC 51-52; World's Fair Park 329; see also state parks
Parson Bald: 300
Parsons Branch Road: 306
Parton, Dolly: 316
passports: 341
Peaks of Otter: 18, 23, 112-114
Peaks of Otter Winery: 117
Penland School of Crafts: 197
performing arts: Asheville 220; Charlottesville 90-91; Cherokee 261; Gatlinburg 311; Horn in the West 177; Knoxville 328; Roanoke 123, 126; Tennessee Theatre 326; Washington DC 48
Peter Chang China Grill: 17, 94
Phillips Collection: 12, 42
Pigeon Forge and Sevierville: 9, 19, 316-324
Pilot Mountain State Park: 150
Pine Tree Loop Trail: 239
Pinnacles Overlook: 70
Pippin Hill Farm and Vineyard: 89
Pisgah National Forest: 244
Pisgah Ranger District: 244-249
Pisgah Ranger Station: 244
planning tips: 8-11
poisonous plants: 343
Poplar Forest: 116
Price Lake Trail: 188
Pride parades: 50
Pritchard Park drum circle: 212
Public Service Building: 212
public transit: 341
Purgatory Overlook: 120

QR

Qualla Arts and Crafts Mutual: 16, 19, 205, 261, 262
Quilt Trails of Western North Carolina: 171
railroads: 182, 265
Rainbow Falls Trail: 288, 289, 298
Ramsey Cascades: 303
Ramsey Cascades Trail: 301, 303
Ramsey Prong: 303

Ramulose Ridge Vineyards: 117
Range View Overlook: 23, 67
Rapidan Camp: 75
Rapidan Camp Trail: 75
Rasika: 12, 29, 32, 54
reading, suggested: 344
rental cars: 11, 30, 337
reservations: 9, 344
resources, Internet: 344-346
Rhythm N Blooms Fest: 328
Richland Balsam Overlook: 16, 18, 251
Richland Balsam Self-Guiding Trail: 252
Rich Mountain: 274
Rich Mountain Loop: 307
Rich Mountain Road: 279, 307
Rich Mountain Trail: 187
Ripley's Aquarium of the Smokies: 309
Riprap Hollow Trail: 80
Riprap Overlook: 80
River and Rail Restaurant: 14, 101, 130
River Arts District: 221
River Bend Farm: 215
Road Prong: 290
road rules: 337-341
Road to Nowhere: 292
Roanoke: 8, 14, 121-133
Roanoke Mountain Summit Trail: 137
Roanoke Pinball Museum: 124
Roanoke Star: 14, 99, 135-137
Roanoke Valley Overlook: 137
Roaring Fork Motor Nature Trail: 279, 288, 296
Roaring Gap: 163-164
Rock Castle Gorge Trail: 142
rock climbing: Boone 179; Chimney Rock State
    Park 235; Fort Windham Rocks 67; Hanging
    Rock State Park 150; Linville Gorge 195; Pilot
    Mountain State Park 150
Rock Creek Park: 51
Rockfish Gap: 103
Rockfish Valley Overlook: 23, 103
Rock House: 295
Rocky Knob Recreation Area: 142-143
Rocky Top: 306
Rocky Top and Thunderhead: 306
roller derby: 92
Rough Ridge: 189
Rumbling Bald Mountain: 235

S

S&W Cafeteria: 212
safety: 338, 342
Salem Red Sox: 129
Sally Mae's on the Parkway: 170
Sandburg, Carl: 236
SAVOR Blowing Rock: 183

Science Museum of Western Virginia: 124
Scott Mountain Trail: 307
Scratch Biscuit Company: 14, 130
senior travelers: 341
Seven Doors Winery: 117
Sevierville: 316-324
Sfoglina: 12, 29, 55
Shakespeare Theatre Company: 49
Sharp Top: 14, 113
Shenandoah National Park: 12, 17, 62-81; fees 9;
    planning tips 8
Shenandoah Valley: 25-95; Charlottesville 84-95;
    driving tips 29; Front Royal 58-62; highlights
    27; Manassas Battlefield National Park 57-58;
    maps 26; planning tips 8, 28; Shenandoah
    National Park 62-81; transportation 29-31;
    Washington DC 31-57; Waynesboro 81-84
Sherando Lake: 104-105
Shindig on the Green: 221
Shining Rock Wilderness: 244
shooting clays: 226
Shut-In Trail: 240
Ski Beech Mountain Resort: 179
skiing: 179, 257, 313
Skinny Dip Falls Trail: 249
skydiving, indoor: 323
Skyland Resort: 12, 17, 72
Skyline Caverns: 59
Skyline-Cliff Trail: 234
Skyline Drive: 8, 12, 13, 17, 62; best views 18; fall
    foliage 23; origin 29
Slacks Trail: 105
Sleepy Gap Overlook to Chestnut Cove
    Overlook: 241
Sliding Rock: 244
Small Creek Trail: 239
Smart View: 137-138
Smart View Loop Trail: 138
Smart View Recreation Area: 137
Smith Mountain Lake State Park: 118
Smithsonian American Art Museum: 42
Smithsonian Castle: 39
Smithsonian Institution: 38-39
Smoky Mountain Alpine Coaster: 323
Smoky Mountain Music Fest: 328
Smoky Mountain Opry: 321
snakes: 342
Soco Gap: 258
Sourwood Inn: 16, 208, 230
Southern District, Shenandoah National Park:
    62, 77-81
Southern Highland Craft Guild: 14, 187
South River Falls: 77
South River Falls Trail: 17, 77
South Street Brewery: 90

Sovereign Remedies: 16, 217
Space Needle: 308-309
spas: 225
speed limits: 11
SpeedZone Fun Park: 19, 323
Spence Field: 306
spiders: 342
spring travel: 9, 209, 339
Spring Wildflower Pilgrimage: 311
Stable Café: 212, 230
Stalacpipe Organ: 70
stand-up paddleboarding: 224, 226
Starr Hill Brewing Company: 90
Star Trail: 135, 136
state parks: Chimney Rock State Park 234; Fairy
    Stone State Park 141-142; Hanging Rock State
    Park 150; Mount Mitchell State Park 199; New
    River State Park 172; Pilot Mountain State
    Park 150; Shenandoah River State Park 61;
    Smith Mountain Lake State Park 118; Stone
    Mountain State Park 164-166
Steven F. Udvar-Hazy Center: 39-40
Stock & Barrel: 22, 331
Stone Mountain Loop Trail: 165
Stone Mountain State Park: 14, 164-166
Stony Man Summit Trail: 72
Storie Street Grille: 14, 161, 185
Story of the Forest Trail: 73
Sugarlands Distilling Company: 16, 309
Sugarlands Visitor Center: 19, 279, 290
Sugarlands Visitor Center and Park
    Headquarters: 280
Sugarloaf Mountain: 152
Sugar Mountain: 179
Sunsphere: 16, 19, 326
Suzanne Farrell Ballet: 48
Sweat Heifer Creek Trail: 286

T

Tanawha Trail: 189
Taubman Museum of Art: 14, 125
Taverna Cretekou: 47
Tennessee Museum of Aviation: 319
Tennessee Theatre: 17, 274, 326, 328
tennis: 52
Texas Tavern: 14, 130
Theodore Roosevelt Island: 52
Thomas Jefferson's Poplar Forest: 116
Thousand Drips Falls: 279, 298
Thunderhead Mountain: 306
ticks: 342
Titanic Pigeon Forge: 319
Tomato Head: 22, 331
Tomb of the Unknown Soldier: 32, 45
Tomkins Knob Trail: 174

Torpedo Factory Art Center: 47
Torry Ridge Trail: 105
Townsend: 303, 307
traffic: 339
Trail of Tears: 262
Trail of Trees Self-Guiding Trail: 109
train travel: 30, 337; Virginia Blue Ridge 102
transportation: 9; see also specific place
Trillium Gap Trail: 288, 303
trolley tours: 43
tubing, river: 241, 263
Tuckaleechee Cove: 307
Tuckasegee River: 266-267
tunnels of the Blue Ridge Parkway: 338
Turchin Center for the Visual Arts: 176
Tweetsie Railroad: 182
Twentymile: 300
Twentymile Loop Trail: 300
200 South Street Inn: 17, 30, 94

UV

United States Capitol: 12, 17, 41
United States Holocaust Memorial Museum:
    27, 40
University of Tennessee Knoxville: 329
University of Virginia: 12, 17, 85
Unto These Hills: 261, 262
U.S. Marine Corps War Memorial: 46
US-29: 18
Vanderbilt, George: 213
viaducts: 338
Vietnam Veterans Memorial: 12, 35
views: best bets: 18; Big Run Overlook 79;
    Brown Mountain Overlook 77; Campbell
    Overlook 290; Chestoa View 196; Chimney
    Rock State Park 234; Cold Mountain Overlook
    243; Crimora Lake Overlook 80; Deep Creek
    Valley Overlook 285; Forest Heritage Scenic
    Byway 244; Hogback Mountain Overlook 67;
    Linn Cove Viaduct 190; Loft Mountain 77;
    Looking Glass Rock Overlook 249; Mabry Mill
    144; Maggie Valley 256; McAfee Knob 128;
    Mount Mitchell State Park 200; Newfound
    Gap Road 283; Otter Creek 107; Pinnacles
    Overlook 70; Purgatory Overlook 120; Range
    View Overlook 67; Richland Balsam Overlook
    252; Rockfish Valley Overlook 103; Skyline
    Drive 62; Space Needle 308-309; Sugarloaf
    Mountain 152; Waterrock Knob Visitor Center
    255
Village Shops: 312
Virginia Blue Ridge: 8, 97-155, 336
Virginia Cavaliers: 92
Virginia Craft Beer Month: 91
Virginia Discovery Museum: 87

Virginia Film Festival: 91
Virginia Museum of Transportation: 125
Virginia Safari Park: 111
Virginia's Explore Park: 133-135
Virginia State Barbecue Championship: 153
Virginia Wine and Craft Festival: 60
Virginia Wine Month: 91
visas: 341
Visitor Center Loop Trail: 233

WXYZ

Walker Camp Prong: 289
Walnut Bottoms: 295
Walnut Cove Overlook to Sleepy Gap Overlook: 240
Walnut Creek Park: 92
Warren County Fair: 60
Warren Rifles Confederate Museum: 59
Washington Capitals: 52
Washington DC: 8, 31-57; accommodations 56-57; day-trip 32; dining 53-56; entertainment/events 46-50; parks and recreation 51-52; shopping 50-51; sights 33-46; sports 52; tours 43; transportation 31-33, 335
Washington, George: 46
Washington Monument: 12, 36
Washington Mystics: 52
Washington National Opera: 48
Washington Nationals: 52
Washington NFL team: 52
Washington Wizards: 52
waterfalls: Abrams Falls Trail 306; Cascade Falls Trail 174; Crabtree Falls 105, 199; Dark Hollow Falls 73; Deep Creek 291; Dupont State Forest 248; Grassy Creek Waterfall 198; Lands Run Falls Trail 67; Laurel Falls Trail 301; Lewis Spring Falls Trail 74-75; Linville Falls 194; Looking Glass Falls 245; Motor Nature Trail 298; Mouse Creek Falls 295; North Carolina High Country 8; Ramsey Cascades 303; Rapidan Camp 75; Riprap Hollow Trail 80; South River Falls Trail 77; Yankee Horse Ridge 107
water parks: 318-319
Waterrock Knob Trail: 256
Waterrock Knob Visitor Center: 16, 18, 255-256
Watson, Merle: 176
Waynesboro: 12, 17, 81-84
Waynesboro Heritage Museum: 81
Waynesville: 251-255
WDVX-FM: 328
weather: 9, 339
weddings, Gatlinburg: 310
Western North Carolina Nature Center: 216
Western Smokies: 299-307

West Jefferson: 170-173
West Jefferson Arts District Gallery Crawl: 171
We the Pizza: 32, 55
Wheels Through Time Museum: 256
Whetstone Ridge: 106
Whetstone Ridge Trail: 106
White House: 12, 41
Whiteoak Canyon: 68-70
Whiteoak Canyon Trail: 68
White Rock Trail: 105
White Rock Vineyards: 117
white-water rafting: 265; Boone: 178-179; Gatlinburg: 313
Wildcat Rocks Overlook: 168
wilderness safety: 342
wildflowers: Balsam Mountain Road 291; Great Smoky Mountains National Park 281; Greenbrier Cove 302; Southern Blue Ridge 209; Spring Wildflower Pilgrimage 311
wildlife viewing: Big Meadows 73; black bears 304; Cades Cove 303; Cataloochee 292; Doughton Park 166; elk 292; Elkmont 301; environmental concerns 342; Grandfather Mountain 191; Great Smoky Mountains National Park 19; Hawksbill Mountain 72; Western North Carolina Nature Center 216
Wild Wolf Brewing Company: 90
wineries: Bedford Wine Trail 117; Biltmore Estate 16, 215; Charlottesville 89; Chateau Morrisette 14, 143; Monticello Wine Trail 17, 88; Roanoke 8; Virginia Wine and Craft Festival 60; Virginia Wine Month 91; Waynesboro 81; Yadkin Valley 163
Wintergreen Resort: 104
winter travel: 9, 281
Wolf Ridge Trail: 300
Women in Service Memorial: 46
Women's Basketball Hall of Fame: 326
WonderWorks: 319
Woodland Walk: 234
Woolworth Walk: 212
World's Fair Park: 16, 329
Yankee Horse Overlook Trail: 107
Yankee Horse Ridge: 107
Zen Tubing: 212, 224, 241
zip lines: 184, 225, 266, 313, 323
zoos: Knoxville Zoo 326; Mill Mountain Zoo 135; National Zoo 39; Natural Bridge Zoo 110

LIST OF MAPS

Front Map
Blue Ridge Parkway Road Trip: 2-3

Discover the Blue Ridge Parkway
route overview: 8

The Shenandoah Valley
The Shenandoah Valley: 26
The National Mall: 34–35
Shenandoah National Park, Northern District: 66
Shenandoah National Park, Central District: 71
Shenandoah National Park, Southern District: 78
Charlottesville: 86

Virginia Blue Ridge
Virginia Blue Ridge - North: 98
Virginia Blue Ridge - South: 98
Downtown Roanoke: 122
Floyd: 138
Mount Airy: 147
Galax: 153

North Carolina High Country
North Carolina High Country: 158
Boone: 177

Asheville and the Southern Blue Ridge
Asheville and the Southern Blue Ridge: 204
Greater Asheville: 211
Downtown Asheville: 213
Waynesville: 253
Maggie Valley: 257
Cherokee: 259

Great Smoky Mountains
Great Smoky Mountains: 272–273
Great Smoky Mountains National Park: 278
Knoxville: 325
Downtown Knoxville: 327

PHOTO CREDITS

Title page photo: © Roanoke Valley CVB; page 4 © Nick Breedlove; page 5 © Robert Stephens | Dreamstime; page 7 (top) © Daveallenphoto | Dreamstime, (bottom) © Daveallenphoto | Dreamstime; page 10 (top left) © Pierre Leclerc | Dreamstime, (top right) © Jason Frye, (bottom) © Sean Pavone | Dreamstime; page 13 © Jason Frye; page 15 (top left) © Orhan Çam | Dreamstime, (top right) © Rita Robinson | Dreamstime, (bottom) © Jason Frye; page 18 © Nick Breedlove; page 20 © Lightscribe | Dreamstime; page 21 (top left) © Jason Frye, (top right) © Benkrut | Dreamstime, (bottom) © Cameron Davidson - Visit Virginia's Blue Ridge; page 24 © Svecchiotti | Dreamstime; page 27 © Joel Gafford | Dreamstime; page 37 (top) © dreamstime.com, (middle) © Wangkun Jia | Dreamstime.com, (bottom) © Jason Frye; page 38 © Wangkun Jia | Dreamstime; page 43 (top) © Jason Frye, (middle) © Izanbar | Dreamstime, (bottom) © Jason Frye; page 44 © Jason Frye; page 54 © Jason Frye; page 58 © Steveheap | Dreamstime; page 63 (top) © Sborisov | Dreamstime, (middle) © Jon Bilous | Dreamstime, (bottom) © Jason Frye; page 68 (top) © Zrfphoto | Dreamstime, (middle) © Jason Frye, (bottom) © NPS; page 74 © Jason Frye; page 82 © Jason Frye; page 88 © Demerzel21 | Dreamstime; page 93 (top) © Jason Frye, (middle) © Jason Frye, (bottom) © Jason Frye; page 96 © Guoqiang Xue | Dreamstime; page 99 © Info68723 | Dreamstime; page 108 (top) © Jason Frye, (middle) © Jason Frye, (bottom) © David Biagi | Dreamstime; page 110 © Botetourt County Tourism - Visit Virginia's Blue Ridge; page 114 © Sarah Hauser - Visit Virginia's Blue Ridge; page 117 (top) © Jason Frye, (middle) © Jason Frye, (bottom) © Jason Frye; page 124 © Jason Frye; page 127 (top) © Jason Frye, (middle) © Jason Frye, (bottom) © Jason Frye; page 132 © Jason Frye; page 136 © Alex Grichenko | Dreamstime; page 139 (top) © Jason Frye, (middle) © Jason Frye, (bottom) © Jason Frye; page 144 © Jason Frye; page 148 (top) © Jason Frye, (middle) © Jason Frye, (bottom) © Jason Frye; page 150 © Jason Frye; page 156 © Kendallwritings | Dreamstime.com; page 159 © Cvandyke | Dreamstime; page 166 © Jason Frye; page 168 (top) © Jason Frye, (middle) © Jason Frye, (bottom) © Jason Frye; page 174 © Jason Frye; page 183 (top) © Jason Frye, (middle) © Jason Frye, (bottom) © Jason Frye; page 190 © Daveallenphoto | Dreamstime.com; page 192 © Daveallenphoto | Dreamstime.com; page 195 (top) © Jason Frye, (middle) © Jason Frye, (bottom) © Kelly Vandellen | Dreamstime; page 202 © Sean Pavone | Dreamstime; page 205 © Robhainer | Dreamstime; page 214 © Inkaone | Dreamstime; page 218 (top) © Jason Frye, (middle) © Jason Frye, (bottom) © Jason Frye; page 227 (top) © Jason Frye, (middle) © Jason Frye, (bottom) © Jason Frye; page 234 (top) © Jason Frye, (middle) © Florentino David | Dreamstime, (bottom) © Cvandyke | Dreamstime; page 240 © Jason Frye; page 250 © Jason Frye; page 260 (top) © Jason Frye, (middle) © Susan Leggett/123RF, (bottom) © Jill Lang/123RF; page 264 © Alex Grichenko | Dreamstime; page 268 © Jason Frye; page 270 © Anthony Heflin | Dreamstime; page 287 (top) © Jason Frye, (middle) © NPS, (bottom) © Jason Frye; page 294 © Jason Frye; page 297 (top) © Sayran | Dreamstime, (middle) © Jason Frye, (bottom) © Jason Frye; page 302 (top) © Jason Frye, (bottom) © Jason Frye; page 314 © Jason Frye; page 318 © Wild Eagle photo shoot for promotions. Photos by http://sbphotos.com; page 330 © Jason Frye; page 332 (top) © Jason Frye, (middle) © Jason Frye, (bottom) © Jason Frye; page 334 © Dfikar | Dreamstime.com

ACKNOWLEDGMENTS

Thanks to the countless readers, friends, industry insiders, and enthusiastic champions for communities up and down the Blue Ridge Parkway and Skyline Drive for letting me know the best of the best places to visit, dine, and include in this book; and thank you to the many people in Washington DC, Great Smoky Mountains National Park, and Knoxville for your help, guidance, and recommendations. As I see each of you over the course of my travels I'll tell you this in person, but until then, know I'm grateful.

Finally, I would like to thank my wife and constant travel companion, Lauren Frye. Without her patience, her excellent road trip DJ-ing, and her support, writing this book would've been impossible.

More Across the South from Moon Travel Guides

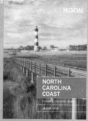

MOON.COM | @MOONGUIDES

Guides for City Escapes!

MOON NATIONAL PARKS

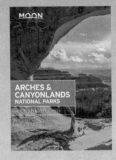

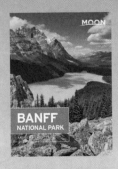

ACADIA
NATIONAL PARK

ARCHES &
CANYONLANDS
NATIONAL PARKS

BANFF
NATIONAL PARK

DEATH VALLEY
NATIONAL PARK

GLACIER
NATIONAL PARK

GRAND
CANYON

GREAT SMOKY
MOUNTAINS
NATIONAL PARK

MOUNT RUSHMORE
& THE BLACK HILLS

ROCKY MOUNTAIN
NATIONAL PARK

In these books:

- Full coverage of gateway cities and towns
- Itineraries from one day to multiple weeks
- Advice on where to stay (or camp) in and
  around the parks